Revolutions and Revolutionary Movements

Revolutions and Revolutionary Movements

THIRD EDITION

James DeFronzo
University of Connecticut

A Member of the Perseus Books Group

Westview Press books are available at special discounts for bulk purchases in the United States by corporations, institutions, and other organizations. For more information, please contact the Special Markets Department at the Perseus Books Group, 11 Cambridge Center, Cambridge MA 02142, or call (617) 252-5298 or (800) 255-1514, or e-mail special.markets@perseusbooks.com.

Designed by Timm Bryson

Library of Congress Cataloging-in-Publication Data
DeFronzo, James.
Revolutions and revolutionary movements / James DeFronzo.—3rd ed.
p.   cm.
Includes bibliographical references and index.
ISBN-13: 978-0-8133-4354-9 (pbk. : alk. paper)
ISBN-10: 0-8133-4354-2 (pbk. : alk. paper)
1. Revolutions. 2. Social movements. 3. Revolutions—Case studies. 4. World politics—20th century. 5. World politics—21st century.   I. Title.
HM876.D44 2007
303.6'4—dc22

2006032493

Contents

List of Maps

Preface

An absence of public knowledge concerning the political histories and socioeconomic characteristics of other societies can permit a government to exercise an excessive influence over citizen perception of its actions in foreign lands. It is possible, for example, that U.S. involvement in Vietnam would not have occurred or at least would not have progressed as far as it did if the American people had been fully aware of the Vietnamese Revolution against French colonial rule, the loss of popular support for France's Indochina war effort, and the terms of the resulting Geneva peace settlement of 1954. Although the U.S. public was too poorly informed to prevent the tragedy in Vietnam, the collective memory of the Vietnam experience probably helped prevent direct U.S. military intervention in several countries in the subsequent years.

But key elements of the Vietnam experience were apparently not passed on to post-Vietnam generations. This situation became especially clear to me through responses to a question that I repeatedly asked students in several large sociology classes. The question was, "How many of you have had any treatment of the Vietnam conflict in high school?" In each case, less than 5 percent raised their hands! Most also indicated on anonymous questionnaires that they knew very little about social movements and political conflicts in other parts of the world. This was particularly noteworthy and disturbing because the large majority were college juniors or seniors preparing to embark on their careers and take on their future political and social responsibilities.

There are probably several causes of Americans' general lack of political knowledge of other societies. As citizens of the richest and most technologically advanced nation, many of us have felt unaffected by other parts of the world, with little need to concern ourselves with the politics of less-developed countries or to become familiar with the traditions of other cultures. Undoubtedly, many people shy away from political topics because they want to avoid controversy. The fear of conflict over how to deal with the subject of Vietnam might have been especially acute within a high school faculty, in which some may be war veterans and others former antiwar activists. The result was probably in many cases a simple avoidance of this potentially explosive topic in history or social science classes.

The mass media, like the educational system, have also generally failed to provide information about foreign societies to the vast majority of the American people. Television networks, in the competition for advertising dollars, are intent on maximizing viewer ratings. Programs dealing with political topics in other lands cannot usually command a respectable percentage of the viewing public (except in times of war or other international emergencies such as the period immediately following the September 11, 2001, terrorist attacks).

Yet many people display a strong interest in learning about political events and conflicts in other parts of the world when an opportunity is provided. I have noted this phenomenon most specifically within the context of a course I have taught called Revolutionary Social Movements Around the World. Through lectures and documentary films, I attempted to explain the development and significance of important twentieth-century and twenty-first-century revolutionary movements and associated political conflicts in Russia, China, Vietnam, Cuba, Central America, Iran, South Africa, and other countries. Since the mid-1980s through 2005, an average of 150 students have taken this course every semester, with about one-third of the enrollment drawn from outside the University of Connecticut's College of Liberal Arts and Sciences (that is, from the Colleges of Business, Engineering, Nursing, Education, and so forth). According to responses on surveys of class enrollees, the course attracted so much interest because it provided students an opportunity to learn about a significant number of political conflicts (and the societies in which they occur) in a single course. I hope to provide a similar opportunity to a wider audience through this book.

In the first chapter, the reader is introduced to factors important for the discussion of modern revolutions, such as the development of revolutionary conditions, relevant theoretical perspectives, the roles of leaders, the functions of ideology, and the meaning of important concepts such as socialism, communism, people's war, guerrilla warfare, and counterinsurgency, which are employed in specific contexts throughout the book. The revolutions, revolutionary movements, and conflicts covered include those of greatest world significance and those of central importance to the development of revolutionary ideology, strategy, and tactics.

The chapters contain book and article references that the reader might consult to broaden his or her knowledge of a particular topic as well as a list of a number of relevant documentary DVDs, videos, and films. The sources from which these documentaries may be obtained are provided at the end of the book.

This volume is intended to fulfill several purposes. First, I hope that it will serve as an instrument through which students and other interested persons can significantly expand their knowledge of the countries covered and of world politics in general. Second, faculty members can utilize the book or parts of it and possibly several of the suggested documentary DVDs, videos, and films in existing sociology, political science, or history courses relating to social movements or political conflicts or to organize a course dealing specifically with revolutionary movements. Finally, this book can also be useful as a reference source for student or civic groups interested in stimulating greater public awareness of, interest in, and knowledge of world developments.

The list of those who played a significant role in the origin of this book must include my own instructors, fellow faculty members, and thousands of students at the University of Connecticut and Indiana University who inspired both the creation of my revolutions course and the concept of a manuscript on the subject. The reviews and advice of the experts in sociology, political science, anthropology, history, and economics who read individual chapters or the manuscript in its entirety have been of immense value. In particular, for kindly consenting to comment on various parts of this manuscript, I would like to thank Juan del Aguila, Robert Denemark, Susan Eckstein, Julie Feinsilver, Darrell Hammer, Peter Klaren, Mohsen Milani, Mark Selden, Thomas Shapiro, William Turley, Kamyar Vala, Mary Vanderlaan, John Walton, Claude Welch, and Ernest Zirakzadeh. I am also appreciative of the fine work done by Raymond Blanchette, who drew the maps used in this book. I would like to express my gratitude to the staff of Westview Press, in particular to Jennifer Knerr for the administrative guidance she provided (for the first two editions) and to senior editor Steve Catalano of Westview and Perseus Books for all his help with preparing this third edition. Finally, I am deeply indebted to the members of my family, in particular my mother, Mary Pavano DeFronzo, and to good friends in Connecticut, Indiana, Massachusetts, Florida, Texas, California, and New Zealand for their past inspiration and their encouragement in the fulfillment of this project.

James DeFronzo

Acronyms

AIDS	Acquired Immune Deficiency Syndrome
ALBA	Bolivarian Alternative for the Americas
ANC	African National Congress
ARDE	Democratic Revolutionary Alliance
ARVN	Army of the Republic of Vietnam
BBC	British Broadcasting Company
BCM	Black Consciousness Movement
CAFTA	Central American Free Trade Agreement
CDRs	Committees for the Defense of the Revolution
CDSs	Sandinista Defense Committees
CIA	Central Intelligence Agency
CNN	Cable News Network
COSATU	Congress of South African Trade Unions
COSEP	Superior Council of Private Enterprise
DR	Revolutionary Directorate
FDN	Nicaraguan Democratic Force
FSLN	Sandinista Front for National Liberation
FTAA	Free Trade Area of the Americas
GDP	Gross Domestic Product
GMD	Guomindang
GNP	Gross National Product
HAMAS	Islamic Resistance Movement
HAPCs	higher-stage agricultural producers' cooperatives
HIV	Human Immunodeficiency Virus
ICP	Indochinese Communist Party
IDF	Israeli Defense Force
IRC	Islamic Revolutionary Council
IRG	Islamic Revolutionary Guard
IRP	Islamic Republic Party
ISCOR	Iron and Steel Corporation
KLA	Kosovo Liberation Army
LAPCs	lower-stage agricultural producers' cooperatives

MAK	Services Office
MDN	Nicaraguan Democratic Movement
MIA	missing in action
MPLA	Popular Movement for the Liberation of Angola
MRS	Sandinista Renewal Movement
MSR	Socialist Revolutionary Movement
M-26-7	26th of July Movement
NACLA	North American Congress on Latin America
NATO	North Atlantic Treaty Organization
NLF	National Liberation Front
OAS	Organization of American States
OSS	Office of Strategic Services
PAC	Pan-Africanist Congress
PCD	Democratic Conservative Party
PLC	Liberal Constitutionalist Party
PLO	Palestine Liberation Organization
PRC	People's Republic of China
SACP	South African Communist Party
SADF	South African Defense Force
SAIC	South African Indian Congress
SAVAK	Organization of National Security and Intelligence
SCIRI	Supreme Council for Islamic Revolution in Iraq
SEZs	Special Economic Zones
SLA	South Lebanon Army
Soweto	South Western Townships
UAE	United Arab Emirates
UDF	United Democratic Front
UIR	Insurrectional Revolutionary Union
UN	United Nations
UNO	National Opposition Union
USSR	Union of Soviet Socialist Republics
VNQDD	Vietnamese Nationalist Party
ZANU	Zimbabwe African National Union

INTRODUCTION

The twentieth century was one of world revolution, characterized first by the Marxist-inspired revolution in Czarist Russia, then Fascist revolutions in Italy and Germany between the world wars, and later anti-imperialist nationalist revolutions in countries such as China, Vietnam, and Cuba. The Iranian Revolution resulted in the victory in 1979 of an Islamic fundamentalist movement, which, like several earlier major revolutions, significantly affected the course of world history. Later in the century, as Islamic fundamentalist movements grew strong in several nations, revolutions for democracy succeeded in Eastern Europe, Russia, and South Africa.

The beginning of the twenty-first century witnessed the devastating September 11, 2001, attacks on the United States and the U.S. overthrow of the extremist Islamic fundamentalist Taliban regime in Afghanistan in late 2001 as well as the March 2003 invasion and occupation of Iraq. During the same period, leftist revolutionary-oriented governments were elected in a number of Latin American nations. The age of revolution and revolutionary conflict continues in the twenty-first century. This book describes and analyzes the development of several major revolutions in an effort to discover their essential features—shared or unique, their individual contributions to revolutionary strategies and practice, and their interactions with and reciprocal effects on the larger world environment.

The revolutions in Russia and China, two of the world's largest and most populous countries, not only had tremendous impacts on their own populations but also affected how other nations and peoples would react to future revolutionary movements. Both the Russian and the Chinese cases constituted models of revolutionary strategy and alerted antirevolutionary ruling elites and governments throughout the world to the need to develop effective counterrevolutionary tactics. The Russian Revolution was the first that resulted in the achievement of state power by revolutionists who aimed to create a socialist society. They succeeded first in urban areas with the support of the nation's industrial working class. Their ideal goal was to reorganize the country into one in which the major resources and industries would be socially owned (that is, collectively owned by all the people) and that would guarantee its citizens equality of opportunity and the satisfaction of the basic needs for food, shelter, clothing, medical services, and education. What was to happen in Russia would serve for some revolutionaries as an inspiration but for others as the prime example of how a revolution could in many ways go wrong.

In particular many critics of the Russian Revolution viewed the installation of a one-party political system as a perversion of revolutionary ideals. The imposition of this form of government on several politically disorganized Eastern European countries at the end of World War II frustrated cherished aspirations both for national independence and for unfettered democracy. Thus a number of Eastern European nations were in a state of readiness for revolution from the moment Communist Party domination was established. The 1989 reversal of past Union of Soviet Socialist Republics (USSR) policy by Soviet leaders, who publicly proclaimed their willingness to allow political self-determination in Eastern Europe, rapidly set a half-dozen revolutionary transformations of governmental structures in motion and set the stage for the disintegration of the USSR itself.

The Chinese Revolution provided revolutionaries in less-developed countries with what appeared to be a model more relevant than the Russian Revolution to largely agrarian societies. Mao Zedong, who eventually emerged as the revolution's central leader, organized a movement based on rural rather than urban warfare. Through the promise of redistribution of land to poor peasants and, more generally, because Mao's revolutionaries directed effective resistance efforts against the 1937 Japanese invasion, Mao's movement attracted massive support.

The military victory of the Communist-led revolution in 1949 was followed in later years by several social movements in China, including the 1966–1968 Great Proletarian Cultural Revolution, which aimed mainly at bringing about a greater level of equality, and the more recent Democracy Movement, whose leaders intended to increase freedom of political expression and participation. The latter movement, although it received significant mass support and was not only tolerated but even encouraged by powerful countries, such as the United States, the USSR, and Japan, was vulnerable to at least temporary suppression.

The Vietnamese Revolution, apart from being a major movement in Asia for political and economic transformation, became a central cold war test case for U.S. opposition to Communist-led revolutions. The Vietnamese, whose homeland had often been attacked and even controlled by foreign powers, waged a mainly rural revolution and eventually adopted a strategy of placing the nationalist aim (of freeing Vietnam from foreign domination) foremost among revolutionary goals. In so doing, Vietnamese revolutionary leaders not only inspired the maximum possible number of people to work for the revolutionary struggle but also, once the foreign presence was eliminated, had an easier task in defeating domestic opponents of their goal of wealth redistribution.

The revolution in Vietnam, however, met with strong resistance from the French and later from the U.S. government, in great part because of the intense hostility between the Western nations on the one hand and the USSR and China on the other. In the context of the cold war it became difficult for U.S. government officials to tolerate the victory of Communist-led revolutions because those officials erroneously (especially in the case of Vietnam) regarded the revolutionaries as puppets or agents of the Soviet Union or China rather than as the organizers of independent and nationalistic movements. The tendencies of both the United States and the USSR to be intolerant of defiance from smaller countries during the cold war and to interfere in their internal political affairs explain why several revolutions in less-developed countries resulted, at least temporarily, in strongly anti-U.S. governments and why revolutions in Eastern Europe in 1989 and 1990 had, in most cases, a distinctly anti-Soviet dimension.

The Cuban, Nicaraguan, and Iranian revolutions were also, in part, reactions to foreign intervention. They illustrate how past interference by a powerful outside country can provide revolutionaries with the advantage of laying legitimate claim to protecting national interests. The Cuban Revolution had special significance as the first in the Western Hemisphere and Latin America resulting in a government committed to building a socialist society. Both the Cuban and the Nicaraguan revolutions, although twenty years apart, were directed against regimes notorious for subservience to foreign interests, internal corruption, greed, and the toleration of unjust economic conditions. The Nicaraguan Revolution, which, like the Cuban, resulted in a new government committed to a redistribution of wealth and expansion of basic services toward the poor, was markedly distinct from the Cuban case in regard to the organization of its postrevolutionary political system. Nicaraguan leaders formally pledged to develop and maintain a multiparty political democracy rather than implement a Leninist-style, one-party system. Although the sincerity of this commitment was often questioned by internal and external critics during the 1980s, United Nations (UN) and Organization of American States (OAS) observers certified Nicaragua's 1989–1990 national election campaign and vote as free and democratic.

The Iranian Revolution was one of the major events in the Middle East during the cold war period. As in the Cuban and Nicaraguan situations, revolutionaries in Iran, an oil-rich and relatively populous nation, rose up against a regime they viewed as a tool of foreign exploitation and a conduit of moral corruption. The anti-imperialist and moralist aspects of the Iranian Revolution, themes present to some extent in other revolutions, contributed to an exceptional outcome, the establishment of the religiously dominated Islamic Republic. As a consequence of this revolution, one of the largest and most powerful countries in the Middle East shifted rapidly from being a reliable ally and implementer of U.S. policies in the region to one whose new government viewed the United States, as well as the USSR, as a "Great Satan." The victory of Islamic fundamentalists in Iran against a U.S.-supported monarchy helped encourage Islamic resistance to the Soviet occupation of Afghanistan during the 1980s. The Soviet inability to defeat Islamic forces in Afghanistan is thought to have played a significant role in undermining the legitimacy of Communist Party rule and in contributing to the democratization of Russia and other Soviet republics and ultimately to the disintegration of the USSR at the end of 1991. And the successful Islamic struggle in Afghanistan also gave birth to Al Qaeda, which later repeatedly attacked the United States, including perpetrating the September 11, 2001, mass killings and destruction. In turn, the September 11 events prompted the United States to intensify its war on terrorism and to invade and occupy both Afghanistan and Iraq, where Al Qaeda played a role in resistance to the U.S. presence.

The final focal point of this volume is the revolutionary struggle to create a nonracial democracy in South Africa. That country's mineral wealth (gold, platinum, uranium, and so forth) and industrial infrastructure are important to the world and potentially critical for the future development of much of the African continent. The struggle against white minority rule led to the election in 1994 of the country's first nonwhite president to lead a transitional government of national unity, in the hope of carrying out a political, social, and economic revolution that is far from finished.

Although attempts were made in the past to formulate universal theories capable of explaining the development of revolutions and predicting their success or failure, such efforts have yielded disappointing results (Coleman 1995; Collins 1995; Foran 2005; 2006; Goldstone 1980; 1982; 1991; 1994; 2001a; 2001b; Goodwin 2001a; Greene 1990; Kiser 1995; Kuran 1995; McAdam, Tarrow, and Tilly 2001; Portes 1995; Selbin 1999; Skocpol 1979; Skocpol and Trimberger 1978; Smelser 1962; Sztompka 1993; Tilly 1978; 1995; Walton 1984; Wickham-Crowley 1992; Wolf 1969). Studies of individual revolutions, however, have identified several key factors that apparently must be simultaneously present for a revolution to succeed. The central flaws of the so-called universal, or general, theories of revolution include their inability to recognize the importance of all the empirically demonstrated factors essential to a revolution's success, their resulting inadequacy in predicting a revolution's development or outcome, and their lack of appreciation for important elements that may be unique to specific revolutions. The approach that I will use here is to explore first the significance of factors that appear necessary to the success of all revolutions. I will then analyze the development of a number of individual revolutionary conflicts, devoting special attention to the history and unique social characteristics generating the essential revolution-promoting factors. Embedded in the historical presentations at appropriate points are references to these factors; readers can anticipate the "Summary and Analysis" section of each chapter by being alert to these references and trying to relate the specific historical and social context to the general revolutionary factors at work. Finally, in the concluding chapter I will attempt to analyze the shortcomings of the general theories of revolution and to identify the reasons why they were inherently incapable of predicting the development of all the key revolution-promoting elements and, consequently, poorly equipped to predict the success of specific revolutions.

References and Further Readings

Brook, Daniel. 2005. *Modern Revolution: Social Change and Cultural Continuity in Czechoslovakia and China*. Lanham, MD: University Press of America.

Coleman, James S. 1995. "Comment on Kuran and Collins." *American Journal of Sociology* 100:1616–19.

Collins, Randall. 1995. "Prediction in Macrosociology: The Case of the Soviet Collapse." *American Journal of Sociology* 100:1552–93.

DeFronzo, James. 2006a. "Introduction." In DeFronzo, ed., *Revolutionary Movements in World History*, 1:xix–xxii.

_____, ed. 2006b. *Revolutionary Movements in World History: From 1750 to the Present*. 3 vols. Santa Barbara, CA: ABC-CLIO.

Foran, John. 2005. *Taking Power: On the Origins of Third World Revolutions*. Cambridge, UK: Cambridge University Press.

_____. 2006. "Theories of Revolution." In DeFronzo, ed., *Revolutionary Movements in World History*, 3:868–72.

Goldfrank, Walter L. 1994. "The Mexican Revolution." In Goldstone, ed., *Revolutions*.

Goldstone, Jack A. 1980. "Theories of Revolution: The Third Generation." *World Politics* 32 (3):425–53.

_____. 1982. "The Comparative and Historical Study Revolutions." *Annual Review of Sociology* 8:187–207.

_____. 1991. "An Analytical Framework." In *Revolutions of the Late Twentieth Century*, ed. Jack A. Goldstone, Ted R. Gurr, and Farrokh Moshiri. Boulder: Westview Press.

_____, ed. 1994. *Revolutions: Theoretical, Comparative, and Historical Studies*. 2nd ed. Fort Worth: Harcourt Brace College Publishers.

_____. 2001a. "Toward a Fourth Generation of Revolutionary Theory." *Annual Review of Political Science*, June, 4:139–87.

_____. 2001b. "An Analytical Framework." In Katz, ed., *Revolutions*, 9–29.

Goodwin, Jeff. 2001a. *No Other Way Out: States and Revolutionary Movements, 1945–1991*. Cambridge: Cambridge University Press.

_____. 2001b. "Is the Age of Revolution Over?" In Katz, ed., *Revolutions: International Dimensions*, 272–83.

Greene, Thomas H. 1990. *Comparative Revolutionary Movements*. Englewood Cliffs, NJ: Prentice-Hall.

Katz, Mark N., ed. 2001. *Revolutions: International Dimensions*. Washington, DC: Congressional Quarterly Press.

Kiser, Edgar. 1995. "What Can Sociological Theories Predict?" *American Journal of Sociology* 100:1611–15.

Kuran, Timer. 1995. "The Inevitability of Future Revolutionary Surprises." *American Journal of Sociology* 100:1528–51.

Lieven, Dominic. 1994. "Western Scholarship on the Rise and Fall of the Soviet Regime." *Journal of Contemporary History* 29:195–227.

McAdam, Doug, Sidney Tarrow, and Charles Tilly. 2001. *Dynamics of Contention.* Cambridge, UK: Cambridge University Press.

Portes, Alejandro. 1995. "On Grand Surprises and Modest Certainties." *American Journal of Sociology* 100:1620–26.

Selbin, Eric. 1999. *Modern Latin American Social Revolutions.* 2nd ed. Boulder: Westview Press.

_____. 2001. "Same As It Ever Was: The Future of Revolutions at the End of the Century." In Katz, ed., *Revolutions.*

Skocpol, Theda. 1979. *States and Social Revolutions: A Comparison of France, Russia, and China.* Cambridge, UK: Cambridge University Press.

Skopal, Theda, and Ellen Kay Trimberger. 1978. "Revolutions and the World Historical Development of Capitalism." *Berkeley Journal of Sociology* 22:101–13.

Smelser, Neil. 1962. *Theory of Collective Behavior.* New York: Free Press.

Sztompka, Piotr. 1993. *The Sociology of Social Change.* Cambridge, MA: Blackwell.

Tilly, Charles. 1978. *From Mobilization to Revolution.* Reading, MA: Addison-Wesley.

_____. 1995. "To Explain Political Process." *American Journal of Sociology* 100:1594–1610.

Walton, John. 1984. *Reluctant Rebels: Comparative Studies of Revolution and Underdevelopment.* New York: Columbia University Press.

Wicham-Crowley, Timothy P. 1992. *Guerillas and Revolution in Latin America: A Comparative Study of Insurgents and Regimes since 1956.* Princeton, NJ: Princeton University Press.

Wolf, Eric. 1969. *Peasant Wars of the Twentieth Century.* New York: Harper and Row.

1

SOCIAL MOVEMENTS AND REVOLUTIONS

A social movement can be defined as a persistent and organized effort on the part of a relatively large number of people either to bring about or to resist social change. Some examples of the many social movements in the history of the United States include the Antislavery movement, antiwar movements (such as the movements against U.S. involvement in the Vietnam conflict and the U.S. invasion of Iraq), the Antipoverty movement, the Civil Rights movement (the movement for equal treatment of minorities), and the Women's Rights movement. These liberal social movements advocated change from existing government policies or traditional patterns of behavior. Other social movements were organized to resist social change and reassert or restore particular traditional institutions, patterns of behavior, norms, or values. These conservative movements have included the Prayer in Public Schools movement, the Pro-life (Anti-abortion) movement, and the Antipornography movement.

Although classifying movements as either primarily change oriented/liberal or change resistant/conservative can be useful in conceptualizing the central goals of particular movements, it is important to understand that in reality few movements can fit perfectly into these categories. For example, although the Women's Rights movement can be viewed as change oriented in the sense of advocating a shift from patterns of male dominance toward greater equality of the genders in the economic and political spheres, it also has qualities that could be perceived as conservative. Among these are the movement's opposition to the sexual exploitation of women, an element of traditional religious morality. Similarly, the Antislavery movement of the nineteenth century and the Antipoverty and Civil Rights movements of the twentieth century, which were change oriented in the sense of fighting for greater equality for minorities, attacked economic and political oppression in part because of their detrimental impacts on family life and child rearing.

The goal of creating optimal economic and political conditions for the maintenance of strong family units and positive family emotional relations can be viewed as conservative: this type of family environment has been an ideal of traditional culture and morality.

Regardless of whether a movement is publicly perceived as predominantly change oriented or change resistant in terms of the direction of its goals, it can be further classified as either a reform or a revolutionary movement on the basis of the scope or magnitude of its goals. A **reform movement** attempts to change limited aspects of a society but does not aim at drastically altering or replacing major social, economic, or political institutions. For example, the Civil Rights movement of the 1960s did not call for changing the form of major U.S. institutions such as the economic system (capitalism) or the political system (representative two-party democracy). The movement instead advocated limited change: the opening up of existing institutions to full and equal participation by members of minority groups. Thus, the Civil Rights movement was a reform rather than a revolutionary movement. Similarly, the anti–Vietnam War movement was a reform movement because its goal involved change in government policy rather than in the structure of government itself or in any other major institution.

A **revolutionary movement**, in comparison, is a social movement in which participants are organized to alter drastically or replace totally existing social, economic, or political institutions. For example, the Communist-led Chinese Revolution transformed China's economy by giving ownership of the country's basic industries to the state rather than private individuals. Besides differing from reform movements regarding which aspects of society are targeted for change, revolutionary movements often use a wider range of means to accomplish change (from legal protest demonstrations to nonviolent civil disobedience to acts of violence). Although revolutionary social change (change in the structure of basic institutions) can be brought about through nonviolent means such as peaceful labor strikes or democratic elections, most revolutionary movements that have succeeded have usually been accompanied by some level of violence on the part of both movement participants and governments and groups opposing revolution (DeFronzo 2006a; 2006b; Greene 1990; Goldstone 1994; 1998; 2001a).

Such violence may be branded **terrorism** by the ruling power being threatened (Cohen 2006; Combs 2005; Howard and Sawyer 2002), but terrorism—the use of force to intimidate for political purposes—is often in the eye of the beholder, and one person's terrorist can be another person's freedom fighter. Forms of revolutionary violence include **people's war** (Giap 1962; Mao [1938] 1965; Mackerras and Knight 1985; Wolf 1969)—characterized by widespread support for the goals of the revolution, so that the established government is fighting an entire people—and **guerrilla warfare** (Guevara 1985; Mao [1938] 1965; Wickham-Crowley 1992; 2006; White 1984)—a form of mobile warfare involving small units of combatants operating even behind enemy lines. Forms of antirevolutionary violence may be generally described as **counterinsurgency techniques** (Calvert 1984; White 1984) and range from arrests and temporary detention to extremes such as the death squads in El Salvador and Guatemala in the 1980s (Binford 2006; Montgomery 1982; Streeter 2000; 2006; White 1984). In several instances since the mid-twentieth century, antirevolutionary forces have, in fact, overturned electoral systems, for example, in Cuba in 1952 (Gott 2004; Szulc 1986), Guatemala in 1954 (Gleijeses 1991; Schlesinger and Kinzer 1982; Streeter 2000; 2006), and Chile in 1973 (Sigmund 2006; Valenzuela 1978), in order to prevent sweeping institutional change or even progressive reforms from being carried out through democratic means.

Sociologists and other social scientists have often attempted to classify revolutions into one of two "ideal types": leftist or rightist. A **left-wing revolution** is one in which the central goal is widely perceived to be to change major social and political institutions in order to alter the dominant economic, social, or political relationships within a society (Greene 1990). Usually involved is a redistribution of valuable resources between the rich and the poor, with more equal access to educational opportunities, medical services, higher wage levels, or, in the case of a predominantly agricultural society, land, a stated goal. A **right-wing revolution** is one in which the primary aim is the restoration of traditional institutions. Right-wing revolutionary movements also generally emphasize the goals of maintaining social order and traditional authority over the goal of achieving greater social equality through institutional change.

Just as social movements in general are difficult to categorize as either totally liberal or totally conservative, many revolutions include both leftist and rightist characteristics. For example, the leaders of a revolutionary movement aimed at achieving greater social equality through radical transformations of a society's economic and political systems (leftist characteristics) might attempt to appeal for mass support by arguing that the redistribution of wealth they propose would help reinforce traditional morality (a rightist element) by eliminating extreme poverty as a cause of social evils, such as prostitution, drug abuse, and predatory crime. A number of revolutions, however, can be placed into one of the two categories on the basis of changes they brought about. Of the revolutions covered in this book, the first Russian and the Chinese, Vietnamese, and Cuban have been widely interpreted as primarily leftist. On the basis of the dominant ideological orientations and policies of the revolutionary leaderships of the two nations that experienced revolutions in 1979, the Iranian Revolution can be classified as a predominantly right-wing revolution and the Nicaraguan as mainly leftist. The South African struggle for revolutionary change was oriented toward achieving greater equality by dismantling the nation's system of white racial domination and by greatly expanding political rights and roles for nonwhite South Africans and can—at least in that sense—be categorized as leftist. The post–Iranian Revolution Islamic movements appeared primarily rightist in terms of their cultural goals, although their economic policies seemed somewhat leftist.

REVOLUTIONARY MOVEMENTS: CRITICAL FACTORS

The factors that can influence the development of revolutionary movements include the extent of inequality and impoverishment within a society's population, degree to which the population is divided along ethnic lines, perception of corruption of governmental officials, level of armament and degree of loyalty of a government's military forces, cultural traditions of violence or nonviolence as means of protesting perceived social injustice, physical size of a country and nature of its terrain, and proximity and level of involvement of other countries that either support or oppose the development and success of a revolutionary movement. But of all possible factors, five stand out as critical and if occurring simultaneously, appear to come close to constituting necessary and sufficient conditions for the success of a revolutionary movement, according to the appraisals of leading academic scholars on the phenomenon of revolution (Foran 2005; 2006; Goldfrank 1986; Goldstone 1994; 2001a; Greene 1990). The order of development and relative importance of these elements differ from one revolution to another.

1. Mass frustration resulting in popular uprisings among urban or rural populations: A large proportion of a society's population becomes extremely discontented, which leads to mass-participation protests and rebellions against state authority. In technologically backward agricultural societies, the occurrence of rural (peasant) rebellion or at least rural support for revolution has often been essential (Foran 2005; 2006; Goldfrank 1986; Goldstone 1991; 1994; 2001a; Greene 1990).
2. Dissident elite political movements: Divisions among elites (groups that have access to wealth or power of various types or are highly educated and possess important technical or managerial skills) pit some elite members against the existing government (Foran 2005; 2006; Goldfrank 1986; Goldstone 1991; 1994; 2001a; Greene 1990).
3. Unifying motivations: The existence of powerful motivations for revolution that cut across major classes and unify the majority of a society's population behind the goal of revolution (Foran 2005, 2006; Goldstone 1994; 2001a; Greene 1990).
4. A severe political crisis paralyzing the administrative and coercive capabilities of the state: A state crisis occurs in the nation experiencing or about to experience the development of a revolutionary movement. The crisis, which may be caused by a catastrophic defeat in war, a natural disaster, an economic depression, or the withdrawal of critical economic or military support from other nations, or by any combination of these factors, may deplete the state of loyal personnel, legitimacy in the eyes of the public, and other resources. The state then becomes incapable of carrying out its normal functions and cannot cope effectively with an opposition revolutionary movement (Foran 2005; 2006; Goldfrank 1986; Goldstone 1991; 1994; 2001a; Greene 1990).

5. A permissive or tolerant world context: The governments of other nations do not intervene effectively to prevent a revolutionary movement from developing and succeeding in a given nation (Foran 2005; 2006; Goldfrank 1994; Goldstone 2001a).

Mass Frustration and Popular Uprisings

Revolution has been described as involving a tremendous increase in mass participation in political activity, participation motivated by widespread opposition to existing conditions. Such popular discontent can result from the development of a gap between people's expectations (regarding the lifestyle they feel they should be able to achieve) and their ability to satisfy those expectations. Social scientists have referred to this phenomenon as **relative deprivation** (Fullerton 2006; Gurr 1970; Greene 1990).

There are several historical processes that can lead to relative deprivation. Among them is rapid deterioration in material living conditions, which may occur for the whole population of a country during an economic depression or for only some population groups during periods of transition in the economic system. A wide breach opens between the way people expect they should be able to live and their capabilities of meeting those expectations— not because of a change in expectations, but because of a decline in capabilities of attaining them. This type of relative deprivation may also result when one country is invaded and conquered by another. The victor nation may exploit the resources and labor power of the defeated people, and a drastic decline in the standard of living ensues. People in the defeated nation may try to resist occupation forces with violence. During World War II many of the peoples whose nations were invaded by Nazi German or Japanese forces organized resistance groups, which, in some instances, grew into revolutionary movements; the latter not only helped expel the invaders but also brought about drastic changes in social, economic, and political institutions after the war.

Another process that can result in the growth of a gap between people's expectations and capabilities involves an increase in expectations rather than a change in capabilities. Expectations are essentially a function of people's beliefs about what is possible and about what is "right." Experiences that alter these conceptions can strongly influence people's expectations. One such experience is communication with people from other societies where the level of material existence is higher or where a past revolution has resulted in a redistribution of wealth. Contact with other societies or with fellow citizens who have themselves been exposed to other ways of life can lead people to believe that improvements are possible. Communication with foreigners can also influence what people consider to be morally acceptable.

A shift in a people's conception of what is morally right, however, can perhaps most easily be brought about if the message is communicated by recognizable moral authorities. The upsurge in revolutionary movements in parts of Latin America during the 1970s and 1980s came about precisely because of the role religious leaders played in changing the conceptions of millions of poor farmers and workers about the moral acceptability of existing social conditions. Many young men and women of the clergy and religious orders began to embrace the idea of an expanded role for the Church in the lives of the poor. Rather than simply to cater to spiritual needs through administering the sacraments and saying Mass, they came to feel it was their religious duty to work for social justice and a redistribution of wealth. This application of Christian values has been called **"liberation theology"** (White 1984; Berryman 1985; 1987). As these ideas were widely communicated, more and more of the poor came to see the poverty and misery they endured as being not God's will but rather the will of some individuals and the result of the systems these people defended. The extreme inequalities that characterized their societies were now considered wrong, even sinful. Peasants and workers began to desire, demand, and expect change. A situation of mass frustration had been created.

Still a third process has evidently operated historically to generate mass discontent. Davies (1962) found that for each of several major revolutions he analyzed, the period of revolutionary upheaval was preceded by several years of economic improvement. The associated rise in material living conditions was likely to have generated an increase in people's expectations because they actually experienced improvements. After the interval of prosperity there was a sudden decline in living conditions, caused by factors such as war or natural or economic catastrophes, which resulted in a wide gap between expectations and capabilities and, consequently, a major increase in mass frustration and support for revolutionary movements.

Dissident Elite Political Movements

Many who have explored the processes involved in the development of revolutionary movements (Goldfrank 1986; Goldstone 1994; 2001a; Gurr 1970; Selbin 2006; Skocpol 1979; Trimberger 1978) have argued that divisions among the elites within a society can increase the probability of the success of a revolutionary movement in a number of ways. First, conflict among elite members, if nothing else, contributes to confusion and disorganization in efforts to suppress a revolutionary movement. Second, if some elite members feel threatened by the actions of other elite members who control their society's government and if these alienated elite members possess important resources required by the state, a decision on their part to withhold or withdraw support from the state can render it too weak and ineffective to cope with revolutionary forces. And finally, some members of the nation's elite families may directly participate in a revolution by providing leadership or other resources to help transform popular discontent and uprisings into an organized and purposeful revolutionary movement. In this capacity, elites usually play a role in formulating an **ideology** for the revolutionary movement: an indictment and criticism of the existing power structure, a set of justifications for the necessity of resorting to a revolutionary movement to bring about social change, and a long-range plan and strategy of action (Greene 1990).

Ideologies may range along a spectrum from those informed by **socialism**—the public ownership of land and capital administered for the community good—to **capitalism**—the private ownership of resources to produce commodities for profit and reinvestment. Ideologies often couple economic aims with powerful unifying goals, such as nationalist resistance to foreign domination or reaffirmation of traditional moral or religious principles, capable of facilitating alliances among a society's major social classes. The primary function of revolutionary ideology is to provide as many people as possible with the same or at least compatible viewpoints on the need to change society so that they will be motivated to cooperate in the revolutionary struggle.

Social theorists and researchers have hypothesized several ways through which elite conflict can develop. Marx and Engels ([1848] 1972; Engels [1880] 1972) argued that technological and economic changes result in one type of economic activity (for example, the manufacture and sale of industrial products) replacing another (such as farming and the sale of agricultural products) as the major source of wealth in a society. The elites involved in the newly dominant economic activity struggle for and eventually win control of the political system from elites representing the previously dominant economic activity. Goldstone (1994), Skocpol and Trimberger (1978), and others, in describing another process for the development of elite conflict, have argued that as a technologically and economically inferior state attempts to compete with more-advanced states, reforms are enacted by some members of its national elite. These reforms are perceived by other elite members to threaten their interests and privileges. Intra-elite conflict and elite opposition to government policies can result.

Huntington (1968), in addition, suggested that as technologically backward societies begin to modernize by expanding educational systems and introducing technologies and learning from the more-advanced countries, they tend to create new, educated, and politically conscious elites that demand participation in government. When traditional elites, such as the case of the royal family and much of the nobility in czarist Russia, resist democratization of the political system, some members of the new elites come to favor revolution. Eisenstadt (1978) further observed that "economic downturns" or other disasters can cause elite conflict in societies with dictatorships based on a patronage system of personal rewards to elite members. When the benefits stop coming or are threatened by a particular dictator's continuation in power, the loyalty of elite members to the regime is greatly reduced. In other situations, some elites may simply feel threatened by the economic and political power of a dictatorship and turn against it. Both these factors applied to a degree in causing the defection of some of Nicaragua's economic elite from support for the Somoza dictatorship (Booth 1985; Walker 1986).

The direct participation of elite elements in the leadership and organizational structure of the dissident political movement has been historically critical for the successful development of a leftist revolutionary movement (Greene 1990; Gurr 1970). Such individuals, representing in some cases only a small minority of elite members, may bring crucial organizational and intellectual skills to a movement. According to Greene (1990), Gill (2006), and myself (DeFronzo 1970), many of the young people from elite families who directly participate in left-wing revolutionary movements appear to have experienced a moral alienation from their society's economic and political systems, often developed or enhanced while attending their nation's colleges and universities. They turn against the very economic and political institutions from which their families have so greatly benefited and reach the conclusion that for some people to live in affluence while the majority of fellow citizens live in abject poverty is unconscionable.

If revolutionaries of upper- and middle-class origin live at a time when there is little or no political discontent among the majority of their society's population, many of them may perish in violent but futile attacks on the armed forces of the government they oppose. But if they live in an era when their frustrations coincide with the aroused discontent of the poor, they may not only participate but also play vital roles in revolutionary movements that have widespread support and, consequently, the potential for victory. There are many examples of revolutionary leaders from relatively privileged families who emerged to lead leftist revolutions that proceeded to dispossess the very classes from which the leaders originated. For example, the Russian revolutionary V. I. Lenin, the Chinese revolutionary Mao Zedong, and the Cuban revolutionary Fidel Castro all came from well-to-do backgrounds.

Unifying Motivations for Revolution

Greene (1990), in his review of various revolutionary movements throughout history, noted that it is extremely rare for a revolution to succeed without the backing of substantial numbers from most major social classes in a society. In other words, for a revolution to triumph, several classes must join forces; thus there must be a shared motivation for revolution that cuts across class lines and possibly additional differing but simultaneous and at least temporarily compatible motivations. Although the concept of redistributing wealth in favor of the poor, often manifested in some form of socialist ideology, has motivated many of the leaders of leftist revolutions, the effective mass appeal of such a goal is usually limited in great part to the members of a society's lower classes. Only a minority of the more affluent classes are likely to rally in support of a revolution intended solely to benefit the poor.

Broad cross-class participation in revolutionary movements has generally been the product of **nationalism** (Chirot 1986; Greene 1990) or of the development of widespread hatred toward a particular dictatorship (Greene 1990). Regardless of class or ideological orientation, people sharing the same language and culture who perceive that their ethnic or national group has been the victim of exploitation by another group or country can join together in an effort to end their domination (Adleman 2006; Braveboy-Wagner 1985; Breuilly 1982; Sathyamurthy 1983; Smith 1983).

Nationalism as a motivating factor that unifies diverse social classes behind the goal of revolution is most likely to emerge in reaction to direct colonial rule or indirect colonial domination through a local regime perceived to be operating on behalf of foreign rather than national interests. The controlling alien power is called "**imperialistic**" because of specific political actions (gaining control over a society and its resources), economic transactions (shaping and developing the society's economy on behalf of the colonizing power), and cultural transformations (inculcating the society with outside religious, educational, linguistic, and aesthetic values based on the foreign culture).

Sometimes the effects of colonization are so thoroughgoing that the overtaken society ends up with a native ruling class not only culturally similar to the imperialist power but also politically loyal to it and economically dependent on it. **Neocolonialism** is the continuing state of political and cultural dependency and economic exploitation present in a former colony even after formal political independence has been declared (Calvert 1984; Cavatorta 2006; Chirot 1986).

Revolutionary movements organized with the stated goal of overthrowing either direct colonial rule or neocolonial governments have been called **national liberation movements** (Calvert 1984; Miller and Aya 1971). Five countries' revolutions covered in this book sprang in great part from such anti-imperialist impulses to national liberation: China, Vietnam, Cuba, and Nicaragua—all organized mainly around socialist goals—and Iran, organized primarily around religious goals.

Beyond nationalism and national liberation, abhorrence of an especially unjust and brutal or incompetent regime can bring several classes together in a movement to oust the detested government. The czar's dictatorial rule coupled with his personal arrogance, incompetence, and disregard for human life in conducting Russia's disastrous war effort eventually brought about a near-universal demand for his abdication and an end to the autocratic monarchy system. Similarly, multiclass aversion to the Batista government in Cuba and Somoza family rule in Nicaragua developed not only because of the widespread belief that these regimes allowed foreign interests to exploit their countries' peoples and resources but also because of the perception of crimes and acts of brutality committed by these dictatorships.

Severe State Crisis

A revolutionary movement may come into being and yet have no reasonable chance for success so long as the government maintains strong administrative capabilities and armed forces to coerce the submission of the dissident elements within its population. But conditions and events, often beyond the control of either government or revolutionary forces, may act to destroy the capabilities of the state to function effectively and permit revolutionary elements to overcome its repressive powers (Goldstone 2001a). Dunn (1972) argued that several successful revolutionary movements of the twentieth century were in part due to state crises caused by either war or the process of decolonization. Economic and military mobilization for war can strain a society's resources, and if the war effort is unsuccessful, the perceived futile loss of life and national wealth can destroy the legitimacy and respect previously bestowed on the government by its population. The shattering defeats suffered by the czar's army during World War I helped generate the state crisis that gave revolutionaries in Russia an opportunity to seize power.

Decolonization involves the withdrawal of one country's official administrative personnel and military forces from another country (the former colony). The resulting postcolonial government may include individuals who previously served the occupying country. Thus, during the period immediately following decolonization, the government of a former colony may be perceived by many of its citizens to be really a mechanism through which the past occupying country continues to control their nation's economy and resources. A postcolonial or neocolonial government may, consequently, lack the support of its own people and perhaps even the loyalty of its armed forces. If this is the case, a postcolonial state can collapse in the face of a revolutionary movement that the population perceives to represent its true national interests.

State collapse may also result from the efforts of economically less-developed states to compete more effectively with more-advanced states in the world economic system or to cope with pressure on food supplies or other resources caused by significant population increase (Goldstone 1994; Skocpol 1979). As a government attempts to achieve these goals through various modernizing reforms (such as an expansion of the educational system, recruitment of administrators and business and military leaders on the basis of talent and achievement rather than on the basis of nobility or some other traditional factor, distribution of land from large estates to the rural poor, and the imposition of higher taxes on the upper classes), some groups may resist, feeling the new policies threaten their wealth, power, or other privileges, even to the point of withdrawing support from the national government. The state may then be so weakened as to provide revolutionary forces with an opportunity to develop and achieve an unstoppable momentum. For example, Chinese rulers who attempted to modernize their country in the late nineteenth century were frustrated by wealthy landowners and other conservative forces who prevented sufficient reforms, weakened the power of the central government, and presented revolutionary forces with a divided, conflict-ridden, and consequently more vulnerable national leadership (Skocpol 1979).

Another type of state structure that is especially fragile is the "neopatrimonial regime" (Eisenstadt 1978). (This concept is similar to what Foran referred to as a "repressive, exclusionary, personalist state" [2005, 20].) Such a government is structured around a particular individual whose rule is based on his or her control of resources that are dispensed as rewards to supporters (such as governmental administrative positions, high-profit business monopolies, high salaries and bonuses to military leaders). Important government supporters in such a society tend to be personally loyal to the particular leader and that leader's system, which rewards them. Such a state is especially vulnerable to several types of problems: economic depression, which reduces the resources available to the chief executive to parcel out to his or her supporters; defeat in war, which can create economic difficulties and also tarnish the reputation of the nation's leader; and events such as illness, accidents, or assassinations, which remove a particular leader from power and thus endanger or destroy the state-supporting patronage system.

Permissive World Context

Because any society exists in a world populated by other societies, some of which may have greater or at least nearly equal military and economic power, a revolutionary movement in one nation that appears to be overcoming the national government might be suppressed, at least temporarily, by other nations opposed to the success of the revolution (Goldfrank 1986). Foran (2005; 2006) and Goldstone (2001a) also recognized the importance of this factor. The U.S. involvements in Vietnam and in El Salvador are examples of foreign intervention in domestic revolutionary situations. Similarly, the USSR intervened in the past in Hungary, Czechoslovakia, and Afghanistan to prevent the success or retard the growth of movements it opposed. Another significant intervention was the sending of military forces by several nations, including Britain, the United States, and Japan, into the Soviet Union in an effort to help White Russian forces overturn the Bolshevik Revolution during the Russian Civil War.

In some situations, outside nations have not intervened to prevent revolutions or have not intervened to the extent necessary to defeat a revolutionary movement. In these cases one of the factors contributing to the victory of a revolutionary movement was, then, a "permissive world context." Reasons for less-than-wholehearted or for no intervention have included: fear of disapproval, economic sanctions, or even military attack from nations that support a given revolutionary movement; concern about provoking a hostile

18 *Revolutions and Revolutionary Movements*

reaction from the potential interventionist country's own citizens; displeasure with the government a revolutionary movement seeks to overthrow; or the fact that despite strong motivation to intervene, recent economic or military hardships or internal political turmoil may have so physically or psychologically exhausted a nation that it is simply unable to intervene effectively.

Several examples of unsuccessful or nonexistent intervention by outside powers against revolutionary movements illustrate the concept of permissive world context. Following World War I, the European capitalist nations and the United States probably were too battered by the years of conflict to mount a large-scale assault on revolutionary Russia, especially given the huge population and vast territory of the country and the level of popular support the revolution enjoyed. During the Cuban Revolution of 1956–1958 and the Nicaraguan and Iranian revolutions of 1978–1979, no nations sent military forces to save the internationally despised regimes of Batista, Somoza, and the shah of Iran. And despite the massive level of intervention in Vietnam and other parts of Southeast Asia during 1963–1973, the United States might have used even greater military power were it not for the development of significant domestic opposition to the Vietnam involvement and the threat of possible direct military confrontation with the USSR or China over Vietnam. Finally, the USSR's 1989 renunciation of the right to intervene in Eastern Europe permitted the swift success of political revolutions in Poland, Hungary, East Germany, Czechoslovakia, Bulgaria, and Romania.

REVOLUTIONS THAT FAILED

The significance of the five critical factors for the success of revolutions can be further illustrated by reference to revolutionary movements that failed to accomplish their goals for sweeping social change. Although they are not inclusive of all the unsuccessful revolutionary situations of the twentieth and twenty-first centuries, the examples presented in Table 1.1 represent most of the important cases for which extensive scholarly analyses are available. In the table the presence of each key factor is indicated by a plus sign, and its absence during the relevant historical period is signified by a minus sign. Even though some students of revolution might question my decision to assign a plus or a minus in one or more individual circumstances, it seems clear that in none of these cases were all of the five key factors present simultaneously. The table refers to the revolutionary movement in South Africa only during the period 1912–1989 and the modern El Salvadoran movement only during the years 1972–1991. Both of these movements, especially South Africa's, achieved at least limited success in the 1990s. Besides South Africa, at least four other revolutions that failed or did not achieve success within the time periods specified—the attempted Russian

TABLE 1.1   Revolutionary Movements That Did Not Succeed During the Time
Periods Specified

	Mass Discontent	Elite Dissent	Unifying Motive	State Crisis	World Permissiveness
Russia 1905	+	+	−	−	−
Zionist 1897–1939	+	+	+	−	−
South Africa 1912–1989	+	+	+	−	−
El Salvador 1932; 1972–1991	+	+	−	−	−
Palestinian 1936–1989	+	+	+	−	−
Guatemala 1944–1954	+	+	+	−	−
Philippines 1946–1956	+	+	−	−	−
Greece 1947–1949	+	+	−	−	−
Hungary 1956	+	+	+	+	−
Czechoslavakia 1968	+	+	+	+	−
Chile 1970–1973	+	+	−	−	−
Poland 1980–1981	+	+	+	−	−

Note: A plus sign means that the factor was judged to have been present during the relevant time period, and a minus sign means that the factor was judged to be absent.

Revolution of 1905 and those of Guatemala (1944–1954), Chile (1970–1973), and Poland (1980–1981)—are dealt with to some extent in later chapters.

Brief accounts of three of the other unsuccessful revolutions, Greece (1947–1949), Hungary (1956), and El Salvador (1932; 1972–1991), may be useful in illustrating the debilitating effect on the progress of revolutionary movements of the absence of one or more of the critical factors.

During World War II, the Greek Communist party and other leftist groups organized the largest and most effective resistance against German Nazi occupation forces and against the Greek politicians and military and police units that collaborated with the Nazis. By 1945, the Communist-led forces controlled much of the countryside and many of the smaller towns and cities. But toward the end of the war, the British, fearing the possibility of the establishment of a leftist government in a nation long considered to be in Great Britain's sphere of interest, turned the reins of power over to conservative Greek political and military leaders, despite the fact that many of them had collaborated with the Nazis (Alexander 1981; Baerentzen and

Close 1993; Close and Veremis 1993; Hondros 1981; Papastratis 1987; Richter 1981; 1986).

Following a number of politically motivated murders and violent skirmishes involving all sides, full-scale civil war broke out in 1947. The revolutionary forces enjoyed some significant popular support, but they also suffered from crucial problems. The most central of these was the lack of a permissive world context in that first Great Britain and then the United States chose, in the context of the developing cold war, to intervene with massive military and economic assistance to aid the conservative-led Greek army in countering Communist-led rebels. The revolutionary forces received much more limited, though significant, assistance, primarily from the newly organized Communist-led government of Yugoslavia.

Since the British refused to remove the large majority of collaborationist military and police but instead incorporated them into the postwar conservative Greek state—which Britain and later the United States supported—the antirevolutionary government did not experience a severe state crisis.

Finally, the revolutionary forces never achieved a stable unifying motivation capable of uniting the majority of Greece's population behind its leadership. This failure was in part due to the intervention of the British. Revolutionary forces were unable to capitalize on their wartime victories as resistance fighters through free elections. British-supported conservatives used repressive measures in the large cities and in areas of the countryside under their control to preclude the establishment of a democratic political system. This policy helped provoke the former resistance fighters to revolt and even to acts of terrorism, which alienated much potential popular support. Furthermore, the revolutionary forces lost much of their nationalist support, which they had enjoyed when fighting the German, Italian, and Bulgarian Axis occupiers, by agreeing to cede significant, largely Slavic-inhabited parts of Greece to Yugoslavia in return for desperately needed military supplies. Divisions within the Greek Communist party that mirrored the split between the USSR and Yugoslavia in 1948–1949 and the subsequent Yugoslav reduction of aid, coupled with crushing military defeats in 1949, resulted in the rout of the rebels and the flight of the survivors to neighboring countries (Close and Veremis 1993; Iatrides 1993; Kalyvas 2006; Smith 1993).

The development of the ill-fated Hungarian Revolution of 1956 followed a different path. Majorities of voters in the 1945 and 1947 parliamentary elections supported a four-party liberal-leftwing coalition, which included the country's Communist party. With the start of the cold war, the pro-Moscow Stalinist faction of the Hungarian Communist party not only seized control of the party but also took over the governing coalition and in effect established a one-party political system. But the death of Stalin in 1953 and the subsequent condemnation of Stalin's crimes of repression in February 1956 by the new leaders in the USSR undermined Hungary's authoritarian pro-

Stalinist regime. A more independent, nationalistic faction gained significant influence in the Hungarian Communist party and government in 1956, a process that also occurred in Poland. Students and citizen groups in both countries demonstrated in favor of more democratic political systems and greater independence from the USSR (Berecz 1986; Byrne 2006; Hoensch 1988; Lomax 1976).

When the newly ascendant, nationalist-oriented leadership of the Polish Communist party began to assert in limited but significant ways its independence from Moscow, thousands of Hungarians held rallies in support of the defiant Poles. After the Soviets accommodated the new Polish government rather than intervening militarily, some nationalist-minded Hungarian Communist Party leaders, including the country's prime minister, declared support for switching to a genuinely democratic multiparty political system and for withdrawing Hungary from its military alliance with the Soviet Union, measures far beyond the concessions the Poles had recently won. The Soviet leaders, whose country had been devastated during World War II by the Nazi-led Axis invasion (in which more than 200,000 Hungarian troops participated) and having witnessed earlier in 1956 the willingness of Britain and France to invade Egypt to protect their perceived interests, decided to intervene militarily in Hungary in order to assist the more hard-line faction of the Hungarian Communist Party in regaining control of the country. Despite massive popular support for revolution, the existence of prorevolution elite elements, the unifying motivation of Hungarian nationalism, and the near collapse of the antirevolutionary state and its armed forces, the lack of a permissive world environment forestalled political revolution in Hungary until 1989.

Much earlier in the twentieth century, El Salvador was characterized by extreme economic inequalities and cultural divisions between the Latinized residents and the other half of the population, which followed the traditional indigenous culture and worked primarily in rural areas, typically for plantation owners engaged in export agriculture. During the 1920s, while the wealthy minority in El Salvador prospered as a result of the relatively high prices on the world market for the country's agricultural exports, leftist intellectuals and labor activists were able to organize socialist-oriented political movements and unions in some towns and among rural workers in the western half of the country. Following a collapse in coffee prices as a consequence of the worldwide depression and increased popular discontent, military leaders, who had long served the interests of the rich, overthrew the country's elected, reform-oriented president in 1931 and prepared to crush the workers' groups and leftist political parties.

An alliance of leaders from the rural and urban unions and some enlisted army soldiers organized an uprising intended to overcome the military leaders and accomplish a socioeconomic revolution. Because of the exposure of the rebels' plans, cultural divisions among the poor majority (which the revolutionary ideology had far from completely overcome), and, most important, the near total monopoly of firearms by the armed forces, the 1932 revolutionary effort lacked a sufficiently unifying motive and confronted a relatively strong state and military. Additionally, the revolutionaries did not enjoy a permissive world environment, although significant foreign intervention was not necessary to defeat the uprising. After they had smashed the revolt through the execution of 10,000 to 30,000 people, a succession of military leaders ruled the country through repression and electoral fraud without effective opposition until the late 1970s (Anderson 1971; Binford 2006; Cockcroft 1989; Montgomery 1982; White [1973] 1982).

Mounting discontent and outrages over rigged elections led to a new leftist revolt, this time accompanied by the development of an effective revolutionary army capable of carrying out sustained combat operations against the El Salvadoran armed forces. Whereas the modern revolution never achieved a unifying motive capable of uniting the majority of the population under its leadership, the most significant barrier to the success of the revolution was a nonpermissive world environment, manifested in the Reagan administration's massive and almost unconditional military and economic support for the antirevolutionary regime. American intervention in El Salvador, coupled with the strength of the revolutionary forces, resulted in a long, brutal civil war during the years 1980–1991. With the end of the cold war and a major reduction of U.S. military assistance, the stalemated El Salvador civil war ended in a negotiated settlement in which only some of the revolutionaries' original aims were satisfied (Binford 2006; Vilas 1995).

THEORIES OF REVOLUTION

Because the five factors—mass frustration, elite dissidence, unifying motivation, state crisis, and permissive world context—appear crucial to the success of revolutionary movements, it is important to evaluate existing theories of revolution in terms of their abilities or inabilities to account for the simultaneous occurrence of these conditions.

Research related to attempts to formulate theories of revolution include the efforts of Edwards ([1927] 1970), Brinton ([1938] 1952), and Pettee (1938) to identify what Goldstone (1982) and Foran (2006) described as a natural history of revolutions: a description of the phases through which a successful revolution almost invariably progresses. These include certain developments in sequence such as

1. a society's intellectuals, most of whom in the past normally supported the existing regime, turn against it;
2. the old regime tries to save itself from revolution by attempting reforms that ultimately fail to protect the old order;

3. the revolutionary alliance that eventually takes power from the old government is soon characterized by internal conflicts;
4. at first the postrevolutionary government is moderate;
5. disappointment with the failure of moderate revolutionaries to fulfill expectations leads to more radical revolutionaries gaining control;
6. the radicals take more extreme actions to fulfill revolutionary aims, including the use of coercive methods against those whom they perceive resist or threaten the fulfillment of revolutionary goals;
7. eventually more pragmatic moderate revolutionaries replace the radicals.

While the discovery of relatively invariant sequences of broad types of events during revolutions is interesting and important, the description of such a chronological sequence is not itself a theory but rather only a description of what must be explained by a theory of revolution. Similarly, the five factors described earlier, which seem both necessary and sufficient for the occurrence and success of a revolution, do not in themselves constitute a complete theory of revolution; instead, they represent factors whose development or presence must be explained by a theory. Greene (1990), in his review of theories of revolution and of studies on participants, ideologies, organizational structures, tactics, and settings for numerous revolutions, identified several major theoretical perspectives, including the Marxist, frustration-aggression, systems, and modernization approaches.

Marxist theory is both too complex to cover here in its entirety and too important to gloss over. Elements of Marxism will be presented here and in several of the following chapters, but for solid overviews, see Robert Tucker's edition of *The Marx-Engels Reader* (1972) and Richard Schmitt's *Introduction to Marx and Engels* (1987). According to Marxist theory, revolution is likely to occur at a point when existing social and political structures and leadership interfere with economic development. Karl Marx traced such economic development through various stages from feudalism to capitalism to socialism and eventually to communism. As technological and economic change takes place during the period of capitalist industrialization, a conflict develops between the new urban industrial working class—**the proletariat**—and the ruling capitalist class. According to Marx, the importance of labor, such as the operating of manufacturing technology, would inevitably supersede that of the ownership of capital (wealth in the form of money, resources, investments, or the physical means of production) in the industrialized economic system. When the government-controlling capitalist class attempts to maintain its grip on power, the working class is driven by frustration and exploitation to revolution. What Marx posited as "the dictatorship of the proletariat" ensues, with the working class taking over governmental power. Many varieties of Marxist theory have developed over the years, but common to all has been the presumption of the need for revolution at certain critical stages in economic history.

According to Foran (2005; 2006) and Goldstone (2001a), during the 1960s attempts to formulate explanations of revolution resulted in two additional types of theories. One of these, which Greene (1990) called the **frustration-aggression theory** of revolution, focused on the development of mass frustration as a cause of mass mobilization for revolution. The frustration-aggression type theory included the relative deprivation theories of popular discontent described by Davies (1962) and Gurr (1970), which were discussed earlier in this chapter (see section "Mass Frustration and Popular Uprisings"). The other type of theory put forth during this period was the **structural functionalist** approach to explaining revolution, exemplified by the work of Smelser (1962) and Johnson (1964), which Greene (1990) referred to as the systems theory of revolution.

Systems theory of revolution, unlike Marxist theory, does not view revolution primarily in terms of progressive historical changes in technology and forms of economic organization. Systems is a more general perspective that assumes that revolution is likely to occur when prerevolutionary social structures fail to perform essential functions, no matter what the cause of such failure might be. Essential functions include not only the carrying out of necessary economic and administrative tasks but also the socialization of society's members to a culture (set of beliefs and attitudes) supportive of existing social structures.

A fourth approach, **modernization theory**, is similar to Marxist theory in that it associates revolution with technological and economic change. But the modernization, unlike the Marxist, perspective does not hypothesize a set historical sequence of stages in economic development and does not specify which particular economic group would be the major proponent of revolutionary transformation. Rather, modernization theory holds that the experience of technological and economic change tends to "mobilize" new or previously apathetic groups by raising both their economic aspirations and their demands for political participation. Revolution is likely to occur when those holding state power are unable or unwilling to meet the demands of groups mobilized by modernization.

During the second half of the 1960s and in the 1970s, a fifth major contemporary theory of revolution, **structural theory**, which like the Marxist perspective emphasized the importance of structural aspects of society, became prominent. Barrington Moore's comparative study (1966) indicated that rebellious movements in peasant societies were most likely to develop when a certain shift in a society's economic structure occurred, that is, as a traditional farming economy was threatened by and beginning to undergo "transition to capitalist agriculture" (Foran 2006, 869). Wolf (1969, 276–302), in analyzing six peasant societies that experienced revolutionary conflicts, also found that a major factor in mobilizing support for rebellion was the situation of increasing commercialization of agriculture threatening "peasants' access to land" (Foran 2006, 869).

The most influential and theoretically comprehensive modern structural theory was developed by Skocpol and Trimberger (Skocpol and Trimberger 1978; Skocpol 1979). It is identified with Marx's view that a revolution is not exclusively the product of subjective characteristics of a society, such as shared cultural values or social or economic expectations, but is in great part dependent on specific objective conditions involving political, economic, and other aspects of social structure. The Skocpol and Trimberger formulation, however, departed from Marx's original perspective in several ways. First, the state was viewed not as the instrument of class domination emphasized by Marx but as a form of social organization that combines administrative and military functions and draws resources from society to use in maintaining social order and in competing against other nations economically and militarily. Second, in contrast to the original Marxist analysis, for which a revolution was the outcome of internal technological and economic factors, this new structural approach was oriented to the larger world environment and perceived revolution as the result of conflict among nations at different levels of technological and economic development.

The Skocpol and Trimberger structural theory specified that the key objective conditions for revolution have in the past occurred in primarily agrarian, technologically inferior states when these were confronted with overpowering military and economic pressures from more-advanced nations. Inability to resist foreign aggression reduced the perceived legitimacy of the prerevolutionary regimes, which were also undermined by divisions within elite population segments regarding how best to deal with external threats. Government policies to cope with foreign pressures, such as attempts to increase state resources by raising taxes on an already largely impoverished population, or the economic effects of foreign exploitation generated mass discontent. The resulting popular support for revolutionary movements overwhelmed the severely weakened prerevolutionary regimes. From the structural point of view, the purpose and outcome of such revolutions was primarily political: the establishment of a new governmental system in a less-developed society, a system that would be better capable of utilizing available resources to counter external threats from more-advanced nations.

The general theories of revolution briefly described here all explicitly or implicitly hold that mass frustration has been an essential element of revolutionary movements. Marxist, modernization, systems, and structural theories also suggest that failure of the state to meet new mass expectations or carry out important economic or other crucial social functions leads to a weakening of government legitimacy and coercive capacity, which heightens the probability of revolution. Modernization, Marxist, and structural

theories specify processes by which certain elites in society may become sufficiently discontented so that they withdraw support for the existing government or even commit themselves to leading a revolutionary effort.

A major inadequacy of the Marxist, frustration-aggression, systems, and
modernization theories, however, is their relative lack of attention to two essential elements of successful revolutionary movements: a unifying motivation capable of bringing together diverse groups behind a common
revolutionary goal and the existence of an international environment permissive of revolution. The Skocpol and Trimberger structural theory, at least
implicitly, confronts the issue of unifying motivation by asserting the primacy of the population-bonding revolutionary aim of creating a new,
stronger government better capable of protecting national interests but, like
the other theories, tends to ignore the world permissiveness factor. These
omissions limit the ability of the major theories of revolution to predict either the development of revolutionary movements or a revolution's chance
for success. Both the unifying motivation factor and the role of a permissive
international environment will be seen at work on many occasions throughout the chapters on individual revolutions. Together with mass frustration,
elite dissidence, and state crisis, these factors go further than general
theories toward explaining and predicting revolutionary action and success.

Summary

This chapter provided an overview of concepts, theoretical perspectives,
and research findings important to the discussion of revolutionary social
movements. A revolutionary movement, in contrast to a reform movement,
is aimed at bringing about change in the basic institutions of a society. Of
all the phenomena specifically relevant to the success of a revolutionary
movement, five appear to be of crucial importance: (1) the growth of frustration among the majority of a population; (2) the existence of elite elements who are alienated from the current government and, more
specifically, of elite members who support the concept of revolution; (3) the
development of unifying motivations that bring together the members of
different social classes in support of a revolution; (4) the occurrence of a
crisis that severely weakens government administrative and coercive capabilities in a society experiencing the development of a revolutionary movement; and (5) the choice on the part of other nations not to intervene or
their inability to do so to prevent the success of a revolutionary movement
in a particular society.

The third point does not exclude the probability that some of the reasons
individuals participate in or support a revolutionary movement are of a
highly personal nature, such as the belief that the success of the revolution
will improve their own material well-being or a desire for revenge, or because of ties to loved ones or friends who support revolution. But as Greene

(1990) pointed out, the participants in a revolution, often drawn from different economic backgrounds, share motivations that bind them together in the common effort. In several revolutions an adherence to a cross-class religious belief or a commitment to freeing one's country from perceived foreign control or from the rule of a despised dictatorship has acted in this way.

Nationalism, often spurred by reaction to imperialist exploitation, has been a powerful unifying sentiment. And although the notion of redistribution of wealth is not necessarily synonymous with socialism, various forms of socialist ideology have figured prominently in the belief systems of many leftist revolutionary movements. The combination of the nationalist goal of liberating one's people from foreign domination and the goal of redistributing wealth to achieve a more egalitarian society has proven to be extremely effective in rallying otherwise diverse social groups to revolutions in Russia, China, Vietnam, and other societies. Nationalism, as a spur to unified action, and economic redistribution, as an antidote to mass frustration, join together with the other major revolutionary factors—elite dissidence, state crisis, and world permissiveness—to explain many sociopolitical upheavals of the past and, perhaps, those of the centuries to come.

References and Further Readings

Adleman, David E. 2006. "Nationalism and Revolution." In DeFronzo, ed., *Revolutionary Movements in World History*, 2:589–94.

Alexander, George M. 1981. "The Demobilization Crisis of November 1944." In Iatrides, ed., *Greece in the 1940s*.

Anderson, Thomas P. 1971. *Matanza: El Salvador's Communist Revolt of 1932*. Lincoln: University of Nebraska Press.

Baerentzen, Lars, and David H. Close. 1993. "The British Defeat of EAM, 1944–5." In Close, ed., *The Greek Civil War*.

Berecz, Janos. 1986. *1956 Counter-Revolution in Hungary*. Budapest: Akadamiai Kiado.

Berryman, Phillip. 1985. *Inside Central America: The Essential Facts Past and Present on El Salvador, Nicaragua, Honduras, Guatemala, and Costa Rica*. New York: Pantheon.

———. 1987. *Liberation Theology: Essential Facts about the Revolutionary Movement in Latin America—and Beyond*. Philadelphia: Temple University Press.

Binford, Leigh. 2006. "The Salvadoran Revolution." In DeFronzo, ed., *Revolutionary Movements in World History*, 3:763–73.

Booth, John A. 1985. *The End and the Beginning: The Nicaraguan Revolution*. Boulder: Westview Press.

Braveboy-Wagner, Jacqueline A. 1985. *Interpreting the Third World: Politics, Economics, and Social Issues*. New York: Praeger.

Breuilly, John. 1982. *Nationalism and the State*. New York: St. Martin's Press.

Brinton, Crane. [1938] 1952. *The Anatomy of Revolution*. New York: Prentice-Hall.

Brook, Daniel. 2005. *Modern Revolution: Social Change and Cultural Continuity in Czechoslovakia and China*. Lanham, MD: University Press of America.

Byrne, Malcolm. 2006. "The Hungarian Revolution of 1956." In DeFronzo, ed., *Revolutionary Movements in World History*, 2:370–78.

Calvert, Peter. 1984. *Revolution and International Politics*. New York: St. Martin's Press.

Cavatorta, Francesco. 2006. "Colonialism, Anti-Colonialism, and Neo-Colonialism." In DeFronzo, ed., *Revolutionary Movements in World History*, 1:163–68.

Chirot, Daniel. 1986. *Social Change in the Modern Era*. San Diego, CA: Harcourt Brace Jovanovich.

Close, David H., ed. 1993. *The Greek Civil War: Studies of Polarization*. London: Routledge.

Close, David H., and Thanos Veremis. 1993. "The Military Struggle." In Close, ed., *The Greek Civil War*.

Cockcroft, James D. 1989. *Neighbors in Turmoil: Latin America*. New York: Harper and Row.

Cohen, Albert K. 2005. "Terrorism." In DeFronzo, ed., *Revolutionary Movements in World History*, 3:862–68.

Combs, Cindy C. 2005. *Terrorism in the Twenty-First Century*. 4th ed. Upper Saddle River, NJ: Prentice-Hall.

Davies, James C. 1962. "Toward a Theory of Revolution." *American Sociological Review* 27:5–19.

DeFronzo, James V. 1970. "Revolution in the Twentieth Century." In *Focus on Sociology: A Book of Sociological Readings*, ed. Arnold O. Olson and Sushil K. Usman, 317–38. Dubuque, IA: Kendall/Hunt Publishing.

———. 2006a. "Introduction." In DeFronzo, ed., *Revolutionary Movements in World History*, 1:xix–xxii.

———, ed. 2006b. *Revolutionary Movements in World History: From 1750 to the Present*. 3 vols. Santa Barbara, CA: ABC-CLIO.

Dix, Robert. 1983. "Varieties of Revolution." *Comparative Politics* 15:281–93.

Dunn, John. 1972. *Modern Revolutions: An Introduction to the Analysis of a Political Phenomenon*. Cambridge, UK: Cambridge University Press.

Edwards, Lyford P. [1927] 1970. *The Natural History of Revolution*. Chicago: University of Chicago Press.

Eisenstadt, S. N. 1978. *Revolution and the Transformation of Societies: A Comparative Study of Civilizations*. New York: Free Press.

Engels, Frederick. [1880] 1972. "Socialism: Utopian and Scientific." In Tucker, ed., *The Marx-Engels Reader*.

Farhi, Farideh. 1990. *States and Urban-Based Revolutions: Iran and Nicaragua*. Urbana: University of Illinois Press.

Foran, John. 2005. *Taking Power: On the Origins of Third World Revolutions*. Cambridge, UK: Cambridge University Press.

———. 2006. "Theories of Revolution." In DeFronzo, ed., *Revolutionary Movements in World History*, 3:868–72.

Fullerton, Andrew. 2006. "Inequality, Class, and Revolution." In DeFronzo, ed., *Revolutionary Movements in World History*, 2:408–12.

Giap, Vo Nguyen. 1962. *People's War, People's Army: The Viet Công Insurrection Manual for Underdeveloped Countries*. London: Praeger.

Gill, Jungyun. 2006. "Student and Youth Movements, Activism and Revolution." In DeFronzo, ed., *Revolutionary Movements in World History*, 3:848–54.

Gleijeses, Piero. 1991. *Shattered Hope: The Guatemalan Revolution and the United States, 1944–1954*. Princeton, NJ: Princeton University Press.

Goldfrank, Walter L. 1994. "The Mexican Revolution." In Goldstone, ed., *Revolutions*.

Goldstone, Jack A. 1980. "Theories of Revolution: The Third Generation." *World Politics* 32 (3): 425–53.

_____. 1982. "The Comparative and Historical Study Revolutions." *Annual Review of Sociology* 8:187–207.

_____. 1991. "An Analytical Framework." In *Revolutions of the Late Twentieth Century*, ed. Jack A. Goldstone, Ted R. Gurr, and Farrokh Moshiri. Boulder: Westview Press.

_____, ed. 1994. *Revolutions: Theoretical, Comparative, and Historical Studies*. 2nd ed. Fort Worth: Harcourt Brace College Publishers.

_____, ed. 1998. *Encyclopedia of Political Revolutions*. Washington, DC: Congressional Quarterly Press.

_____. 2001a. "Toward a Fourth Generation of Revolutionary Theory." *Annual Review of Political Science*, June, 4:139–87.

_____. 2001b. "An Analytical Framework." In Katz, ed., *Revolutions*, 9–29.

Goodwin, Jeff. 2001a. *No Other Way Out: States and Revolutionary Movements, 1945–1991*. Cambridge, UK: Cambridge University Press.

_____. 2001b. "Is the Age of Revolution Over?" In Katz, ed., *Revolutions*, 272–83.

Gott, Richard. 2004. *Cuba: A New History*. New Haven, CT: Yale University Press.

Greene, Thomas H. 1990. *Comparative Revolutionary Movements: Search for Theory and Justice*. Prentice-Hall Contemporary Comparative Politics. 3rd ed. Englewood Cliffs, NJ: Prentice-Hall.

Guevara, Che. 1985. *Guerrilla Warfare: Selected Case Studies*. Ed. Brian Loveman and Thomas M. Davies Jr. Lincoln: University of Nebraska Press.

Gurr, Ted Robert. 1970. *Why Men Rebel*. Princeton, NJ: Princeton University Press.

Hoensch, Jorg K. 1988. *A History of Modern Hungary, 1867–1986*. New York: Longman.

Hondros, John L. 1981. "The Greek Resistance, 1941–44." In Iatrides, ed., *Greece in the 1940s*.

Howard, Russell D., and Reid L. Sawyer, eds. 2002. *Terrorism and Counterterrorism: Understanding the New Security Environment*. Guilford, CT: McGraw-Hill/Dushkin.

Huntington, Samuel P. 1968. *Political Order in Changing Societies*. New Haven, CT: Yale University Press.

Iatrides, John O., ed. 1981. *Greece in the 1940s: A Nation in Crisis*. Modern Greek Studies Association 4. Hanover, MA: University of New England Press.

_____. 1993. "Britain, the United States, and Greece, 1945–1949." In Close, ed., *The Greek Civil War*.

Johnson, Chalmers. 1964. *Revolution and the Social System*. Hoover Institution Studies 3. Stanford, CA: Hoover Institution on War, Revolution, and Peace, Stanford University.

Kalyvas, Stathis. 2006. "The Greek Civil War." In DeFronzo, ed., *Revolutionary Movements in World History*, 1:316–25.

Katz, Mark. N. 1997. *Revolutions and Revolutionary Waves*. New York: St. Martin's Press.

_____, ed. 2001. *Revolutions: International Dimensions*. Washington, DC: Congressional Quarterly Press.

_____. 2006. "Transnational Revolutionary Movements." In DeFronzo, ed., *Revolutionary Movements in World History*, 3:872–76.

Lomax, Bill. 1976. *Hungary, 1956*. New York: St. Martin's Press.

Mackerras, Collin, and Nick Knight, eds. 1985. *Marxism in Asia*. New York: St. Martin's Press.

Mao Tse-Tung. [1938] 1965. "Problems of Strategy in the Guerrilla War Against Japan." In *Selected Works of Mao Tse-Tung*, vol. 2. Beijing: Foreign Languages Press.

Marx, Karl, and Frederick Engels. [1848] 1972. "The Communist Manifesto." In Tucker, ed., *The Marx-Engels Reader*.

McAdam, Doug, Sidney Tarrow, and Charles Tilly. 2001. *Dynamics of Contention*. Cambridge, UK: Cambridge University Press.

Miller, Norman, and Roserick Aya, eds. 1971. *National Liberation: Revolution in the Third World*. New York: Free Press.

Montgomery, Evan Braden, and Stacie L. Pettyjohn. 2006. "Ideology, Propaganda, and Revolution." In DeFronzo, ed., *Revolutionary Movements in World History*, 2:379–83.

Montgomery, Tommie Sue. 1982. *Revolution in El Salvador: Origins and Evolution*. Boulder: Westview Press.

Moore, Barrington, Jr. 1966. *Social Origins of Dictatorship Democracy: Lord and Peasant in the Making of the Modern World*. Boston: Beacon Press.

Paige, Jeffery M. 1975. *Agrarian Revolution: Social Movements and Export Agriculture in the Underdeveloped World*. New York: Free Press.

Papastratis, Procopis. 1987. "The Purge of the Greek Civil Service on the Eve of the Civil War." In *Studies in the History of the Greek Civil War, 1945–1949*, ed. Lars Baerentzen, John O. Iatrides, and Ole L. Smith. Copenhagen: Museum Tusculanum Press.

Parsa, Misagh. 2000. *States, Ideologies, and Social Revolutions: A Comparative Analysis of Iran, Nicaragua and the Philippines*. Cambridge, UK: Cambridge University Press.

Pettee, George Sawyer. 1938. *The Process of Revolution*. Studies in Systematic Political Science and Comparative Government 5. New York: Harper.

Richter, Heinz. 1981. "The Varkiza Agreement and the Origins of the Civil War." In Iatrides, ed., *Greece in the 1940s*.

_____. 1986. *British Intervention in Greece: From Varkiza to Civil War, February 1945 to August 1946*. Trans. Marion Sarafis. London: Merlin.

Sathyamurthy, T. V. 1983. *Nationalism in the Contemporary World: Political and Sociological Perspectives*. London: Frances Pinter.

Schlesinger, Stephen, and Stephen Kinzer. 1982. *Bitter Fruit: The Untold Story of the American Coup in Guatemala*. Garden City, NY: Doubleday.

Schmitt, Richard. 1987. *Introduction to Marx and Engels: A Critical Reconstruction*. Boulder: Westview Press.

Scott, James C. 1976. *The Moral Economy of the Peasant: Rebellion and Subsistence in Southeast Asia*. New Haven, CT: Yale University Press.

Selbin, Eric. 1999. *Modern Latin American Revolutions*. 2nd ed. Boulder: Westview Press.

_____. 2001. "Same as It Ever Was: The Future of Revolutions at the End of the Century. In Katz, ed., *Revolutions*.

_____. 2006. "Elites, Intellectuals, and Revolutionary Leadership." In DeFronzo, ed., *Revolutionary Movements in World History*, 1:253–58.

Sigmund, Paul. 2006. "The Chilean Socialist Revolution, Counter-Revolution, and Restoration of Democracy." In DeFronzo, ed., *Revolutionary Movements in World History*, 1:107–16.

Skocpol, Theda. 1979. *States and Social Revolutions: A Comparison of France, Russia, and China*. Cambridge, UK: Cambridge University Press.

Skocpol, Theda, and Ellen Kay Trimberger. 1978. "Revolutions and the World Historical Development of Capitalism." *Berkeley Journal of Sociology* 22:101–13.

Smelser, Neil. 1962. *Theory of Collective Behavior*. New York: Free Press.

Smith, Anthony D. 1983. *Theories of Nationalism*. 2nd ed. New York: Holmes & Meier.

Smith, Ole L. 1993. "The Greek Communist Party, 1945–9." In Close, ed., *The Greek Civil War*.

Streeter, Stephen M. 2000. *Managing the Counterrevolution: The United States and Guatemala, 1954–1961*. Athens: Ohio University Press.

_____. 2006. "Guatemalan Democratic Revolution, Counter-Revolution, and Restoration of Democracy." In DeFronzo, ed., *Revolutionary Movements in World History*, 1:325–35.

Szulc, Tad. 1986. *Fidel: A Critical Portrait*. New York: Morrow.

Thaxton, Ralph. 1983. *China Turned Rightside Up: Revolutionary Legitimacy in the Peasant World*. New Haven, CT: Yale University Press.

Tilly, Charles. 1978. *From Mobilization to Revolution*. Reading, MA: Addison-Wesley.

Trimberger, Ellen Kay. 1978. *Revolution from Above: Military Bureaucrats and Development in Japan, Turkey, Egypt, and Peru*. New Brunswick, NJ: Transaction Books.

Tucker, Robert, ed. 1972. *The Marx-Engels Reader*. New York: W. W. Norton.

Valenzuela, Arturo. 1978. *Chile. The Breakdown of Democratic Regimes*. Baltimore: Johns Hopkins University Press.

Vilas, Carlos M. 1995. "A Painful Peace: El Salvador After the Accords." *NACLA* 28:6–11.

Walker, Thomas W. 1986. *Nicaragua: The Land of Sandino*. 2nd ed. Boulder: Westview Press.

Walton, John. 1984. *Reluctant Rebels: Comparative Studies of Revolution and Underdevelopment*. New York: Columbia University Press.

White, Alastair. [1973] 1982. *El Salvador*. Boulder: Westview Press.

White, Richard. 1984. *The Morass: United States Intervention in Central America*. New York: Harper and Row.

Wickham-Crowley, Timothy P. 1992. *Guerrillas and Revolution in Latin America: A Comparative Study of Insurgents and Regimes since 1956*. Princeton, NJ: Princeton University Press.

_____. 2006. "Guerrilla Warfare and Revolution." In DeFronzo, ed., *Revolutionary Movements in World History*, 1:336–40.

Wolf, Eric. 1969. *Peasant Wars of the Twentieth Century*. New York: Harper and Row.

_____. 1971. "Peasant Rebellion and Revolution." In Miller and Aya, eds., *National Liberation*.

2

THE RUSSIAN REVOLUTIONS
AND EASTERN EUROPE

The 1917 Russian October Revolution was the first in history won by revolutionaries who advocated the establishment of a socialist society. By early 1917 the majority of the Russian people were extremely discontented with the czar's regime. Various revolutionary groups sought to mobilize popular frustration in support of a massive effort to transform Russian society. An extraordinary opportunity for the leaders of revolutionary movements to seize control of their nation's destiny was provided by the relatively sudden collapse of the coercive power of the czarist state in early 1917. Soldiers and sailors refused orders to repress rebellious street demonstrations and instead went over to the side of the revolutionaries. As the institutions of the czarist government rapidly deteriorated, workers, military personnel, and peasants elected revolutionary administrative councils, or "soviets," from among their own numbers, to exercise power. In fall 1917 soldiers, sailors, and workers loyal to the Bolshevik-led citywide soviet of the capital, Petrograd (later Leningrad and after 1991, St. Petersburg), established a new national revolutionary government and soon proclaimed the existence of the Union of Soviet Socialist Republics.

GEOGRAPHY AND POPULATION

The USSR, at 8,649,489 square miles (22,402,200 square kilometers), was the federation of ethnically diverse states that was the successor to the czar's vast empire. The majority of the USSR's territory, the largest country in the world until its dissolution in December 1991, was a vast plain extending from Eastern Europe to the Pacific Ocean, interrupted occasionally by low mountain ranges. This huge plain is characterized by three distinctive sectors running east and west: the Arctic section is a frozen marshy tundra, the middle band of the country is heavily forested, and the southernmost area is composed of extensive arid grassy plains that in the far south become sandy deserts.

The population of the Soviet Union, which was about 150 million at the time of the revolutions in 1917, exceeded 287 million during the last year of its existence. The USSR was composed of fifteen "union republics," the largest of which was Russia (now an independent nation), which was home to 52 percent of the USSR's population and included 76 percent of the USSR's land area. The second most populous republic was the now-independent Ukraine, which had about 18 percent of the USSR's citizens. The remaining republics each contained less than 6 percent of the USSR's population.

In 2006 the Russian Federation, at 6,592,741 square miles (17,075,200 square kilometers), had a population of 142,893,540. The country's people were ethnically about 80 percent Russian, with small minorities of Tatars, Ukrainians, and others.

THE SETTING FOR REVOLUTION

Before the Bolshevik Revolution, Russia was a vast empire ruled by a hereditary emperor called the czar. The czar governed not only the Russian people but also many of the other nationalities and lands that later were incorporated into the USSR. At the time of the revolution, only about 15 percent of the population lived in cities. Russia had begun to industrialize considerably later than other European societies, but the process was well under way by 1917.

Large factories were mainly concentrated in eight industrial regions, including Petrograd (which was the capital at the time of the revolution) and Moscow (which was the old capital and which the revolutionary government established as the capital of the USSR). Approximately half the industrial plants were owned by foreign companies from the more technologically advanced nations. In 1917 at least one-half of all Russia's industrial workers had peasant parents or had themselves been peasants or rural laborers before migrating to urban areas.

The rural mass of peasants had considerable reason to be discontented with their lot in czarist Russia. Before the seventeenth century many had lived a nomadic existence, traveling about the countryside seeking optimal conditions, such as the highest possible wages or more fertile land, or simply enjoying new experiences and environments. Peasant freedom of movement proved intolerable to many large landowners who desired a more reliable labor force. Thus, in 1649, serfdom, which bound individuals and their families to particular landowners or, in some cases, to the state, under penalty of law, was established. By the 1760s about 52 percent of those living in rural Russia were serfs (Wolf 1969).

ARCTIC OCEAN

FINLAND

Kronstadt

● Leningrad
(Petrograd)

Baltic
Sea

ESTONIA

LATVIA

LITHUANIA

● Minsk

BYELORUSSIA

POLAND

● Kiev

UKRAINE

MOLDAVIA

ROMANIA

BULGARIA

GREECE

**RUSSIAN SOVIET
FEDERATED SOCIALIST
REPUBLIC**

● Moscow

KAZAKHSTAN

● Volgograd
(Stalingrad)

Caspian
Sea

Black Sea

GEORGIA

AZERBAIJAN

ARMENIA

IRAN

TURKEY

EUROPEAN USSR

After the Russian defeat in the 1854–1856 Crimean War, Czar Alexander II decided to strengthen the nation through a modernization program, which included reforms in the countryside. In 1861 serfdom was abolished, and parcels of land were distributed to former serfs. However, in many instances the emancipation from serfdom generated more economic hardship than it alleviated. Most had to pay "redemption" fees, which stretched out over decades, for their land. Many former serfs awaited a "second emancipation" that would free them from the burden of redemption payments. Peasants also suffered from heavy taxes, which, especially during the tenure of Finance Minister Sergei Witte (1882–1903), a primary architect of the nation's industrial drive, were a major source of government investment capital (Von Laue 1971). Many fell further and further into debt because they often could not produce enough to feed their families, meet their redemption payments, and pay taxes simultaneously (Wolf 1969). Intense peasant discontent with the czar's regime constituted one of the essential elements of the revolutionary situation in the early twentieth century.

Many peasants did not own their land independently but rather were members of rural collectives called *mirs*. The *mir* assigned individual parcels of land to be worked by particular peasants and established taxation rates for individual households. In some areas, the parcels of land were passed down from father to son on a hereditary basis; in other areas the *mir* had the power to reassign parcels of land on a periodic basis. The existence of the *mir* in the Russian countryside helped prepare much of the rural population not only for participation in a socialist revolution but also for the collectivization of agriculture that occurred during the late 1920s and early 1930s.

Achieving the goals of industrialization and technological development required that thousands of upper- and upper-middle-class Russians receive modern educations. But since the source of advanced technological learning was Western Europe (by attending a university there or being instructed by a Western European or someone who had been educated there), education inevitably meant exposure to political and economic concepts that were alien to the Russian autocratic system of national government.

By favoring more democratic forms of government and a redistribution of wealth and opportunity, many young people came to constitute a dissident element within Russia's educated elite. During the mid-nineteenth century some proponents of social change, influenced by the Russian revolutionary activist Mikhail Bakunin, who advocated anarchism, organized the Populist movement. Anarchism included the concept that all productive wealth should be owned by the workers and peasants in collective associations. Economic inequality was to be minimized and people's basic needs satisfied. Since the participants in such an economic system would, ideally, coordinate activities and accomplish important tasks on a cooperative basis, there would be no need for society to employ force through the police or the military. In other words, there would be no need for a centralized formal government. This was important, according to anarchists, because government had always functioned, in part, as an instrument of oppression used by the rich to exploit the labor of the majority of the population.

Many Populist activists went into the countryside to attempt to "educate" the rural masses about the possibility and desirability of revolutionary change. Their efforts met with only very limited success, as many villagers viewed them as outsiders and meddlers. Other Populists, concluding that violent attacks on the czar's government and its supporters would help topple the dictatorship, secretly organized Narodnaia Volia (People's Will) to carry out numerous assassinations and acts of anti-government terrorism (Dmytryshyn 1984, 25). People's Will, along with other branches of the Populist movement, supported the creation of national and local elected assemblies; economic and administrative freedom of action for the village communes; bestowing ownership of all land on those who worked it; workers' control of industrial plants; complete freedom of speech, press, and political activity; granting all adults, regardless of gender, wealth, or landownership, the right to vote; and the replacement of the existing professional army with a people's militia (Dmytryshyn 1984). The major victim of People's Will terrorist activity was Czar Alexander II, who was assassinated on March 13, 1881. After the assassination, the government increased police repression, effectively destroyed People's Will, and made it extremely difficult for other revolutionary groups to operate in Russia.

The Populist movement helped formulate the concept of the totally dedicated revolutionist. In a book written in 1869 by the anarchists Sergei Nechaev and Bakunin, *Catechism of the Revolutionary*, the ideal revolutionary was described as a person with no inhibiting personal bonds or emotional concerns and only one dominant passion—accomplishing the revolution (Wolf 1969). Another important element of Populist thought was the belief that traditional communal institutions among Russian peasants, such as the *mir*, could serve as the basis for a direct transition in Russia from rural collectivism to modern socialism without having to undergo what the Populists considered to be the brutalizing and dehumanizing experience of capitalist industrialization. The program of the Russian revolutionaries who eventually succeeded, the Marxist Bolsheviks led by Lenin, incorporated some of the Populist concepts, including the need for an organization of dedicated professional revolutionaries and the possibility of industrializing under a socialist system without having to go through a period of capitalist development. Versions of the Populist movement grew and faded away repeatedly over several decades. At the time of the 1917 Revolutions, populism was manifested in the countryside through the Socialist Revolutionary Party, which was then the most popular political party among the peasants.

THE RUSSIAN SOCIAL DEMOCRATIC PARTY

Among the educated elite, some advocates of sweeping social change in Russia rejected terrorist methods. Such actions, they argued, not only intensified police repression but also morally alienated large numbers of citizens and caused them to reject the message of the revolutionaries without ever giving it serious attention. One organization that condemned terrorism, Osvobozhdhenie Truda (Liberation of Labor), was founded in 1883 in Geneva, Switzerland, by Russian exiles who were interested in the ideas of Karl Marx. This group included Georgi Plekhanov, the man who translated Marx's works into Russian.

Marx's analysis of history had led him to conclude that capitalism (the period of social development during which private ownership of resources, industry, and commerce characterizes the economic system and the owners of industrial and commercial enterprises control the government) would inevitably be succeeded by socialism (the phase of society theoretically characterized by public ownership of resources and productive institutions and by working-class control of government). In Marx's view, socialism would eventually lead to the final and highest developmental stage of history, communism, which was to be characterized by material abundance, cooperative social relations, and the end of the need for suppressive governmental institutions such as armies or police forces.

Marx predicted that capitalist society would create both the political means and the motivation for the exploited and toiling masses of the world finally, for the first time in history, to seize control and redirect the resources of society toward benefiting the needs of the great majority rather than catering to the interests of a numerically small ruling element (Marx and Engels [1848] 1998). According to Marx, capitalism provided the political means for the working class to seize power by physically concentrating working people in large cities where they could interact, organize, and develop a shared consciousness concerning the cause of their economic exploitation and the desirability of replacing capitalism with socialism. The motivation for the urban industrial working class, or proletariat, to strive for revolutionary change would be what Marx thought was a continuous characteristic of capitalism, the impoverishment and miserable living conditions of the working class. Once capitalism had been overcome, the new socialist society, as described by Marx ([1875] 1994) and later, Lenin ([1917] 1975), would be characterized by collective rather than private ownership of the economy, greater economic and social equality, an attempt to provide employment for all people able to work, and the provision of basic foods, medical services, education, and other necessities of life either free or at low cost to the entire population.

Although advocating many of the goals of the Populists, such as a democratic political system and absolute freedom of speech, press, and assembly, the Russian Marxists did not initially feel that the village commune of traditional peasant society could form the basis of a future socialist Russia. They argued, strictly adhering to Marx's concepts, that Russia first had to undergo industrialization at the hands of privately owned companies. Once capitalism had transformed much of the peasantry into an urban industrial working class, the transformation to socialism could occur.

During the 1890s the Liberation of Labor group evolved into a critically important political organization, the Russian Social Democratic Party (complete title: Russian Social Democratic Labor Party). At its 1903 meeting, the party publicly supported goals almost identical to those previously advocated by the Liberation of Labor movement. However, at the same meeting a split developed within the party. One divisive factor was an argument concerning control of the party itself. An important party leader, Lenin (born Vladimir Ilich Ulyanov in 1870), tried to persuade the other delegates that only the hard-core activists in the party (lifelong committed revolutionaries and certain dedicated participants in the underground revolutionary organizations) should have a voice in governing the party. Lenin, whose older brother Alexander, a brilliant university science student, was executed at age twenty-one for involvement in a plot to assassinate Czar Alexander III when Lenin was seventeen (Volkogonov 1994), claimed that a fully open and democratic party system would be hopelessly vulnerable to infiltration and manipulation by the czar's secret police and easily repressed in autocratic Russia (Wilson 1972). He was defeated 28 to 23 on this issue (Dmytryshyn 1984). But in the election for control of the party's central committees and the editorial board of its newspaper, *Iskra* (The Spark), candidates favored by Lenin won. From that point on, the supporters of Lenin called themselves "Bolsheviks" (the majority), and Lenin's opponents in the Social Democratic Party were called "Mensheviks" (the minority).

The division within the Russian Social Democratic Party grew and became permanent after the 1912 Party conference in Prague. The Mensheviks continued to support the notion that the transition to socialism would occur gradually and in stages in Russia. First the monarchy would be destroyed and replaced by a political democracy with a capitalist economic system. As the capitalist business investors transformed the economy of Russia through industrialization, the Mensheviks would take advantage of the open democratic political system to educate the members of the industrial working class to the desirability of the fairer, more efficient economic system and society that the Mensheviks (as well as the Bolsheviks) felt socialism represented.

In contrast, the Bolsheviks, under Lenin's influence, concluded that once the monarchy had been overthrown, the postrevolutionary political system should immediately become a **dictatorship of the proletariat,** in which the government would be in the hands of leaders truly committed to the interests of the worker-peasant majority of the population and the rapid implementation of socialism (Fitzpatrick 1982; Rabinowitch 1976; Von Laue 1971).

Marx had asserted that socialist society would be characterized by the dictatorship of the proletariat, by which he meant the political domination of the working class over the government. He, however, never clearly defined how the working-class majority would control the political system and the institutions of governmental coercion, such as the army and the police. Lenin, in contrast, provided his own operational definition of the concept. He argued that the expanding Bolshevik organization should seize power in order to effect change rapidly and defend the revolution and the working class from opponents (Bottomore 1983; Fitzpatrick 1982). Thus for Lenin the dictatorship of the proletariat meant the rule of the revolutionary party in a one-party political system.

Lenin believed that although the industrial workers were to be the basis of the revolution, on their own they could develop only what was called "trade union consciousness" (that is, a concern about limited job-related objectives, such as wages, benefits, number of working hours, and working conditions). He argued that the workers required the leadership and inspiration of revolutionary intellectuals (whether they had risen from the working class to attain an education or came from middle- or upper-class backgrounds) to achieve "revolutionary consciousness" (the commitment to a transformation of society to socialism). The Bolsheviks, who before the 1917 Revolutions officially referred to themselves as the Russian Social Democratic Labor Party and in 1918 adopted the title Communist Party, would, according to Lenin, lead the masses to socialism and then through the stage of socialist development to communist society (Lenin [1902] 1975; [1917] 1975). Whether Lenin would have come up with a more democratic system in a different political context or whether he would have modified his concept of government after the threat to the revolution had subsided will never be known: he died soon after the end of the Russian Revolution.

The Attempted Revolution of 1905

At the turn of the century, discontent with the czar's dictatorship was manifested not only through the growth of political parties dedicated to the overthrow of the monarchy but also through industrial strikes for better wages and working conditions, protests and riots among peasants, university demonstrations, and the assassinations of government officials, often by Socialist Revolutionaries (both the Bolsheviks and the Mensheviks opposed terrorist violence). But when in 1904 hostilities broke out between Russian and Japanese forces in the Far East, Russian government and military figures felt that domestic tensions could be reduced by rallying the country for a war that they were confident Russia would win. Instead, the Japanese inflicted one military disaster after another on Russian forces until the United States mediated a settlement.

Hardships caused by the war intensified worker discontent. In January 1905 a peaceful procession of thousands of workers, led by an activist priest named George Gapon, attempted to present the czar a petition listing grievances and calling upon him for assistance. But soldiers fired on the demonstrators, killing scores of people. Following the massacre, known as Bloody Sunday, strikes and peasant uprisings spread through many areas of Russia. Even some units of the army and navy rebelled. These events are known collectively as the Revolution of 1905. Industrial workers in Petrograd elected a workers' governing parliament called the Soviet (council) of Workers' Deputies (representatives).

In fear that the revolution might succeed, Czar Nicholas II promised reforms. Specifically, he pledged to allow (1) freedom of conscience, speech, and assembly; (2) the creation of a national parliament, or State Duma, which would have the power to confirm or block the implementation of any law; and (3) the right of even men who did not own property to participate in the election of the Duma (Dmytryshyn 1984; Salisbury 1981). The proclamation of these reforms caused great celebration among liberals of aristocratic background, capitalist businessmen, and many highly educated professionals. Workers and peasants who wished to continue the revolution were deprived of the support of the upper- and middle-class elements that had been opposed to the czar's dictatorial style of government. The czar then sent military units (most of the army had remained loyal) to those towns and peasant villages still in rebellion. Thousands of people were executed, and many thousands more, especially Jewish socialists, were forced to leave Russia. Some of the Russian Jewish exiles migrated to Palestine, where they established collective-farming communes (*kibbutzim*), which embodied their socialist ideals.

In order to pacify the growing industrial working class, the czar's government legalized labor unions and introduced health and accident insurance programs for some categories of workers. Plans were developed to provide free elementary education. The government also launched an agrarian-reform program intended to encourage more individual peasants to own parcels of land rather than participate in village communes. One purpose of this policy, named the Stolypin Land Reform, after its director, Premier Peter Stolypin, was to eliminate the *mir*, which had been a source of revolutionary organization during the 1905 revolution, and to institute capitalist business relationships among farmers in place of the cooperative and collectivist relationships of the traditional village commune. This effort was intended to greatly expand the class of land-owning peasants, especially the number of rich peasants (*kulaks*), in order to use them as a protection against further revolutionary developments in the countryside. The regime claimed that half or more of the peasants were private landowners by 1915.

The czar later refused to honor some of his promised reforms. Election laws were structured so as to prevent most of the adult population (including those most prone to revolutionary ideas, such as many of the industrial workers) from voting (Dmytryshyn 1984; Von Laue 1971). When those permitted to vote still elected a Duma that the czar could not totally control, he responded to the legislature's measures and demands by ignoring them or periodically disbanding it. Thus the czar continued to exercise dictatorial power.

The attempted revolution in 1905 had failed for a number of reasons. Most revolutionary leaders were taken by surprise by the uprisings of workers and peasants and were not in a position to coordinate the individual rebellions throughout the Russian Empire, making them easier to suppress. Furthermore, the creation of a national elected parliament persuaded upper- and middle-class liberals to desert the revolutionary cause. And the majority of army and naval units remained loyal to the czar's government. Each of these factors would be reversed in 1917.

THE REVOLUTIONS OF 1917

The February Revolution

During the early part of the twentieth century, tensions among European nations intensified over a number of issues, including competition for control of the resources of the less-developed parts of the world and the worsening of traditional ethnic hostilities. When Archduke Ferdinand of Austria was assassinated by a Serb and the Austro-Hungarian army attacked Serbia, Russia, declaring its readiness to aid the Serbians, a fellow Slavic people, plunged into war against the Austro-Hungarian Empire and its more powerful ally, Germany. Despite earlier commitments not to obey if ordered by "capitalist governments" to take up arms against working-class brothers in neighboring countries, most socialist leaders, apparently swept away on tides of nationalist fervor, pledged support for their nations' war efforts. Among Russian socialists, Lenin and his fellow Bolsheviks were virtually alone in condemning the war as a "capitalist atrocity" perpetrated by the ruling classes of Europe, an atrocity that would result in the mass slaughter of millions of peasants and workers. Although he opposed the war, Lenin recognized it as a potential opportunity for a new and successful revolution. In fact, he argued that Russia's defeat in the war would be the best possible outcome because such a catastrophe would deprive the czarist state of its remaining aura of legitimacy and the loyalty of its armed forces and generate the level of mass discontent necessary to topple the regime (Fitzpatrick 1982).

Russian armies soon suffered a series of devastating defeats in battles against the better-armed German forces. Millions of Russian soldiers perished; the call-up of fifteen million men into military service caused serious industrial and agricultural labor shortages, which disrupted not only army supplies but also the availability of food for the entire population. In Petrograd, extreme shortages led to accelerated inflation. Between the start of World War I and 1917, the real (inflation-adjusted) wages of Petrograd workers declined to about one-third of prewar levels, owing largely to increases in the price of necessities (Rabinowitch 1976). As conditions worsened, hundreds of thousands of soldiers, sailors, workers, and peasants elected "soviets" to demand change and to provide organization for a building revolutionary upsurge. By early March 1917 (late February according to the Julian calendar, which Russia followed at the time), mass industrial strikes had broken out in major urban centers. The czar, who was at the front, sent troops to Petrograd to subdue the strikers. However, most of the soldiers refused to fire on the demonstrators, and many joined the protests.

As the coercive power of the czarist state rapidly disintegrated, it became clear that not only the civilian workers and peasants but also the bulk of the armed forces (drawn from those classes), as well as most of the middle class and some in the upper class, were now united in opposition to the czar's continuation in power. Units of the Petrograd garrison mutinied, and soldiers, under the direction of the Petrograd Soviet of Soldiers' and Workers' Deputies, took control of the capital on March 12 (February 27 on the Julian calendar). On March 16 the czar was forced to abdicate, and Russia became a republic. The czar's parliament, the Duma, then drew from its numbers individuals to serve in a new "provisional government," which was at first headed by an aristocrat, Prince Lvov, and eventually by the moderate socialist Alexander Kerensky (Katov 1967; Rabinowitch 1976).

But the immediate postczarist national government suffered from critical weaknesses. Members of the provisional government reflected the social-class composition of the Duma: they were largely wealthy businessmen, aristocrats, or employed in the professions. Although moderate socialists served in the provisional government along with conservatives and liberals, it represented primarily upper-income interests and was viewed with some suspicion by workers and peasants, many of whom in the capital recognized only the authority of their Petrograd Soviet. Despite the fact that the Petrograd Soviet initially supported the right of the provisional government to exercise the power of the state, a system of "dual power" actually existed, with the provisional government and the Petrograd Soviet as the two centers of authority. The Petrograd Soviet agreed to share power with and support the provisional government until national political power could be handed over to a Constituent Assembly that was to be elected by all male citizens.

All over the country, class hostility intensified. Soldiers no longer automatically obeyed their officers, who typically had higher-class backgrounds. Rather, soldiers and sailors debated issues and continued to elect self-governing soviets from their own numbers. Initially, the Petrograd Soviet was dominated by Mensheviks and Socialist Revolutionaries. But from spring 1917 on, the Bolsheviks gained members—including many Mensheviks and Socialist Revolutionaries who defected—faster than any other group (Dmytryshyn 1984; Fitzpatrick 1982; Greene 1990; Rabinowitch 1976). The Bolsheviks achieved majorities in both the Petrograd and the Moscow soviets by early fall.

The October Revolution

The provisional government made several crucial decisions that rapidly dissipated its initially limited coercive capability, which had been based on the willingness of military personnel and the Petrograd Soviet to accept its authority. First, it decided to continue the war against Germany. Those in favor of maintaining Russia's war effort, including the Mensheviks and the more conservative of the Socialist Revolutionaries in the Petrograd Soviet, were motivated by several factors: patriotism, hatred of Germany, and the perceived need for future economic and technical aid from England and France, Russia's allies against Germany. The Bolsheviks and the pro-Bolshevik Socialist Revolutionaries (called Left Socialist Revolutionaries) opposed the war. The provisional government's other crucial failings were its policy of delaying major economic reforms, including the redistribution of lands to the poor peasants, until after the war, and postponing the election of the national Constituent Assembly. The decision to delay land reform outraged many peasants, who suspected the upper-class members of the provisional government were not going to go through with a land-reform program at all. But the provisional government feared mass desertions if land redistribution occurred while the war was still going on: peasant soldiers would not want to miss out on the opportunity to obtain distributed land. So once the decision to continue the war had been made, the provisional government was forced to make the extremely unpopular declaration that land reform would be delayed.

When the czar was overthrown, two important advocates of revolution were not in Russia. Lenin was in exile in Geneva, and Leon Trotsky (born Lyov Davidovich Bronstein in the Ukraine in 1879), who had participated in the Petrograd Soviet during its brief 1905 existence, was in New York. Lenin realized the opportunity for a sweeping socioeconomic revolution was developing in his homeland and determined that he must get to Petrograd as soon as possible. Assistance came from a remarkable source: the imperial German government. German capitalist leaders detested the ideology of socialism, especially the ideas of the Bolsheviks concerning redistribution of wealth and worldwide revolution. But Germany was at war and fighting on two fronts. If Russia were to give up the war, Germany could concentrate on the western front and perhaps deliver a knockout blow. The German leaders correctly concluded that the chances of Russia's leaving the conflict would be much greater if the charismatic Lenin, long an opponent of the war, were to return to Petrograd. The German government transported him in a railroad car through Germany to Sweden, from which Lenin made his way to Petrograd in April.

Trotsky arrived in Petrograd in May and declared that he was in favor of Lenin and the Bolshevik program rather than that of the Mensheviks, who continued to support Russian involvement in the war and the concept of a gradual evolution toward socialist transformation. Trotsky, Lenin, and other Bolshevik leaders argued, in contrast, that there must be a second revolution, one in which the workers and peasants would take power away from the upper class. Throughout Russia, Bolshevik speakers proclaimed: "End the war"; "All land to the peasants"; and "All power to the soviets" (Dmytryshyn 1984; Fitzpatrick 1982; Rabinowitch 1976).

The provisional government in early July launched a new offensive against the Germans, which predictably ended in disaster. Then the Germans launched a successful counterattack. Thousands of deserting Russian soldiers flocked to Petrograd. These events encouraged some Bolshevik leaders to attempt an uprising. Lenin apparently was uncertain whether the conditions were yet right for a Bolshevik seizure of power and may even have opposed an insurrection at that point. In any case, the uprising failed, and Trotsky and several other Bolsheviks were jailed by soldiers still loyal to the provisional government. Lenin went into hiding. At that time, Kerensky, representing a group of moderate socialists, became head of the provisional government.

The unsuccessful Bolshevik insurrection of July was followed in September by the attempt of a conservative general, Lavr Kornilov, to seize power. Expecting the attack, the provisional government released Trotsky and other imprisoned Bolshevik leaders and called upon the growing ranks of the Bolsheviks to defend Petrograd. As it turned out, Kornilov's attempted takeover proved an utter failure, since most of his forces refused to carry out their orders and many joined the Bolsheviks. Rapidly increasing numbers of workers, soldiers, and sailors concluded that any further counterrevolutionary attempts to crush the revolution and working-class power must be prevented. Therefore, the popularly elected soviets, led by those committed to establishing a socialist economic system, must be granted total power.

Bolshevik majorities, by the end of September, had been elected in both the Petrograd and the Moscow soviets. Lenin concluded that the time had come for the Bolsheviks to seize power on behalf of the workers and peasants and decisively commit the country to socialism. On November 7 (October 25 according to the Julian calendar), soldiers, sailors, and armed workers of the Petrograd Soviet, under Trotsky's command, occupied transportation and communication centers, government buildings, and the czar's winter palace (Greene 1990). There was little bloodshed, since few military personnel in the capital still recognized the authority of the provisional government. Kerensky fled, and the provisional government was at an end. Soviet workers and soldiers under Bolshevik leadership also took control in Moscow and other large cities. The Bolshevik-led new revolutionary government instructed local village soviets to seize large private estates and church-owned land, abolished private ownership of industry, and announced its intention to end the war with Germany.

The election of the previously agreed-upon Constituent Assembly was held shortly after the Bolshevik overthrow of the provisional government. Bolshevik popularity had been increasing, but the party was still not well known to most people in the countryside or in the southern part of the country. Votes of the five million soldiers and sailors were counted separately. The Bolsheviks won absolute majorities in the armies in the north and west and among the sailors of the Baltic Fleet, but the Socialist Revolutionaries and the Ukrainian ethnic parties won among the armies of the south and the Black Sea Fleet (Fitzpatrick 1982). The Bolsheviks also won majorities in Petrograd and Moscow and probably took most of the country's urban vote. The Bolsheviks received 24 percent of the total (9,800,000 votes), placing them second to the relatively loosely organized revolutionary party popular among the peasants, the Socialist Revolutionaries, which received 41 percent (17,100,000 votes) (Dmytryshyn 1984). A number of other political parties and several parties representing minority ethnic interests won much lower percentages. For example, the Constitutional Democrats (Cadets), who favored a parliamentary constitutional monarchy system and moderate economic reforms, received 5 percent (2,000,000), and the Mensheviks' vote was 3 percent (1,360,000).

At the time of the election, the positions of the Bolsheviks and the Socialist Revolutionaries on the issue of central concern to the peasants, redistribution of land, were basically identical. Consequently, in the minority of villages that were close enough to cities, towns, military bases, or rail depots for the inhabitants to know the Bolshevik program, the peasants voted in equal numbers for the Bolsheviks and the Socialist Revolutionaries. But in most villages where the people were not familiar with the Bolsheviks or their land policy, the rural-based Socialist Revolutionaries achieved majorities (Fitzpatrick 1982). When the assembly convened in January 1918, many of the delegates began criticizing the Bolsheviks. Before the assembly had been in existence for twenty-four hours, soldiers loyal to the Bolshevik-controlled Petrograd Soviet forced it to disband.

In the following months, power shifted more and more from the elected soviets to the Bolshevik Party organization (Daniels 1988; Dmytryshyn 1984; Fitzpatrick 1982; Rabinowitch 1976). Some who had supported the revolution to overthrow the provisional government objected to Bolshevik domination and demanded that major power be returned to the soviets. Most notably, in 1921 many of the sailors at the Kronstadt Naval Base rebelled and demanded a "true soviet republic of workers and peasants." The Kronstadt rebellion was quickly crushed by Bolshevik-led military units. The soviets, although still in existence, assumed a role in influencing local community affairs. But not until the major democratization reforms in 1989 and 1990 did a soviet exercise effective power at the national level.

ASSESSING THE BOLSHEVIK SEIZURE OF POWER

According to most interpretations of Marx's theories, the Bolsheviks were wrong to seize power in 1917. Marx felt that the transformation to socialism would first occur in the most-advanced countries because they had the large urban industrial working classes that he thought would constitute the basis of support for socialism. The Russian industrial working class in 1917 was revolutionary but made up only a small fraction of the total population. Lenin realized, however, that an extraordinary political situation had provided a unique opportunity for revolutionists in Russia. In the face of rebellious armed forces and revolutionary peasants and workers desperate for relief from the miseries of war and economic exploitation, the Russian state had collapsed. Most competing political groups were handicapped by ineffectual leaders and confused or unappealing ideologies. Lenin believed that the Bolsheviks had a scientifically based understanding of human history and a realistic plan to create the first truly just human society. He and other Bolshevik leaders felt that history would not excuse a failure to take advantage of such a remarkable set of circumstances.

But Lenin and his associates also realized their "premature" seizure of power would result in several problems. For example, the revolutionary leadership was attempting to carry out a socialist revolution in a primarily agrarian society. Marxist theory assumed that socialist revolution was impossible without the support of the majority. But in Russia the majority of the population was not the industrial proletariat but the rural peasantry. Lenin, incorporating some concepts from the tradition of the old Populist movement, argued that the majority of peasants could be convinced to support the revolution. Mobilization of the peasants would proceed, Lenin argued, in the following sequence. The Bolsheviks, originally composed mainly of revolutionary intellectuals from generally upper-middle or middle-class backgrounds, would initially awaken and recruit the Russian industrial working class to the revolution. Then the revolutionary working class, hundreds of thousands of whom would join the Bolshevik organization (Communist Party after 1918) and many having relatives who were peasants or had once been peasant themselves, would provide leadership and inspiration to the population's discontented peasant majority, many of whom would soon also join the Party. Most of the peasants, according to Lenin, could be won over for several reasons. First, the lands of the big private owners and the Church were to be given over to the peasants. Second, the Bolsheviks anticipated that the peasant communes (*mirs*), with their traditions of collectivism and cooperation, could provide the basis for peasant incorporation into the socialist revolution. Thus Lenin thought that whereas the industrial working class would constitute the core of the revolution in Russia, most of the peasants would also support the revolution (Fitzpatrick 1982).

Another major concern was the question of how to industrialize without capitalism. Industry and modern technology were necessary to make the economy produce the wealth needed to provide a materially satisfying life for all of society's members. But according to Marx, industrialization was to be accomplished under the system of private ownership, investment, and profit making. If the revolution preceded complete industrialization, the latter would have to be accomplished under socialism. But this would seem to mean that the improvement of the material well-being of the population would have to be postponed while the system accumulated enough wealth (capital) to bring about industrialization.

Could a harsh transition to industrial society under socialism be avoided? Remarkably, Lenin, Trotsky, and some of their associates initially anticipated that once the Bolshevik Revolution succeeded, revolutionary Russia would provide inspiration and perhaps assistance to the working classes of the advanced industrial nations to accomplish their own socialist revolutions (Rabinowitch 1976). Then the revolutionary advanced societies could use some of the wealth produced by their industries to create an assistance fund for Russia and other less-developed countries so that they could undergo industrialization without imposing harsh austerity or repressive measures on their populations. But although industrial workers in several of the nations defeated in World War I, including Germany and Hungary, tried to organize revolutions, their efforts were unsuccessful. In these countries the armed forces, who were not won over to the side of the revolutionaries, suppressed the uprisings. Furthermore, the peasants of other European societies were more conservative than those in Russia and generally opposed revolution (Greene 1990).

When it became clear that no advanced nations of the World War I era would experience a socialist revolution, the leaders of revolutionary Russia confronted serious problems. Industrialization would have to be achieved through the Soviet Union's own resources. This meant that extreme austerity measures would be necessary for the Soviet state to accumulate the capital necessary to transform the economy. The hostility of the more-industrialized societies toward the Soviet Union intensified the motivation to industrialize as quickly as possible. In the event of military attacks from capitalist nations, heavy industry would be crucial for producing the weapons needed for defense (Von Laue 1971).

THE CIVIL WAR

The Bolshevik Revolution of November 7, 1917, did not result in an immediate revolutionary victory throughout the czar's vast empire. On the periphery of European Russia, various forces gathered, some to overthrow the revolution and some to establish different versions of revolutionary society than that proposed by the Bolsheviks. Former czarist generals rallied anti-Bolshevik officers and soldiers and organized so-called White Armies. The more conservative elements of the Socialist Revolutionary Party attempted to set up a separate revolutionary government. An anarchist group that opposed any strong central state government, czarist or Bolshevik, attempted to maintain control of much of the southern Ukraine (Palij 1976). Several capitalist countries, including Britain, the United States, and Japan, sent troops to various parts of Russia and provided military assistance to anti-Bolshevik armies.

The Bolshevik leadership responded to these attacks by organizing the Red Army, which first was made up of volunteers; later a draft was imposed. The core of the army included hundreds of thousands of industrial workers and Communist Party members. Trotsky provided it with energetic and charismatic leadership. Eventually numbering more than five million, by 1923 the Red Army had defeated all the White Armies and other anti-Bolshevik forces.

The years of civil war and foreign capitalist military intervention instilled a siege mentality in Bolshevik supporters and helped militarize the Communist

Party itself (Daniels 1988; Fitzpatrick 1982). The attempted assassination and wounding of Lenin in 1918 by Fanya Kaplan, a member of the Socialist Revolutionary Party who objected to the disbanding of the Constituent Assembly and feared that Lenin's approach would be self-defeating for the cause of socialism, and the actual killings of thousands of Communist Party members and supporters by anti-Bolshevik forces were accompanied by the growth of the Bolshevik internal security forces (secret police), which executed thousands of people without trial during the civil war (Fitzpatrick 1982; Volkogonov 1994).

There were several reasons why anti-Bolshevik forces failed. Probably of greatest importance was the fact that the Whites had political and economic goals that were far less appealing to the vast majority of Russia's population than those of the Bolsheviks. For example, most of the White Army leaders proposed immediately returning the land distributed to peasants to the former big landowners and the Church. The peasants were further alienated from the Whites by the conduct of the White soldiers toward the civilian population, which was worse than the behavior of the Red Army (Dmytryshyn 1984; Fitzpatrick 1982). Moreover, the anti-Bolshevik forces were not unified, nor were their efforts, for the most part, coordinated (Von Laue 1971). Their receiving aid from foreign nations made them appear agents of imperialism to many Russians. The Red Army, in contrast, was usually perceived of as defending the country against the rich and their foreign allies. Finally, the assistance provided to White Armies and other anti-Bolshevik forces was limited both by the vast size of the country and by the fact that capitalist governments were confronted with domestic populations and economies still recovering from the devastation of World War I.

LEADERSHIP STRUGGLE

The death in 1924 of Lenin, who had been ill for some time, prompted a struggle for control of the revolution. The future course of development of the Russian Communist Party and the Soviet Union was at stake. Lenin had evaluated in writing some of the top Bolshevik leaders and had at one time singled out Trotsky and Stalin as outstanding. Trotsky, the educated son of a rich peasant, was a brilliant organizer and leader; he had engineered the Bolshevik overthrow of the provisional government in 1917 and then led the Red Army to victory in the civil war.

Stalin (born Iosif Vissarionovich Dzhugashvili in 1879) was the son of a cobbler, who reportedly used alcohol heavily and was prone to violence, and a washerwoman, former serfs in Georgia, a small mountainous state that had been conquered by the czar's army and then incorporated into the Russian Empire. Stalin was one of the few top Bolshevik leaders to have come from the lowest classes of prerevolutionary czarist society. Although he had trained for the priesthood, Stalin left the seminary to become a revolutionary activist among oil-industry workers. The czar's government imprisoned him and exiled him to Siberia. Although neither a charismatic speaker nor a war hero, Stalin became a top-level and very effective Party organizer. After the Civil War, much of the Red Army was demobilized, but the Communist Party continued to grow in membership as well as in political dominance. Controlling the Party machinery (Party leaders, bureaucracy, and newspapers) was a more significant source of power than past military glory. In 1922 the leading Party officials appointed Stalin to the new position of general secretary of the Communist Party to oversee the rapidly expanding membership. This was of crucial importance to Stalin's later rise to dictatorial power because, while other Party leaders held top government posts, Stalin frequently provided their staff personnel who often felt more loyal to him than to the heads of their ministries. In his final days, Lenin wrote a letter to the Communist Party in which he suggested that Party members "find a way to remove Stalin," whom he now considered too prone to violence and "too rude" to be Party leader (*New York Times*, May 10, 1987, E3). But Lenin's final disapproval came too late to block Stalin's ascent to power.

Trotsky and Stalin agreed on some important issues, such as the need to industrialize the Soviet Union rapidly and the dominant political role of the Communist Party. However, they disagreed on two major points (Dmytryshyn 1984; Dunn 1972; Fitzpatrick 1982; Von Laue 1971). First, Trotsky, a former Menshevik, claimed that Stalin was imposing a type of dictatorial control over the Communist Party. Trotsky argued that freedom of expression and more open and democratic methods of leader selection and policy development should exist within the Party. Stalin and his associates could assert that Lenin was responsible for or accepted some of the limitations on democracy within the Party, such as the 1922 Party congress resolution that permitted the Central Committee to expel by a two-thirds vote any Party members involved in an organized faction opposing the policies of the governing majority (Von Laue 1971). But Trotsky and his supporters argued that Lenin's restrictions were a reaction first to the police-state repression of the czar's regime and later to the threat posed by the civil war, the accompanying foreign military intervention, and other serious postrevolution problems and that they were not meant to be permanent, let alone tightened by Stalin's measures.

The second major disagreement had to do with Russia's role in regard to revolutionary movements in other countries. Trotsky argued that Russia should provide them all possible encouragement and physical assistance. His supporters used the slogan "World revolution now!" to express this point of view. According to Trotsky, "true" socialism would be impossible to achieve, particularly in a primarily agricultural society like Russia in the 1920s, without revolutions throughout the world, including in the advanced capitalist nations. An isolated revolutionary but economically backward society without substantial industrialization assistance from the advanced countries and, in fact, militarily threatened by them would, Trotsky predicted, tend to develop a repressive government for defensive reasons. And instead of improving the material well-being of the people, the state would be forced to limit political freedom and consumption in order to ensure a disciplined and reliable labor force and also to accumulate the capital needed for industrialization. The hardships could be avoided if worldwide revolution occurred. Fostering international revolution was an element of Trotsky's general theory of "permanent revolution." Trotsky borrowed this expression from Marx and Engels and used it to refer to what he considered to be a necessary worldwide series of revolutionary upheavals, which together would bring about the conditions necessary for the achievement of socialism throughout the world (Bottomore 1983).

Stalin, in contrast, argued that events had proven that the political circumstances in most other countries were simply not right for the occurrence of socialist revolutions, even with the meager assistance the new, economically struggling Soviet Union might be able to provide to revolutionaries. In light of these realities, Soviet aid to revolutionary movements in the more technologically advanced societies could well have the effect not of bringing about more revolutions but of provoking a new and even more determined military intervention against the Soviet Union. Rather, the Soviet Union should limit assistance for the time being and devote its energies toward rapidly industrializing and increasing the efficiency of agricultural production. Then, once the Soviet Union was a mighty industrial power, not only could the country produce the weaponry necessary to defend its own revolution against capitalist intervention, but it would also be in a better position to aid foreign revolutionary movements. Stalin's supporters represented this position by the slogan "Build socialism in one country first!" That made sense to many in the Soviet Union.

Trotsky suffered from several additional handicaps in the power struggle. First, many people apparently associated the initial limitations on internal Party democracy with Lenin rather than with Stalin, even though Stalin extended them and made them permanent. Also, many Bolsheviks were students of past revolutions and feared that, as happened after the French Revolution, a successful army officer could seize power and become a "Russian Napoleon." Even though it was Stalin who eventually assumed dictatorial power, in the 1920s many Bolsheviks feared that Trotsky, charismatic leader of the Red Army, represented the real danger of a one-man dictatorship. As noted earlier, Stalin's position as general secretary of the Communist Party provided him with a major organizational advantage over Trotsky. Also significant was the fact that as the Communist Party greatly expanded, it became more worker and peasant in composition than the original small Communist Party dominated by intellectuals. Stalin, from peasant background, was often better able to communicate with the vast new membership than highly educated members like Trotsky. Finally, although Stalin himself was not a Russian but a Georgian, many Bolsheviks and other Soviet citizens were not certain about Trotsky's nationalist commitment to the Soviet Union because he had spent considerable time outside the country and because he was Jewish. Some feared that Trotsky's commitment to "world revolution" might mean sacrificing the well-being or even the existence of the Soviet Union. In the struggle for control of the Communist Party, Stalin's supporters were often able to portray Trotsky as an elitist cosmopolitan intellectual with only a weak nationalist loyalty to the Soviet Union (Fitzpatrick 1982). In 1929 Trotsky, after losing several political confrontations with Stalin's supporters, was expelled from the Soviet Union. He continued to write and critically evaluate developments in the Soviet Union until he was assassinated in Mexico City in 1940 by a supporter of Stalin.

THE SOVIET UNION UNDER STALIN

Stalin and the Communist Party were confronted with the task of industrializing the Soviet Union as rapidly as possible. As revolutions had not occurred in the more-advanced industrial nations, the Soviet Union was on its own. This meant that industrialization was going to be a painful experience under socialism, as it would have been under capitalism. The only advantages, hypothetically, would be a more equal distribution of the burden under socialism, and a more-organized, centrally directed industrialization process. Unfortunately for the peasants, the Soviet Union would have to rely on its agricultural productivity to finance the further development of heavy industry.

During the late 1920s and the early 1930s virtually all agriculture was collectivized. Collectivization, by increasing efficiency, would theoretically make much of the previous agricultural labor force available for the growing needs of industry. The introduction of more machinery, better management, and farming methods that were more scientific were also supposed to raise productivity. For many peasants, collectivization was not much more than a technicality because they were already members of village communes. But for many of those who farmed their own land independently, it was a disagreeable and often traumatic process.

According to Von Laue (1971, 198–99), "the transition from private to collective farming was pushed forward with utter recklessness in 1929 and early 1930. For the countryside it meant a far more brutal upheaval than any previous agrarian measure since the imposition of serfdom." Vast rural areas were characterized by widespread "class warfare," in which many of the poorer peasants and Party activists championed the collectivization cause by attempting to force the most affluent peasants (the *kulaks*), often among the hardest working and most productive, to surrender their land, livestock, and costly farm equipment to the collectives. But many rich peasants killed their animals or sold them for slaughter rather than contribute them to the collective farms. The number of farm animals declined significantly (Dmytryshyn 1984). In retaliation, the government arrested and deported perhaps one million *kulak* families to Siberia (Fitzpatrick 1982). Hundreds of thousands of others who resisted collectivization were forcibly separated from their families and sent as forced labor to new industrial centers (Von Laue 1971).

The Soviet government demanded large portions of peasant production for grain export in order to earn the capital needed to purchase the industrial technology and machinery for industrialization. The loss of farm animals, the large share of agricultural production taken by the state to finance industrialization, poor weather conditions, and the social disorganization, conflict, and disruption of agriculture caused by collectivization combined to generate a famine in certain areas during the early 1930s. According to various sources, at least several million people starved to death (Dmytryshyn 1984; Fitzpatrick 1982; Von Laue 1971).

The push for rapid industrialization also meant hardships for the industrial workers. Trade union freedoms were reduced so that "labor discipline" could be maintained and industrial productivity raised as quickly as possible. Improvement in living standards occurred at a slow pace because the state stressed reinvestment in heavy industry rather than development of consumer goods. The Communist Party inspired a "cultural revolution," which generated literary works, cultural events, and works of art supportive of the revolution, collectivization of agriculture, and the crash industrialization program (Dmytryshyn 1984; Fitzpatrick 1982). The Soviet state's control over education, labor unions, peasant collectives, and the mass media and the government's marshalling of the arts and literature in support of its economic and political goals within the context of a one-party political system have been characterized as a form of totalitarianism (total government domination of all major social institutions) both by international critics of the Soviet regime and by later generations of Soviet and Russian leaders and citizens. Many Communist leaders reportedly objected to the forced collectivization of agriculture, but their misgivings on that policy were more than offset by their satisfaction with the spectacularly rapid growth in industry (Fitzpatrick 1982).

Stalin continued to lead the Soviet Union until his death in 1953. His fear of counterrevolutionary or anti-Stalinist plots motivated "purges" of many government and Party officials and army officers in the mid- and late 1930s. Thousands of people were executed, and millions were deported to remote regions of the country, often to labor camps, where many died. After Stalin died, Soviet leaders condemned his excesses and brutally repressive tactics. Yet Stalin's leadership did accomplish rapid industrialization. And the Soviet Union's heavy industry was a critical factor in helping the Soviet people repel the Nazi German invasion, launched in 1941.

THE RUSSIAN REVOLUTION: LONG-TERM CONSEQUENCES

When a revolution develops, often individuals and groups with somewhat differing philosophies and plans for the future join forces. Once the old order has been overthrown, disagreements among former allies are likely to resurface. During the Russian Revolutions of 1917 some of the most popular slogans were "All power to the soviets," "Soviet democracy," "All land to the peasants," and "Power to the working class." When among the contending revolutionary groups the Communist Party emerged victorious, its leaders determined what these slogans were to mean in practice. "All power" or at least most power went not to the soviets but to the Communist Party. "Soviet democracy" was relegated mainly to local community concerns. Elections for Party officials provided Party members with a role in exercising political power, but ordinary citizens were allowed only to vote yes or no for individuals nominated by the Party for government positions. "All land to the peasants" meant land to peasant collectives and state farms, rather than to individual peasants. And "Power to the working class" meant the direct exercise of political power not by all industrial workers and peasants but by those workers and peasants who were Communist Party members.

In fall 1917 when the Bolsheviks—theoretically on behalf of workers and peasants—assumed control of Russia, they were no longer simply an organization of middle- and upper-class intellectuals. They had by then admitted to their ranks tens of thousands of workers and peasants. In the succeeding years, the Communist Party recruited millions of individuals who were from these groups or had parents in these groups, provided them with educations and ideological instruction, and gave them access to political and economic power both through Communist Party membership and through admission to managerial and technical occupations and positions of authority in government. The victory of Marxism in Russia meant not only the alienation and even the flight of members of the former elite and privileged classes but also an extraordinary increase in social and economic mobility for industrial workers and peasants (Fitzpatrick 1982).

In later years, students of Soviet society noted that the causes of economic and scientific shortcomings in the USSR included a political system that restricted freedom of expression and therefore inhibited creativity as well as an economic system that was overly constrained by bureaucracy and central planning and did not provide enough incentive for productive individuals. By the mid-1980s, Soviet leaders acknowledged such problems and launched a series of reforms (*New York Times*, Jan. 28, 1987, A1; June 26, 1987, A1), which ultimately led to the dissolution of the USSR itself.

But there were additional reasons for the technological differences between the USSR and the United States. Czarist Russia began its industrial development later; the process was disrupted by the attempted revolution in 1905; the devastation of World War I, in which several million Russians died; and the Revolutions of 1917 and the accompanying 1918–1922 Civil War, in which hundreds of thousands more perished. The economic achievements of the 1920s and 1930s were rocked by the horrible Nazi German invasion of the early 1940s. An estimated twenty-six million Soviet citizens were killed and hundreds of cities and towns destroyed. Following the war, the Soviet people had to devote enormous resources to reconstruction. In response to the U.S. use of atomic bombs (against Japan), the Soviet Union diverted much of its own resources toward developing nuclear weapons. All these elements conceivably contributed to retarding the growth of the Soviet economy and nonmilitary technology.

The relative lack of civil liberties and political freedom in the USSR in comparison to the United States probably had multiple causes. First, the Soviet people had never really experienced a stable democratic political system. The country went almost directly from the dictatorship of the czar to the dictatorship of the proletariat. Moreover, the closed, authoritarian system of government that developed in the Soviet Union, especially during the 1927–1953 Stalinist era, was in part a reaction to the threats and hostilities directed against socialist movements and against the first self-proclaimed socialist state. During the Russian Civil War, the White Armies were financed and armed by the great capitalist powers and further assisted by troops from these nations. Twenty years later, capitalist Germany under a fascist government launched a devastating invasion of the Soviet Union with the goals not only of destroying "Bolshevism" but also of exterminating the Russian Jews, colonizing the Ukraine, and enslaving the Slavic peoples, whom the Nazis considered racially inferior.

Almost immediately following World War II, the Soviet Union was confronted with a rekindled hostility from the other major capitalist powers, which proceeded to introduce one new and potentially devastating strategic weapons system after another: the hydrogen bomb, long-range jet bombers, missile-firing submarines, and so forth. The leaders and people of the Soviet Union from 1917 until relatively recent times experienced a series of events and hardships that contributed to the development of a siege mentality. That in turn provided justification for restrictions on civil liberties and political freedoms as well as for the USSR's political and military domination of Eastern Europe. Reduction of international hostilities in the late 1980s likely played a major role in promoting the creation of a more democratic political system in the Soviet Union and in other Communist Party–led states.

THE SOVIET UNION AND REVOLUTION IN EASTERN EUROPE

At the conclusion of World War II, Soviet armies occupied most of the states in Eastern Europe. The presence of Soviet forces strengthened the position of local Communist parties, many of whose members had played significant roles in wartime resistance movements against German Nazis and other fascist elements. In some cases anti-Communists in these countries had disgraced themselves by tolerating or even supporting and assisting Nazis in the suppression, imprisonment, and mass murder of Jews and political leftists during the war.

After the war left-wing political coalitions, usually involving Communist and Socialist parties and sometimes Peasant and Liberal parties, tended to dominate the governments of Eastern Europe (Goldman 1990). With the onset of the cold war between the United States and the USSR in 1947, the Soviet Union encouraged and assisted local Communist parties in seizing exclusive control in several Eastern European countries and in the establishment of repressive regimes similar to the Stalinist system then in place in the USSR. In the process hundreds and perhaps thousands of competent administrators and technically skilled persons were denied positions of authority, which were instead filled by less-qualified individuals who were judged more loyal to local pro-Moscow Communist leaders.

Stalinist-type governments subservient to Moscow were undermined by Stalin's death in 1953 and by the condemnation of Stalin's repressive policies by the Soviet leader Nikita Khrushchev in February 1956. As a consequence of these changes in the Soviet Union, some Stalinist regimes in Eastern Europe were replaced in the second half of the 1950s by Communist Party governments that were less repressive, often relatively nationalistic, and thus somewhat more independent of the USSR.

The Soviet Union, however, invaded Hungary in 1956, when Hungarians attempted to withdraw from Moscow's influence totally, and occupied Czechoslovakia in 1968 when that nation's liberal Communist leaders acted to increase freedoms of expression and assembly. Soviet leaders attempted to rationalize these military interventions by reference to the combined British, French, and Israeli invasion of Egyptian territory in 1956 and U.S. interventions in Latin America and Vietnam. The Soviet leader at the time of the 1968 occupation of Czechoslovakia, Leonid Brezhnev, proclaimed the right of other "socialist countries" (those whose governments were controlled by the Communist Party) to intervene militarily elsewhere to protect "socialism" (in his meaning, Communist Party control of the state). The Brezhnev Doctrine inhibited democratization of the Eastern European countries for the next two decades.

By the late 1980s, however, changes had occurred within the Soviet Union that contributed to a dramatic public abandonment of the Brezhnev Doctrine in 1989. Possibly the most important development leading to the new permissive orientation of the USSR toward Eastern Europe was the transition in national leadership embodied in the selection of Mikhail Gorbachev as general secretary of the Communist Party in 1985 and as president of the nation in 1988. Members of the new cohort of Soviet leaders displayed a greater historical and psychological distance from both the early external and internal threats to the revolution and the trauma and devastation of the Nazi invasion of World War II. Gorbachev and his associates, as well as large sectors of the Soviet population, tended to view their repressive political system, excessively large and inefficient bureaucracies, and overly centralized economy as obsolete relics of a more hostile era and of Stalinist paranoia. Many apparently felt that Soviet economic progress would require a more-decentralized, market-oriented economy, greater trade with and technological assistance from the advanced capitalist nations, a reduced drain on the economy for military expenditures, and a more democratic political system. President Gorbachev, consequently, called for perestroika (restructuring) of the USSR's economic and political systems and increased glasnost (public disclosure or openness) and freedom throughout Soviet society. The perceived advantages of more positive economic and political relations with the United States and Western Europe, the incentive to decrease military spending, and the growing view that political control over Eastern Europe was no longer necessary for the security interests of the USSR contributed to the decision to allow the nations of Eastern Europe to select their own forms of government.

For most of the Eastern European countries Communist Party rule had come about as the result of primarily external factors, such as Soviet occupation and the pressures of the cold war, rather than as the outcome of an internal revolution, as had been the case in the Soviet Union. Many of the people in these countries considered Communist Party rule an aspect of Russian domination and a suppression of both nationalist aspirations and democratic ideals. Although Communist Party–led governments often accomplished some popular reforms such as land redistribution and improvements in access to education and medical services, frustrated nationalism, lack of democratic political systems, and, especially after 1980, stagnated economic development were significant causes of mass discontent.

Poland, which in summer 1989 became the first Eastern European nation to end Communist Party domination of its government, had experienced a steady deterioration in its economy and huge increases in its foreign debt since 1975. Polish economic difficulties were widely viewed as resulting from a combination of factors, including poor planning, lack of sufficient market incentives, and the devastating impact of the 1973 Arab oil embargo, which unexpectedly and drastically increased the cost of the Western technology and machinery on which Polish development had been designed to rely. It became clear that economic austerity measures would be necessary to rescue Poland from further economic decline. But in return for sacrifices (such as higher prices for food and higher risk of unemployment), large sectors of the Polish population demanded the right to participate in governmental decision making. In 1980 workers' protests at Gdansk and Szczecin led to the formation of the Solidarity Labor Union, an organization independent of Communist Party control (Ascherson 1982; Craig 1987; Kunicki 2006; Rensenbrink 1988).

The Solidarity movement, an expression of nationalist, democratic, and economic aspirations, spread rapidly to all parts of the nation and enlisted more than nine million people, including approximately one-third of the members of the Polish Communist Party (called the Polish United Workers' Party). Although an implied threat of Soviet intervention kept Solidarity suppressed during most of the 1980s, the continued inability of Polish

Communist leaders to solve the nation's economic crisis led to the Party's acceptance of Solidarity's demand for revoking the guarantee of Communist Party control of the Polish government. Solidarity, centered in the Polish working class, undermined the Communist Party's claim to be the sole legitimate representative of the workers and set an example whose ultimate success in transforming the Polish government undoubtedly had powerful impacts elsewhere in Eastern Europe and on the USSR itself.

In 1989 in the face of massive support for the Solidarity movement and the Polish Communist Party's agreement to give up control of the government if defeated in free elections, Soviet leaders announced their decision to abandon the Brezhnev Doctrine and allow all Eastern European nations to select their own forms of government. This constituted the advent of the only remaining necessary condition for the success of political transformations in Eastern Europe, the existence of a permissive world context for revolution. When Polish national elections in summer 1989 resulted in the defeat of the Communist Party, the Soviet Union proved its willingness to allow the establishment of the first non-Communist (Solidarity)-led government in Eastern Europe since the late 1940s (*New York Times*, Aug. 25, 1989, A8).

The populations of other Eastern European countries, including Hungary, Czechoslovakia, East Germany, Bulgaria, and Romania, were themselves encouraged by both Poland's achievement and the USSR's permissiveness and rapidly disposed of their own Communist Party–dominated governmental systems (Brook 2005; Chirot 1994; *New York Times*, Feb. 18, 1990, E2). In the elections that followed (which were internationally evaluated as free and democratic), Communist parties (even after being reorganized and renamed) lost to non-Communist parties in three countries that had experienced Soviet interventions in the 1950s or 1960s: Hungary, East Germany, and Czechoslovakia (*New York Times*, June 17, 1990, E1). But a reform coalition dominated by former Communist Party members, the National Salvation Front, won by a wide margin in Romania in May 1990, and in Bulgaria during the following month, the Communist Party (renamed the Socialist Party) achieved a majority of the vote (*New York Times*, May 21, 1990, A1; June 12, 1990, A12). In addition, a number of republics within the USSR itself also initiated multiparty political systems, and newly elected governments in Lithuania, Estonia, and Latvia, which had been forcibly incorporated into the USSR at the beginning of World War II, resolved to secede from the Soviet Union (*New York Times*, Oct. 26, 1990, A6; Jan. 11, 1991, A1).

The Soviet Union's willingness to allow Eastern European nations to establish new forms of government was apparently in part a manifestation of Soviet leaders' reanalysis and restructuring of the USSR's own political system. In February 1990, Soviet leaders agreed to surrender the Communist Party's monopoly on power and to construct a Western-style form of government in which parties would compete for popular support and in which a president would be elected directly by the people (*New York*

Times, Feb. 8, 1990, A1). The USSR and Eastern European nations also made plans to move toward greater market orientation of their economies and even private ownership and operation of businesses and industries (*New York Times*, Oct. 17, 1990, A1).

THE SOLIDARITY MOVEMENT AND THE ROOTS OF CONFLICT IN POST–COMMUNIST PARTY STATES

In August 1980 thousands of striking workers at the Gdansk Shipyard in Poland formulated a list of twenty-one demands, which they presented to the country's Communist Party–dominated government. An analysis of the demands, a major document of the then-developing political revolution in Eastern Europe, not only illustrates the range of aspirations that motivated the opponents of the old one-party system but also provides important insights into central reasons for major social conflicts in post–Communist Party states and for the disintegration of anti-Communist alliances and coalitions, including the Solidarity movement itself.

Among the twenty-one demands in the Gdansk Solidarity proclamation was one demanding greater efficiency and effectiveness in Poland's economic institutions through elimination of the Stalinist-era practice of appointing administrators of economic enterprises on the basis of Party membership and loyalty. Instead, the workers wanted executives and decision makers chosen on the basis of proven expertise and technical knowledge. The first six demands called for more political democracy, including the right to form labor unions independent of the government or the Communist Party, legalization of the right to strike, and the granting of various forms of freedom of information, expression, and communication. (In 1980, when the Soviet Union was still controlled by leaders who both supported the one-party system and claimed for the Soviet Union the right to intervene in Eastern European countries to maintain Communist Party control of those governments, the Solidarity movement activists did not dare to demand immediately a totally democratic, multiparty political system.)

Virtually all of the other fourteen Solidarity items, however, were demands for increased economic security, social welfare measures, and government-provided economic benefits, including guarantees of automatic increases in wages parallel to rises in prices and inflation, lowering the age for retirement eligibility, complete medical care, availability of day care facilities for all working families, and guarantees of longer maternity leaves.

After replacement of Poland's old Leninist structure with a more-democratic multiparty political system and the Solidarity Party's victory in the 1989 parliamentary election, major disagreements arose within the movement concerning what democracy really meant (for example, did it mean not only political democracy but also a particular type of economic system?), which goals of the movement alliance should have priority, and even whether the movement should abandon a major proportion of its original goals: the workers' aspirations for greater economic security and a more humane society.

As the Solidarity Party achieved the leading role in the Polish government, some Solidarity figures who assumed government leadership roles, apparently enamored of capitalist ideology and themselves insulated from the economic hardships their policies would bring to many workers, retired persons, and other disadvantaged groups, began to implement procapitalist economic policies. Their program involved privatizing much of the economic system, closing down or reducing the staff of unprofitable or inefficient enterprises, and limiting funding for social services, health care, and other government expenditures.

Although such measures enabled a minority of Poles to significantly increase their incomes and improve their lifestyles, the unpleasant consequences of such policies for many of the workers and their families who had formed a large segment of the mass support for the prodemocracy movement began to generate major divisions in Solidarity. A large group of workers, apparently thinking their fate would improve if a person from a genuine working-class background became head of state, pressed Lech Walesa, the former electrician and leader of Solidarity, to run for the presidency, which he won in 1990.

Still, much of the former Solidarity constituency remained dissatisfied with their lot after their apparent Pyrrhic victory over the old political system. The pervasiveness of disillusionment was manifested in the 1991 parliamentary election in which only 40 percent of the potential electorate chose to vote. In this election Solidarity split into five factions, and twenty-nine parties won seats in the parliament, with no party receiving more than 12 percent of the votes cast.

In 1993 the successor to Poland's Communist Party and its allied leftist Peasant Party, promising to continue market-oriented economic reforms but with more concern and safeguards for the welfare of the country and the working class, won back control of the parliament.

Electoral victories inspired by concern over similar issues were achieved by renamed and restructured former Communist parties and allied leftist parties in other Eastern European countries, including Lithuania, Bulgaria, and Hungary (*New York Times*, Dec. 19, 1994, A5; Jan. 8, 1995, 5; Feb. 5, 1995, 10; Smolar 1994). And in November 1995, Aleksander Kwasniewski, a former member of the old Communist Party and the candidate of Poland's leftist parties, defeated Lech Walesa in the presidential election (*New York Times*, Nov. 12, 1995, 10; Nov. 21, 1995, A1) and was reelected president in 2000. But in 2005, an alliance of center-right parties won control of the parliament from the former Communists, the Democratic Left Alliance, who had been unable to reduce the country's 18 percent unemployment rate and some of whom had been accused of corruption. A noncommunist, Lech Kaczyñski, was elected president.

RUSSIA, EASTERN EUROPE, AND NEIGHBORING STATES (after 1991)

THE DISINTEGRATION OF THE SOVIET UNION

In February 1990, as democracy blossomed in Eastern Europe, the government of the USSR proclaimed that it, too, would abandon the one-party system. In the future the Communist Party would compete with other political parties in free multiparty elections. The democratization process led to the first free, multicandidate election for president of the Russian Republic (Russian Federation) of the USSR in June 1991. Boris Yeltsin, a former regional Communist Party leader who had previously resigned from the Party, won and thereby became the first democratically elected leader in the hundreds of years of Russia's existence. This event created a remarkable political incongruity in that the president of the USSR's largest component republic (as well as the presidents of several other republics) could claim a higher level of political legitimacy than could Gorbachev, the president of the entire Soviet Union, who held power by virtue of the old Communist Party–dominated political process rather than through a totally democratic election.

Gorbachev envisioned not only democratizing the USSR but also preserving it in a looser form, which would gratify its constituent republics' growing demands for more autonomy and local control of their resources and economies. But Gorbachev, a leading architect of the democratization process, witnessed the movement surge beyond his or any of the other Soviet leaders' control and result in the destruction of the USSR itself. The catalyst for this event was the attempted coup by government, military, and Communist Party "hard-liners" opposed to aspects of the democratization process in August 1991.

Prior to the coup attempt, Gorbachev had held a referendum, which took place in Russia and eight other USSR republics (Rutland 2006), on the issue of preserving the USSR, in which a large majority of citizens (76 percent) had expressed support for maintaining a reformed Soviet Union. To accomplish this, Gorbachev had apparently succeeded in reaching agreements with the leaders of a number of the USSR's republics to ratify a modified, more decentralized constitution. Days before the scheduled signing of the new constitution, while Gorbachev was on a short vacation to the Crimea, the coup was initiated by several top Soviet leaders, including the head of the KGB, a high-ranking army general, and the Soviet Union's vice president. Apparently fearing that the new constitution of the USSR would lead to its destruction, further economic disorganization, continued rapid growth of crime and other social problems, and loss of their own power and status, these men and their associates placed Gorbachev under house arrest and announced to the world that he had taken ill, requiring their assuming control of the nation.

But Yeltsin and the parliament of the Russian Republic refused to recognize the authority of the coup plotters, condemned them as criminals, and called upon Russian citizens to defend the government of the Russian Republic at its parliament building, the so-called "Russian White House." There, Russian President Yeltsin, many parliamentarians, and tens of thousands of citizens resisted the coup and the tanks, which were mostly manned by confused soldiers who had been ordered to Moscow to seize the White House. The coup plotters, in the face of massive peaceful popular resistance and the refusal of most military commanders around the country to acknowledge their authority, gave up after three days and were placed under arrest.

Gorbachev returned to Moscow only to see his dream of a new democratic USSR destroyed. The parliaments of all of the USSR's republics, fearing that some future coup could lead to their resubjugation to a new totalitarian Soviet government, rapidly announced plans to secede from the USSR. On December 31, 1991, the USSR formally went out of existence. The one nation was replaced by fifteen independent countries (the former republics of the USSR), three of which besides Russia (Belarus, Ukraine, and Kazakhstan) initially had nuclear weapons. As the USSR came to an end, so did Gorbachev's office as president of the Soviet Union, reducing him to the status of a private citizen of Russia (Cohen 1994; Kipp 1994; McFaul 1994).

The collapse of the USSR contributed to further economic calamities and social conflicts in part as a result of the harm done to previously established patterns of economic exchange among the republics. The surge of nationalism enhanced by the new independent status of the former republics led to ethnically based wars between and within several of the new nations, including Russia itself, where the Chechens attempted to secede (Aslund 1995; Colarusso 1995; Desai 1994; Goldman 1995; Katz 1994; Lieven 2006; *New York Times*, Jan. 9, 1995, 1; Feb. 7, 1995, A1; Sept. 25, 1995, A1).

Mounting ethnic strife, concern over Yeltsin's alleged authoritarian tendencies and excessive use of alcohol, rising street crime, infiltration of many of Russia's new privately owned businesses by organized-crime groups, and the transfer of incredibly valuable state property, including mineral resource companies, to well-connected political supporters of Yeltsin ("crony capitalism") contributing to the creation of an enormously wealthy and powerful group of oligarchs, some of whom reportedly sent billions of dollars out of Russia to foreign banks, led to hostility between Yeltsin and the Russian parliament. Many parliament members blamed the president's policies for creating these problems or making them worse. Some parliamentarians expressed concern that Yeltsin's administration was also allowing foreign-based corporations to gain control over much of Russia's enormous natural resources. The growing enmity of most of the parliamentarians toward Yeltsin led to an attempt by the parliament to impeach Yeltsin and replace him with the Russian vice president, Rutskoi, who sided with the parliament. In October 1993, after days of confrontation, supporters of the parliament stormed and seized several other government buildings, including the Moscow mayor's office, and then attacked the main TV broadcasting center, which was controlled by Yeltsin supporters. The proparliament forces apparently intended to use the TV center to broadcast their views to other parts of the nation. A number of people were killed in the battle for the television building, which Yeltsin supporters succeeded in defending.

After the initial violence both Yeltsin and the parliament's leaders ordered the military to intervene against the other side. The army decided to obey Yeltsin, who claimed that the process by which he was elected was more democratic than that by which the parliament members had achieved their positions. The military also might have been influenced because the parliament supporters were the ones who first resorted to violence and because Yeltsin enjoyed the open support of the U.S. government, in particular, President Clinton. On orders from Yeltsin, army troops and tanks commenced a morning assault on the Russian White House, from which Yeltsin and the parliament had resisted the August 1991 attempted coup. The defenders initially refused to surrender. After a day of fighting during which more than one hundred people were killed and the building was bombarded by tanks, set on fire, and partially destroyed, the remaining parliamentarians surrendered and were arrested.

Months later, elections for a new parliament resulted in a legislative body perhaps just as anti-Yeltsin as the one that Yeltsin had destroyed. The new parliament, dominated mainly by anti-Yeltsin Russian nationalists and leftists, forced the president to modify some of his policies and promise to take action against governmental corruption in his own administration. And over Yeltsin's protests the new parliament proceeded to pardon all the participants in the previous parliament's rebellion against Yeltsin and also those who had participated in the attempted 1991 coup against Gorbachev and Yeltsin. By 1996 several parliamentarians had been assassinated, as was the head of the nation's major television network, a famous news anchor, with organized-crime groups suspected in most of these murders. Many businesspeople and bankers, thought either to have been resisting extortion or corruption or to have had, in some cases, disputes with organized criminals, had also been murdered (Fish 1995; Handelman 1994; *New York Times*, Oct. 29, 1994, 1; Dec. 11, 1994, E1; Feb. 19, 1995, 1; Feb. 22, 1995, A8; Mar. 2, 1995, A10; Mar. 3, 1995, A8; Mar. 10, 1995, A10; Apr. 11, 1995, A3; May 23, 1995, A1; June 7, 1995, A10). And the health and life expectancy of many Russians underwent a rapid and drastic decline (CBS, May 19, 1996).

Discontent among Russian voters appeared to intensify in the mid-1990s, and in fall 1995 public opinion surveys appeared to indicate that the main Communist Party, publicly embracing the new democratic political system, enjoyed more popular support than any other party (*New York Times*, Oct. 1, 1995, E4; Nov. 8, 1995, A1; Dec. 11, 1995, A1). In the December 17, 1995, election for the Russian parliament, the leading Communist Party won a greater number of seats and a much larger share of the popular vote than any of the many other participating parties (*New York Times*, Dec. 19, 1995a, A24; Dec. 19, 1995b, A1; Dec. 20, 1995, A1; Dec. 30, 1995, A1). Yeltsin was, however, with the assistance of wealthy oligarchs and the resources and media outlets they controlled, able to win reelection as president in 1996, defeating the candidate of the Communist Party, Gennady Zyuganov.

ECONOMIC AND POLITICAL TRENDS

Yeltsin's policies during the 1990s were aimed in great part at transforming Russia's economy as quickly as possible from one that was state owned and centrally planned to one that was largely privately owned and would be characterized by market forces and fair competition. Supporters of the "shock therapy" changeover thought that privately owned competing businesses would increase efficiency and productivity and lead to rapid economic development (Goldman 2003, 320; Thompson 2004, 304). In the view of many observers, however, the privatization process was extremely flawed.

According to Goldman (2003), there were three main types of owners of the new private businesses. One group were former factory directors or members of their staffs who together received about 50 percent of the stock in the newly privatized companies. Many of these, after obtaining more stock through various relatively inexpensive means from poorly informed workers, became affluent participants in the new Russian economy. But a number of persons in the second and third categories became enormously wealthy. One group was composed of former government or Communist Party officials who were powerful and/or politically well connected, especially to President Yeltsin. Some of these obtained hugely valuable previously state-owned energy resources for far below their real value and became billionaires in a very short time. For example, Yukos Oil, estimated to be worth about $20 billion or more in 2003, was obtained for about $300 million; Sibneft Oil, worth about $10 billion in 2003, was obtained for about $100 million. The third major group of new business owners came from among those involved in illegal, but often highly profitable, private business activity under the old soviet system. With the sudden change in laws regulating economic activity, many of these persons found that their previous illegal business activity was now legal. And their years of experience in locating and bringing together resources, products, and customers gave them a huge advantage over others in the new legal market economy. Some of these individuals became extremely wealthy, sometimes reportedly by intimidating or even physically eliminating business rivals.

Although privatization helped create a small percentage of affluent persons and a tiny group of Russian billionaires, the Russia economy as a whole deteriorated dramatically, and millions of Russians became impoverished. According to President Vladimir Putin (Millar 2000, 330), during the 1990s Russian Gross Domestic Product (GDP) plunged by 45 percent resulting in GDP per capita that was about one-tenth of that in the United States. In comparison, the decline in per capita GDP in the United States during the Great Depression, 1929–1933, was "a little less than 25 percent"

(Millar 1999, 323). Much of the new business activity was not competitive but in reality monopolistic, with the new monopolies controlled not by the state as in the Soviet era, but instead by private individuals dedicated to maximizing their profits. Prices rose dramatically in the early 1990s, and by 1999 an estimated 40 percent of Russians found themselves living in poverty (World Bank 2004). The economy was further impaired by the drain on resources for the largely unsuccessful 1994–1996 War in Chechnya. The entire foundation of privatization of major resources in Russia was considered a form of legalized theft on a scale virtually unheard of in human history by many millions of Russian citizens. Some business leaders shipped billions of dollars to secure investments in Western or other countries instead of investing in developing their own nation's economic infrastructure and used their wealth in part to influence government officials and assure their favored politicians superior resources during elections.

When Putin succeeded Yeltsin as president at the end of 1999, his major policies, besides responding to popular sentiment by launching a new invasion of Chechnya to suppress terrorist attacks against Russia thought to be originating there, included attempting to rein in and even prosecute some of the oligarchs, to renationalize some of the most valuable previously state-owned energy resources, and to restore public faith in the new economic system. Because so many of those benefiting from the post-Soviet economic reforms used deceptive means to avoid paying the 35 percent tax rate on high-income persons, Putin instituted a universal 13 percent tax rate that, while many claimed was unfair to lower-income people, seemed more effective in the collection of tax revenue (Goldman 2003). Much of the Russian economic infrastructure was in need of modernization, and the economy itself was heavily dependent on the export of energy resources, similar to the economies of several mineral-rich, less-developed countries. But Russia benefited enormously from the surge in the price of oil after 1999. The growth in Russia's energy export revenue was thought to make up about half of Russia's approximately 6 to 7 percent annual GDP increase during the early 2000s. By the end of 2002 some observers estimated that the percent of Russians living in poverty had been greatly reduced—to around 20 percent.

Economic improvement, Putin's actions against certain oligarchs, and his war on terrorism helped maintain his personal popularity at 70 to 80 percent (Goldman 2003, 324). A pro-Putin political party, United Russia, was created, and Putin's supporters began to dominate the parliament and weaken the influence of the Communist deputies. Besides reducing the political threat from the Communists and somewhat curbing the power of the economic oligarchs, Putin acted to reduce the power of regional Russian authorities relative to that of the central government in part as a means of preventing local interference with the implementation of central government policies intended to cope with continuing challenges, such as Russia's need to diversify its economy from heavy reliance on the export of energy resources, improve the country's industrial and communications infrastructure, significantly reduce corruption, increase agricultural production, and structure a fairer legal system.

According to Thompson (2004) the Russian Revolution of 1991 was a quadruple revolution: a shift from a state-controlled and state-owned economy to one that was in great part privately owned and governed by market forces; the replacement of a one-party state with a multiparty democratic political system; the displacement of Marxist-Leninist ideology with a political culture stressing democratic freedoms and emphasizing individual rights over collective responsibilities; and replacement of a previous conflict-oriented stance toward many other nations with a more integrative and cooperative international approach. However, the actions of the George W. Bush administration in using the war on terrorism as part of its justification for invading and occupying Iraq in 2003 and its relatively hostile orientation toward several countries (such as Iran and certain nations with leftist governments in Latin America, such as Venezuela) likely contributed to a reduction in the willingness of the Russian government to collaborate with the United States on certain issues. But Russia's behavior in this regard was similar to that of other nations whose rebellious voters used elections to reverse their countries' policies of supporting the U.S.-led occupation of Iraq by removing from power Bush-allied governing elites.

CORRUPTION

As Goldman (2005) observed, bribery of public officials was common during the czarist era, and certain forms of graft characterized the era of Communist Party rule. But post-Soviet Russia earned the reputation of being one of the most corrupt nations in the world. The corruption of the post-Soviet period was multifaceted, including most prominently the previously mentioned ability of politically well-connected persons to acquire at little cost billions of dollars of former state property, especially energy companies. According to Sun (2005, 259), Yeltsin depended on economic oligarchs for help in his 1996 reelection, "rendering the government vulnerable to the group's demand for economic and political concessions." The willingness of public officials to accept bribes was related to the rampant inflation during 1992, which wiped out many people's savings. Government salaries did not keep pace with price increases, and many publicly employed professionals and officials, including traffic cops, began to demand bribes to supplement their meager and often inadequate government salaries. Judges were accused of selling their court decisions and university officials of accepting bribes in return for admitting certain students. Putin's anticorruption efforts were considered by some to be inadequate. Many claimed that in effect, while strengthening central government power, he concurrently weakened the ability of regional governments to exercise independent, local anticorruption initiatives. And by intimidating the press with regard to criticizing him or his policies, he also may have reduced its ability to function in an independent role as a weapon against corruption. Yet Sun noted that in China many people came to support the idea of strengthening central government power to intervene in the economy as a necessary anticorruption measure. Putin and his supporters apparently reached a similar conclusion regarding how to curb the massive and diverse forms of corruption in Russia.

HEALTH AND RELATED ISSUES

According to Powell, the birth rate in Russia fell significantly, so that by 2002 the death rate exceeded the birthrate by 70 percent (2002, 344). The decline in the birthrate was due, in part, to the perception of many people that they lacked the resources to raise children in Russia's new economic environment.

Increasing inequality, drug use, deterioration in much of the health care and welfare systems, and growth in criminal behavior, including organized crime, contributed to a rapid reduction in life span, particularly for men. Powell noted that many observers and researchers in Russia believed that a drastic rise in alcoholism since the end of the Soviet Union, perhaps due to the growth in economic hardships, dismal expectations for the future, and/or moral or ideological disillusionment contributed to a surge in diseases and forms of death closely linked to alcohol. Homicides, about 80 percent of which appeared to be associated with alcohol use, rose dramatically during the 1990s (Chervyakov, Shkolnikov, Pridemore, and McKee 2002). In 1999, the homicide rate (age standardized) was about 81 percent higher than in 1990. This was estimated to represent generally about double the rate of increase for other causes of death. The number of murders by hired killers was one form of homicide that rose in the 1990s. During the period 1993–1998 the murders of six members of parliament, nineteen journalists, ninety-five bankers, and hundreds of other businessmen were thought, in great part, to be related to the fact that as many as one-half of private businesses were either controlled by criminals or the victims of extortion by criminal groups.

Researchers estimated that there was also a dramatic rise in injection drug use, which contributed to the spread of the HIV virus and AIDS deaths. In 2006, women's life span was 74.1 years, while for men it was only 60.5 years (it had been 64.9 years in 1987). For decades before the end of the USSR, the male-female differential had been about ten years (Powell 2002, 345), but in 2006, the gap had grown to over thirteen years. In 2006, Belarus, Ukraine, and Kazakhstan—other former major components of the USSR—also had large gender mortality gaps of about eleven years. In contrast, the United States, United Kingdom, and Australia all had more narrow gender differentials in mortality of five to six years. And two remaining Communist Party–dominated states had even smaller gender differences in death rates. For Cuba, with an average life expectancy nearly identical to that of the United States, the men's life span in 2006 averaged only 4.74 years less than women, and in China, with an average life span about five years less than the United States, the difference between women's and men's longevity was only 3.57 years.

The rapid decline in the male life span in Russia, virtually unprecedented in history, and the wide range of other enormous social problems afflicting large sections of the population under the new economic and political systems, while a small minority of Russians prospered or even accumulated immense wealth, undoubtedly had major international impacts. To many of those in lesser-developed countries, the negative developments in Russia confirmed their hostility toward neoliberal economic policies. And the fate of the Russians undoubtedly caused large numbers of people in China and Cuba to be extremely cautious regarding whether and how to change their countries' political systems. In May 2006, President Putin called on the Russian parliament to launch a program to stop the drastic decline in Russia's population—losses of almost 700,000 annually, which demographers claim threatened the future viability of the Russian nation—in part by offering subsidies and financial incentives to Russian women to have more children (Chivers 2006).

THE DISINTEGRATION OF YUGOSLAVIA AND THE TRAGEDY OF BOSNIA

The most violent political events in Europe during the 1990s included the death of the Yugoslav nation and the civil war within the former Yugoslav republic of Bosnia-Hercegovina. Yugoslavia, the land of the "Yugo" (or "South") Slavs, first became a reality at the conclusion of World War I. Croatia and Slovenia, which had been components of the Austro-Hungarian Empire, agreed to unite with other South Slav states, in particular Serbia and largely Serbian-populated Montenegro, to preserve their individual cultures from the threat of powerful non-Slavic neighbors such as Italy, Germany, and Turkey. The first Yugoslavia, the Kingdom of Serbs, Croats, and Slovenes (1918–1941), incorporated peoples who spoke three Slavic languages—Slovene, Macedonian, and Serbo-Croatian—as well as residents who spoke other languages such as Hungarian and Albanian. Yugoslavia's major religions included Orthodox Christianity, practiced by most Serbs; Roman Catholicism, practiced by the large majority of Croats; and Islam, to which many Serbs and Albanians had converted during hundreds of years of Turkish occupation (Akhavan and Howse 1995; Bennett 1995; Djilas 1991; Dragnich 1992; Luk 1995; Necak 1995; Sahara 1994).

During World War II Nazi Germans and Italian Fascists invaded and destroyed the first Yugoslavia and placed a Croatian terrorist group, Ustasha (Croatian Revolutionary Organization), in charge of most of what is today Croatia and Bosnia. The Ustasha government, characterized by adherence to extreme Croat nationalism and fanatical Catholicism, apparently murdered hundreds of thousands of Serbs in "ethnic cleansing" of large areas, as well as thousands of Jews and gypsies (although Croat historians cite lower numbers of victims). Several top Serb military leaders accused of brutalities against non-Serbs in the 1990s were raised on stories of Ustasha or other Fascist World War II atrocities or personally witnessed them as children.

Many Yugoslavians joined the multiethnic, Communist-led resistance against the Italian and German Fascists and the Ustasha. The leader of this anti-Fascist guerrilla movement was a charismatic revolutionary, Tito, whose father was Croatian and whose mother was Slovene. At the end of World War II, Tito and his movement created a new Yugoslavia (1945–1991) (Vujaèic 2006a).

The second Yugoslavia, especially as structured by its 1974 constitution, was a federation consisting of eight "federal units": six republics—Bosnia-Hercegovina, Croatia, Macedonia, Montenegro, Serbia, and Slovenia (which technically had the right of secession from the federation)—and two "autonomous" regions within the republic of Serbia, Vojvodina (with a Serbian majority and a large Hungarian minority) and Kosovo (which was over 85 percent Albanian and approximately 13 percent Serbian) (Bennett 1995; Dimitrijevic 1995; Dragnich 1992; Vojnic 1995). In each of Yugoslavia's federal units one particular ethnic group was a majority, except in Bosnia, where, since Muslims regardless of language were characterized as a separate ethnic group, about 44 percent were Muslims, 33 percent were Serbs, 17 percent were Croats, and 6 percent labeled themselves simply "Yugoslavs." In all of Yugoslavia about 36 percent were Serbs, 20 percent Croats, 9 percent Muslims, 8 percent Slovenes, 8 percent Albanians, 6 percent Macedonians, 3 percent Montenegrins, 2 percent Hungarians, and 5 percent "Yugoslavs."

Tito served as president of Yugoslavia for life. Following his death in 1980, the presidency was, in effect, to rotate annually among leaders from each of the eight federal units. According to the 1974 constitution, a consensus of all eight federal units was necessary for determining Yugoslav federal policies. Tito continuously mediated problems that arose among Yugoslavia's ethnic groups and, by most accounts, attempted to prevent any one ethnic group from becoming dominant in the federation.

Besides Tito's charisma, leadership, and the aura of the wartime, multiethnic "equality and brotherhood" struggle against foreign and domestic fascism, several other factors played significant roles in helping to maintain the Yugoslav federation. All Yugoslavian school children were taught the official state sponsored "universalist" ideology of the equality of Yugoslavia's peoples, coupled with lessons concerning appreciation of their individual cultures and histories. Another key factor that helped to perpetuate the Yugoslav state was the cold war and the role Tito's Yugoslavia played in it as a regional stabilizing factor and as a sort of bridge between East and West. Because after World War II Tito's pursuit of policies somewhat independent of those of the USSR provoked Stalin's displeasure, Yugoslavia's peoples began to fear the possibility of an invasion from Russia, a threat that kept them bound together. Later, Tito, along with the leaders of several other nations, including India, established the organization of "nonaligned states," countries that were not formally allied to either the United States or the USSR. Because Yugoslavia led the large block of nonaligned nations, defied the USSR, and attempted with limited success to introduce a greater level of democracy and economic freedom through "worker self-management" and "market socialism," it received large amounts of economic assistance from capitalist nations. Eventually, even the USSR, sharing the West's goal of preserving stability in the Balkans, began to support Yugoslavia.

After the death of Tito in 1980 and the end of the cold war later in the decade, however, a number of developments contributed to increasing tensions among Yugoslavia's ethnic groups. The economy suffered greatly from the phenomenal rise in oil prices during the 1970s. Since Yugoslavia's leaders feared that economic hardships such as the threat of unemployment or increasing economic inequality would likely promote hostility and nationalist urges among the country's diverse population groups, the federation began to borrow heavily from Western nations to maintain an acceptable domestic living standard. By the 1980s Yugoslavia was more than $20 billion in debt, and the more prosperous republics, Slovenia and Croatia, began to resist providing assistance to poorer regions of the country. Furthermore, with the end of the cold war, neither fear of possible foreign attack nor pride in leading the increasingly irrelevant nonaligned movement acted to bind Yugoslavia's peoples together, as had once been the case.

As antagonisms among several of Yugoslavia's ethnic groups began to rise during the 1980s, events in Serbia and the Kosovo autonomous region of the Serbian Republic accelerated the process of Yugoslavia's disintegration. Slobodan Milošević, a Serbian nationalist, assumed leadership of the Serbian Communist Party and proceeded to appeal to Serbians to redress perceived grievances allegedly inflicted on them in several parts of Yugoslavia. In 1987 Milošević traveled to Kosovo, viewed by many as "the cradle of the Serb nation," the site of a heroic battle in 1389 in which the Serbs were conquered and then ruled by the Turks until 1867. He intervened decisively on the side of the Serb minority there. Milošević's apparent exaggeration of Serb difficulties in Kosovo and his overt appeal to Serb nationalism, an act that was in direct opposition to past Communist Party internationality policies, were widely reported by the Serb media. Milošević's popularity among Serbians increased, and his opponents within the Serbian Communist Party were unable to turn back the nationalist tide (Bennett 1995; Janjic 1995; Pajic 1995; Puhovski 1995; Pupovac 1995).

In 1989 Milošević helped bring about a new constitution for the Serb Republic. It was interpreted as effectively depriving Kosovo, and therefore its large Albanian-speaking majority, of its autonomy and, further, as proclaiming that the government of the Serb Republic was the legitimate representative of all Serbs throughout Yugoslavia, including the 30 percent of Yugoslavia's Serbs who lived in Bosnia and Croatia. Essentially these actions permanently split the already deeply divided federation-wide Communist Party, the League of Communists of Yugoslavia, into separate ethnically based parties. Individual republics, influenced by popular support for the political revolutions in the nations of Eastern Europe in 1989 and 1990, all held multiparty elections. In Slovenia and Croatia, nationalist parties won over the local Communist parties, but in Serbia the nationalist-oriented Communist Party was victorious.

Alarmed over a Serbian-sponsored plan to strengthen the Yugoslavian federal government at the expense of limiting the authority of individual republics and perhaps fearful of the possibility of future Serbian repression (as had befallen the Kosovo Albanians), Slovenia declared its independence in 1991, followed quickly by Croatia. After Germany and Great Britain recognized the independence of Slovenia and Croatia, Bosnia followed suit and declared independence as well. Only Montenegro, with its Serbian majority, decided to stay federated with Serbia in a much-reduced Yugoslavia. Many non-Serbian personnel resigned from the Yugoslav army and helped build new armies for their particular ethnic homelands.

Whereas the Serbs put up little resistance to Slovenia's secession (since few Serbs lived there), war broke out between Serbs and Croatians in Croatia and among Serbs, Muslims, and Croatians in Bosnia. The early Serbian advantage in heavy weaponry may have promoted the fighting and certainly contributed to initial Serbian military successes (Bennett 1995; Jost 1995; Pajic 1995).

After four years of warfare, brutality, forcible relocations of hundreds of thousands of one nationality from territories seized by another nationality ("ethnic cleansing"), and the reported deaths of possibly over 250,000 persons, the opposing parties in Bosnia accepted an internationally sponsored peace settlement in 1995.

The peace accords maintained Bosnia technically as a united and independent nation but assigned 49 percent of its territory to a Bosnian Serb Republic, with its own parliament and its own armed forces, and 51 percent of Bosnia's territory to a Bosnian Muslim-Croat "federation," also with its own parliament and armed forces. In addition, there was to be a nationwide parliament and elected president (*New York Times*, Nov. 22, 1995, A1; Dec. 15, 1995, A1). Separation of the opposing military units and enforcement of the peace agreement were to be carried out through an international force of 60,000, including the participation of 20,000 U.S. soldiers (a stipulation demanded by all warring parties).

As with the 1989 and 1990 revolutions in Eastern Europe and the USSR, the political transformations of Yugoslavia and its individual republics can be analyzed in terms of the five factors critical to the success of all revolutions. In the late 1980s, widespread decline in living standards and the increasing threat of unemployment contributed to the development of discontent among large sectors of Yugoslavia's population. Some among the ethnic elites, once united by an ideology of universal equality, anticipating the likely appeal of nationalistic (ethnic) collectivism to an increasing economically threatened population, tended to foster individual ethnic interests and views. South Slavs, once motivated to unify in the face of perceived threats from non-Slavic nations and later from the USSR, reverted to individual ethnic unity once external threats had clearly dissipated.

The previous sense of unity that had once characterized much of the Yugoslav population was further undermined by initial acts of violence, often committed by extremists from more-backward, poverty-stricken, and less-educated elements of individual ethnic groups, whose brutality provoked much more pervasive and intense levels of interethnic hostility. The Yugoslav state had arisen in great part in reaction to past and continuing foreign invasions and external threats and was sustained by its prestigious cold war status as a valuable, peace-sustaining bridge between East and West. Once the cold war ended, the legitimacy of the Yugoslav federation eroded to a point at which it could not survive the mounting internal interethnic antagonisms. The realization of the first Yugoslavia was partially a product of world permissiveness in that the non-Slavic powers that had previously dominated the South Slavs were defeated in World War I. Later, the end of the cold war left no major power with serious commitment to preventing the breakup of the Yugoslav federation.

After the agreements signed at Dayton, Ohio, brought an end to most of the armed conflict in the territory of the former Yugoslavia, fighting broke out in 1998 in Kosovo, the southern province of Serbia. There the Kosovo Liberation Army (KLA) launched an effort to separate Kosovo, with its overwhelmingly Albanian population, from Serbia, and transform it into an independent nation. Due to the conflict, approximately 200,000 Kosovo Albanians were forced to leave their homes (Vujaèic 2006b, 971). A new peace conference focusing on the situation in Kosovo was held at Rambouillet, France. But the Serbian delegation refused to accept the U.S.-drafted peace plan, which put Kosovo under North Atlantic Treaty Organization (NATO) control and allowed NATO troops free movement within Serbia. In retaliation, NATO initiated a bombing campaign against Serbia. On March 24, 1999, NATO forces began bombing Serbia and Montenegro, and on May 27 the International War Crimes Tribunal indicted Milošević for crimes against humanity, along with a number of high-level Serbian military and civilian leaders. In June, after eighty-eight days of bombing, Serbia agreed to withdraw its forces from Kosovo. The UN approved Resolution 1244, which, while technically referring to Kosovo as still a province of Serbia, allowed it to become self-governing under the protection of NATO and the UN. Opposition in Serbia to Milošević's leadership grew, and he was defeated in the October 2000 presidential elections. In June 2001 the new Serbian government sent Milošević to stand trial in the Hague, Netherlands, but he died in 2006 before the trial ended. On June 3, 2006, Montenegro declared independence, ending its federation with Serbia.

Summary and Analysis

For several decades before the Revolutions of 1917, thousands of young educated Russians had joined revolutionary movements and even engaged in terrorist violence in efforts to topple the czar's government. Elite radicalism eventually led to the formation of the Russian Social Democratic Party and, more significant, of its Bolshevik faction under Lenin's leadership. The Bolsheviks steadfastly condemned Russia's participation in World War I but perceived a great opportunity for revolution in Russia's likely defeat.

Inadequate land reforms and subsequent hardships had fostered deep-seated peasant frustration. Industrial development led to the growth of a large urban working class, many of whose members were dissatisfied with their working and living conditions. Though nationalism inflamed by the onset of World War I temporarily suppressed interclass hostilities, catastrophic military losses and war-caused social and economic disorganization resulted in widespread and intense discontent among both peasants and workers.

The monarchy was steadily undermined in the latter half of the nineteenth century in great part because of governmental efforts to spur industrialization and modernization. Many of those young Russians schooled in the technologies of the more advanced societies also learned of the relatively democratic political systems in Western Europe. As increasing numbers of educated Russians rejected autocracy in favor of the establishment of a freer and more participatory form of government, the prerevolutionary state was progressively weakened. Russia's military defeat during World War I and the accompanying social unrest finally forced the czar's abdication. Soldiers ordered to put down the protests of their fellow workers refused or openly joined the demonstrators, as did peasants. Faced with massive popular opposition and army and navy mutinies, and deserted by much of the middle- and upper-class minorities, the czarist state collapsed, providing a historic opportunity for the establishment of new political, social, and economic institutions.

A number of groups initially cooperated to accomplish the overthrow of the monarchy. But although the contending revolutionary movements and most members of the major social classes were temporarily united in the goal of ousting the czar, they were divided over other issues. Various political movements favored divergent programs ranging from constructing a constitutional monarchy and carrying out moderate social reforms to abolishing private ownership of major industries. The Bolsheviks demanded additional changes for which most people yearned, including a quick end to the war, an immediate redistribution of land to the peasants, and workers' control of industry. When other parties and factions, through the provisional government, attempted to continue the war and delayed land redistribution, popular support swung rapidly to the Bolsheviks in the large urban areas, permitting them to seize control of the national government in fall 1917.

The czar's capitalist allies were unable to assist effectively in repressing revolutionaries as long as their resources were absorbed in fighting World

War I. In 1918 several nations sent troops and military supplies into the Soviet Union to aid White Armies attempting to reverse the Bolshevik Revolution. The White Armies, however, lacked unity, were notorious for engaging in more brutality toward civilians than the Red Army, and further alienated any significant popular support by offering those peasants dissatisfied with Bolshevik policies the even-less-appealing alternative of a return to czarist-era landownership patterns. The fact that the capitalist nations were either unwilling or unable to launch major invasions of the Soviet Union in support of White forces facilitated the Bolshevik defeat of counterrevolutionaries. After the Bolshevik seizure of power and the end of the Russian Civil War, Stalin and his supporters established an authoritarian governmental structure, which characterized the USSR until the democratizing reforms of the late 1980s.

At the end of 1991 the USSR disintegrated into fifteen independent nations. Russia's president Boris Yeltsin launched economic reforms that privatized much of the economy but in the process allowed politically connected individuals and Yeltsin supporters to acquire vast wealth that was once state property. The economy temporarily spiraled downward, inequality increased, and by 1999 approximately 40 percent of Russians lived in poverty. Observers claimed that alcoholism, drug use, major forms of crime, including homicide and organized crime, and corruption dramatically increased, while health care deteriorated and life span, especially that of men, declined rapidly. Russia's population began to decrease by more than 500,000 people each year, as death rates far exceeded birthrates. This trend continued through 2006. President Putin, who first took office at the end of 1999, attempted to continue economic reforms but also to reduce the level of corruption and the power of the economic oligarchs spawned by Yeltsin's deeply flawed privatization scheme and to cope with a number of other major problems. Putin was accused of shifting governmental practices back toward authoritarianism, but some observers thought that his actions were necessitated by the nature and scope of the problems his nation faced.

RUSSIAN REVOLUTIONS: CHRONOLOGY OF MAJOR EVENTS

1898	Formation of the Russian Social Democratic Party
1903	Split develops within the Russian Social Democratic Party between the Bolshevik and Menshevik factions
1904–1905	Russia defeat by Japan; attempted revolution
1914	Russia enters World War I
1917	March (February by Julian calendar) Revolution: the establishment of the provisional government; November (October by Julian calendar) Revolution: Bolsheviks seize power
1918–1922	Civil War and foreign intervention
1924	Lenin dies

1927–1929	Trotsky expelled from the Communist Party and then exiled from the Soviet Union; Stalin becomes the dominant Soviet leader
1929–1940	Forced collectivization of agriculture and rapid industrialization; development of Stalin's repressive regime
1941–1945	Nazi German invasion devastates USSR but results in Soviet victory
1953	Stalin dies
1991	First democratically elected president of Russia; USSR divides into separate nations
1991–1999	Much of the Russian economy is privatized; some Russians prosper while many sink into poverty; mortality rates climb while birthrates decline, resulting in huge annual population losses
1993	In October, President Yeltsin orders the military to attack and arrest members of the Russian parliament for opposing him and certain of his policies
1994	War against rebellious Chechnya begins
1996	With the help of the new economic oligarchs, Yeltsin is re-elected president
1999–2000	At the end of 1999, Yeltsin resigns, making Prime Minister Putin acting president; Putin elected president in 2000
2004	Putin elected to a second term as president of Russia

References and Further Readings

Abdullaev, Nabi. 2004. "Chechnya Ten Years Later." *Current History*, October, 332–36.

Akhavan, Payam, and Robert Howse, eds. 1995. *Yugoslavia: The Former and Future*. Geneva: United Nations Research Institute for Social Development.

Ascherson, Neal. 1982. *The Polish August: The Self-Limiting Revolution*. New York: Viking Press.

Aslund, Anders. 1995. "The Russian Road to the Market." *Current History*, October, 311–16.

Beissinger, Mark. 2002. *Nationalist Mobilization and the Collapse of the Soviet State*. New York: Cambridge University Press.

Bennett, Christopher. 1995. *Yugoslavia's Bloody Collapse: Causes, Course and Consequences*. New York: New York University Press.

Bottomore, Tom, ed. 1983. *A Dictionary of Marxist Thought*. Cambridge, MA: Harvard University Press.

Breslauer, George W. 2002. *Gorbachev and Yeltsin as Leaders*. New York: Cambridge University Press.

Brook, Daniel. 2005. *Modern Revolution: Social Change and Cultural Continuity in Czechoslovakia and China*. Lanham, MD: University Press of America.

CBS. May 19, 1996. "Facts of Life in Russia." *60 Minutes*.

Charance, Bernard. 1994. *The Transformation of Communist Systems: Economic Reform since the 1950s.* Boulder: Westview Press.

Chervyakov, V. V., V. M. Shkolnikov, W. A. Pridemore, and M. McKee. 2002. "The Changing Nature of Murder in Russia." *Social Science and Medicine,* November, 55 (10):1713–24.

Chirot, David. 1994. "The Eastern European Revolutions of 1989." In Goldstone, ed., *Revolutions.*

Chivers, C. J. 2006. "Putin Urges Plan to Reverse Slide in the Birth Rate." *New York Times,* May 11.

Cohen, Stephen. 1994. "America's Failed Crusade in Russia." *The Nation,* February, 261–63.

Colarusso, John. 1995. "Chechnya: The War Without Winners." *Current History,* October, 329–36.

Craig, Mary. 1987. *Lech Walesa and His Poland.* New York: Continuum.

Daniels, Robert V. 1988. *Is Russia Reformable? Change and Resistance from Stalin to Gorbachev.* Boulder: Westview Press.

DeFronzo, James, ed. 2006a. *Revolutionary Movements in World History: From 1750 to the Present.* 3 vols. Santa Barbara, CA: ABC-CLIO.

_____. 2006b. "The Russian Revolution of 1917." In DeFronzo, ed., *Revolutionary Movements in World History,* 3:721–38.

Desai, Padma. 1994. "Aftershock in Russia's Economy." *Current History,* October, 320–23.

Dimitrijevic, Vojin. 1995. "The 1974 Constitution and Constitutional Process as a Factor in the Collapse of Yugoslavia." In Akhavan and Howse, eds., *Yugoslavia.*

Djilas, Aleksa. 1991. *The Contested Country: Yugoslav Unity and Communist Revolution, 1919–1953.* Cambridge, MA: Harvard University Press.

Dmytryshyn, Basil. 1984. *The USSR: A Concise History.* New York: Scribner.

Dragnich, Alex N. 1992. *Serbs and Croats: The Struggle in Yugoslavia.* New York: Harcourt Brace Jovanovich.

Dunn, John. 1972. *Modern Revolutions: An Introduction to the Analysis of a Political Phenomenon.* Cambridge, UK: Cambridge University Press.

Evangelista, Matthew. 2003. "Chechnya's Russia Problem." *Current History,* October, 313–19.

Fish, M. Steven. 1995. "Democracy Begins to Emerge." *Current History,* October, 317–21.

Fitzpatrick, Sheila. 1982. *The Russian Revolution: 1917–1932.* New York: Oxford University Press.

Ganev, Venelin G. 2006. "Eastern European Revolutions of 1989." In DeFronzo, ed., *Revolutionary Movements in World History,* 1:217–35.

Getty, J. Arch, and Oleg Naumov. 1999. *The Road to Terror: Stalin and the Self-Destruction of the Bolsheviks, 1932–1939.* New Haven, CT: Yale University Press.

Gill, Jungyun. 2006. "Student and Youth Movements, Activism and Revolution." In DeFronzo, ed., *Revolutionary Movements in World History,* 3:848–54.

Goldman, Marshall I. 1995. "Is This Anyway to Create a Market Economy?" *Current History,* October, 305–10.

_____. 2003. "Render Unto Caesar: Putin and the Oligarchs." *Current History,* October, 320–26.

_____. 2005. "Political Graft: The Russian Way." *Current History*, October, 313–18.

Goldman, Minton F. 1990. *Global Studies: The Soviet Union and Eastern Europe.* 3rd ed. Guilford, CT: Dushkin Publishing.

Goldstone, Jack A., ed. 1994. *Revolutions: Theoretical, Comparative, and Historical Studies.* 2nd ed. Fort Worth, TX: Harcourt Brace College Publishers.

Greene, Thomas H. 1990. *Comparative Revolutionary Movements: Search for Theory and Justice.* Prentice-Hall Contemporary Comparative Politics. 3rd ed. Englewood Cliffs, NJ: Prentice-Hall.

Handelman, Stephen. 1994. "The Russian Mafiya." *Foreign Affairs*, March/April, 83–96.

Hill, Fiona. 2004. "Siberia: Russia's Economic Heartland and Daunting Dilemma." *Current History*, October, 324–31.

Janjic, Dusan. 1995. "Resurgence of Ethnic Conflict in Yugoslavia: The Demise of Communism and the Rise of the 'New Elites' of Nationalism." In Akhavan and Howse, eds., *Yugoslavia.*

Jost, Kenneth. 1995. "War Crimes." *Congressional Quarterly Researcher*, July 5, 5 (25): 585–608.

Katov, George. 1967. *Russia 1917: The February Revolution.* New York: Harper and Row.

Katz, Mark N. 1994. "Nationalism and the Legacy of Empire." *Current History*, October, 327–31.

Kipp, Jacob W. 1994. "The Zhirinovsky Threat." *Foreign Affairs*, May/June, 72–86.

Kotkin, Stephen. 2003. *Armageddon Averted: The Soviet Collapse, 1970–2000.* New York: Oxford University Press.

Kunicki, Mikolaj Stanislaw. 2006. "The Polish Solidarity Movement." In DeFronzo, ed., *Revolutionary Movements in World History*, 2:698–711.

Lavelle, Peter. 2004. "What Does Putin Want?" *Current History*, October, 314–18.

Lenin, V. I. [1902] 1975. "What Is To Be Done?" In Tucker, ed., *The Lenin Anthology.*
_____. [1917] 1975. "The State and Revolution." In Tucker, ed., *The Lenin Anthology.*

Lieven, Anatol. 2006. "Chechen Revolt Against Russia." In DeFronzo, ed., *Revolutionary Movements in World History*, 1:99–107.

Luk, Albina Necak. 1995. "The Linguistic Aspect of the Ethnic Conflict in Yugoslavia." In Akhavan and Howse, eds., *Yugoslavia.*

Marx, Karl. [1875] 1994. "Critique of the Gotha Program." In Lawrence H. Simon, ed., *Karl Marx: Selected Writings*, 315–32. Indianapolis: Hackett Publishing.

Marx, Karl, and Friedrich Engels. [1848] 1998. *The Communist Manifesto.* New York: Signet Classics.

McFaul, Michael. 1994. "Russian Politics: The Calm Before the Storm?" *Current History*, October, 313–19.
_____. 2005. "Russia and the West: A Dangerous Drift." *Current History*, October, 307–12.

Millar, James R. 1999. "The De-development of Russia." *Current History*, October, 322–27.
_____. 2000. "Can Putin Jump-Start Russia's Stalled Economy?" *Current History*, October, 329–33.

Necak, Dusan. 1995. "Historical Elements for Understanding the 'Yugoslav Question.'" In Akhavan and Howse, eds., *Yugoslavia.*

New York Times, January 28, 1987, A1, "Gorbachev, Citing Party's Failures, Demands Changes, Asks Secret Votes, A Choice of Candidates."

_____, May 10, 1987, E3, "Kremlin Reinterprets and Re-emphasizes the Legacy of Lenin."

_____, June 26, 1987, A1, "Gorbachev urges 'Radical' Changes to Spur Economy."

_____, August 25, 1989, A8, "Soviet Congratulations Sent to New Premier of Poland."

_____, February 8, 1990, A1, "Soviet Leaders Agree to Surrender Communist Party Monopoly on Power."

_____, February 18, 1990, E2, "Up-to-the-Minute Scores from the Revolution in the East Bloc."

_____, May 13, 1990, E3, "Catching Up with Change in Eastern Europe: First Steps and Second Thoughts."

_____, May 20, 1990, E3, "In Search of Capitalism with a Human Face."

_____, May 21, 1990, A1, "Front in Romania Seems Victorious in Free Elections."

_____, June 12, 1990, A12, "Bulgarian Voting Stuns Opposition."

_____, June 17, 1990, E1, "Free Choice Revives the Best and the Worst of Eastern Europe."

_____, October 17, 1990, A1, "Gorbachev Offers His Plan to Remake Soviet Economy But Includes No Timetable."

_____, October 26, 1990, A6, "In Soviet Union, Dizzying Disunion."

_____, January 11, 1991, A1, "Gorbachev Warns the Lithuanians to Halt Defiance."

_____, October 29, 1994, 1, "Russian Miners Become Victims of the Upheaval They Helped Start."

_____, December 11, 1994, E1, "The Long Shadow of the Russian Mob."

_____, December 19, 1994, A5, "Bulgaria's Communists Claim Parliament Election Victory."

_____, January 8, 1995, 5, "In Modern Polish Politics, It's Still Solidarity vs. the Communists."

_____, January 9, 1995, 1, "Hundreds Killed in Chechen Strife."

_____, February 5, 1995, 10, "Poland's Leaders: Old Communists But with a Difference."

_____, February 7, 1995, A1, "Russians in Central Asia, Once Welcome Now Flee."

_____, February 19, 1995, 1, "Russia's Declining Health: Rising Illness, Shorter Lives."

_____, February 22, 1995, A8, "Yeltsin Bans Advertising of Tobacco and Alcohol."

_____, March 2, 1995, A10, "Russian Journalist Is Slain; Profits May Be the Motive."

_____, March 3, 1995, A8, "Celebrity's Killing Stirs Talk of Intrigue in Russia."

_____, March 10, 1995, A10, "Yeltsin Vows Crackdown on Gangsters."

_____, April 11, 1995, A3, "Latest Films for $2: Video Piracy Boom in Russia."

_____, May 9, 1995, A11, "In Russia, Nostalgia and Edginess."

_____, May 23, 1995, A1, "Russia's New Rulers Govern, and Live, in Neo-Soviet Style."

_____, June 7, 1995, A10, "Images of Lawlessness Twist Russian Reality."

_____, September 25, 1995, A1, "After Long Slide, Russia's Economy Nearing Stability."

_____, October 1, 1995, E4, "Russia's Voters Turn Cranky."

_____, November 8, 1995, A1, "Russia's Political Miracle: A Red Comeback."

_____, November 12, 1995, 10, "Young Poles View Walesa as Passé: Generation X Votes for Ex-Communist."

_____, November 21, 1995, A1, "Walesa's Nemesis: Aleksander Kwasniewski."

_____, November 22, 1995, A1, "Accord Reached to End the War in Bosnia; Clinton Pledges U.S. Troops to Keep Peace."

_____, December 11, 1995, A1, "Once Key Allies of Yeltsin, Miners Turn Against Him."

_____, December 15, 1995, A1, "Balkan Foes Sign Peace Pact, Dividing an Unpacified Bosnia."

_____, December 19, 1995a, A24, "The Communist Comeback."

_____, December 19, 1995b, A1, "Communists Lead the Ruling Party by 2 to 1 in Russia."

_____, December 20, 1995, A1, "Communists Gain in Second Tier of Russia's Vote."

_____, December 30, 1995, A1, "Russian TV, Freed of Communism, Gilds It."

Pajic, Zoran. 1995. "Bosnia-Herzegovina: Multiethnic Coexistence to 'Apartheid' . . . and Back." In Akhavan and Howse, eds., *Yugoslavia.*

Palij, Michael. 1976. *The Anarchism of Hector Makhno, 1918–1921.* Seattle: University of Washington Press.

Powell, David E. 2002. "Death as a Way of Life: Russia's Demographic Decline." *Current History*, October, 344–48.

Puhovski, Zarko. 1995. "Yugoslav Origins of the Post-Yugoslav Situation and the Bleak Prospects for Civil Society." In Akhavan and Howse, eds., *Yugoslavia.*

Pupovac, Milorad. 1995. "Piecing Together the Balkan Puzzle." In Akhavan and Howse, eds., *Yugoslavia.*

Rabinowitch, Alexander. 1976. *The Bolsheviks Come to Power: The Revolution of 1917 in Petrograd.* New York: W. W. Norton.

Rapport, Mike. 2006. "French Revolution." In DeFronzo, ed., *Revolutionary Movements in World History*, 1:285–305.

Rensenbrink, John. 1988. *Poland Challenges a Divided World.* Baton Rouge: Louisiana State University Press.

Ross, John. 1994. "Economic Reform: Success in China and Failure in Eastern Europe." *Monthly Review*, May, 19–28.

Rutland, Peter. 2006. "The Russian Revolution of 1991 and the Dissolution of the U.S.S.R." In DeFronzo, ed., *Revolutionary Movements in World History*, 3:739–52.

Sahara, Tetsuya. 1994. "The Islamic World and the Bosnia Crisis." *Current History*, November, 386–89.

Salisbury, Harrison E. 1981. *Black Night, White Snow: Russia's Revolutions, 1905–1917.* New York: Da Capo.

Selbin, Eric. 2006. "Elites, Intellectuals, and Revolutionary Leadership." In DeFronzo, ed., *Revolutionary Movements in World History*, 1:253–58.

Smolar, Aleksander. 1994. "A Communist Comeback? The Dissolution of Solidarity." *Journal of Democracy* 5:70–84.

Sun, Yan. 2005. "Corruption, Growth, and Reform: The Chinese Enigma." *Current History*, September, 257–63.

Suny, Ronald G. 1993. *The Revenge of the Past: Nationalism, Revolution, and the Collapse of the Soviet Union.* Stanford, CA: Stanford University Press.

Thompson, John M. 2005. *Russia and the Soviet Union: An Historical Introduction from the Kievan State to the Present.* 5th ed. Boulder: Westview Press.

Tucker, Robert C., ed. 1975. *The Lenin Anthology.* New York: W. W. Norton.

Ulam, Adam B. 1965. *The Bolsheviks: The Intellectual and Political History of the Triumph of Communism in Russia.* New York: Macmillan.

_____. 1978. *A History of Soviet Russia.* Orlando, FL: Harcourt Brace Jovanovich.

Vojnic, Dragomar. 1995. "Disparity and Disintegration: The Economic Dimension of Yugoslavia's Demise." In Akhavan and Howse, eds., *Yugoslavia.*

Volkogonov, Dmitri. 1991. *Stalin: Triumph and Tragedy.* London: Weidenfeld & Nicolson.

_____. 1994. *Lenin: A New Biography.* New York: Free Press.

_____. 1996. *Trotsky: The Eternal Revolutionary.* New York: Free Press.

_____. 1998. *Autopsy for an Empire: The Seven Leaders Who Built the Soviet Regime.* New York: Free Press.

Von Laue, Theodore H. 1971. *Why Lenin? Why Stalin?* New York: Lippincott.

Vujaèic, Veljo. 2006a. "Yugoslav Communist Revolution." In DeFronzo, ed., *Revolutionary Movements in World History,* 3:955–63.

_____. 2006b. "Yugoslavia: Dissolution." In DeFronzo, ed., *Revolutionary Movements in World History,* 3:963–74.

Watson, Samuel. 2006. "Armed Forces, Revolution, and Counter-Revolution." In DeFronzo, ed., *Revolutionary Movements in World History,* 1:77–82.

Wilson, Edmund. 1972. *To the Finland Station: A Study in the Writing and Acting of History.* New York: Farrar Straus Giroux.

Wolf, Eric. 1969. *Peasant Wars of the Twentieth Century.* New York: Harper and Row.

World Bank. 2004. *Poverty Assessment Report on Russia.* http://www.world bank.org.

Selected DVD, Film, and Videocassette Documentaries

See "Purchase and Rental Sources" at the end of this volume for information on how to obtain the following resources and for full names of media companies and other organizations listed here as abbreviations.

After Gorbachev's USSR. 1992. 60 min. Video. PBS. Reforms, political revolution, and other social change in Russia.

After Stalin. 1998. CNN Cold War Series Episode 7. 46 min. Eastern European resistance to Soviet domination, including the 1956 Hungarian Revolution.

The Bolshevik Victory. 1969. 20 min. Black-and-white film. KSU, PSU, SYRU, UARIZ, UI. Kerensky to the October Revolution.

Boris Yeltsin. 50 min. BIO. Russia's first elected president.

Death of Yugoslavia. 2005. 50 min. DVD. AETV.

Forgotten Wars. 50 min. Video. AETV, HC. Includes U.S. military intervention in the Russian Civil War along with interventions in other countries.

History 1917–67, Unit II, No. 5: Lenin's Revolution. 1970. 20 min., Black-and-white film. KSU, UI, UMONT, UWASH.

History 1917–67, Unit II, No. 6: Stalin's Revolution. 1971. 22 min. Black-and-white film. KSU, UI, UMONT, UWASH. Explains how Stalin shunned Lenin's goal of world revolution but built the Soviet Union into a great industrial power.

Joseph Broz Tito. 50 min. DVD. BIO. Yugoslavian Communist leader.

Lech Walesa. 50 min. Video, DVD. BIO. Solidarity leader and president of Poland.

Lenin. 1980. 39 min. Black-and-white film. KSU, UI, UWASH, UWISC-M. Lenin's life.

Lenin and Trotsky. 1964. 16 min. Black-and-white film. KSU, SYRU, UI, UWY. Traces the roles of Lenin and Trotsky in the Bolshevik Revolution.

Mikhail Gorbachev: A Man Who Changed the World. 50 min. DVD. BIO. Russian reformer.

Pope John Paul II: Statesman of Faith. 50 min. DVD. BIO. The Polish pope and his impact.

Rasputin. 50 min. Video. BIO. Monk blamed for helping to destroy the Romanov dynasty.

The Rise and Fall of the Soviet Union. 124 min. SEG.

The Romanovs. 50 min. DVD. AETV. Last years of the Romanov dynasty.

Russia: Land of the Tsars. 200 min. Video, DVD. AETV. Russia's past.

The Russian Revolution: Czar to Lenin. 1966. 33 min. Black-and-white film. PSU. Outstanding documentary of the Russian revolution.

The Soviet Union: Gorbachev's Reforms and the Eastern Block. 30 min. Video. PBS. Political and economic reforms in Eastern Europe.

Stalin: Man of Steel. 100 min. DVD. BIO.

Stalin and the Modernization of Russia. 1982. 29 min. Color film or video. Films, Inc. Covers Stalin's rise to power, the industrialization drive, and the collectivization of agriculture.

Stalin and Russian History (1879–1927). 1974. 29 min. Black-and-white film. PSU, UARIZ, UI, UWASH. Stalin's early life and his role in the Bolshevik Revolution.

Stalin vs. Trotsky: Struggle for Power. 1964. 16 min. Black-and-white film. KSU, UARIZ, UI. The conflict between Stalin and Trotsky.

Struggle for Russia. 1994. 120 min. Video. AFSC. Problems of "shock economic therapy," economic and social chaos, and political conflict in Russia.

Vladimir Lenin: Voice of Revolution. 50 min. DVD. BIO.

Vladimir Putin. 50 min. DVD. BIO. Russia's second elected president.

World Revolutions for Students: The Russian Revolution. 2005. 23 min. Video, DVD. LVC.

3

REVOLUTION IN CHINA

The world was shaken in 1917, when czarist Russia, the largest nation in the world, was swept by socialist revolution. In 1949 another revolution triumphed, this one in the world's most populous country. Just as the success of the Russian Revolution owed much to Lenin's ideas, the Chinese Revolution was, in part, the result of innovations introduced by a charismatic revolutionary genius, Mao Zedong (Mao Tse-Tung).

Mao realized that the sudden collapse of prerevolutionary governmental authority and coercive capability that provided a unique opportunity for Russian revolutionaries at the close of World War I was unlikely to occur in China. He correctly predicted that in his nation the major cities would remain under antirevolutionary control almost until the conclusion of the revolution. According to Mao's analysis, the accomplishment of sweeping social change in China depended on wedding the frustration of the country's huge rural majority to a genuinely revolutionary ideology. Thus during the 1927–1949 period the peasant rebellion, the traditional mechanism for the expression of rural discontent, became a revolution that, more than simply replacing national government leaders, radically transformed the basic structure of China's economic, political, and social systems.

Chinese terms used in this chapter are written according to the "pinyin" (combination of sounds) procedure, the official system introduced by Chinese authorities in the late 1970s. In pinyin most letters are pronounced approximately the same as in those languages using the Latin alphabet, including English. Exceptions include c, which is pronounced as "ts" (as in "its"); x, as "sh" (as in "show"); zh, as "j" (as in "jump"); e, as "e" (as in "her"); and q, as "ch" (as in "cheese") (Chance 1985, xix). Each time a Chinese term first appears in the text, the Wade-Giles spelling follows in parentheses. The latter system was widely used in Western academic books on China before 1979 (Domes 1985).

GEOGRAPHY AND POPULATION

The People's Republic of China (PRC) has a land area of 3,705,390 square miles (9,596,960 square kilometers), making it the fourth largest country in the world after Russia, Canada, and the United States. Most of the country is mountainous, and only about 15 percent of the land is arable. The population in 2006 was 1.3 billion, with approximately 59 percent living in the countryside. About 92 percent were Han Chinese. The remaining 8 percent included fifty-five ethnic groups, such as Manchus, Mongols, Tibetans, and Zhuang. The relative ethnic homogeneity of China's population facilitated the mobilization of large numbers into periodic peasant rebellions and later into the peasant-based revolution of the twentieth century.

SOCIAL AND HISTORICAL SETTINGS FOR REVOLUTION

When China entered the twentieth century, 90 percent or more of its people were involved in agricultural activities. The approximately 10 percent who did not work the land included servants, urban laborers, soldiers, craftsmen of various types, merchants, government administrators, and members of the economic elite. In rural China the top level of the class system was occupied by the landlord gentry. Families in this class gained wealth primarily through renting parcels of land to poor and landless peasants and through interest on loans. Several students of Chinese society have estimated that the landlord gentry families constituted from 2 to 4 percent of the population and owned from 30 to 50 percent of all cultivated land until 1949 (Blecher 1986; Clubb 1978; Wolf 1969). China's landlords were usually in close contact with the peasants, typically living in or near the market towns, which served surrounding villages and hamlets.

Four economic categories, rich, middle, poor, and landless, were distinguishable among peasants. In general, rich peasants owned enough land not only to provide for their families but also to rent to others. Middle peasants owned enough land to satisfy their own families' needs but lacked any significant surplus to rent. Poor peasants did not have sufficient land to grow the food or generate the income needed to feed their families. Whereas a rich or middle peasant might choose to engage in work activity in addition to cultivating his or her own land, such extra labor was a necessity for subsistence for poor peasants. Supplementary labor might involve renting land from a rich peasant or a landlord, hiring out as a farm hand to do work on someone else's land, or engaging in handicrafts to make articles for sale to other peasants, merchants, or landlords. A fourth group of peasants owned no land at all and simply rented land or worked as farm hands for others. The percentage of rural families in each of the peasant categories appears to have varied from one part of China to another. It also varied over time owing to factors such as land fertility, amounts of rainfall or irrigation, land availability relative to population size, and external economic burdens such as levels of government taxation. During the late nineteenth and early twentieth centuries, anthropologists estimated that nationally about 10 percent were rich peasants, 30 percent middle peasants, 50 percent poor peasants, and 10 percent landless peasants (Bianco 1971; Thaxton 1983; Wolf 1969).

The considerable inequality in the distribution of land and other resources and forms of wealth meant that wars and natural calamities, such as floods or periods of drought that disrupted agricultural production, could have quite negative effects on the majority of peasants who lived near or at the level of subsistence. Famines occasionally killed millions. To prevent an entire family from starving, poor and landless peasants sometimes resorted to selling children, prostitution, or some form of predatory criminal activity, such as banditry. Poverty and hardships of nature in the countryside constituted a continuing source of mass frustration that would eventually combine with other critical factors to bring about a sweeping peasant-based socioeconomic revolution.

Prerevolutionary China

The official political-religious culture of China, Confucianism, functioned, in conjunction with the Chinese state and its military apparatus, to help maintain the traditional structure of society in the face of periodic surges of peasant discontent. Confucius was a philosopher (551–479 BCE) who believed that respect for one's ancestors and obedience to one's parents constituted the foundations of society and formal authority (the state) and fostered social harmony. Confucianism promoted a sense of fatalism, or accepting one's lot in life as heaven's will, and obedience to various authority figures. The Confucian stress on the individual's obligations to family and state provided a cultural and psychological receptiveness among many Chinese to the later Communist emphasis on the desirability of a collective rather than a self-centered value system.

The emperor, who exercised absolute authority over his subjects, merited the "mandate of heaven" as long as his rule embodied "justice" and "goodness." Through its recorded history, China had twenty-four imperial dynasties. Replacement of a corrupt or incompetent regime was consistent with the Confucian doctrine that unworthy rulers lose their mandate and should be overthrown.

Although the emperor was divinely selected to rule, his governmental administrators were chosen on the basis of a set of examinations that tested knowledge of the classical Confucian writings as well as administrative skills. The theory was that thorough comprehension of Confucian wisdom would result in officials who were morally good men and, consequently, government that was fair and effective in maintaining social harmony. It was estimated that during the late nineteenth century the national government comprised approximately forty thousand imperial officials, or "mandarins" (Skocpol 1979). Although entrance into the mandarinate was theoretically open to all, in the vast majority of cases only relatively wealthy families could afford the tutors and years of study required for preparation for the examinations and the loss of a son's labor and potential income for the educational period.

Mandarins delegated authority at the local level to members of the land-lord gentry class. Landlords assumed leading roles in extended family net-works, or clans. Poor peasants might refuse to join in a protest against a landlord or government official from their own clan in order to avoid dis-honoring the family. Furthermore, prestige rivalries among some clans often meant that peasants of different clans who had similar economic interests might not readily cooperate with one another (Wolf 1969).

Traditional Forms of Peasant Resistance

Peasant and working-class hardships and consciousness of subordinate so-cial status fostered the development of various forms of opposition to the dominant Confucian system. Anti-Confucian secret societies, such as White Lotus, Red Spear, and Big Knives, were characterized by distinctive belief systems, oaths of allegiance, and other rituals. These organizations were generally polytheistic and often combined elements of several religious tra-ditions, for example, the Buddhist concept of reincarnation and the Taoist emphasis on individual happiness and rejection of the value of Confucian scholarship (Chesneaux 1971; 1972b). Chinese scholars noted distinctions between the folk sects, which were older and primarily religious in pur-pose, and other groups, which included secret brotherhoods and the pro-tection societies, both of which functioned mainly to provide members with mutual assistance (Eastman 1988).

Secret societies were usually more egalitarian than the dominant social or-der, and often members took an oath to help the poor. Most of the members of these illegal organizations were poor peasants in the countryside and "marginal and destitute elements of the towns and villages," such as porters, laborers, peddlers, boatmen, poor artisans, and smugglers (Ches-neaux 1972b, 8). In the countryside secret societies often carried out a peas-ant self-defense function against marauding imperial forces, bandits, or even attacks by rival societies (Bianco 1971). In the cities some societies, such as the Green Gang in Shanghai, capitalized on their group network and mem-bers' loyalty to develop into mafia-style organized crime associations in-volved in drug trafficking, smuggling, control of prostitution, and similar activities (Lust 1972; Posner 1988).

Unusually high levels of peasant unrest occasionally resulted in a peasant rebellion. These uprisings were sometimes preceded by the development of widespread banditry, with the mass of the peasantry finally driven to rebel-lion by the same conditions that earlier had provoked the poorest into ban-ditry. In some instances rebellions were in part inspired by charismatic or visionary leaders. But often natural calamities played a precipitating role. When an earthquake, a flood, or a period of drought killed large numbers and endangered many more by significantly reducing agricultural productivity, many peasants interpreted the disaster as a sign that heaven had withdrawn its support for the governing regime.

Whatever the causes, peasant uprisings were only rarely successful in overthrowing a ruling dynasty. And on the few occasions when a peasant rebellion played a role in actually toppling an emperor (in these cases, elements of the national elite, military and administrative, were known to desert a crippled dynasty to assume leadership roles in a popular rebellion), postrebellion changes tended to be limited to establishing a new ruling dynasty and temporary improvements in the efficiency and fairness of government actions; meanwhile, the Confucian system was maintained. That was because although peasant rebels often fought for social justice within the Confucian framework, they almost never had the goal of transforming the traditional structure (political, economic, and social institutions) or supporting cultural system of Chinese society (Blecher 1986; Wolf 1969). Participants apparently felt that their goals could be achieved mainly by getting rid of "bad" or incompetent leaders and replacing them with virtuous men who would bring back "the good old days" of some real or mythical period of China's past. Since the basic economic and political relationships remained unchanged, the factors that caused the victorious rebellion would eventually surface again and result in still further peasant uprisings (Thaxton 1983; Wolf 1969).

The Manchu Dynasty

In 1644 the warlike Manchus, a Sinified tribal people from beyond the Great Wall in northeastern China (constituting less than 0.5 percent of China's population), took advantage of incompetence among the Ming dynasty rulers and disunity and rivalries among provincial administrators and military leaders to sweep down and seize Beijing, China's capital. The Manchus established their own Qing (Ch'ing) dynasty, which would be China's last, 1644–1911. Since according to the Confucian belief system, a dynasty could not be overthrown and replaced by another unless heaven had removed the mandate from the defeated and bestowed it on the victorious, many Chinese accepted the rule of the Manchus, although military resistance continued for years in southern China. Many of China's secret societies took upon themselves the defense of Chinese ethnic honor by opposing Manchu authority and advocating a return to Ming dynasty rule.

Several Manchu emperors, however, proved to be effective rulers and two had exceptionally long reigns (covering 1683–1796) during which social stability returned to much of the country, Chinese military and political power achieved high levels, agricultural productivity increased, and

there was peace. The latter two factors contributed to an apparent dou-
bling of the population between 1700 and 1900 to more than 400 million
(Blecher 1986; Clubb 1978).

During the nineteenth century, various pressures and momentous events
heightened peasant discontent and undermined the traditional Chinese
state. Among these were increased strain on China's agricultural resources
because of previous decades of large population growth; military defeats by
European nations and later Japan, which humiliated the Chinese, inflamed
Chinese nationalism, and burdened China with huge war indemnities and
unfavorable trade relationships; and massive, though unsuccessful, peasant
rebellions, which resulted in millions of deaths and further depleted the resources of the central government (Bianco 1971; Blecher 1986; Eastman
1988; Skocpol 1979; Wolf 1969).

Foreign Involvement in China

The Opium War (1839–1842) severely weakened China's ability to resist foreign imports. During the 1830s Great Britain's leaders were appalled by the
flow of their hard currency into China to purchase tea, silk, porcelains, and
other exports. They proposed to pay for Chinese goods by increasing sales in
China of a product of their Burma and India colonies, opium. China's government reportedly feared an increase in drug dependency if the British were
allowed to sell opium freely. After the Chinese destroyed an opium shipment,
Britain sent military expeditions, whose advanced weaponry devastated the
Chinese. As a result, the Chinese were forced to agree to (1) allow the British
to sell opium and other products in China; (2) allow European missionaries
to preach Christianity; (3) pay large war indemnities to the British; (4) provide the British with certain cities or sections of cities as treaty-ports or concessions, within which they could establish economic enterprises, deploy
military personnel, and provide exclusively European living quarters and
recreational facilities. Later other European nations and Japan forced similar
concessions and war-indemnity payments and eventually carved China into
spheres of influence, often making specific deals for cooperation with local
governmental and military leaders. The six nations that had developed significant economic interests and military presence in China by the end of the
nineteenth century were Great Britain, France, Germany, Japan, czarist Russia, and the United States (Harrison 1967).

Apart from the harmful effects of opium addiction, foreign victories over
China had negative economic consequences. The Chinese government was
forced to raise taxes in order to pay war indemnities and also to help cope
with other debts that stemmed from the country's unfavorable economic relationship with Europe. The burden fell disproportionately on the relatively
powerless mass of poor peasants because, in order to pay taxes, the landlords and rich peasants tended to increase the rents they charged for land
use as well as interest rates on loans. The poor were further victimized by

the fact that sources of supplemental income needed to make ends meet, such as handicrafts, were partially undermined by the influx of manufactured articles from the industrialized countries. These developments contributed to the discontent among the rural masses. Many Chinese blamed the Manchu dynasty (and soon the Confucian system itself) for China's inability to resist foreign domination and for conditions in the countryside.

Nineteenth-Century Rebellions

Economic deprivation and hostility toward the Manchu rulers contributed to the development of two major peasant rebellions, the Nian (Nien) Rebellion (1853–1868) in central China and the Taiping (T'aip'ing) Rebellion (1851–1864), which began in south China and spread northward, eventually establishing the Taiping capital at Nanjing (Nanking). Both rebellions advocated a redistribution of wealth in favor of the poor; at times the Taiping units advancing northward allied with Nian forces in battles against the Manchu army.

The Nian were members of a secret society devoted to overthrowing the Manchu dynasty. They were defeated in part because their decentralized military effort permitted the Manchus to concentrate large forces against isolated rebel towns (Wolf 1969). Nevertheless, the Nian Rebellion provided the peasants of central China with a tradition that helped prepare them culturally to support and participate in the Communist-led peasant revolution of the twentieth century.

The Taiping (Great Peace) Rebellion was ideologically unique and more massive than the Nian. The Taiping Rebellion and its repression by the Manchus resulted in an estimated twenty million deaths. The Taiping movement had been begun by a man from peasant background of the Hakka minority group, Hong (Hung) (1814–1864), who was born near the city of Guangzhou (Canton), a major site of early foreign influence. The culture of the Hakka people was characterized by more equalitarian gender and income norms than the dominant Confucianist system. Hong's family made sacrifices to accumulate the funds to provide him with an education, but he failed in several attempts to pass state exams for a position as a state official. In Guangzhou, however, Hong received Christian religious instruction from an American missionary.

During a serious illness Hong, possibly in a state of delirium, had a dream in which two men spoke to him. Later he interpreted this experience as a visitation from God the Father and his Son Jesus. Hong began to explain to his associates that there was only one God, not the multitude of deities to which many Chinese offered sacrifices. Hong claimed it had been revealed to him that he was God's younger son, the brother of Jesus Christ. He proclaimed that he had been instructed to gather followers and organize an army that would "destroy the demons on earth in order to create a new Kingdom of God" (Wolf 1969, 120). Much of the Confucian value system and power structure, including the landlord gentry class, was to be eradicated. Land parcels would be assigned to peasants to farm, but ownership would be retained by the Taiping state. Any production beyond that required to feed individual families would become a collective resource. Advancement in the political hierarchy was to be based on meritorious performance, not heredity, family wealth, or Confucian scholarship.

The Taipings granted extensive rights to women and forbade foot binding of female children and prostitution. Men were to have only one wife, and marriage was to be on the basis of mutual attraction rather than arranged by parents for financial gain. Women were allowed access to the Taiping leadership grades and were given the right to serve as soldiers. The Taipings also attacked the practice of ancestor worship: they wanted to de-emphasize family lineage and clan membership, which had been one of the main causes of division among the lower classes and a major source of power and social control for the landlord class (Li 1956; Wolf 1969).

The major weaknesses of the Taipings included their sweeping attacks on all three of China's main religions (Confucianism, Buddhism, and Taoism), which provoked opposition from many traditionalist Chinese strongly influenced by their religious training. Furthermore, the implemented Taiping land reforms were in reality limited and did little to improve the lot of most peasants, who soon began to resent the heavy tax burden placed on them by the Taiping regime (Wolf 1969).

Moreover, foreign interests in China, having won by force of arms favorable treaties, concessions, and trade relations from the Manchu dynasty, saw their privileges endangered by the possible countrywide victory of the Taipings. Consequently, the industrialized nations provided the anti-Taiping Manchu ("Ever-Victorious") army with weapons, technical assistance, and mercenary officers and advisors, which contributed significantly to the defeat of the Taiping movement and execution of its leaders in 1864 (Bohr 2006; Payne 1969).

The Taiping peasant rebellion and the later Communist-led peasant revolution had important parallels. Both enjoyed mass support from intensely frustrated rural populations, and both were characterized by ideologies that incorporated ideas from the West and called for sweeping changes in major economic, social, political, and cultural institutions. (Had the Taipings won and succeeded in accomplishing transformations in the basic structures of Chinese society, their movement would have been later referred to as a revolution.) The Taiping plans for wealth equalization and collective ownership as well as the measures directed at liberating women and minimizing the factor of family prestige as a source of social status were remarkably similar to several of the basic goals proclaimed by the Communist revolutionaries sixty years later (Bohr 2006). And the twentieth-century peasant revolutionaries succeeded in establishing their first rural bases in areas of south China formerly supportive of the Taipings (Skocpol 1979; Wolf 1969).

THE DEVELOPMENT OF THE REPUBLICAN MOVEMENT

By the latter part of the nineteenth century, many Chinese realized that to regain its independence their country would have to modernize its political and social systems and industrialize. But the Confucian culture and political system constituted powerful barriers to social change. Since a rationalized and technologically advancing society would have little use for leaders whose authority was based on antiquated and nonutilitarian scholarship, most mandarins resisted modernization.

Large landholders throughout the country were also in general not inclined to support modernization because it would likely shift China's economy toward industry and commerce (Moore 1966; Skocpol 1976). Confucian culture assigned maximum prestige to agriculture as an economic activity, ideally coupled with training in the Confucian classics, and bestowed much less honor on merchants or others involved in nonagricultural or nonscholarly endeavors (Blecher 1986). Many Chinese businessmen had turned to commerce or industry as a means of developing wealth because they did not possess large landholdings. But instead of using their profits to expand commercial or industrial operations, they often purchased land in order to gain entrance to the most time-honored status recognized in Confucian culture (Blecher 1986). This was an important reason why China did not develop a strong and independent national business class, which might have constituted the leadership element to bring about a rapid modernization. Consequently, much of the major industry of prerevolutionary China was foreign owned, and many of the smaller industrial enterprises were owned by Westernized Chinese often shunned by their country folk as cultural apostates or lackeys of foreign interests.

Any modernization attempted by the central government had to confront not only the absence of a powerful Chinese business class but also the woeful inadequacy of imperial finances. The government had spent enormous sums in the suppression of the Taiping and Nian rebellions and in paying indemnities to victorious foreign powers. Because of their role in raising the resources and forces to crush the Taipings, the power of provincial authorities had been greatly enhanced. Few provincial leaders were willing to support any major national effort for modernization that might threaten their new political and economic prerogatives.

When war broke out between China and Japan in 1894–1895, China's navy was easily defeated, a very traumatic event for many Chinese, who had previously viewed Japan as almost a vassal state. Japan had been able to accomplish this feat largely because of its reaction to its own humiliation in 1853, when it was militarily unable to resist being opened to world trade by a U.S. naval force. The event disgraced a traditionalist, isolationist dynasty and precipitated its fall and replacement by a dynasty committed to rapid technological modernization (Gurley 1983). The new regime succeeded in freeing the Japanese in a few decades from cultural impediments to industrialization, commercial development, and military modernization. Many Chinese began to look to Japan as a model.

In 1898 the Chinese Emperor Guangxu (Kuang Hsu), then in his late twenties, and a very small group of advisors attempted to introduce a sweeping package of reforms that included the abolition of Confucian exams as a requirement for administrative posts and a plan for adopting a parliamentary form of government (a constitutional monarchy). All towns were to create free schools for the poor, and all existing governmental and military officeholders were to be reevaluated. However, the "one hundred days reform" movement was abruptly halted by a palace coup in which the traditionalist majority of government ministers, along with the conservative and exceptionally ruthless dowager empress, Ci Xi (Tz'u Hsi), placed the emperor under house arrest and ordered the execution of his reform-oriented advisors (Payne 1969; Skocpol 1979).

In 1900 the antiforeign Fists of Harmony and Justice Society (called Boxers by the Europeans because of their clenched fist symbol), encouraged by the dowager empress, murdered several missionaries and hundreds of Christian Chinese and besieged the foreign embassies in Beijing. After several months, the siege was lifted by an international relief force. Once again, victorious foreigners imposed on China new reparations payments. After this humiliation, the central government finally decided that major reforms were necessary to facilitate modernization. Among the changes was the establishment of provincial parliaments in 1908. The legislators were selected through elections in which the economic elite voted. A national parliament was to be elected in 1917. The traditional Confucian examinations for admittance to the government bureaucracy were ended in 1905. Another reform involved the establishment of technical training centers for young army officers, who were to constitute the leadership of China's "new army" (Eastman 1988; Skocpol 1979).

Sun and the Republican Revolution

Much of the ideology for the revolution to establish a Chinese republic was developed by Sun Yixian (Sun Yat-sen), eventually honored by the title "Father of the Chinese Republic." Sun, whose father was a poor peasant, was born in a village forty miles from Guangzhou in 1866. He, like Hong, the leader of the Taiping Rebellion whom he came to admire, was of Hakka ancestry. Sun told friends that as a child he was deeply impressed by the stories he heard from a village teacher who was a surviving soldier of the Taiping rebel armies (Schiffrin 1989). Sun's older brother left the family for Hawaii when Sun was six and, using savings from his wages, bought a farm and later established a store. Sun eventually traveled to Hawaii, where he worked for his brother and attended the English-language Anglican College of Honolulu. When Sun, after converting to Christianity, returned to China, he made his way to Xianggang (Hong Kong) and spent the years 1884–1892 obtaining a medical degree at Queen's College (Payne 1969).

Sun, like many young Chinese of his era, especially those with some exposure to the benefits of Western technology, was outraged by China's backwardness and became determined to play a role in ridding China of the ineffective Manchu dynasty and in revitalizing and modernizing the nation. In 1905 Sun combined an organization he had helped found with another republican revolutionary group and formed the United Revolutionary Society, initially established among Chinese exiles in Japan. Thousands secretly joined the group inside China, along with many Chinese throughout the world. Thus, within China's educated minority profoundly intense divisions developed. Depriving the state of many of its most capable and skilled citizens, these divisions also provided effective leadership for the growing revolutionary movements aimed at overthrowing the monarchy and establishing a republic form of government.

Sun and most of his associates either had professional careers or were students from upper-income families. Since they lacked a mechanism for directly incorporating the mass of China's population into the republican movement, they allied themselves with the anti-Manchu secret societies (Lust 1972). But Sun viewed these groups as backward looking and a possible impediment to social, economic, and political modernization. He asserted that he supported alliances with secret societies only as a temporary and expedient method of extending mass involvement in the republican movement (Borokh 1972).

In 1908 the dynasty was weakened by the deaths of both the villainous Empress Dowager Ci Xi and her unfortunate nephew, the deposed former emperor Guangxu. The monarchy fell into the hands of Prince Chun, who ruled as regent on behalf of the three-year-old Emperor Fu Yi (Pu Yi). As anti-Manchu riots broke out in south China, Prince Chun called on General Yuan Shikai (Yuan Shih-K'ai) to restore order.

On October 10, 1911, several thousand soldiers, fearing exposure and execution for their secret membership in republican revolutionary groups, staged a rebellion in Hubei (Hupei) Province in central China. The uprising was soon followed by similar mutinies against imperial rule in more than a dozen southern and central provinces. Local military commanders (or their successors) declared the independence of their provinces from Manchu rule. The insurrections resulted in part from the successful efforts of Sun and his associates in "forging a powerful coalition" that included their revolutionary organization; "southern Chinese secret societies; regional interest groups in Hunan, Hubei, Guangdong, Sichuan; and some of the modern crack military units" (Domes 1985, 29).

Yuan Shikai seized the opportunity to advance his ambition to be China's new leader by convincing the members of the royal family that they faced the possibility of execution if they failed to compromise with the republican forces. The Manchu rulers abdicated on February 12, 1912. At Nanjing,

Sun was declared provisional president of the Republic of China. But in an effort to prevent a civil war, Sun resigned after fifteen days and agreed to accept Yuan Shikai as president if Yuan would declare support for the republic. Yuan consented and became president on March 10, 1912.

Sun's United Society was transformed into the Guomindang (GMD) (Kou-min tang, KMT) National Party, in fall 1912. But in the new parliament the GMD members soon fell into conflict with Yuan Shikai's supporters over issues such as Yuan's assertion that his authority was above that of the parliament. The GMD's parliamentary leader was assassinated by Yuan's agents, and Sun temporarily fled. Yuan outlawed the Guomindang Party and then dismissed the national parliament in 1914. The following year he installed himself as China's new "emperor," only to die in 1916. After Yuan's death, central state authority effectively ceased to exist, and most of the nation disintegrated into its component provinces. Each of these was ruled by local landowning elites in combination with the general in charge of the provincial armed forces, the local "warlord."

Sun, who had been forced to leave the country, returned to south China and began to reorganize the republican movement. He appealed to the United States and several other nations for financial assistance, weapons, and military advisors to train a republican army that could subdue the warlords. But these countries, some having made trade arrangements with individual warlords and perhaps fearful of the power of a unified China and the potential radical or antiforeign tendencies of the republican revolutionaries, declined to provide aid. Only the new revolutionary government in the Soviet Union agreed to send weapons and advisors (Jordan 1976; Wolf 1969).

Sun dispatched a young republican officer, Jiang Jieshi (Chiang Kaishek), to Moscow to report on the Soviet political and military systems. He returned impressed by the success of the Bolsheviks in carrying out and defending their revolution and in unifying the Soviet Union. But Jiang, son of a merchant in a family with claims to royal ancestry (Ming dynasty) and well schooled in Confucian traditions, disagreed with the social revolution occurring in the Soviet Union. Sun, however, rejected the more negative aspects of Jiang's report and proceeded to pattern the Guomindang's organizational structure after that of the Russian Communist Party (Bianco 1971).

The ideological foundation of the Guomindang was the widely cited and applauded "Three Principles of the People," formulated by Sun. The first principle was that of Independence, or Nationalism, which meant freeing China from foreign domination and exploitation. Although it can be argued that this was the most clearly defined of the three principles, in reality Chinese political factions disagreed over which types and what degrees of economic and political association with other nations constituted manifestations of imperialism.

The second principle was Democracy. Sun called for a strong central government but, by the early 1920s, was disillusioned with the representative (parliamentary) democracies of the European states. He felt that these governments were dominated by capitalist ruling classes willing to tolerate poverty in their own countries as well as exploit the peoples of less-developed societies. Sun favored the direct election of the nation's leaders by its citizens—who would also have the right to recall public officials and the right to propose laws and vote on proposals through referendums. However, Sun advocated a period of "tutelage," during which the Guomindang would be the only political party able to exercise state power. When China had achieved independence and political stability and had a powerful postrevolutionary central state government structure, full democracy would be established (Cheng 1989).

The third principle, People's Livelihood, was even less completely defined than the first two, and its interpretation was a main point of contention among China's rightists and leftists in the years after Sun's death. In his earliest formulations of the third principle, Sun seemed to disagree with the Marxist concept that redistribution of wealth would be achieved through a process of class conflict and instead proposed that it could be accomplished peacefully and involve cooperation among the classes. People's Livelihood would include the provision of employment and the necessities of life for all. The government was to bring about an equalization of rural landownership gradually. How this could occur without the resistance of the landlords and, consequently, class conflict, was not adequately explained. Sun appeared to become more and more influenced by policies in the Soviet Union, his revolution's only source of external military assistance, and at one point confounded conservative members of the Guomindang by responding to a question about People's Livelihood with the puzzling statement, "It is communism and it is socialism" (Ch'ien 1964, 75). With the republican revolution still in progress, Sun died of cancer in March 1925.

China's Communist Party

Despite Sun's attempts to develop a unified movement, the republican revolutionary elite was deeply divided. Rightist figures in the GMD typically came from the upper-income families of China's coastal provinces and had little interest in redistributing the nation's wealth toward the poor. Rather, they favored the retention of capitalist property relations along with much of the Confucian cultural system. In contrast, leftists in the GMD, particularly Communist Party members, viewed the revolution as both nationalistic and socioeconomic. Thus the emergent republican state was to be immediately characterized by a dissident elite movement of leftists favoring a further profound socioeconomic revolution.

China's Communist Party had its origins in the New Youth movement, in which many of the nation's Western-educated students participated during the period 1915–1919 (Meisner 1986). The movement's leaders had become convinced that the future development and independence of China depended upon a near-total rejection of traditional culture and the rapid substitution of Western norms and values. In particular, New Youth advocates called for a radical shift in education: schools should teach methods of rational inquiry and scientific research and convey information about modern technologies. The movement also advocated the creation of a democratically elected parliament.

The apogee of the New Youth movement occurred after the disclosure of the terms of the Versailles Treaty ending World War I that transferred German colonial holdings in China to Japan instead of returning them to the Chinese. To many it appeared that the victorious Western nations were bribing the Japanese to collaborate in the mutual exploitation of China and betraying the often-stated promise that the defeat of Germany in World War I would bring democracy and the right of national self-determination to the entire world. On May 4, 1919, three thousand students, proclaiming "Democracy and Science," the slogan inspired by the New Youth movement, demonstrated in Beijing to protest both the treaty provisions and their nation's inability to resist foreign domination.

Many participants in the New Youth movement abruptly altered their perceptions of the Western nations. "The intellectuals' views of the West underwent a rapid and dramatic transformation. The bitter nationalist resentments aroused by the fateful decision at Versailles coupled with growing nationalist political activism at home, led to a rapid erosion of faith that the 'advanced' Western nations would instruct China in the principles of democracy and science" (Meisner 1986, 17). Former leaders of the New Youth movement proclaimed a new movement, the May Fourth movement, whose participants continued to look to the West for inspiration, but less to the dominant ideologies that justified capitalist economic systems and the perceived imperialism of the Western nations and Japan toward China. Instead movement activists began to turn to Marxism, which some viewed

> as the most advanced intellectual product of the modern West, but one that rejected the Western world in its capitalist form and its imperialist relationship with China. The latter was most forcefully demonstrated through the nationalist appeal of Leninist theory of imperialism (which offered the colonial and semi-colonial lands a crucial international revolutionary role) and the new Soviet government's renunciation of old Czarist imperialist privileges in China. (Meisner 1986, 18)

Lenin, in his analysis of the international function of modern imperialism, attempted to explain the failure of Marx's prediction that the industrialized capitalist societies would be the first in the world to experience transformations to socialism. Imperialism involved the efforts over several hundred years of the technologically advanced societies to establish political, economic, and cultural control over less-developed parts of the world. Lenin noted that through imperialism several capitalist countries gained access to huge land areas with vast agricultural and mineral resources as well as the labor power of much of the world's population. The countries dominated by foreign imperialism, especially the more affluent classes among the indigenous populations, also constituted significant new markets for products manufactured in the advanced countries. Lenin argued that the capitalist ruling classes of the advanced nations used some of the "superprofits" from their capital investments in the less-developed parts of the world to improve the living conditions of their own working classes, thus reducing the workers' inclination to join political movements advocating revolution and socialism (Lenin [1916] 1975). As a result, Lenin concluded, in reality revolutions would tend to occur first in less-developed, economically exploited societies and would involve not only the relatively small native industrial working class but also the participation of peasants (Bottomore 1983).

As such revolutions occurred, new leaders would demand more wealth in return for the use of their countries' mineral, agricultural, and labor resources and limit the size of the profits foreign capital could generate through business activity in their lands. Thus, the exploitive relationships between the advanced capitalist nations and underdeveloped societies would gradually come to an end. As this change in international economic relationships began to cause shortages in the advanced capitalist societies, the capitalist ruling classes would try to force their working classes to bear most of the economic hardships. Then, according to Lenin, the people of the advanced societies would want to change from capitalism to socialism. Thus revolution in China could conceivably play a major role in causing revolution eventually in the more technologically advanced countries.

In 1920 young Marxists established a number of political organizations in major cities, and in July 1921 twelve delegates from the various groups met in Shanghai to found China's Communist Party. The Party initially attempted to recruit members of the country's small urban working class, following Marx's theory that this class would constitute the social basis for a socialist transformation (Bianco 1971). The Russian Communist Party pressured the Chinese Communists into uniting with the Guomindang and collaborating with its landlord and capitalist elements. Sun, enamored of the Bolsheviks' achievements, accepted the growing Communist movement into the GMD in January 1924 despite the objections of Jiang and other conservatives. The purpose of the alliance was to achieve the common goals of unifying the country, freeing it from foreign control, and, at least in terms of formal proclamations, eventually establishing a Western-style parliamentary democracy.

98

CHINA (1927–1949)

CIVIL WAR IN CHINA

In summer 1926 Jiang, who had become a prominent GMD general, launched the Northern Expedition (1926–1928), through which the Guomindang intended to defeat the provincial warlords and unite China under its rule. The Northern Expedition involved an unstable coalition among conservative landlords and coastal merchants who helped finance the enterprise, the Communist Party and allied leftist activists, and military forces led by Jiang and other mostly rightist officers. In this situation, as in the later revolutionary struggle, nationalism in the sense of the desire to construct a unified and powerful China free of foreign domination constituted the main unifying motivation bringing different groups together on behalf of the revolutionary effort.

Young GMD activists, many of them Communists, attempted to mobilize workers and peasants in the cities and territories as the republican armies approached with the hopeful message that republican victory would result in relief from both political and economic oppression. Enlisted workers, when able to defy physical intimidation, showed support for the revolution by striking and shutting down factories and services, thereby hastening warlord surrender. But Jiang was able to "subdue" one warlord after another by bribery (offers of money and/or senior ranking positions in the republican army) as much as through military or economic pressures (Jordan 1976; Wei 1985).

By the time Jiang's forces moved on Shanghai in 1927, he had decided to begin an all-out repression of the Communist movement. Jiang first secured promises of funding from Shanghai financiers and businessmen who were eager to see the militant workers' movement eliminated (Bianco 1971; Eastman 1988; Meisner 1986). He also negotiated with Shanghai's mafialike Green Gang secret society. Green Gang members were knowledgeable of the city's working-class sections and could help in the identification and liquidation of labor groups and Communist workers who, only days before their annihilation, had played a substantial role in helping the GMD forces capture the city (Clubb 1978). Before dawn on April 12, GMD soldiers and members of the Green Gang attacked the headquarters of Communist-oriented labor unions and proceeded to destroy the workers' militia (Jordan 1976). In addition to the workers killed in the day-long battle, hundreds more were executed after capture.

Surviving Communist activists went into hiding. Jiang's forces soon repeated these measures in other major Chinese cities. The left-leaning GMD civilian government was appalled at hearing of the murders of workers and the spreading persecution of the Communists. But Jiang, because he controlled the armed forces, was soon able to assume governmental as well as military control. Some civilians in the GMD government also supported Jiang's seizure of power because they were alarmed at reports that the

Communists planned to take land from large landholders and factories from Chinese and foreign capitalists and turn these over to poor peasants and workers. Despite the reverses, most surviving Communist leaders still dogmatically held to the belief that the Communist movement must establish control of the cities and base the revolution on China's relatively minute urban working class. Some Communist leaders, however, felt that in China a revolution could be based on the rural population. The most important of these was Mao Zedong.

Mao and People's War in the Countryside

Mao (1893–1976) was born in Hunan Province, the son of a rich peasant. At seventeen, he left school to join republican revolutionary forces attempting to overthrow the Manchu dynasty. In 1912 Mao resumed his education, earning a teaching degree, and then briefly joined the library staff at the University of Beijing. Later in 1920, the same year that he became a Marxist, Mao got a position as an elementary school principal in Changsha, Hunan Province. In 1921 he traveled secretly to Shanghai to participate with eleven other delegates from other locations in the founding congress of the Chinese Communist Party (Short 2000, 119). Unlike many other early members of the Chinese Communist Party, Mao, influenced by his knowledge of peasant support for the Taiping Rebellion and its popularity in his home province, favored a peasant-based socialist revolution in China. But after the 1927 Shanghai massacre, Mao and others were ordered by Party leaders to assemble Communist forces (which included armed workers and peasants and a number of GMD regiments that had sided with the Communists) in the countryside and then attack and seize several cities. These efforts, as well as attempts of Communist-led workers to stage urban uprisings or resist GMD military takeovers, failed. Mao's forces retreated to heavily forested areas of Jiangxi (Kiangsi) Province in southeast China. There he and his associates first recruited several hundred rural bandits to their cause and soon began to make inroads with local peasants (Wei 1985).

Mao developed the theory—a modification of earlier Marxist revolutionary thought—that in China, where the vast majority of the population was rural and where relatively strong anti-Communist military forces, GMD or warlord, held the cities, the revolution would be based on the peasants (Bianco 1971; Mackerras and Knight 1985; Skocpol 1979). Marx had originally concluded that most peasants would not be receptive to revolutionary goals because of their relative ignorance of the world beyond their villages, their sense of powerlessness, and their ties to tradition. He anticipated that only after capitalist industrial economies had brought about the migration of millions of peasants to urban areas (and in the process caused tremendous adaptive changes in their cultural values and norms) would conditions be right for the transformation to socialism. The masses of urban-industrial workers would hypothetically be much more willing than their rural ancestors to participate in a revolutionary movement to improve their economic condition. This would be true not only because of their ability to interact in large numbers in urban areas and carry out unified political actions but also because their recent alteration in livelihood and living environment would provide them with a sense of the possibility of further sweeping social changes, which the preindustrialization rural population was supposedly incapable of comprehending.

But Mao, in contrast to many Marxists, put faith in the power of ideas to transform the consciousness of the Chinese peasants. Aware of how receptive the peasants of south and central China had been to the very untraditional ideology of the mid-nineteenth-century Taipings, Mao was certain that the similar but more "scientific" concepts of Marxism could transform China's historically rebellious peasants into a massive revolutionary force. The key, as Mao saw it, was to fuse the tradition of peasant rebellion with the ideology of Marxism, which proposed a new plan for society in which major sources of wealth would be collectively owned and in which socioeconomic inequality would be greatly reduced. Mao's innovation, referred to as the "Sinification of Marxism," proved to be a major reason for the revolutionary victory in China.

Mao also extracted from his knowledge of past military conflicts the concept of "people's war" and adapted it to the revolutionary struggle in China. The most essential aspect of people's war was the goal of achieving widespread popular support for the revolutionary effort. Antirevolutionary forces would then confront not just the revolutionary army but also the hostility of large numbers of noncombatants rendering whatever assistance possible to the revolutionary fighters. Another central element of the people's war concept was to create politicized armed forces that would manifest the ideals of the revolution in their interaction with and treatment of noncombatants. The revolutionary soldier was to be motivated by the belief that he or she was fighting for the creation of a morally just society and against the oppression of the landlords, exploitive capitalists, and their instrument of violence, the GMD army. The intended result of politicalization of combatants was an armed revolutionary force driven by high ideals to courageous acts and to waging a determined struggle.

The people were to be educated to the goals of the revolution through both word (speeches and political instruction) and deeds, such as land reform and the exemplary conduct of revolutionary leaders and soldiers. If the people supported the revolution, the revolutionaries could overcome their disadvantages in armament and military training. This concept was expressed in the slogan, "The people are the water, the (revolutionary) army are the fish; without the water, the fish will die" (Fairbairn 1974, 99). The revolutionary forces were to be nourished, hidden, informed about enemy troop dispositions, and in other ways aided by the people.

The GMD waged five successive military campaigns against the Communists' main base area (called the "Jiangxi Soviet"). During the fifth campaign in 1934, 700,000 GMD troops under Jiang's command, following a plan conceived by a German military adviser, closed in on the Communist-controlled areas, constructing stone forts, or "blockhouses," along road-ways to reduce the revolutionaries' freedom of movement. The main Communist forces in the province, thought to number about 100,000, were forced to abandon Jiangxi. They slipped out of the encirclement and began a long and tortuous retreat, first generally toward the west, then north, and then northeast to the remote north-central town of Yan'an (Yennan). The journey covered about six thousand miles and lasted over a year. During that time Communist units were pursued by GMD forces and attacked by hostile warlord armies along the way. Fewer than 20,000 completed the entire Long March and made it to Yan'an in late 1935 (Blecher 1986; Domes 1985; Salisbury 1985).

The reform program at the new rural base differed in several respects from the Jiangxi Soviet and came to be known as the Yan'an Way. At Jiangxi Mao had advocated a land-reform policy in which the rich peasants, who were generally the most productive, would retain an amount of land at least equal to the size of the farms of the poor peasants after land redistribution. In this way he hoped to minimize resistance and maximize agricultural output by continuing to have the rich peasants make major contributions to production (Wei 1985). Mao had also favored providing dispossessed land-lords with land to work. But at Jiangxi more radical and vengeful thinking had prevailed. Although the rich peasants received some land of poor quality, the landlords were transformed into landless laborers. These measures not only helped decrease agricultural production, they also drove outraged landlords and rich peasants to provide important assistance to GMD forces in the successful encirclement campaign (Wei 1985). But in the Yan'an program both the rich peasants and the landlords were allowed to retain much of their land under conditions that restricted profit levels and the exploitation of poor and landless peasants (Thaxton 1983).

The mass-line approach to revolutionary leadership was also established at Yan'an. This method, while leaving ultimate decision making to the Communist Party, reflected Mao's conviction that Party policy and its mode of implementation must stem from the people and be based on popular support. According to Mao in 1943: "All correct leadership is necessarily 'from the masses, to the masses.' This means: take the ideas of the masses (scattered and unsystematic ideas) and 'concentrate' them (through study turn them into concentrated and systematic ideas), then go to the masses and propagate and explain these ideas until the masses embrace them as their own" (Mao 1967, 117–19). The mass-line approach became a lasting characteristic of Chinese socialism and was adopted to some extent by revolutionary movements or governments in other countries, such as Vietnam and Cuba. It distinguished policymaking in these nations from the more elitist procedures characteristic of most Eastern European states before 1989 (Blecher 1986).

Mao and other leaders took part in manual labor alongside peasants and were expected to submit to regular public criticism by colleagues, followed by public self-criticism. These mechanisms were intended to prevent excessive concentration of power or development of feelings of superiority.

Japanese Invasion and Revolutionary Victory

The establishment of the Yan'an base coincided with Japanese attacks on China south of the Great Wall in 1937. The Communists proposed an end to the civil war and the formation of a coalition with Jiang's GMD army in order to fight Japan jointly. Jiang, having long ignored the Japanese occupation of Manchuria and other parts of China to devote his attention to crushing the Communists, was coerced by his associates into stopping the civil war and agreeing to a United Front of Communist and GMD forces against the Japanese.

The land-reform program during the United Front struggle against the Japanese (1937–1945) in Communist-controlled areas was relatively mild: landlords who were not collaborating with the Japanese generally did not experience land expropriation but rather were subject to a rent-control program for the land they rented to poor or landless peasants and were limited in the amount of interest they could charge on loans. These wartime reforms were still significant because under Guomindang rule many landlords had increased rents and interest rates, with little concern for the welfare of the peasants. Such a trend indicated that the norms of unfettered capitalist business relations had begun to erode the collective responsibility aspects of the Confucian system, which in the past had somewhat moderated landlord avarice (Bianco 1971; Eastman 1988; Thaxton 1983).

During the war nationalist sentiment swung increasingly in favor of the Communists (Blecher 1986; Dunn 1972). Jiang, anticipating that the United States and its allies would defeat Japan, held some of his best divisions out of the conflict so that they could be employed after the war against the Communists. This choice of action was partly dictated by other factors, such as the widespread corruption of the GMD officer corps and the low morale of many of the GMD enlisted men. The latter were subject to abuse and exploitation by their often profiteering officers (Blecher 1986). The GMD military's efforts and successes against the Japanese were far less than those of the Communist-led army, and many members of the classes most supportive of Jiang's regime (the landlords and the merchants) collaborated with the Japanese in occupied areas of China in order to preserve their assets and comfortable lifestyles. Because of those factors, as the war progressed, more and more people began to recognize Mao's forces (which expanded from 80,000 in 1937 to 900,000 in 1945) as the real army of China (Bianco 1971). GMD army abuse of peasants also alienated many. Consequently, when the war ended, the legitimacy of the GMD state was severely weakened, and nationalist sympathy was more on the side of the Communists than on the side of Jiang's government. All these things helped the Communist leadership to draw together diverse population segments.

Other factors reduced the appeal and moral authority of the GMD state. It seemed clear to many that the GMD under Jiang had effectively abandoned Sun's Three Principles of the People. As for fighting for independence and against imperialism, Jiang, who obtained much of his knowledge of warfare while a cadet at a military academy in Japan, was possibly so convinced that his forces could not effectively combat the Japanese that he preferred to leave the fight to the United States and the Communists. His regime had become heavily influenced by foreign advisors and technicians. Western-educated Chinese played major roles in the GMD, and Jiang's wife, Song Meiling (Soong Meiling), the daughter of a wealthy family, grew up in the United States and often seemed to manifest more allegiance to U.S. culture than to Chinese. As a condition of marriage, Jiang became a Methodist; soon he was a great exponent of the church's teachings. His New Life movement, launched in 1934 supposedly to "rejuvenate" the Chinese, was a mixture of Confucian tenets and Methodist doctrine, propagated by a GMD youth movement (Payne 1969). Thus the goal that had acted to unify various groups in the republican revolution of the early twentieth century, that of ridding China of foreign domination, united increasing numbers behind the Communist-led revolution, which appeared to be capable of and likely to establish a genuinely Chinese-controlled national government.

Jiang's conception of advancing the second of Sun's principles, Democracy, was apparently to crush the Communists. But his own government became essentially a conservative military dictatorship with Jiang in control of the single party, the Guomindang, still patterned after the old Russian Communist Party organizationally but, unlike the Communists, functioning to preserve rather than reduce basic inequalities in the socioeconomic system.

The GMD regime attempted to attract and maintain the support of the traditional elites, the rural landlords, by promising to protect their landholdings. Consequently, the GMD did little to bring about the redistribution of wealth that Sun had proposed as the way to fulfill his third principle, that of People's Livelihood. Because inequalities and oppressive conditions persisted or even worsened in GMD-controlled areas, discontent among the rural population found its expression in the Communist-led, peasant revolutionary army (Bianco 1971; Blecher 1986; Moore 1966; Skocpol 1979).

After World War II and the failure of U.S.-mediated attempts to forestall the renewal of the civil war, the conflict between the immensely strengthened Communist movement and Jiang's huge but largely demoralized and incompetently led army resumed in 1947. Popular support in the countryside and massive defections from the GMD military helped the Communist forces achieve a relatively quick victory. Other nations, awed by the gigantic proportions of the conflict in China and recovering from the devastations of the war, chose not to intervene militarily to try to prevent or reverse the outcome of China's civil war. On October 1, 1949, Mao proclaimed the establishment of the People's Republic of China in Beijing.

Jiang and remnants of the GMD armies fled from the mainland to Taiwan. There, protected by U.S. naval forces, Jiang claimed to represent the legitimate government of China. With U.S. support, the Taiwanese state, calling itself the Republic of China, held China's seat at the United Nations until 1971. At that point President Richard Nixon visited China—probably in an attempt to gain Chinese support in the U.S. international competition with the USSR and to obtain Chinese assistance in pressuring the Vietnamese into agreeing to a peace settlement acceptable to U.S. leaders. The Nixon administration decided to accept admission of the People's Republic into the United Nations and to agree that Taiwan is a part of China and must someday be reunited with the mainland.

THE PEOPLE'S REPUBLIC OF CHINA: 1949–1990

After the civil war ended in victory for the revolutionaries, a national revolutionary government was established, dominated by the Communist Party but including many non-Communists, such as Madame Song Qing Ling (Soong Ghing-ling) (1891–1981), the widow of Sun. Counterrevolutionary efforts and serious nonpolitical criminal acts were harshly dealt with. This was especially true after China began to fight in Korea against the United States in 1950. More than 100,000 official executions occurred in the first half of 1951, and many more people were sent to prison or forced labor camps.

China in 1949 had a gigantic urban drug problem in part as a result of previous corruption among GMD police and GMD use of "secret societies and gangster organizations which profited from the drug trade" for the political purpose of repressing revolutionaries (Meisner 1986, 90). Revolutionary authorities quickly launched anticrime and antivice campaigns, which over a two-year period succeeded in drastically reducing opium addiction, prostitution, gambling, and alcohol abuse. The antidrug drive "employed a combination of drastic criminal penalties (including execution) for major suppliers and dealers, amnesty for petty traffickers, rehabilitation for addicts, and a massive nationwide campaign of education and public 'ban opium' rallies appealing to patriotic sentiments by stressing the nineteenth century imperialistic origins of the drug problem" (Meisner 1986, 90–91). Actions taken by the revolutionary leadership involving redistribution of wealth and resources toward the poor, providing jobs to the previously unemployed, asserting Chinese nationalism in defiance of former imperialist powers, and the ideology of the revolution that exalted the roles of peasant and worker in society tended to elevate the self-esteem of many Chinese and reduce several important psychological and economic causes of drug abuse.

The new government's land-redistribution program tended to reinforce support for the revolution among most poor peasants, and the successful anticrime measures appealed to much of the urban population. The confrontation with the United States in Korea beginning in November 1950 also strengthened the revolutionary government.

> For over a century, China had been humiliated repeatedly by Western military forces, but now, for the first time, a Chinese army had defeated a Western army—and then fought the strongest military power in the world to a stalemate in a major conventional war. This event, perhaps more than any other in China's modern history, served to stimulate intense feelings of national pride and confidence among the Chinese people. (Meisner 1986, 79)

And it helped rally nationalist sentiment throughout China in support of the revolutionary government.

Rural Change

Mao was often cited in the West for making the statement "political power grows out of the barrel of a gun" (Mao 1965, 224). Some erroneously interpreted the expression to mean that according to Mao political power was identical with violence and that the revolutionary program would be forced on the majority of China's people. The intended meaning of the statement, however, was that in order for the poor majority of the people to pursue their aspirations, the instruments of institutionalized force (army, police) must support their right to political power rather than protect the privileges and wealth of China's landlord class, as they had in the past. Once the people no longer had to fear repression by warlord or GMD armies, they would feel secure in demanding and carrying out the redistribution of land they longed for (Blecher 1986; Meisner 1986).

After the revolution, landownership patterns in the countryside went through a series of changes. During the years 1950–1953 land was taken from landlords and some rich peasants and distributed to the poor. But both landlords and rich peasants retained amounts of land to cultivate in approximate proportion to their percentage in the population. After land redistribution, 80 percent of the rural population were classified as middle peasants (average 2.3 acres), 5 percent as rich peasants (average 3 acres), and 15 percent as poor peasants (average 2.1 acres) (Domes 1985, 44). The continued existence of the category of poor peasant was partly due to the lack of sufficient arable land in certain areas to permit each household a parcel large enough to provide its minimum income requirements.

The process of land reform itself was at once economically, politically, socially, culturally, and psychologically transforming and, at times, violent. Throughout rural China village meetings were held in which the community participated in confiscating and redistributing land. The poor were encouraged to confront landlords directly and vent their feelings about past injustices. The reform process was intended to provide the poor, previously conditioned to a self-acceptance of inferiority and subordinate status, an experience of successful use of power against the landlords who had formerly controlled their lives (Blecher 1986). Village confrontations were typically emotionally explosive, with peasants "speaking bitterness" in recounting the deaths from starvation of children or other loved ones or the loss of friends or relatives in the struggles against the Japanese and the Guomindang.

Although Mao had called for an end of the landlord class as an economic and political entity, he had argued that landlords should not be physically eliminated, and the majority survived the land-reform process. But where emotions were particularly intense, poor peasants often vented their outrage through violence. The exact number of landlords killed is variously estimated at between 0.5 and 1 million (China's 1950 population was approximately 600 million) (Blecher 1986).

In the years following the first land reform, it became clear to many peasants that they could not significantly increase agricultural productivity on their small farms since as individuals they lacked the resources to purchase machinery or improve irrigation systems. This led to the formation of local mutual assistance organizations ("mutual aid teams") and then in the mid-1950s to the movement to combine land, livestock, and equipment to form "lower-stage agricultural producers' cooperatives" (LAPCs), which averaged about thirty households. In the LAPCs peasants received wages in proportion to their group-evaluated work contribution to farm production and in proportion to the amount of land and livestock and the value of equipment they contributed to the cooperative. Membership in the LAPCs was voluntary. Finally, in the late 1950s the government, encouraged by increased agricultural productivity throughout the earlier stages of land reform, decreed the transition to the "fully socialist," or "higher-stage agricultural producers cooperatives" (HAPCs), in which all property was equally owned by participants and individuals received shares of produce and profits only in proportion to their labor as evaluated by their coworkers. Membership in the HAPCs seems to have been voluntary on the part of many but involved coercion for some who had contributed the most in property to the LAPCs (Blecher 1986).

Urban Change

In 1953, after the conclusion of the Korean conflict with the United States—in which China suffered approximately one million persons killed or wounded, including the death of one of Mao's sons—government leaders prepared to launch a rapid industrialization program. Because intense mutual hostility existed at the time between China and United States and most capitalist European nations, the Chinese could not turn to the West for assistance. China had no alternative but to rely on the Soviet Union.

The Chinese were encouraged by Russian advisors to adopt the model for industrialization that had worked for the USSR, the Stalinist strategy of the late 1920s and the 1930s. This approach called for the development of powerful bureaucratic structures to control various aspects of industrialization through comprehensive central planning; for concentration of investment in heavy industry, such as steel production, rather than in the agricultural sector or in the production of consumer goods; and for obtaining financing through selling agricultural surpluses, made possible by the anticipated greater efficiency and profitability of cooperative over individual farms. The system placed economic authority primarily in the hands of technically skilled personnel rather than relying on participatory democratic styles of management, in which workers share in decision making.

During the years 1953–1957 China graduated 130,000 engineers and achieved a healthy annual growth rate of 8 percent. But Mao and others were not satisfied with this pace or with the increase in urban unemployment, the de-emphasis on political education in favor of technical training, and the low priority assigned to agricultural sector development. Furthermore, many of the revolutionaries whose concepts of political authority and exercise of power had been shaped by the popular input characteristics of the mass-line approach to leadership objected to the bureaucratic elite's monopoly on decision making. Mao and like-minded leaders decided to depart from the Stalinist model and launch a new program, the Great Leap Forward, intended to achieve more rapid growth and more worker and peasant participation in decision-making processes.

The Great Leap: 1958–1960

The new policy involved several components. First, heavy industry, light industry, and agriculture were to be developed simultaneously. Second, the distinction between urban and rural was to be minimized by locating industrial enterprises in the countryside and recruiting urban workers for periodic agricultural work. Dispersing industry to rural locations was also viewed as a way to insure that a significant amount of industrial capacity could survive a possible nuclear attack on China's major cities. Third, to make up for China's deficiency in industry-building capital and equipment, the Great Leap was to substitute the resource of its vast population: it would provide jobs in new projects for the unemployed, and large numbers of women would be recruited into the labor force. Fourth, central planning was to give way to decentralization of authority to release the forces of creativity and to provide greater adaptability to local conditions and greater popular participation in policymaking.

The Great Leap also involved the shift in many rural areas from the fully socialist cooperative farms (HAPCs), which averaged about 160 households, to communes, which included several thousand households. Communes, unlike LAPCs and HAPCs, were much more than agricultural economic institutions. Many communes constructed their own industrial plants and functioned politically as local government units within the state framework. The communes also provided their members with social services such as child care, medical treatment, education, and food services (Blecher 1986).

The Great Leap registered some positive achievements. Many previously unemployed men, as well as many women never before in the labor force, gained jobs and a new sense of purpose. Massive improvements were made to the agricultural infrastructure, including dams and irrigation systems, and many rural industrial plants were established. Those plants eventually accounted for more than 20 percent of industrial output.

However, the negative consequences of the Great Leap seem to have outweighed the gains. The quality of the output of the rural factories was often too low to be useful. And in the agricultural sector, productivity fell because of the reduction of material incentives: food and important social services were free in the new commune system, and the practice of farming private plots for individual profit making was discontinued. Moreover, the years 1959, 1960, and 1961 were among those with the worst weather conditions in the century, and there were disastrous declines in farm output. During 1960 and 1961 food shortages contributed to a net loss in population of twenty to twenty-five million people, including deaths and deferred or unsuccessful pregnancies (Blecher 1986; Meisner 1986). The crisis in agriculture affected industrial productivity, which decreased by 38 percent in 1961 and 17 percent in 1962.

The deterioration of the economy also resulted from the abrupt cutoff of Soviet economic and technical assistance, ordered by Premier Khrushchev. This measure signaled the beginning of more than two decades of hostility between the USSR and China. Whereas some disagreements between Russian and Chinese Communist leaders dated from the 1920s, the more immediate antagonisms preceding the break included Soviet displeasure with Chinese abandonment of the Russian model of development and with the disruptive or impractical policies of the Great Leap, and Chinese criticisms of the elite Soviet political system and aspects of Soviet foreign policy. The suspension of Soviet aid not only halted dozens of industrial construction projects but also forced the shutdown of several existing power and industrial plants because of the lack of replacement parts for Russian-made machinery.

Retreat from the Great Leap: 1961–1965

In an effort to bring about economic recovery the government increased reliance on centralized economic planning, canceled a number of costly construction projects, and reduced the size of communes, limiting the economic management units to about 160 households each. Peasants were again allowed to cultivate their own private plots in addition to collectively farmed land. In both agriculture and industry, differential reward levels (material incentives) were increased. And within industrial plants worker participation in management was curtailed, and more power was restored to factory managers (Blecher 1986; Meisner 1986).

However, the shift back toward a concentration of power in the government and Party bureaucracies and the emphasis on material incentives versus revolutionary idealism provoked the animosity of Mao and various other leftists. Prior to the 1960s Mao seemed to have argued that any resurgence of capitalist traits was due to the effects of lingering feudalistic and capitalistic cultural values, largely sustained by those still active in the remaining private businesses, and that these elements would gradually be eroded as collective ownership and other economic changes strengthened socialist culture and collectivist psychology.

But in the early 1960s Mao formulated a new theory about the reemergence of capitalist traits. He said that in any social system that allowed one population element to become specialized in the function of exercising power, "capitalist tendencies" would begin to emerge. Greater power would lead to feelings of superiority, the desire for and rationalization of having a higher standard of living than others had, and the development of mechanisms, such as elitist schools for the children of power holders, to perpetuate the concentration of power in the hands of certain groups and families, which could come to constitute a new ruling class. Unlike traditional Marxist thinking, Mao was arguing that changing the nature of the economic system did not preclude, even after some lengthy period of time, the reemergence of capitalism because such a phenomenon would be fostered whenever power differentiation occurred. In other words, he located the "material basis" for capitalist tendencies "not in *property* relations . . . but in *political* relations between leaders and masses" (Blecher 1986, 78; emphasis in original). He argued, therefore, that the people must be constantly ready to mount new revolutions or at least new mass movements to prevent the domination of new privileged classes and to redistribute power more democratically throughout society.

These propositions essentially constituted Mao's theory of the need for "permanent revolution" (Blecher 1986; Mackerras and Knight 1985). Such mass movements would, as in the case of China's Communist revolution, involve the combination of leftist revolutionary intellectuals and the masses. In China in the mid-1960s Mao and others attempted to rally the masses against those perceived to be seeking a monopoly on power and privilege. Such persons included, in Mao's view, much of the bureaucratic elite of the government and the Communist Party. The occurrence of a mass movement led or at least inspired by the leader of a Communist revolution against the Party elite in the postrevolutionary period was unique. The Chinese refer to it as the Great Proletarian Cultural Revolution.

THE GREAT PROLETARIAN CULTURAL REVOLUTION: 1966–1968

A publicly asserted objective of the Cultural Revolution was to redistribute power to the people. Concentration of power in institutional elites was viewed as being a characteristic of both U.S. capitalist society and the Soviet socialist system. The worst offenders were to be removed from their positions and assigned employment at manual labor jobs in the cities or in the countryside. In general, all persons involved in nonmanual tasks were in the future expected also to perform manual labor part of the time in order to maintain an appreciation of that form of work and to identify with the large mass of workers and peasants. Wage differentials were to be reduced and rural development projects reemphasized lest China develop parasitic urban centers relying on the economic exploitation of the surrounding countryside, as, it was argued, was the case in virtually all other primarily agrarian societies.

Mao in early 1965 began explaining the need for a cultural revolution in which leftist intellectuals would work through literature and the arts and in other areas to erode the harmful residue of "bourgeois culture" present in Chinese society and more rapidly develop cultural elements congruent with socialism and the future "Communist" stage of society (Blecher 1986). Mao anticipated that the new culture would generate a new psychology, or "consciousness," among the people favorable to the development of Communist economic and social relations even before the advanced technology and material wealth assumed by Marx to be necessary conditions for communism were present (Meisner 1986).

The movement developed after a series of exchanges among leftist and rightist intellectuals over a play dealing with domineering officials and victimized peasants in a much earlier era in Chinese history. Many viewed this play as, in certain ways, critical of Mao's Great Leap program for rearranging the lives and livelihood of the nation's rural population. "A radical Beijing University philosophy instructor . . . denounced the university president" for attempting to suppress leftist criticism and called "upon students and intellectuals to join the battle" against rightists (Blecher 1986, 82). Students, faculty, and other citizens became involved in the conflict. Mao sided with the philosophy instructor and had his arguments broadcast throughout the nation. Inspired students organized Red Guard committees to begin movements in their cities against rightists in positions of authority.

Often during the Cultural Revolution Red Guards in individual communities would lead huge crowds in a march to a particular site, for example, the local Communist Party headquarters, and demand the presence of "guilty" officials, who would then be subjected to public criticism. The charges might include past behavior aimed at self-enrichment, acting in "elitist" and "antidemocratic" ways, advocating policies emphasizing material incentives, or any other practices or stated opinions that reflected the "capitalist road" to economic development. In individual industrial plants revolutionary committees of workers were elected to act as managers; many past executives were reassigned to machine work or other manual tasks. According to Chinese government estimates made in the 1980s, between 700,000 and 800,000 officials lost their positions during the years 1966–1968. The Cultural Revolution also attacked elements of traditional Chinese culture, which were seen as sources of counterrevolutionary values.

In late 1966 factions began to develop among Red Guard members over issues such as whether particular sets of local, regional, or national officials should be attacked or defended. And in 1967 the Cultural Revolution surged beyond the control of any particular leader or group, including Mao. Violent conflicts broke out in a number of locales between movement supporters and opponents, both of whom were armed with militia weapons, and in some places even among rival Red Guard factions.

Mao called on the People's Liberation Army, whose commanders were loyal to him and largely had not been the targets of Red Guard purges, to restore order. He stated that "capitalist roaders" constituted only a minority among the Communist Party's leadership. Estimates of the number of people who died in the turbulent 1966–1968 period as a result of fighting among different factions, Red Guard persecution, and army efforts to repress Red Guard forces in several parts of the country range from 40,000 to 400,000 (Blecher 1986; Meisner 1986).

After 1968, the turmoil subsided, but the movement still exercised influence over wide sectors of the population until the mid-1970s. Several top Chinese leaders died around then; most important of course was Mao's death on September 8, 1976. A month later, on October 6, Hua Guofeng (Hua Kuo-feng), premier and Party chairman, while professing support for the Cultural Revolution, had four top leftist leaders (the so-called Gang of Four), including Mao's wife, arrested on charges of "trying to foment civil war by allegedly arming the Shanghai militia and planning an attack on the organs of state" (Blecher 1986, 90). In general, Hua attempted to work out a compromise between left (Maoist) and right factions in the Chinese Communist Party. But these efforts failed, and the right wing won control of the Party Central Committee in December 1978. The apparent leader of the right-wing faction, Deng Xiaoping (Teng Hsiao-p'ing), assumed the vice premiership and the leadership of the Party committee that oversees the armed forces (Blecher 1986; Domes 1985).

POST-1978 REFORMS

The new rightist atmosphere in China was accompanied by the demotion of prominent Maoists and the "rehabilitation" of many who had been removed from their positions during the Cultural Revolution. Mao was subjected to posthumous criticism and accused of major errors, such as his grandiose and unsound plans during the Great Leap of the late 1950s and his role in helping to launch the Great Proletarian Cultural Revolution. But he was still officially recognized as "a great Marxist and a great proletarian revolutionary" whose "contributions to the Chinese Revolution far outweigh his mistakes" (Blecher 1986, 92).

The Cultural Revolution itself was interpreted by the new leadership as largely a catastrophe. Although the movement helped bring about a redistribution of resources to the rural areas, resulting in better education and health care and more industry there, the goal of increased and lasting "democratization" of national, local, and workplace authority structures was not achieved (Meisner 1986). Furthermore, economic development became stagnant because of social conflict; the interruption of the educational system and thus a reduced output of new engineers, technicians, and other skilled professionals; and the large number of incompetent administrators and other key personnel recruited during the Cultural Revolution, when emphasis was on loyalty to Mao's ideas rather than on expertise (Blecher 1986; Domes 1985).

In the 1980s changes were instituted in the economy to bring about increases in productivity. These included greater reliance on material incentives and legalizing the establishment of small-scale private businesses and industries in such areas as restaurants, clothing manufacture and sales, and transport services. A process of decollectivization of agriculture was also carried out, permitting individuals to withdraw from cooperative farming by leasing parcels of land from the cooperatives. The leasing party would then farm independently, being allowed to keep the profits (the farmer had to sell a set quantity of crops to the state at a fixed price but could sell the surplus beyond the quota at market prices).

Reforms relevant to state-owned industries included allowing such enterprises to "produce for the market demand as long as they fulfilled the assigned state quota ... purchase needed raw material through the market, rather than remaining dependent on central allocation ... [and allowing that] prices for the products ... be set by the supply and demand mechanism" (Theen and Wilson 1986, 448). Another important innovation involved allowing foreign corporations to build plants in specific restricted-access sites inside China (initially in coastal areas) called Special Economic Zones (SEZs). In 1989, 450 U.S. corporations were involved in joint ventures with the Chinese government, including projects such as aircraft assembly, nuclear power plants, and coal mining (CNN, May 24, 1989). Renewed emphasis was placed on higher education and technical training and on obtaining technology and scientific knowledge from the more-advanced industrial nations. To this end, tens of thousands of Chinese students were allowed to go to the United States, Japan, and other nations for graduate school.

China's internal politics were reshaped in part by the 1982 constitution, which attempted to shift citizen political participation away from the postrevolutionary phenomena of mass mobilization and mass movements (viewed by the 1980s leadership as potentially too disruptive and chaotic) and toward reliance on political expression through representative governmental mechanisms. Although the Communist Party remained dominant, under the new constitution citizens voted for representatives to local assemblies in multicandidate elections. Those elected voted in turn for the next level of officials. This process continued up to the national level.

China's post-Mao leadership contended that capitalism could not be reestablished so long as the land—even if leased to individuals—and certain other forms of national wealth were ultimately owned collectively. Rather, they hoped that under the reforms "some will get rich faster so that all may get rich" (Schell 1985, 16) and that individual initiative and effort would be maximized within an essentially socialist framework (Blecher 1986; Mackerras and Knight 1985; Meisner 1986; *New York Times*, Dec. 31, 1990, A7).

THE 1989 PRODEMOCRACY DEMONSTRATIONS

The changes in China's political system were insufficient to satisfy the demands for greater democracy put forth by millions in the late 1980s. Among the factors leading to the movement for more political freedom were the historic desire of Chinese intellectuals for a genuinely democratic political system, the decentralization and increase in freedom of initiative in the economic system, higher levels of cultural contact with societies that have relatively open political expression, and the example of democratizing political reforms in the USSR promoted by President Gorbachev. In the years prior to the democratic movement, relaxation of international tensions and economic progress had apparently also reduced public perception of the need for an authoritarian regime. The Communist Party had reportedly lost considerable prestige because of the failure of a number of its pre-1980s programs and allegations of corruption of some Party and government officials (Kristof 1989). And many young people began to anticipate a greater level of freedom of expression and political participation as necessary components of economic change and technological modernization.

A series of remarkable prodemocracy protests began in April 1989 (*New York Times*, May 20, 1989, 6). On April 15 Hu Yaobang, the ousted Communist Party leader who had advocated reforms to bring about greater freedom of expression, died. Beijing University students put up posters praising him and criticizing Party and government officials who had forced his resignation after blaming him for fomenting student demonstrations in 1986 and 1987. On April 17 thousands of students marched in Beijing and Shanghai, chanting the slogan "Long live Hu Yaobang! Long live democracy!" After further demonstrations, students began a boycott of classes at Beijing universities and demanded a dialogue with government officials concerning further democratization.

On May 4 tens of thousands marched in Beijing and other cities to commemorate the anniversary of China's first modern student demonstration, which had occurred seventy years earlier, in 1919. Two thousand students began a hunger strike on May 13 in Tiananmen Square in Beijing, asking for increased political and media freedom. Within a few days, hundreds of thousands, including journalists, intellectuals, and workers, joined the protests. The students appeared to enjoy widespread popular sympathy in urban areas and even some support among Party, government, and military leaders as well as encouragement from powerful countries including the United States and the USSR. One development during the sequence of demonstrations was a rapid increase in effective freedom of the press to cover the protests.

The majority of the nation's leaders, however, were unwilling to grant all the demands of the students and eventually lost patience with continued protestor occupation of Tiananmen Square. After unarmed police and soldiers were unable to clear the square, heavily armed troops, untrained and ill equipped for dealing with civilian protests, brutally repressed the demonstrators. At a minimum, hundreds were killed, apparently mainly nonstudent residents of the city attempting to block the advance of troops in the streets leading to Tiananmen Square, and in the weeks following the June 3 crackdown, thousands were arrested across the country. Several high-ranking officials accused of encouraging prodemocracy activism were demoted from public leadership roles. The government also enacted measures intended to heighten political loyalty, increase citizen commitment to the welfare of the entire nation, and intensify student identification and social bonds with the urban working class, the peasants, and the People's Liberation Army. The policies designed to accomplish these goals included more political education in the colleges and universities and the requirement that students spend at least one year working at manual labor jobs. In addition, egalitarian ideals championed by Mao were again officially emphasized.

The suppression of prodemocracy activists was in part a reaction to the dangers that many government and Communist Party leaders perceived to be embodied in the movement. They feared that the conflicts and uncertainties that might result from a rapid transition to full democracy could lead to a Chinese government too weak and divided to protect national interests effectively. According to this view, a fully democratic China might be too feeble to defend itself against economic exploitation by the more technologically advanced nations, resulting in a new era of subservience to and humiliation by neoimperialist powers. Some Party and government officials complained that many student activists were overly concerned with personal gain and with attaining the relatively comfortable lifestyles characteristic of the affluent classes of Western Europe and the United States at the expense of the peasant and worker majority. Finally, government and Party leaders who had been victims of the Great Proletarian Cultural Revolution feared the spread of a new, uncontrolled mass social movement that not only might cost them their positions but also might again plunge the nation into a state of social chaos, conflict, and economic disruption.

The weaknesses of the prodemocracy movement were to some extent the opposite of several of the strengths of the earlier Communist-led revolution. Although in 1989 over 70 percent of China's people continued to reside in the rural areas where Mao's revolution had thrived, the prodemocracy movement was almost totally urban based. Its core social constituency was highly educated young persons, an elite sector of the population, whose goals movement opponents could portray to the larger public as reforms that would mainly benefit an already advantaged minority to the detriment of the rural majority's well-being. Furthermore, the factor of nationalism, instead of operating in support of the movement as had been the case in the Communist-led revolution, was employed with some success to mobilize public opinion against proponents of the prodemocracy movement. Anti-movement government officials depicted the most radical of the activists as foreign inspired and argued that rapid unconditional democratization of China would leave the country, while still relatively underdeveloped economically, too divided politically to resist domination by the advanced Western nations and Japan.

By late June 1990 many of those arrested during the previous summer had been released (*New York Times*, May 11, 1990, A1), and a number of prodemocracy movement organizers were later given relatively short sentences (*New York Times*, Jan. 6, 1991, A3). And the attempt of pro-crackdown elements in the then forty-eight-million-member Communist Party to purge the organization of prodemocracy movement sympathizers apparently had very little impact (*New York Times*, June 23, 1990, A3). Additional reforms, including gradual steps toward greater democracy, seemed likely in the future.

CHINA'S ECONOMIC AND POLITICAL SYSTEMS IN THE 1990S

Between 1982 and the mid-1990s real wages in China approximately doubled, apparently reflecting the success of China's approach to economic reform (Yabuki 1995). Economic progress was greater in coastal areas than in inland provinces, which tended to increase regional inequalities and promote migration to certain urban areas. Some observers noted that China's development policies of fostering private enterprise, maintaining a leading role for the state in economic planning and coordination, and a relatively closed, disciplined, one-party political system characterized by only a gradual democratization process seemed to resemble past development programs pursued by U.S.-supported Asian "success stories" such as Taiwan, Hong Kong, Singapore, South Korea, and post–World War II Japan (Overholt 1993; Ross 1994; Yabuki 1995).

Since the institution of market-oriented reforms and the creation of non-state-owned economic enterprises, the share of China's gross national product (GNP) generated by the state sector declined between 1978 and 1992 from 56 percent to less than 40 percent, while the share of collectively owned enterprises (those owned by town or village residents or by groups of people in urban areas) climbed from 42 percent to 50 percent. The share contributed by private businesses and "joint" ventures (corporations with stock owned partly by the Chinese government and partly by foreign companies) rose from 2 percent to 10 percent (Yabuki 1995; Zhang 1994). By the mid-1990s, the prices of most consumer goods (with certain exceptions such as medicines and salt) were set by market forces. Most private businesses tended to be modest operations with average assets of about $20,700, with an average of seventeen employees. The occupational structure of the country shifted significantly from the late 1970s to the early 1990s with the percentage of agricultural, livestock, and fishing and related industry workers declining from 69 percent to less than 58 percent, while the percentage of nonfarm workers rose from 31.5 percent to 34 percent, and self-employed and private businesspeople rose from .04 percent to 3.7 percent (Zhang 1994).

By late 1994 the Chinese government appeared committed to revitalizing rather than privatizing major state industries (*New York Times*, Dec. 16, 1994, A1; June 18, 1995, 8; Ross 1994) and, in so doing, avoiding the widespread unemployment, essential resource scarcities and price destabilizations, and the crime and corruption that had accompanied privatization in Russia. China's leaders also wanted to avoid the development of a large, welfare-supported population segment, such as that which characterized the United States. Chinese officials increased the amount of government investment in state-owned industries, many of which were losing money, anticipating that reorganization, improved training and technology, and competition with nonstate businesses would improve the productivity and efficiency of state-owned enterprises.

China's government in the mid-1990s remained a Leninist-inspired, one-party political system, criticized by the United States and other Western nations as well as by organizations such as Amnesty International for human rights violations against political dissidents and for an overly harsh criminal justice system. One significant innovation in political procedures involved providing Chinese voters not only the opportunity to approve or disapprove a party-nominated candidate but also the capacity to select a set of choices from a set of candidates larger than the number of positions to be filled (Fewsmith 1994). This modification resulted in the replacement through voter action of several members of the Communist Party's governing Central Committee.

CHINA'S ECONOMIC SUCCESS RELATIVE TO THE FORMER USSR

China's economy generally made steady and impressive gains during the 1980s and the 1990s, suffering mainly from periodic bouts of inflation. In contrast, Russia's economy and society were plagued by sluggish growth, massive involvement of mafialike organized-crime groups in thousands of supposedly legitimate businesses, gigantic levels of corruption—resulting in dozens of murders, including killings of journalists, major television personalities, members of parliament, and legitimate businesspeople opposed to corruption and organized-crime infiltration as well as some deeply involved in it (*New York Times*, Dec. 11, 1994, E1; March 2, 1995, A10; March 7, 1995, A10).

Opinions on the reasons for the contrasts between the performance of China's and Russia's reform programs have varied and even shifted over time. By the mid-1990s it was possible to identify differences in both political and economic policies between the two countries that apparently contributed to the divergent outcomes.

In terms of economic policies, prominent social and economic scientists (Dittmer 1994; Overholt 1993; Yabuki 1995; Zhang 1994) tend to conclude that China's decisions were superior in terms of timing, order, and perhaps dimension of reforms in comparison to Russia's. China determined to change economic policies gradually and piece by piece and to reflect cautiously on past performance before deciding on where, when, and how to make the next change. Russia's initial post-Communist leaders, in contrast, allegedly advised by U.S. professors (Overholt 1993), attempted to employ "economic shock therapy," which tended to be characterized by multiple, near-simultaneous changes, often with catastrophic results.

Another major difference between the Chinese and Russian approaches was in terms of the order of changes. Chinese policy involved first altering regulations regarding areas of the economy in which simple and relatively inexpensive changes were likely to produce large, rapid economic gains, leaving more complex, difficult issues for later evaluation. In China, the private enterprise option was first introduced in agriculture, thereby allowing farmers to cultivate for private profit, and this option quickly resulted in rapid increases in productivity and higher income levels and improved lifestyles for hundreds of millions of farmers. Next, profit-oriented small- and medium-sized enterprises in the areas of service and light industry were now permitted, again resulting in rapid productivity and income gains for the overall economy. The Chinese also experimented with creating and modifying economic infrastructures necessary to substantial privatization of the economy, in particular stock markets at which investors could purchase shares in the ownership of companies, a seemingly logical step before considering the sale of large state-owned industries.

Foreign investment was allowed, including totally foreign-owned enterprises, under terms set by the Chinese government. Whereas there were fewer than five thousand foreign-affiliated businesses in 1987, there were almost 50,000 by 1992. Just over 16 percent of these were totally foreign owned (compared to near zero in 1987); 18.6 percent operated under a contract system between the Chinese government and foreign interests, which apportioned risks, responsibilities, and profits and set management structure; and 64.9 percent were joint ventures in which the enterprise's stock was owned in part by the Chinese state and in part by the foreign entity (Yabuki 1995).

Russia, in contrast, tended to avoid agricultural reforms, waffled over the issue of large-scale foreign investments (a touchy issue for nationalists in the Russian parliament concerned with allowing increased foreign control over the domestic economy), and instead attempted rapidly to privatize a substantial number of large state-owned industries, which often required significant infusions of capital for retooling, technological updating, and reorganization, with any substantial economic gains perhaps years off. In the meantime, this approach meant that tens of thousands of workers faced layoffs, contributing to declining social morale, increasing inequality, drug use, and street and organized crime. Furthermore, the disrupted supply and increased prices of critical materials produced by newly privatized major industries (formerly controlled by the state) contributed to the failure of many small- and medium-sized businesses and to the deterioration of Russia's agricultural sector, which suffered substantially from the loss of machinery and fertilizers previously provided by the state.

China in the mid-1990s appeared ready to reject the concept of completely privatizing large state-owned heavy and related industries, apparently preferring instead to transform some into joint stock enterprises and to maintain state control over improved, profitable industries. These options might avoid or minimize the massive layoffs and social disorganization, protests, and welfare burdens that would otherwise likely result. Further, state control over supply and prices of certain critical materials produced by state-controlled industries could help insure an economically healthy environment for the continued steady growth of collectively and privately owned market-oriented businesses.

Politically, a major difference between China and Russia had to do with the level and point in time of democratization relative to economic reform and development. Gorbachev attempted to fully democratize the political system in the former USSR and Russia before attempting economic reforms. Some prominent Russian leaders, as well as foreign advisors, believed this was a necessary political step for economic reforms to succeed, a somewhat dubious hypothesis given the impressive economic performance of certain capitalistic nations such as Singapore, Taiwan, and South Korea, which developed under authoritarian political systems.

In Russia, especially after the failed coup attempt by Communist hard-liners in August 1991, democracy provided the means for nationalistic tensions to overcome the old political framework and ideology and destroy the USSR and the system of economic integration of industries and resources that was the organic foundation of the Soviet Union. This situation contributed to massive economic disruption in several new nations that had previously been republics of the USSR and provided huge opportunities for organized-crime smuggling operations, at least temporarily, to satisfy supply demands across borders and simultaneously to avoid arrest by taking advantage of new international boundaries and divisions in police jurisdiction.

China, however, at least temporarily, opted to maintain the one-party state system. Or as Deng, a leader of China's economic reform program put it, to achieve economic development by adhering to the "four cardinal principles": (1) maintain the political system that puts the interests of the worker-peasant majority first—the "people's democratic dictatorship"; (2) maintain the political leadership of the Communist Party; (3) adhere to "Marxist-Leninist-Maoist" thought; and (4) pursue the "socialist road" to development (Fewsmith 1994). The potential advantages of a one-party system, assuming a party leadership genuinely committed to the welfare of the majority of China's people and to national interests, theoretically include: maintaining a strong, united state capable of preventing the type of social chaos that ensued from Russia's economic reforms; planning and carrying out economic change in a measured, cautious, and integrated way (avoiding or minimizing policies that might result in regional, occupational, or economic sector-centered depressions); and countering economic, diplomatic, or covert measures by foreign powers aimed at weakening China or generating internal conflict, such as that which occurred in the former USSR or the former Yugoslavia.

Beyond the maintenance of the one-party state another major political strategy pursued by Deng and his associates was to carry out economic and other reforms in ways that tended to build or reinforce popular support for reform policies and the reforming government (Overholt 1993). This meant attempting a process of modernization and change through consensus building rather than one that, in trying to do many things at once, risked alienating large population segments from supporting the modernizing government. Thus, once China's agricultural reforms had succeeded in substantially raising income for almost 800 million rural Chinese, the government, enjoying their support, could move securely to the next phase of reform.

Deng and associates viewed economic failure as being the central cause of the collapse of the European Communist Party states, and they believed that economic growth was necessary to the survival of a socialist system, at least during periods when the society's citizens feel free from major external threats. An implication of this interpretation is that, following a successful economic development program, popular support might help to sustain the Chinese Communist Party, even in a more-democratic political system. Among the major challenges to the successful continuation of the development program were: limiting population growth; insuring an adequate food supply; maintaining the prosperity of farmers; revitalizing state-owned industries; minimizing unemployment, underemployment, and the growth of economic inequality; and limiting and suppressing corruption (which seemed, at least at certain points, to flourish as many low-paid party and government officials and supposedly legitimate businesspeople used their power or other advantages and opportunities to extort bribes or commit financial frauds).

MORALITY AND THE FUTURE OF THE CHINESE REVOLUTION

Chirot (1994) and I (DeFronzo 1991) have argued that the collapse of the Eastern European Communist Party states was due in great part to their lack of moral legitimacy. According to Chirot, the lack of legitimacy had multiple causes, including the fact that the Communist Party governments in Eastern Europe were largely the result of World War II and the Soviet occupation of those nations, periodic repression to maintain Communist Party–dominated systems, and widespread corruption and tendency of officials to act in an authoritarian and inconsiderate manner toward fellow citizens. The Stalinist-era economic systems and bureaucratic personnel of these societies proved too rigid to adjust adequately to market mechanisms, to develop and employ new technologies, and to display the flexibility necessary to move successfully into the electronic-bio-technical phase of modern industrialization. Because traditional Marxist ideology failed to anticipate and adapt to the impact of technological innovations, it also failed to live up to its claim to be a scientifically valid belief system. Also contributing to the demise of the East European Communist Party states was the spread of knowledge among the people of these societies concerning the material wealth and democratic political systems of Western Europe and the United States and the existence of sizable educated middle classes, which became morally disillusioned and even outraged against their counries' leaders and political systems. Once the threat of Soviet intervention was removed, the one-party governments were quickly dismantled in largely nonviolent political revolutions.

Chirot (1994) concluded that citizenry's moral perception of their societies and political systems, as reflected in the Eastern European situations, was likely to be a dominant cause of "revolutionary instability" in the future. This hypothesis has implications for the potential preservation or extinction of the Communist Party's leadership role in China.

The first moral issue concerns economic development. To maintain the legitimacy of Communist Party leadership, the Party leaders believe that they must maintain a successful economic development program. For Deng and his associates, China's "socialist stage of development" apparently did not necessarily mean either a "planned" economy or a "state-owned economy" but rather the government pursuit of economic policies that promote great economic and technological growth and lifestyle improvement while enhancing the basic welfare of the vast majority of China's people. Permitting a significant degree of private ownership, profit-making motivation, and market mechanisms to set prices and stimulate efficiency could be partially rationalized as consistent with Marxist ideology because China did not undergo economic development to an advanced level under capitalism, as traditional Marxist theory claimed was necessary (although Mao suggested that capitalism was not necessary to accomplish this). Therefore "capitalistic" elements of China's "socialist" economy may be interpreted as a necessary and tolerable way to utilize the motivational and efficiency-fostering aspects of capitalism while maintaining or developing major social benefits and state-coordinating capacities of socialism.

In the process, the leadership proposed that the development of further inequality in income, wealth, and opportunity must be limited and, in particular, must not lead to the creation of an impoverished "underclass," as occurred in the United States. Such a development would likely critically erode the moral basis of the country's official "socialist ideology." Similarly, maintenance of moral legitimacy implies the harsh suppression of corrupt government officials or businesspeople.

The moral stature of China's political leadership in the perceptions of China's growing percentage of highly educated citizens may be protected or heightened to the extent that former Communist party–dominated countries such as Russia are characterized by economic stagnation, corruption, flourishing organized crime, debilitating internal political conflict, and other social ills under their new capitalistic systems. Finally, but importantly, the moral basis of China's government can be enhanced to the extent that it successfully demonstrates the capacity to defend the country's national interests and resist foreign exploitation and intimidation.

CHINA'S PROGRESS, PROBLEMS, POLICIES, AND PLANS FOR THE FUTURE

Economic Growth and Energy Needs

Since the start of major economic reforms, China's gross domestic product (GDP) has grown at an average of about 9 to 10 percent per year, and has now become the fourth largest economy in the world after the United States, Japan, and Germany. If adjusted for domestic purchasing power, China in 2006 ranked second. GDP per capita rose from $1,071 in 1978 to $4,726 in 2003. China's spectacular economic growth has been based primarily on its expanding "vast and diverse manufacturing sector" (Sharma 2006, 170). By 2006, China was consuming about one-third of the world's steel and close to half of the world's cement.

China's dramatic economic growth drastically increased its demand for energy from multiple sources including oil, coal, natural gas, hydro power, nuclear, solar, and wind. The projected enormous increase in the utilization of its abundant coal resources poses the threat of increased environmental hazards unless technologies for reducing pollutants from burning coal are widely employed (Economy 2005; Klare 2006). Up until 1993 China produced enough oil to satisfy its own needs. But since then its importation of oil has soared. By 2004 China was importing 48 percent of the oil it consumed (Klare 2006, 181). China's increased demand for oil contributed to the surge in the price of oil in 2006. To meet its oil needs, China has expanded its international sources from Indonesia, Yemen, and Oman to include Saudi Arabia, Iran, Angola, and Sudan and has entered into agreements to explore for or develop and extract oil reserves in Venezuela and coastal Cuba (Hennock 2005).

China's international search for oil and trade partners has been paralleled by its growing international political influence, particularly in Africa and Latin America, where many nations are still characterized by widespread poverty. China has offered assistance to nations such as Brazil in coping with its social problems (Hawksley 2006). The developing ties between the growing economic power house of China and a large number of Latin American nations, several of whose populations had elected left-wing governments by the end of 2006, was of concern to conservative political leaders in the United States.

Inequality and Poverty

China's phenomenal economic growth has been accompanied by increases in inequality between cities and rural areas, among regions, and among citizens. Privatization of much of the economy has even permitted some businessmen to become U.S. dollar billionaires (BBC News, November 4, 2005). But at the same time that economic inequality increased significantly, absolute poverty—in terms of people lacking certain basic minimum physical and service requirements—declined drastically. According to Sharma (2006, 172), the proportion of China's population living in poverty in 1981 was 53 percent but only 8 percent in 2001. Thus, any significant economically rooted mass discontent in China's foreseeable future would likely be due to relative deprivation rather than absolute want.

In the early twenty-first century many of China's rural residents staged protests over issues such as land appropriations for commercial purposes, economic problems, or concern over corruption. Rural discontent alarmed many government officials and Communist Party leaders for a number of reasons, the most important including the fact that the majority of China's population, about 59 percent, still lived in rural areas and that peasant support was responsible for the victory of the Communist revolution. The government responded to protests by taking steps to promote economic progress in the countryside, reduce corruption, and develop a universal social welfare safety net for the entire population, urban and rural (Hussain 2005). The welfare reforms were also in part designed to meet the needs of China's so-called floating population, an estimated one hundred million formerly rural residents who had migrated to urban areas in search of better opportunities.

Corruption

China's economic liberalization has been accompanied by a surge in corruption "afflicting almost all" transitions to market economies (Sun 2005, 257). The corruption has interfered with economic and social development, particularly in certain regions, infuriated tens of millions of citizens, and "cast doubt on the neoliberal logic" (Sun 2005, 257). Corruption-related losses to state revenue may have amounted to about 4 percent of GDP and corruption related capital flight to about 2 percent of GDP in the early years of the twenty-first century (Sun 2005, 258). Yet China's economy has continued to grow at an enormous pace despite significant corruption because, according to Sun (2005, 259), China "has avoided the most destructive kinds of corruption at the national level": "kleptocracy," in which a national leader uses his power for personal material gain, and "bilateral monopoly," in which the ruler and "a few private interests share in the spoils." According to Sun, bilateral monopoly was the damaging form of corruption that characterized the Yeltsin government in Russia, in which a number of Yeltsin's associates became "economic oligarchs." In contrast, according to Sun, China's leadership at the national level has been relatively free from this type of corruption. "In post Mao China, the top leadership has been clean and devoted to national development, as has most of the top leadership at the provincial level" (Sun 2005, 259).

The most serious corruption in government, with a few exceptions, has occurred among the lower level of provincial government, especially in more remote areas of the country less closely monitored in the past by the central government. A number of these corrupt officials have been imprisoned and some executed. The "dominant form of corruption" in China in 2005 was what Sun called "competitive corruption," in which a businessman offers someone, often a lower-level state official, a bribe to secure benefits such as a business contract, a loan, access to markets, ability to avoid paying taxes, or the capacity to influence regulatory decisions (Sun 2005, 259–60). But according to Sun, extortion, which was common in post-Soviet Russia, seems rare in China. So-called New Left intellectuals and political leaders in China believe that strengthening the power of the central state is the best way to combat corruption spawned by excessive neoliberal economic policies.

Democracy and Human Rights

In 2006 China's national government was controlled in effect exclusively by the sixty-eight-million-member Communist Party. Since 1988, however, China has mandated that individual villages hold direct elections each three years for village committees, which have the power to determine important local issues such as land rights (Luard 2005). In recent years, often in situations in which existing village officials were thought guilty of unfairly acquiring land or abusing resources, they were voted out of power. But as of 2006, direct voting for political officials has not been extended to higher levels of government. The Communist Party–controlled government monitors the Internet, censoring it to a significant degree (Thompson 2006). While in important respects the Chinese political system lacks the levels of political freedom identified as human rights in Western capitalist democracies, Chinese leaders emphasize benefits that it views as essential economic human rights but that they accuse capitalist-oriented governments of relegating to the realm of market forces both on the domestic and on the international level. Apparently expressing this point of view, Charles Tang, head of the Brazil-China Chamber of Commerce, stated: "The Chinese government has achieved the greatest victory in the history of human rights. It has removed 400 million Chinese people from poverty and enabled them to live with dignity and take part in economic life. That is the true measure of human rights" (Hawksley 2006, 4).

As Jeffrey Wasserstrom (2001) has noted, a people's view of human rights is shaped by their experience and their knowledge (or ignorance) of history. When Western leaders discuss human rights abuses in China, they generally refer to limitations on political activities and freedom of speech. But from the official Chinese point of view, the memory of massive human rights abuses by foreign powers can dwarf issues such as limitations on freedom of expression. The British victory over the Chinese in the 1839–1842 Opium Wars is blamed, as noted earlier, for the spread of opium addiction to tens of millions. The multinational Boxer Protocol, the military mop-up campaign that followed the defeat of the Boxer Rebellion in 1901, reportedly involved many killings, rapes, and lootings. And the Japanese invasion and occupation during the 1930s and the first half of the 1940s inflicted massive atrocities. Chinese leaders credit the revolution and its Communist leadership with freeing the Chinese people from the abuses of foreign aggression and exploitation and, despite major and sometimes disastrous mistakes, eventually successfully lifting the large majority of the people out of dire poverty. Thus Wasserstrom suggests a "history driven" human rights policy (2001, 267). Such an approach, coupled with continued trade and increased international communication, might attempt to advance human rights by first recognizing all past human rights abuses from which a society's people have suffered and a public acknowledgement of Western and other foreign responsibility for such abuses, along with recognition of China's achievements in dealing with certain types of human rights abuses, including the repressive aspects of imperialism. Then the quest for future human rights progress could proceed in an atmosphere of historical integrity and openness and could be potentially more effective than a Western-biased human rights campaign that might be portrayed as deceptive, hypocritical, and racist.

Future Political Change: Conditioning Factors

According to Tim Luard (2005, 5), "former Chinese leader Deng Xiaoping was quoted as saying there would be national elections in 50 years—by 2037." For advocates of multiparty democracy, that seems a long time to wait. And some might expect that China's rapidly developing market economy and increasing levels of communication might hasten the process of democratization. But Wasserstrom's (2002) analysis identified several factors that affect the pace of political change and the forms it may take. China's immense size makes the organization of a nationwide anti-government movement difficult as long as "factional disputes within the top leadership are kept under control," "relatively good cooperation" exists between civilian and military leadership and between the central and provincial governments, and "the flow of information through systems of mass communication is tightly held" by the central government (2002, 258). Wasserstrom claimed that the Chinese government has been relatively tolerant of small-scale or local protests but has "been ruthless toward anything that seems to have the potential to provide an organizational framework for collective action by people from different regions and walks of life."

One reason for the continuing legitimacy of Communist Party rule among wide sectors of the population is the relatively strong "link between patriotism and communism" in that "the Chinese Communist Party has a historical record of anti-imperialist accomplishment" and "national liberation" (Wasserstrom 2002, 258). This is a similar strength of the Communist parties of Cuba and Vietnam, just as the lack of a strong link between Communist parties and patriotism in countries such as Poland, Hungary, and East Germany, where Communist Party rule was widely perceived as the result mainly of Soviet military occupation in the last part of World War II and after, was a major reason for the overthrow of these Communist-led governments in 1989.

Another element in the preservation of Communist Party rule in China has been the reaction of Chinese leaders to what they perceive as the mistakes of Communist-led governments in Eastern Europe and the Soviet Union, which contributed greatly to their downfall. As noted earlier, Communist leaders viewed economic failure as a primary reason for the fall of European Communist states. Therefore they pursued economic reforms in a way planned to achieve maximum success and growth despite the associated problems such as at least temporary surges in inequality among individuals and regions and between cities and rural areas. Privatization and market processes were introduced first in sectors promising quick success. When these experiments worked, more reforms were introduced in other selected sectors of the economy. The resulting tremendous economic growth, in significantly improving the lives of hundreds of millions of people, has apparently led to tolerance of increases in inequality and perhaps—to some extent—of corruption. Leaders learned from the failed Communist states the importance of providing increasing availability of consumer goods to the people, reducing government intrusiveness in their lives, and launching "high-profile anti-corruption campaigns" (Wasserstrom 2002, 258). Another important factor inhibiting political change in China is the awareness by many of China's people of the serious problems that afflicted large numbers of people in a number of post-Communist countries including Russia: drastic declines in life span; large increases in organized crime, homicide, and other street crimes; drug use; prostitution; the most damaging forms of corruption; ethnic strife; and terrorism, along with the deterioration of health care and social services for many, while a minority grew enormously wealthy. This is different from the Chinese experience, in which the lifestyle of the majority of the population markedly improved. Millions of China's people questioned the value of the flawed type of democracy introduced in some of the post-Communist nations in comparison to China's existing political system.

SUMMARY AND ANALYSIS

A number of factors contributed to the increase in discontent among China's peasants during the late nineteenth and early twentieth centuries, including massive population growth, intense poverty in rural areas, and humiliating military defeats and exploitation by foreign powers. The impoverished millions among China's rural population, culturally inclined to the historic mechanism of rebellion as a means of expressing outrage, were attracted to the Communist-inspired program for land redistribution and formed the basis of the peasant revolution.

Within the republican movements of the early twentieth century, two types of revolutionary elites developed: the relatively conservative leadership of the GMD and the more radical leadership of the Communist Party. Most individuals in these elites came from the socioeconomic upper 10 percent of China's population and had achieved a relatively high degree of education. GMD leaders were drawn largely from the merchant and other business classes of the coastal cities and often had considerable contact with Western culture and economic interests. The leadership of the Communist Party tended to emerge from among the "radicalized" children of rich peasants and landlords. Ideologically, these two sets of leaders developed strikingly different interpretations of Sun's Three Principles of the People. The main point of contention was the meaning of the third principle, People's Livelihood. For GMD leaders who relied on the urban backing of merchants and foreign business interests and the rural support of the landlord classes, People's Livelihood could not mean a substantial redistribution of wealth toward the poor.

The GMD's failure to implement meaningful economic reform after the death of Sun not only alienated large segments of the impoverished majority but also affected the GMD's ability to fulfill the first and second of Sun's principles, Independence and Democracy. Failing to carry out significant land reform and, consequently, forced to repress popular aspirations, the GMD became a conservative military dictatorship exercising power through force of arms and a one-party government. The GMD reliance on weapons and other assistance from Western nations to maintain its military apparatus compromised its claims to nationalism.

After the abdication of the Manchus in 1911 and the death of the military dictator Yuan in 1916, China dissolved into separate provinces ruled independently by warlords. But though a central government no longer exercised control over most of China until after 1927, conservative province-level governments and armed forces remained essentially intact. Jiang and the GMD succeeded in unifying most of China partly through military efforts but also by offering acceptable financial, political, and military arrangements to warlords, landlords, and urban merchants and other businessmen, domestic and foreign. The primary limitations on state power were a lack of sufficient resources and of coordination among military commanders to crush insurgency in the countryside and later the inability to resist the Japanese. Because the GMD state, its armed forces, and allied provincial governments and warlord armies were relatively strong in the 1920s and 1930s, Communist revolutionaries were defeated in urban areas, unlike their Russian predecessors, and turned to organizing a peasant-based rural revolution.

Other nations of the world did not directly intervene in China to stop the revolution. Their role was largely limited to providing weapons and advisors to Jiang's GMD forces. The Japanese invaded China to conquer and possibly colonize it, but not specifically to prevent a revolution. Later, after the defeat of the Japanese, a war-weary world was loath to intervene in the internal conflict among 600 million Chinese.

By advocating the seizure and redistribution of landlord property, the Chinese Communists took advantage of the lack of GMD land reform to attract peasants to their cause. However, although this policy received an enthusiastic response from many, an additional powerful cause for peasant support and a more general unifying motivation for participation in the revolution was the nationalism inspired by the Japanese invasion. Not only did the Japanese attack reduce Jiang's ability to combat Communist rebels, but it also provided an opportunity for Communist forces to display their nationalist commitment. Jiang's GMD armies faired poorly against the Japanese and often retreated. In contrast the Communist forces in north China organized an effective peasant-based guerrilla war against the Japanese and Chinese collaborators, often pro-GMD landlords and merchants, and largely isolated them in cities. After the withdrawal of the Japanese, the combination of the Communists' proven nationalist fervor and their program for wealth redistribution resulted in a mounting tide of popular support. This support facilitated the relatively quick defeat of the GMD and the October 1, 1949, establishment of the People's Republic of China.

After the military victory of the revolution, China collectivized its agricultural, industrial, and commercial systems. But following the death of Mao in 1976, China's new leaders embarked on a policy of economic reform, aspects of which were referred to as the "personal responsibility system" and "market socialism." Innovations involved allowing farmers to cultivate land for personal profit at prices set by market demand (once state quotas were met), permitting privately owned businesses, and allowing state-controlled foreign investment. Although China carried out major economic changes, it maintained a one-party-dominated political system.

The economic reforms and related government policies unleashed spectacular economic growth. As China's economy rapidly expanded, so did its need for energy, and after 1993 China began to dramatically increase its importation of oil. China's booming economy permitted some citizens to become enormously rich while also drastically reducing the percentage of the country's people living in poverty.

CHINESE REVOLUTION: CHRONOLOGY OF MAJOR EVENTS

1839–1842	Opium War, resulting in British victory; beginning of process of Chinese subjugation to foreign economic and political interests
1851–1864	Taiping Rebellion
1911	Republican Revolution, led by Sun
1912	Sun organizes republican revolutionary groups into the Guomindang
1921	Formation of the Chinese Communist Party
1925	Sun dies
1926	Guomindang armies under General Jiang launch campaign to subdue warlords and unify China
1927	Jiang attacks Communists, precipitating a new civil war
1934–1935	Communist forces retreat in the Long March; Mao, advocate of a peasant-based revolution, becomes the dominant Communist leader
1937–1945	The Guomindang and the Communists halt civil war and form an alliance to fight Japanese invaders
1947–1949	Civil war resumes; Communists win
1958–1960	Great Leap Forward
1966–1968	Great Proletarian Cultural Revolution
1976	Mao dies
1989	Prodemocracy movement develops and is suppressed

1994   China's dramatic economic growth drastically increases its demand for energy, and after 1993, China begins to import oil

2003   China's technological progress results in it becoming the third nation to launch an astronaut into Earth's orbit and successfully recover him

2004   China is importing 48 percent of the oil it consumes

2006   China's economy, depending on the method used, is rated as either the fourth or the second largest in the world; poverty, according to international standards, is reportedly reduced to below 10 percent of the population

References and Further Readings

Barme, Geremie. 1994. "Soft Porn, Packaged Dissent, and Nationalism: Notes on Chinese Culture in the 1990s." *Current History*, September, 270–75.

BBC News, November 4, 2005, "Chinese Billionaires on the Rise." http://news.bbc.co.uk/2/hi/business/4406922.stm.

Bianco, Lucien. 1971. *Origins of the Chinese Revolution, 1915–1949.* Trans. Muriel Bell. Stanford, CA: Stanford University Press.

Binyan, Liu. 1994. "Tiananmen and the Future of China." *Current History*, September, 241–246.

Blecher, Marc. 1986. *China, Politics, Economics, and Society: Iconoclasm and Innovation in a Revolutionary Socialist Country.* Marxist Regimes series. London: Pinter.

Bohr, Richard. 2006. "The Taiping Revolution." In DeFronzo, ed., *Revolutionary Movements in World History*, 3:855–62.

Borokh, Lila. 1972. "Notes on the Early Role of Secret Societies in Sun Yatsen's Republican Movement." In Chesneaux, ed., *Popular Movements and Secret Societies in China.*

Bottomore, Tom, ed. 1983. *A Dictionary of Marxist Thought.* Cambridge, MA: Harvard University Press.

Brown, Roger H. 2006. "The Japanese New Order Movement." In DeFronzo, ed., *Revolutionary Movements in World History*, 2:489–98.

Cavatorta, Francesco. 2006. "Colonialism, Anti-Colonialism and Neo-Colonialism." In DeFronzo, ed., *Revolutionary Movements in World History*, 1:163–68.

Chance, Norman. 1985. *China's Urban Villagers: Life in a Beijing Commune.* New York: Holt, Rinehart and Winston.

Cheng, Chu-yuan, ed. 1989. *Sun Yat-sen's Doctrine in the Modern World.* Boulder: Westview Press.

Chesneaux, Jean. 1971. *Secret Societies in China in the Nineteenth and Twentieth Centuries.* Trans. Gillian Nettle. Ann Arbor: University of Michigan Press.

_____, ed. 1972a. *Popular Movements and Secret Societies in China, 1840–1950.* Stanford, CA: Stanford University Press.

_____. 1972b. "Secret Societies in China's Historical Evolution." In Chesneaux, ed., *Popular Movements and Secret Societies in China.*

Ch'ien, Tuan-sheng. 1964. "The Kuomintang: Its Doctrine, Organization, and Leadership." In *Modern China*, ed. Albert Feuerwerker. Asian Civilization. Englewood Cliffs, NJ: Prentice-Hall.

Chirot, Daniel. 1994. "What Happened in Eastern Europe in 1989?" In Wasserstrom and Perry, eds., *Popular Protest and Political Culture in Modern China*.

Clubb, O. Edmund. 1978. *20th Century China*. 3rd ed. New York: Columbia University Press.

CNN, May 24, 1989, "U.S.-China Joint Economic Ventures."

DeFronzo, James. 1991. *Revolutions and Revolutionary Movements*. 1st ed. Boulder: Westview Press.

———. 2006a. "The Chinese Revolution." In DeFronzo, ed., *Revolutionary Movements in World History*, 1:126–39.

———, ed. 2006b. *Revolutionary Movements in World History: From 1750 to the Present*. 3 vols. Santa Barbara, CA: ABC-CLIO.

Dittmer, Lowell. 1994. *China Under Reform*. Politics in Asia and the Pacific. Boulder: Westview Press.

Domes, Jürgen. 1985. *The Government and Politics of the PRC: A Time of Transition*. Boulder: Westview Press.

Dreyer, June Teufel. 1994. "The People's Army: Serving Whose Interests?" *Current History* September, 265–69.

Dunn, John. 1972. *Modern Revolutions: An Introduction to the Analysis of a Political Phenomenon*. Cambridge, UK: Cambridge University Press.

Eastman, Lloyd E. 1988. *Family, Fields, and Ancestors: Constancy and Change in China's Social and Economic History, 1550–1949*. New York: Oxford University Press.

Economy, Elizabeth. 2005. "China's Environmental Challenges." *Current History*, September, 278–83.

Eisenman, Joshua, and Joshua Kurlantzick. 2006. "China's Africa Strategy." *Current History*, May, 219–24.

Fairbairn, Geoffrey. 1974. *Revolutionary Guerrilla Warfare: The Countryside Version*. Middlesex, UK: Penguin.

Fewsmith, Joseph. 1994. "Reform, Resistance, and the Politics of Succession." In *China Briefing, 1994*, ed. William A. Joseph. Boulder: Westview Press.

Gill, Jungyun. 2006. "Student and Youth Movements, Activism, and Revolution." In Defronzo, ed., *Revolutionary Movements in World History*, 3:848–54.

Gurley, John G. 1983. *Challenges to Communism*. San Francisco: Freeman.

Harrison, John A. 1967. *China Since 1800*. New York: Harcourt, Brace & World.

Hawksley, Humphrey. 2006. "Chinese Influence in Brazil Worries US." BBC News, April 3. http://news.bbc.co.uk/2/hi/americas/4872522.stm.

Hennock, Mary. 2005. "China's Global Hunt for Oil." BBC News, March 9. http://news.bbc.co.uk/2/hi/business/4191683.stm.

Hough, Jeffrey F. 1994. "America's Russian Policy: The Triumph of Neglect." *Current History*, October, 308–12.

Hussain, Athar. 2005. "Repairing China's Social Safety Net." *Current History*, September, 268–71.

Jordan, Donald A. 1976. *The Northern Expedition: China's National Revolution of 1926–1928*. Honolulu: University Press of Hawaii.

Klare, Michael T. 2006. "Fueling the Dragon: China's Strategic Energy Dilemma." *Current History*, April, 180–85.

Kristof, Nicholas D. 1989. "China Erupts." *New York Times Magazine*, June 4.

Kwong, Julia. 1994. "Ideological Crisis Among China's Youths: Values and Official Ideology." *British Journal of Sociology* 45 (June): 245–64.

Lenin, V. I. [1916] 1975. "Imperialism, The Highest Stage of Capitalism." In *The Lenin Anthology*, ed. Robert C. Tucker. New York: W. W. Norton.

Li, Chien-Nung. 1956. *The Political History of China, 1840–1928*. Trans. and ed. Ssu-Teng and Jeremy Ingalls. Princeton, NJ: Van Nostrand.

Luard, Tim. 2005. "China's Village Democracy Skin Deep." BBC News, October 10. http://news.bbc.co.uk/1/hi/world/asia-pacific/4319954.stm.

Lust, John. 1972. "Secret Societies, Popular Movements and the 1911 Revolution." In Chesneaux, ed., *Popular Movements and Secret Societies in China*.

Mackerras, Collin, and Nick Knight, ed. 1985. *Marxism in Asia*. New York: St. Martin's Press.

Mao Zedong. 1965. *Selected Works of Mao Tse-Tung*. Vol. 2. Beijing: Foreign Languages Press.

_____. 1967. *Selected Readings from the Work of Mao*. Beijing: Foreign Languages Press.

Meisner, Maurice. 1986. *Mao's China and After: A History of the People's Republic*. The Transformation of Modern China. New York: Free Press.

Moore, Barrington, Jr. 1966. *Social Origins of Dictatorship and Democracy: Lord and Peasant in the Making of the Modern World*. Boston: Beacon.

Mulcahy, Michael. 2006. "Human Rights, Morality, Social Justice, and Revolution." In DeFronzo, ed., *Revolutionary Movements in World History*, 2:365–70.

New York Times, May 20, 1989, 6, "China's Upheaval: Five Weeks of Student Demonstrations."

_____, May 11, 1990, A1, "China Announces Release from Jail of 211 Dissidents."

_____, June 23, 1990, A3, "China Ends Purge of Party's Ranks."

_____, December 31, 1990, A7, "China Offers Cautious Economic Plans."

_____, January 6, 1991, A3, "7 Sentenced in First Tiananmen Square Protest Trials."

_____, November 14, 1994, A17, "Beijing's Polite Politics."

_____, December 4, 1994, 24, "Never Far from Power, China's Military Is Back."

_____, December 11, 1994, E1, "The Long Shadow of the Russian Mob."

_____, December 16, 1994, A1, "Overhaul of China's Industry at a Standstill."

_____, January 26, 1995, 1, "12 Intellectuals Petition China on Corruption."

_____, February 1, 1995, A1, "Report by the State Department Faults Beijing on Rights Abuse."

_____, February 27, 1995, A1, "U.S. and China Sign Accords to End Piracy of Software, Music Recordings and Films."

_____, March 2, 1995, A10, "Russian Journalist Is Slain; Profits May Be the Motive."

_____, March 6, 1995, A1, "Chinese Leader Says Mistakes by Government Fueled Inflation."

_____, March 7, 1995, A10, "Yeltsin Vows Crackdown on Gangsters."

_____, April 10, 1995, A4, "On the Farms, China Could Be Sowing Disaster."

_____, April 30, 1995, 12, "6 Years After Tiananmen Massacre, Survivors Clash Anew on Tactics."

_____, May 8, 1995, A10, "Beijing Party 'Decapitated' by President."

_____, June 4, 1995, A9, "Tiananmen Milestone Prompts New Activism."

_____, June 18, 1995, 8, "With Deng's Influence Waning, Privatizing of China's State Industry Stalls."

Nusbaumer, Michael. 2006. "War and Revolution." In DeFronzo, ed., *Revolutionary Movements in World History*, 3:931–36.

Overholt, William. 1993. *The Rise of China: How Economic Reform Is Creating a New Superpower*. New York: W. W. Norton.

Payne, Robert. 1969. *Chiang Kai-shek*. New York: Weybright & Talley.

Perry, Elizabeth J. 1994. "Casting a Chinese Democracy Movement: The Roles of Students, Workers and Entrepreneurs." In Wasserstrom and Perry, eds., *Popular Protest and Political Culture in Modern China*.

Posner, Gerald L. 1988. *Warlords of Crime: Chinese Secret Societies—The New Mafia*. New York: McGraw-Hill.

Ross, John. 1994. "Economic Reform: Success in China and Failure in Eastern Europe." *Monthly Review*, May, 19–28.

Saich, Tony. 1994. "The Search for Civil Society and Democracy in China." *Current History*, September, 260–64.

Salisbury, Harrison E. 1985. *The Long March: The Untold Story*. New York: McGraw-Hill.

Schell, Orville. 1985. *To Get Rich Is Glorious: China in the 1980s*. New York: Mentor.

Schiffrin, Harold Z. 1989. "Sun Yat-sen: His Life and Times." In Cheng, ed., *Sun Yat-sen's Doctrine in the Modern World*.

Sharma, Shalendra. 2006. "Asia's Challenged Giants." *Current History*, April, 170–75.

Short, Philip. 2000. *Mao: A Life*. New York: Henry Holt.

Skocpol, Theda. 1976. "Old Regime Legacies and the Communist Revolutions in Russia and China." *Social Forces* 55 (2): 284–315.

_____. 1979. *States and Social Revolutions: A Comparison of France, Russia, and China*. Cambridge, UK: Cambridge University Press.

Sun, Yan. 2005. "Corruption, Growth, and Reform: The Chinese Enigma." *Current History*, September, 257–63.

Thaxton, Ralph. 1983. *China Turned Rightside Up: Revolutionary Legitimacy in the Peasant World*. New Haven, CT: Yale University Press.

Theen, Rolf H. W., and Frank L. Wilson. 1986. *Comparative Politics: An Introduction to Six Countries*. Englewood Cliffs, NJ: Prentice-Hall.

Thompson, Clive. 2006. "Google in China: The Big Disconnect." *New York Times Magazine*, April 23.

Wasserstrom, Jeffrey N. 2001. "Human Rights and the Lessons of History." *Current History*, September, 263–68.

_____. 2002. "Waiting for China's Lech Walesa." *Current History*, September, 256–58.

Wasserstrom, Jeffrey N., and Elizabeth J. Perry, eds. 1994. 2nd ed. *Popular Protest and Political Culture in Modern China*. Politics in Asia and the Pacific. Boulder: Westview Press.

Watson, Samuel. 2006. "Armed Forces, Revolution, and Counter-Revolution." In DeFronzo, ed., *Revolutionary Movements in World History*, 1:77–82.

Wei, William. 1985. *Counterrevolution in China: The Nationalists in Jianxi during the Soviet Period*. Michigan Studies on China. Ann Arbor: University of Michigan Press.

Wickham-Crowley, Timothy P. 2006. "Guerrilla Warfare and Revolution." In De-
Fronzo, ed., *Revolutionary Movements in World History*, 1:336–40.
Wolf, Eric. 1969. *Peasant Wars of the Twentieth Century*. New York: Harper &
Row.
Wright, Teresa. 2006. "Chinese Democracy Movement." In DeFronzo, ed., *Revolu-
tionary Movements in World History*, 1:117–25.
Yabuki, Susumu. 1995. *China's New Political Economy: The Giant Awakes*. Trans.
Stephen M. Harner. Boulder: Westview Press.
Zhang, Jialin. 1994. "Guiding China's Market Economy." *Current History*, September,
276–80.

Selected DVD, Film, and Videocassette Documentaries

See "Purchase and Rental Sources" at the end of this volume for information on how
to obtain the following resources and for full names of media companies and
other organizations listed here as abbreviations.

The Boxer Rebellion. 50 min. HC.

Chiang Kai Shek. 50 min. HC, BIO.

China: 1949–1972. 1998. 46 min. CNN Cold War, Episode 15. Truman Library.
Revolution and later movements.

China: A Century of Revolution. 1989–1997. 1: *China in Revolution, 1911–1949*.
2: *The Mao Years, 1949–1976*. 3: *Born Under the Red Flag, 1976–1996*. AEMS.

China After Tiananmen. 1992. 90 min. Video. PBS. Economic reform, political conservatism, and social conflict in China.

China: Century of Revolution, Part 1: Agonies of Nationalism, 1800–1927. 1972.
24 min. Film. UC-B, UI, ISU, KSU, UMISSOURI, SUNY-B, PSU, PU, UT-A, WSU.
Impacts of foreign interventions in China, the republican movement, and the
Communist Party.

China: Century of Revolution, Part 2: Enemies Within and Without, 1927–1944.
1972. 26 min. Film. UC-B, UI, ISU, KSU, UMISSOURI, SUNY-B, PSU, PU, UT-A,
WSU. Chinese civil war and Japanese invasion.

*China: Century of Revolution, Part 3: Communist Triumph and Consolidation,
1945–1971*. 1972. 20 min. Film. US-B, ISU, KSU, UMISSOURI, SUNY-B, PSU,
PU, WSU. Communist victory in the late 1940s.

China in the Red. 2003. 50 min. PBS Frontline. China's economy.

China Rising. 150 min. HC. Modern Chinese history.

China: Unleashing the Dragon. 1995. 200 min. FRIF. China's cultural and economic
changes.

China Yellow, China Blue. 1998. 104 min. FRIF. Twentieth-century China.

Democracy Crushed: Tiananmen Square. 50 min. HC.

Emerging Powers: China. 1996. AEMS.

The Gate of Heavenly Peace. 1995. 50 min. NAATA. Demonstrations at Tiananmen
Square and repression.

Mao: Long March to Power. 1978. 24 min. Color film. BU, UI, IU, UIOWA, KSU,
SYRU. Mao's political philosophy and rise to power.

Mao: Organized Chaos. 1978. 24 min. Color film. BU, UI, IU, UIOWA, KSU, SYRU.
Postrevolutionary China through the Cultural Revolution.

Mao Tse Tung. 50 min. BIO.

Morning Sun. 2003. 117 min. NAATA. Growing up during the formation of the People's Republic.

Small Happiness: Women of a Chinese Village. 1984. 58 min. Video. Highly acclaimed unrestricted investigation of changes in rural women's lives since the revolution as well as the persistence of traditional views.

Sprouts of Capitalism in China. 1997. 20 min. AEMS.

Sunrise over Tiananmen Square. 1998. 29 min. FRIF. China's modern history.

Through the Consul's Eyes. 1999. 50 min. FRIF. China 1896–1905.

World Revolutions for Students: The Chinese Revolution (1911–1989). 2005. 23 min. Film. LVC.

4

THE VIETNAMESE REVOLUTION

While Mao and his associates were building their initial rural bases in south-central China, revolutionary ideas were taking root in another part of Asia. In 1930, several groups of Marxist-inspired Vietnamese nationalists formed the Indochinese Communist Party (ICP). The Party members vowed to accomplish a social revolution in Vietnam, then under French colonial control. After years of organizational efforts, localized rebellions, and repression, the ICP made paramount the achievement of independence from foreign rule and united various sectors of Vietnamese society behind this nationalist goal. The Party established a network of mass organizations, the Viet Minh (League for Vietnamese Independence), which it led. In 1941 the Party launched a war of resistance against both the French and the Japanese armed forces, which at the time jointly occupied Vietnam. The Vietnamese were to be involved in armed conflict almost continuously for more than three decades.

GEOGRAPHY AND POPULATION

Vietnam, which has a land area of 127,246 square miles (329,566 square kilometers), is a long, narrow country situated along the eastern side of the Indochinese peninsula in Southeast Asia. China lies to the north and Laos and Cambodia to the west. The South China Sea borders Vietnam's entire coastline. Heavily forested mountain and plateau regions constitute most of the country's territory. Two fertile river delta areas are located at opposite ends of Vietnam, the Red River Delta (about 5,800 square miles, or 15,000 square kilometers) in the north and the Mekong River Delta (about 14,000 square miles, or 36,250 square kilometers) in the south. The population, which numbered approximately 84.4 million in 2006, is about 85 percent ethnic Vietnamese. The remaining 15 percent include residents of Chinese and Cambodian (Khmer) ancestry as well as tribal peoples in the lightly populated highland areas. Most of the ethnic Vietnamese live in the fertile lowlands of Vietnam below the three-hundred-foot-altitude level and are concentrated in the two large river deltas and in smaller river deltas and coastal plains along the length of the country. Those areas constitute about 20 percent of the land area but contain about 85 percent of the population.

EARLY CULTURAL AND POLITICAL CHARACTERISTICS

The Vietnamese are apparently of Mongol ancestry and originated as a distinctive ethnic group thousands of years ago. They gradually moved south from the Red River Delta, assimilating the local residents (or forcing them to seek refuge in the mountains). The Chinese attacked and defeated the Vietnamese in 111 BCE and occupied the country, despite repeated rebellions, until 939 CE. In that year, Viet forces finally inflicted a devastating defeat on the Chinese, forcing their withdrawal and an end to direct Chinese control (except for a twenty-year Chinese reoccupation of Vietnam during the years 1407–1427). The Vietnamese completed occupation of the southernmost region of the country, which had been Cambodian territory, in 1780.

Often afflicted by internal dynastic wars and other conflicts, the country was finally ruled as a unified political entity within its current borders under Emperor Gia Long in 1802. Despite subsequent Chinese invasions, the Vietnamese retained their independence until conquered by the French during the nineteenth century. The Chinese often referred to Vietnam as *Annam* (the pacified south), a term most Vietnamese detested. Later the French adopted this expression, referring to the Vietnamese as Annamites, and outlawed use of the word "Vietnam."

Prior to Chinese conquest the Vietnamese were a tribal people whose king was one of the more powerful tribal chiefs to whom other chiefs owed feudal obligations. Religious practice was a form of animism in which ritual sacrifice and veneration were directed toward spirits thought to control natural phenomena, such as the soil and water, and toward the "souls" of dangerous or powerful animals, such as tigers. During the more than thousand years of Chinese domination, the Vietnamese adopted a Confucian political system (see chapter 3), along with the Chinese writing system, clothing styles, and technology. But they retained their own language (related to the Mon-Khmer and Thai linguistic families), and most steadfastly refused to relinquish their separate ethnic identity and their desire for independence. Throughout the period of Chinese rule, Viet leaders (such as the Trung sisters in 39–43 CE) mounted heroic rebellions.

The peasant culture that evolved under Chinese domination combined previously ingrained rural customs and beliefs with ideologies brought by the Chinese, including Confucianism (with its emphasis on obedience and social order), Buddhism (stressing morally right behavior and denial of self-importance in order to achieve nirvana and escape the cycle of reincarnation), and Taoism (emphasizing the individual's search for the tao, the path or way, to happiness and enlightenment in this world and the hereafter). Although these belief systems contained elements that were conflicting (such as Taoism's rejection of the importance of Confucian scholarship in favor of seeking harmony with nature), the Vietnamese tended to select and blend compatible or complimentary aspects of the imported doctrines with indigenous folkways (Bain 1967).

FRENCH CONQUEST

In 1516 Portuguese explorers visited Vietnam. They referred to the country as Cauchichina, deriving this term from the Chinese characters for Vietnam, giao chi, and adding "china" to distinguish it from their "Cochin" colony located in India. Later the French came to play the dominant European role in Vietnam after it became clear that Portugal was simply too weak to master the task of "Christianizing" and colonizing Asia. The French, who attempted to portray Vietnam to the world as three separate countries, modified the Portuguese misnomer and referred to the southernmost part of Vietnam, within which the Mekong Delta and Saigon were located, as "Cochinchina." They labeled the long middle section of the country, with the old imperial capital Hue, "Annam," and called the northernmost part of Vietnam, which included the Red River Delta and the cities of Hanoi and Haiphong, "Tonkin."

French missionaries, originally entering Vietnam under Portuguese auspices, enthusiastically embraced the goal of converting the Vietnamese and returned to France with stories of immense wealth and excellent harbors to entice the support of French businessmen and military leaders. Eventually a mutually supportive relationship evolved among French missionaries, merchants, and the navy, which developed an interest in the potential usefulness of Vietnamese ports for extending its operational combat range. Some Vietnamese monarchs craved the modern weapons and other technologies or products the Europeans could provide and periodically tolerated missionary work in order to obtain benefits or avoid French displeasure. But inevitably Vietnamese officials became alarmed that the spread of Christianity reflected the threat of a massive expansion of French imperial presence in Vietnam.

In 1847, outraged by Vietnamese campaigns against Christian missionaries and envious of Britain's gains in its successful Opium War against the Chinese, the French defeated Vietnamese naval forces and obtained concessions from the emperor. Further disputes led to a French assault in 1858 and the seizure of Saigon and its surrounding provinces in 1861. In 1863 the Vietnamese gave up their control of Cambodia to the French, and in 1867 the emperor surrendered the provinces west of Saigon. The French soon established Cochinchina as a colony, displacing Vietnamese administrators with French officials. Later a series of military conflicts resulted in French "protectorates" over Annam and Tonkin. In these areas many Vietnamese mandarins (those willing to collaborate) maintained their positions under the authority of French civil and military officials. By the end of 1883 the French conquest of Vietnam was complete.

THE FRENCH IMPACT ON VIETNAM

Economic Effects

Few Frenchmen had as great an impact on Vietnam as Paul Doumer, who arrived in Vietnam as governor-general of Indochina in 1897. The measures that Doumer instituted, although harmful to the welfare of many Vietnamese, transformed Vietnam into a colony that not only paid for the cost of its own military occupation but also generated great wealth for France and many of its citizens.

In some instances Doumer merely accelerated French colonial programs begun earlier, whereas in other cases he innovated. Confronted initially with a country composed of an enormous number of basically self-sufficient agricultural communities, the French resolved to utilize Vietnamese resources in such a way as to generate products for the world market and construct a regionally complimentary economic infrastructure. Because mineral deposits were discovered in the north and labor could be readily obtained from the densely populated Red River Delta, mining and industry were developed primarily in the northern third of Vietnam. Recognizing the potential of the much larger Mekong Delta, the French government constructed hydraulic projects there to control water levels, opened huge tracts to cultivation, and sold large sections cheaply to French and Vietnamese investors in order to pay the cost of the water control program and to bring the new land under cultivation quickly. As a consequence, landownership, which was very unequal in Tonkin and Annam, was even more highly concentrated in Cochinchina. Of 6,530 landholders in all of French Indochina (Vietnam, Cambodia, and Laos) with more than 125 acres, 6,300 resided in this southernmost part of Vietnam: there 2.5 percent of the population owned 45 percent of the cultivated land (Duong 1985; McAlister 1969). Tenant farmers and landless agricultural laborers made up more than half of the rural population in Cochinchina (many of the landless had migrated from the overpopulated Red River Delta area in search of employment).

The French succeeded in massively increasing the amount of rice exported from Vietnam—from about 57,000 tons in 1860 to more than 1,500,000 tons in 1937 (Wolf 1969). They also developed large rubber plantations (over 1,000 in Cochinchina and Cambodia), which employed tens of thousands of Vietnamese workers under generally harsh conditions. The colonial authorities also introduced heavy taxes. Since many peasants could not make ends meet, they fell into debt and were forced to sell their

CHINA

Red River

TONKIN

Hanoi ● ● Haiphong

← Red River Delta

LAOS

GULF OF TONKIN

Mekong

River

THAILAND

Hue ●

CAMBODIA

ANNAM

GULF OF THAILAND

Saigon ●

← Mekong Delta

COCHINCHINA

SOUTH CHINA SEA

FRENCH INDOCHINA

land, contributing to the growth of the landless rural segment and greater concentration of landownership. By 1930, even before the hardships inflicted by the international economic depression, an estimated 70 percent of the country's rural population either were landless or lacked sufficient land to meet minimal survival requirements. These people were forced to rent additional land or to engage in other work activity to supplement family income (Duong 1985; Karnow 1983; Popkin 1979).

Moreover, in the effort to expand produce for export, the percentages of land and harvested grain that had traditionally been held communally to assist peasants in times of hardship were significantly reduced, depriving rural Vietnamese of their state-sponsored aid system (Duong 1985; Popkin 1979). Doumer's agents recruited many of the landless to work in the mines, on the rubber plantations, or in the building of roads and railways, sometimes making use of laws against "vagrancy" or "vagabondism" to coerce potential laborers. In general, as the majority of Vietnam's population could no longer maintain a self-sufficient existence because of loss of land, lack of enough land, or inability to pay taxes, their material well-being became dependent on the international market prices for Vietnam's exports. These prices affected the wages of landless workers, farm income, and consumer prices for food and other necessities. Thus the development of an export-oriented economy under colonialism, while benefiting the French and Vietnamese large landholders and industrial and commercial elite by providing them with a high money income, often had negative consequences for the larger population, particularly in times of low international prices for Vietnam's products (McAlister 1969; Wolf 1969).

When Doumer reached Vietnam, only its Chinese residents smoked opium. He proceeded to build an opium refinery that produced a quick-burning mixture that proved popular. Opium addiction spread extensively among the Vietnamese, and profits from the sale of the drug eventually accounted for one-third of the colonial administration's income (Karnow 1983). Doumer's success in generating large profits for his country and its agricultural, industrial, and commercial enterprises helped put an end to significant criticism of imperial policy in France. And the publicity given to the views of wealthy Francophile Vietnamese, who visited Paris and expressed gratitude for France's role in their nation, contributed to the self-serving illusion among the French that most Vietnamese were happy with colonial status.

For the approximately 0.3 percent of Vietnamese who had received five or more years of schooling in the French colonial educational system by 1931 (French education was a key to social mobility in colonial Vietnam), opportunities for high-paying careers and access to political power were limited. The French dominated the major positions in the colonial bureaucracy and in commerce, along with Vietnam's Chinese minority, the product of past Chinese colonial rule and repeated invasions (McAlister 1969). The lack of sufficient social and economic mobility may have motivated some in Vietnam's French-educated elite to work for independence, since access to political power and high-paying positions would presumably be greater once the French left.

By 1929 the French colonial process had also generated a Vietnamese working class, composed of about 140,000 (probably under 5 percent of the working population), which provided labor for industry, commercial operations, and mining. A 1931 analysis of the overall income structure of Vietnam showed that the top 1 percent of the population (composed of French administrators, large landholders, and well-to-do Vietnamese) enjoyed an annual money income level that was about eight times the average income of the 9 percent who were largely urban, nonpeasant employees and workers and twenty-four times the income of the 90 percent who were peasants. Although landowning peasants were usually able to raise at least part of their own basic food requirements, money income reflected their ability to pay taxes and purchase equipment and other commodities, especially imported goods (McAlister 1969).

Cultural and Social Changes

French colonialism precipitated the rapid erosion of the Confucian system, which was blamed for Vietnam's inability to resist French conquest. Many in the Vietnamese elite, schooled in the Confucian scholarship that had in the past constituted the means to governmental and economic opportunity, now sought a French education for their children. French culture soon enveloped the upper levels of Vietnamese society and, in varying ways, affected the larger population.

The colonial educational system was intended to propagate an admiration for French culture and achievements among the Vietnamese and to recruit a French-educated elite that would collaborate with colonial authorities and businesspeople. But many Vietnamese took their lessons on French history and political ideologies to heart: the French Revolution and concepts of political democracy and socialism eventually would help inspire an effective revolutionary movement in Vietnam. Prominent among future revolutionary figures was a brilliant history teacher, Vo Nguyen Giap, who enthralled his students with accounts of the French Revolution and the unjust society against which it was directed. In the late 1930s he left the classroom to organize and lead the revolutionary armies that would drive the French from Vietnam.

Among the social consequences of French economic policies was the movement of large numbers of landless Vietnamese away from their home villages to mining areas, industrial centers, plantations, and the newly developed and fertile agricultural land in the Mekong Delta. Migration apparently had great emotional and moral consequences for many of the uprooted poor because their traditional culture provided few satisfactory interpretations of their new experiences and because they were isolated from their extended-family networks. Many Vietnamese succumbed to opium addiction or became involved in prostitution, both of which were promoted by the French colonial administrative and military presence. Other Vietnamese turned to new religions. In the Mekong Delta, where many migrants, separated from past social ties and lacking the status and security of landownership, had established villages, the appeal of new religions, which provided a feeling of community and a sense of prestige and personal worth through membership in the "true faith," was especially strong. Cao Dai, an eclectic, or syncretic, cult founded by a mystic in 1926, and a Buddhist reformist sect, Hoa Hao, formally established in 1939, gained many adherents.

Cao Dai, named for a spirit who communed with its founder, was based on the concept that the ideal religion should combine the best elements of all faiths and secular philosophies and included among its "saints" Jesus, Buddha, Joan of Arc, and Sun Yixian (Karnow 1983). However, Cao Dai leaders, while attempting to incorporate what they perceived as beneficial elements from Western cultures, strongly emphasized Vietnamese nationalism. Their religion centered on an explicit integration of the three major faiths of Vietnam—Buddhism, Confucianism, and Taoism—in an effort to present a sort of united religious-cultural front to French imperialism (Tai 1983; Woodside 1976; Werner 1981). Hoa Hao (named after the Mekong town where it was invented by a prophetic faith healer) was a kind of "Buddhist Protestantism"; part of its attraction for the poor was its simplicity and rejection of expensive rituals or religious artifacts. Hoa Hao manifested strong nationalistic tendencies: it stressed traditional Vietnamese Buddhist doctrine and customs and opposed the adoption of certain Western values and even some forms of Western technology (Tai 1983).

Both Cao Dai and Hoa Hao developed into political-religious organizations with their own armed militias. The leadership of these two religions (both of which eventually fragmented into feuding subdivisions) strove for autonomous political control over certain districts in the Mekong Delta. At times they allied with Communist-led independence forces and at other times with the French, depending on which course of action seemed to maximize their goal of localized political authority. By the mid-1950s the Cao Dai and the Hoa Hao apparently each numbered over 1 million (together about 6 to 8 percent of the population), while 10 percent of the Vietnamese embraced Catholicism, and 80 percent claimed varying degrees of association with one of the dozen or so other Buddhist sects.

Political Consequences

As noted earlier, the French chose to rule the southernmost part of Vietnam, Cochinchina, which the Vietnamese called Nam Bo (south territory, also called Nam Ky) as a directly administered colony. This part of Vietnam was controlled for the longest period by France and was most influenced by

French rule. In contrast, the middle section of Vietnam, Annam (Trung Bo or Trung Ky), and the northernmost region, Tonkin (Bac Bo or Bac Ky), were technically protectorates of France. The Vietnamese emperor, with his court at Hue, served primarily as a figurehead, and scholarly mandarins continued to exercise political authority on the condition of serving French colonial interests. But even in these provinces the old political system was gradually phased out. As the French-educated elite gradually replaced the Confucian mandarins in Tonkin and Annam, the distinction between direct rule (in Cochinchina) and indirect rule (in Tonkin and Annam) became "virtually meaningless" by the time the revolution began in the early 1940s (McAlister 1969, 43).

The French also changed the system of government at the local level. Traditionally a village had been governed by a "council of notables" composed of the local Confucian scholars and the village elders. The new system provided that elections be held to select a council with a strong executive who had to be approved by the province governor and who was directly responsible for carrying out colonial policy in his village (McAlister 1969; Wolf 1969). Many Vietnamese did not accept the new system and viewed it as a mechanism of colonial control; thus the French in reality had destroyed the popularly supported and understood form of local government without replacing it with one that was similarly accepted by the majority of the population. A political vacuum developed; it persisted in the countryside until it was filled by the new forms of political and social organization developed by Vietnamese revolutionaries (McAlister 1969).

The strongest base of political support for the French presence in Vietnam was in Cochinchina and consisted of the wealthy and powerful French settlers and Francophile Vietnamese large landholders there. This group organized the pro-French Constitutionalist Party, which eventually ran candidates for the Saigon city council and other local government posts. A reflection of the degree of loyalty the French enjoyed from affluent Vietnamese in this southernmost section of Vietnam was the fact that in 1937, of the 2,555 largely wealthy Vietnamese who had received French citizenship, 1,474 resided in Cochinchina, which then had only about 20 percent of Vietnam's population (McAlister 1969).

A major mechanism through which the French sought to control the Vietnamese colony was the Colonial Militia, composed of Vietnamese in service to the French. This institution became a channel of social and economic mobility for those Vietnamese willing to improve their lot at the probable expense of their country folk. It also served as the nucleus of the antirevolutionary Vietnamese armies that fought first alongside the French and later alongside U.S. forces in attempts to crush the Vietnamese Revolution.

A final but critically important political consequence of French colonial policy was the development of a Vietnamese revolutionary elite from among the French-educated fraction of the colony's population. This group would make use of concepts derived from their Western educations, fuse them with Vietnamese nationalism, and organize the successful movement to oust the French.

RESISTANCE TO FRENCH RULE

Analyses provided by McAlister (1969), Wolf (1969), and Khanh (1982) suggest four phases of Vietnamese resistance: a period of tradition-based rebellion; a transitional phase involving the integration of traditional goals with new concepts; the creation of modern but unsuccessful nationalist movements; and the development of a successful revolutionary effort, the Viet Minh.

Tradition-Based Rebellion: 1883–1900

During the period of tradition-based rebellion, many Confucian scholars refused to serve in collaboration with the French and organized protests and even rebellions against colonial rule. But these were localized episodes that were relatively easy for the French to suppress. Furthermore, in these efforts traditional leaders were attempting to rally Vietnamese nationalism through a reliance on the Confucian system of the past, which had proven to be oppressive and ineffective.

Transition: 1900–1925

After 1900 several Vietnamese scholars, originally educated in the Confucian classics in preparation for mandarinal exams, attempted to organize Vietnamese independence movements that incorporated concepts from the more technologically advanced societies. Most important of these leaders were Phan Boi Chau (1867–1940) and Phan Chu Trinh (1872–1926), who represented a transitional generation between the tradition-oriented pre-1900 rebellions and the modern nationalist movements, which began to develop in the 1920s. Although both advocated independence and had become convinced that traditional Confucian learning had failed miserably in providing Vietnam the ability to resist Western colonialism, they advocated significantly different methods in the pursuit of nationalist goals.

Phan Boi Chau was concerned with developing a model for a modified Vietnamese state that would integrate useful modern concepts into traditional Vietnamese culture. Over time he advocated traditional monarchy, then a constitutional monarchy based on the Japanese model, then a totally republican form of government. Many of his ideas were understood only by the best-educated Vietnamese, a number of whom viewed some of his major proposals, such as blending traditional Vietnamese social forms with more efficient Japanese innovations, as ill suited to Vietnam's local conditions. In the end Phan Boi Chau was valued not for the soundness of his proposals but for being a fervent nationalist who exalted the intellectual capabilities, resourcefulness, and stubborn determination of the Vietnamese people and who supported the tradition of violent resistance to colonialism (Duiker 1976; Marr 1971; Woodside 1976).

Phan Chu Trinh, in contrast, refused to advocate armed rebellion, which, given Vietnam's technological inferiority, he viewed as a senseless waste of life. He held that modernization of Vietnam's technology, culture, and political and social systems was an absolute necessity even if this required an extended period of colonialism. He somewhat optimistically called on the French to modernize Vietnam rapidly and assist in building mechanisms of self-government leading to full Vietnamese independence. Although in the end colonialism was thrown off not through a reformist process but through the method of armed revolution advocated by Phan Boi Chau, Phan Chu Trinh was credited with encouraging many young Vietnamese to learn from Western societies those concepts that could one day make Vietnam a strong and independent nation.

Phan Chu Trinh, whom the French treated in a relatively lenient manner because his protests against colonial injustices were tempered by his nonviolent reformist approach and his advocacy of French-Vietnamese harmony, died of natural causes in March 1926. Phan Boi Chau was arrested by the French secret police in 1925. He spent the rest of his life under detention and died in 1940.

Modern Nationalist Attempts: 1925–1940

By the late 1920s a significant number of Vietnam's educated young people had traveled abroad, some hoping to discover new ideas and methods for bringing independence to Vietnam. Several groups coalesced to form two nationalist organizations, the Vietnamese Nationalist Party (VNQDD) in 1927 and the ultimately much more important Indochinese Communist Party in 1930.

The VNQDD, loosely patterned after the Chinese GMD (Guomindang), attempted to incorporate within its program several of the ideas of Sun Yixian. In particular, its platform proclaimed the goals of national liberation and social revolution. But the meaning of "social revolution" was never clearly defined within the party, and many of its members had differing interpretations of it (Khanh 1982). The party recruited mainly among students and urban, middle-income, nonmanual employees, such as teachers, clerks, and journalists. The VNQDD also gained the support of significant numbers of Vietnamese soldiers in the French-organized and -controlled colonial militia. Among the limitations of the VNQDD was its being primarily urban based; consequently, it had almost no organized support among the 90 percent of Vietnam's population who were peasants. Instead of developing an ideology and program for redistribution of wealth that would appeal to the peasants and patiently working to build revolutionary support and organizational structures in the countryside, the VNQDD created special units to carry out attacks and assassinations against French officials. The VNQDD leaders apparently thought that using terrorist violence against colonial agents would arouse Vietnamese patriotism and win mass support.

The VNQDD was largely crushed after the failure of the Yen Bay Mutiny in February 1930. In Yen Bay, VNQDD-organized Vietnamese colonial militia soldiers mutinied and killed their French officers. But the military rebels were overwhelmed in one day. More than one thousand VNQDD party members were arrested. In the trials that followed, about one hundred were given life sentences, and eighty were sentenced to death. The VNQDD lost most of its best leaders during this repression and ceased to be a credible and genuinely Vietnamese nationalist movement. More than a decade later the French would desperately try to establish a significant non-Communist nationalist movement, only to be faced with the realization that they had destroyed in 1930 the sole organization that could have competed with the Communist-led movement's nationalist credentials. Following the destruction of the VNQDD, some of its members joined Marxist-led movements, and others escaped to China or Japan, where they reorganized under foreign sponsorship and entered Vietnam during or immediately after World War II. But many Vietnamese tended to view the resurrected versions of the VNQDD as mainly extensions of foreign imperialism (Khanh 1982).

During the latter half of the 1920s several Marxist-inspired groups, including Thanh Nien (Youth) and Tan Viet (New Vietnam), were organized by university students and young, educated urban Vietnamese employed mostly in nonmanual professions, such as teaching or office work. These Marxist-oriented nationalists called for both "anti-imperialism" (independence for Vietnam) and "antifeudalism" (social revolution). When these groups, along with peasant activists, united in 1930 to form a Communist Party, the membership was mostly a combination of middle-class and peasant revolutionaries with only a small representation of urban industrial workers.

At first the goal of independence assumed priority within the new party; this fact was reflected in the title "Vietnamese Communist Party." But during the same year, the international congress of Communist parties (the "Communist International," or "Comintern") decided that throughout the world Communist parties should emphasize class conflict and achievement of social revolution rather than nationalism and criticized the Communist parties in less-developed countries for cooperating in nationalist alliances with political parties that opposed social revolution. The Comintern encouraged Communist parties to break relations with other parties, including socialists, in order to communicate Party concepts more effectively to the masses and organize them for the class conflict viewed as necessary to achieve a social revolution.

This shift in the orientation of the international Communist movement influenced the Vietnamese Communist Party to change its name to the Indochinese Communist Party within a few months of its founding. The name change also reflected Party members' acceptance of the Comintern's policy of matching Communist Party organizations to colonial jurisdictions (in this case French Indochina) rather than to ethnic divisions. The ICP was at least nominally given the task of bringing social revolution to Cambodia and Laos as well as Vietnam, although there were only a few Cambodians and Laotians in the Party during its early years. As the ICP turned energetically to the task of mobilizing peasants and workers for class conflict and social revolution, neglecting the independence struggle, the Party lost much of its appeal to educated Vietnamese in urban nonmanual occupations (who had previously been rallied by the call to fight against foreign domination, even if the movement was led by Communist revolutionaries).

In 1930 and 1931 the economic well-being of many Vietnamese abruptly worsened because of the worldwide depression, which lowered prices for Vietnam's exports. ICP agitation among peasants and workers led to strikes and protests in many parts of Vietnam. During this period there was a peasant insurrection in Nghe An, a province traditionally rebellious against foreign rule, and the neighboring province, Ha Tinh, in north-central Vietnam (northern Annam colonial region). The movement began with unarmed peasants staging demonstrations demanding the abolition or postponement of certain taxes and higher prices for their produce from the colonial government. Soon peasants began electing local revolutionary councils ("soviets") to take the place of collaborationist and French authorities and to enact reforms. The national leadership of the ICP had little role in planning the insurrection and considered it premature in the sense that, outside of Nghe An and Ha Tinh provinces, most peasants in Vietnam were not yet politically committed to revolution.

Repression of the rural soviets was carried out in summer 1931. Hundreds lost their lives in the rebelling provinces and thousands of ICP members or supporters were incarcerated throughout Vietnam. But the commitment demonstrated by the ICP to social revolution in the countryside and the examples of heroism on the part of individual ICP members (important to public perception in a land inspired by myths of heroic resistance to foreign invaders and oppression) won further support from many of Vietnam's peasants and workers (Karnow 1983; Khanh 1982; McAlister 1969; Wolf 1969). The concept of communism itself, *cong san* in Vietnamese, was popularly defined as taking all property and equally dividing it among the population (Khanh 1982), a notion well received by Vietnam's impoverished classes.

Political developments in the international Communist movement and in France contributed to a considerable improvement in the ICP's situation. The leaders of the world's Communist parties had become alarmed at the growth and success of Fascist movements, which espoused extreme nationalism and concepts of racial and cultural superiority. The election victory of the Nazi Party in Germany in 1933 was blamed in part on the division and

hostility between the German Communist and Socialist parties. Consequently, in the mid-1930s Communist parties advocated the formation of
Popular Fronts involving leftist and antifascist parties. In France a Popular
Front coalition including the French Socialist and Communist parties was
elected and ordered the release from Vietnamese prisons of many ICP members. The period of 1936–1939 was one of growth for the ICP throughout
Vietnam. In Saigon, the major city in Cochinchina, members of the Communist Party and other revolutionary-oriented leftists (followers of Trotsky)
were even elected to the city council.

But in 1939 the French government, in response to shifts in policy by both
the USSR and the French Communist Party, made a new attempt to crush the
ICP. The Soviets had been outraged when the Western democracies failed to
help the elected leftist Spanish government prevent the victory of conservative forces and Fascist armies (Italian and German) in the 1936–1939
Spanish Civil War and when the British and the French decided to grant Nazi
Germany effective control of Czechoslovakia at Munich in 1938. The Soviets
suspected that the capitalist democracies were attempting to appease Hitler
so that he would turn east and launch an invasion of the USSR; he could then
seize and colonize Soviet territory as he had advocated years earlier in his
book, *Mein Kampf.* To forestall an expected attack, the Soviet leader, Stalin,
signed a "nonaggression pact" with Germany, which greatly increased the
probability of a German attack on France. After Germany, with Soviet acqui-
escence, invaded Poland in September 1939 and France and Britain declared
war, the new French government outlawed the pro-Moscow, temporarily antiwar, French Communist Party and ordered the repression of the ICP in
Vietnam. But by this point many ICP members had already gone underground and, consequently, escaped imprisonment (Khanh 1982).

Ho Chi Minh and the Formation of the Viet Minh

No other person contributed so much individually to the development of the
revolution in Vietnam as Ho Chi Minh. According to official accounts, he
was born May 19, 1890, the third child in a prominent anticolonial family
in rebellious Nghe An Province in northern Annam. His scholar father was
eventually dismissed from his government position when, consistent with
his belief in administering the law fairly for the rich as well as the poor, he
was accused of being too harsh in the punishment of a prominent person
(Duiker 2000, 41). Ho's parents named him Nguyen Sinh Cung at birth,
and "following a common tradition," his father chose a new name for him,
Nguyen Tat Thanh, when he was eleven (Duiker 2000, 22–23). His mother
died soon after giving birth to another son.

Both at home and abroad and in writing his hundreds of articles and political analyses, he used as many as seventy-six aliases. However, he became
famous among the Vietnamese (and internationally) under two names. Dur-

ing 1919–1945, the world knew him as Nguyen Ai Quoc (Nguyen who loves his country), energetic Vietnamese nationalist and most prominent organizer of the Vietnamese Communist movement. After the Viet Minh–led revolution in August 1945, when he became the first president of the Democratic Republic of Vietnam, he was known as Ho Chi Minh ("He who enlightens") (Duiker 2000, 248–49).

True to his family's political leanings, Ho became involved in anticolonial activities at age fifteen, working as a courier and contact for pro-independence scholars. He later told friends that after he learned the French slogan "Liberty, equality, and fraternity," he was confused by the lack of application of these ideals in Vietnam, and he yearned to understand better the civilization behind both the concepts and the imperialism Vietnam experienced. His interest in traveling to France and other advanced nations reflected a Vietnamese saying popular with the youth of the period, "Go abroad to study to come home to help the country" (Khanh 1982, 59). After acting as an interpreter for a group of peasants protesting to French authorities about high taxes and forced labor in May 1908, shortly before his eighteenth birthday, Ho was expelled from the National Academy (Duiker 2000, 36–37). In December 1911 he left Vietnam for France, earning his way as a laborer on the SS *Latouche-Treville*. He would not return to Vietnam for thirty years.

Ho traveled to a great number of ports and countries and learned that Vietnam was only one of many European colonies. Sensing that many of the French and other Europeans did not really regard the peoples of Asia and Africa as equal human beings, he began to understand imperialism and racism as worldwide phenomena. Ho also visited the United States, living and working in Boston and New York for at least several months. Ho was favorably impressed that Asian immigrants to the United States enjoyed political and other rights that the Vietnamese did not have in their own country, and he viewed the United States as a nation born from a successful revolution against British imperialism. Later he patterned Vietnam's September 1945 Declaration of Independence after the corresponding American Revolutionary War document. Ho left the United States in 1913. In England he worked as a snow shoveler for the London school system (Lacouture 1968) and as a dishwasher and then a chef at the Carlton Hotel (Duiker 2000, 52).

In 1917 Ho arrived in France, where 80,000 Vietnamese were serving in the French armed forces or working in defense industries as part of the war effort. He remained there until 1923. Ho was reportedly surprised to find that most of the French at home were "good people," while "the French in the colonies were cruel and inhuman" (Khanh 1982, 60). This observation, along with similar conclusions regarding Americans and the British, led him to the erroneous assumption that the governments of the Western democracies would honor the World War I commitment of President Wilson and other world leaders to national self-determination around the globe.

Ho attempted to present a list of moderate proposals for Vietnamese self-government, initially within the colonial system, to the world leaders attending the 1919 Paris Peace Conference. This effort made him an instant national hero among many Vietnamese (Khanh 1982; Lacouture 1968). But when the proposals were not even granted a hearing, he soon became disillusioned with the concept of reforming colonialism peacefully from within. Ho instead concluded that independence would probably come only as the result of an autonomous effort in Vietnam, without reliance on a change of heart on the part of the colonial power, and that decolonization, like colonial enslavement, would likely be a violent process (Khanh 1982).

In December 1920 Ho, who was affiliated with France's Socialist Party, as its program seemed most beneficial toward the colonized peoples, voted with the majority of its members to form the French Communist Party. Ho's decision was reportedly a simple one. He discovered that the Socialists inclined to follow Lenin had the greatest concern with freeing the colonial peoples. Once Ho read Lenin's works on imperialism and colonialism, he was reportedly overcome with emotion and the feeling that Lenin had formulated conceptually the reality that he and all the colonial peoples he had encountered actually experienced. For Ho, the path to independence for Vietnam was through the international Communist movement.

In 1924 Ho went to Moscow to study revolutionary theory and organizational methods and to prepare to build a revolution in Vietnam. In December he left for China to act as a translator for the Soviet advisory mission under Mikhail Borodin. In southern China in 1925 Ho introduced the members of a previously created Vietnamese anticolonial resistance organization to Marxist thinking and Leninist concepts concerning imperialism. Together they organized the Marxist-oriented group Thanh Nien (Youth), which would be the primary forerunner of the ICP. During the years 1925–1927 Ho provided lecture programs and training sessions covering world history, colonial history, Marxist theory, Lenin's analyses of imperialism, and revolutionary theory and method to about three hundred Vietnamese exiles (Khanh 1982). Many of them returned to Vietnam to create local Thanh Nien organizations.

After the Chinese civil war broke out between General Chiang Kaishek's wing of the GMD and the Chinese Communists in 1927, Thanh Nien members fled from Canton to Hong Kong. There Ho and others founded the Vietnamese Communist Party in 1930, which, as we have seen, in a few months became the Indochinese Communist Party. But on June 5, 1931, Ho was arrested by Hong Kong police and incarcerated. His health deteriorated, and he was hospitalized. He evidently convinced hospital personnel to allow him to leave. A story spread that he had died from tuberculosis. Memorial services were held for him in Paris and Moscow. With the help of friends, including in Shanghai a visiting French Communist and, according to Duiker (2000, 210), Sun Yat Sen's wife, Soong Qingling, who secretly had "a close relationship" with the Chinese Communist Party, Ho eventually made his way to Moscow, where he spent the years from 1934 to 1939 recuperating, studying, writing, and teaching history and political theory to Vietnamese students being educated in the Soviet Union. During these years Ho seems to have played no direct role in the ICP in Vietnam. The Party, at the time, was pursuing the goal of social revolution through class warfare over the nationalistic, independence-first strategy Ho favored.

Ho returned to China in 1939, during the period in which the GMD and the Communist Party had halted the civil war in order to join forces to fight the invading Japanese; in 1941 he reentered Vietnam. In a mountain cave in a northern province of Tonkin, Ho and several other ICP members held a meeting to establish the League for Vietnamese Independence, the Viet Minh. The formation of the Viet Minh represented the completion of the shift in ICP strategy back to an emphasis on the primacy of national liberation. It also represented the reestablishment of Ho's leadership of the ICP.

Ho had long emphasized that the "elimination of imperialism" in Vietnam, or independence, had to take precedence over the "elimination of feudalism" (breaking the hold of the landlord class and redistributing wealth, largely land, to the mass of the population). He and his supporters argued for his formula on two major grounds. First, since many peasants and workers were already inclined to support the social revolution program of the ICP, advocacy of nationalism would appeal not only to peasants but also to other patriotic Vietnamese of all classes who wanted to free their country from foreign domination. Second, Ho's analysis indicated that foreign imperialism was the main ally and source of strength for the feudalistic system in Vietnam and that a major step toward accomplishing a social revolution had to be first severing the old social and economic order from its powerful outside support. Consequently, in 1941 the Viet Minh program gave priority to achieving the goal of independence and delayed enacting a sweeping land reform until 1953.

The Viet Minh was designed to combine mass-membership organizations, whose participants were committed to an independent Vietnam and generally also to social revolution, under the leadership of the ICP, which would act, in part, as a coordinating mechanism. The ranks of the ICP were to be filled from among those members of the mass organizations willing to devote all their time to working for the revolution and developing an understanding of Marxist and Leninist concepts and theories of revolution. Actually, the linkage of the ICP with mass-membership organizations had begun long before the specifically independence-oriented Viet Minh was formulated. Through the development of mass organizations, the ICP had succeeded in providing a meaningful opportunity for large-scale political participation and mobilization. Thus in many areas the ICP not only filled the vacuum created by the French destruction of the traditional village political mechanisms but also brought many more people than ever before into the political process (McAlister 1969).

The revolutionary village councils and mass-membership organizations were considered by many rural residents to be truly Vietnamese rather than under the control or serving the interests of some foreign occupying power. The mass organizations established by ICP activists and supporters were based on social categories easily understood by Vietnam's peasants and workers. These included national women's, youths', peasants', and workers' associations and other groups with local chapters and national leadership; they were linked at all levels to the ICP through mechanisms such as interlocking membership. Many of the nationalists who joined the Viet Minh were not specifically interested in social revolution or in working their way into ICP membership. Some, especially recruits from the well-to-do classes, opposed communism or at least expressed little support for the ICP's plans for wealth redistribution. But they joined the Viet Minh and accepted ICP leadership because they recognized the ICP, especially under Ho Chi Minh, as a truly nationalist organization and because they felt that the ICP, and the movement and network it had created, represented the only viable means for establishing an independent Vietnam (Khanh 1982; McAlister 1969).

THE IMPACT OF WORLD WAR II

Events during World War II had profound effects on the development of the Vietnamese Revolution. In June 1940 Germany defeated France, and in the unoccupied sector of the country an extremely conservative government based in the town of Vichy assumed power. The Vichy regime collaborated with the Nazi Germans and their allies, the Japanese, when the latter became interested in occupying Indochina to exploit its agricultural and mineral resources and to use it as a staging area for troop deployments elsewhere. The Vichy government allowed Japan to occupy Indochina in September 1940. But the Japanese left the French colonial administration, armed forces, and French-controlled Vietnamese colonial militia intact. Thus the French were able to maintain a repressive stance toward Vietnamese rebels, smashing a Communist-organized uprising in Cochinchina in late 1940 (Khanh 1982).

The Japanese presence did, however, gradually weaken French control. And on March 9, 1945, for specific political and military reasons, the Japanese attacked French colonial forces, and most French units surrendered within twenty-four hours. The ability of the Japanese, an Asian people, to dictate to the previously all-powerful French and cast them aside at will had a significant effect on many Vietnamese. Just as the French conquest had destroyed the concept of a heavenly mandated, immutable Confucian system, the Japanese victory annihilated the myth of European racial superiority. Many more Vietnamese were thereafter encouraged to resist the French actively.

While some Vietnamese supported the Japanese, and others, mostly among the 10 percent Catholic minority and the wealthy landowners, continued to support the French, the Viet Minh opposed both imperialist intruders. Under the military leadership of former history teacher Vo Nguyen Giap, the Viet Minh began to educate peasants politically and organize them in the northern highlands of Vietnam. Giap and other Viet Minh leaders, who had been exposed to Chinese Communist concepts of "people's war" and who, in their own history, had repeatedly witnessed the defeat of urban or lowland insurrections against the French, realized that a key element in gaining independence would be the establishment of secure base camps in the northern mountains, where tanks and heavy weapons would be of little use to the enemy. Giap's plan for a people's war called for obtaining the support of the people in base area regions and developing intensely motivated revolutionary soldiers before fighting began. According to this approach, revolutionary combatants, highly committed to the goal of establishing a more just moral, social, economic, and political order, would constitute the fighting arm of a mobilized supportive population. Such a combination could conceivably overcome the imperialist's advantage in weaponry (Giap 1962; Karnow 1983).

ICP activists won the support of many of the Tay and Nung tribal peoples, who lived in a mountainous region extending from northern Vietnam to southern China. Leaders of these groups were hostile toward the French, who had intervened in their affairs, and many were favorably inclined to the ICP's program because relatives in China, having already been in contact with Chinese Communist activists, had told them of the perceived benefits for most peasants of Communist-led revolution. Support from the Tay and Nung, several of whom became prominent generals in the Viet Minh army, and from other minority groups in the northern Tonkin highlands was a key factor in constructing secure base areas within which the Viet Minh could organize and train a revolutionary armed force (Khanh 1982; McAlister 1969).

As World War II continued, the Viet Minh network expanded throughout most of Vietnam. Even groups tolerated or encouraged by the Japanese or the French, such as the Advanced Guard Youth militia in Cochinchina (transformed by the Japanese from the French-sponsored Sports and Youth movement into a paramilitary group [McAlister 1969]) and the University of Hanoi Student Association in Tonkin, affiliated with the Viet Minh. The success of the Viet Minh and the wide popular support it enjoyed were soon obvious to the nations fighting against Japan. GMD military leaders in southern China recognized the Viet Minh as the only effective countrywide anti-Japanese intelligence and resistance network in Vietnam and worked with the Viet Minh despite its Communist leadership. U.S. military forces came to a similar conclusion and air-dropped weapons, along with Office of Strategic Services (OSS, predecessor of the CIA) advisors, to Giap's forces (Karnow 1983; Khanh 1982). At one point when Ho became seriously ill, it is possible that medicine provided by one of the U.S. agents saved his life. The presence of U.S. advisors indicated to some Vietnamese that the United

States actually supported the Viet Minh's goal of attaining national power, further improving the movement's appeal to Western-educated Vietnamese.

INSURRECTION

The conditions for revolutionary insurrection improved dramatically in March 1945, when Japanese forces, anticipating a possible Allied invasion, imprisoned the French colonial administration and captured or routed French military forces. The advantage for the Viet Minh was that the repressive French colonial apparatus in the countryside was destroyed without its being replaced by Japanese forces. For the next five months, "the most important period in the history of the ICP" (Khanh 1982, 309), the Viet Minh were relatively unimpeded in their organizational and mobilization efforts. During this period, Viet Minh military forces expanded rapidly. In the northern provinces of Tonkin, local authorities who had previously served the colonial administration threw their support to the Viet Minh, fled to areas under Japanese control, or, in some cases, were assassinated as collaborators of foreign imperialists. By August 1945 the Viet Minh had secured control of six northern provinces in Tonkin and had as many as 5,000 men and women under arms (to increase to 75,000 within a year and more than 350,000 by the early 1950s). The movement also had a countrywide network of 200,000 Viet Minh activists, led by the ICP, which had 5,000 members (it was also rapidly expanding). The Viet Minh's membership was many times greater than the 5,000 to 10,000 estimated to be associated with the largely elite urban, foreign-sponsored, alternate "nationalist" groups of the period (Khanh 1982; McAlister 1969; Wolf 1969).

Acts of terrorism, such as assassinations, were characteristic of several political groups in Vietnam, not just the Viet Minh. The previously discussed latter versions of the VNQDD and a number of other organizations used terror against Viet Minh activists and sympathizers. The French, for their part, had used terror in various forms, including mass executions and aerial and artillery bombardments of civilians, to control the Vietnamese for decades.

The Viet Minh violence tended to be selective. Targets were usually individuals who were clearly identifiable as agents of the colonial regime or colonial military or police personnel. The acts were terrifying to the small category of Vietnamese who shared the collaborationist characteristics of the victims. But the violence was intended to win popular support from the majority of the population who had suffered hardships and the loss of friends and family members as a result of French, as well as Japanese, imperial policies and who longed to strike back and win a truly independent Vietnam (Dunn 1972).

At about the same time as the Japanese overthrow of the French administration, a terrible famine reached its height in parts of Tonkin and northern Annam. At least several hundred thousand and possibly over one million of Tonkin's 1945 population of eight million perished (Karnow 1983; Khanh

1982). The food shortage was in part due to unusually heavy rainfall, which caused flooding of many cultivated areas, and to Allied bombing, which reduced the rice shipments sent from the Mekong Delta to relieve the starving north. But the famine was blamed primarily on the French and the Japanese. The Japanese had presented the French with a quota of the rice production to feed troops; the French authorities then demanded the rice from the northern peasants (who barely produced enough for their own needs). The Japanese also directed the French to require the planting of industrial-use crops, such as peanuts, other oilseed crops, and cotton, in place of some food crops (Khanh 1982; McAlister 1969). The Viet Minh organized peasants and attacked landlord and Japanese grain storage buildings, rationing out what they found. The famine greatly intensified hostility in the countryside toward both the French and the Japanese and increased respect and support for the Viet Minh.

By summer 1945 the Viet Minh were immensely more powerful and had more popular support than any of the other Vietnamese groups who labeled themselves nationalists despite their foreign sponsorship. Besides the flaws listed previously, the anti–Viet Minh groups generally lacked charismatic or heroic leadership and put forth ideologies and programs that were very narrow in scope and unappealing in content. They basically offered the Vietnamese people the concept of a partially independent Vietnam run by a foreign-educated urban elite under the sponsorship of China, Japan, or France (depending on the particular clique). Furthermore, their programs contained virtually no proposals for improving the social and economic conditions of the majority of Vietnamese (largely because to do so would endanger the economic interests of the small but relatively wealthy classes they represented, the interests of the foreign countries that sponsored them, or both). The Viet Minh, in contrast, offered not only genuine nationalism (an independent Vietnam controlled by Vietnamese) but also a plan for redistribution of wealth in favor of the nation's majority. Since their program embodied the aspirations of most of the rural population and much of the urban working class, the Viet Minh fostered the participation of peasants and workers in local government as well as in local chapters of the mass organizations.

Maximally favorable conditions for a revolutionary uprising developed suddenly on August 15, 1945, when Japan surrendered shortly after two of its cities were destroyed by atomic bombs. At this point, with French troops still incarcerated and the Japanese demoralized and unlikely to resist the efforts of another Asian people to seize their independence before the return of European imperialists, the likelihood that the insurrection would succeed was high. By mid-August (before the Japanese surrender) many villages surrounding Hanoi were under Viet Minh control, and the stage was set for the "August revolution." In the major cities leaflets urging preparations for insurrection were circulated, movies and plays were interrupted so that announcements could be made concerning the national liberation struggle, and the flag of the Viet Minh with its gold star and red background suddenly appeared flying from prominent buildings throughout the country (McAlister 1969). On August 18 the insurrection began. For the next ten days uprisings swept the Viet Minh and allied groups into power in sixty-four major cities in Vietnam, including Hanoi on August 19, Hue on August 23, and Saigon on August 25 (Khanh 1982). In essence, the Japanese turned Vietnam over to the Viet Minh without violent resistance (Karnow 1983).

In the Tonkin and Annam regions, the Viet Minh met little in the way of organized opposition from other Vietnamese political groups. The situation was more complicated in Saigon and the rest of Cochinchina. The Viet Minh won over the support of the Japanese-armed youth militias. But there also existed the armed political-religious sects, which had organization and popular support in certain areas of the Mekong Delta, and the Trotskyite Communists, who had no network of mass organizations but enjoyed some popular support (Khanh 1982). Consequently, the insurrection in Saigon involved an alliance of several groups, in which the Viet Minh was most prominent. But the coalition proved unstable, and participants soon began to feud among themselves. Cochinchina, which had been under French rule the longest of the three regions, also had a well-organized pro-French party, the Constitutionalists. This group desired to maintain close ties with France (McAlister 1969). In the weeks that followed the "August revolution," scores of Vietnamese were assassinated, usually by fanatical members of rival groups. Those groups with limited membership and little mass organization or popular support could not survive the loss of a few prominent figures. But the Viet Minh could endure terrorist acts directed against it precisely because it had thousands of members, a resilient organizational structure, and widespread popular support.

On August 30, after representatives of the pro–Viet Minh Students Association of the University of Hanoi petitioned the figurehead emperor, Bao Dai, to support the revolution, the latter abdicated in favor of the Viet Minh provisional government. Two days later, on September 2, Ho Chi Minh addressed several hundred thousand people at a Hanoi rally to proclaim Vietnam's Declaration of Independence and announce the establishment of the Democratic Republic of Vietnam. No other nation at that point recognized Vietnam's independence.

The victorious Allied powers instead decided to occupy Vietnam. British and Indian troops (under British control) entered the southern half of Vietnam, while approximately 125,000 anti-Communist Chinese GMD troops were sent into the northern half of the country. In late September 1945 the British commander in Saigon rearmed the 1,400 French soldiers the Japanese had arrested there in March. In a surprise move the French troops quickly seized the city's government buildings and with British assistance drove the Viet Minh from Saigon. In October an additional 25,000 French troops arrived and reoccupied all the major cities in Cochinchina. In the northern part of Vietnam, the Viet Minh resorted to bribing Chinese commanders (with gold from rings and other jewelry donated by thousands of Vietnamese) to prevent repression of their new government. And in December 1945 elections were held for a national assembly in Tonkin and Annam; the Viet Minh appeared to receive about 90 percent of the vote (Khanh 1982; McAlister 1969). French military authorities refused to allow elections in Cochinchina, where almost 25 percent of Vietnam's 1945 population of twenty-two million resided. The national assembly elected Ho Chi Minh president. Ho, asserting his intention to create a government of national unity, included Socialist and Catholic politicians as well as Communists among his cabinet ministers (Karnow 1983).

To Ho the Chinese presence in the north represented a greater danger than the French reoccupation in the south. China had long threatened Vietnam with its immensity and power. It appeared that Ho, lacking any significant international support for immediate independence, would have to take the risk of making a deal with the French, the more distant imperialist power, to get the Chinese out. As Ho put it, "Better to sniff a bit of French shit briefly than eat Chinese shit for the rest of our lives" (Karnow 1983, 100). In a move evidently intended to gain greater acceptance of their movement by the GMD Chinese and the French, the members of the ICP publicly dissolved their organization in October 1945 (although the Party continued to function covertly through its extensive and still intact social network). The Party was formally reestablished in 1951 as the Vietnamese Communist Party (officially labeled the Vietnam Labor Party).

Early in 1946 the Chinese decided to withdraw and allow the French to reenter northern Vietnam, provided that the French relinquish their colonial claims to territory within China. The Viet Minh government agreed to allow the French to reintroduce military forces into northern Vietnam on the condition that these units be withdrawn in five years. According to this proposal, the French were then to grant Vietnam independence within the framework of the so-called French Union, which would keep Vietnam economically associated with France (Karnow 1983; Lacouture 1968; McAlister 1969). The future status of the southernmost part of Vietnam, Cochinchina, was a major point of contention. Neither the French nor many of the wealthy Vietnamese residents of this region wanted unification with the other parts of Vietnam, whereas the Viet Minh demanded that Cochinchina be joined to the middle section of Vietnam (Annam) and the northernmost section (Tonkin) in one independent Vietnamese state. The compromise was an agreement to hold a referendum in which the people of Cochinchina would vote either to unify with the other parts or to remain separate. The Viet Minh were certain the majority would vote for unification. But the Cochinchina colonial administration, ignoring the pledge of the French government, refused to hold the referendum.

Tensions continued to rise. The government of France, despite its leftist slant, was staunchly nationalistic and interested in restoring French pride through reclaiming imperial territory. The French, subjugated so recently by the Germans, were now attempting to reestablish their national machismo by reasserting domination over the colonies. On November 23, 1946, a dispute over who controlled customs collections in the Port of Haiphong precipitated skirmishes between Viet Minh and French units. French naval forces opened an artillery bombardment of the city, resulting in hundreds, perhaps thousands, of deaths.

THE FRENCH INDOCHINA WAR: 1946–1954

The French proceeded to seize major cities and towns and to build a colonial Vietnamese militia of more than 300,000 to help fight the Viet Minh. But the local allies of the French were largely composed of the most Europeanized Vietnamese, some anti-Vietnamese members of minority groups, the political-religious sects in the south, and the Binh Xuyen criminal "mafia," which controlled much of the Saigon-area drug business and organized prostitution. France's military leaders, however, anticipated that their professional army and much superior firepower would bring them victory in only a few weeks. But the Viet Minh chose to fight largely on terrain that reduced the effectiveness of the French advantage in weaponry. Throughout the war with the French (and later in the war with the United States) the Vietnamese revolutionary forces, in addition to the small-unit harassment tactics characteristic of guerrilla warfare, often employed the technique of attacking many widely dispersed targets simultaneously, forcing the enemy to scatter its forces. Then, when possible, revolutionary forces would use large units to attack individual positions that had been drained of manpower to meet attacks elsewhere. The Viet Minh usually enjoyed popular support in the areas of military operation and were more highly motivated than the typical Vietnamese who fought alongside the French, often as a mercenary.

At the beginning of the war the Viet Minh emphasized the goal of winning independence in an attempt to unite as many people as possible from all social classes in support of the Communist-led forces confronting the French. Rather than alienate potentially patriotic landlords and rich peasants by giving some of their land to poor peasants, the Viet Minh delayed land redistribution in the areas they controlled throughout most of the war. The Viet Minh rural economic policy until 1953 was to leave landownership patterns relatively intact while easing the economic burdens of the poor by reducing the rent that landlords could charge for land parcels cultivated by tenant farmers.

But the Viet Minh promised the poor that the anti-imperialist struggle against the French would also be antifeudalist and eventually result in both a transfer of much of the land owned by landlords to the landless and nearly landless peasants and the destruction of landlord political dominance in the countryside. And in the later stage of the war the demands of the poor for land ownership and the need for their increased involvement in the revolutionary effort as combatants and in transporting by foot large quantities of ammunition and other equipment prompted the Viet Minh in 1953 to begin significant land redistribution in much of the countryside (Moise 1983).

Realizing they were badly in need of a legitimate nationalist image for their Vietnamese supporters, the French invited back the ever-opportunistic Bao Dai to resume the role of emperor in a partially "independent" French-sponsored Vietnamese state in which Frenchmen continued to control, among other things, the country's economy and army. The men willing to serve the French in Bao Dai's cabinet were characterized by a U.S. diplomat in Hanoi in 1952 as "opportunists, nonentities, extreme reactionaries, assassins, hirelings, and, finally, men of faded mental powers" (Karnow 1983, 180). As Communist-led rebellions began to develop in Laos and Cambodia with Viet Minh assistance, the French allowed non-Communist governments in these countries to declare independence from France in 1953.

By the 1950s the French were experiencing extreme difficulties in Indochina. After the 1949 culmination of the Chinese Revolution, China began to provide the Viet Minh with valuable assistance, such as training services and shipments of weapons, including artillery. The French economy could not support the war effort, and consequently, the United States, determined to help the French succeed in defeating the Communist-led Viet Minh, was paying 78 percent of the cost of the war at its conclusion, including Bao Dai's $4 million per year "stipend" (Karnow 1983; Turley 1986). The French military was eventually losing more officers in combat than were being graduated from the nation's main military academy. And army morale was deteriorating, not only because of battlefield losses, but also because much of the French public turned against the war.

In 1953 both the French and the Viet Minh were considering negotiations to end the fighting. But each side sought a final battlefield triumph that would give it the stronger bargaining position. General Giap, commander of the Viet Minh forces, had sent three divisions toward Laos, taking the village of Dienbienphu on the Vietnamese-Laotian border. French commanders, eager to protect the pro-French Laotian government from the Viet Minh, decided to recapture the town and then use it as a fortress from which to attack Viet Minh base camps. Despite its remote location, the French were confident it could be supplied by aircraft, if necessary.

The first of 12,000 French paratroopers entered Dienbienphu in November 1953. Simultaneously, 50,000 Viet Minh, including artillery, antiaircraft, and engineering units, moved to encircle them. In March 1954 Viet Minh forces attacked and quickly destroyed French artillery bases and the airfield. The Viet Minh then closed in by digging tunnels and trenches ever closer to French positions. In desperation the French appealed unsuccessfully to the United States for heavy bomber attacks to break the siege. On May 7, 1954, the day the Geneva negotiations to settle the fighting in Indochina convened, the Viet Minh's red and gold banner was raised over the French command center at Dienbienphu.

THE 1954 GENEVA ACCORDS ON INDOCHINA

As the Geneva Conference opened, the Viet Minh were in control of most of the countryside in the northern two-thirds of Vietnam, with base camps, sizable "liberated" areas, and large forces active in the remaining southern third of the country (Karnow 1983; Turley 1986). The Viet Minh concluded they had won the war and expected essentially to negotiate terms for the French departure. But they did not anticipate the compromise stance that would be taken by the two Communist giants. The USSR leadership was attempting to establish better relations with the West after the death of Stalin in 1953 and avoided pushing for a settlement favorable to the Viet Minh. And the Chinese had suffered approximately one million casualties in fighting against U.S. forces in Korea and were determined not to risk another violent confrontation. Both the USSR and China pressured the Viet Minh to settle for a partial victory (Karnow 1983; 1990; Turley 1986).

The key provisions of the Geneva settlement included a temporary division of Vietnam at latitude 17 degrees north—the 17th parallel—which explicitly was not to be viewed as a national boundary. French military units were to be withdrawn south of this line and Viet Minh forces to the north. No foreign military forces were to be introduced into Vietnam. And in a provision by which the post-French Saigon regime refused to be bound, the settlement stipulated that elections were to be held throughout Vietnam in 1956 to unify the entire country under one government (Bergerud 1991; Duiker 1995, 2000; Karnow 1983; Lacouture 1968; McAlister 1969; Turley 1986; Wolf 1969).

The fulfillment of the terms of the Geneva Accords was to be supervised by a commission composed of observers from Canada, India, and Poland. During a three-hundred-day "regroupment period," about 900,000 Vietnamese moved south of the 17th parallel (about two-thirds were Catholics fearing Communist persecution and encouraged by CIA-supplied leaflets stating, "Christ has gone to the South," while the rest were largely businessmen and employees of the French); approximately 87,000 Viet Minh combatants and 47,000 civilians headed north (Turley 1986, 11).

U.S. INVOLVEMENT IN VIETNAM: 1954–1975

The U.S. decision to provide aid to the French in Indochina was based, in part, on the conception of a monolithic Communist movement expanding outward from its "origin" in European Russia. In this formulation, Communist China represented the success of "Communist aggression" against China, and Ho Chi Minh and the Viet Minh represented a new Communist

VIETNAM (1954–1975)

aggression against Vietnam (supposedly directed from China). Ignoring the nationalistic character of the Viet Minh movement and the fact that Vietnam's unique history and political and economic characteristics had brought about an essentially nonexportable revolution (except, in a sense, to the two other countries that had also been components of French Indochina), the Eisenhower administration resolved to stop the "spread of communism."

President Diem: An Anti-Communist Leader

An important aspect of the plan to prevent the southern part of Vietnam from reuniting with the north was the selection of a leader for the south who was both an anti-Communist and recognized as a nationalist. The anti-Communist leader chosen for South Vietnam was Ngo Dinh Diem. Diem was born to a wealthy Catholic family at Hue in 1901 and attended the French School of Administration in Hanoi, where he finished first in his class. He rose rapidly through governmental ranks and in 1933 was appointed minister of the interior to Emperor Bao Dai. He subsequently resigned because of French interference in his official duties. This action earned him the reputation of being a Vietnamese patriot within Vietnam's elite circle of middle- and upper-class anti-Communist nationalists. Diem, who at one time considered becoming a priest, was a religious ascetic throughout his life. His conception of holding and exercising political authority was akin to the absolute power exercised by Vietnam's ancient emperors, and "concepts of compromise, power-sharing and popular participation" were alien to him (Turley 1986, 13).

The Viet Minh captured Diem in 1945 and sent him to a remote village for six months. In 1946 Ho Chi Minh offered him a governmental position, but he refused to work with Communists, and he blamed the deaths of a brother and a nephew on the Viet Minh. In 1950, after residing for four years in seclusion at Hue, he left Vietnam and eventually settled at the Maryknoll Seminary in Lakewood, New Jersey. Diem came to the attention of the influential Catholic leader Cardinal Spellman and was later accepted by the Eisenhower administration as a possible anti-Communist leader for the southern part of Vietnam.

In July 1954 Diem was appointed prime minister of South Vietnam by Emperor Bao Dai and quickly returned to Saigon. By 1955 the Eisenhower administration was pouring economic assistance and military aid into South Vietnam and reorganizing and training the soldiers who had served in the French colonial armed forces into what was eventually called the Army of the Republic of Vietnam (ARVN). The weapons and military advisors the United States sent to Vietnam were in direct violation of the Geneva Accords. During the same year, Diem consolidated his power by intimidating and bribing the leaders of the political-religious sects and through military action against the French-supported Binh Xuyen organized-crime group. He also turned on Bao Dai, eliminating the position of emperor through a rigged referendum in October 1955 (Karnow 1983).

Diem decided not to hold the reunification elections scheduled for 1956 because he, like virtually everyone else, realized that Ho Chi Minh and the Viet Minh would almost certainly win (Karnow 1983; Turley 1986; Wolf 1969). Diem's police even helped burn the Geneva commission's office in Saigon. He proceeded to launch the fierce Denunciation of Communists Campaign, in which thousands of Viet Minh supporters, relatively unprotected since most of the revolutionary soldiers had gone north as called for by the Geneva Accords, were arrested and imprisoned. Many were tortured to obtain information about their compatriots, and some were killed. Morale among Viet Minh sympathizers in the south deteriorated because the government in the north would not immediately give consent for armed resistance to Diem's repression. Without effective means of defense against persecution, membership in the southern branch of the Vietnamese Communist Party declined to about five thousand in 1959.

Ho Chi Minh and the government of the Democratic Republic of Vietnam in the north were hesitant to consent to a renewal of armed revolutionary conflict in the south. Among their reasons was the hope that international pressure would eventually force the Diem regime to hold the reunification elections. The leaders in the north clung to this increasingly remote possibility because they anticipated the devastation a war with the United States would bring. They also were unsure of what assistance the USSR and China would be willing to provide in the event of large-scale U.S. intervention. This apprehension was in part prompted by the Soviet Union's startling 1957 proposal that both North and South Vietnam be admitted to the United Nations, in effect granting recognition to the south as a separate nation. Ironically, the United States helped kill this measure at the time because it objected to the implied recognition of the government of North Vietnam (Karnow 1983).

The North Vietnamese government also became preoccupied in the mid-1950s with the mishandled land-reform program, which had been designed largely by urban Party leaders and had created chaos in parts of the north. The planners selected mainly poor, semiliterate rural youth to implement the reform at the village level. These young zealots, often recruited from the revolutionary army, had thrown the countryside into an uproar by organizing other poor peasants to denounce landlords for past crimes, such as collaborating with the French and exploiting the poor. Seized lands were distributed to 75 percent of the region's peasants. But 5,000 to 15,000 landlords and "collaborators" were killed by peasants who blamed them for the deaths of loved ones and other past hardships (Moise 1983).

Distressed by disruptions, protests, and injustices resulting from the poorly executed land-reform program, the North Vietnamese government initiated a period of self-criticism and reassessment. Eventually many of

North Vietnam's peasants were organized into lower-stage, or "semisocialist," cooperatives, in which the participants retained individual ownership of their pooled land, livestock, and equipment. The cooperative paid them "rent" in proportion to their contributed assets as well as a share of the profits in proportion to their labor (Duiker 1983; Moise 1983). During the 1960s most cooperatives became higher stage, or "fully socialist," in that land and productive agricultural property were owned collectively by all members of the cooperative, with an individual paid only in proportion to the amount of work he or she performed.

In the south the Saigon regime's efforts to repress Viet Minh activists and suspected Communist Party members by imprisonment or execution seriously damaged the revolutionary social network. Surviving Communist Party members began to demand that the government to the north of the 17th parallel consent to their right to engage in all-out armed resistance against Saigon military and police forces, perhaps as much out of a desire to fight for self-preservation as anything else (Bergerud 1991; Turley 1986; Race 1972).

The call for violent opposition to the South Vietnamese government was well received by large numbers of peasants who since 1954 had been outraged and alienated by many of Saigon's policies. Among the measures provoking widespread discontent, particularly significant was the Saigon regime's effective reversal of the land reform that the Viet Minh had carried out in much of the countryside toward the end of the war with the French. Saigon forced poor peasants to return ownership of the land to their former landlords and then pay rent for its use. In some instances those given land by the Viet Minh were forced to pay for it. The urban-based Saigon government, in attempting to assert its control over the countryside, allied itself with the rural landlord class, which had fled to the relative safety of cities during the war. The Saigon regime returned the landlords to the villages, some in the role of village council administrators, protected by armed guards, and therefore largely reinstituted the economic and political domination of the traditional rural elite (Bergerud 1991; Race 1972). Saigon authorities further antagonized many among the poor majority by coercing them to work on government projects, by persecuting many non-Communists who supported the Viet Minh reforms, and by often engaging in corruption and abusive behavior.

Formation of the National Liberation Front

On December 20, 1960, resistance forces proclaimed the formation of the National Liberation Front (NLF) of South Vietnam, an organization of southern nationalists united under the leadership of the southern branch of Vietnam's Communist Party for the purpose of bringing about a reunification of Vietnam (Turley 1986). The Diem government quickly branded the NLF

the "Viet Cong" (Viet Communists). The leaders of the Communist Party evidently hoped that the actions of the NLF, together with expected mass uprisings against Diem, would precipitate the formation of a coalition government
in the south that would include representatives of the NLF. The new government would then hold negotiations with the north to reunify Vietnam. The
decision to mobilize the southern nationalists for armed resistance to the
Diem regime under the banner of the NLF resulted in a rapid revitalization of
both the revolutionary effort and Communist Party membership in the
south, which reached 70,000 by 1963 (Turley 1986). NLF armed forces grew
at a dramatic pace, and attacks on Saigon forces multiplied.

As the NLF expanded, the Diem regime, with U.S. support, launched the
so-called strategic hamlet program, which involved in some cases the relocation of peasants from their homes to fortified sites and in others the fortifi-
cation of existing hamlets (Bergerud 1991; Duiker 1983; Turley 1986).
According to Saigon authorities, the peasants in their new or modified living
environments would be safe from Viet Cong terrorism. They would also be
inhibited from supporting or joining the NLF, if they were so inclined. The
policy, in effect, was a counterinsurgency technique intended to deprive the
revolutionary forces of their popular support by physically removing its
source—the peasants—from the open countryside (an attempt to starve the
guerrilla "fish" by drying up the popular "sea" that nourished them). However, many peasants resented being displaced from their ancestral villages
and compelled to build hamlets and fortifications so that they could reside
under the surveillance of the Saigon regime and be subjected to its coercive
measures. The strategic hamlet program was apparently so unpopular with
most peasants that it influenced many to join the NLF. In fact, the ARVN
army colonel in charge of implementing the program for the Saigon regime
was, throughout the war, secretly a member of the National Liberation
Front (Karnow 1983), and it is very likely he was willing to carry out the
policy precisely because of its positive impact on NLF recruitment.

Diem favored the Catholic minority, of which he was a member. This orientation prompted opposition from some Buddhists, to which Diem responded characteristically with violent repression. After several Buddhist
monks set fire to themselves in further protests in June 1963, Diem's special
forces, under the command of his brother, donned regular army uniforms
and raided several Buddhist pagodas. The counterproductive nature of these
actions outraged many ARVN officers, most of whom were at least nominally Buddhists like 80 percent of their compatriots. Saigon's top military
leaders, most inherited from the French colonial army, also resented Diem's
interference in the handling of the war against the NLF. Fearing the possibility of a military plot against his government, Diem regularly rotated officers
around the country so that they could not stay long enough in any one place
to organize a conspiracy. But consequently, they also often lacked the time
to gain the experience necessary to adapt to one command situation before

they were shifted to another. Moreover, incompetence in the military ranks was heightened by Diem's tendency to promote those he deemed most loyal to him rather than those most able (Karnow 1983; Turley 1986).

Most important, Diem's regime was clearly losing the war with the NLF. Both Washington and the Saigon general staff decided that Diem had to go. On November 1, 1963, most of Diem's generals, assured of support or at least noninterference by U.S. officials, rebelled against him (Karnow 1983). Diem and his brother were executed the next day. President John F. Kennedy, although anticipating that Diem would be forced out, was reportedly shocked at the news of his killing. On November 22, 1963, Kennedy was himself assassinated in Dallas.

By the end of 1963 some 15,000 U.S. military advisors were in South Vietnam. Several thousand former Viet Minh had moved south to help organize and strengthen the growing NLF ranks, but these were almost all individuals born in the south who had gone north as Viet Minh soldiers, in line with the 1954 peace accords (Karnow 1983; Turley 1986). In Saigon a council of generals replaced Diem, but this was followed by seven changes in leadership during 1964, as Saigon military figures struggled for power. According to Turley (1986, 52), Saigon's military leaders were "mostly products of French education and bourgeois families, holdovers of the colonial system who made up the South's anti-Communist elite" and were usually unconcerned with the economic and social hardships of the majority of the population. After Diem, corruption in the military appeared to increase. And the NLF continued to expand its areas of control. U.S. advisors concluded that only large-scale U.S. military action could save the Saigon regime (Karnow 1983; Turley 1986).

Massive U.S. Military Intervention

On August 2, 1964, an American destroyer, the *Maddox*, engaged in close surveillance in the Gulf of Tonkin off the coast of North Vietnam, was attacked by North Vietnamese patrol boats. ARVN units had earlier raided several positions in the area. The patrol boat incident, which inflicted no damage on the U.S. vessel, and a second alleged but unconfirmed incident involving another destroyer two days later, were represented to Congress and the U.S. public as "unprovoked Communist aggression." On August 7, 1964, the U.S. Congress passed the Gulf of Tonkin Resolution (unanimously in the House of Representatives and with only two dissenting votes in the Senate), giving President Lyndon Johnson the power to take whatever military action necessary to defend U.S. forces. This vote constituted the essential congressional authorization for the war in Southeast Asia, and Congress would continue until 1973 to vote appropriations for various aspects of the conflict (Karnow 1983; McNamara 1995).

In February 1965 the United States initiated continuous bombing raids over North Vietnam, and by December U.S. troop strength had reached 200,000. Regular North Vietnamese army (People's Army of Vietnam) units were also entering the south along the "Ho Chi Minh Trail" (a network of mountain and jungle paths extending through Laos into Vietnam's central highlands as well as into its southern regions) to assist several hundred thousand NLF (Viet Cong) fighters organized into village militia, regional defense units, and main combat units. U.S. force levels continued to rise, eventually approaching 500,000 by the end of 1967. The Soviet Union provided the north with weapons, including anti-aircraft missiles, and China contributed weapons and rice.

In a highly constrained 1967 South Vietnamese "election" without NLF participation—but in which there were eleven slates of candidates—General Thieu, a former major in the French army who had married into a wealthy Catholic family and converted from Buddhism to Catholicism, and his running mate, General Ky, won with 34.5 percent of the vote (Karnow 1983; Kolko 1985). Toward the end of that year, U.S. military leaders assured President Johnson and the U.S. public that the war was being won and that enemy forces in the south would be hard-pressed to mount any significant attacks. This assessment was highly inaccurate. Communist Party leaders devised a plan for an offensive that would significantly affect the course of the war. It was set for the Vietnamese new year, or Tet, January 31, 1968.

The planners of the Tet offensive had several potential goals. The basic ones were to disrupt the Saigon regime's efforts to expand control over the countryside by forcing its forces to fall back toward the cities into defensive positions; to destroy the confidence and sense of security of the Saigon government's urban supporters, who had been long removed from the violence of the war; and to disrupt any plans of the U.S. or Saigon government to launch an invasion of the north. The organizers were also hopeful that Tet would disillusion U.S. governmental and military leaders and the U.S. public and demonstrate that the conflict would last indefinitely if U.S. troops were not withdrawn. The most optimistic potential outcome of the Tet offensive, which few of its planners felt was realistic, was to provoke widespread uprisings throughout the south to bring a quick end to the war and reunify the country before the death of Ho Chi Minh (who was ill and would die in 1969) (Karnow 1990; Kolko 1985; Turley 1986).

On January 31 approximately 80,000 National Liberation Front soldiers simultaneously attacked about one hundred cities and towns (North Vietnamese units took part only in assaults in the northernmost sections of South Vietnam) (Duiker 1995; Karnow 1983; Turley 1986). Four thousand NLF fighters invaded Saigon itself, and one unit seized the grounds of the U.S. embassy before being annihilated. Hue, the old imperial capital, was captured and held for weeks against a tremendous counterattack organized by U.S. and Saigon forces. In the end, all the major cities and towns captured by the NLF were retaken.

The NLF suffered as many as 40,000 casualties, a devastation that would take years of recovery. The offensive, however, did weaken Saigon's control over areas of the countryside previously thought to have been secured from the NLF. But probably the most important consequence of Tet was the powerful demoralizing effect it had on the U.S. public and government. Top military leaders who had previously claimed the war was being won now appeared incompetent or deceitful. The war itself seemed destined to go on without end. While Vietnamese revolutionaries were prepared to keep fighting for decades, if necessary, the U.S. public was willing to endure the sacrifices of warfare only if a limit could be set and victory assured (Karnow 1983).

Although virtually all the observable military targets in North Vietnam had been repeatedly bombed, some U.S. political figures called for the use of even greater armed might, such as an invasion of North Vietnam by U.S. forces or even tactical nuclear weapons. However, this demand ignored important realities. The publicly asserted purpose for the U.S. presence in Vietnam was to promote democracy, the expression of the people's will. But the massive resistance to U.S. intervention by millions of Vietnamese, hundreds of thousands of whom perished, suggested that the high level of military violence used was necessary precisely because U.S. policy ran counter to the aspirations of the majority of Vietnamese. Since many of the people of other nations not directly involved in the conflict interpreted the situation in exactly this manner, the U.S. government received very little support from its major allies for its actions in Vietnam. Greater levels of military force might have further isolated the United States. Of critical importance moreover, all the presidents and Congresses of the Vietnam era feared the possibility of direct military intervention by the USSR and China. That could have forced the United States to choose between accepting an enormous military catastrophe for its forces in Vietnam or using nuclear weapons in an attempt to protect them, possibly precipitating a world war.

In any case, public opinion in the United States turned decisively against the war after the Tet offensive. The reasons for antiwar sentiment varied greatly. Some who voted for peace candidates in the 1968 presidential primary campaign (Eugene McCarthy and Robert Kennedy, who was assassinated after winning the California Democratic Primary) felt the war was an immoral intervention. Others supported antiwar candidates out of a belief that U.S. armed forces were not allowed to use all their potential destructive might to win the war (Karnow 1983). But clearly, after 1968 the majority of Americans demanded an end to the conflict.

Richard Nixon, inaugurated president in January 1969, pledged to end the war "with honor." Thirty thousand Americans had died in Southeast Asia before Nixon took office, and more than 26,000 would perish before the final U.S. departure in 1975. Nixon's approach to ending the war involved greatly increasing the size and level of armament of the Saigon armed forces while at the same time gradually withdrawing U.S. units. This process was referred to as Vietnamization. Another aspect of the Nixon plan involved threats and massive bombing attacks against the North Vietnamese to pressure concessions during negotiations (Karnow 1983).

1973 Peace Agreement

The peace agreement worked out between the Nixon administration and the government of North Vietnam permitted North Vietnamese troops to remain in place in South Vietnam. The Saigon government of President Thieu (the North Vietnamese and the NLF had dropped the demand that Thieu be ousted as part of a peace agreement) was to enter into negotiations with the NLF's Provisional Revolutionary Government to form a coalition government in South Vietnam. The new provisional coalition government would, in turn, negotiate the possibility of reunification with the north. U.S. prisoners of war would be returned, and the U.S. would provide economic assistance to Vietnam. In essence, the peace agreement was very much in line with what the National Liberation Front had hoped to achieve when taking up arms in the early 1960s. Thieu and many in his Saigon government were outraged by the peace accords (Kolko 1985).

Nixon promised Thieu that any Communist offensive in violation of the treaty would be countered with massive U.S. air attacks. Saigon's own air force was, at the time, the fourth largest in the world (Karnow 1983). Thieu, who ignored the cease-fire in certain areas of South Vietnam, ordered the Saigon army to begin attacking NLF units and seizing territory. His plan was evidently to expand the land area (and population) under his control gradually until that held by the NLF was insignificant, thereby making the formation of a coalition government appear unnecessary (Karnow 1983).

The Communist-led forces, however, had expanded the Ho Chi Minh Trail and were pouring equipment and men into the south in preparation for the final campaign to reunify Vietnam. The offensive was launched in earnest in March 1975 with the expectation that a year's fighting might be necessary. Since Nixon had previously been forced to resign in disgrace (in August 1974) over the Watergate affair, and the U.S. Congress had proceeded to ban any further U.S. military action in Southeast Asia, including air attacks, Saigon's forces were on their own. Initial Communist victories in Vietnam's central highlands precipitated an ARVN retreat, which turned into a rout. As ARVN generals and some other officers fled the country with whatever wealth they had accumulated, enlisted soldiers surrendered or changed into civilian clothes and simply went home (Karnow 1983; Kolko 1985; Turley 1986). With the exception of a few South Vietnamese army and air units, the startlingly sudden collapse of Saigon's forces in the face of the determined advance of their opponents appeared to testify to the inherent weakness, artificiality, and moral shallowness of the Saigon government. Communist-led forces accepted the surrender of Saigon on April 30, 1975, and renamed it Ho Chi Minh City. The two halves of Vietnam, separated at the 17th parallel since the 1954 Geneva Accords, were then once again joined into a single nation. In retaliation for the Communist offensive, the United States canceled proposed assistance and enforced an economically damaging trade embargo on Vietnam, which was in effect until lifted by the Clinton administration in 1994. The United States and Vietnam finally established formal ties in August 1995 (*New York Times*, Aug. 6, 1995, 3).

AFTERMATH AND RELATED DEVELOPMENTS

Following the fall of Saigon and the reunification of Vietnam in April 1975, at least 200,000 former South Vietnamese government officials and military officers were sent to "reeducation camps" for periods generally ranging from a few months to several years. Upon release, many of these men and their families joined the more than one million people who emigrated from Vietnam after the end of the war.

After years of destruction, Vietnam was left with staggering problems. The tasks of repairing war damage, clearing unexploded mines and bombs, and coping with the medical and ecological catastrophe caused by the spreading of thousands of tons of herbicides over the countryside (the U.S. military had attempted to defoliate large areas to reveal or inhibit the movement of enemy forces) retarded development of the economy. The country also had to care for hundreds of thousands of injured soldiers and civilians and thousands of war orphans. Inefficiency, over-centralization, and corruption created further problems in administrative and economic functions. Population growth of 3 percent per year put additional strains on resources.

Vietnam never received the several billion dollars in aid from the United States that was part of the 1973 peace settlement (the U.S. view was that the agreements had been broken, so assistance was no longer merited). And Vietnam was soon further burdened with the cost of its invasion and military operations in Cambodia after December 1978 and of defending against a punitive attack from Cambodia's ally, China, in 1979.

U.S. treatment of Vietnam after 1975 tended to be relatively punitive. The officially stated U.S. government conditions for considering the establishment of diplomatic and commercial relations with Vietnam were the removal of Vietnamese troops from Cambodia (where they had intervened in 1978) and the formulation of a peace settlement there, freedom for all remaining political prisoners, permission to leave Vietnam for any Amerasian offspring of U.S. citizens, and assistance in resolving questions concerning more than 2,200 U.S. personnel who were still listed as missing in action (MIA).

The MIA issue was of considerable emotional significance in the United States, and opinion surveys in the early 1990s indicated that a majority of U.S. citizens, especially Vietnam veterans, believed MIAs were still alive in

Vietnam. But according to U.S. government officials, no reports of MIA sightings were ever confirmed after investigation, at least up to 2006. Most Vietnamese had little hope of finding the remains of their estimated 300,000 loved ones who were also MIA (*New York Times*, Oct. 10, 2002, A1). U.S. authorities surmised that the persons some Vietnamese refugees reported as Americans in Vietnam were either Eastern Europeans or Amerasians. In any case, attitude surveys also showed that by the 1990s many more U.S. citizens favored than opposed reestablishing relations with Vietnam.

The constitution of the Socialist Republic of Vietnam specified that the nationally elected legislature, the National Assembly, with 492 members in the mid-1990s, was the supreme governing body of the state. But observers noted that in reality the legislature tended to be subservient to decisions made by the executive branch of government (Duiker 1995). The executive branch initially consisted of a presidency with strong powers, an office once occupied by Ho Chi Minh. But the 1980 constitution created an executive committee, the Council of State, which replaced the position of president as chief of state.

Following the end of the war, the southern branch of the Vietnamese Communist Party was joined with the northern branch. The Vietnamese 1980 constitution clearly stipulated that the Vietnamese Communist Party was the leading political force in Vietnamese society. Although some Vietnamese protested against the persistence of the Leninist-inspired "dictatorship of the proletariat" political system, most observers estimated that although the country continued to pursue the fruits of a "market economy," in the foreseeable future it would experience "minimal challenges to central political authority" (*New York Times*, Aug. 6, 1995, 3). The Communist Party's ability to maintain political dominance in Vietnam was probably due to several factors. Duiker (1995) suggested that one reason was the "paternalistic character of Vietnamese political culture," which "idealizes benevolent despotism and a hierarchal view of social relationships" (Duiker 1995, 122, 123). Duiker's second reason may be even more significant: that the Communist Party enjoys its dominant position since the Party has played a "historically central role in the creation of an independent and united Vietnam" (Duiker 1995, 123). Any significant persistence of the perception that Vietnam continues to be threatened by foreign powers militarily or economically is likely to enhance the Communist Party's chances of holding on to its leading role.

The leaders of post-1975 Vietnam maintained state ownership of industry and utilized centralized economic planning up to the mid-1980s. But inadequate economic progress caused the country's leaders to implement "renovation" reforms (*doi moi*) in 1986. Similar to reforms adopted earlier in China, these new policies allowed farmers to have greater control over which crops they grew and permitted some direct foreign investment. Once the reforms were in place, economic growth accelerated to about 8 percent per year. Vietnam emerged as the second largest exporter of rice, as its agricultural production increased by 100 percent. By 2001 privately owned enterprises produced about 20 percent of industrial output, foreign investment about 30 percent, and state-owned companies approximately 50 percent (Manyin 2003, 12–13). Poverty in rural areas of Vietnam was estimated to have declined from 66 percent in 1993 to 36 percent in 2002 (World Bank 2005, 1). The 2006 CIA country report for Vietnam indicated that in 2004 slightly under 20 percent of the entire population was living in poverty.

Like the Chinese Communist officials, Vietnamese leaders undoubtedly recognized the role that economic failure played in the fall of Communist-led governments in Eastern Europe and the USSR, which had provided large amounts of military aid, including anti-aircraft missiles, for the war against the United States. Now without the support of these nations, it was all the more important for Vietnam to adopt economic policies that would accelerate the country's economic development and improve the lives of its people. The significance of business enterprise and market economics for the welfare of the Vietnamese people and the continued leadership of the Communist Partly led to the Party's central committee deciding to allow, as China's party had done in 2001, private businessmen to be considered for Communist Party membership in 2005 (BBC News, July 18, 2005).

As has been the case in other countries that have shifted away from centrally controlled economies to market systems, private ownership of businesses, and permitting large-scale foreign investment, Vietnam has apparently experienced expanded and new forms of corruption. The reasons appeared to be both the new opportunities for corruption inherent in competition among enterprises, as the proprietors of some attempted to gain unfair advantages through bribery, and the tendency for a decrease in the state's ability to deter corruption through effective detection and punishment in a decentralizing economy. Some of the worst corruption was tied to organized crime. In 2004 a major organized crime figure, Troung Nam Cam, charged earlier with murder, assault, extortion, drug trafficking, organizing bribery, and other offenses, was executed by firing squad along with four of his gang members (BBC News, July 16, 2002; June 3, 2004a; June 3, 2004b). Some 150 people stood trial in connection with the case including two expelled members of the 150-member Communist Party central committee, the former head of the state radio system, and the former director of police in Troung Nam Cam's base of operation, Ho Chi Minh City, who was accused of allowing the gang to operate without fear of police interference.

Like other countries in Southeast Asia, Vietnam has also been a destination for Western sex tourists seeking young prostitutes or even sex with children. The prosecution, conviction, and prison sentence handed out to British rock star Gary Glitter for offenses with young girls was considered part of a crackdown on this type of activity (BBC News, Mar. 3, 2006).

Government and Party leaders appear to have reacted to the extent of corruption within their own ranks, resulting popular rage and anxiety, and the threat posed to the existing political system by handing out strong punishments to convicted officials and by allowing an increased level of public criticism of the government and the Party (BBC News, Mar. 2, 2006; Apr. 18, 2006a; Apr. 18, 2006b). Some prominent citizens and Party members called for even more criticism of the government and Party and for a need to move toward a more democratic political system. Despite the potential challenge to continued Communist Party domination of the state posed by disclosures of high-level corruption from 2002 through 2006, Communist leadership in Vietnam benefited from some of the same factors that Jeffrey Wasserstrom (2002) identified in his evaluation of the strengths and weaknesses of the Communist government in China. As in China, there is a historic link between national liberation and the Communist Party. Since it was Ho Chi Minh and his associates who led the successful struggle against foreign invasion and occupation, there was an identification in the minds of millions of Vietnamese of patriotism with Communist Party leadership.

Many Vietnamese became aware of the social devastation that afflicted millions of people in post-Communist regimes in Russia and Eastern Europe and of the consequences of the seemingly unbridled pursuit of neoliberal economic policies by procapitalist regimes, democratically elected or authoritarian, in a number of developing countries. Despite the shortcomings of Vietnam's current political system, the fear of similar social disasters may inhibit consideration of sweeping political changes in Vietnam. Since they are citizens of a nation that throughout much of its history was invaded and occupied by foreign powers, the perception of deception and hypocrisy by the Bush administration in its invasion and occupation of oil-rich Iraq on the apparently false pretext of a threat of weapons of mass destruction undoubtedly reminded most Vietnamese of the Gulf of Tonkin incident that was used by a previous U.S. administration to justify its catastrophic intervention in Vietnam. This U.S. policy, coupled with its seemingly inconsistent support for democracy, namely advocating "democracy" for uncooperative authoritarian regimes while seemingly tolerating the lack of democracy in cooperative monarchies or other types of nondemocratic regimes, has likely undermined the possibility of democratic changes in a number of countries, including Vietnam. The perception of international lawlessness and unjustified resort to violence by the world's most powerful nation probably strengthens existing governments that use the threat of foreign imperialism to prevent political change. One implication is that democratization in Vietnam or other nations is partially dependent on the political choices of voters in the United States.

Laos

Laos, to the west of Vietnam, a country of approximately 6.4 million in 2006, had been plagued by civil war among right-wing, neutralist, and leftist factions and had experienced French and U.S. military interventions since

World War II. The leftist forces, the Pathet Lao, were originally trained by the Viet Minh and adopted much of the Viet Minh organizational structure in the areas they controlled, mostly the regions bordering the northern part of Vietnam (Adams and McCoy 1970; Zasloff 1973). In 1973 a cease-fire was negotiated, and a neutral coalition government assumed power. Later the Pathet Lao movement, enjoying organizational networks and support among many of the country's peasants, inspired local seizures of power by "people's committees," followed by elections, which forced the abdication of the Laotian king and resulted in the establishment on December 2, 1975, of the Communist-led People's Democratic Republic of Laos (Turley 1986).

A greater proportion of prerevolutionary elites in Laos survived war and revolution in comparison to those in Vietnam and Cambodia. They and the postrevolutionary elites of the governing Communist Party appeared to en-joy distinct lifestyle and opportunity advantages compared to most Laotians (*New York Times*, July 30, 1995, 10). The Laotian leadership apparently patterned its political and economic policies after those of Vietnam. Thus Laos embarked on a program of market reforms beginning in 1986, while preserving the state-dominating role of the Communist Party. Laos became a member of the Association of Southeast Asian Nations (ASEAN) in 1997 (Stuart-Fox 2006). During the 1990s the economy grew at an annual rate of 6.3 percent, and the World Bank forecast a growth rate of 7.1 percent for 2006 (Nualkhair 2006). Yet Laos continued to be one of the poorest nations in the world, with about two-thirds of the population living on less than US$2 per day. The World Bank in 2005 provided financing for the major Nam Theun Two hydroelectric dam project, and Vietnam was assisting with construction of several smaller dams. But in 2006 Laos continued to lag be-hind Vietnam and many other nations in terms of economic development, educational opportunities, and health care.

Cambodia

On April 17, 1975, two weeks before the end of the Vietnam conflict, the Khmer Rouge (Red Khmer, or Red Cambodians) captured the capital of Cambodia, Phnom Penh. The Cambodian Communist movement had devel-oped with Viet Minh assistance during the French Indochina War. At the Geneva Conference, however, the Cambodian Communists (as well as the Laotian Party) had been left out of the peace accords, a fact some Cambodi-ans blamed on the Viet Minh (Chandler 1983; Etcheson 1984). Cambodian Communist displeasure with the Vietnamese increased because the Viet-namese Communist forces were reluctant to help arm the Khmer Rouge in its efforts to topple the non-Communist Cambodian government of Prince Sihanouk. Sihanouk, who had helped lead Cambodia to independence from French colonial rule in 1953 through a negotiation process, had tried to keep his nation relatively neutral regarding the conflicts in Vietnam. The prince, however, was critical of U.S. intervention and had permitted the

Vietnamese National Liberation Front and North Vietnamese units to use Cambodian territory for base camps and storage of food and war matériel.

Whereas many members of the original Cambodian Communist Party had taken refuge in North Vietnam after the Geneva Accords in 1954, another faction, formed mainly by Cambodian students radicalized while studying in France, returned to Cambodia with an ideology that combined ultranationalism with some extreme-Maoist concepts. The intense nationalist orientation of this group, led by individuals such as Saloth Sar (later called Pol Pot), was reflected in its hostility not only to European and U.S. influences but also to the Vietnamese, who in the late eighteenth century had deprived Cambodia of the Mekong Delta area. Inspired by their interpretation of Mao's concepts, Pol Pot Communists intended to depopulate what they viewed as the "parasitic" and "corrupt" cities and then organize the people into rural farming collectives.

The neutralist Prince Sihanouk, however, was also threatened from the right. His establishment of diplomatic relations with the NLF's Provisional Revolutionary Government of South Vietnam disturbed conservative Cambodian generals, government officials, and businessmen. Many in these groups, along with thousands of other urban Cambodians, advocated allying Cambodia with the United States and anticipated that such a move would result in a beneficial massive infusion of U.S. assistance. On March 18, 1970, while Prince Sihanouk was out of the country, General Lon Nol seized control of the government and proceeded to establish himself as chief executive (Etcheson 1984; Turley 1986). The Lon Nol government soon became totally dependent on U.S. economic and military aid and air power for survival.

On April 29, 1970, President Nixon ordered U.S. military forces, accompanied by South Vietnamese troops, into Cambodia for sixty days to destroy North Vietnamese and NLF supplies and bases in order both to provide the Saigon government with more time to build its forces and to shield remaining U.S. units in Vietnam from major attacks before their final departure (Bergerud 1991; Duiker 1995; Etcheson 1984; Turley 1986). Vietnamese Communist forces responded by moving large amounts of equipment away from invaded territory and by occupying large interior sections of Cambodia, which they soon turned over to the Khmer Rouge. The U.S. invasion and simultaneous massive bombing campaign drove tens of thousands of Cambodians into the ranks of the Khmer Rouge and strengthened the ultranationalist faction in the Cambodian Communist Party, which benefited from the intensified hatred of foreigners (Etcheson 1984). Because the U.S. Congress had banned bombing in Cambodia in August 1973, U.S. air power was not available to slow the Communists' 1975 "final offensive." General Lon Nol fled to Hawaii on April 1. Phnom Penh fell on April 17.

The Khmer Rouge, dominated by Pol Pot, quickly moved hundreds of thousands of urban Cambodians to agricultural settlements, killed thousands accused of supporting Lon Nol and the Americans, and purged and executed many Cambodian Communists thought to be "contaminated" by

Vietnamese influence. In addition to those killed in fighting during the years 1970–1975, many more (estimates range from several hundred thousand to more than one million, out of Cambodia's then eight million total population) died between 1975 and 1979 from persecution, starvation, or disease (Etcheson 1984).

After the fall of Phnom Penh, Khmer Rouge units began attacking Vietnamese communities in border areas to the west of Saigon, possibly hoping to evict the Vietnamese from territories that two hundred years earlier had belonged to Cambodia. After repeated assaults and failed negotiations, Vietnamese military forces invaded Cambodia on December 25, 1978, accompanied by thousands of Cambodian Communists opposed to the Pol Pot regime. The Vietnamese offered three major reasons for their occupation of Cambodia: providing protection for Vietnamese civilians from Khmer Rouge border attacks; preventing the possibility of a two-front war with the Khmer Rouge attacking from west of Saigon and China, Cambodia's ally, attacking from the north; and halting the brutality of the Pol Pot extremists (Etcheson 1984). In retaliation for the Vietnamese occupation of Cambodia, the Chinese attacked the northern section of Vietnam in February 1979 and, after reportedly suffering considerable losses, withdrew.

Despite the opposition of the United States, China, and most members of the United Nations, Vietnamese forces, harassed by Khmer Rouge and some non-Communist Cambodian guerrillas, remained in Cambodia for over a decade. Finally, after negotiations involving several Cambodian factions and representatives of Vietnam and China, a tentative agreement was reached to end the war. The pact centered on the establishment of a coalition government of national unity. Vietnamese leaders announced that all their remaining troops would leave Cambodia by the end of September 1989 (*New York Times*, Apr. 6, 1989, A1). Vietnam's intervention in Cambodia, although at least partially achieving the original aims, had cost the Vietnamese 18,000 killed and 37,000 wounded (*New York Times*, Apr. 9, 1989, A1).

The Cambodian peace negotiations, however, repeatedly broke down, leading to renewed civil war. The coalition of three Cambodian organizations (of which the Khmer Rouge was by far the largest and militarily most effective), supported by China and the United States, opposed the Vietnamese-backed Cambodian government in Phnom Penh. But in the face of mounting successes by the Khmer Rouge, the U.S. government, apparently fearing that this movement, already held responsible for as many as a million deaths, could again seize power with the aid of its indirect U.S. assistance, dramatically shifted its position in July 1990. The Bush administration withdrew its previous diplomatic recognition for the anti-Vietnamese Cambodian rebel alliance and stopped referring to the Cambodian government as a puppet of Vietnam. Instead the United States agreed to negotiate with Vietnam (for the first time since 1975) in an effort to bring about an end both to the Cambodian conflict and to the threat of the establishment of a new brutal regime in that nation (*New York Times*, July 19, 1990, A1, A10; Jan. 13, 1991, E3).

By the late 1980s Vietnam had become increasingly interested in pressuring the government it had helped to install in Cambodia to agree to a final settlement of the country's civil war. Vietnam's leaders anticipated the loss of assistance from its once-mighty ally, the USSR, which would disintegrate into fifteen nations in December 1991. This development intensified Vietnam's motivation to help solve the Cambodian conflict so as to improve the chances for aid from and trade with European and other nations, including the United States and China, which had objected to Vietnam's involvement in Cambodia. The final agreement was signed on October 23, 1991, with UN peacekeeping forces and election observers helping to provide security and legitimacy for the country's first democratic elections in May 1993 (Chandler 2006; Duiker 1995). With the Khmer Rouge boycotting the election and even attacking UN units, the party associated with Prince Sihanouk received the largest share of the popular vote and formed a coalition government with the party that had governed Cambodia during the years of Vietnamese occupation. The new Constituent Assembly voted to establish a constitutional monarchy, with the former Prince Sihanouk as king.

Despite the election results, Khmer Rouge units operating mainly in the western part of the country continued to attack Cambodian government forces and even to kidnap and murder foreigners in an attempt to weaken the country's economy by discouraging foreign investment and tourism and thus perhaps pave the way for a return to power (*New York Times*, Feb. 6, 1995, A1). Although thousands defected from the Khmer Rouge to the government during the mid-1990s as part of an amnesty program, elements of the Khmer Rouge and much of its original leadership continued to survive, funded, it appeared, through the selling of gems and timber from Khmer Rouge–controlled territories to business interests in Thailand. Although many Cambodians perceived their government officials, though democratically elected, to be generally corrupt (enjoying relatively luxurious lifestyles in an otherwise impoverished nation), the Khmer Rouge leaders were often seen as brutal but honest and fervently nationalistic. Thus internal conflict was expected to persist in Cambodia for years to come (*New York Times*, Feb. 6, 1995, A1). According to David Chandler, Khmer Rouge guerillas continued to be armed in the northwestern area of the country, yet some 300,000 Cambodians were resettled in Cambodia from refugee camps in Thailand, and the Cambodian government allowed "local human rights organizations . . . to flourish" (2006, 97). Further elections were held in Cambodia in 1998 and 2004.

"During 1994–2004, economic growth averaged 7.1 percent per annum," based mainly on increasing "garment manufacturing and tourism" (World Bank 2006, 53). The shift to a more market-oriented economy coupled with "preferential access to the US and EU markets from the mid-1990s drove the growth of garment exports." Aspects of Cambodia (whose population was estimated at about 13.9 million in 2006), such as the Ankor temples, attracted many tourists, benefiting the growth of services related to tourism such as restaurants, hotels, transportation, and construction. Like growth in the garment industry, tourism-related development occurred primarily in urban areas. Poverty was estimated to have declined in Cambodia from 45 percent of the population in 1994 to 35 percent in 2004 (World Bank 2006, 17).

Summary and Analysis

The prime unifying motivation for revolution in Vietnam was the goal of throwing off perceived foreign subjugation. The Vietnamese people for hundreds of years manifested a desire for independence in rebellions and wars against a multitude of enemies, taking on and often defeating Chinese armies, the forces of Kubla Khan, and numerous other foes before the twentieth century. Vietnamese nationalism, although temporarily checked by the modern weaponry of Western nations, experienced a rapid resurgence in the 1920s and, heightened further by colonial repression, contributed greatly to the development of the revolution.

Frustrated nationalist aspirations, along with widespread economic hardships, were a major source of mass discontent and a basis for popular participation in revolution. Traditional inequalities present in Vietnamese society had occasionally spurred rebellions against the big landlords and the exploitation and oppression of the mandarin elite. In many ways the French colonization of Vietnam, while elevating a small percentage of the Vietnamese to great wealth and extending the benefits of Western education and technology to a larger minority, brought dislocation, a loss of self-sufficiency, and dependence on the world market to much of the peasantry. Many rural residents were transformed into propertyless tenant farmers, plantation workers, or mine or factory laborers. Downturns in the world economy meant lower prices for exports and hardships for those at the bottom of Vietnam's economic pyramid. Occupying powers so disrupted agriculture during World War II that mass starvation occurred in the northern half of Vietnam. This disaster greatly intensified hostility against the French and the Japanese and against those Vietnamese who supported the foreigners.

During the twentieth century a small percentage of Vietnamese obtained access to the French colonial educational system, and some even studied in France itself. After the 1920s at least three major divisions could be identified among the educated. First, French colonization had generated a small but significant Francophile elite among the Vietnamese, including large landowners, some members of the Catholic minority, officers in the Vietnamese colonial army, which was organized and trained by the French, and some businessmen. These individuals supported close ties with France, if not outright colonial status, and hundreds were granted French as well as Vietnamese citizenship. Most members of this group would transfer allegiance to the United States after the French defeat in the 1946–1954 war.

A second elite element claimed the title "nationalist" (that is, they claimed to be neither front men for a foreign power nor Communists) but were anti-Communists or at least non-Communists. Ngo Dinh Diem, wealthy and French educated, was viewed as a nationalist by virtue of his resignation from Emperor Bao Dai's French puppet administration during the 1930s. But Diem represented the limited appeal of this type of nationalist to most Vietnamese. Self-centered and dictatorial, he and his supporters manifested little interest in the welfare of the majority of the population and appeared even less concerned with paying attention to popular views and national aspirations. Reflecting this approach, the Diem regime not only did little to redistribute wealth toward the masses but even reversed land-distribution programs set in motion by the Viet Minh. The lack of a commitment to social revolution reduced the appeal of non-Communist nationalists to the peasants, and sponsorship by foreign powers undermined their claims to nationalism.

The third elite element to develop in Vietnam during the 1920s and 1930s was composed of Marxist-oriented, largely urban, middle-class, educated individuals who in 1930 unified most of their various groups into the Indochinese Communist Party. Ho Chi Minh did more than anyone else to organize the ICP and develop its basic revolutionary program. The ICP fused traditionally fierce and resilient Vietnamese nationalism with Marxist-Leninist concepts. The result was an ideology that called for both the defeat of "imperialism" (meaning the attainment of true independence for Vietnam) and the defeat of "feudalism" (social revolution involving redistribution of wealth and abandonment of the remaining oppressive aspects of Confucian culture). The Party's reform program, including land redistribution to poor and landless peasants, won broad support in the countryside and provided the basis, along with nationalism, for mass membership in organizations tied to and coordinated by the ICP. Eventually the ICP, accepting Ho Chi Minh's position, put primary emphasis on achieving independence from foreign domination.

During the period of revolutionary conflict, the antirevolutionary state apparatus was always flawed in terms of its legitimacy to govern the Vietnamese people because it was either the creation of some foreign power or dependent on foreign support for its existence. From the early 1930s to 1955, the playboy emperor, Bao Dai, occupied the role of puppet for whichever outside power was paying the bills. Diem, dependent on U.S. economic and military aid, which was used to suppress revolutionaries and Buddhist religious leaders alike, also failed to gain the respect, much less the support, of most Vietnamese. The succession of generals who followed Diem, including General Thieu during the period 1967–1975, had previously served in the French colonial army, and some succeeded in greatly enriching themselves during their periods of military and governmental service.

The coercive and administrative capabilities of the antirevolutionary state in Vietnam fluctuated over time. On paper these were high at the time of the victorious Communist offensive in 1975. Saigon had one million soldiers under arms and outnumbered its adversaries in the south by about 3 to 1. But South Vietnam's army was, especially by 1975, riddled with corruption. After the final departure of U.S. combat troops in 1973, the South Vietnamese economy went into a decline, deprived of its U.S. military customers for shop goods, bars, drugs, and prostitutes. Urban unemployment rose to 40 percent, and inflation increased. Many Saigon officers embezzled army funds and even charged "tolls" for other military units to cross through areas their garrisons controlled. By 1975 the large majority of South Vietnam's enlisted soldiers were not earning enough to support their families, and morale was low (Karnow 1983; Kolko 1985; Turley 1986). Once deprived of unconditional U.S. support, the Saigon government and military could hardly withstand the onslaught of highly motivated revolutionary forces.

The developing Vietnamese revolution experienced periodic "windows of permissiveness" regarding the larger world context and involvement of other nations in Vietnam's affairs. The 1936–1939 Popular Front government in France precipitated the release of many ICP members from Vietnamese prisons and presented an opportunity for the ICP to organize openly after earlier repression. The Japanese overthrow of French colonial authority in March 1945 provided the Viet Minh with a five-month period of relative freedom of movement in the countryside, during which base areas and the foundations of the revolutionary armed forces were securely established. The several weeks between the mid-August surrender of the Japanese and the arrival of Chinese and British (and later French) occupation forces provided the maximum favorable conditions for revolutionary insurrections. These were carried out with virtually no resistance from the demoralized Japanese in more than sixty Vietnamese cities. After that time, the huge coercive power of the French (400,000 Vietnamese killed during the years 1946–1954) and the even more massive military strength of the United States (over one million Vietnamese dead between 1956 and 1975) were inadequate to reverse a revolution that long before had succeeded in achieving widespread popular support. The steadily declining commitment of the U.S. government to supporting the Saigon regime after 1973 resulted in nonintervention during the spring 1975 Communist offensive and a relatively quick end to the military conflict.

Following almost twenty years of estrangement and sometimes overt hostility, the U.S. lifted its economic embargo against Vietnam in 1994, and in 1995 the two nations established diplomatic relations. Like China, Vietnam enacted market-oriented economic reforms and permitted foreign investment. As its economy grew at a strong pace in the early twenty-first century, Vietnam experienced new forms of corruption, increased criticism of government and Communist Party officials, and popular demands for greater democratization of its political system.

VIETNAMESE REVOLUTION: CHRONOLOGY OF MAJOR EVENTS

1847–1883 In a series of wars, French forces defeat the Vietnamese and establish control over Vietnam, Cambodia, and Laos; the French then call these countries French Indochina
1919 Ho Chi Minh proposal for Vietnamese autonomy rejected at Paris Peace Conference
1930 French suppress non-Communist Vietnamese nationalists; Vietnamese Communist Party (called the Indochinese Communist Party) founded
1940 France defeated by Germany; Japanese forces occupy Vietnam
1941 Communist-led nationalist movement, Viet Minh, established
1945 August revolution results in Vietnamese declaration of independence
1946–1954 French Indochina War, resulting in victory for the Viet Minh
1954 Geneva Peace Conference temporarily divides Vietnam
1954–1959 Diem becomes leader of South Vietnam and uses U.S. support to suppress opponents and prevent reunification
1960 Formation of the National Liberation Front
1963 Diem assassinated; Johnson becomes U.S. president after Kennedy assassination
1964 Gulf of Tonkin Resolution passed by U.S. Congress
1965–1973 Major commitment of U.S. armed forces to conflict in Vietnam
1968 Tet offensive increases antiwar sentiment in the United States
1975 Vietnam reunified
1994 United States lifts trade embargo
1995 United States and Vietnam establish full diplomatic relations
2000 U.S. President Bill Clinton becomes the first U.S. president to visit Vietnam since reunification
2005 Prime Minister Phan Van Khai makes the first visit by a Vietnamese leader to the United States since the end of the war
2006 Vietnamese economy continues rapid growth as national leaders promise intensified crackdown on corruption

References and Further Readings

Adams, Nina S., and Alfred W. McCoy. 1970. *Laos: War and Revolution*. New York: Harper & Row.

Bain, Chester A. 1967. *Vietnam: The Roots of Conflict*. Englewood Cliffs, NJ: Prentice-Hall.

BBC News, July 16, 2002. "Vietnam Officials Sacked for Mob Links." http://news .bbc.co.uk/2/hi/asia-pacific/2129842.stm.

_____, June 3, 2004a. "Vietnam Executes Gang Leader." http://news.bbc .co.uk/2/hi/asia-pacific/3772037.stm.

_____, June 3, 2004b. "Nam Cam: Vietnam's Godfather." http://news.bbc .co.uk/2/hi/asia-pacific/2794607.stm.

_____, July 18, 2005. "Vietnam Party Eying Capitalists." http://news.bbc .co.uk/2/hi/asia-pacific/4693449.stm.

_____, March 2, 2006. "Communist Debate Grips Vietnam." http://news.bbc .co.uk/2/hi/asia-pacific/4766846.stm.

_____, March 3, 2006. "Vietnam Shows Stance with Glitter Case." http://news.bbc .co.uk/2/hi/asia-pacific/4769946.stm.

_____, April 18, 2006a. "Crisis Dogs Vietnam Congress." http://news.bbc .co.uk/2/hi/asia-pacific/4917466.stm.

_____, April 18, 2006b. "Vietnam Party to Tackle Graft." http://news.bbc .co.uk/2/hi/asia-pacific/4917576.stm.

Bergerud, Eric M. 1991. *The Dynamics of Defeat: The Vietnam War in Hau Nghia Province*. Boulder: Westview Press.

Bourdet, Yves. 2000. *The Economics of Transition in Laos: From Socialism to ASEAN Integration*. Cheltenham, UK: Edward Elgar.

Butler-Diaz, Jacqueline, ed. 1998. *New Laos, New Challenges*. Program for Southeast Asian Studies Monograph series. Tempe: Program for Southeast Asian Studies, Arizona State University.

Chandler, David P. 1983. *A History of Cambodia*. Boulder: Westview Press.

_____. 1999. *Brother Number One: A Political Biography of Pol Pot*. Boulder: Westview Press.

_____. 2000. *A History of Cambodia*. 3rd ed. Boulder: Westview Press.

_____. 2006. "Cambodian Revolution." In DeFronzo, ed., *Revolutionary Movements in World History*, 1:91–98.

CIA. 2006. *The World Factbook: Vietnam*. http://www.cia.gov/cia/publications/ factbook/geos/vm.html (accessed June 19, 2006).

DeFronzo, James, ed. 2006a. *Revolutionary Movements in World History: From 1750 to the Present*. 3 vols. Santa Barbara, CA: ABC-CLIO.

_____. 2006b. "The Vietnamese Revolution." In DeFronzo, ed., *Revolutionary Movements in World History*, 3:912–30.

Duiker, William J. 1976. *The Rise of Nationalism in Vietnam, 1900–1941*. Ithaca, NY: Cornell University Press.

_____. 1983. *Vietnam: Nation in Revolution*. Boulder: Westview Press.

_____. 1995. *Vietnam: Revolution in Transition*. Boulder: Westview Press.

_____. 2000. *Ho Chi Minh*. New York: Hyperion.

Dunn, John D. 1972. *Modern Revolutions: An Introduction to the Analysis of a Political Phenomenon*. Cambridge, UK: Cambridge University Press.

Duong, Pham Cao. 1985. *Vietnamese Peasants Under French Domination, 1861–1945*. Monograph Series 24. Berkeley: Center for South and Southeast Asia Studies, University of California.

Elliott, Duong Van Mai. 1999. *The Sacred Willow: Four Generations of Life in a Vietnamese Family*. Oxford: Oxford University Press.

Etcheson, Craig. 1984. *The Rise and Demise of Democratic Kampuchea*. Westview Special Studies on South and Southeast Asia. Boulder: Westview Press.

Evans, Grant. 1998. *The Politics of Ritual and Remembrance: Laos since 1975*. Chiang Mai: Silkworm Press.

Giap, Vo Nguyen. 1962. *People's War, People's Army: The Viet Công Insurrection Manual for Underdeveloped Countries*. Praeger: New York.

Karnow, Stanley. 1983. *Vietnam: A History*. New York: Viking.

_____. 1990. "Hanoi's Legendary General Giap Remembers." *New York Times Magazine*, June 24.

Khanh, Huynh Kim. 1982. *Vietnamese Communism: 1925–1945*. Ithaca, NY: Cornell University Press.

Kolko, Gabriel. 1985. *Anatomy of a War: Vietnam, the United States, and the Modern Historical Experience*. New York: Pantheon.

Kurlantzick, Joshua. 2005. "Laos: Still Communist After All These Years." *Current History*, March, 114–19.

Lacouture, Jean. 1968. *Ho Chi Minh: A Political Biography*. New York: Random House.

Manyin, Mark E. 2003. *CRS Issue Brief for Congress: The Vietnam-U.S. Normalization Process*. Washington, DC: Congressional Research Service.

Marr, David G. 1971. *Vietnamese Anticolonialism: 1885–1925*. Berkeley: University of California Press.

McAlister, John T., Jr. 1969. *Vietnam: The Origins of Revolution*. New York: Knopf.

McNamara, Robert S. 1995. *In Retrospect: The Tragedy and Lessons of Vietnam*. New York: Random House.

Moise, Edwin E. 1983. *Land Reform in China and North Vietnam: Consolidating the Revolution at the Village Level*. Chapel Hill: University of North Carolina Press.

New York Times, April 6, 1989, A1, "Vietnam Promises Troops Will Leave Cambodia by Fall."

_____, April 9, 1989, A1, "Vietnam's Vietnam: Scars of Cambodia."

_____, April 9, 1989, E2, "Vietnam Still Lives Hand to Mouth, But Less Collectively."

_____, April 24, 1989, A1, "Vietnam, Drained by Dogmatism, Tries a 'Restructuring' of Its Own."

_____, July 19, 1990, A1, "U.S. Shifts Cambodian Policy; Ends Recognition of Cambodian Rebels; Agrees to Talk with Hanoi."

_____, July 19, 1990, A10, "Behind U.S. Reversal: Gains by Khmer Rouge."

_____, January 13, 1991, E3, "Cambodia's Uneasy Truce with the Future."

_____, November 21, 1994, A4, "In the Free Market, Vietnam's Poor Pay."

_____, December 5, 1994, A1, "Former Refugees See Opportunity in Vietnam."

_____, February 6, 1995, A1, "Rebels Still Torment Cambodia 20 Years After Their Rampage."

_____, April 9, 1995, 1, "McNamara Recalls and Regrets Vietnam."

_____, April 23, 1995, 12, "20 Years After Victory, Vietnamese Communists Ponder How to Celebrate."

_____, April 30, 1995, 1, "On Saigon's Day of Defeat, Glitter of Rebirth."

_____, July 2, 1995, 3, "Back in Vietnam, Boat People Both Sink and Swim."

_____, July 12, 1995, A1, "U.S. Grants Full Ties to Hanoi; Time for Healing, Clinton Says."

_____, July 30, 1995, 10, "Communism in Laos: Poverty and a Thriving Elite."

_____, August 6, 1995, 3, "In a War-Haunted Hanoi, U.S. Opens Formal Ties."

_____, October 10, 2002, A1, "Vietnam Seeking to Identify 300,000 MIAs from War."

Nualkhair, Chawadee. 2006. "Laos Votes with Eye on Anti-Poverty Goals." Reuters, April 30. http://go.reuters.com.

Popkin, Samuel L. 1979. *The Rational Peasant: The Political Economy of Rural Society in Vietnam.* Berkeley: University of California Press.

Race, Jeffrey. 1972. *War Comes to Long An: Revolutionary Conflict in a Vietnamese Province.* Berkeley: University of California Press.

Stuart-Fox, Martin. 1997. *A History of Laos.* Cambridge, UK: Cambridge University Press.

_____. 1999. "Laos: From Buddhist Kingdom to Marxist State." In *Buddhism and Politics in Twentieth Century Asia,* ed. Ian Harris, 153–72. London: Continuum.

_____. 2001. *Historical Dictionary of Laos.* 2nd ed. Lanham, MD: Scarecrow Press.

_____. 2002. *Buddhist Kingdom, Marxist State: The Making of Modern Laos.* Bangkok: White Lotus.

_____. 2006. "The Lao Communist Revolution." In DeFronzo, ed., *Revolutionary Movements in World History,* 2:529–38.

Tai, Hue-Tam Ho. 1983. *Millenarianism and Peasant Politics in Vietnam.* Harvard East Asian Series 99. Cambridge, MA: Harvard University Press.

Time, April 30, 1990, 18, "Vietnam: Fifteen Years Later."

Turley, William S. 1986. *The Second Indochina War: A Short Political and Military History, 1954–1975.* Boulder: Westview Press.

Turner, Robert F. 1975. *Vietnamese Communism: Its Origins and Development.* Hoover Institution Publication 143. Stanford, CA: Hoover Institution Press, Stanford University.

Wasserstrom, Jeffrey N. 2002. "Waiting for China's Lech Walesa." *Current History,* September, 256–58.

Werner, Jayne Susan. 1981. *Peasant Politics and Religious Sectarianism: Peasant and Priest in the Cao Dai in Viet Nam.* Monograph Series 23. New Haven, CT: Yale University Southeast Asia Studies.

Wolf, Eric. 1969. *Peasant Wars of the Twentieth Century.* New York: Harper & Row.

Woodside, Alexander B. 1976. *Community and Revolution in Modern Vietnam.* Boston: Houghton Mifflin.

World Bank. 2005. "Accelerating Rural Development in Vietnam." http://siteresources.worldbank.org/vietnam/resources_vietnam_brochure18aug05.pdf (accessed May 7, 2006).

_____. 2006. "Cambodia: Halving Poverty by 2015? Poverty Assessment 2006." http://www.worldbank.org.

Zasloff, Joseph J. 1973. *The Pathet Lao: Leadership and Organization.* Lexington, MA: Lexington Books.

Selected DVD, Film, and Videocassette Documentaries

See "Purchase and Rental Sources" at the end of this volume for information on how to obtain the following resources and for full names of media companies and other organizations listed here as abbreviations.

Cambodia: Return to Year Zero. 1993. 60 min. Video. AFSC. Analysis of UN Peace Plan for Cambodia.

Cambodia: Year 10. 1989. 45 min. Video. AFSC. Interesting analysis of U.S. and British involvement in Cambodia's civil war.

From the Killing Fields. 1990. 50 min. Video. AFSC. Peter Jennings analyzes the civil war in Cambodia and U.S. involvement.

Guerrilla Warfare: Vietnam. 1997. 46 min. Amazon.com. Masters of War Series: General Vo Nguyen Giap versus General William Westmoreland.

Guns, Drugs and the CIA. 1988. PBS-Frontline. Possible connections between the CIA and drug trafficking in Southeast Asia and Central America.

Hearts and Minds. 1974. 112 min. Color film. UMICH, UT-D. Award-winning documentary of the effects of the Vietnam War on both the Vietnamese and American peoples. This film should be preceded by lecture or reading material on the factors that led to the Vietnam conflict.

Ho Chi Minh. 1968. 26 min. Black-and-white film. UMINN, UWISC-M. CBS documentary on the life of Ho Chi Minh.

Ho Chi Minh. 1998. 50 min. BIO. Life of the leader of the Vietnamese Revolution.

LBJ and Vietnam. 100 min. BIO.

Passage: Journeys from War to Peace. 60 min. PBS. Impact of the war on the Vietnamese.

Pol Pot. 50 min. BIO. Life of the Khmer Rouge leader.

Pol Pot's Shadow. 2002. 60 min. PBS Frontline.

The Road from Kampuchea. 1998. 44 min. FRIF. Aiding the Cambodian people.

S21: The Khmer Rouge Killing Machine. 2002. 105 min. FRIF.

Time of the Locust. 1966. 13 min. Black-and-white film. FRIF. U.S., Japanese, and National Liberation Front coverage of the violent conflict in Vietnam.

Vietnam: A Chronicle of War. 89 min. Amazon.com. Extended CBS documentary history of U.S. involvement in Vietnam.

Vietnam: An Historical Document. 1975. 56 min. Color film. UARIZ, UC-B, USF, UIOWA, KSU, PSU. CBS documentary history of U.S. involvement in Vietnam.

Vietnam: A Television History. 1983. 60 min. per part. Color video. 13 parts. Parts 1–12 available from UIOWA, PSU, Films Inc; part 13 from PSU, Films Inc. This highly acclaimed series includes: 1—Roots of War; 2—First Vietnam War, 1946–1954; 3—America's Mandarin, 1954–1963; 4—LBJ Goes to War, 1964–1965; 5—America Takes Charge, 1965–1967; 6—America's Enemy, 1954–1967; 7—Tet, 1968; 8—Vietnamizing the War, 1968–1973; 9—No Neutral Ground: Laos and Cambodia; 10—Peace Is at Hand, 1968–1973; 11—Homefront USA; 12—End of the Tunnel; 13—Legacies.

Vietnam: Faces of Development. 1994. 24 min. Video. AFSC. Vietnam in the 1990s.

Vietnam: The Ten Thousand Day War. 1980. Color film. 26 parts. Part 1 available from UI, ISU; Parts 2–26 from IU. America in Vietnam. Part 1, 55 min.; Parts 2–26, 26 min. each. 1—America in Vietnam; 2—France in Vietnam; 3—Dien Bien Phu; 4—Early Hopes; 5—Assassination; 6—Days of Decision; 7—Westy's War;

8—Uneasy Allies; 9—Guerrilla Society; 10—Ho Chi Minh Trail; 11—Firepower; 12—Village War; 13—Airwar; 14—Siege; 15—TET!; 16—Frontline America; 17—Soldiering On; 18—Changing the Guard; 19—Wanting Out; 20—Bombing of Hanoi; 21—Peace; 22—Prisoners; 23—Unsung Soldiers; 24—Final Offensive; 25—Surrender; 26—Vietnam Recalled.

Vietnam: The Vietnam Conflict. 1998. CNN Cold War Series, Episode 11. 46 min. Truman Library.

The World Below the War. 1996. NAATA. Vietnamese live underground to escape the fighting.

Year Zero: The Silent Death of Cambodia. 1979. 60 min. Video or color film. AFSC. Describes Khmer Rouge attainment of power, policies, and resulting conflict.

5

THE CUBAN REVOLUTION

In the 1950s, as the United States became increasingly involved in Vietnam, the nearby island nation of Cuba was torn by civil war. Many Cubans took up arms in the hope of winning a fairer distribution of the island's wealth for the poor, while others aimed primarily at establishing a truly democratic political system. Of critical significance for the success of the revolution, however, was the unity of virtually all the revolutionaries and their supporters in the goal of ridding Cuba of the corrupt Batista dictatorship, a regime widely viewed as an antidemocratic protector of the economic status quo and, perhaps most important, as the mechanism through which foreign interests dominated and exploited the Cuban people.

The Cuban Revolution had important consequences not only for the Cuban people but also for the United States, the other countries of the Americas, and even, in certain ways, other parts of the world. The success of the movement led by Fidel Castro resulted in the establishment of the first predominantly socialist economy in the Western Hemisphere. Radical social change and the coercive measures utilized to achieve change polarized Cuban society. A majority of Cubans, craving social justice, inflamed by nationalist fervor, and inspired by Castro's charismatic leadership, supported the revolution (Aguila 1988; 1994; Quirk 1993; Szulc 1986). A minority, disproportionately urban upper- and middle-class in composition, objected to aspects of the revolutionary program and especially to the dominant role of the Communist Party. Since 1959 more than one million Cubans have left their homeland.

The revolution, however, succeeded in virtually eliminating the desperate poverty characteristic of most Latin American countries and in providing hundreds of thousands with educational opportunities, medical services, and other benefits that they never would have enjoyed without the overthrow of the Batista government. These accomplishments contributed to consolidating the support of most of the island's working and peasant classes for the postrevolutionary government and its policies and the development of a relatively strong and resilient sociopolitical system (Aguila 1988; 1994).

Cuba's success in providing the large majority of its population with essential needs undoubtedly contributed significantly to explaining the country's phenomenal achievements in the world of sports, as evidenced by its fifth-place finish in total medals at the conclusion of the 1992 Olympics in Barcelona (after Russia, the United States, Germany, and China, and with more than ten times as many medals as the next highest and much more populous Latin American nations, Brazil and Mexico [*Hartford Courant*, Aug. 10, 1992, D6]). Cuban dominance among Latin American countries continued through later Olympics in 1996, 2000, and 2004.

The Cuban regular armed forces, including reservists, were estimated in the 1990s to number about 300,000, with an additional 1,300,000 men and women in militia units. But by 2006 the active forces had been reduced to an estimated 46,000, with "39,000 reservists and a militia of at least one million" (International Institute for Strategic Studies 2005). During the 1970s and 1980s more than 50,000 Cuban troops and military advisors were deployed around the world, most notably in Angola, where they helped turn back military forces of the then-white minority government of South Africa (Aguila 1994; PBS 1985). Apart from military personnel, thousands of Cuban doctors, nurses, teachers, and engineers, whose expenses and salaries were paid by the Cuban government, served as volunteers in at least twenty-five developing countries. This program, which provided much aid over a number of years to African peoples, began in 1963, when fifty-three Cuban health workers arrived in Algeria (Gott 2004, 221). The goodwill that Cuba enjoyed from many other nations was in great part responsible for Fidel Castro's election to the presidency of the Organization of Non-Aligned States ("non-aligned" in the sense of not being a member of a formal alliance with either the United States or the USSR).

In the early 1990s, immediately after the fall of the Communist Party–dominated governments in Eastern Europe and the end of most of the assistance Cuba had previously received from these societies, the island nation was under greater economic and political pressure than at any time since the 1960s. But in the second half of the 1990s, despite the U.S. Helms-Burton Act of 1996, which was intended to discourage foreign companies from doing business with Cuba, its economy began to recover, benefiting from investment from other nations, increased tourism, money sent by Cuban-Americans to their relatives on the island, and, in the first decade of the twenty-first century, Venezuelan oil provided to Cuba by Hugo Chavez's leftist government.

Without a doubt, Cuba has been the subject of world attention and controversy far out of proportion to its physical size or its population. This chapter will address a number of important questions: Why did the revolution succeed in Cuba? Why did the revolution lead to the domination of the Communist Party? How has Cuba affected, assisted, and reacted to revolutionary movements in other societies? What effects did the fall of the European Communist Party states have on Cuba? How did the Cuban system adapt to the loss of aid from its former allies? What role did Cuba play in the transnational revolutionary movements of the twenty-first century?

GEOGRAPHY AND POPULATION

Cuba has a land area of 42,803 square miles (110,860 square kilometers—about the same size as Pennsylvania) and a population in 2006 of about 11.4 million. The island, 90 miles (145 kilometers) south of Key West Florida, is 744 miles (1,197 kilometers) long, with an average width of 60 miles (97 kilometers). The nation's capital is Havana, which has about 2.1 million residents. According to the Cuban census, about 51 percent of Cubans are of mixed racial ancestry ("mulatto"). Eleven percent are classified as of African ancestry, 1 percent as Asian, and 37 percent of European origin (Aguila 1994). Unlike several other Latin American societies, no indigenous subcultures exist in Cuba. The health and educational levels of the Cuban population improved significantly after the revolution. By 2006 about 97 percent of the population was literate, the infant mortality rate was 6 per 1,000 live births, and life expectancy was about 77 years. These statistics were comparable to those of advanced European societies.

PREREVOLUTIONARY POLITICAL HISTORY

Columbus discovered Cuba in 1492 on his first voyage to the New World. The Spanish settlers forcibly recruited thousands of Taino Arawak Indians, the indigenous people of Cuba, to work mining gold and clearing land for agriculture. As harsh conditions of servitude, poor nutrition, and diseases transmitted by the Spanish rapidly depleted the indigenous population, African slaves were brought to Cuba. Early agriculture involved tobacco and later coffee, but after war and rebellion had disrupted the economies of French colonies in the Caribbean, wealthy migrants established large sugar plantations in Cuba and spurred a rapid increase in the importation of slaves. From 1792 to 1821, 250,000 slaves passed through Havana customs, and an estimated 60,000 were brought in illegally (Wolf 1969). Unsuccessful slave rebellions occurred in 1810, 1812, and 1844. The African heritage of the slaves blended with Spanish culture, so that later the Cuban government described the nation's overall culture as Afro-Latin.

When other Spanish colonies were gaining their independence in the 1820s, many Cubans preferred to remain under Spanish military occupation. Because at the time the majority of Cuba's population was black,

members of the dominant European minority might have feared that without the assistance of the Spanish army they would be overwhelmed in a
slave rebellion. Cuba's independence movement did not gain support until
the last third of the century, when Cubans of European ancestry were clearly
a majority of the island's inhabitants. But Spain's loss of its major colonies
strengthened its determination to retain control of Cuba as a valuable trade
and military asset.

A reformist movement, which developed in the early 1860s, was motivated in part by the desire of "Creole" planters (agriculturalists born in
Cuba) to gain greater economic influence on the island. After negotiations
with Spain failed, a group of planters in Cuba's easternmost province, Oriente, demanded total independence. The reasons given to justify the rebellion included Cuba's lack of effective political representation in the Spanish
parliament (the Cortes), limitations on freedom of speech and other civil
rights, an unfair tariff system that put Cuban planters at a disadvantage,
and discrimination against native-born Cubans in business and government.
The rebel group also called for an end to slavery, upon which the wealthiest
planters, located in the western more often than in the eastern part of the
country, depended for their prosperity. In 1868 a ten-year war of independence broke out. But because of arguments among rebel leaders, lack of
support from the United States, and strong resistance by Spanish forces, the
conflict—after the loss of more than 200,000 Cuban and Spanish lives—
ended in stalemate (Aguila 1988).

Martí and the Struggle for Independence

After 1878, Spain introduced some reforms and abolished slavery. But many
Cubans continued to crave full independence. A second war (1895–1898)
was inspired in part through the efforts of Cuban writer José Martí
(1853–1895). Martí was born in Havana, the son of Spanish immigrants.
He enthusiastically embraced the cause of Cuban independence and at seventeen was sentenced to six years at hard labor for writing pro-independence
literature. After serving a few months, he was exiled to Spain, where he
earned university degrees in law, philosophy, and literature. Martí returned
to Cuba in 1878, after the Pact of Zanjón had ended ten years of warfare.
But since he immediately resumed pro-independence activities, Spanish authorities again expelled him. Martí settled in New York and worked as an
art critic for the *New York Sun* (Ruiz 1968).

During the period Martí lived in the United States (1881–1895), he
wrote prolifically and inspired many others who later would lead Cuba
through the struggle for independence. At first he extolled capitalism and
found fault with the labor movement. But after 1883 some of Martí's views
changed. Witnessing the hardships of U.S. workers and experiencing deprivation himself, he became critical of the capitalist society of his era and

CUBA

much more favorable toward labor unions. Martí supported some of the ideas of Karl Marx and praised Marx's concern for the welfare of workers. Martí expressed the belief that poverty, racism, and other forms of oppression could and should be eliminated. One of his favorite sayings was "I will stake my fate on the poor of the earth" (Ruiz 1968, 67). And Martí expressed fear of possible U.S. economic imperialism toward Cuba. But according to most scholars, Martí never became a Marxist revolutionary. His first passion was to liberate Cuba. Whatever plans he had for social revolution would presumably have followed the achievement of independence. Because Martí's views changed in reaction to his experiences, the full range of his writings contain contradictory concepts and attitudes. Consequently, later Cubans with diverse and even conflicting political and economic philosophies could find some support for their particular ideologies in Martí's works (Ruiz 1968; Szulc 1986).

Martí's nationalism led him to land in eastern Cuba in 1895 in an effort to join rebel guerrilla groups. He was soon killed in an ambush. Despite Martí's death, a new war for Cuban independence was under way. The Spanish army erected fortified barriers to seal off one part of the country from another and forcibly relocated much of the rural population to special camps or to the cities in an effort to separate independence fighters from civilian supporters (Wolf 1969). Rebel forces burned sugar plantations in the western part of Cuba to deprive Spain and its supporters of revenues. Tens of thousands on both sides perished in the conflict. But by 1898 the Spanish army had been driven from most of the rural areas. Many Cubans felt that through their sacrifices Spain had been defeated and would shortly be forced to withdraw.

At that point the United States, motivated by popular support for the rebels, reports of Spanish atrocities, a desire to protect U.S. interests in Cuba, and, finally, the sinking of the battleship *Maine* while it was visiting Havana harbor, entered the war. Once U.S. naval forces destroyed the Spanish fleet, Spain's armies could not be resupplied and were quickly forced to surrender. As a result of the Spanish-American War, the United States assumed control of Cuba, the Philippines, and Puerto Rico.

When President William McKinley requested the authority to "end the hostilities between the government of Spain and the people of Cuba," Congress approved the measure, but only after attaching the Teller amendment, which asserted that the United States would not attempt to "exercise sovereignty, jurisdiction or control" over Cuba once peace was restored (Aguila 1994, 17). The occupation forces, however, established a military government, which then restructured Cuba's economic, administrative, and political systems. Of critical significance was U.S. encouragement of the rehabilitation and expansion of Cuba's sugar industry. A number of Cuban political figures argued that Cuba would be locked into a dependent status if a "monoculture" based on sugar were revived and extended. They advocated greater diversification in agriculture and in the economy in general so that Cuba would become economically self-sufficient instead of tied to an external market for sale of a single crucially important crop. Through sugar, however, foreign investors in good times could obtain sizable returns on their capital, and Cuban growers could earn foreign currency with which to purchase luxury items from other nations.

After bringing about significant improvements in health, education, sanitation, public administration, and finance, U.S. authorities turned over the reins of government. But before granting Cuba independence in 1902, the U.S. Congress forced Cuban political leaders to incorporate the so-called Platt amendment into their constitution. The amendment, drafted by Senator Orville Platt and Secretary of State Elihu Root as part of an army appropriations bill, declared that the United States could exercise the right to intervene for the preservation of Cuban independence and for the maintenance of a government capable of protecting life, property, and individual liberty (Ruiz 1968; Szulc 1986). The Platt amendment also prevented Cuba from contracting any foreign debt that could not be serviced from existing revenues, barred Cuba from entering into treaties with other governments that compromised its sovereignty, and gave the United States the right to buy or lease land for naval facilities (Wolf 1969). Although some Cubans supported U.S. involvement in Cuba and even requested U.S. military interventions, many others deeply resented the Platt amendment and the growing U.S. role in Cuba's economy and political life. Under terms of the Platt amendment, the United States intervened militarily in Cuba during the years 1906–1909, 1912, and 1917 to protect business interests or to reestablish order (Aguila 1988; 1994). Frustrated Cuban nationalism and widespread abhorrence of corrupt and authoritarian regimes perceived as prostituting the nation for the benefit of foreigners would in the mid-twentieth century constitute the overwhelming unifying emotional sentiment welding Cubans of diverse backgrounds into a powerful revolutionary coalition.

Discontent and the Emergence of Batista

Following several unstable governments, the candidate of the Liberal Party, Gerardo Machado, a popular veteran of the independence war, was elected president in 1924. Machado had promised voters that he would work for the elimination of the Platt amendment and free the government of corruption. But after his election Machado dropped his campaign to abolish the Platt amendment, financed his corruption-plagued projects with loans from U.S. financial institutions, and in general was compliant in relation to U.S. business interests (Ruiz 1968). In 1928 Machado had the national congress, which was under his control, change the constitution to permit him to win an additional six-year presidential term. Supported by the army and U.S. business interests, he instituted a repressive and bloody dictatorship (Aguila 1988; 1994).

The negative effects of the Great Depression on the Cuban economy intensified popular protest against Machado's regime. Middle-class reformers, students, and professors from Havana University and many workers, whose unions were often led by members of the growing Cuban Communist Party, joined forces against the dictatorship. As disorders and violence reached extraordinary levels, the Franklin Roosevelt administration intervened and convinced Machado to resign in order to restore stability. Once Machado was out, frenzied mobs attacked and killed many of his supporters, who were accused of torture and murder. Machado's successor, Carlos Manuel de Céspedes, was quickly overthrown by a coup of noncommissioned officers led by a sergeant, Fulgencio Batista. The soldiers supporting Batista had been outraged by pay cuts, troop reductions, and other grievances.

Batista initially supported a five-man revolutionary government led by a professor of physiology at Havana University, Ramón Grau San Martín. The revolutionary government attempted to enact reforms, such as establishing the eight-hour workday, cutting utility rates, granting land to some poor peasants, limiting land purchases by foreigners, taking control of some foreign-owned properties, and mandating that a minimum of 50 percent of a factory's employees be Cuban citizens (some employers imported foreign workers willing to work for less pay). These reforms were strongly opposed by the Cuban upper class and U.S. business interests. Grau, an anti-Communist, also faced opposition from the Communist Party. And the Roosevelt administration refused to recognize his government. After serving in office for four months, Grau, under pressure from Batista, who declined to continue supporting a government opposed by the United States, resigned on January 15, 1934.

Following Grau's resignation and the cancellation of certain reforms, the U.S. government, stating that political stability had returned to Cuba, abolished the Platt amendment. But many Cubans came to feel that the 1933 rebellion, like that of 1895, had failed to achieve its most important goals of eliminating corruption, significantly redistributing wealth, and freeing Cuba from foreign control. This perception was to foster both further mass discontent and elite dissidence. Some of those craving more significant reforms formed the Auténtico Party, which pledged to make an "authentic revolution," faithful to the concepts of José Martí.

With Batista holding real power through control over the army, Cuba was governed by a succession of puppet presidents until 1940. After a new constitution was enacted, Batista defeated Grau in what historians regard as a free election (Aguila 1988; 1994; Perez-Stable 1993; Ruiz 1968; Szulc 1986). As the new constitution limited the presidency to a single four-year term, Batista could not succeed himself. He was followed by the Auténtico administrations of Ramón Grau (1944–1948) and Carlos Prío (1948–1952). These governments enacted some reforms in agriculture, education, and labor but avoided measures that could be viewed as challenging U.S. business interests; the administrations were themselves characterized by massive graft, political patronage, and theft and abuse of public funds.

In protest, a leading charismatic though emotionally unstable Cuban senator, Eduardo Chibás, quit the Auténtico Party in 1947 in order to organize a new reform movement, the Orthodoxo Party, which Chibás claimed was dedicated to the true (orthodox) principles of the Cuban hero Martí. Chibás, who formulated the slogan "honor against money," exposed corruption through his very popular weekly radio program. Despite the fact that many viewed him as the probable victor in the 1952 presidential election, Chibás, apparently bitterly disappointed by the failure of colleagues to provide him with the evidence needed to prove, as he had promised the public, a charge of corruption, shot himself during a broadcast in August 1951 (Ruiz 1968). The Orthodoxo Party continued to campaign for reform and still might have won the 1952 elections, including the congressional seat sought by a young activist lawyer, Fidel Castro. But before the elections could be held, the army, again under Batista's leadership, seized power. Batista installed an authoritarian regime, which lasted until he fled Cuba on New Year's Day, 1959.

ECONOMY AND SOCIAL CLASSES

Sugar came to represent over 80 percent of Cuban exports, most of which went to the United States. In the 1950s U.S.-owned companies controlled nine of the ten largest sugar mills and twelve of the next twenty in size and accounted for almost 40 percent of the island's sugar crop (Wolf 1969). U.S. businesses also had hundreds of millions invested in utilities, manufacturing, mining, and oil refineries (Aguila 1988; 1994). Organized-crime figures based in the United States played a significant role in casinos and hotels in Havana, which was a major international gambling resort before the revolution (PBS 1985).

Approximately 160,000 Cubans were employed by U.S.-owned businesses, and 186,000 worked for the Cuban government. The regularly employed nonagricultural working class included about 400,000. Another 250,000 people worked as waiters, servants, entertainers, and gift shop proprietors and in other occupations serving tourists and well-to-do Cubans. The poorest stratum in urban Cuba included several hundred thousand underemployed or part-time workers (Wolf 1969). Official statistics indicated that during the period 1943–1957, national unemployment averaged 20 to 30 percent (Amaro and Mesa-Lago 1971). As a result of consumer-price increases, real per capita income fell during much of the decade preceding the revolution (Ruiz 1968).

The Cuban economy, prone to suffer from fluctuations in the world market price for sugar, was ranked fifth among Latin American countries in per capita income. Other measures of development during the 1950s, such as life expectancy (about 60 years), infant mortality rate (32 per 1,000 live births), and literacy (between 75 and 80 percent literate), all placed Cuba among the top five Latin American societies before the revolution (Aguila 1988; Ruiz 1968; Wolf 1969). But the island's wealth was unevenly distributed, fostering a feeling of social injustice. Although in 1956 the per capita income for Cuba's then approximately 6 million people was 336 pesos, the majority of rural families (representing about 44 percent of the population) survived on about 90 pesos. Eight percent of the farms controlled 75 percent of the farmland (and 0.5 percent, mostly large sugar concerns and cattle ranches, held one-third of the land). Eighty-five percent of the farms had only 20 percent of the land (Aguila 1988; 1994).

Medical personnel, hospitals, teachers, and schools were concentrated in urban areas, where most of the wealthy and middle class resided. The illiteracy rate in the countryside was approximately 42 percent; it was about 12 percent in the cities. In rural areas about 500,000 were employed as sugarcane cutters and 50,000 as sugar mill workers. Between sugar harvests, all the cane cutters were laid off, as were two-thirds of the mill workers. During the periods of unemployment, many rural families subsisted in part on raw sugarcane. Sugar workers who desired to end the debilitating cycle of seasonal unemployment constituted a major source of support for the revolutionary government after the 1959 victory (Wolf 1969). In general, perception of foreign dominance and exploitation of the Cuban economy, high unemployment, declining real income for many in the 1950s, and the poverty of the rural population all contributed to the growth of mass discontent preceding the revolution.

Several social scientists have argued that Cuba never developed a large, independent native capitalist class because of the dominant role played by U.S. business interests and the dependency of many Cuban capitalists on U.S. financial institutions (Wolf 1969). Furthermore, both Cuba's upper class and its middle class, which together appear to have constituted perhaps 25 percent of the population, were generally enamored of U.S. lifestyles and culture. Members of the Cuban middle class were often unsatisfied with their status and yearned to be rich. Highly educated Cubans, trained mainly in the legal and medical professions, often turned to government for employment and enrichment. Some without sugar holdings viewed political office, with its access to public moneys and opportunities for graft, as their only potential source of wealth (Ruiz 1968). By the 1950s so many politicians had failed the public trust that government officials received little respect from the general population, a fact that constituted a critical flaw in the prerevolutionary state apparatus.

Upper- and middle-class Cubans were disproportionately represented among practicing Catholics. Unlike the case in other Latin American countries, the Catholic Church in Cuba was relatively weak and did not provide an effective bond among the island's various classes and social groups. Although most Cubans were nominally Catholic, only about 10 percent practiced their religion (Ruiz 1968). Part of the reason for the Church's limited influence was the fact that the Church in Cuba was Spanish dominated and during the nineteenth century had opposed Cuban independence, which provoked harsh criticism by José Martí and alienated much of the Cuban people. Martí further accused the clergy of being unconcerned with the plight of Cuba's rural poor. Even in the 1950s the large majority of Cuba's eight hundred priests were Spaniards and very conservative (*New York Times*, May 15, 1987, A4). The Catholic Church was especially weak in rural Cuba, particularly among Afro-Cubans.

The subordinate social and economic status of mulattoes and blacks was a major reason why many nonwhite Cubans became prominent in two rather distinct institutions, the army and the Communist Party. The prerevolutionary army had originally been organized by occupation authorities early in the century and was trained and equipped by the United States. As was the case with most armies in Latin America, it functioned not to defend Cuba from foreign enemies but to preserve order and, by and large, protect traditional institutions and the interests of the privileged classes. The Cuban armed forces, which numbered about 40,000 in 1958, provided a source of steady employment, relative economic security, and an opportunity for social mobility for lower-income groups.

Following Batista's takeover of the army in 1933, 384 of its 500 officers resigned, in great part because they were unwilling to accept a mulatto commander (Batista was of Chinese, African, Amerindian, and European ancestry). Batista then granted commissions to 527 enlisted men, expanded the army, and increased military pay levels (Ruiz 1968). After 1933 about one-third of the officers were Afro-Cuban. Under Batista, the army was often not as directly responsive to conservative upper-class interests as in the past. Batista occasionally supported limited reforms that benefited the poor or organized labor but that did not threaten the basic interests of the upper class. Consequently, many nonwhite Cubans identified positively with Batista before the late 1950s. The army, however, because of its origin as a product of occupation, its hindering of major reforms proposed by leaders of the 1933 revolution against Machado, and its use of repressive measures, which greatly intensified during the 1950s, was generally unpopular with many Cubans (Ruiz 1968).

In the 1860s Spanish political refugees had introduced socialist concepts in Cuba. After the 1917 Bolshevik Revolution, Leninist ideas began to spread among some Cuban intellectuals and within the working class. In 1925 several union activists joined militant students from Havana University to form the Cuban Communist Party. A popular university student leader, Julio Antonio Mella, became the Party's first secretary-general. Despite the fact that the Machado regime outlawed the Communist Party and apparently paid assassins to murder Mella, the Party grew in membership and influence (Ruiz 1968). The success the Party enjoyed was due to worker frustration with corrupt business and government officials, the exploitive conditions under which many Cubans labored, and the fact that Communists generally proved to be among the most effective union leaders in their ability to win improvements from management and government.

The Communists gained thousands of members from among Cuba's especially impoverished nonwhite population. Afro-Cuban Communist leaders included Lázaro Peña, the most powerful labor leader in the island's history; Blás Roca Calderío, ideological spokesperson for the Party; and Jesús Menéndez Larrondo, who headed the Sugar Workers' Federation until he was assassinated in 1947 (Ruiz 1968). The Communists were able to obtain about 10 percent of the vote in the 1946 legislative elections. But the level of membership and public support varied over time, stemming from a combination of factors, such as periodic government repression and the occasional willingness of Party leaders to compromise principles for short-term political gains. The Communist Party generally supported Batista during the 1930s and early 1940s and especially discredited itself by accepting Batista's military regime in the 1950s, with some Party members even serving in the dictator's government. Most of the Communist leadership initially refused to support Fidel Castro's movement to get rid of Batista by force of arms, claiming that it would result in useless bloodshed; those people did not endorse Castro until 1958, when the revolution was clearly gaining momentum (Aguila 1988; Ruiz 1968; Szulc 1986).

REVOLUTION

Fidel Castro and the M-26-7 Movement

Fidel Castro was born in 1926 in the town of Biran in eastern Cuba. His father, Angel Castro y Argiz, was a Spanish immigrant who became a peddler selling lemonade and other items to sugar workers and their families. With his savings he rented and later purchased land to grow sugar. Eventually the Castro holdings amounted to some 26,000 owned or permanently rented acres (Szulc 1986). Fidel's mother was his father's second wife, Lina Ruz Gonzalez, who had worked as a maid or cook in the Castro household and was at least twenty-five years younger than her husband. Lina was illiterate until well into adulthood and, though religious and devoted to her five children (Fidel was the third), did not marry Angel until several years after Fidel's birth.

Fidel, competitive and physically active, studied and played with the children of the rural poor at the little country school near his home. He later recalled realizing that his barefoot classmates would soon leave school and that their parent's impoverishment would condemn them to lives of ignorance and abject poverty. Castro claimed this early experience set him on the path toward becoming a revolutionary. After a few years Fidel was enrolled in a Jesuit-run private school in Santiago. Later he entered Cuba's best preparatory school, Belén College, in Havana. At Belén, Jesuit instructors, who were usually conservative politically, considered Castro perhaps the most intelligent student and certainly the best all-around athlete in his class. But although prone to rebelliousness, Castro claims he knew little of political parties and their ideologies until he entered law school at Havana University (Szulc 1986).

At the university, political activity was intense. Major activist organizations included the student branch of the Communist Party and two reportedly revolutionary but anti-Communist armed groups, the MSR (Socialist Revolutionary Movement) and the UIR (Insurrectional Revolutionary Union). These organizations and others competed for control of the student government. Physical intimidation, beatings, and even assassinations occurred. Because the university was autonomous and self-governing, neither the army nor the police could enter the campus (Szulc 1986). The fact that so many of the children of Cuba's educated classes were drawn to revolutionary groups at the university and passionately devoted to radical change reflected the acute elite discontent in the nation. That discontent was to be a critical element in the development and success of the revolution. Once Castro became involved in politics on and off campus, he, like other student activists, often carried a gun.

Although not yet twenty-one years old but already recognized as an eloquent speaker, Castro was invited (the only university student asked), along with six senators, ten congressmen, and about eighty other government and business figures, to the May 15, 1947, founding of the Orthodoxo Reform Party. Although Castro claimed he became interested in Marxist socialist concepts during his third year at the university, he felt that the Cuban Communist Party was too politically isolated to garner the popular support necessary to bring about revolutionary change. He preferred to work with the Orthodoxos because of their greater potential mass appeal and the greater freedom of action this course allowed him. His younger brother Raúl, in contrast, decided to join the Communists.

After passing law school exams, Fidel started handling cases for lower-income people in Havana. He built a base of support that appeared to assure him election to congress on the Orthodoxo ticket in the scheduled 1952 elections. Castro claimed he intended to work within the democratic system and campaign for high public office. He would have then used his political and oratorical skills to prepare the Cuban people gradually for the advent of a socialist economic system, which he had become convinced was necessary for the welfare of the large majority of the island's population (Szulc 1986; Quirk 1993).

Batista's seizure of power before the 1952 elections could be held changed Castro's plans. Fidel, Raúl, and a number of other militant activists decided to resort to armed insurrection. Over a number of months scores of young working-class people, many with only a primary education, met for training sessions with university-educated radicals to organize an attack on Batista's

army. The target was the Moncada barracks in Santiago at the eastern end
of the island, about 533 miles from Havana. The participants hoped to surprise the base's approximately four hundred soldiers and seize its store of
weapons. After distributing captured arms to supporters in Santiago, the
rebels planned to take the city and call for a general uprising against Batista
throughout the island.

On the morning of Sunday, July 26, 1953, about 125 men and women
crowded into sixteen automobiles and drove to the Moncada complex. Unfortunately for the attackers, they immediately encountered an army patrol.
When firing broke out, soldiers in the base were alerted. Several of the rebels
were killed in the fighting, more were captured, and the rest fled. During the
next few days almost all the rebels were caught, and about half were executed. The Castro brothers had the good fortune to be captured by a squad
under the command of Afro-Cuban Lieutenant Pedro Manuel Sarria Tarta-
bull, who, despite the demands of some of his men and the anticipated displeasure of several of his superiors, refused on ethical grounds to kill the
surrendering rebels. (Years later Sarria would be arrested for refusing to fight
against Castro's new rebel band. But after the 1959 victory Sarria was promoted to captain and proclaimed a "Hero of the Revolution" [Szulc 1986].)

Castro was brought to trial. But at his defense he delivered a stinging indictment of the dictatorship, governmental corruption, and social ills of
Cuba, ending with the words "History will absolve me." Fidel was sentenced to fifteen years imprisonment. The Castro brothers were confined to
the maximum-security prison on the Isle of Pines. Feeling secure in power
and hoping to improve his public image, Batista declared an amnesty and
freed the Moncada rebels after they had served one year and seven months
(Szulc 1986). The Castro brothers and several associates, fearing assassination by Batista agents and impeded in efforts to organize a new rebel organization while they remained in Cuba, left for Mexico, Raúl on June 24 and
Fidel on July 7, 1955.

Shortly after arriving, Castro announced formation of the 26th of July
movement (M-26-7), which included several Orthodoxo Party members,
liberals, socialists, and some Communist Party members (although Party
leaders had condemned both the Moncada attack and plans for armed revolution). Castro soon contacted the Cuban-born Alberto Bayo, a guerrilla-
warfare expert who had served in the Spanish Civil War with the Republican
forces against the conservative Spanish military and its Italian and German
Fascist allies. Castro convinced Bayo that it was his patriotic duty to help
prepare the members of M-26-7. While a training base was being established, Castro traveled to the United States and addressed anti-Batista Cuban
exiles in New York and Florida. He raised thousands of dollars for the purchase of weapons, supplies, and a wooden, hurricane-damaged thirty-eight-
foot yacht, the *Granma*, to transport his revolutionaries to Cuba.

"Che" Guevara and the Lesson of Guatemala

In Mexico the Castro brothers met a young Argentine physician, Ernesto (later nicknamed "Che") Guevara. After becoming a specialist in allergies (he suffered from asthma himself), Guevara had traveled from Argentina to several other Latin American countries. Che became possibly the most radical of the revolution's central figures. Before joining M-26-7, he had lived in Guatemala, where an elected government was attempting progressive reforms (Gott 2004). Mass protests followed by an army coup in 1944 had toppled a brutal military dictatorship. Genuinely free elections resulted in the overwhelming victory of a government under the leadership of President Juan José Arevalo, a former university professor, who was dedicated to improving the lot of the poor. Arevalo's reforms offended wealthy conservative interests, which repeatedly tried to overthrow him. He left office in March 1951 worried that fascism, though militarily defeated in Europe in World War II, permeated Latin America and was even growing stronger there (Schlesinger and Kinzer 1982). Arevalo was succeeded in office by the second democratically elected president, Jacobo Arbenz Guzmán, one of the officers who had overthrown the previous dictatorship.

President Arbenz enacted a sweeping land-redistribution program that involved parceling out uncultivated acreage to poor peasants. A major target for land appropriation was the United Fruit Company, based in Boston. The Arbenz government confiscated over 300,000 unused acres from United Fruit (which planted only 15 to 20 percent of its approximately 600,000 acres annually), offering to pay compensation, which the company considered inadequate. The Eisenhower administration became convinced that the Arbenz government was influenced by Communists and a threat to U.S. interests. The CIA proceeded to recruit several hundred conservative opponents of Arbenz, arm them, and provide them with a mercenary air force, flown by U.S. pilots, and a CIA-run radio station to broadcast false news reports intended to demoralize and disorganize Arbenz supporters. Some Guatemalan generals were persuaded either to support the 1954 CIA-sponsored invasion or simply not to resist it. Arbenz was forced to resign and flee the country. The right-wing military governments that followed Arbenz murdered many of his supporters, reversed some of the reforms, and engaged in repressive measures for decades to prevent the growth of leftist revolutionary or reform movements (*New York Times*, Apr. 9, 1994, E5; July 24, 1994, 3; Gleijeses 1991; Schlesinger and Kinzer 1982; Streeter 2000a; 2000b; 2006).

Guevara was present in Guatemala and witnessed firsthand the overthrow of an elected progressive government. The tragedy of Guatemala undoubtedly convinced many who supported change in Latin America that future U.S. administrations would most likely again take advantage of the vulnerabilities inherent in open democratic systems in poorer, less-powerful states and, through the CIA, frustrate disagreeable policies or even destroy elected governments. Guatemala convinced Guevara of the "necessity" for armed struggle. It also taught him a lesson about Latin American armies. He felt that the Guatemalan army had deserted and betrayed Arbenz. Guevara concluded, and emphasized to Castro, that a revolution could not be secure until the armed forces were purged of conservative, corrupt, and unreliable officers and soldiers and brought firmly under revolutionary control.

Revolutionary Struggle

On November 25, 1956, eighty-two men set sail aboard the *Granma* for a landing in Oriente Province in eastern Cuba. The bad weather and mechanical problems that delayed their arrival by two days until December 2 led to failure to connect with a waiting supply party on shore and inability to coordinate with a planned uprising by the M-26-7 underground in Santiago. Within a few days the rebel band was betrayed by a peasant guide, who helped an army unit stage a successful ambush. Most in the landing party were killed, captured, or dispersed. At least sixteen survivors, including the Castro brothers and Guevara, reassembled in the Sierra Maestra (mountain range). With help from friendly peasants and reinforcements from Santiago and from among the local rural population, the rebel army began to grow.

In the mountains many of the peasants were small landowners who had settled there to avoid having to work as farmhands or seasonal employees for the big landholders. Though economically more independent than the sugarcane workers, they were subject to bullying and other forms of exploitation by Batista military units (Szulc 1986; Wolf 1969). Many were inclined to support the rebels but at first were reluctant because the army executed peasants who assisted Castro's guerrillas.

The rebels followed the policy of releasing captured Cuban soldiers who were only doing what they perceived to be their patriotic duty. The guerrillas, however, regularly executed captured military personnel guilty of murder, rape, or torture, as well as any civilians who informed on revolutionary forces to the army (Szulc 1986; Wolf 1969). The rebels tended to fight harder than their opponents because they were aware that they would most likely be tortured and executed if captured, whereas the army's enlisted soldiers knew their lives would be spared if they surrendered. Tactics used by the guerrillas involved high mobility, attacking vulnerable military outposts that could be looted for weapons, staging ambushes in terrain unsuitable for heavy weapons, and relying on peasant supporters for information regarding enemy troop movements. As peasants witnessed the defeats suffered by the dictator's army and learned of the revolutionaries' plans for land reform, schools, and health care, more were encouraged to join or assist the rebel forces. Eventually, most Batista army units refused to venture into the hostile mountains.

Soon after the rebel landing, Batista announced that Fidel Castro had been killed. To expose this falsehood the rebels invited *New York Times* reporter Herbert Mathews to the Sierra Maestra to interview Castro in February 1957. The interview brought Castro to the attention of the U.S. media as a patriot fighting against a brutal and corrupt dictatorship. Castro appeared to be a non-Marxist, moderate nationalist with U.S.-style democratic ideas. Although he displayed hostility to the U.S. government for providing bombers, weapons, and munitions to Batista, he claimed the rebels wanted friendship with the United States. Publicity from the interview provided hope and encouragement for rebel sympathizers throughout the country.

M-26-7 organized a National Directorate with Castro at its head; it included representatives from both urban-movement units and rural guerrilla bands, united to achieve the goal of ousting the Batista regime. The urban resistance appeared genuinely more moderate in political goals and plans for social change and often was more middle- and upper-class in composition than the rebel guerrilla bands in the mountains. One of the several anti-Batista revolutionary groups outside of Castro's M-26-7 was the urban-based Revolutionary Directorate (DR). The members of the DR, which was anti-Communist, were drawn from university students and the middle class. On March 13, 1957, the DR launched an unsuccessful assault on the National Palace in Havana in an attempt to kill Batista. Thirty-five DR members died at the palace, and scores of others were hunted down, tortured, and killed.

Throughout 1957–1958 urban assaults against the dictatorship met with defeat and bloody suppression, which probably both promoted the success of the revolution and increased the likelihood of a radical outcome. First, urban repression eliminated some of the moderate revolutionary leaders, making Fidel Castro an even more dominating figure. Second, defeats in the cities made the rural guerrilla strategy seem more effective and intelligent, bestowing greater prestige on this wing of the revolution. Third, torture and killing by Batista security forces provoked immense popular outrage and alienated much of the middle class from the Batista government, since the victims were often from this class. The carnage, coupled with perception of Batista's unpopularity and a lack of appreciation for Castro's plans for sweeping social change, also resulted in the U.S. Eisenhower administration's stopping arms shipments to Batista's military in March 1958, although Batista's planes were still allowed to refuel at the U.S. naval base at Guantanamo while on bombing missions against the rebels (Szulc 1986, 438–39). Eisenhower's action not only contributed to creating a severe state crisis for Batista's regime through accelerating the deterioration of army and government morale but also essentially constituted the advent of a permissive stance of the U.S. government toward the developing revolution.

The M-26-7 urban units planned to precipitate Batista's fall by means of a general strike set for April 9, 1958. When large-scale participation in the strike failed to materialize, partly because organizers kept the strike date secret until the last moment, the urban moderates in M-26-7 lost much of their remaining political influence (Szulc 1986). Meanwhile, the rebel units in the mountains were scoring repeated successes. The morale of the Cuban army was sinking because of the defeats in the Sierra Maestra and the U.S. cutoff of new weapons to the Batista government. Other demoralizing factors probably included growing popular opposition to the army, the sympathy of a number of soldiers for the revolution, the disgust of many at the brutality of some of their fellow soldiers, and the knowledge that many officers were corrupt. Several officers refused to go into combat against the rebels and even organized mutinies against Batista. Partly as a result of the army's deteriorating confidence and spirit, Batista's 1958 summer offensive against the rebels failed miserably.

In the fall Castro ordered two guerrilla units, with a total of 230 combatants, under the command, respectively, of Che Guevara and Camilo Cienfuegos, to advance into the lowlands. Remarkably, the army withdrew in the face of the oncoming rebels. At the end of December Guevara's force was victorious at the city of Santa Clara, about 168 miles east of Havana, the first major city taken by the rebels, while Castro's forces surrounded Santiago and negotiated a surrender of the city's garrison on December 31, with the troops being placed under Castro's command (Szulc 1986). Batista fled the country on January 1, 1959.

REVOLUTIONARY CUBA

When Castro assumed control of Cuba in January 1959, he enjoyed the enthusiastic support of the great majority of the Cuban people. He invited anti-Batista moderates and liberals to join with M-26-7 in organizing a provisional government under his leadership. The new government soon increased the wage levels of workers and lower-middle-class employees. In May an agricultural reform act limited the size of farm holdings to a maximum of 966 acres, with sugar, rice, and cattle-raising enterprises allowed to be as large as 3,300 acres (Szulc 1986). This measure destroyed the very large landholdings (latifundia), including U.S.-owned sugar properties, several of which exceeded 400,000 acres. Land was distributed to tens of thousands of rural workers, and support for the revolution increased throughout the countryside. A literacy campaign sent an estimated 100,000 young volunteers to rural areas in 1961 to teach people to read and write (Gott 2004, 189). The government also began building hundreds of new schools and training thousands of additional teachers. Similarly, new clinics and hospitals were constructed, many in rural areas where such facilities had been almost nonexistent. Private beaches and resorts were opened to the entire public. All these changes were immensely popular with most Cubans.

Szulc claims that Castro decided to attempt developing Cuba into a Marxist-Leninist one-party state during 1959 or even earlier. Castro's reasons apparently included the belief that a centrally controlled government was necessary to counter anticipated U.S. opposition to his planned socio-economic changes (Szulc 1986; Ruiz 1968). Castro viewed the U.S. government as capitalist dominated and was sure that it would not easily accept the establishment of a socialist economic system in Cuba not only because of the negative impact on U.S. investments there, but also out of fear that other Latin American countries might follow Cuba's example. Castro's experience with self-seeking and corrupt political figures in Cuba and the country's shifts between elective politics and pro-U.S. dictatorships probably convinced him that a multiparty democratic system would be too vulnerable to economic and military pressures from the United States or to covert actions by the CIA, such as the bribery, intimidation, or assassination of key leaders ("The CIA Hit List" 1975). Another factor influencing Castro's decision was his belief that Marxist-Leninist-style socialism could solve Cuba's socioeconomic problems, such as its high levels of inequality, unemployment, crime, and corruption (Ruiz 1968). Control of Cuba's government by a revolutionary party would enable major structural social change to be carried out quickly.

Castro and many of his associates felt that past revolutions had bitterly disappointed the economic and nationalist aspirations of most Cubans. In contrast, the new revolutionary government's rapid redistribution of wealth rallied enthusiastic support for the revolution among the majority of Cuba's rural and urban populations. Revolutionary leaders concluded that a nationally owned (rather than foreign-dominated) economic infrastructure would give Cuba the ability to resist economic control from other countries more effectively. The possibility that Cuba, having alienated the United States, might become economically dependent on the USSR seemed less onerous because the Soviet Union was very distant and presumably could not exercise the same level of control over Cuba as the military and economic giant only ninety miles away.

By the end of 1959 the more radical elements from Castro's M-26-7 movement had consolidated control over the Cuban army. This accomplishment involved the removal of conservative officers and soldiers and the trials and executions of about 550 Batista military and police personnel accused of murder and torture. The firing squads offended some North Americans but won the strong approval of the thousands of Cubans whose family members or friends had suffered Batista's repression (Quirk 1993; Szulc 1986; PBS 1985). Members of M-26-7 also assumed positions in the government bureaucracy. During 1959 Castro held negotiations with leaders of the Communist Party; his goal was to fuse his M-26-7 movement and their organization to create a new Communist Party under his leadership.

Revolutionary Instruction Schools were established not only to train young recruits in how to run revolutionary institutions but also to teach Marxist-Leninist concepts and interpretations of Cuban history (Szulc 1986). Castro concealed his plans to transform Cuba into a Communist Party–dominated state in an attempt to delay the expected furious opposition from the United States and to provide time to strengthen the revolutionaries' control over the army and prepare the Cuban people psychologically to accept the new system. Later Castro cited Martí's advice to revolutionaries that to achieve desired goals, deception must sometimes be used because to state those goals openly might provoke powerful opposition that revolutionaries might not yet be able to overcome. When in April 1961 Castro revealed to the Cuban people that the revolution was going to result in socialism, he used Martí's demands for social justice and the elimination of poverty and racism as the basis for the proclamation.

When moderates in the provisional government, M-26-7, and the rebel army realized that the revolution was moving toward a socialist economy and a political system dominated by a rejuvenated Communist Party, they began to resign in protest. Castro condemned such resignations as counterrevolutionary and called upon supporters to stage mass demonstrations. Some opposed to Castro's plans launched a new guerrilla war in the Escambray Mountains in central Cuba. The counterrevolutionary guerrillas included former Batista soldiers, some landowners opposed to the agrarian reform, a number of individuals with rightist political views, and even some disillusioned former rebel army members, all loosely bound together under the banner of anticommunism (Szulc 1986). They numbered as many as five thousand in the early 1960s, but the revolutionary government was able to mobilize many times more men and women. Castro sent tens of thousands of revolutionary militia into the mountains, positioning one person every few hundred yards along trails and roads. This made movement of opposition forces extremely difficult, except in small groups, and most of the weapons and supplies the CIA airdropped to them fell into the hands of Castro's people. In a few years, the counterrevolutionary guerrilla threat was eliminated.

In the cities, hundreds of thousands joined neighborhood Committees for the Defense of the Revolution (CDRs) to carry on organized surveillance, which brought an end to violent attacks on the government in urban areas. In the 1980s an estimated 66 percent of the total population and over 80 percent of adults belonged to CDRs (Aguila 1994; Szulc 1986). The efforts of the revolutionary armed forces and the CDRs were aided by Castro's intelligence service, which had agents placed in virtually every counterrevolutionary group. Several hundred thousand discontented Cubans, mostly urban upper- and middle-class individuals and families, left Cuba in the first half of the 1960s. Castro's program of "exporting dissent" reduced security problems but also hurt the economy because many of those who departed possessed important skills.

U.S. REACTIONS TO THE REVOLUTION

In April 1959 Fidel Castro visited the United States and expressed a desire for friendship and continued trade. But by late 1959 the CIA began sending weapons to anti-Castro guerrillas in the Escambray Mountains. And by mid-1960 the Eisenhower administration had decided to organize and arm an exile military force to overthrow Castro's government (Quirk 1993; Szulc 1986; Wyden 1979). In September 1960 the CIA recruited several U.S. Italian-American organized-crime figures, formerly involved in Havana casinos, to assassinate Castro. It is very possible that Eisenhower and later presidents were not specifically informed of plans to kill Castro; the CIA often neglected to inform a president about a controversial operation in order to give him "plausible deniability" if the matter ever came to light (Szulc 1986).

During 1959 the revolutionary government began buying arms for its new army, purchasing 25,000 rifles, fifty million rounds of ammunition, and 100,000 grenades from Belgium, and mortars, cannons, and heavy machine guns from Italy. The United States would not sell Cuba weapons and soon pressured Western European countries into refusing arms sales. Revolutionary Cuba could then only obtain military equipment from the Soviet Union and its Eastern European allies. According to Szulc (1986), the first weapons from Czechoslovakia and the USSR began reaching Cuba in late 1960, several months after President Eisenhower had severed economic relations. Deliveries of jet military aircraft began in mid-1961, after the U.S.-organized "Bay of Pigs" invasion of Cuba had failed.

When the revolution succeeded in January 1959, the Soviet Union was at first not very enthusiastic about Castro's government because for years Cuba's Communist Party had portrayed Castro as an irresponsible adventurer precipitating pointless bloodshed before objective conditions were right for revolution. But certain events during the year 1960 greatly increased Soviet interest in aiding Cuba (Szulc 1986). First, relations with the United States worsened markedly following the downing of a U.S. U-2 spy plane over the Soviet Union. As tensions increased, the Soviets quickly recognized that given their significant inferiority to the United States in nuclear weapons and delivery systems, Cuba could be a valuable strategic asset. Furthermore, in 1960 the ideological conflict between the USSR and the People's Republic of China became public knowledge. The Soviets and the Chinese were thereafter in competition for influence among less-developed countries. Cuba provided the USSR an opportunity to demonstrate its concern with aiding a developing nation attempting to free itself from what its revolutionary leaders viewed as imperial domination.

As ties between Cuba and the USSR were developing, Cuban relations with the United States rapidly worsened. In June 1960 oil refineries in Cuba owned by U.S. citizens, under pressure from the U.S. government, refused to refine crude oil delivered to Cuba from the Soviet Union. Cuba, in turn, nationalized the refineries and all remaining U.S. properties. The United States then cut its purchase of Cuban sugar by 95 percent; it soon imposed a virtually complete economic embargo and for years convinced all Latin American countries except Mexico to refuse trade with Cuba. Cuba responded to scarcities with a rationing system intended to ensure that basic commodities were directed toward families with the greatest need, generally those with the most children.

The Bay of Pigs invasion, a major attempt to overthrow the revolutionary government, was initiated by the Eisenhower administration. By the latter half of 1960 the CIA had recruited hundreds of anti-Castro Cuban exiles and established bases for them in Guatemala (Gott 2004). The plan, in fact, was modeled on the CIA's successful 1954 overthrow of the elected reform government in Guatemala. Some CIA instructors evidently promised many of the exiles direct U.S. military intervention, apparently assuming that Nixon, a strongly anti-Communist conservative and Eisenhower's vice president, would be elected president instead of Kennedy in fall 1960 (Wyden 1979).

After Kennedy was elected, the CIA informed the new president of the invasion plan and attempted to convince him to approve it (Quirk 1993; Wyden 1979). The agency suggested that if Kennedy refused to let the invasion go forward, he would be seen as a weakling unwilling to confront a Communist threat, perhaps encouraging more revolutions in Latin America. Furthermore, the CIA misinformed the president, evidently through mistaken intelligence, that Castro was no longer popular and an invasion would spark mass uprisings against him. This erroneous view may have resulted from the agency's relying too heavily on the opinions of middle- and upper-class exiles, among whom Castro was certainly unpopular. The revolution, however, was immensely popular with other sectors of the population, and Castro was apparently strongly supported by a large majority (Quirk 1993; Szulc 1986; Wyden 1979). Besides 25,000 in the regular army, 200,000 had volunteered to join militia forces all over the island and trained day and night to learn how to use newly arrived Soviet weapons. When the invasion, preceded by the detentions of several thousand Cubans suspected of counterrevolutionary activity, occurred, no uprisings materialized. Kennedy, also incorrectly informed that the Cuban air force would be destroyed before the assault, gave the go ahead, but on the condition that once the landing force was deposited on Cuban soil, there would be no direct U.S. military involvement.

The CIA signed up Cuban-American-owned ships to transport the invasion force and assembled a secret air force composed of a number of B-26 World War II–era twin-engine bombers, with Cuban-exile air crews, along with several pilots on loan from the Alabama Air National Guard (four U.S. pilots were shot down and killed in the assault). Cuban air force markings were put on the CIA planes so that it would appear during the invasion that the country's own pilots had mutinied and joined the counterrevolutionary attack. The function of the CIA air force was both to provide air support for the invasion and to destroy the small Cuban air force on the ground through bombing attacks. Two days before the invasion, eight CIA B-26s conducted a raid on Cuban airfields. After the attack the CIA attempted to stage a false defection by having an anti-Castro Cuban impersonate a Cuban air force pilot. Wearing a Cuban uniform, he landed his B-26 in south Florida and announced that he had defected and bombed his own air base on the way out. The purpose of the charade was probably to persuade the U.S. public that Castro was so unpopular that the loyalty of his armed forces was disintegrating, and perhaps to confuse or demoralize the Cubans. But the revolutionary government quickly pointed out that the front ends of its few B-26s were Plexiglas, whereas on the falsely defecting plane the front end was metal, a detail the CIA had apparently overlooked (Quirk 1993; Szulc 1986; Wyden 1979).

After the CIA bombing raid, which destroyed five planes, the Cuban air force consisted of eight operational aircraft, including four British-made Sea Fury light attack bombers (propeller driven), one B-26, three T-33 jet trainers, and seven pilots. Unknown to the CIA, the Cubans had been able to equip the T-33 jets with two 50-caliber machine guns each and used them as fighter interceptors during the invasion to destroy or drive off the CIA's B-26s. The Sea Fury bombers were directed against the invasion transport ships, sinking or disabling two and forcing the others to flee, thereby isolating more than 1,300 counterrevolutionaries on the beach (more than one hundred of these would be killed, along with about 160 defenders [Gott 2004, 194]).

Following the raid, on April 16, 1961, Castro publicly proclaimed for the first time that Cuba's revolution was a socialist one. He had planned to make the announcement in a speech on May 1, but realizing the invasion was about to occur, he made the statement just before the April 17 landing. Later Castro said that he felt those who were preparing to give their lives in defense of the revolution had the right to know what they were fighting for (Szulc 1986).

Immediately attacked by local militia forces and then surrounded by thousands of Cuban army and militia, cut off from resupply or evacuation and with its air force neutralized, the invasion brigade surrendered after about forty-eight hours. Later, more than 1,100 members of the brigade were sent back to the United States in return for about $53 million worth of medicine and food. The successful defeat of the Bay of Pigs invasion further consolidated Castro's revolution by demonstrating that it had given Cuba the strength to defeat U.S. intervention. Cuban nationalism soared, and Castro's popularity was greater than ever. On December 1, 1961, Castro went beyond his April speech to announce that Cuba would proceed along a "Marxist-Leninist" course of development (Szulc 1986).

The Soviet Union, taking advantage of Cuba's fear of another invasion, perhaps directly involving U.S. armed forces, offered to station nuclear missiles in Cuba, precipitating the October 1962 Cuban Missile Crisis (Gott 2004). The Kennedy administration demanded that the missiles be removed and placed a naval blockade around the island. The USSR, at the time weaker than the United States in nuclear military capability and fearing world war, withdrew the missiles. The Kennedy administration, for its part, pledged that the United States would not invade Cuba. But the CIA recruited scores of brigade veterans and other Cuban exiles; they waged a secret war of infiltration and sabotage against Cuba through the early 1970s and continued efforts to assassinate Castro (Brenner 1988; "The CIA Hit List" 1975; PBS 1985; Szulc 1986).

CUBA AND REVOLUTION IN LATIN AMERICA

The Quest for a Continental Revolution

The success of the Cuban Revolution in resisting U.S. economic and military pressures encouraged revolutionaries throughout Latin America. Many came to Cuba to train in guerrilla tactics. The United States, which for its part had trained and armed thousands of soldiers of rightist governments in Latin America, intensified its efforts, adding specialized counterinsurgency instruction to its military aid programs.

The Kennedy administration also launched a major economic assistance project, the Alliance for Progress, intended to improve the life of the poor, increase the size of the middle class in Latin American societies, and support the efforts of anti-Communist reform movements, especially the region's Christian Democratic parties, to accomplish constructive social change. The alliance contributed to significant improvements in education, health, and housing but failed to achieve most of its objectives. It did succeed in raising the expectations of millions of the disadvantaged, thereby helping to generate frustrations when expectations were inadequately gratified, and it threatened the interests of ruling elites. These consequences, coupled with the continuing threat of violent revolution, probably brought about the overthrow of democracies by conservative military leaders in Brazil (1964), Argentina (1966), Peru (1968), Chile (1973), and Uruguay (1973). The fear of Cuban-style revolutions was undoubtedly a major factor motivating several U.S. administrations to provide recognition and military and economic assistance to these conservative dictatorships despite their elimination of democratic systems and their human rights violations, which some observers characterized as state terrorism.

Several leaders of the Cuban Revolution initially called for a "continental revolution" to liberate all of Latin America from "imperialism" and social injustice. Che Guevara became the major public proponent of this concept through his speeches and his widely read works, *Guerrilla Warfare* (1960) and *Guerrilla Warfare: A Method* (1963) (Guevara 1985). Guevara, along with the French philosopher Regis Debray (1967), formulated the so-called theory of the guerrilla *foco*. The *foco* concept contradicted the policies of the established Marxist-Leninist leadership around the world regarding the justifiability and prospects for success of revolutionary violence to accomplish structural change and redistribution of wealth. The leaders of the Soviet Union, China, and most Communist parties took the position that violent revolution was not justifiable and could not be successful if the society in question had a democratic political system. In such a situation, in which there was at least a theoretical possibility that a revolutionary party or leaders could be elected to power, people would likely view individuals who resorted to violence as terrorists, and armed revolutionaries would be unable to achieve popular support and, therefore, unable to win.

Furthermore, traditional Marxist thinking held that political work among the population had to precede any armed revolutionary effort, even if a society was governed by a rightist dictatorship rather than by an elected government. The notion was that the people had to be educated about the desirability and possibility of revolutionary change and organized into mass-support networks before revolutionary war commenced. Only in a situation in which the revolutionaries enjoyed the support of a majority of their countrymen and -women could they hope to overcome the superior weaponry of the ruling element's professional army. Finally, Russia's Lenin, China's Mao, and Vietnam's Giap all stated that the revolutionary armed forces must be under the leadership of the nation's "revolutionary political party."

In contrast, Guevara argued that in a society in which the majority of the people suffered from extreme economic inequality, the injection of an armed revolutionary band of as few as thirty to fifty combatants could, through violent attacks on the state's instruments of repression, create the objective conditions necessary for a successful revolution. Guevara and Debray claimed that even if the majority of a nation's population was apathetic and culturally conditioned to view deprivation as unavoidable, the actions of the guerrilla *foco* would gain people's attention and begin to make them aware that their rulers were not all-powerful but were vulnerable to popular resistance. Once having "awakened the people," many of whom would tend to identify positively with the revolutionaries who were striking against the rich or hated army or police officials, the guerrillas would spread their concept of revolution. Eventually they would convert a majority of the nation's people to the desirability of the revolution's goals. Popular support would constitute the necessary condition for revolutionary victory. Because virtually all the Communist parties of Latin America criticized the guerrilla *foco* concept, revolutionaries following Guevara's strategy would have to proceed, at least in the beginning, without the support of their nation's supposedly revolutionary party.

In his 1960 work, *Guerrilla Warfare*, Guevara stated that his approach was applicable to Caribbean-style personalist dictatorships, which openly used violent repression and which no citizens really accepted as democratic governments. But in his 1963 book, *Guerrilla Warfare: A Method*, he argued that the *foco* strategy could work in almost any Latin American country, even those that were formally (in Guevara's thinking, superficially) democracies but in reality dominated by wealthy oligarchies. In November 1966 Guevara entered Bolivia under a false identity and formed a guerrilla *foco* with a number of Cubans, who had also infiltrated Bolivia, and Bolivians. Guevara thought that Bolivia provided good physical terrain for guerrilla warfare and that if he were successful, it could serve as a base of operations for similar efforts in several of the countries it borders. However, the Bolivian Communist Party refused to endorse his effort. And many of the Bolivian peasants his guerrillas encountered were not inclined to support the "outsiders." After a few months Bolivian rangers, trained and assisted by U.S. military and CIA advisors, wounded, captured, and executed Guevara. A few of the Cubans were able to escape to Chile and eventually made it back to Cuba. In 1997 Guevara's remains were located, retuned to Cuba, and reburied at Santa Clara, Cuba, the site of his greatest victory during the Cuban Revolution.

The Attempt at Democratic Revolution in Chile

Cuba's seemingly unqualified support for leftist guerrilla movements in the 1960s, which according to Gott (2004, 231) reached a "high tide" at the January 1966 Havana Tricontinental Conference attended by revolutionaries from around the world, created a host of problems for Castro's government. Many Latin American governments used Cuba's aid to revolutionaries as the reason for participating in the U.S. economic embargo. To demonstrate displeasure with some of Castro's policies, both foreign and domestic, the Soviet Union slowed oil shipments to Cuba in the late 1960s. Possibly because of this pressure and because of Guevara's failure in Bolivia, Castro declared in the early 1970s that Cuba recognized alternative paths to socialism. Local conditions could dictate methods other than armed revolution. In particular Castro expressed his willingness to support the attempt of Salvador Allende to achieve a socialist revolution in Chile through democratic means.

Allende, leader of the Socialist Party, had obtained a plurality (36.3 percent) of the vote for president on September 4, 1970, in a three-way race. He had been the candidate of the Popular Unity coalition involving the Socialist, Communist, and Radical parties and was a self-avowed Marxist (though not a Marxist-Leninist in the sense that he did not advocate a one-party state). Since he had not received more than 50 percent of the popular vote, Allende was not formally elected until seven weeks later, when many Christian Democrats joined Popular Unity legislators in voting for Allende in a joint session of the Chilean Senate and Chamber of Deputies (Davis 1985; Oppenheim 1993; Petras and Leiva 1994; Valenzuela 1978). Allende's dream was to establish socialism in Chile not through armed revolution but through elections in a multiparty democratic political system. He was committed to preserving the multiparty system and to allowing opposition political forces to express their positions through the mass media. Allende and Popular Unity anticipated that the improvements and greater social equality they planned to bring to Chile would win the electoral support of the majority of Chileans.

But President Allende faced enormous and, in the end, insurmountable obstacles. The economy was dominated by domestic capitalists opposed to his government and by foreign corporations, which owned copper mines, 70 percent of the Chilean telephone company, and other significant investments (Davis 1985). The Nixon administration, outraged at Allende's election, proceeded to wage economic warfare against Chile (greatly restricting aid, trade, and credit) to generate scarcities and hardships intended to increase the Chilean people's discontent with the Allende government. The CIA engaged in covert operations, such as the financing of opposition media, political parties, and even violent right-wing extremist groups that carried out acts of terrorism such as the murder of army commander General Schneider, who supported the democratic constitution and refused to block Allende's election (Davis 1985; Oppenheim 1993; Petras and Leiva 1994; "The CIA Hit List" 1975). The Chilean army, which continued to receive assistance and training from the Nixon administration, was generally under conservative leadership hostile to Allende. Those high-ranking officers who supported Allende or were firm defenders of the country's democratic constitution were gradually removed from positions of effective authority through various means, including pressure from the rightist generals.

The Allende government enacted reforms that benefited working-class and poor Chileans and nationalized the foreign-owned copper mines, which won widespread approval. But many well-to-do Chileans opposed Allende's plans to extend the role of state-owned enterprises in the country's economic system (Oppenheim 1993; Petras and Leiva 1994). And growing economic difficulties adversely affected the lifestyles of middle- and upper-class Chileans, many of whom rallied against the Popular Unity government. In the 1971 municipal elections Popular Unity received slightly more votes than the combined Christian Democrat and National (conservative) party opposition, and in 1973, despite worsened economic conditions, Popular Unity received about 44 percent of the vote in congressional elections. But a major weakness of Popular Unity was that it never achieved the clear and stable support of a majority of Chilean voters.

Allende did not have the opportunity to utilize the second half of his six-year term to build more support for Popular Unity. On September 11, 1973, the armed forces overthrew the Allende government and Chile's democratic constitution, ending the longest continually functioning democratic political system in the history of South America. The presidential building was hit with bombs and rockets; as a result, Allende apparently committed suicide rather than surrender. Many other Chileans died resisting the military takeover.

Through the 1970s international human rights monitoring groups gave Chile's conservative military dictatorship one of the worst ratings in the world. General Augusto Pinochet's regime even carried out assassinations of critics in Argentina, Italy, and the United States (Dinges and Landau 1980; Freed and Landis 1980). Finally, General Pinochet, perhaps overestimating his popularity outside of his circle of conservative advisors and friends, permitted a plebiscite on October 5, 1988 (*New York Times*, Oct. 7, 1988, A1). By an official tally of 55 to 43 percent, Chilean voters rejected extending the general's presidency for another eight years. This outcome led to a multicandidate presidential election in December 1989. The Socialist Party did not field its own candidate but rather backed the nominee of the Christian Democratic Party, Patricio Aylwin. Aylwin easily defeated the candidate favored by the military and was inaugurated in 1990 as Chile's first civilian president since the 1973 armed forces takeover. But the constitution, originally drafted under the auspices of the Pinochet dictatorship, provided for a continued role of the military in overseeing the Chilean government. The Christian Democrat–Socialist alliance again won the presidency in 1993 with the election of Christian Democrat Eduardo Frei Jr. but seemed unable or unwilling to amend the constitution significantly, punish human rights abusers, or challenge the economic domination previously achieved by powerful domestic and foreign corporations during the period of direct military rule.

The tragic and violent overthrow of Allende's Popular Unity movement provided yet another bitter lesson to those who favored peaceful and democratic means for accomplishing revolutionary change in Latin America. And just as U.S. economic pressure and CIA intervention in Guatemala had influenced Cuban revolutionaries in the early 1950s, similar actions in the early 1970s against Chile's elected government had a significant impact on revolutionaries who achieved victory in Nicaragua in 1979 (see chapter 6).

Cuba and Revolutions in Latin America and Africa

During the 1970s and 1980s Cuba provided training and weapons to the Sandinista revolutionaries, who achieved power in Nicaragua in summer 1979, to leftist rebels in El Salvador, and to anticolonial leftist revolutionaries who came to power in Angola after the Portuguese withdrew in 1975. Estimates of the number of Cuban military advisors in Nicaragua during the 1980s ranged from several hundred to more than one thousand. The Popular Movement for the Liberation of Angola (MPLA), some of whose members had been trained in Cuba, requested Cuban advisors and troops to assist them in resisting invasions by South African forces (Quirk 1993; Szulc 1986). According to Gott (2004, 254), several hundred Cuban special forces soldiers played a major role in helping the MPLA turn back a South African invasion in November 1975. The knowledge that the white South African army had been defeated by Angolans is thought to have encouraged the 1976 Soweto uprising against apartheid by black school children. Cuba was estimated to have had about 45,000 troops in Angola by 1988, the year of another victory of Angolan and Cuban forces over invading South African troops at the Battle of Cuito Cuanavale. (The Cuban troops were later withdrawn over a period of about thirty months as part of a peace settlement.) The Cubans also assisted members of the anti-apartheid African National Congress (ANC), which in 1994 won the first postapartheid elections in South Africa. Nelson Mandela, speaking in Cuba on July 26, 1991, on the anniversary of the 1953 Moncada attack, stated that the victory of Angolan and Cuban forces at Cuito Cuanavale protected Angolan independence, helped bring about the liberation of Namibia, showed again that white racist forces could be defeated, and encouraged the anti-apartheid struggle in South Africa (Gott 2004, 279).

International developments in the late 1980s and the 1990s had major implications for revolutionary movements in terms of ideological goals, methods, and any future Cuban role in revolutionary efforts in other countries. First, the cold war ended in a defeat for the authoritarian socialist model based on a one-party state and the centrally planned, government-owned-and-controlled economic systems that had characterized the pre-Gorbachev USSR and the Eastern European states. Following the end of these one-party systems, the shift of their economies toward market systems, and the disintegration of the USSR and Russia's economic distress, revolutionary ideologies advocating state-controlled economies or nondemocratic political systems tended to lose favor among discontented intellectuals.

Revolutionaries in countries such as El Salvador reformulated their ideologies to focus on achieving several goals: first, the achievement of genuine political democracy and guarantees of respect for basic human rights; second, an economic system that would allow for the operation of market forces, individual initiatives, and substantial private ownership of economic enterprises; and third, the development of policies increasing economic security, opportunity, and welfare for the poor (Vilas 1995).

The Cuban model was attractive to post–cold war revolutionaries primarily with regard to the third goal. But Cuba, having lost its previous economic and military aid from the Soviet Union and Eastern Europe, was in no position during much of the 1990s to provide significant assistance to any revolutionary movement but rather struggled to assure the survival of major elements of its own postrevolution achievements.

The shift in revolutionary economic ideology of political groups formerly oriented toward rapid structural social change can also be illustrated by Chile's Socialist Party (Oppenheim 1993; Petras and Leiva 1994). The Chilean Socialist Party and its Allende-era Popular Unity allies had been driven from power by a brutal, democracy-destroying military coup in part for attempting to expand the role of the Chilean state in the nation's economy. In the 1990s, as a condition of being allowed to participate in electoral politics and also because of genuine changes in many of its leaders' points of view, the Chilean Socialist Party—along with its new political ally, the Christian Democratic Party—appeared explicitly or implicitly to adopt the following guidelines: first, maintain a commitment to a market economy and the primacy of pursuing policies to insure continued economic growth; second, in the context of capitalist domination of the world economy, maintain cooperative rather than conflict-oriented relations with multinational corporations and financial institutions; and third, preserve commitment to a consensus-oriented approach to developing government policy, which operationally meant avoiding significant conflict with either the Chilean military or Chile's wealthy capitalist elites (Petras and Leiva 1994).

The changes in goals and means on the part of major leaders of Chile's Socialist Party came about in light of modern world economic realities, the proven willingness of some U.S. administrations to intervene overtly or covertly against regimes or political movements that advocated revolutionary change (structural change) viewed as damaging to U.S. economic or security interests, a Chilean military establishment virtually totally unpunished up through the early 1990s for past human rights abuses and really not under effective civilian control, and also the incentive of the relatively high level of economic growth associated with the privatization of formerly state-owned industries and resources, market-oriented economic policies, and proforeign corporate relationships structured during the period of direct military rule (Aguero 1993; Oppenheim 1993; Petras and Leiva 1994).

In 1999 (for the first time since Allende) another Socialist Party leader, Ricardo Lagos, supported by the Christian Democrats and other parties of the Concert Coalition and also aided by Communist votes, won the presidential election. Lagos worked to remove some of the nondemocratic aspects of the Chilean constitution that had been written during the period of military rule. His administration also entered into free trade agreements with the United States and the European Union, increased foreign investment, and extended medical coverage to lower-income groups. In 2006 Michelle Bachelet, a medical doctor like Allende and also a Socialist Party leader, was elected Chile's first woman president. The daughter of an air force general who supported the Allende government and was tortured and died in prison under the right-wing military regime, Bachelet, who along with her mother had also been temporarily imprisoned by the former dictatorship, pledged to work to solve Chile's social problems, including its apparently largely disastrous privatized pension system.

The positive achievements and persistence of the Cuban Revolution appear to have played a significant role in inspiring the Venezuelan Bolivarian Revolution of Hugo Chavez (Gott 2000). Chavez, a leftist former officer in an army paratrooper unit, was able to resist an attempted coup in 2002 partly because of his strong support in a sector of the military coupled with his continued popularity with about 58 percent of voters (Ewell 2006). President Chavez began to supply Cuba with large quantities of much needed oil. Under Chavez's leadership Venezuela formed an alliance with Cuba intended to accomplish sweeping international economic and social goals in Latin America and the Caribbean.

Cuba and Venezuela's Bolivarian Revolution and the Democratic Shift to the Left in Latin America

For years Cuba stood alone as the sole surviving socialist revolution in the Western Hemisphere. Allende's Popular Unity government in Chile was destroyed by a violent right-wing military overthrow on September 11, 1973, and the Sandinista revolutionaries were defeated in Nicaragua's 1990 elections. But in 1998 Hugo Chavez was elected president of oil-rich Venezuela, pledging to bring about a Bolivarian Revolution to aid the poor and resist foreign imperialism (Ewell 2006; Gott 2000; McCoy and Neuman 2001). Chavez was an admirer of Fidel Castro for what he perceived were the benefits the Cuban Revolution had brought to Cuba's poor. Within a short time Venezuela was shipping oil to Cuba, and Cuba was sending thousands of its doctors and nurses to provide medical services to Venezuela's people. The combination of the revolution-promoting efforts of Venezuela and Cuba, the use of Venezuelan oil money by the Chavez government to aid the poor in many countries in the Western Hemisphere, the devastating impact of neoliberal economic policies on wide sections of Latin American populations, and the intense unpopularity of the U.S. George W. Bush administration in the region, all contributed in varying degrees to the democratic elections of left or left-leaning governments in a number of Latin American nations during the early part of the twenty-first century (Carlson 2005; Shifter 2004).

In 2006 Bolivians elected their first indigenous president, Evo Morales, an admirer of Venezuela's Hugo Chavez. Morales pledged to pursue similar policies in Bolivia and use the mineral and other resources of his country to more effectively serve the interests of the Bolivian people. On May 1 Morales met with Chavez and Fidel Castro in Havana to make Bolivia a member of the Bolivarian Alternative for the Americas (ALBA), founded by Cuba and Venezuela on May 1, 2005, in an effort to counter the U.S.-sponsored Free Trade Area of the Americas (FTAA) project (Salazar 2006). Critics of the U.S. FTAA claim that it would benefit U.S. multinational corporations but "threaten Latin American economic development" (Williams 2006). In contrast, ALBA was described by its supporters as promoting socially beneficial and constructive trade among nations. Other countries with more mildly left governments in 2006 included Argentina, Brazil, Chile, and Uruguay. Some observers predicted that the voters of more Latin American nations would bring additional left-wing governments to power, possibly creating the potential for continental social revolution dreamed of in the past by Fidel Castro and Che Guevara—not by the strategy of the guerilla *foco*, but instead through mass participation movements and democratic elections. The Venezuelan-Cuban alliance may come to constitute a new variety of transnational revolutionary movement to be added to those previously analyzed by Mark Katz (1999; 2002; 2006).

CUBAN ECONOMY AND POLITICAL SYSTEM

Cuba's economy suffered crippling losses during the early 1960s because of the cutoff of trade with the United States and almost all the other Latin American countries as well as the flight of middle- and upper-class Cubans with valuable technical and managerial skills. Development of the economy was also impeded by the idealistic but impractical approach of relying heavily on moral appeals and commitment to the revolution rather than use of differentiated wage scales to provide material incentives for good work performance. Castro's personal interference in economic development through the proposal of inappropriate or inadequately planned projects, such as the drive to harvest ten million tons of sugar in 1970, also periodically resulted in inefficiency and dislocations in the economy.

Beginning in the early 1970s Cuban leaders, in an effort to utilize resources better, attempted to develop the economy in a more organized fashion, with greater material incentives. In 1976 Cuba introduced limited market mechanisms, more autonomy in decision making for state enterprises, and even a system of free markets in which farmers could sell some of their produce outside the state-controlled rationing structure. During the period 1970–1979 the nation sustained an average annual economic growth of over 5 percent.

President Castro and others, however, feared that continued reintroduction of capitalist free market practices and private profit-making activities would progressively undermine revolutionary collectivism and idealism and promote excessively self-centered individualism. Because of this concern and in reaction to alleged cases of mismanagement and corruption, Cuban authorities again shifted economic policies. The 1984 Campaign of Rectification of Errors and Negative Tendencies was launched "to rectify vices and antisocialist attitudes spawned by the reforms of the 1970s. . . . Once again moral incentives are emphasized, private gain is chastised, labor discipline is sanctioned severely, and sacrifices are demanded" (Aguila 1988, 108–9). But during the late 1980s Cuba still experienced problems in fulfilling its trade obligations and paying its foreign debts (Brenner 1988).

The Soviet Union provided major assistance to the Cuban economy in a number of ways (Eckstein 1986). In particular, the USSR agreed to purchase large quantities of sugar at relatively stable prices that were usually well above world market prices. Although the arrangement benefited Cuba by billions of dollars, the Cuban government portrayed this trade agreement as a positive example of the way all advanced industrial powers should economically interact with developing nations.

In the 1990s Cuba faced serious economic problems brought on primarily by two factors: first, the loss of favorable trade relations and economic and military assistance from the former USSR and Eastern Europe, and, second, continued U.S. hostility, manifested most significantly through the maintenance of the U.S. economic embargo and other financial pressures against Cuba (Aguila 1994; "Cuba in Crisis" 1991). One of Cuba's advantages, however, was the refusal of the large majority of the world's nations to cooperate with the U.S. campaign against Cuba, as manifested by the November 8, 2005, United Nations vote against the embargo, with 182 nations condemning the embargo (only the United States, Israel, the Marshall Islands, and Palau supported the embargo) (Leopold 2005). This was the fourteenth year in a row that the UN had voted overwhelmingly against the U.S. embargo.

Nonetheless, Cuba suffered huge reductions in its ability to pay for imports, including oil, which resulted in a major energy crisis. Manufacturing activity declined, and electric service was severely rationed. Farmers stored useless tractors and returned to animal and human power and to organic farming techniques that avoided the need for scarce chemical fertilizers (Rosset 1994).

To spur production internally, Cuba again legalized small-scale capitalist business activity and negotiated scores of joint industrial and other ventures with companies based in Spain, Mexico, Italy, Canada, and other nations (Fedarko 1995; *New York Times*, Feb. 3, 1994, A4; Sept. 7, 1995, A12). A major and growing source of foreign currency for Cuba was its expanding tourist industry involving hundreds of thousands of visitors annually (Aguila 1994). Other sources of foreign revenue were the sale of Cuban crops and resources, including sugar, nickel, tobacco, citrus, seafood, and products such as biotechnological agricultural, industrial, and medical-pharmaceutical products (Feinsilver 1993).

The U.S. Congress's Cuban Democracy Act of 1992 attempted to tighten the embargo against Cuba by, among other measures, specifically banning the export to Cuba of anything that could assist the development of its biotechnology program (Feinsilver 1993). In March 1996 Congress passed the Helms-Burton Act (The Cuban Liberty and Solidarity Act), which was intended to increase pressures on Cuba by forcing other nations' business-people and corporations to stop doing business with or investing in Cuba. The most controversial aspect of the Helms-Burton Act, Title III, would allow U.S. citizens or companies to use U.S. courts to sue foreign companies using property in Cuba that once belonged to them. If victorious, U.S. courts could provide compensation to the former owners by seizing some of the U.S. assets of the accused foreign companies. The governments of many countries staunchly opposed the Helms-Burton Act, and a number warned of economic retaliation against the U.S. if it was fully implemented. Apparently out of concern with provoking international economic warfare, U.S. presidents Bill Clinton and George W. Bush repeatedly delayed activation of

Title III of the Helms-Burton Act (*New York Times*, Feb. 21, 1997, A1; PBS Online News Hour Update, July 17, 2001).

The Clinton and the later Bush administration justified their continuation of the U.S. embargo against Cuba on the grounds that Cuba's political system was not democratic. Important Cuba scholars, such as Juan del Aguila, expressed support for the view that "many of the reasons for Cuba's isolation stem from its refusal to grant ordinary civil and political rights" (Aguila 1994, 125). But this argument appears incomplete for at least two reasons.

The first problem concerns the operational definitions of democracy and civil rights. Were states such as Guatemala and Chile "democratic" when their military personnel were neither under effective elected civilian control nor accountable for past human rights abuses, including thousands of murders? Where did political dissidents have the greatest fear of being "disappeared" or otherwise killed for their views in the 1980s, in Cuba or in the nonembargoed "democracies" of Guatemala and El Salvador? Second, it is obvious that totally undemocratic nations, such as certain oil-rich dictatorial monarchies, did not suffer U.S.-orchestrated isolation and economic pressure but rather enjoyed U.S. support because these dictators and their nondemocratic forms of government assured the United States and its allies easy and affordable access to important resources. Cuba's "isolation" may have been due less to its lack of "democracy" than to its lack of submission.

Instead of attempting to isolate Cuba economically, the goals of increasing liberty and developing a more democratic Cuban political system might have been better and more quickly achieved by instituting trade, investment activity, and cultural exchanges between the United States and Cuba. U.S. administrations appeared disinclined to employ this approach because of fear of the political power of anti-Castro Cuban-American groups and, in particular, concern with the importance of Florida's electoral votes, which proved crucial in both the 2000 election, when George W. Bush lost the popular vote by approximately 500,000 votes but became president because he apparently won Florida by about 500 votes, and the 2004 election.

Another potential misjudgment by some students of Cuban society, certain of whom have in the past offered repeated but inaccurate predictions of the fall of Cuba's government, is the notion that the "legitimacy" of the Cuban regime is derived primarily from its past ability to provide the Cuban people with a significant level (especially by the standards of less-developed countries) of social benefits, such as easy access to health care, educational opportunities, and basic nutrition (McFadyen 1995). The implication was that Cuba's economic problems would seriously deteriorate its social welfare system, leading to a drastic delegitimization of the government and its overthrow. But this point of view neglected other factors that can continue to provide popular support and legitimacy for a government, such as the public perception of the reasons for hardships, whether burdens are shared fairly equally, and whether the government is viewed as committed to defending national interests and protecting the majority of citizens from even worse consequences that could result from capitulation to foreign pressure.

The Cuban Constitution of 1976, which, according to the government, had been approved by an overwhelming majority of the population in secret ballot elections, institutionalized the dominant role of the Communist Party and set the structure of Cuba's political system. The Constitution was revised in 1992 to permit direct elections of the members of the National Assembly (from lists of candidates approved by the Communist Party). "At the same time, references in the constitution to Marxism-Leninism were quietly dropped and the ban on Christians joining the Party was also abandoned" (Gott 2004, 294). Cuba was further declared a "secular" rather than an "atheist" state (Gott 2004, 308). The top executive branch of government is the Council of State of thirty-one members (last elected in 2003), which includes the president (Castro in 2006), vice presidents, and the heads of several major government agencies. The members of the Council are elected by the National Assembly of People's Power, the country's national legislature. The 609 members of the National Assembly were directly elected by the voters in 2003 to serve a five-year term (all candidates were nominated by or acceptable to local branches of the Communist Party, which had about 780,000 members). The Communist Party's Central Committee had 150 members.

At the beginning of the twenty-first century Cuba's economy and its regional influence were reinvigorated through an alliance with Venezuelan president Hugo Chavez's government as well as the election of leftist governments in a number of other Latin American nations (Monreal 2006). As Cuba became less isolated internationally, ongoing hostility toward Cuba by the U.S. government, certain other unpopular actions by the Bush administration in the name of fighting terrorism, and the Bush government's dogged pursuit of neoliberal economic policies worldwide provoked anger not so much from Latin America's traditional economic and political elites, but in many countries from the majority of voters. Ironically, the creation of a supportive leftist political environment in Latin America, long a goal of the Cuban Communist Party, may be a crucial factor in the future democratization of Cuba if it is accompanied by increased security and economic progress for the Cuban people.

SUMMARY AND ANALYSIS

Repeatedly during the nineteenth and twentieth centuries, Cubans of various social classes took up arms on behalf of the goal of national independence. In the 1950s a broad coalition developed in opposition to the Batista government, a regime widely viewed as not only authoritarian but also corrupt and subservient to foreign interests. The pervasive hatred for the Batista dictatorship and for its collaboration in the foreign domination and exploitation of the Cuban people was the key factor motivating a desperate and heroic revolutionary struggle.

Members of Cuba's educated elite historically initiated or joined revolutionary movements. José Martí led the generation that launched the 1895 fight for independence. The outcome of that costly struggle, a political and economic system dominated by the United States, alienated many intellectuals not only from the political leaders who ran the country but also from the entire corrupt political apparatus, especially after the betrayal of the major reform goals of the 1933 rebellion. During the 1950s other rebellious children of the elite, led by Fidel Castro, launched a violent revolution against the Batista dictatorship. Apart from those members of Cuba's privileged classes who were openly revolutionary, others withdrew support from Batista due to his regime's brutal, repressive tactics.

Popular discontent grew. The dependency of the Cuban economy on a single export crop, sugar, meant both seasonal unemployment for hundreds of thousands of rural workers and cycles of prosperity and depression for much of the general population as world sugar prices rose and fell. The 1933 rebellion was sparked, in part, by a fall in sugar prices. And during the 1950s, after the prosperity of the World War II period, real income in Cuba declined. In addition to the discontent related to high unemployment and other economic problems, nationalism was often inflamed by various displays of subservience on the part of Cuban military, economic, and political figures toward foreign interests.

Batista's state apparatus was inherently weak: First, many Cubans viewed Batista's regime as strongly influenced by foreign governmental, business, and even organized-crime figures and, consequently, not truly representative of Cuban national interests. Second, as Batista had blocked an election and used military force to seize power, his government lacked legitimacy. Batista's government was weakened further by the growing hostility of the island's middle class, in great part owing to the torture and murder of hundreds of young middle-class activists and revolutionaries by Batista's security forces. Finally, the army became increasingly demoralized by guerrilla successes, the growth of popular hostility toward the army, the defection of army personnel to the rebel cause, and other factors, such as the decision of the Eisenhower administration to stop sending new weapons to the Cuban armed forces in March 1958.

Since the Spanish-American War the United States had played an active role with regard to the Cuban economy and political system. In the early part of the twentieth century the U.S. government ordered troops into Cuba and later helped precipitate changes in the country's leadership by withholding, bestowing, or withdrawing support. Before 1958 the United States supported Batista for years with arms, military advisors, and other forms of assistance. But recognition of intense popular opposition to Batista and his regime's human rights violations, coupled with a belief that the revolutionary leadership was not dominated by Marxists, influenced President Eisenhower's decision to end arms shipments to Batista's army and not to intervene militarily to prevent the victory of the revolution.

Soon, however, the Eisenhower administration reversed its permissive stance toward the Cuban Revolution, instituted an economic boycott of the island, and engaged in a series of efforts to alter the revolution's outcome. The defeat of the most dramatic of these—the 1961 Bay of Pigs invasion, which was permitted to go forward by the Kennedy administration—generated increased nationalistic support for the revolutionary government.

Fear of future revolutions stimulated a new U.S. economic aid program for Latin America as well as more military assistance and covert CIA activities such as those directed against the Popular Unity movement in Chile. In the 1960s and 1970s U.S. administrations recognized and aided conservative military dictatorships that had seized power in a number of Latin American countries. Measures taken by U.S. administrations after the Cuban Revolution helped prevent the victory of any further Latin American revolutionary movements until the Carter presidency. Carter's policy of making military assistance to governments contingent on their human rights behavior in effect constituted a new period of permissiveness for social change in Latin America and contributed to the success of the Nicaraguan Revolution.

In the 1990s, after the loss of most of its aid from Russia and Eastern Europe, Cuba faced a difficult economic situation. In response, the island's leaders moved to access the productivity and technological benefits available by encouraging private enterprise and cooperating with foreign-owned capitalist corporations while maintaining Cuba's independence and its impressive educational, health care, and social service systems. The conservative U.S. Congress attempted to inhibit Cuban economic recovery through the Helms-Burton Act of 1996, which was designed to prevent companies of other nations from doing business with Cuba. In contrast, the vast majority of countries voted repeatedly in the United Nations that the United States should end its economic embargo against Cuba. Cuba's international influence began to increase at the beginning of the twenty-first century in part through its alliance with Venezuela and as a result of the election of leftist governments in a number of other Latin American countries.

CUBAN REVOLUTION: CHRONOLOGY OF MAJOR EVENTS

1868–1878	First war of Cuban independence
1895–1898	Second war of Cuban independence
1902	Cuban independence, but limited by Platt amendment
1933	Revolution ousts Machado; Batista gains control of Cuban armed forces
1947	Orthodoxo Party founded
1952	Batista stages military takeover

1953	Moncada attack fails
1954	Democratically elected reform government in Guatemala overthrown with CIA assistance, providing starkly different lessons for the CIA and Cuban revolutionaries
1955	Castro organizes M-26-7
1956–1958	Cuban Revolution
1959	Castro assumes power in January
1961	Bay of Pigs invasion, patterned after the CIA's successful operation in Guatemala in 1954, is defeated; Castro declares Cuban Revolution socialist
1962	Cuban Missile Crisis; United States pledges not to invade Cuba
1966	Revolutionaries from many countries attend the Tricontinental Conference in Havana
1967	Che Guevara captured and executed in Bolivia
1970	Cuba recognizes alternate paths, such as democratic elections, to social revolution, including the election of Marxist Socialist Salvador Allende in Chile
1973	On September 11 Chilean military overthrows the elected Allende government and establishes a right-wing dictatorship
1975–1989	Cuban troops aid Angolan revolutionaries to defeat repeated South African invasions of Angola
1980	More than one hundred thousand Cubans leave Cuba for the United States during the Mariel boat lift
1988	At the conclusion of the Battle of Cuito Cuanvalle, Angolan and Cuban forces defeat the invasion by the South African army; Nelson Mandela describes this victory as a major event in the process of destroying apartheid
1991	USSR disintegrates, and Cuba loses valuable financial assistance
1992	Cuba's revised constitution permits direct popular election of the members of the National Assembly and describes Cuba as a secular rather than an atheist nation; the Cuban Communist Party allows practicing Christians to join
1993	Cuba allows some private business activity
1996	U.S. Congress passes the Helms-Burton Act to try to prevent companies of other nations from doing business with Cuba
1997	Che Guevara's remains transported from Bolivia and reburied at Santa Clara, Cuba
1998	Pope John Paul II visits Cuba, sparking renewed interest in Catholicism among some Cubans, and calls for the United States to end its economic embargo against Cuba; leftist Hugo Chavez, an admirer of Fidel Castro and the achieve-

ments of the Cuban Revolution, is elected president of Venezuela

2000   The government of Hugo Chavez provides oil to Cuba; Cuba provides thousands of doctors and nurses to Venezuela

2005   Cuba and Venezuela create the Bolivarian Alternative for the Americas (ALBA), an economic alliance for socially beneficial trade

2006   Bolivia, under newly elected leftist president Evo Morales, joins the ALBA trade alliance

References and Further Readings

Aguero, Felipe. 1993. "Chile: South America's Success Story?" *Current History*, March, 130–35.

Aguila, Juan M. del. 1988. *Cuba: Dilemmas of a Revolution*. Westview Profiles: Nations of Contemporary Latin America. Rev. and updated ed. Boulder: Westview Press.

_____. 1994. *Cuba: Dilemmas of a Revolution*. Nations of Contemporary Latin America. 3rd ed. Boulder: Westview Press.

Alfonso, Haroldo Dilla. 2006. "Cuban Civil Society: II. Future Directions and Challenges." *NACLA Report on the Americas—Cuba in the Americas*, January/February, 37–42.

Amaro, Neson, and Carmelo Mesa-Lago. 1971. "Inequality and Classes." In *Revolutionary Change in Cuba*, ed. Carmelo Mesa-Lago. Pittsburgh: University of Pittsburgh Press.

Anderson, Jon Lee. 1998. *Che Guevara: A Revolutionary Life*. New York: Grove/Atlantic.

Arreaza, Teresa. 2004. January 30. *ALBA: Bolivarian Alternative for Latin America and the Caribbean*. http://www.venezuelanalysis.com/docs.php?dno=1010 (accessed June 19, 2005).

Binford, Leigh. 2006. "Salvadoran Revolution." In DeFronzo, ed., *Revolutionary Movements in World History*, 3:763–73.

Brenner, Philip. 1988. *From Confrontation to Negotiation: U.S. Relations with Cuba*. Boulder: Westview Press.

Brenner, Philip, and Marguerite Jimenez. 2006. "U.S. Policy on Cuba Beyond the Last Gasp." *NACLA Report on the Americas—Cuba in the Americas*, January/February, 15–22.

Carlson, Laura. 2005. "The Continental Drift of the Left." *NACLA Report on the Americas, War on Terror—Target: Americas*, May/June, 13–17.

"The CIA Hit List." 1975. *Newsweek*, December 1, 28–35.

CNN, June 25, 1990, "A Conversation with Fidel Castro."

Corrales, Javier. 2005. "Cuba After Fidel." *Current History*, February, 69–76.

"Cuba in Crisis." 1991. *Congressional Quarterly Researcher* 28:897–920.

Davis, Nathaniel. 1985. *The Last Two Years of Salvador Allende*. Ithaca, NY: Cornell University Press.

Debray, Regis. 1967. *Revolution in the Revolution? Armed Struggle and Political Struggle in Latin America*. Trans. Bobbye Ortiz. New York: Monthly Review Press.

DeFronzo, James. 2006a. "The Cuban Revolution." In DeFronzo, ed., *Revolutionary Movements in World History*, 1:177–91.

_____, ed. 2006b. *Revolutionary Movements in World History: From 1750 to the Present*. 3 vols. Santa Barbara, CA: ABC-CLIO.

_____. 2006c. "The South African Revolution." In DeFronzo, ed., *Revolutionary Movements in World History*, 3:784–801.

Dinges, John, and Saul Landau. 1980. *Assassination on Embassy Row*. New York: Pantheon.

Eckstein, Susan. 1986. "The Impact of the Cuban Revolution: A Comparative Perspective." *Comparative Studies in Society and History* 28 (July):502–34.

Ewell, Judith. 2006. "Venezuelan Bolivarian Revolution of Hugo Chavez." In DeFronzo, ed., *Revolutionary Movements in World History*, 3:903–12.

Fedarko, Kevin. 1995. "Open For Business." *Time*, February 20, 51–53.

Feinsilver, Julie. 1993. "Can Biotechnology Save the Revolution?" *NACLA* 26 (May): 7–10.

Flakus, Greg. 2005. "Chavez Establishes Oil Office in Havana." *Voice of America*, April 29. http://www.voanews.com/english/archive/2005–04/2005–04–29–voa9.cfm?CFID=32815185&CFTOKEN=80894983.

Freed, Donald, and Fred Simon Landis. 1980. *Death in Washington: The Murder of Orlando Letelier*. Westport, CT: Lawrence Hill.

Fullerton, Andrew. 2006. "Inequality, Class and Revolution." In DeFronzo, ed., *Revolutionary Movements in World History*, 2:408–12.

Gill, Jungyun. 2006. "Student and Youth Movements, Activism and Revolution." In DeFronzo, ed., *Revolutionary Movements in World History*, 3:848–54.

Gleijeses, Piero. 1991. *Shattered Hope: The Guatemalan Revolution and the United States, 1944–1954*. Princeton, NJ: Princeton University Press.

González, Jorge Luis Acanda. 2006. "Cuban Civil Society: I. Reinterpreting the Debate." *NACLA Report on the Americas—Cuba in the Americas*, January/February, 32–36.

Gott, Richard. 2000. *In the Shadow of the Liberator: Hugo Chavez and the Transformation of Venezuela*. London: Verso.

_____. 2004. *Cuba: A New History*. New Haven, CT: Yale University Press.

Guevara, Ernesto Che. 1968a. *Episodes of the Revolutionary War*. New York: International Publishers.

_____. 1968b. *The Diary of Che Guevara*. New York: Bantam Books.

_____. 1969a. *Guerilla Warfare*. New York: Vintage Press.

_____. 1969b. *Che: Selected Works of Ernesto Guevara*. Ed. Roland E. Bonachea and Nelson P. Valdes. Cambridge, MA: MIT Press.

_____. 1985. *Guerrilla Warfare: Selected Case Studies*. Ed. Brian Loveman and Thomas M. Davies Jr. Lincoln: University of Nebraska Press.

_____. 2000. *The African Dream: The Diaries of the Revolutionary War in the Congo*. Trans. Patrick Camiller. New York: Grove Press.

Hakim, Peter. 1994. "NAFTA . . . and After: A New Era for the U.S. and Latin America?" *Current History*, March, 97–102.

Hartford Courant, August 10, 1992, D6, "Barcelona '92 Medals Table—All 257 Events Completed."

International Institute for Strategic Studies. 2005. "Dec 2nd—Associated Press—Cuba's Military Celebrates 49 Years."

Kampwirth, Karen. 2002. *Women and Guerilla Movements: Nicaragua, El Salvador, Chiapas, Cuba.* University Park: Pennsylvania State University Press.

Katz, Mark N. 1999. *Revolutions and Revolutionary Waves.* New York: St. Martin's Press.

_____. 2002. "Osama bin Laden as Transnational Revolutionary Leader." *Current History*, February, 81–85.

_____. 2006. Transnational Revolutionary Movements." In DeFronzo, ed., *Revolutionary Movements in World History*, 3:872–76.

Leopold, Evelyn. 2005. "UN Casts Record Vote Against US Embargo on Cuba." Reuters, November 8.

Mbeko Tali, Jean-Michel. 2006. "The Angolan Revolution." In DeFronzo, ed., *Revolutionary Movements in World History*, 1:575–82.

McCoy, Jennifer, and Laura Neuman. 2001. "Defining the 'Bolivarian Revolution': Hugo Chavez's Venezuela." *Current History*, February, 80–85.

McFadyen, Deidre. 1995. "The Social Repercussions of the Crisis." *NACLA* 29 (September/October): 20–22.

Monreal, Pedro. 2006. "Cuban Development in the Bolivarian Matrix." *NACLA Report on the Americas—Cuba in the Americas*, January/February, 22–26.

New York Times, May 15, 1987, A4, "Man and God in Cuba: A Castro-Church Detente?"

_____, October 7, 1988, A1, "Regime of Pinochet Accepts Defeat in Chile's Plebiscite."

_____, October 10, 1988, A1, "4 Nations Agree on Cuban Pullout from Angola War."

_____, January 7, 1991, A9, "Czechs Will No Longer Represent Cuba in U.S."

_____, February 3, 1994, A4, "On the Street Cubans Fondly Embrace Capitalism."

_____, April 3, 1994, 3, "Senior Judge Is Assassinated in Guatemala."

_____, April 9, 1994, E5, "Guatemala's War: Ideology Is the Latest Excuse."

_____, July 24, 1994, 3, "Guatemalan Police Find 1,000 Bodies."

_____, September 7, 1994, A1, "Latin American Speed Up Leaves Poor in Dust."

_____, December 12, 1994, A8, "Chile Is Admitted as North American Free Trade Partner."

_____, December 13, 1994, A1, "An Evening with Castro: 36 Years Later and No Regrets."

_____, March 14, 1995, A9, "Castro Given Big Welcome by Mitterand."

_____, April 13, 1995, A9, "Allies of U.S. Seek to Block Bill on Cuba."

_____, May 23, 1995, A3, "Congress Move on Cuba Irks Canada and Mexico."

_____, September 7, 1995, A12, "Cuba Passes Law to Attract Greater Foreign Investment."

_____, October 8, 1995, 9, "Republicans Attack Shift in Cuban Policy."

_____, November 3, 1995, A8, "U.N. Urges U.S. to End Ban on Cuba."

_____, March 3, 1996, 8, "Curbs Expected to Have Little Effect."

_____, February 21, 1997, A1, "U.S. Rejects Role for World Court in Trade Dispute."

Oppenheim, Lois Hecht. 1993. *Politics in Chile: Democracy, Authoritarianism, and the Search for Development*. Boulder: Westview Press.
Parenti, Christian. 2006. "Venezuela's Revolution and the Oil Company Inside." *NACLA Report on the Americas*, January/February, 8–13.
PBS. 1985. "Frontline: Crisis in Central America—Castro's Challenge."
PBS Online NewsHour Update, July 17, 2001, "Bush Renews Waiver of Helms-Burton Provision." http://www.pbs.org/newshour/updates/july01/cuba_7–17.html (accessed June 15, 2005).
Perez-Stable, Marifeli. 1993. *The Cuban Revolution: Origins, Course, and Legacy*. New York: Oxford University Press.
Petras, James, and Fernando Ignacio Leiva. 1994. *Democracy and Poverty in Chile: The Limits to Electoral Politics*. Series in Political Economy and Economic Development in Latin America. Boulder: Westview Press.
Quirk, Robert E. 1993. *Fidel Castro*. New York: W. W. Norton.
Rosset, Peter. 1994. "The Greening of Cuba." *NACLA* 28 (November/December):37–41.
Ruiz, Ramon Eduardo. 1968. *Cuba: The Making of a Revolution*. Amherst: University of Massachusetts Press.
Salazar, Luis Suárez. 2006. "Cuba's Foreign Policy and the Promise of ALBA." *NACLA Report on the Americas—Cuba in the Americas*, January/February, 27–32.
Schlesinger, Stephen, and Stephen Kinzer. 1982. *Bitter Fruit: The Untold Story of the American Coup in Guatemala*. Garden City, NY: Doubleday.
Shayne, Julie. 2006. "Women and Revolution." In DeFronzo, ed., *Revolutionary Movements in World History*, 3:936–40.
Shifter, Michael. 2004. "The US and Latin America through the Lens of Empire." *Current History*, February, 61–67.
Sigmund, Paul. 2006. "Chilean Socialist Revolution, Counter-Revolution, and the Restoration of Democracy." In DeFronzo, ed., *Revolutionary Movements in World History*, 1:107–16.
Stahler-Sholk, Richard. 2006. "Nicaraguan Revolution." In DeFronzo, ed., *Revolutionary Movements in World History*, 2:609–22.
Streeter, Stephen M. 2000a. "Interpreting the 1954 U.S. Intervention in Guatemala: Realist, Revisionist, and Postrevisionist Perspectives." *History Teacher* 34 (1): 61–74.
_____. 2000b. *Managing the Counterrevolution: The United States and Guatemala, 1954–1961*. Athens: Ohio University Press.
_____. 2006. "The Guatemalan Democratic Revolution, Counter-Revolution, and Restoration of Democracy." In DeFronzo, ed., *Revolutionary Movements in World History*, 2:325–35.
Szulc, Tad. 1986. *Fidel: A Critical Portrait*. New York: Morrow.
"U.N. Condemns Blockade." 1994. *Cuba Update*, February, 11.
Valenzuela, Arturo. 1978. *The Breakdown of Democratic Regimes: Chile*. Baltimore: Johns Hopkins University Press.
Vilas, Carlos M. 1995. "A Painful Peace: El Salvador After the Accords." *NACLA* 28 (May/June): 6–11.
Wickham-Crowley, Timothy P. 2006. "Guerilla Warfare and Revolution." In DeFronzo, ed., *Revolutionary Movements in World History*, 1:336–40.

Williams, Howard. 2006, May 1, CNSNEWS.com, International. "Chavez, Castro Political Alliance Grows with Bolivian Entry." http://www.cnsnews.com/viewfor-eignbureaus.asp?page=/foreignbureaus/archive/200605/for20060501d.html.

Wolf, Eric R. 1969. *Peasant Wars of the Twentieth Century.* New York: Harper & Row.

Wyden, Peter. 1979. *Bay of Pigs: The Untold Story.* New York: Simon & Schuster.

Selected DVD, Film, and Videocassette Documentaries

See "Purchase and Rental Sources" at the end of this volume for information on how to obtain the following resources and for full names of media companies and other organizations listed here as abbreviations.

Americas in Transition. 1982. 29 min. Color film. AFSC. Interesting overview of political developments in Cuba, Guatemala, and other Latin American states.

Americas, Number 5: In Women's Hands: The Changing Roles of Women. 1993. 60 min. Video. EMC. Women's roles and actions in Chile during the military dictatorship.

Americas, Number 9: Fire in the Mind. 1993. 57 min. Video. EMC. Revolutionary movements and conflicts in El Salvador and Peru.

Approach of Dawn: Portraits of Mayan Women Forging Peace in Guatemala. 1997. 52 min. AFSC. Women working for peace and shortcomings of the 1998 Guatemalan Peace Accords.

Battle for Chile. 1976. 184 min. Black-and-white film. FRIF. Parts 1 and 2. Efforts at peaceful democratic social revolution and the violent military seizure of power by the right-wing military on Sept. 1, 1973, and the aftermath.

Battle for El Salvador: A Country in Crisis. 1981. 60 min. PBS Frontline. Part four in the Crisis in Central America Series. Development of the conflict.

Bay of Pigs Declassified. 50 min. AETV (History Undercover). Failed CIA-organized Bay of Pigs invasion of Cuba.

Castro's Challenge. 1985. 60 min. Video. Films Inc. PBS account of the Cuban Revolution and its aftermath.

Chile: Hasta Cuando? 1987. 57 min. Color film or video. Filmakers Library. Academy Award–nominated documentary of the overthrow of the Allende government in 1973 and Chilean society under the Pinochet military dictatorship.

Chile: Obstinate Memory. 1997. 58 min. FRIF. Chile years after the military takeover.

CIA Secret Files: Part 3, Executive Action. 45 min. Time Machine. Describes CIA actions regarding Cuba, Che Guevara, and the Allende government in Chile. Includes interviews with former CIA personnel.

Conflict in Cuba: The Bay of Pigs and the Cuban Missile Crisis. 50 min. AETV.

Controlling Interests. 1978. 40 min. Color film. AFSC. Modern classic on the influence of multinational corporations in less-developed societies, with specific coverage of Latin America.

Cuba and Castro. 50 min. AETV. Castro as leader of Cuba.

Cuba: In the Shadow of Doubt. 1987. 58 min. Color film or video. Filmakers Library. Documents the Cuban Revolution, developmental successes and failures, and U.S.-Cuba relations.

The Cuban Missile Crisis of October 1962. 1998. 46 min. CNN Cold War Series, Episode 10. Truman Library.

Cuba: The Uncompromising Revolution. 1990. 54 min. Video. AFSC. Describes the Cuban Revolution and life in the island nation. Discusses policy, progress, and problems.

Denial. 1993. 57 min. FRIF. El Mossote Massacre.

Dirty Secrets: Jennifer, Evardo, and the CIA in Guatemala. 1998. 56 min. AFSC. Jennifer searches for her disappeared husband and makes discoveries about the CIA in Guatemala.

Discovering Dominga. 2002. 60 min. ITVS. A Guatemalan woman returns home to learn about both her own and her country's history.

Don't Threaten Me. 1990. 52 min. FRIF. Rebuilding democracy in Chile.

El Salvador in Crisis. 1989. 33 min. Video. AFSC. Analysis of the roles of inequality, liberation theology, and U.S. policy in El Salvador.

Enemies of War. 1993. 60 min. ITVS, PBS. The El Salvadoran civil war.

Fidel. 2001. 91 min. FRIF. Fidel Castro and Cuban history.

Fidel Castro. 2004. 120 min. DVD, video. PBS. Fidel Castro as leader of Cuba.

Fidel Castro: El Comandante. 50 min. DVD, video. BIO. Castro as revolutionary and president of Cuba.

Focus on Cuba. 1983. 25 min. Video. AFSC. History of Cuba, revolution, U.S. embargo, and Cuba's attempts to cope.

Guatemala: Deadly Connections. 1993. 13 min. AFSC. The U.S. role in Guatemala and corruption of the Guatemalan military.

The Last Communist. 1992. 60 min. Video. PBS (Frontline). The life of Fidel Castro and the Cuban Revolution.

Maria's Story. 1991. 58 min. POV, Filmakers. The El Salvadoran guerrilla leader Maria Serrano.

People's Power. 1989. 53 min. FRIF. People's power movements in Chile, in the Philippines, and among the Palestinians.

The Pinochet Case. 2001. 109 min. FRIF. General Pinochet, leader of the military government of Chile, 1973–1989.

Remembering Romero. 1992. 28 min. FRIF. Archbishop Romero of El Salvador, who was assassinated after calling for an end to military repression and an end to U.S. assistance to the El Salvadoran military.

Under the Gun: Democracy in Guatemala. 1987. 40 min. FRIF. Military influence in Guatemala.

Venezuela: Revolution in Progress. 2005. 50 min. DCTV. President Hugo Chavez and conflict over his policies.

World Revolutions for Students: Castro and the Cuban Revolution. 2005. 23 min. LVC.

The Yankee Years. 1985. 60 min. Video. Films Inc. PBS documentary on Cuba, Guatemala, Nicaragua, and El Salvador during the first half of the twentieth century.

6

REVOLUTION IN NICARAGUA

In the 1930s, as Fulgencio Batista assumed leadership of the Cuban army and effective control of the island's political system, Anastasio Somoza García used his command of Nicaraguan armed forces to seize the government of that Central American nation. The murder of the rebel nationalist leader Sandino in 1934 permitted the Somoza family and its primary mechanism of coercion, the National Guard, to dominate Nicaragua for decades. The Somozas amassed a huge fortune, while the gap between the nation's privileged and poor classes continued to widen. By the mid-1970s many Nicaraguans, enraged by the greed and brutality of the Somoza regime, were willing to set aside, at least temporarily, their differences and unite in a revolution to oust Somoza. During 1978 and 1979, 30,000 to 50,000 Nicaraguans perished in the conflict before the last of the Somozas fled the country. Following the July 19, 1979, victory, the new Sandinista government became a major concern of successive U.S. administrations. The Democratic majority in Congress at the time repeatedly clashed with Presidents Reagan and Bush over issues such as CIA aid to counterrevolutionaries (contras) trying to overthrow Nicaragua's government and the question of how much, if any, danger the Nicaraguan Revolution posed to the United States.

GEOGRAPHY AND POPULATION

Nicaragua (49,998 square miles, or 129,494 square kilometers) is about the size of New York State and had approximately 5,570,000 residents in 2006 (about three million at the time of the 1979 revolution). The population was estimated to be 69 percent of mixed ancestry, 17 percent European, 9 percent African, and 5 percent Amerindian (indigenous). About half the country's inhabitants were under sixteen. Approximately 90 percent lived on the Pacific side of the country and shared a Spanish culture. Those among the 10 percent of the population on the Atlantic (Caribbean) side were characterized by diverse cultural heritages. The largest indigenous group there was the Miskito, with about 70,000 members. Other inhabitants of the Atlantic Coast included the descendants of former African slaves who fled to Nicaragua from other lands. Britain had controlled the Atlantic side of Nicaragua until the 1890s, so many in the region spoke English and were Protestants.

NICARAGUA BEFORE THE REVOLUTION

The early political history of Nicaragua was characterized by frequent civil strife. After Nicaragua obtained its independence from Spain in the 1820s, the country was ruled by a small number of well-to-do families. Economic and regional conflicts and ideological disagreements often resulted in civil wars in which wealthy Nicaraguans hired small armies of only a few hundred men each. One important early rivalry was that between the prominent families of the cities of León and Granada. The leading citizens of León supported social change in the direction of greater personal liberty and an economic shift toward commerce, industrialization, and other modern business activity. Calling themselves Liberals, in the classical sense of favoring increased freedom from Church or state controls, they organized Nicaragua's Liberal Party. In contrast, the landowning families of Granada, who founded the Conservative Party, supported the values of traditional Spain and the dominance of the Church in social and political life and tended to favor an economy based on agriculture.

In the mid-nineteenth century U.S. citizens became interested in Nicaragua as a means of travel from the eastern part of the United States to California. North Americans sailed down the Atlantic to the Nicaraguan coast and then traveled up the San Juan River to Lake Nicaragua, where employees of the American industrialist Cornelius Vanderbilt operated a steamship. After the fifty-mile crossing of the lake, stagecoaches carried the passengers the remaining fifteen miles to the Pacific and another sea voyage up to California.

During a civil war in 1855 the Liberal faction recruited about sixty heavily armed North American mercenaries led by an adventurer from Tennessee named William Walker. After his men and modern weapons helped the Liberals temporarily defeat the Conservatives, Walker used his control of the Liberal army to declare himself president of Nicaragua. Walker decided to promote North American colonization of Nicaragua, establish slavery, and possibly later annex Nicaragua to the United States as a slave state to help increase the South's representation in the U.S. Senate. In 1857, once Walker's plans became clear, Nicaraguans, aided by other Central Americans, drove him out of the country. When Walker attempted to repeat his intervention in 1860, he was captured and executed in the neighboring country of Honduras.

NICARAGUA

After 1857 Nicaragua technically functioned as a republic with a president and a national legislature; many outside observers, however, did not consider Nicaragua a democracy, but rather a society governed exclusively by a group of wealthy families. As the Liberal Party had disgraced itself by inviting in North American mercenaries, members of the Conservative Party held the presidency during the years 1858–1893. A Conservative Party dictatorship enacted laws in 1877 intended to end indigenous ownership of communal lands and to force peasants to work as laborers harvesting coffee crops and cutting mahogany trees for European and U.S. markets. These measures helped provoke rebellions that were repressed in 1881 with the loss of several thousand lives (Cockcroft 1989). In 1893 General José Santos Zelaya of the Liberal Party took over the government. Although many Nicaraguans considered Zelaya a dictator, most felt that he was also a staunch nationalist who attempted to reduce the country's dependence on foreign business interests (Cockcroft 1989; Millett 1977; Diederich 1981).

The fact that a river and a lake cut through all but about fifteen miles of the country inspired the idea that Nicaragua would be an ideal location for a canal to link the Atlantic and the Pacific. However, certain disagreements between Nicaragua and the United States, coupled with an exaggerated fear of volcanic eruptions and earthquakes, which was promoted by business interests favoring a canal through Panama, resulted in the U.S. selection of that country rather than Nicaragua as the canal site. When President Zelaya considered negotiating with the British and the Japanese about their building a Nicaraguan canal that would compete for inter-ocean traffic with the upcoming Panama Canal, U.S. officials encouraged Conservatives to rebel against Zelaya. Military intervention by the U.S. navy and marines, along with the rebellion, forced Zelaya to resign in 1909. After fighting resumed among Liberal and Conservative factions, the United States again intervened militarily in 1912 and helped install a pro-U.S. Conservative government. A marine contingent stationed in Nicaragua during the period 1912–1925 helped maintain Conservatives from the Chamorro family in the presidency. In 1913 and 1914 new treaties gave the United States the right to build a canal through Nicaragua and to lease Nicaraguan land for U.S. army and naval bases.

Sandino, Somoza, and the Nicaraguan National Guard

U.S. officials publicly supported the establishment of a real democracy in Nicaragua. One measure theoretically instituted to achieve a democratic system was the organization of the Nicaraguan National Guard during the 1920s. The guard, trained and equipped by the United States, was to take the place of all the small personal armies and political-party militias that had previously constituted Nicaragua's factionalized armed forces. The National Guard, it was hoped, would be loyal not to any one man or political party but to a democratic national constitution. U.S. advisors selected as leader for the new army Anastasio Somoza García (nicknamed "Tacho"). Somoza was the U.S.-educated son of a coffee plantation owner. Although he had apparently been previously accused of being involved in a counterfeiting scheme, he spoke English well (initially serving as a translator for U.S. officials), was familiar with U.S. customs and popular sports, and had an appealing personality (Macaulay 1967; Millett 1977).

In 1924 U.S. officials helped supervise a national election that appeared to be relatively free and resulted in the victory of an anti-Chamorro Conservative, Carlos Solorzano, for president and a Liberal named Juan Bautista Sacasa for vice president. In 1925 the marines withdrew. Within a few months a new civil war broke out when Chamorro Conservatives rebelled and attempted to seize power. When U.S. marines landed in 1926 to force a settlement of the conflict, one liberal general, Augusto César Sandino, a farm owner whose ancestry was half indigenous and half European, refused to lay down his arms as long as U.S. troops occupied Nicaragua. He argued that the United States was trying to impose terms that would benefit foreign, not Nicaraguan, interests and would result in the installation of another U.S. puppet as president. Rejecting attempted bribes, including the offer of regional governmental posts, Sandino and his initial band of perhaps fifty men fought on. Between 1926 and 1933, Sandino's forces, which eventually grew to more than three thousand combatants, battled both several thousand marines and the Nicaraguan National Guard. Although newsreels shown in U.S. movie theaters at that time portrayed Sandino as a bandit leader, many Latin Americans viewed him as a nationalist fighting heroically against foreign military invasion.

Finally, facing U.S. public pressure to end a foreign intervention, whose cost during the Great Depression made it even more unpopular, as well as opposition from many Latin American countries, U.S. marines withdrew in 1933. Sandino then agreed to a settlement of the war that involved allowing Juan Bautista Sacasa, a Liberal, to serve as president. The agreement, which would have allowed Sandino's forces to control much of Nicaragua and effectively compete for national political power, proved unacceptable to General Somoza. After having had dinner with President Sacasa one evening in 1934, Sandino and two of his aides were kidnapped and executed by officers of Somoza's National Guard. President Sacasa was outraged at the cowardly murder of his friend Sandino and demanded that those guilty be punished. They never were. Two years later, in 1936, Somoza used the National Guard to install himself as president (Macauley 1967; Millett 1977; Stahler-Sholk 2006). Anastasio Somoza García ("Tacho I") ruled Nicaragua until he was assassinated by a Nicaraguan poet in 1956; he was succeeded by his eldest son, Luis Somoza Debayle, who died apparently of natural causes in 1967. The younger, West Point–educated son, Anastasio Somoza Debayle ("Tacho II," or "Tachito"), took over until the 1979 revolution forced him to flee, first to the United States and then to Paraguay, where he was assassinated in 1980, evidently by Argentinean leftists.

Somoza Family Rule

The Somozas dominated Nicaragua through a number of methods. Most important was family control of the National Guard. Men of lower-middle-class, working-class, and peasant background joined the guard as a means of social and economic mobility in a land of limited opportunity. In return for loyal service, the guard provided steady pay, food, medical care, and eventually a pension following retirement. The retiree could often obtain a job in a Somoza-owned business to supplement his pension or might receive assistance in opening his own small business (Millett 1977). However, the fact that the nation's military became very much the personal army of the Somoza family meant that the end of the family dynasty would likely severely weaken the coercive capacity of the Nicaraguan state.

The Somozas were also clever politicians who could keep the opposition divided and ineffectual through a combination of bribery, intimidation, or, if necessary, imprisonment and death (some dissidents were supposedly shot while trying to escape). In some "elections" vote buying, ballot box stuffing, or both reportedly occurred, and the Somozas even went so far as to rewrite the country's constitution to maintain power (Booth 1985; Diederich 1981; Walker 1986).

Anastasio Somoza García often adapted to changing political conditions to protect his regime. During the years 1936–1938, when upper-class groups sponsored a Nazi-style "brown shirt" organization, he adopted a pro-Fascist position. In contrast, during World War II Somoza allied with the United States against Germany, and as European fascism was going down to defeat in 1944, he convinced leaders of the nation's labor unions to support continuation of his rule instead of joining the prodemocracy movement then attempting to oust him. His prolabor policies during the period 1944–1948 won him the temporary backing of Nicaragua's Communist Party (called at that point the Nicaraguan Socialist Party), some of whose members were union activists. But once Somoza had succeeded in co-opting leaders of his major upper-class opposition in the Conservative Party by giving them subordinate roles in his government and once his major foreign sponsor, the United States, became increasingly hostile to the Soviet Union, he abandoned many of his previous labor reforms. Somoza then "violently purged former union leaders and forced many unionists and socialists into exile" (Booth 1985, 65).

Through control of the government the family was able to accumulate massive wealth. One scheme involved charging foreign and domestic business interests special fees for the privilege of exploiting the nation's gold and timber resources. During World War II the Somoza government confiscated German estates, some of which the Somoza family obtained at little expense. The Somozas also reportedly profited from illegally shipping cattle to other Central American countries and by violating a number of trade-restriction laws by which other businessmen were bound. By 1979 the family owned between 10 and 20 percent of the cultivated land, more than 150 factories, several banks, an airline, and port facilities (property in Nicaragua valued in the hundreds of millions of dollars) and was thought to have placed $500 million or more in foreign bank accounts and other foreign investments (Booth 1985; Walker 1986).

Despite the huge gap in lifestyle between the mass of the Nicaraguan population and the Somoza family and its business associates, the U.S. government staunchly supported the dynasty because of its friendliness toward North American business interests and its strong and consistent anti-Communist stance. Because the Somoza family's hold on power was in great part the result of foreign intervention and sponsorship, its control was based on repression coupled with opportunistic political alliances and bribes, and its continuous goal was to increase personal and family wealth, Somoza rule generally lacked moral legitimacy. The Somoza regime, consequently, was vulnerable to the loss of U.S. support and of the ability to buy off opposition elements.

The Nicaraguan Economy

When Sandino was murdered in February 1934, Nicaragua was suffering the effects of the worldwide depression, which resulted in a drastic decline in the prices paid internationally for the nation's major exports (coffee prices in 1933 were only one-third their 1929 level and did not recover fully until 1947). Many indebted owners of small farms lost their land to wealthy landowners, who proceeded to expand coffee planting to compensate for lower prices. As landownership became more concentrated, displaced peasants joined the ranks of landless agricultural laborers and urban workers. Many agricultural laborers were effectively bound to the plantations where they were employed through laws that prevented departure of any workers who owed money to the plantation stores. Because such stores usually sold food or tools at very high prices and provided credit only at very high interest rates, many rural workers remained mired in long-term debt and were forbidden from seeking alternate employment.

During World War II the economy improved, as the United States became somewhat more dependent on Central America's resources (such as rubber, metals, and wood). Following the war, the economy fluctuated in response to changes in the demand and prices paid for Nicaragua's exports. But in the early 1960s fear of further Cuban-style revolutions in Latin America prompted the United States to increase economic assistance to Nicaragua greatly and led to the formation of the Central American Common Market to spur trade among nations within the region. Partly as a result, Nicaragua's GNP rose by 250 percent between 1960 and 1975, and manufacturing's share rose from 15.6 to 23 percent. Although aggregate growth was impressive, benefits reaching the majority in the lower classes were limited by the Somoza government's restrictions on labor unions, maintenance of low wages for many workers, and failure to implement extensive agrarian-reform measures. Because of Nicaragua's high rate of population growth (the population doubled between 1950 and 1970) and the nature of the country's prerevolutionary economic system, which disproportionately benefited the upper- and middle-class minorities, inequality among social groups increased (Booth 1985).

By the start of the revolutionary decade of the 1970s, 50 percent of economically active Nicaraguans were employed in agriculture, 10 percent were industrial workers, and about 20 percent were employed in other largely urban, nonagricultural blue-collar jobs such as construction, transportation, and domestic labor. The nation's middle class included between 15 and 20 percent of working Nicaraguans with managerial, sales, and clerical jobs, small businesses, government functions such as administrative development planning, and the performance of other technical functions. In the 1970s the lower half of Nicaraguan income earners received a total of 15 percent of all income, whereas the top 5 percent received 30 percent of the national income. These statistics indicate that the average income earner in the upper 5 percent had an income twenty times that of the average income earner in the lower 50 percent of the population (Booth 1985). With respect to agricultural wealth, the largest 0.6 percent of farms had 31 percent of the farmland, and the bottom 58 percent had only 3.4 percent. Of the rural population 75 percent was illiterate (compared to 25 percent in urban areas).

In the 1960s the upper class prospered, and much of the middle class and some in the urban working class enjoyed economic improvements. Many wealthy and middle-class individuals flaunted their good fortune through the conspicuous consumption of luxury items. Among urban workers industrial employees experienced an 81 percent increase in real wages (adjusted for inflation) between 1961 and 1968. By the mid-1970s, however, there was an economic downturn. The devastating 1972 earthquake had caused 5,000 to 10,000 deaths and destroyed thousands of homes, businesses, and manufacturing jobs. Within a few years the economy was negatively affected by lowered international coffee prices, labor unrest, and intensified Somoza political repression, which discouraged new investments in business and industry. The economic decline was reflected in drops in real wages between 1968 and 1975 of 29 percent for industrial workers, 15 percent for construction workers, and 26 percent for communications and transportation workers (Booth 1985). Economically generated frustration, especially dangerous to a government lacking moral legitimacy, was increasing in the years leading up to the revolution.

THE REVOLUTION

Formation of the FSLN

Widespread poverty, along with Somoza corruption, greed, apparent sub-servience to foreign interests, and repressive measures, earned the regime many enemies. Survivors of Sandino's army repeatedly attempted to launch guerrilla wars against the Somoza dynasty. But in 1961 a small group of younger anti-Somoza militants, led by Carlos Fonseca Amador, Tomás Borge, and Silvio Mayorga, created a new organization, the Sandinista Front for National Liberation (FSLN) (Stahler-Sholk 2006). Of the original founders only Borge survived to witness the overthrow of the Somoza regime. FSLN leaders, who viewed the Somoza dynasty as a creature of U.S. intervention, an instrument of foreign exploitation, and the embodiment of corruption and unrestrained greed, were inspired in part by the example of a number of national liberation movements around the world. Taking the name of the nationalist hero Sandino for their revolutionary movement, FSLN organizers intended both to rid the country of the Somozas and to launch a social revolution that would redistribute much of the nation's re-sources toward the poor and create a society without extremes of wealth and poverty (Cockcroft 1989; Booth 1985; Walker 1986). The formation of the FSLN reflected not only the development of dissident elements within Nicaragua's educated elite but also the increasing commitment of young elite members to the view that an armed revolution was the only feasible means of social transformation.

Although most of the leaders of the FSLN from 1961 to 1979 came from middle- and upper-class families, Carlos Fonseca, widely recognized as the "prime mover" in the formation of the FSLN, was the illegitimate son of a poor single mother who worked as a cook (Zimmermann 2000). Excelling as a student and a leader at Matagalpa High School, Fonseca was attracted to Marxist concepts such as the view that the flow of history involved a struggle among economic classes, that the majority of Nicaragua's people were the victims of greedy U.S. corporations and an exploiting Nicaraguan capitalist class, and that there was a need for a revolutionary redistribution of wealth and power (Booth 1985; Pastor 1987). Fonseca, who would die in combat against Somoza's National Guard in 1976, became a leftist activist at the National Autonomous University and joined the Nicaraguan Socialist Party (the country's Communist Party).

Fonseca, Borge, Daniel Ortega and Lidia Saavedra de Ortega, parents of the Ortega brothers (one of whom, Camilo, was to die in the revolution; an-other, Daniel, to become the first president of the revolutionary government; and a third, Humberto, to become commander of the Sandinista army), and thousands of others suffered imprisonment and often torture for openly op-posing the Somoza regime (Pastor 1987; Booth 1985). Following the assassi-nation of Anastasio Somoza García in 1956, Fonseca was one of more than two thousand arrested. In 1957 Fonseca was released from prison, and the Nicaraguan Socialist Party sent him to the Soviet Union. But in 1960 Fonseca quit the Party in part because of its refusal to support a violent revolution to oust Somoza. Fonseca and others in the FSLN received training in jungle warfare from Santos López, a surviving veteran of Sandino's original army.

The Nicaraguan people in the 1960s, however, were not yet ready to make the sacrifices that getting rid of the Somozas and their system would require. Mass discontent had not reached the critical level. The Sandinistas had also not succeeded in communicating to most people the purpose and the desirability of the revolutionary movement before launching their guerrilla war. Therefore, another of the necessary conditions for revolutionary victory, a shared motivation for revolution capable of uniting the largely urban-born, middle-class Sandinistas with the impoverished national majority composed of workers and peasants did not exist when the Sandinistas first initiated armed struggle. Thus the FSLN in the 1960s was little more than a small group of highly committed radicals bent on armed revolution but lacking the enthusiastic support of the people, the only possible means of victory against the well-trained and well-equipped National Guard. The result was that Somoza's army, bolstered by U.S. aid given in fear of another Cuban-style revolution, devastated the Sandinistas militarily (Stahler-Sholk 2006; Zimmermann 2000).

Partly in reaction to initial failures, disagreements arose within the FSLN concerning which approach would be most effective in overthrowing the Somoza regime. During the years 1975–1977 three distinct divisions were identifiable (Booth 1985; Pastor 1987). The Guerra Popular Prolongada (Prolonged People's War) faction, led by Tomás Borge and Henry Ruíz, held that a strategy of rural warfare was the key to success. The members of this group, influenced by the examples of China's Mao and Vietnam's Giap, planned to build up peasant support gradually and to construct a large revolutionary army, which over a lengthy period would wear down, demoralize, and defeat Somoza's forces. The Proletarios (Proletarians) believed that mobilizing the urban working class would be the most effective way to achieve victory. The Proletarios, one of whose leaders was Jaime Wheelock, sought to organize labor unions and many residents of urban Nicaragua's poor neighborhoods for an anticipated campaign of workers' strikes and mass demonstrations that would bring down the Somoza system. The Terceristas (Third Force), also called the Insurrecionales (Insurgents) and the Christian Wing, included Daniel and Humberto Ortega. This group differed from the others in two major ways. First, the Terceristas de-emphasized the original FSLN Marxist point of view and rapidly expanded their ranks with members who were non-Marxist socialists, Catholic and Protestant social activists (including priests), and other diverse anti-Somoza advocates of social reform and democracy. Second, this FSLN faction advocated and carried out much bolder attacks than the other two and was eventually successful in provoking widespread insurrections against the Somoza regime.

As the tactics employed by the Terceristas proved effective and the majority of the population clearly committed itself to revolution, the primary points of disagreement among the FSLN factions disappeared. This led to provisional reunification in December 1978. Formal reunification occurred in March 1979, with each faction contributing three representatives to a nine-person FSLN overall governing directorate (Stahler-Sholk 2006; Zimmermann 2000). Partly in response to the success of the concepts employed by the Terceristas and the growth of the FSLN by 1979 into a mass movement with philosophically diverse members, the ideology of the FSLN evolved in a moderate direction. FSLN policy after the victory was "Marxist" in the sense of promoting a "profound socioeconomic transformation to benefit the working classes but was also innovative in that it institutionalized political opposition, preserved a large private sector [in the economy], and established traditional civil liberties" (Booth 1985, 147).

Increased Popular Discontent

During the late 1960s and early 1970s, certain changes and events occurred in Nicaragua that drastically increased dissatisfaction with the Somoza dictatorship and set the stage for the development of a Sandinista-led mass insurrection against the dynasty. One major factor was the growth of social activism among the younger priests and religious workers. As happened in other Latin American countries, the philosophy of liberation theology was taking hold. The clergy, often central to the cultural and emotional life of the poor, began to tell impoverished workers, peasants, and farmhands that education, medical care, and decent wages were not unrealistic fantasies but rights to which they were morally entitled. The spread of these ideas helped generate the demand for change that would assure the victory of the revolution (Berryman 1987; Walker 1986).

The 1972 earthquake that devastated the capital, Managua, a city of more than 600,000 at the time, further increased mass discontent. In the following months millions of dollars in international aid poured into Nicaragua. But the Somozas and their friends were ready to take advantage of what they evidently viewed as a good business opportunity and reportedly siphoned off huge amounts of relief aid through schemes involving real estate speculation, mortgage financing, and steering reconstruction projects to Somoza-owned land. Elements of Somoza's National Guard reportedly engaged in the theft and sale of donated reconstruction supplies.

In the years following the earthquake, the real wages of many Nicaraguan urban workers declined significantly, and unemployment grew to almost 30 percent by 1979. The deprivation that many felt because of the worsening economic conditions was intensified by the knowledge of the luxuriant lifestyles pursued by the Somozas and other members of the country's upper class. But even some wealthy individuals began to feel that Somoza's greed could simply not be satisfied. Using his enormous economic resources and political clout to unfair advantage, Somoza was steadily absorbing more and more of the economy. The desire for self-preservation prompted an increasing number of businesspeople to demand an end to the dictatorship (Walker 1986). Thus diverse population segments, which in some cases had differing economic interests, became at least temporarily united by the motivation to end Somoza family rule.

State of Siege: 1974–1977

On December 27, 1974, a group of thirteen armed Sandinistas seized several politically prominent hostages at the home of a wealthy cotton exporter. The thirteen, who acted in part to protest Somoza's reelection to the presidency on his Liberal National Party's ticket, captured the mayor of Managua, the country's foreign minister, the ambassador to the United States, and other foreign and domestic celebrities, some of whom were Somoza family members. The FSLN released the hostages in exchange for eighteen Sandinista prisoners (including Daniel Ortega, later president of Nicaragua), a payment of $5 million, publication of a message from the FSLN to the Nicaraguan people, and safe passage to Cuba. Somoza, however, declared martial law under a "state of siege," which lasted until September 1977. During this period the FSLN lost many of its personnel and top leaders, including Fonseca in combat in 1976 (Stahler-Sholk 2006; Zimmermann 2000). And Somoza's National Guard tortured and murdered hundreds of peasants suspected of being sympathetic to the FSLN, greatly increasing hatred for the regime.

In 1977, however, several factors prompted Somoza to lift the state of siege. Most important was the U.S. election of Jimmy Carter, who made an improvement in Nicaragua's human rights situation a necessary condition for continued military assistance. While Somoza was recovering in Miami from a July 28, 1977, heart attack, Amnesty International released a report condemning the behavior of his armed forces. To counter the negative publicity and prevent a cutoff of aid from the Carter administration, and also because he apparently thought that his military had crushed the Sandinista threat in rural areas, Somoza ended the state of siege on September 19, 1977.

Somoza's temporary cessation of martial law allowed the FSLN to organize more freely and extend its support network around the country. Since the relaxation of repression was in part a response to President Carter's human rights ultimatum, Somoza's regime was significantly weakened by the widespread impression that his government and his National Guard no longer enjoyed the unconditional support of the United States. It now appeared that the United States might not intervene to prevent Somoza's overthrow. Thus Carter's human rights policy simultaneously meant a giant increase in the level of international permissiveness toward a revolution in Nicaragua and a substantial weakening of the prerevolutionary state.

The Revolution Intensifies

By the mid-1970s other groups and individuals besides the FSLN called for an end to Somoza rule, including some members of the Conservative Party. Pedro Joaquín Chamorro, the well-known Conservative Party editor of the opposition newspaper, *La Prensa*, was a leader of upper-class critics and attacked the Somoza regime in several articles. Chamorro's final assault exposed the greedy activities of several Somoza supporters who ran a blood plasma-exporting business in Managua. Blood was purchased from poor Nicaraguans to sell at considerable profit to hospitals in the United States. Evidence suggested that the owners of the business hired assassins to murder Pedro Chamorro on January 10, 1978 (Booth 1985; Christian 1985). Although perhaps not directly responsible, Somoza was blamed, and anti-Somoza businesspeople declared a strike in protest.

On August 22, 1978, an FSLN unit seized the National Palace and took more than 1,500 people hostage, including most of the government's officials. The raid was led by Edén Pastora, who held a deep personal animosity toward Somoza's National Guard, which he blamed for the death of his father in a land dispute. In exchange for the hostages, the Sandinistas received the release of more than fifty FSLN members, $500,000, publication of revolutionary proclamations, and safe passage out of the country (Christian 1985; Diederich 1981).

After the National Palace episode, excited and inspired teenagers in several Nicaraguan towns grabbed what weapons they could and began spontaneous insurrections. Somoza reimposed martial law in early September and ordered his National Guard to attack with planes, tanks, and artillery. Perhaps five thousand were killed in fall 1978, many shot after capture by Somoza's soldiers. But many more fled to Sandinista camps to organize and train for a coordinated revolutionary offensive.

Until 1978 the FSLN received only very limited foreign assistance. Cuba was initially reluctant to send arms, fearing that the United States would view such a move as a provocation and a reason to intervene to crush the FSLN while it was still weak. But once mass uprisings demonstrated the real possibility of ousting the Somoza regime, Venezuela, Panama, Costa Rica, and Cuba provided major aid to the Sandinistas. In 1979 Cuba commenced large-scale arms shipments to the FSLN.

FSLN full-time guerrilla fighters, despite heavy losses, usually averaged about 150 in the period from the mid-1960s through 1976. During 1977 the number rose, reaching an estimated five hundred to one thousand in early 1978 and climbing to three thousand by early 1979. In the climactic combat of summer 1979, the FSLN had approximately five thousand regular soldiers, one-quarter of them women (Booth 1985; Kampwirth 2002; Pastor 1987; Reif 1986; Shayne 2006). FSLN mainline forces at the local fronts were typically increased several times over by untrained or minimally

trained volunteers wanting to join the revolutionary struggle against Somoza's National Guard.

Since Somoza refused any compromise deemed acceptable by even the
most moderate of the opposition to his government, the Carter administration decided to restrict the flow of U.S. weapons to Somoza's National
Guard in February 1979. Much of Somoza's ammunition and weapons were
later provided by Argentina, Guatemala, and Israel (Pastor 1987).

On May 29, 1979, the Sandinistas launched the "final offensive"
against Somoza's regime. After weeks of combat, several major towns and
cities were under FSLN control and fighting had commenced in the capital, Managua. Somoza's air force repeatedly bombed FSLN-held cities and
neighborhoods, killing thousands and destroying tens of thousands of
homes and many factories and businesses. After the June 20 videotaped
murder of ABC news reporter Bill Stewart by Somoza's National Guard
(guardsmen felt that press coverage was aiding the Sandinistas) was seen
by millions of Americans on news programs, the Carter administration essentially ordered Somoza to leave Nicaragua. Support for Somoza's departure was overwhelmingly expressed by the Organization of American
States (OAS) on June 23, which voted 17 to 2 (Paraguay voted with Somoza) to demand Somoza's resignation. The OAS also rejected a Carter
administration plan to send an OAS military force into Nicaragua because
the organization viewed such an action as unwarranted interference in
Nicaragua's internal affairs. At that point, with the U.S. withdrawing support for Somoza and several regional nations assisting the Sandinistas, a
maximally permissive international environment existed with regard to
the revolution.

When a Carter administration plan to preserve a restructured National
Guard failed because of a misunderstanding by Somoza's temporary replacement, Francisco Urcuyo, and after the National Guard panicked at the
flight of Somoza and a lack of ammunition, the dictator's military disintegrated on July 17 and 18. On July 19, 1979, Sandinista fighters took control
of Managua. Several thousand National Guardsmen were captured, and
hundreds more fled north to Honduras. In the months following the revolutionary victory, the behavior of each captured guardsman was reportedly
examined. Those for whom there was no evidence of personal involvement
in torture or murder were let go. Hundreds thought guilty of war crimes
were kept in prison, but most were released before the end of 1989.
Nicaragua's criminal justice system did not have the death penalty.

POSTREVOLUTIONARY GOVERNMENT,
CHANGES, AND CONFLICTS

Although the Sandinista Front controlled the revolutionary armed forces, it
did not assume exclusive responsibility for governing Nicaragua. The

FSLN joined with other anti-Somoza groups to establish a revolutionary executive committee of five persons to run the country until elections were held. The governing committee included top Sandinista leaders (who favored the concept of at least a partially collectively owned economy rather than one based exclusively on private ownership) and two non-FSLN opponents of the Somoza regime: multimillionaire businessman, Alfonso Robello Callejas, a leader of an organization called the Nicaraguan Democratic Movement (MDN), and Violeta Barrios de Chamorro, widow of the assassinated editor of *La Prensa*.

At the outset the revolutionary leadership faced immense problems. The struggle to oust Somoza and the National Guard had been devastating. In addition to the tens of thousands (estimated variously at 30,000 to 50,000) killed, many more had been injured or made homeless. Many industries and businesses had been destroyed or badly damaged. Somoza and his associates not only had made off with their liquid assets and most of the state's treasury (except for about $3 million) but had also left Nicaragua a $1.6 billion debt (Booth 1985; Walker 1986). Moreover, the revolution faced the task of reducing the vast inequalities in wealth distribution, landownership, education, and health care that had characterized Nicaragua.

The revolution did, however, possess certain strengths and advantages. As Thomas Walker notes, one great asset was the fact that the dictator's National Guard had been destroyed and replaced by a new armed force that was "explicitly sandinist—that is, revolutionary and popularly oriented" (1986, 43). This meant that, unlike the situation in many other Latin American countries, conservative and counterrevolutionary elements, whether internal or external, would not be able to use Nicaragua's military to block progressive change. But Sandinista domination of the postrevolution military, ostensibly to ensure the implementation of the goal of socioeconomic transformation to benefit the poor, was to be continually criticized by many outside the FSLN on the grounds that one political party's control over the armed forces interfered with the realization of the fully democratic political system also promised by the revolution.

Another major strength was that "the mass organizations created in the struggle to overthrow the dictator gave the FSLN a grass-roots base that dwarfed the organized support of all potential rivals" (Walker 1986, 43). The prerevolutionary mass organizations had provided and would continue to provide hundreds of thousands of Nicaraguans with their first experiences of direct political organization and participation. By 1984 almost half of all Nicaraguans aged sixteen years or older were members of pro-Sandinista voluntary membership mass organizations (Cockcroft 1989; Walker 1986). The knowledge and experience gained through involvement in these groups inspired a feeling of political competency and empowerment among many of the Nicaraguan people. No longer were politics and the exercise of political power likely to be limited to Nicaragua's wealthy minority. Neither would political power be exclusively a male prerogative. Women constituted a large proportion of members in both the mass organizations as well as the revolutionary armed forces.

The revolutionary government moved quickly to improve the lot of impoverished Nicaraguans. Somoza family land, along with the land of several Somoza associates who had fled, was confiscated; some large holdings were turned into state farms, and more than six million acres were distributed to poor peasants and landless rural workers (Cockcroft 1989). Banks and industries owned by the Somoza family were nationalized. But more than half of all farms, businesses, and industries continued to be privately owned. The revolutionary government asserted that it would attempt to (1) maintain a mixed economy and encourage investment by the private sector; (2) institutionalize political pluralism (a multiparty political democracy) and solicit feedback from all classes; and (3) establish diplomatic and economic relations with "as many nations as possible, regardless of ideology" (Walker 1986, 44).

Young educated people were called upon to volunteer to combat widespread rural illiteracy. Tens of thousands, primarily urban high school and college students, spent months living with farm families and taught, with varying degrees of success, family members to read and write (Arnove 1986). With the aid of hundreds of doctors, nurses, and health care workers from many countries, including Western and Eastern European nations, Cuba, the United States, and Canada, scores of health clinics were established all over the country and several hospitals were built, primarily with international funding (Booth 1985; Donahue 1986; Walker 1986). In 1982 the World Health Organization declared revolutionary Nicaragua a model for primary health care.

Opposition to the FSLN

Despite its policies and achievements and, in some instances, because of them, internal and external opposition to the leading role played by the FSLN began to develop. The opposition included elements of the business elite as well as much of the middle class. Before the revolution, economic class reportedly constituted the most significant social division in Nicaragua. About 20 percent of economically active persons were engaged in nonmanual businesses, professions, or other careers, whereas 80 percent worked with their hands. The division between manual and nonmanual labor was accompanied by status differences more pronounced than those existing in North America or Europe. The norms of interclass relations required individuals in the lower-class majority to address members of the middle and upper classes by family name or with specified terms of respect such as *don* or *dona* (Walker 1986).

The victorious FSLN, in contrast, encouraged Nicaraguans to treat one another as social equals and promoted other changes that irritated many members of Nicaragua's privileged minority. Beyond land redistribution, some nationalizations of properties that the Somozas owned in partnership with other businesspeople prompted angry reactions from those who felt they were given inadequate compensation. Confiscations of private country clubs and their conversion to public recreational centers and other uses, the reduction of imports of luxuries, and the taxation of domestically produced luxury items as well as new taxes on income and property upset many of the well-to-do. Some economically advantaged Nicaraguans, though, agreed with these policies and supported the goal of social revolution, even to the point of granting the necessary parental permission for their children to take part in the National Literacy Crusade of 1980.

Some businesspeople, however, began to liquidate their assets in order to free up capital for investment outside Nicaragua, and a number left the country. Within Nicaragua much of the opposition toward the FSLN was expressed through the Superior Council of Private Enterprise (COSEP). The leadership of COSEP objected to some of the central policies of the revolutionary government such as the literacy crusade (evidently fearing prorevolutionary indoctrination of the peasants by the young volunteers), the participation and political mobilization of hundreds of thousands of Nicaraguans in prorevolutionary mass organizations, and the fact that the new Nicaraguan army was politicized in that it was led by FSLN members dedicated to the goal of economic and social revolution and was serving as an instrument of political indoctrination of recruits and draftees (Booth 1985; Christian 1985; Walker 1986).

The Nicaraguan Catholic Church, divided before the revolution between old-line conservative and liberation theology proponents, manifested intense internal conflict after Somoza's ouster (O'Shaughnessy and Serra 1986). Some priests supported the FSLN, many of whose members, while espousing Marxist concepts in some respects, were also practicing Catholics. In the revolutionary leadership priests served as foreign minister, cultural affairs minister, and head of the Literacy Crusade (Booth 1985; Christian 1985; Walker 1986). A number of clergy formed the Popular Church movement, which explicitly advocated progressive economic and social change, proclaiming that "between Christianity and revolution there is no contradiction" (Christian 1985, 221). But much of the hierarchy of the Catholic Church, represented by the nine-member Council of Bishops led by Archbishop (later Cardinal) Miguel Obando y Bravo, evolved into a major source of criticism of the FSLN. The archbishop objected to the efforts of some priests and Sandinista activists to combine Christian values and Marxist concepts and repeatedly voiced fear of Russian and Cuban "ideological imperialism" (Booth 1985, 214). He also objected to the draft on the grounds that draftees would be exposed to Sandinista ideological indoctrination. The Catholic hierarchy in general expressed outrage at what the bishops perceived to be disrespectful treatment of the pope during his 1983 Nicaragua visit. After the pope had publicly criticized priests holding high positions in the revolutionary government and refused—possibly wanting to avoid an act that could be interpreted as taking sides—to bless several Nicaraguan soldiers killed by counterrevolutionaries, though entreated to do so by the fallen soldiers' mothers, pro-Sandinista crowds at the pope's Managua Mass began chanting "we want peace" (Booth 1985, 213).

Opposition to the FSLN also emerged from within the nation's news media. A split developed in *La Prensa*, the newspaper owned by the Chamorro family, over the course of the revolution under Sandinista leadership. The Chamorro family, historically associated with Nicaragua's Conservative Party, had long opposed the Somoza dictatorship. During 1980, however, political differences and contrasting sympathies within the Chamorro family intensified (Christian 1985). Carlos Fernando Chamorro, youngest son of the martyred Pedro Joaquín Chamorro and Violeta Chamorro, had joined with the Sandinistas during the revolutionary war and became editor of the Sandinista newspaper, *Barricada*. The editor of *La Prensa* following the revolution was Xavier Chamorro Cardenal, brother of the assassinated former editor, Pedro. But by spring 1980 the majority of the Chamorro clan became convinced that Xavier was too favorable toward the FSLN. Xavier, in turn, accused several other Chamorro family members of becoming hostile toward the revolution and of slanting news coverage in attempts to slander or undermine the FSLN, promoting public discontent with the revolutionary government by printing false rumors and exaggerating real problems and giving disproportionate coverage to government critics like COSEP. On April 20, 1980, the family decided to replace Xavier, but most of *La Prensa*'s staff staged a protest strike in an attempt to force the Chamorros to keep Xavier as editor. The conflict eventually resulted in the departure of Xavier and much of the staff to establish a new independent newspaper, *El Nuevo Diario* (Christian 1985). Violeta Chamorro and other family members assumed total control of *La Prensa* and proceeded to use the newspaper to launch continuous attacks on the FSLN.

In April 1980 Alfonso Robelo and Violeta Chamorro resigned from the revolutionary governing committee. Both had opposed changes in the makeup of a national assembly, the Council of State, which was to assume the role of a legislature until elections could be held. At first it appeared that the assembly would have a majority of delegates representing business and union groups that had existed during the Somoza dictatorship and that were not involved in the FSLN. But the Sandinista majority on the revolutionary governing committee decided to include representatives from the newly created revolutionary neighborhood committees, called CDSs (Sandinista Defense Committees), and from new labor unions (several times more workers joined labor unions after the revolution than had been unionized under the Somoza regime) and other groups that had organized or greatly expanded only after the overthrow of Somoza. The Sandinistas argued that only with the addition of delegates from new organizations would the various social classes be proportionally represented to any reasonable degree in the Council of State (Booth 1985; Walker 1986). The resulting Council of State had forty-seven delegates instead of the originally intended thirty-three, with twenty-four seats assigned to pro-Sandinista groups. The ruling executive committee after the departure of Alfonso Robelo and Violeta Chamorro was reduced in size from five to three members, with two from the FSLN and one from the Democratic Conservative Party (PCD).

The hostility of anti-FSLN businesspeople, bishops, and other opposition elements intensified with the 1980 election of Ronald Reagan, a hard-line conservative U.S. president, who some thought might help rid them of the Sandinistas. The opposition protested that the FSLN was postponing elections to use the intervening years to rally youth to its cause and thus assure the FSLN of victory once elections were held. The Sandinista leadership, in turn, claimed that planning and implementing the literacy crusade, the land-redistribution process, and the health care program and carrying out other basic reforms all took priority over the organization and holding of elections (Booth 1985; Walker 1986).

Atlantic Coast Opposition

Perhaps the biggest error made by the revolutionary Nicaraguan government was its flawed initial policy regarding attempts to integrate the Atlantic Coast region with the much more populous Spanish side of the country. Foreign-owned companies had reaped the mineral and timber resources of the area since the nineteenth century. The various indigenous groups (Miskito, Sumu, Rama, and others, who resided largely in the northern section) and the English-speaking, Protestant blacks (largely in the southern section) historically viewed Spanish-speaking Nicaraguans as "alien exploiters" (Booth 1985, 234). To make matters worse, Somoza had supported the efforts of the conservative, anti-FSLN Moravian Protestant sect in the region. After the revolution, scores of mostly very young Spanish-speaking, pro-FSLN Nicaraguans, many of whom had never been to the Atlantic Coast, arrived to take over nationalized mines, lumber operations, and fisheries, as well as to open new schools and health clinics.

Sandinista militants came to the region expecting to find enthusiastic support for the revolution among the impoverished inhabitants. Instead they found unfamiliar peoples and cultures that had remained relatively isolated from Hispanic Nicaragua for generations (Dishkin 1987). The Atlantic Coast residents relished the freedom to live according to their own customs, even if in poverty. Although some indigenous people were friendly to the Sandinistas, others viewed the new schools, clinics, and public works projects as part of a plan by the central government to destroy indigenous and other local cultures. Disputes broke out in the early 1980s, and in the violent skirmishes that followed more than 150 local people and dozens of

Sandinistas were killed (Walker 1986). Later the revolutionary government tried and punished many soldiers guilty of human rights violations of Atlantic Coast residents. In 1987, after evaluating reports from hundreds of town and village meetings, the Nicaraguan government devised and approved limited autonomy status for the Atlantic Coast and, in effect, granted an amnesty to the indigenous guerrillas who had taken up arms against the Sandinista-led army. By spring 1987 fighting between Atlantic Coast people and Nicaraguan government forces had largely come to an end (Cockcroft 1989; *New York Times*, Apr. 14, 1987, A12).

U.S. AND WORLD REACTIONS TO THE REVOLUTION

Initially President Carter decided to provide over $100 million in aid to Nicaragua after Somoza's departure, although much of the sum was intended to assist private businesses rather than the revolutionary government. Carter's administration took the view that providing aid would allow the United States to influence the development of the Nicaraguan Revolution nonviolently. According to Robert Pastor, a member of Carter's National Security Council, the Carter administration objectives were:

(1) internal: to assist the revolution to fulfill its stated promises of political pluralism, elections, and a vigorous private sector, and conversely, to reduce the chances that the revolution would become Communist [result in a Leninist-style one-party state]; (2) strategic: to deny the Sandinistas an enemy and thus a reason for relying on Cuban and Soviet military assistance; and (3) regional: to make clear that a good relationship with the United States was contingent on Nicaraguan noninterference in the internal affairs of its neighbors. (1987, 194)

But when convinced that at least some Sandinistas were transporting arms to leftist rebels in nearby El Salvador, Carter suspended aid.

The Reagan administration, which took office in January 1981, assumed a much more hostile and violent stance toward the revolution. President Reagan permanently canceled the previously suspended assistance and pressured all U.S. businesses to stop buying Nicaraguan coffee, cotton, sugar, and other goods and to stop selling U.S. products to Nicaragua, eventually making all remaining trade illegal in May 1985 (Conroy 1987). As a result, from 1980 to 1986 the percentage of Nicaraguan trade (imports and exports combined) with the United States fell from 30.4 percent to 0 and with other Central American nations from 28.1 to 7.4 percent. In contrast, the percentage of Nicaragua's trade with Western European countries (almost all of which opposed the hostile measures of the Reagan administration and the later Bush administration) rose from 17.6 to 37.7 percent, while trade with Eastern Europe increased from 1.0 to 27.2 percent and with Japan from 3.0 to 9.0 percent (Kornbluh 1987).

The Contras

Beyond economic pressure, the major strategy employed by the Reagan administration to attack the revolutionary government and impede the development of Nicaragua under FSLN leadership was the sponsorship, recruitment, and arming of the contras (short for "counterrevolutionaries"), who operated primarily out of bases in Honduras supplied by the CIA (White 1984; Walker 1986). The initial counterrevolutionary units were organized by several former officers of the Somoza National Guard after their flight from Nicaragua and were funded by wealthy Nicaraguan exiles (PBS 1987). Following past strategies designed to overturn "undesirable" governments in Guatemala and Cuba, the CIA, bolstered by Reagan, provided the funds, weapons, and advisors to expand the contras dramatically.

The contras drew recruits and supporters from several groups with grievances against the Sandinista movement. First, most of the top military leadership consisted of former Somoza National Guard members. These were individuals who had staked their futures on the Somoza system. When Somoza was overthrown, their status, privileges, and careers were destroyed. Their goals were generally to eliminate the Sandinista government, take revenge, and restore their dominant position in Nicaragua (Booth 1985; PBS 1986; White 1984). Second, many affluent businesspeople opposed the Sandinista government because they viewed it as undemocratic and possibly also because it prevented people like them from controlling Nicaragua politically and economically. Some initially worked against the Somoza dictatorship and cooperated with the provisional revolutionary government, but they were usually individuals who had never been members of the FSLN. Often with reputations among U.S. officials as political moderates or conservatives, they provided the contras with a civilian political wing and a public image of respectability (PBS 1987). These elements together formed in August 1981 the largest and longest-enduring contra organization, the Nicaraguan Democratic Force (FDN), which in the latter half of the 1980s had between 6,000 and 12,000 soldiers. The FDN was assisted at times by mercenaries from Honduras, Chile, and Argentina paid by the CIA (Kornbluh 1987).

One prominent Sandinista figure, Edén Pastora, did desert the revolutionary government and chose to start his own contra group based to the south in Costa Rica. He felt that the Sandinistas had betrayed the goals of the revolution and had failed to establish a pluralist democracy. Pastora's background (his family had been involved in the Conservative Party) and past political associations indicated that he was considerably more conservative than other Sandinistas (Christian 1985). He had successively joined and quit several anti-Somoza movements of varying ideological characteristics and eventually committed himself to the FSLN when he perceived it to be the organization actually capable of leading and winning a revolution against the

Somoza regime. His statements suggested that his motives for turning against the FSLN might have been as much personal as ideological. After the revolution he appeared to be upset because he was not being accepted as a true Sandinista (PBS 1985) and did not receive a desired government appointment.

Pastora, however, refused to enter into an alliance with the main contra army based in Honduras because it was under the influence of the CIA. As most of the popular support he had enjoyed as a Sandinista hero quickly evaporated once he took up arms against the revolution and as his resources were limited compared to the CIA-funded group, his movement, founded in September 1982 under the title Democratic Revolutionary Alliance (ARDE), became insignificant by 1985 (*New York Times*, Sept. 4, 1985, A3). In summer 1986 Pastora turned himself in to Costa Rican authorities and retired from the contra war to run a fishing business. During spring 1987 he told a CNN correspondent that he believed the FDN counterrevolutionaries had tried to assassinate him because he would not unite his forces with theirs and that the only reason he would again take up arms would be to help defeat the CIA-backed contras (CNN, May 22, 1987). In 1989 Pastora, benefiting from Nicaragua's amnesty program, returned to Nicaragua and announced his intention to resume peaceful political activities.

By the mid-1980s many of the contra soldiers were very young and thus could not have been members of Somoza's National Guard. And whereas 90 percent of the top fifty officers in the FDN had been in Somoza's army, 80 percent of contra field officers had not (Vanderlaan 1986). Motives for joining the contras appeared to vary. Some volunteers were the younger brothers of National Guard soldiers or relatives of former Somoza supporters. Others were recruited from among the religiously conservative peasants of northeastern Nicaragua who, largely because of contra misinformation, feared a Sandinista attack on their religious institutions and beliefs. Many independent farmers turned against the Sandinistas because of Managua's restrictions on their ability to market their produce freely or because of harsh measures that were part of the FSLN anticontra effort, such as the forcible relocation of some peasants away from homes and farms. The salaries paid to contra soldiers from the scores of millions of dollars provided by the Reagan administration and other sources constituted a significant incentive for some farmers of northeastern Nicaragua to join the contras—the pay levels were often far above their usual incomes.

Other Nicaraguans of indigenous ancestry were provoked into hostility against the revolutionary government by heavy-handed tactics used in the early 1980s by Sandinista soldiers to counter opposition in the Atlantic Coast region. Some anti-Sandinista indigenous rebel groups allied for a time with the FDN and others with Pastor's ARDE. But by spring 1987 most of the indigenous guerrillas had withdrawn from the contra war, and several indigenous leaders, who had initially organized armed resistance against the Sandinistas, supported the government's autonomy plan and accused the CIA-sponsored contra army of lacking any significant popular support (*New York Times*, Apr. 14, 1987, A12).

Opposition to Reagan Administration Policy on Nicaragua

The conduct of contra forces in Nicaragua provoked condemnation from international human rights monitoring organizations, which noted in 1986 and in 1987 that although the Sandinistas committed violations of human rights (such as the jailing of Miskito Indian dissidents), the Sandinista offenses were generally of a lesser magnitude and far less frequent than those of the contras (Americas Watch Committee 1985; PBS 1986; *New York Times*, Feb. 10, 1987, A10). Furthermore, a news story revealed that as many as 125 citizens of Honduras (the site of contra bases) who opposed the contras were assassinated by contra death squads after being identified by the CIA as subversives (CBS, March 29, 1987).

The CIA and various U.S. government officials not only knew about contra atrocities, including the murders of mayors, teachers, doctors and nurses, and captured Nicaraguan militia soldiers but had actually prepared and distributed to contras two thousand copies of an instructional booklet entitled "Psychological Techniques of Guerrilla Warfare." This manual, among other things, provided explicit instructions on how to carry out public executions of captured military or civilian leaders (Cockcroft 1989; *Providence Journal*, Oct. 20, 1984, 1).

The behavior of contra forces and leaders caused the disillusionment and resignation of several individuals recruited by the CIA to serve as the civilian political leadership for the contras. They included Edgar Chamorro, who had been FDN public relations director during the years 1981–1984. In a letter to the *New York Times* (Jan. 9, 1986, A22), Chamorro stated that the contras had a policy of terrorizing civilian noncombatants to discourage support for the FSLN-dominated government. He also noted that the Sandinistas, despite serious shortcomings, had created a national atmosphere of social equality for the first time in the country's history and had made huge improvements in health care, education, and housing, much of which was destroyed by the contra war. He concluded that the Nicaraguan economy had been devastated primarily by the effects of the contra war and the U.S. economic embargo. According to Chamorro, the goals of the contra leaders, as revealed in their conversations with him, had been to recover their wealth and restore their previous dominant social status.

Western European allies of the United States almost unanimously refused to cooperate with the Republican administration's economic embargo and instead provided assistance to and increased trade with Nicaragua. International opposition to the contras and the CIA war against the Nicaraguan government was reflected in the overwhelming ruling of the United Nations World Court in 1984 to condemn the January-

February CIA mining of Nicaragua's harbors. In 1986 the World Court, again by a large majority, found the Reagan administration's support for the contras in violation of international law and ruled that the United States must cease its assault on Nicaragua and pay reparations to Nicaragua for the loss of life, property damage, and other costs of the contra war (Cockcroft 1989; Gutman 1988; Sklar 1988).

Despite President Reagan's references to the contras as "freedom fighters," a majority of U.S. citizens consistently opposed aid to the contras. A 1986 ABC/*Washington Post* national survey of U.S. adults, who were reminded that the United States was supporting the contras, found that 62 percent opposed U.S. efforts to overthrow the Nicaraguan government, while 28 percent supported such measures, and 10 percent had "no opinion" (Kornbluh 1987). CBS/*New York Times*, Harris Polls, and other surveys obtained similar results throughout the decade.

Contra atrocities and the mining of Nicaragua's harbors outraged many members of the U.S. House of Representatives as well as the leaders of most major religious denominations in the United States. Typical was the evaluation of Rep. Berkley Bedell (a Democrat from Iowa), who reported, "If the American people could have talked with the common people of Nicaragua whose women and children are being indiscriminately tortured and killed by terrorists (contras) financed by the American taxpayer, they would rise up in legitimate anger and demand that support for this criminal activity be ended at once" (*New York Times*, Apr. 14, 1983, 1). The House of Representatives refused, in October 1984, to provide further military aid to the contras (Booth 1985; Gutman 1988).

But in June 1986 a few members of the House, under administration pressure and angered by reports of Sandinista army incursions into Honduras in pursuit of contras, shifted their position, resulting in a close 221 to 209 vote victory for the Reagan administration's proposal to provide $70 million in military assistance (and $30 million in nonmilitary aid) to the contras (Sklar 1988). The contras had received tens of millions of dollars in the two-year period during which Congress blocked U.S. government funds (Cockburn 1987; Sklar 1988). It was disclosed in 1986, 1987, and 1988 that Reagan administration personnel had sold weapons to Iran (involved then in its war with Iraq) at two to three times the cost, evidently diverting some of the huge profits to the contras (*New York Times*, Nov. 26, 1986, 1). The Reagan administration had also convinced other governments, such as Saudi Arabia and Brunei, to contribute millions to the contras (*New York Times*, Apr. 25, 1987, 1). Finally, a Senate investigative committee found evidence of a $10 million contribution to the contras from Colombian drug traffickers and other revenues derived from the transportation of drugs into the United States on planes returning from delivering weapons to contras (Cockburn 1987; PBS 1988; Sklar 1988). Public knowledge of these disclosures, a larger Democratic majority in Congress following legislative elections, and increased congressional sentiment in favor of nonviolent resolution of Central American conflicts led Congress to vote again in February 1988 to ban U.S. military assistance to the contras (Cockcroft 1989).

Impacts of the Contra War and the Economic Embargo

The contra war took at least 30,000 lives and strained the Nicaraguan economy in several ways. First, over half of the national budget was shifted to defense (including the purchase of weapons, largely from the only available sources willing to antagonize the United States by aiding Nicaragua militarily—the Soviet Union, Cuba, and several Eastern European nations), thus impeding further development of the economy and social programs. Second, contras and non-Nicaraguan mercenaries (reportedly paid by the CIA) inflicted significant damage on several industrial installations and repeatedly interfered with the coffee harvest in some parts of Nicaragua. Third, out of an adult (sixteen or over) population of approximately 1.5 million, Nicaragua had to mobilize a regular army of more than 60,000 and local militia units numbering more than 200,000 (PBS 1987; Walker 1986). The huge proportion of Nicaraguans under arms was one of the strongest indications that the Sandinista government enjoyed considerable popular support. But the large number of citizens committed to military operations or intermittent guard duty contributed to a labor shortage that was only partially offset by the assistance of international volunteer workers. The low-intensity warfare waged by the Reagan administration through the contras, the CIA, and the economic embargo appeared intended to motivate an overthrow of the Sandinista-led government by a population exhausted and desperate for peace at any price (*New York Times*, Mar. 23, 1987, A10; Oct. 16, 1988, A1; PBS 1987).

Nicaraguan Defensive Measures and International Assistance

The Nicaraguan government not only mobilized army and militia forces in its own defense. In November 1984 elections were held for a national legislature and a president. In a seven-party, secret ballot competition, the Sandinista Party won about 62 percent of the vote, both for the presidency and for seats in the legislature (which were awarded in proportion to the popular vote). The Democratic Conservative Party finished second, with 13 percent, Independent Liberals received about 10 percent, People's Social Christians 5 percent, and three parties to the left of the Sandinistas (the Socialist, Communist, and Marxist-Leninist parties) received 4 percent. About 6 percent of the ballots were filled out incorrectly and declared invalid. Approximately 80 percent of those eligible to vote (those at least sixteen years old) had done so, although not required to by law. The political parties that participated had been given weekly radio and TV time and were able to post signs and distribute campaign literature. International observers from several democracies, although noting that conditions were far from perfect, provided favorable evaluations of the election procedures, especially in comparison to elections in other nations in the region that the Reagan administration viewed as acceptably democratic (*Manchester Guardian*, Nov. 5, 1984, 6; Nov. 6, 1984, 7; Walker 1986).

Some political groups had refused to appear on the ballot. Although their spokesperson, Arturo Cruz, claimed that campaign conditions were unfair, lack of participation probably stemmed from a realistic anticipation of very poor performance, coupled with, as some later admitted, inducements from U.S. agents to encourage boycotting the election in an effort to make it appear that Nicaraguans had no choices but left-wing parties (Booth 1985; Walker 1986). The election was held just before the 1984 U.S. presidential vote in order to ensure that Nicaragua would have an elected government before the virtually certain reelection of President Reagan. Some FSLN leaders feared that once Reagan no longer had to worry about running for a second term, he would militarily intervene if Nicaragua did not have an internationally recognized, popularly elected government.

Still another defensive action taken by the Nicaraguan government was limiting civil liberties, including imposing press censorship. Such restrictions were suspended during the election campaign period but reinstituted shortly afterward. *La Prensa* was shut down temporarily in 1986 (in order to prevent, according to the Nicaraguan government, publication of militarily useful information or rumors that might incite panic hoarding of essential goods). And labor strikes were banned during the contra war. As the war continued, Sandinista activists often attempted to mobilize the mass organizations, which had earlier served in part as social centers of participatory democracy, on behalf of government policies and the anticontra effort. The increasing FSLN- and government-directed character of mass organizations reduced their popularity, and participation in them declined markedly in the late 1980s (Vickers 1990).

The Sandinista government justified its limitations on civil liberties by appealing to the precedents set by other nations at war, noting, for example, that during World War I and World War II the U.S. government restricted freedom of the press and freedom of speech, imposed a ban on strikes, and, specifically during World War II, forcibly relocated tens of thousands of Japanese-American citizens, all to be more effective in a fight against enemies thousands of miles away—who never came close to invading U.S. national territory. Also, the Sandinistas were painfully aware of how the CIA and its conservative Chilean allies had made use of the wide-open democracy during Allende's presidency to prepare to overthrow not only the Allende government but also the entire democratic system in Chile (see chapter 5). The Sandinistas and many other Nicaraguans vowed to prevent Nicaragua from becoming another Chile. The Nicaraguan government asserted that the true cause of limitations on civil liberties was the war being waged on Nicaragua by the Reagan administration and that full civil liberties would be restored once that war ended.

Outside assistance bolstered Nicaragua's ability to cope at least partially with the effects of the U.S. economic embargo and the contra war. As the Reagan administration shut down U.S. commerce with Nicaragua, Western and Eastern Europe dramatically increased their trade and sent economic and technical assistance. The Soviet Union provided weapons, and Cuba sent military advisors. Assistance from the USSR was estimated to be about $400 million annually in the late 1980s (Cockcroft 1989).

1989 Peace Agreement and 1990 Election

The revolutionary Nicaraguan government's diplomatic successes went beyond obtaining aid and increasing trade with Europe. Nicaragua in 1989 won the cooperation of the presidents of the other four Central American states and the support of the Organization of American States and the United Nations for a comprehensive peace plan (*New York Times*, Feb. 16, 1989, A14; Aug. 8, 1989, A1; Oct. 2, 1989, A10). The agreement called for dismantling the contra camps in Honduras and amnesty and repatriation for all those who wished to return to Nicaragua. National and municipal elections were scheduled to be held by the end of February 1990. Voter registration, the participation of existing and new political parties, campaigning, and the election itself were to be supervised by officially designated observers from the UN and the OAS. The involvement of those organizations in the election process was meant to provide irrefutable evidence and an impartial judgment regarding the fairness of the election to a potentially hostile or skeptical Bush administration.

In the campaign for the February 25, 1990, election, fourteen political parties formed a coalition, the National Opposition Union (UNO), to run against the FSLN party. UNO included (in alphabetical order) the Central American Integrationist Party, the Communist Party of Nicaragua, the Conservative National Action Party, the Conservative Popular Alliance (one of the largest parties in the coalition), the Democratic Party of National Confidence, the Independent Liberal Party (another of the largest parties in UNO), the Liberal Constitutionalist Party (PLC), the Liberal Party, the National Action Party, the National Conservative Party, the Nicaraguan Democratic Movement, the Nicaraguan Socialist Party, the Popular Social Christian Party, and the Social Democratic Party (*New York Times*, Mar. 1, 1990, A20). UNO was also supported by Yatama, a Miskito Indian organization. Several leaders within the UNO coalition had at one time been associated with the contras, while other leaders and parties in UNO, although critical of the FSLN, had also opposed the contras and the violent attempt to overthrow the Nicaraguan government. The UNO coalition selected Violeta

Barrios de Chamorro, widow of the assassinated anti-Somoza newspaper editor, Pedro Chamorro, as its presidential candidate. She did not officially belong to any of the individual parties in the UNO alliance. The Social Christian Party and a number of other parties ran independently.

In the election, in which an estimated 93 percent of those eligible participated, the UNO group of parties received approximately 55 percent of the vote, while the FSLN received about 41 percent and other parties about 4 percent. This outcome resulted in the election of Violeta Chamorro over the incumbent president and FSLN presidential candidate Daniel Ortega (*New York Times*, Feb. 27, 1990, A1; Feb. 28, 1990, A1). The seats in the new parliament were awarded in approximate proportion to the votes received by the UNO coalition, the FSLN, and other competing parties. The FSLN won thirty-nine seats, and one each was won by two parties not in the UNO alliance, the Revolutionary Unity Movement and the Social Christian Party. Among the parties within the UNO coalition, the three conservative parties received a total of thirteen seats, the three liberal parties, twelve; the socialist and social democratic parties, eleven; the three social Christian parties (the Democratic Party of National Confidence, the Popular Social Christian Party, and the National Action Party) received ten seats; the Communist Party, three seats; and the Central American Integrationist Party, two seats (Vilas 1990).

Pre- and postelection voter surveys and interviews identified several major reasons for the defeat of the FSLN. The most important appeared to be concern about the Nicaraguan economy, which had 1,700 percent inflation in 1989 (following over 33,000 percent inflation in 1988) along with an estimated 30 percent unemployed or underemployed (*New York Times*, Mar. 4, 1990, A1). Some observers claimed the austerity measures imposed by the FSLN-dominated government in 1988, designed to rescue the economy, hurt low-income workers and peasants more than the middle or upper classes (Vilas 1990). Since many FSLN leaders were somewhat insulated from economic hardships by virtue of their government jobs and privileges, such as cars and housing, resentment among the poor grew. As a result, electoral support for UNO came not only from the most politically conservative and wealthy sectors in the population but also from the most impoverished. The discontented among the poor typically knew little of UNO proposals or policies but desperately hoped for economic salvation under a new government and perhaps also desired to punish the Sandinistas for failing to deliver on past promises (O'Kane 1990). As many as 150,000 voters were estimated to have shifted from their 1984 vote for the FSLN and Daniel Ortega to UNO and Violeta Chamorro in 1990.

The military draft under the Sandinista government was also unpopular, along with the war against the contras, which had taken an estimated 30,000 lives by 1990 and resulted in the destruction of much of the early postrevolutionary educational and medical gains in the countryside. Some voters felt that Sandinista economic policies and hostility toward the United States government were largely responsible for both the economic problems and the war. Others opposed the Sandinistas because of their periodic repressive measures toward opponents.

Many voters blamed the U.S. economic embargo and contra war for most of Nicaragua's problems but concluded that the only way to save Nicaragua would be to replace the FSLN with a government more acceptable to the United States and likely to receive immediate U.S. economic aid. Some Nicaraguans opposed the Sandinista presidential and vice-presidential candidates, Ortega and Sergio Ramírez, simply because these men were running for reelection to new six-year terms instead of accepting lesser political roles and supporting other FSLN members for the top offices (Vilas 1990). Finally, many voters admired and positively identified with Violeta Chamorro, whose husband had been martyred in the struggle against the Somoza dictatorship and whose own family, like so many in Nicaragua, had divided over the issue of support or opposition to the governing Sandinista Party (one son and one daughter on each side). Chamorro was also respected for having remained in Nicaragua to pursue her ideals and her conception of the Nicaraguan Revolution.

President Daniel Ortega and other Sandinista leaders peacefully surrendered governmental power and control of the military to President Chamorro and the new parliament on April 25, 1990 (*New York Times*, Apr. 26, 1990, A1). To the surprise of many, President Chamorro reappointed Humberto Ortega, the brother of the former president, as head of the armed forces (*New York Times*, Jan. 10, 1991, A6). Following the election, President Bush quickly ended the U.S. trade embargo against Nicaragua and announced plans to send $300 million in assistance to help restore Nicaragua's devastated economy (*New York Times*, Mar. 14, 1990, A15). Violeta Chamorro, Daniel Ortega, and President Bush within days of the election all called for the contras to disband. In accordance with the peace agreement, most contras turned in their weapons to UN peacekeeping troops, who had been deployed in the Nicaraguan countryside to prevent further violent conflict (*New York Times*, June 11, 1990, A3).

Although the FSLN lost the 1990 presidential election, it remained the country's largest, best-organized, and most popular individual political party, with many supporters in the military, the police, and the major labor unions and among government employees and teachers. Daniel Ortega, an FSLN member of parliament after the 1990 elections, and other prominent Sandinista leaders vowed to "rule from below" and to fight in parliament and through the threat of labor strikes and demonstrations to defend what they viewed as the positive achievements of the revolution for the nation's disadvantaged (*New York Times*, May 30, 1990, A1). By mid-1990 there had been major strikes in Nicaragua for higher wages and against proposed government policies that many viewed as benefiting the economically privileged to the detriment of the less fortunate (*New York Times*, July 11, 1990, A3). And in general the poverty, inequality, and other economic factors that initially had led to the formation of the FSLN, the Nicaraguan Revolution, and the development of other conflicts in Central America appeared in 1990 as bad as or worse than they were in 1970 (*New York Times*, June 24, 1990, E3).

NICARAGUA IN THE 1990S

Violeta Chamorro's presidency was characterized by several major developments. First, President Chamorro pursued neoliberal economic policies that included downsizing government agencies and expenditures (including the country's armed forces), creating conditions favorable to business enterprises, attempting to privatize some government-owned enterprises, and seeking to compensate former owners of many properties confiscated by the previous Sandinista administration (*New York Times*, Dec. 8, 1994, A17). These measures, though benefiting some relatively affluent Nicaraguans, tended to create hardships for many more, provoking major strikes, demonstrations, and even some localized rebellions against the government. Many Nicaraguan soldiers who lost their jobs when the armed forces were greatly reduced from a contra war high of about 96,000 down to about 15,000 in 1990 and many contras who fought them, also without jobs or land, again took up arms, many resorting to criminal activity to survive, such as theft, kidnapping, extortion, or weapons or drugs trafficking (Rogers 2001, 13–14.

At the same time, President Chamorro tended to maintain a conciliatory orientation toward the Sandinista Party and the Sandinista-led armed forces. She retained former Sandinista president Daniel Ortega's brother, Humberto, as head of the armed forces until mid-1995. President Chamorro cooperated with Sandinista politicians and military and police officials. There was evidence that certain Sandinistas were assisting revolutionary movements in other countries and rumors that some Sandinistas might have been involved in the 1991 murders of several former contras, including contra commander Enrique Bermudez. These developments turned most of the UNO coalition members of parliament, who had supported Chamorro's victorious presidential campaign, against her (Burbach 1994; LaRamee 1995; McConnell 1993; Millett 1994; 1995; Vilas 1994). Similarly, major U.S. political figures, in particular Senator Jesse Helms, head of the U.S. Senate Foreign Relations Committee, objected to Ortega continuing as commander of the army and campaigned against U.S. aid going to Nicaragua (Wilson 1994).

As President Chamorro's administration came under pressure from both the majority of her own UNO coalition and powerful U.S. politicians, she formed an alliance with the remaining minority of UNO parliamentarians who supported her and the Sandinista parliamentary delegation, which together constituted a slight majority. But by 1993 a national survey indicated that 61 percent of Nicaraguans said they had "no faith in any political party." Only 21 percent expressed support for the Sandinistas, and only 18 percent backed the UNO coalition. UNO appeared to lose support in great part for pursuing policies that appeared to favor the rich, such as returning public-use properties to former owners and enacting austerity measures blamed for increasing unemployment and limiting social services.

The Sandinistas appeared to lose support for several reasons. One factor was that by simply being a large component of the parliament and often supporting President Chamorro, the Sandinistas suffered from some of the population's general animosity toward the government. Second, as members of parliament or recipients of some of the properties previously confiscated from wealthy Somoza or contra supporters in the so-called *piñata* or "candy grab" (Stahler-Sholk 2006), some high-ranking Sandinistas seemed relatively insulated from the economic hardships afflicting so many Nicaraguans and were discredited in the eyes of many people. Another development that caused significant disillusionment among many Sandinista sympathizers was that the Sandinista-led army of Nicaragua, the Sandinista People's Army, was forced to obey orders to suppress disorders resulting from popular protests, often led or encouraged by Sandinista Party activists, against the Chamorro administration. This included the retaking of the town of Esteli (with the loss of forty lives), which had been seized by former Sandinista soldiers objecting to certain government policies. The Sandinista army, in following President Chamorro's orders, was sometimes forced to confront, arrest, or even fight other Sandinistas and large numbers of Nicaraguans who had previously constituted a component of the mass support for the Sandinista movement.

By the mid-1990s conflicts within the Sandinista Party resulted in the development of two distinct factions. One group, led by the former president of Nicaragua, Daniel Ortega, was called the "Democratic Left." This faction claimed to maintain a strong commitment to a genuine revolutionary reconstruction of Nicaraguan society, a project that its leaders claimed had been sabotaged by U.S. intervention in the form of both economic warfare and the contra war that devastated the country, destroying much of the 1979 revolution's early achievements. In the 1990s this group pledged to remain dedicated to defending the interests of the poor and resisting foreign imperialism, including foreign corporate exploitation of Nicaragua. Most of those elected by Sandinista Party members to the party's governing council were Democratic Left Sandinistas. But only a minority of the Sandinistas in parliament were members of this faction. Most of the Sandinistas in parliament belonged to the "Sandinista Renewal Movement" faction (MRS). The MRS faction criticized the Democratic Left side of the Party for running the Party in a too authoritarian manner, for losing touch with the masses, and for not appreciating the importance of foreign investment for Nicaragua's future development (LaRamee 1995; *New York Times*, Dec. 28, 1994, A9.).

In 1995 the Sandinista members of parliament from the MRS faction joined their votes with those of conservative UNO parliamentarians to force significant modifications of the Nicaraguan constitution, which limited presidential power while enlarging that of the parliament, claiming that this would make the country's political system more democratic (*New York Times*, June 16, 1995, A11). Another major development in 1995 was the retirement of General Humberto Ortega from command of the nation's army and his replacement by his former second in command, General Joaquin Cuadra Lacayo, also a Sandinista (*New York Times*, July 26, 1995, 10). In the same year, the army, which had been reduced to less than 20 percent of its highest level during the contra war to about 15,000 in the mid-1990s, was officially renamed from its original "Sandinista People's Army" to the "Nicaraguan Army." Government leaders hoped that these measures would help reduce domestic conflict and encourage foreign investment and aid, including U.S. assistance, to help rebuild the economy and reduce Nicaragua's debt, which had reached $12 billion by the mid-1990s.

Why Were Republican Administrations So Hostile?

What could possibly have accounted for the intense hostility and violent responses of the Reagan and Bush administrations toward the Nicaraguan Revolution, while at the same time they took nonviolent and much more tolerant approaches to regimes internationally evaluated as undemocratic, brutally repressive, or even racist (such as the pre-1990 military dictatorship in Chile or the white minority government in South Africa)? The government first rationalized aid to the contras by stating that the contras were being used to stop arms shipments across Nicaragua to leftist rebels in El Salvador. But soon it became clear that the real goal was to overthrow the Nicaraguan government. The Reagan administration's negative attitude toward Nicaragua was undoubtedly partly due to the president's tendency, which persisted until at least the latter half of his second term, to view the world largely in terms of a bipolar East-West competition. According to this rigid logic, because the Nicaraguan revolutionary government was not clearly in the U.S. camp and was receiving military and other assistance from the Soviet Union and Cuba, it was an ally or even a clone of the enemy superpower, not the product of a revolution unique to its own culture and history. By 1983 President Reagan accused Nicaragua of having become a totalitarian Communist dictatorship, a charge rejected not only by most of the world's other democracies but also by the leadership of major religious denominations in the United States (*Hartford Courant*, May 19, 1985, A12).

Reagan also claimed that the Nicaraguan government was persecuting minorities and religions and that Nicaragua was serving as a base for international terrorism. The charges were criticized as either falsehoods or exaggerations (*New York Times*, June 18, 1985, A27). Furthermore, the Reagan administration claimed that the large Sandinista army and militia constituted a potential invasion threat to neighboring countries. The Nicaraguan government responded by inviting members of the U.S. House of Representatives, Senate, and news media to inspect its military and armaments in order to prove that its capabilities and deployment of armed forces were for defensive purposes (CBS, Oct. 27, 1985).

A major reason for the Reagan administration's animosity toward Nicaragua may have been the fear that a successful Nicaraguan Revolution could serve as an inspiration for other less-developed societies. The Cuban Revolution succeeded in redistributing wealth toward the poor majority and in creating a social and economic system more egalitarian than any other society in Latin America (Eckstein 1986). But the Cuban model was not very appealing to other American peoples because its one-party, Marxist-Leninist government ran counter to aspirations for an open and free political system. The victory of Popular Unity in Chile in 1970 suggested that a more attractive alternative might be possible. Through elections in a multiparty system, a movement advocating radical redistribution of wealth and the retention of an open, democratic political system had come to power. But for a variety of reasons, including the economic pressures applied by the Nixon administration, CIA intrigues, and the opposition of conservative Chilean military, business, and political leaders, the Chilean experiment ended, at least temporarily, in disaster.

In Nicaragua, after a violent revolution, another government advocating radical redistribution of wealth achieved power. But unlike Chile the army that served the past conservative regime was destroyed, and the new national army was supportive of the goal of social and economic revolution. Furthermore, the willingness of the government to distribute arms to hundreds of thousands of citizens and the results of the 1984 election reflected widespread popular support for the Nicaraguan government (in Chile, among the contending parties, Popular Unity was never able to achieve an absolute majority of the vote). All these factors indicated that Nicaragua was on the verge of achieving that dreamed of, but elusive, combination of socioeconomic revolution and democracy in a Third World country. Nicaraguan success might have threatened the interests of multinational corporations, for which economic stability and certainty of favorable investment conditions were viewed as prerequisites for profit-making ventures in less-developed societies.

Real political democracy in nations of impoverished workers and farmers constitutes a risk factor many multinationals have been content to do without. Truly democratic elections might result in governments that respond to popular aspirations by raising minimum wage levels (thereby increasing the cost of labor and reducing profits) or by expropriating foreign holdings (as occurred in Chile). The loss of political and economic control over Nicaragua was of little direct significance to most multinational corporations or the economies of their homelands. But if, having been encouraged by the Nicaraguan example, movements advocating socioeconomic revolution and real democracy (meaning the mobilization and political participation of the poor majority) come to power in the larger and more populous nations of Latin America or certain other less-developed parts of the world, the impact on the multinationals could be very significant.

NICARAGUA AFTER THE VIOLETA CHAMORRO PRESIDENCY

Following Violeta Chamorro, conservative populist Arnoldo Alemán of the Liberal Constitutionalist Party (PLC), a former mayor of Managua, became president in 1997, after defeating FSLN candidate Daniel Ortega. This administration was later accused of corruption, resulting in Alemán's arrest, conviction, and imprisonment. During the Alemán administration a controversial agreement, disapproved of by a wide section of the Nicaraguan population, was made between the Liberal Constitutional Party and the FSLN, the "El Pacto" (Bendaña 2002, 14; SSHL, UCSD 2005, 16). The purpose of the pact seemed to be an attempt to insure that future presidents would be candidates of either the PLC or the Sandinista Party. Since Nicaragua had a number of political parties, it was possible that in the first round of presidential elections, no candidate would get enough votes to win without having a second run-off election between the top two vote getters in the first round. But in order to have a chance to win, the remaining two candidates would be forced to make agreements with and likely promise positions or other benefits to members of the smaller parties to gather enough votes for victory in the second round. El Pacto greatly reduced the possibility that a run-off election for the presidency would be needed. Under El Pacto the election law was changed to allow the top vote getter in the first round to win with only 40 percent of the popular vote. Furthermore, it even permitted a top vote getter with as low as 35 percent of the popular vote to win the presidency, so long as that candidate's vote total was at least 5 percent of the total vote higher than the percentage for the next highest candidate. Many people viewed El Pacto as a partial betrayal of democratic principles by Alemán of the PLC and Ortega of the FSLN. Furthermore, many current or former supporters of the FSLN became disappointed that Ortega and the FSLN seemed to adopt some neoliberal economic policies rather than attempting to do more to directly assist the hundreds of thousands of poor and under- or unemployed people in the country.

In 1998 Nicaragua was devastated by hurricane Mitch, which killed about three thousand people and made hundreds of thousands at least temporarily homeless. Intensified economic desperation seemed to increase the political appeal of the FSLN. Polls indicated that Daniel Ortega, again running as the FSLN candidate, might win the presidential election in November 2001, despite the accusation by his stepdaughter that he sexually abused her as a child and even though some party members preferred that the FSLN select a different candidate. But the September 11, 2001, terrorist attacks in the United States assured that the FSLN would be defeated again. President Bush's post–9/11 national speech, in which he stated that the U.S. would intensify the war against terrorism and deal harshly with any country that aided or harbored terrorists, terrified many Nicaraguans and played into the hands of the PLC and its candidate, Enrique Bolaños, a former contra. Bolaños's presidential campaign proclaimed the strong probability that a victory by the FSLN, a party that a previous U.S. Republican administration had accused of supporting terrorism when it was in power, would provoke the Bush administration into punishing Nicaragua economically and perhaps even more harshly. The threat of additional economic hardships and possible U.S. military intervention likely helped to insure the Bolaños victory.

President Bolaños shocked many members of his own PLC by allowing the party's outgoing president Alemán to be charged in 2002 with embezzlement while in office and money laundering. In 2003 Alemán was sentenced to twenty years' confinement. In January 2004 the World Bank wrote off 80 percent of the debt owed by Nicaragua, and in July Russia similarly forgave billions of dollars in loans (BBC News, April 21, 2006). In 2005 many PLC members of congress, angered at Bolaños over the imprisonment of Alemán, collaborated in an alliance with the Sandinista representatives against the president and attempted to pass constitutional reforms to limit his power. But in October the Nicaraguan congress agreed to postpone the reforms until the following president's term began in 2007. The congress in 2005 also approved the Central American Free Trade Agreement (CAFTA) with the United States.

The World Bank (2004, 1) estimated that the proportion of the population in Nicaragua living in poverty was 45.8 percent, although this was down from 50.3 percent in 1993. Apparently attempting to improve the electoral prospects of the FSLN while at the same time provide assistance to many among Nicaragua's large proportion of low-income residents, leftist Venezuelan President Hugo Chavez's government agreed to supply oil to Nicaragua's municipalities on favorable payment terms (Rogers 2006).

In the 2006 presidential election scheduled for November 5 there were five candidates: Eduardo Montealegre, candidate of both the Nicaraguan Liberal Alliance and the Conservative Party (Montealegre had previously been a member of the PLC), Daniel Ortega of the FSLN, Eduardo Jarquín of the Sandinista Renewal Movement, José Rizo of the PLC, and Edén Pastora of the Alternative for Change Party. In a September 2006 public opinion poll Ortega was in the lead, but an earlier survey indicated that in a possible run-off election Montealegre might defeat any of the other candidates (Angus Reid Global Scan: Polls and Research 2006a, b).

Although the revolution failed to achieve the original socioeconomic transformation goals of Carlos Fonseca and the other founders of the FSLN, it has been credited with dramatically increasing the level of political participation and building a far more democratic political system. According to Richard Stahler-Sholk (2006, 618),

> The Sandinista revolution began democratizing Nicaragua, ending an era when the U.S. controlled client states by designating autocratic leaders who lacked popular support. The Nicaraguan revolution also helped shift the focus of revolution itself, from the seizure of state power to the longer-term process of social transformation. That shift continued with the rise of diverse social movements, confronting not so much the state as transnational capital in the era of globalization.

Summary and Analysis

The major unifying motivation for and central cause of the Nicaraguan Revolution—the widespread desire to end Somoza family rule—served as the basis for joining diverse political and economic groups in the FSLN-led anti-Somoza movement. Later, conflicting class interests and differing conceptions of a post-Somoza government and society caused many Nicaraguans to desert the revolutionary alliance with the FSLN.

The FSLN was formed initially by young dissident members of Nicaragua's educated classes who intended not only to oust the dictator but also to bring social revolution to Nicaragua. Other elements of Nicaragua's elite, moderates and conservatives, had periodically mobilized against the Somoza dictatorship. The assassination of an outspoken critic of the Somozas, wealthy newspaper editor Pedro Chamorro, convinced more upper-class Nicaraguans that the family dictatorship must end. In 1978 and 1979 many business and church leaders helped weaken the Somoza government by withdrawing their support.

Popular discontent developed in response to the vast economic inequalities in Nicaragua and in reaction to the avarice, corruption, and repression of the Somozas. Discontent was considerably widened and intensified by the spread of liberation theology, by the misuse of earthquake relief aid, and by the increasing acts of brutality, such as the torture and murder of hundreds of suspected Sandinista sympathizers and the assassination of Pedro Chamorro. Finally, mass frustration reached explosive levels that found expression in the urban insurrections of 1978 and 1979.

For decades U.S. administrations had supported Somoza family control of the Nicaraguan government and had provided weapons and training to the dictatorship's armed forces. But, in contrast, President Carter's emphasis on human rights and his policy of making military aid contingent on improvements in the recipient nation's treatment of its citizens caused Anastasio Somoza Debayle to end a state of siege. This relaxation of repression allowed opposition forces greater freedom of movement. Later, as evidence of the Somoza regime's brutality increased, the Carter administration pressured

Somoza to leave, thereby precipitating the final collapse of the National Guard and the remaining prerevolutionary state structure. Neither the United States nor any other country intervened militarily to prevent the revolutionary victory. The Reagan administration later altered the level of U.S. permissiveness and attempted to change the outcome of the revolution.

The disintegration of Somoza's regime occurred in stages: The initial withdrawal in 1977 of unconditional U.S. support for the Somoza government was a central factor. The result was that the people of Nicaragua no longer viewed the strength of the Somoza government as identical to the economic and military power of the United States. The Somoza state was probably also weakened by perception of the dictator's serious health problems following the heart attack he suffered in July 1977. Acts of repression intended to buttress Somoza rule actually weakened the regime by further alienating not only ordinary Nicaraguans but also moderate and some conservative members of Nicaragua's economic elite. Eventually, support for Somoza's government narrowed to a small number of rightist Nicaraguans and the Nicaraguan National Guard, whose officers correctly anticipated its extinction in the advent of an FSLN victory. Loss of U.S. support in summer 1979, coupled with the flight of the dictator to Miami, caused the final destruction of the Somoza system. Demoralized members of the battered National Guard disbanded and were either captured or fled to neighboring countries.

The Republican administrations' strategy of low-intensity warfare appeared to involve inflicting hardships on the Nicaraguan people and of provoking postrevolution authorities into enacting unpopular measures, such as the military draft and restrictions on civil liberties, in order to foster mass discontent, which would lead either to an overthrow of the Sandinista-led government or to a critical erosion of its popular support. The military and economic pressures brought against Nicaragua did not succeed in violently overthrowing the revolution but did have catastrophic effects on health care, education, social welfare, and general living standards, which contributed to the 1990 election defeat of the FSLN.

Following the inauguration of Violeta Chamorro as president of Nicaragua in 1990, both her winning coalition of UNO parties and the Sandinista Party experienced significant internal divisions. Economic development was a difficult goal for Nicaragua to achieve, and hardship, continuing political conflicts, and perceived betrayals by elected officials caused massive disillusionment with all political parties among many Nicaraguans. The September 11, 2001, terrorist attacks in the United States contributed to the electoral defeat of the FSLN that year, when Nicaraguan voters were warned that electing the FSLN might make Nicaragua a target in the U.S. war on terrorism. In the 2006 election year internal conflict seriously divided the major political parties, and the country, with almost half its population still living in poverty, was subject to international political influences from both the right and the left.

Nicaraguan Revolution: Chronology of Major Events

1912–1925	U.S. troops stationed in Nicaragua
1926–1933	U.S. troops return to Nicaragua during civil war and train and support the Nicaraguan National Guard in the conflict against forces led by nationalist rebel leader Sandino
1934	Sandino is murdered
1936	Somoza uses National Guard to seize Nicaraguan government
1956	Anastasio Somoza García assassinated
1961	Sandinista Front for National Liberation founded
1977	Carter makes U.S. aid conditional on improved human rights situation; Anastasio Somoza Debayle ends state of siege
1978	Pedro Joaquín Chamorro murdered; Sandinista unit seizes National Palace; insurrections and strikes against Somoza regime
1979	Civil war intensifies; Somoza flees July 17; Sandinistas control Managua and declare victory July 19
1980	Divisions occur in revolutionary coalition
1981	Reagan provides U.S. support for counterrevolutionaries
1981–1989	Contra war
1990	Following peace agreements, internationally supervised vote results in election of Violeta Chamorro as president of Nicaragua
1990–2005	FSLN repeatedly defeated in presidential elections while continuing to hold about 40 percent of the seats in the Nicaraguan legislature and controlling many of the country's municipal governments

References and Further Readings

Americas Watch Committee. 1985. *An Americas Watch Report: Violations of the Laws of War by Both Sides in Nicaragua, 1981–85*. New York: Americas Watch.

Angus Reid Global Scan: Polls and Research. 2006a. "Montealegre, Ortega Almost Tied in Nicaragua." June 1. http://www.angus-reid.com/polls/index.cfm/fuseaction/viewItem/itemID/12074.

———. 2006b. "Ortega Gets 15-point Edge in Nicaragua." September 18. http://www.angus-reid.com/polls/index.cfm/fuseaction/viewitem/itemID/13178.

Arnove, Robert F. 1986. *Education and Revolution in Nicaragua*. New York: Praeger.

BBC News, April 21, 2006, "Country Profiles, Timeline: Nicaragua." http://news.bbc.co.uk/2/hi/americas/country_profiles/1225283.stm.

Bendaña, Alejandro. 2002. "Washington and the Caudillos: Calculation and Miscalculation in Managua." *NACLA: Report on the Americas, Post Cold War Latin America*, January/February, 12–16.

Berryman, Phillip. 1987. *Liberation Theology: Essential Facts about the Revolutionary Movement in Latin America—and Beyond*. Philadelphia: Temple University Press.

Binford, Leigh. 2006. "Salvadoran Revolution." In DeFronzo, ed., *Revolutionary Movements in World History*, 3:763–73.

Booth, John A. 1985. *The End and the Beginning: The Nicaraguan Revolution*. Westview Special Studies on Latin America and the Caribbean. 2nd ed. Boulder: Westview Press.

Burbach, Roger. 1994. "The Pot Boils Over." *NACLA* 27 (January): 4–7.

CBS. October 27, 1985. "Invade Nicaragua?" *60 Minutes*.

_____. March 29, 1987. "Contra Country." *60 Minutes*.

Christian, Shirley. 1985. *Nicaragua: Revolution in the Family*. New York: Random House.

CNN. May 22, 1987. "Interview with Edén Pastora."

Cockburn, Leslie. 1987. *Out of Control: The Story of the Reagan Administration's Secret War in Nicaragua, the Illegal Arms Pipeline, and the Contra Drug Connection*. New York: Atlantic Monthly Press.

Cockcroft, James D. 1989. *Neighbors in Turmoil: Latin America*. New York: Harper & Row.

Conroy, Michael E. 1987. "Economic Aggression as an Instrument of Low-Intensity Warfare." In Walker, ed., *Reagan versus the Sandinistas*.

DeFronzo, James, ed. 2006. *Revolutionary Movements in World History: From 1750 to the Present*. 3 vols. Santa Barbara, CA: ABC-CLIO.

Diederich, Bernard. 1981. *Somoza and the Legacy of U.S. Involvement in Central America*. New York: Dutton.

Dishkin, Martin. 1987. "The Manipulation of Indigenous Struggles." In Walker, ed., *Reagan versus the Sandinistas*.

Donahue, John M. 1986. *The Nicaraguan Revolution in Health: From Somoza to the Sandinistas*. South Hadley, MA: Bergin & Garvey.

Eckstein, Susan. 1986. "The Impact of the Cuban Revolution: A Comparative Perspective." *Comparative Studies in Society and History* 28 (July): 502–34.

Ewell, Judith. 2006. "Venezuelan Bolivarian Revolution of Hugo Chavez." In DeFronzo, ed., *Revolutionary Movements in World History*, 3:903–12.

Fullerton, Andrew. 2006. "Inequality, Class and Revolution." In DeFronzo, ed., *Revolutionary Movements in World History*, 2:408–12.

Gill, Jungyun. 2006. "Student and Youth Movements, Activism and Revolution." In DeFronzo, ed., *Revolutionary Movements in World History*, 3:848–54.

Gutman, Roy. 1988. *Banana Diplomacy: The Making of American Policy in Nicaragua, 1981–87*. New York: Simon & Schuster.

Hartford Courant, May 19, 1985, A12, "U.S. Churches Called Formidable Foe in Fighting Aid to Nicaraguan Contras."

Kampwirth, Karen. 2002. *Women and Guerilla Movements: Nicaragua, El Salvador, Chiapas, Cuba*. University Park: Pennsylvania State University Press.

Kornbluh, Peter. 1987. *Nicaragua: The Price of Intervention*. Washington, DC: Institute of Policy Studies.

LaRamee, Pierre. 1995. "Differences of Opinion: Interviews with Sandinistas." *NACLA* 28 (March/April): 11–14.

Macaulay, Neil. 1967. *The Sandino Affair*. Chicago: Quadrangle.

Manchester Guardian, November 5, 1984, 6, "Nicaraguans Pack Polling Stations."

_____, November 6, 1984, 7, "Huge Vote of Confidence for Sandinistas, But Conservatives' Showing a Surprise."

McConnell, Shelly. 1993. "Rules of the Game: Nicaragua's Contentious Constitutional Debate." *NACLA* 27 (September/October):20–25.

Millett, Richard. 1977. *Guardians of the Dynasty*. Maryknoll, NY: Orbis Books.

_____. 1994. "Central America's Enduring Conflicts." *Current History*, March, 124–28.

_____. 1995. "An End to Militarism? Democracy and the Armed Forces in Central America." *Current History*, February, 71–75.

New York Times, April 14, 1983, 1, "Key House Member Fears U.S. Breaks Law in Nicaragua."

_____, June 18, 1985, A27, "Reagan's Untruths About Nicaragua."

_____, September 4, 1985, A3, "Pastora Beleaguered."

_____, January 9, 1986, A22, Letter to the Editor, by Edgar Chamorro.

_____, November 26, 1986, 1, "Iran Payment Funds Diverted to Contras."

_____, February 10, 1987, A10, "U.S. Group Finds No Improvements in Contras' Human Rights Records."

_____, March 23, 1987, A10, "Casualties in Nicaragua: Schools and Health Care."

_____, April 14, 1987, A12, "Sandinistas Test Autonomy in East Province."

_____, April 25, 1987, 1, "Contra Suppliers Reportedly Got U.S. Military Help."

_____, October 16, 1988, A1, "Nicaragua's Economic Crisis Seen as Worsening."

_____, February 16, 1989, A14, "Text of Accord by Central American Presidents."

_____, August 8, 1989, A1, "5 Latin Presidents Defy U.S. and Urge Contras' Eviction."

_____, October 2, 1989, A10, "In Nicaragua, the Election Observers Are Coming!"

_____, February 27, 1990, A1, "Nicaraguan Opposition Routs Sandinistas: U.S. Pledges Aid, Tied to Orderly Turnover."

_____, February 28, 1990, A1, "Chamorro and Sandinista Rulers Begin Delicate Transition Talks."

_____, March 1, 1990, A20, "The Parties That Beat the Sandinistas."

_____, March 4, 1990, A1, "Message for Nicaraguan Victors: Things Must Get Better, and Fast."

_____, March 14, 1990, A15, "Nicaraguans on Both Sides Praise Embargo's End."

_____, April 26, 1990, A1, "Chamorro Takes Helm; Hails a New Era."

_____, May 30, 1990, A1, "Ruling Nicaragua: Almost a Daily Battle with Foes."

_____, June 11, 1990, A3, "Contras Continue to Surrender Arms."

_____, June 24, 1990, E3, "Can Central America Win a War on Poverty?"

_____, July 11, 1990, A3, "Managua Police Raze Roadblocks."

_____, January 10, 1991, A6, "Managua Defends Army Chief in Missile Uproar."

_____, December 8, 1994, A17, "Confiscations by Leftists Still Embroil Nicaraguans."

_____, December 28, 1994, A9, "Bitter Feud Is Dividing Sandinistas."

_____, June 16, 1995, A11, "New Nicaraguan Constitution."

_____, July 26, 1995, 10, "Critics Question Nicaraguan Army's Makeover."

O'Kane, Trish. 1990. "The New Old Order." *NACLA* (June): 28–36.

O'Shaughnessy, Laura Nuzzi, and Louis Serra. 1986. *The Church and Revolution in Nicaragua*. Monographs in International Studies, Latin America series, 11.

Athens: Ohio University, Center for International Studies, Latin American Studies Program.

Pastor, Robert A. 1987. *Condemned to Repetition: The United States and Nicaragua*. Princeton, NJ: Princeton University Press.

PBS. 1985. "Crisis in Central America: Revolution in Nicaragua." *Frontline*.

_____. 1986. "Who Runs the Contras." *Frontline*.

_____. 1987. "War on Nicaragua." *Frontline*.

_____. 1988. "Guns, Drugs, and the CIA." *Frontline*.

Providence Journal, October 20, 1984, 1, "Top Aide in CIA Defended Killings in Nicaragua."

Reif, Linda L. 1986. "Women in Latin American Guerrilla Movements: A Comparative Perspective." *Comparative Politics* January, 147–69.

Rogers, Tim. 2001. "Silent War in Nicaragua: The New Politics of Violence." *NACLA Report on the Americas, Well of Contention: Oil in the Americas*, January/February, 11–15.

_____. 2006. "Chavez Plays Oil Card in Nicaragua." *The Christian Science Monitor*, May 5.

Shayne, Julie. 2006. "Women and Revolution." In DeFronzo, ed., *Revolutionary Movements in World History*, 3:936–40.

Sigmund, Paul. 2006. "Chilean Socialist Revolution, Counter-Revolution, and the Restoration of Democracy." In DeFronzo, ed., *Revolutionary Movements in World History*, 1:107–16.

Sklar, Holly. 1988. *Washington's War on Nicaragua*. Boston: South End Press.

SSHL (Social Sciences and Humanities Library), UCSD (University of California, San Diego). 2005. "Nicaragua: Elections and Events 1996–1999." http://sshl.ucsd.edu /collections/las/nicaragua/1996.html.

Stahler-Sholk, Richard. 2006. "Nicaraguan Revolution." In DeFronzo, ed., *Revolutionary Movements in World History*, 2:609–22.

Streeter, Stephen. 2006. "Guatemalan Democratic Revolution, Counter-Revolution, and Restoration of Democracy." In DeFronzo, ed., *Revolutionary Movements in World History*, 1:325–35.

Vanderlaan, Mary B. 1986. *Revolution and Foreign Policy in Nicaragua*. Westview Special Studies on Latin America and the Caribbean. Boulder: Westview Press.

Vickers, George R. 1990. "A Spider's Web." *NACLA* (June): 19–27.

Vilas, Carlos M. 1990. "What Went Wrong." *NACLA* (June): 28–36.

_____. 1994. "The Sandinistas." *NACLA* 27 (May/June): 4.

Walker, Thomas W., ed. 1982. *Nicaragua in Revolution*. New York: Praeger.

_____. 1986. *Nicaragua: The Land of Sandino*. 2nd ed. Boulder: Westview Press.

_____, ed. 1987. *Reagan versus the Sandinistas: The Undeclared War on Nicaragua*. Boulder: Westview Press.

White, Richard. 1984. *The Morass: United States Intervention in Central America*. New York: Harper & Row.

Wickham-Crowley, Timothy P. 2006. "Guerilla Warfare and Revolution." In DeFronzo, ed., *Revolutionary Movements in World History*, 1:336–40.

Wilson, David L. 1994. "The Sandinistas." *NACLA* 28 (September/October): 4.

World Bank. 2004. "Nicaragua Poverty Assessment." http://www.worldbank.org.

Zimmermann, Matilde. 2000. *Sandinista: Carlos Fonseca and the Nicaraguan Revolution*. Durham, NC: Duke University Press.

Selected DVD, Film, and Videocassette Documentaries

See "Purchase and Rental Sources" at the end of this volume for information on how to obtain the following resources and for full names of media companies and other organizations listed here as abbreviations.

Deadly Embrace: Nicaragua, the World Bank, and the International Monetary Fund. 1996. 28 min. AFSC.

Did They Buy It? Nicaragua's 1990 Elections. 1990. 45 min. Video. AFSC. U.S. media's behavior analyzed with regard to both the 1990 and the 1984 elections.

Fire from the Mountain. 1988. POV. Story of a student activist who becomes a revolutionary guerrilla and then eventually a government official.

Forgotten Wars. 50 min. AETV, HC. U.S. military intervention in Nicaragua in the 1920s and 1930s and other U.S. military interventions including during the Russian Civil War.

Guns, Drugs and the CIA. 1988. 60 min. PBS (Frontline). Possible connections between CIA activities and drug operations in Central America and Southeast Asia.

Revolution in Nicaragua. 1985. 60 min. Video. PBS, AFSC. Documentary of the revolution, produced by PBS.

Second Revolution: Women in Nicaragua. 1983. 27 min. AFSC. Women's lives in Nicaragua after the revolution.

The Secret Government: The Constitution in Crisis. 1987. 90 min. SUN. Investigation into secret government activities, including the Iran-Contra operation.

Ten Days/Ten Years: The Nicaraguan Elections of 1990. 1990. 54 min. Video. AFSC. Penetrating exploration of the factors contributing to the election results.

U.S. Foreign Policy: Projecting U.S. Influence. 30 min. Video. PBS. U.S. foreign policy toward Nicaragua.

War on Nicaragua. 1987. 55 min. Video. AFSC. PBS traces the development of the contra war.

7

THE IRANIAN REVOLUTION AND
ISLAMIC FUNDAMENTALISM

As the Sandinistas and their allies battled to defeat the Somoza regime in Nicaragua, another revolutionary coalition mobilized to attempt the overthrow of the shah of Iran. In the mid-1970s Iran's economy seemed to be prospering from the high price paid by European nations, Japan, and the United States for Iranian oil. But the oil-derived wealth disproportionately benefited a minority of Iran's people and contributed to increased inequality and disruptions of traditional social and economic patterns. Much of the expanded national income was channeled into grandiose military and economic development projects conceived by Muhammad Shah Pahlavi and his advisors. The repressive aspects of the shah's regime, its ties to foreign interests, and certain of its economic and cultural policies fostered a pervasive hatred of the monarch.

Animosity toward the shah and the intensification of Iranian nationalism, aroused by the perception of the shah's regime as an instrument of foreign imperialism and moral corruption, united otherwise incompatible groups into a powerful and determined revolutionary alliance. In the course of one year, 1978, the shah's regime and the legacy of 2,500 years of Persian monarchy were swept away. But the revolutionary process continued beyond the January 16, 1979, flight of the shah. Among the contending revolutionary forces, religious leaders possessed a greater cultural affinity with Iran's masses and better access to extensive social networks for mobilizing large numbers of people than any other component of the original anti-shah coalition. The result was a startling innovation in the history of world governments, the creation of the Islamic Republic.

GEOGRAPHY AND POPULATION

Iran is a Middle Eastern nation located to the south of the Caspian Sea and to the north of the Persian Gulf and the Gulf of Oman. It is bordered by Iraq, Armenia, Azerbaijan, Turkmenistan, Afghanistan, and Pakistan. At 636,293 square miles (1,648,000 square kilometers), it is more than twice the size of Texas. Much of the country is a plateau averaging 4,000 feet (1,219 meters). A large desert stretches 800 miles (1,217 kilometers), but there are also many oases and forests. In 2006 Iran's population was approximately 68,700,000. The capital, Tehran, had an estimated 7.5 million residents in 2006, with as many as 6.5 million more in the surrounding metropolitan area. About 58 percent of Iran's people were Persian speaking. The remainder included Turkish-speaking minorities (about 26 percent, primarily the Azeris), Kurdish (9 percent), and other language groups about 7 percent, including Arab, Balochi, and Luri.

NATIONAL CULTURE

Until 1934 Iran was known to the world as Persia, the Greek word for Pars, a part of ancient Iran. In the sixth century BCE, Cyrus the Great established the Persian Empire, which reached its greatest extent around 525 BCE, spanning territory from the Indus to the Nile. The Arab conquest in 637 CE resulted in the conversion of most of Iran's population from the Zoroastrian religion to Islam.

Islam, an Arabic word, means the state of submission to the one and only God (Allah), and **Muslim** refers to a person who has submitted to the will of Allah. Muslims share a faith in the teachings of the Prophet Muhammad, who was born in 571 in Mecca. When he was about forty years old, he began preaching to the local people, who previously had worshipped several deities, saying that he had been given messages from God through the Archangel Gabriel. Muhammad's verbal expositions of God's revelations were recorded by the Prophet's followers in 114 chapters (of greatly varying length), which together constituted the Quran (Koran). By the time of Muhammad's death in 632, Islam was prevalent in much of contemporary Saudi Arabia.

Leaders of the Islamic community elected a successor to the Prophet called the *caliph*. The first caliph died after only two years, and the next two were criticized for rendering unfair judgments and favoring the interests of the rich. Both were assassinated. The fourth elected caliph was Ali, a cousin of the Prophet and husband of the Prophet's daughter, Fatima. Ali, revered by many as a champion of the poor and exploited, was opposed by several powerful Muslims and was also assassinated in 661. A belief had developed among some Muslims, however, that Ali had originally been chosen as successor by Muhammad. According to this line of reasoning, only descendants of Ali and

Fatima were to rule the community of Islam. Believers in this concept came to be known as Shiat Ali ("Partisans of Ali") or more simply Shia. The Shia Muslims referred to Ali and certain male descendants of Ali and Fatima whom they recognized as having the right to rule on behalf of Allah as imams.

The imams were thought by the Shia to be infallible. Other Muslims rejected this notion and instead held the view that the faithful were to consider infallible only the Quran, the Word of Allah and the most-central element of the Sunna ("tradition") of Islam. According to the Sunnis, no person after Muhammad was infallible. Religious leaders could only attempt to interpret the Quran to the faithful in the particular context of each historical era. In the twenty-first century the large majority within Islam were Sunni, and about one-sixth were Shia.

The Shia attached special significance to the martyrdom of Imam Hussein in 680. Hussein was the grandson of the Prophet and, according to the Shia, the third imam (the first being Hussein's father, Ali, and the second, Hussein's brother Hassan). Following the death of Ali, the caliphate was assumed by Muawiya Abi Sufian, governor of Syria and antagonist of Ali. During the course of his nineteen-year reign, Muawiya attempted to alter the basis for ascendancy to the caliphate from election by the Islamic community to that of heredity (the dynastic principle). However, Muawiya's plan was for the line of descent to follow from him rather than from the Prophet. Muawiya designated his son Yazid as the successor to the caliphate. Yazid demanded that Ali's son, Hussein, pledge his allegiance to him. When Hussein refused, Yazid's army surrounded and killed him and many of his seventy-two companions in the Karbala desert in Iraq. In subsequent years Hussein's death while resisting Yazid's tyranny came to symbolize the major example of "jihad" (a struggle conducted on behalf of the Islamic community) and martyrdom for the Shia (Hussain 1985). The concept of martyrdom thus became especially powerful among the Shia.

Despite the inflammatory issue of what constituted the right to govern the Islamic community after the death of the Prophet, the Sunnis and the Shia otherwise had very similar sets of beliefs based on the Quran and the Sharia, Islamic law derived from the Quran. However, several divisions developed among the Shia concerning how many imams had actually followed Muhammad. The Twelver Shias hold that the last imam, the infant son of the eleventh Imam, vanished in 873. With the disappearance of the last imam there was no longer an infallible interpreter of the Quran and Islamic law. This situation will only change when the twelfth imam, the "hidden imam," or "Mahdi," returns to the faithful. Twelver Shia adherents believe that in the absence of the infallible imams Islamic scholars (mujtahid) qualified to issue authoritative, though fallible, opinions in all matters relating to Islam were to govern the Islamic community (Hussain 1985).

Prior to the sixteenth century the people of Iran were mostly Sunni. The spread of Twelver Shiism was occasioned by the Safavid conquest of Iran at the beginning of that century. The Safavids decided to foster a distinct religious culture in order to maintain the population's loyalty in the conflict against the powerful Sunni Ottoman Empire expanding from Turkey. Consequently, the Safavid rulers adopted Twelver Shiism as Iran's state religion. They imported Shia religious experts on Islamic law ("ulama") from southern Iraq, as well as from Syria and Lebanon, and provided them with wealth and status. In return the ulama accepted the Safavid dynasty and provided the new rulers with a Shia clerical infrastructure. By 1700 most Iranians were Shia. In 2006 approximately 89 percent of Iran's population was Shia, 9 percent Sunni, and 2 percent other religions such as Christian, Baha'i, Jewish, and Zoroastrian.

THE QAJAR DYNASTY AND FOREIGN INFLUENCE

In 1779 Aga Muhammad Khan Qajar, leader of the Qajars (a Shia tribe), conquered almost all of Iran. In return for Shia religious leaders' support, the Qajars confirmed the ulama's right (originally established during the Safavid dynasty) to accept and administer religious endowments, or *waqfs*, donated by wealthy Iranians. This provided the clergy with a significant measure of economic independence. The ulama were also allowed to collect religious taxes.

The Qajar rulers often cooperated with Britain and Russia. The British began work in 1859 on a thirteen-year project to put a telegraph system through Iran to link Britain with its colonial interests in India. And in 1879 Nasser al-Din Shah accepted Russian military assistance to organize and train an elite Iranian military unit, the Iranian Cossack Brigade. Both Britain and Russia were granted economic privileges that many Iranians perceived as detrimental to their country.

Early in the twentieth century a number of Iranian intellectuals, thinking that a parliament could protect national interests from the foreign imperialists who exercised so much influence over the Qajar shahs, organized a movement for a constitutional monarchy. The first parliament, or Majlis, convened in October 1906 but was prevented from fully confronting the British and the Russians by internal strife and foreign military intervention. By World War I Great Britain's interest in Iran intensified; the British navy had begun to switch from coal to oil fuel, much of which was obtained from the British-owned Anglo Persian Oil Company's Iranian wells at secretly lowered prices (Hussain 1985). When the Bolshevik Revolution succeeded, Russian officers left the Iranian Cossack Brigade to return to their homeland. The British then took control of the brigade and the Ministries of War and Finance.

In 1921 the new Soviet government and Iran signed a treaty stating that neither the USSR nor Iran would allow its territory to be used as a platform for launching aggression against the other. The British, who had been aiding counterrevolutionaries trying to overthrow the Soviets, became alarmed and worried that Bolshevism might spread not only to Iran but also to the huge British colonial possession, India. To counter the threat of socialist revolution, the British considered helping to oust the ineffective and corrupt Qajar dynasty and supporting a new leader committed to modernization and the organization of a strong Iranian government with a military capable of defeating potential revolutionary movements (Abrahamian 1982; Milani 1988).

The British-backed candidate for post-Qajar leadership of Iran was forty-two-year-old Colonel Reza Khan, commander of Iran's British-advised Cossack Brigade. On February 21, 1921, Reza Khan led three thousand soldiers to Tehran, forced the resignation of the Qajar government's prime minister, and soon assumed the position of minister of war. For the next four years, Reza Khan, while manipulating the government and greatly expanding the standing army he commanded to 40,000 men, pretended to back Ahmad Shah Qajar. Reza Khan increased his support among the Persian-speaking majority by successfully suppressing tribal rebellions and unifying the nation. Finally on October 25, 1925, the parliament voted (80 to 5 with 30 abstentions) to depose the Qajar dynasty. Reza adopted the name of a pre-Islamic Iranian language, "Pahlavi," as the name for his dynasty and crowned himself shah-en-shah (king of kings) in 1926.

The Pahlavi Dynasty

Reza Shah Pahlavi quickly enacted measures that were aimed at modernizing the economy and speeding the development of a new middle class, including engineers, doctors, lawyers, businesspeople, civil servants, secular teachers, and other professional and technical workers. Because Reza Shah came to view traditional Shia influence in the social and political systems as an impediment to social change, he decided to reduce the power of the clergy. But he attempted to minimize opposition to this policy by simultaneously carrying out popular economic reforms and pro-nationalist actions.

During the 1930s new laws restricted the number of seminaries, placed several theological centers under state supervision, and gave the state approval power over religious endowment expenditures. The shah ordered all state institutions to accept women, and he reversed the previous requirement that women appear in public wearing the veil. At the same time he gratified Iranian nationalism by renegotiating the British oil concession, resulting in more favorable terms for Iran. Although the shah restricted candidacy for the national legislature to individuals of whom he approved, the basis of his political strength was his growing army and police and his development of an extensive patronage system (continued and expanded by his son), through which loyal military officers, businesspeople, and even some religious figures were rewarded for their allegiance. The shah's government built thousands of miles of roads, the trans-Iranian railroad, and 230 factories, providing opportunities for the shah and his associates to enrich themselves both within the law and illegally.

IRAN AND NEIGHBORING STATES (during the Revolution and the Iran-Iraq War)

The concerns of vastly more powerful nations locked in the conflict of World War II and aware of Iran's strategic importance led to Reza Shah's loss of power. The shah had been favorably impressed by the German Nazi government, which came to power in 1933. Adolf Hitler had referred to Iran as an Aryan nation, inhabited by people racially related to Germans. In 1934 the shah proclaimed that the country should in the future be referred to by the rest of the world as Iran, "land of the Aryans," the name used by most of Iran's people, rather than Persia. The shah also invited hundreds of German advisors to Iran to assist in construction projects and in the organization of an Iranian Youth Corps.

When the Germans invaded the Soviet Union in June 1941, both the Russians and the British feared the shah would side with Germany, possibly deny them Iran's oil and bestow this resource on their enemy, and forbid the use of Iranian territory as a weapons supply route to the Soviets. On August 25, 1941, the Soviets occupied northern Iran and the British seized sections in the south. Fearing that the Allied invaders would depose him and also terminate the Pahlavi dynasty, Reza Shah abdicated in favor of his twenty-year-old son, Muhammad Reza, a course of action acceptable to the British, who were apparently concerned for the future stability of Iran and the possibility of expanded Russian influence if the monarchy was not preserved (Abrahamian 1982).

Reza was quickly transported to the British island colony of Mauritius and then to Johannesburg, South Africa, where he died in 1944. The first Pahlavi shah, however, left behind an Iran containing two distinct and antagonistic cultures.

> The upper and new middle classes became increasingly Westernized and scarcely understood the traditional or religious culture of most of their compatriots. On the other hand peasant and urban Bazaar classes [traditional middle-class merchants, craftsmen, and their employees] continued to follow the ulama, however politically cowed the ulama were. . . . These classes associated "the way things should be" more with Islam than with the West. (Keddie 1981, 111)

Muhammad Reza Shah Pahlavi

The new shah in 1941 was a Western-educated playboy who lacked his father's charisma, forcefulness, and physical stature; he ascended to the "peacock throne" under British sponsorship, with his exercise of governmental power limited by Allied occupation authorities. Following the end of the war, he was in desperate need of increased internal as well as external support. Leftist political parties had attempted to establish independent republics in the Kurdistan and Azerbaijan sections of Iran while Russian forces were present in those areas. In particular, Russian troops delayed their departure from Azerbaijan. The U.S. government, fearful of either

Russian imperialism or the establishment of new nations in the region controlled by leftist governments, backed the shah's demand that the Russians withdraw. When they did, the shah's army marched in and suppressed the separatist governments. The shah's actions not only rallied significant nationalist support for his leadership but also seemed to identify him as an effective anti-Communist Third World leader.

The shah attempted to appeal to the ulama by portraying himself as both a defender of Islam and a foe of communism. Eventually, pronounced divisions came to exist within the ulama regarding the monarchy. The majority of the clergy prior to the revolutionary turmoil of the 1970s, the "orthodox" ulama, were accepting or supportive of the monarchy and rejected involvement in politics unless government actions threatened Islam or violated Islamic law. A significant minority, the "fundamentalist" ulama, held the position that Islam and the clergy must be involved in politics and government and that, in fact, any concept of separating church and state was un-Islamic and a key element of foreign imperialist strategy against Muslim societies intended to subvert them morally, culturally, politically, and economically (Hussain 1985; Milani 1988). Until the 1970s this group sometimes supported the shah as a bulwark against the spread of Iran's Communist movement. But after 1971 the fundamentalists, by then led by Ayatollah Khomeini, openly attacked the monarchy form of government.

Following World War II, the shah feared the further growth of the Iranian Communist Party, called the Tudeh (Masses), which during the wartime period of Russian influence had increased its membership to more than 50,000, drawing recruits from both the modern middle class and industrial employees, particularly oil-field workers (Abrahamian 1982). The shah repeatedly predicted, especially after the 1963 protests, which were religiously inspired for the most part, that his government would be attacked by an alliance of Islamic fundamentalists and leftists, in effect anticipating that these otherwise mutually hostile groups could be united by their hatred of his regime. The unsuccessful attempt on the shah's life on February 4, 1949, in which he was shot and wounded, appeared to justify his concern. The attacker, immediately killed by the shah's bodyguards, was carrying identification papers indicating that he was a reporter for an Islamic newspaper and that he also belonged to a journalists' union affiliated with a Communist-led union federation (Abrahamian 1982). In reaction, the government temporarily imprisoned Ayatollah Kashani, then leader of the fundamentalists, and enacted repressive measures against the Iranian Communist Party.

The 1953 National Front Government

The ouster of Reza Shah during World War II had revived the vitality of the national parliament and had helped to shift the balance of power toward it and away from the monarch. Smarting from the humiliating wartime foreign occupations, parliamentary leaders of the National Front coalition of political parties soon attempted to assert Iranian national interests through a proposed expropriation of the British-controlled Anglo Iranian Oil Company. In March 1951 the parliament voted 79 to 12 in favor of nationalization and demanded that the shah name as premier Muhammad Mossadeq, leader of the National Front.

The National Front was composed primarily of secular nationalists, drawn mainly from the urban, educated, new middle class, who favored an end to foreign political influence and economic exploitation. National Front leaders proclaimed that they were also dedicated to strengthening democracy by shifting control of the military from the shah to elected government leaders and by reducing other monarchal prerogatives and ending what they viewed as the Pahlavis' repeated autocratic violations of the provisions of the 1906 constitution. But the National Front had little in the way of grassroots organization among either the industrial working class or the peasants. Mossadeq, in fact, attempted unsuccessfully to bar illiterate men from voting (women did not have the right to vote) because he thought they could be too easily manipulated by traditional authorities such as the heads of families with large landholdings in the countryside (Abrahamian 1982). The support Mossadeq received from the masses was based primarily on the popularity of his nationalist appeals to the people and his charisma. When confronted with obstacles from the shah or opponents in parliament, Mossadeq's solution was often to speak directly to the nation and provoke marches and demonstrations in support of his policies. The temporary ally of Mossadeq's National Front was Ayatollah Kashani's fundamentalist Islamic movement, which advocated anti-imperialism on behalf of purging un-Islamic foreign influences. The Tudeh, while not allied with the National Front, also stated its support for an end to foreign economic exploitation but in addition wanted to achieve an extensive redistribution of wealth.

Mossadeq seized control of the military from the shah, confiscated royal lands, and reduced the palace budget, giving the savings to the country's Health Ministry. With emergency powers granted him by the parliament, Mossadeq increased the peasants' share of agricultural produce by 15 percent and shifted the burden of taxation away from the poorer classes (Abrahamian 1982).

Great Britain, however, was outraged by the Iranian seizure of its oil holdings. And although Mossadeq looked to the United States for support, the British convinced the Dwight Eisenhower administration that the Mossadeq government was a threat to Western interests and had to be eliminated. The British got major Western oil companies to cooperate in a largely successful international boycott of Iranian oil, which resulted in a deterioration of Iran's economy. The traditional middle class, whose members' businesses were harmed by both the worsening economic conditions and Mossadeq's emergency regulatory measures, became increasingly dissatisfied. In January

1953 Ayatollah Kashani, troubled by the complaints of the strongly Islamic merchants and shopkeepers, and the increasing strength of the Tudeh and other leftist elements, ended his alliance with the National Front.

When Mossadeq's ability to control the parliament was impaired by opposition from conservative, pro-shah, and some clerical legislators and the filibustering tactics (unending debates) they employed, National Front parliamentarians (thirty of the seventy-nine members of parliament) resigned their seats, which reduced the size of the legislative body below its necessary minimum and in effect disbanded it. Mossadeq then held a national referendum, a measure not in accordance with the country's constitution, in July 1953, to provide proof that the majority of Iran's people backed his actions (Abrahamian 1982; Diba 1986). The vote, which he won overwhelmingly, was interpreted by him as supporting both the dissolution of parliament and his continuation in power (although referendum procedures were criticized as unfair by Mossadeq opponents).

Several groups conspired to eliminate the Mossadeq government. Most important were the royalist officers in the military who had received special benefits that might be threatened if anti-shah civilian authorities succeeded in permanently gaining control over the armed forces. British agents and the U.S. CIA worked with pro-shah officers during 1953 to organize and coordinate the overthrow of the National Front government. Other Mossadeq opponents included many in the upper class who had profited through their association with the shah or Western businesses and feared that future reforms might harm their interests. Finally, a number of high-ranking clerics, in addition to Kashani, began to look again to the monarchy as a mechanism for suppressing the Communist movement (Abrahamian 1982; Keddie 1981).

On August 12, 1953, the shah announced the dismissal of Mossadeq as premier and the appointment of General Fazlollah Zahedi as his successor. Troops in the Imperial Guard moved to carry out the shah's order. However, soldiers loyal to the Mossadeq government surrounded and arrested the pro-shah unit. Faced with a failed takeover attempt, the shah fled in his private plane to Rome. His departure sparked wild street celebrations and demonstrations, which deteriorated into three days of rioting, often with strong anti-British and anti-American aspects. Mossadeq's order for the army to end civil disorders provided the cover for General Zahedi to launch the coup. As troops suppressed pro-Mossadeq demonstrators, pro-shah civilians including anti-left clerics and pro-shah merchants and their employees marched into central Tehran and joined with pro-shah military units, which proceeded to attack the prime minister's residence. After nine hours and 164 deaths, the shah's forces prevailed.

The shah quickly returned to Iran to assume dictatorial power. Mossadeq and other members of his government were arrested and tried for crimes against the monarchy by a military court. In the next two years hundreds of the shah's opponents were executed, given long prison sentences, or driven into exile. Many of these were from among six hundred army personnel who had secretly been members of the Tudeh (Milani 1988).

The shah lavishly rewarded businessmen and military officers who had organized or supported the coup. CIA assistance was instrumental in helping the shah create a new secret police force to gather information and harass or destroy political opposition groups. The Sazman-e Amniyat Va Ittilaat-e Keshvar (Organization of National Security and Intelligence), or SAVAK, formally organized in 1957, would be accused of the torture and deaths of thousands of Iranians. The shah decided to provide a degree of primarily elite political participation through a parliament with two controlled parties—both led by his own cronies. The new two-party system was apparently also meant to demonstrate to concerned members of the U.S. government that the shah was "democratizing" his regime.

The White Revolution

In November 1961 the shah temporarily dispensed with the formality of parliament and decided to rule by decree in order to carry out a significant reform program rapidly. The so-called White Revolution, or "Shah-People Revolution," eventually included six publicly announced goals: (1) distribution of many of the large landholdings among former sharecroppers; (2) government ownership of forests; (3) sale of government-owned factories to private interests in order to raise the funds to be used to compensate those who gave up land; (4) providing women the right to vote; (5) encouragement of profit sharing between workers and management; and (6) creation of a Literacy Corps to reduce illiteracy and promote acceptance of compulsory education (Graham 1979).

The purposes of the White Revolution, apart from the six explicitly stated aims, were to promote modernization (for example, by encouraging dispossessed large landholders to use compensation money to invest in industry and commerce), to extend state control in the countryside in place of the political power previously held by landlords, and to set in motion changes, such as mechanization of farming, that would motivate much of the rural population to migrate to urban centers where labor was needed for construction projects and growing industry. The shah also hoped to win support for his regime from previously disadvantaged population groups, mainly peasants and women, gratify middle-class progressives who advocated land redistribution and greater equality for women, and accommodate pressures for economic reform emanating from Iran's powerful ally, the United States, during the Kennedy administration.

Landowners were allowed to retain "mechanized" farms, as the productivity of these enterprises was considered too important to sacrifice by division into less efficiently exploitable small holdings. Recipients of distributed land were scheduled to pay for their parcels in equal annual installments over fifteen years (these payments were usually less than the previously paid rent). The 40 percent of rural residents who lacked cultivation rights under the old system, the large majority of whom had worked as farm laborers or in various nonagricultural service occupations, were not eligible to benefit from the reform and, consequently, were to be permanently barred from acquiring land. Many from this large group abandoned the countryside to seek employment in urban areas. To blunt opposition from the ulama, land held by clergy-controlled religious organizations was not sold but instead leased to peasants on a long-term basis (up to ninety-nine years) to farm for profit, with rent paid to the clergy.

At the conclusion of the various phases of the land-reform program in the early 1970s, about half of the nation's cultivated land had been distributed to half of the rural families. However, most of the parcels owned or leased by individual peasants were actually below the minimum necessary for subsistence. Many new landowning families were required to supplement their income by additional labor. But opportunities in the countryside were limited because greater availability of manufactured goods progressively eroded the market for traditional peasant handicrafts, and increased mechanization of the large farms reduced the demand for part-time agricultural laborers (Hooglund 1982; Najmabadi 1987). Thus migration to cities of the landless and even of many members of families that had received land accelerated. Social surveys indicated that approximately 85 percent claimed their main reason for leaving the countryside was the unsatisfactory employment and income opportunities there, although many were also drawn to cities by relatively high urban wage levels (Najmabadi 1987). In Tehran most of the hundreds of thousands of rural migrants lived on the south side of the capital in primitive conditions. Many of these would join the anti-shah revolutionary upsurge in 1978.

The 1963 Protest

The White Revolution provoked serious opposition from several sectors. Some secular opponents of the shah objected to the totally unconstitutional way the program was implemented. A number of religious leaders attacked the land reform as un-Islamic because it violated what they viewed as the landlord's right to maintain his private property and weakened the independent economic resources of the clergy and its staunchest contributors. Other clerics objected to the establishment of new rights for women. Ayatollah Khomeini, who in the early 1960s was emerging as the main spokesman for the fundamentalists, also found fault with the shah's program.

Ruhollah Khomeini, born September 24, 1902, the son and grandson of religious scholars, had been oriented toward a theological career from an early age. When he was only five months old, his father was murdered, possibly in revenge for enforcing a death penalty on a man who had publicly violated an Islamic fast. Khomeini's religious education was supported by members of his landowning extended family. As a member of the clergy, he became widely known for his integrity, scholarship, teaching ability, and charismatic personality (Bakhash 1984).

In his attack on the White Revolution, Khomeini criticized the shah for not calling for the election of a new parliament but rather carrying out the reforms by decree. Behind this indictment was Khomeini's belief that a parliament would have at least partially represented the view of the Islamic clergy. By ignoring parliament and the religious leadership, the shah was conducting government in an un-Islamic manner, that is, without the consent or even the guidance of the ulama (Hussain 1985). Khomeini also accused the shah and his wealthy supporters of being corrupt and of reaping huge and undeserved profits from their access to the nation's oil income.

In a courageous speech Khomeini asked:

And those who have filled foreign banks with the wealth produced by our poverty-stricken people, who have built towering palaces but still will not leave the people in peace, wishing to fill their pockets . . . are they not parasites? Let the world judge, let the nation judge who the parasites are! Let me give you some advice, Mr. Shah! . . . Don't you know that if one day some uproar occurs and the tables are turned, none of those people around you will be your friends? They are friends of the dollar; they have no religion, no loyalty. They are hanging responsibility for everything around your miserable neck! (Algar 1981, 178, 180)

The shah had Khomeini arrested on June 5, 1963. The news provoked anti-shah demonstrations and rioting in Qom, Tehran, and other cities. The shah proclaimed martial law and temporarily jailed twenty-eight prominent clergymen. In crushing the protest movement, troops killed at least eighty-six.

Khomeini was released from prison to placate both the public and other major religious leaders. By January 1964 "Khomeini had emerged as the most popular religious leader in Iran" (Milani 1988, 93). When a new pro-shah parliament voted to grant legal privileges to U.S. citizens engaged in military projects in Iran, Khomeini proclaimed:

If some American's servant, some American's cook, assassinates your religious leader in the middle of the bazaar . . . the Iranian police do not have the right to apprehend him! Iranian courts do not have the right to judge him! The dossier must be sent to America, so that our masters there can decide what is to be done! . . . Americans . . . are to enjoy legal immunity, but the ulama of Islam, the preachers and servants of Islam, are to live banished or imprisoned. (Algar 1981, 181, 182, 186)

In retaliation, Khomeini was rearrested and exiled, and in 1965 he took up residence in the Shia holy city of Najaf in Iraq.

Economic Development and Class Structure

After the White Revolution was inaugurated, the government and private investors expanded irrigation projects and the subsidized use of farm machinery. But agricultural production increased by only 2.5 percent per year, which could not keep pace with the 3 percent annual gain in population. Iran began to purchase and import grain and other food products. Industrial productivity, however, rose dramatically from 5 percent per year in 1963, with 1,902 factories, to 20 percent in 1977, with 7,989 factories. During the same period the number of doctors tripled, and hospital capacity doubled. College enrollment increased by more than 700 percent.

The financing for Iran's rapid overall growth in industry and services came primarily from rising oil income, which was $450 million in 1963 but $4.4 billion in 1973. After the October 1973 Arab-Israeli War, the Arab nations imposed an oil blockade on the United States and European nations aiding Israel. Consequently, the price of oil rose dramatically from $2.55 per barrel in September 1973 to $11.65 in December. As Iran was not cooperating in the boycott, its oil income climbed to $11.7 billion in 1974 (Hiro 1987). The shah and many of his advisors decided to expand both industrialization and the acquisition of military hardware rapidly. Much of the expertise in using advanced machinery and weapons was imported in the form of an estimated 60,000 foreign technicians and military advisors. The very high salaries paid to these individuals, as well as to Iranians with technical expertise, contributed to a dramatic rise in inflation and to a widening income gap between the technical and professional employees and the rest of the population (Graham 1979).

Economic development during the 1960s and 1970s had significant impacts on labor force and social class composition. At the top of the prerevolutionary class system was the aristocratic core, including the shah and his brothers, sister, and cousins, totaling about sixty families. Several hundred other families were ranked in the nobility in terms of closeness of relationship to the monarch. These, as well as the nonaristocratic upper-class families, derived wealth from landholdings and investments in urban projects. Many directed companies that benefited from government contracts. The entire upper class was estimated to constitute less than 0.01 percent of the population (Abrahamian 1989).

Approximately one million families made up the traditional middle class (about 13 percent of the population in 1976). These were headed by individuals in the types of middle-income occupations that existed before the modernization drives of the twentieth century. About 500,000 in this class were bazaaris, in that their occupations were associated with the bazaar system of trade and craft industries. The bazaar structure involved a network of guilds or associations for all its participants. By 1926 there were more than one hundred guilds for craftsmen, about seventy for merchants, and forty for various types of unskilled bazaar employees. A guild-dominated district (bazaar) in a town or city typically contained one or more mosques, traditional religious schools, businesses, craft workshops, and several tea-houses. The percentage of the labor force who were bazaaris declined slightly from 6.8 percent in 1966 to 6.4 percent in 1976 (Milani 1988, 107, 116). The other half of the traditional middle class included families that owned one or more of the nation's 420,000 village workshops that were not part of the bazaar guild system (many of these were carpet-weaving shops employing women workers) or one or more of the several hundred thousand moderate-sized farms.

Both branches of the traditional middle class contributed money and sons (as theological students and future clergy) to Islam. Major categories among the Shia clergy included mullahs (preachers), who were thoroughly versed in the Quran and Islamic traditions and laws. Those mullahs who memorized the entire Quran and the Islamic traditions merited the title *ho-jatolislam* (proof of Islam). Of these some were considered learned enough to qualify as mujtahids (interpreters) and were entitled to issue judgments and interpretations concerning both religious affairs and events occurring in other areas of life. Those mujtahids who achieved wide recognition and large popular followings were awarded the title "ayatollah" (sign of Allah) (Graham 1979; Hussain 1985). At the time of the modern Iranian Revolution, Iran was estimated to have more than five thousand mosques and at least 23,000 mullahs (and probably thousands more who were not officially certified as clergy by the shah's government), of whom as many as five thousand were hojatolislam and fifty were ayatollahs (estimate of mullahs from Milani 1988; estimates of hojatolislam and ayatollahs from Abrahamian 1982).

The modern middle class included white-collar professionals, engineers, skilled technicians, bureaucrats, managers, teachers, other intellectuals, and the large majority of students whose educations were preparing them for future careers in these occupations. Iran's process of modernization resulted in a massive expansion during the period 1966–1976 of the high school population, from 158,798 to 482,042, and college enrollment, from 52,943 to 437,089. The percentage of the labor force actually employed as professional workers, technicians, administrators or managers, and teachers increased from 2.8 percent (201,577) in 1966 to 6.5 percent (571,068) in 1976 (Milani 1988, 107, 114).

The industrial working class (including those employed in such areas as manufacturing, mining, oil operations, and construction) climbed from 26.5 percent (1,886,988) of the labor force in 1966 to 34.2 percent (3,012,300) in 1976. The fastest-growing component of this category was the lowest stratum of urban wage earners, which included primarily construction workers, who were 7.2 percent (509,778) of the labor force in 1966 but 13.5 percent (1,188,720) in 1976 (Milani 1988). Most of these were relatively recent migrants to the cities, poorly educated but usually deeply imbued with religious values. They sought continuity with their traditional culture through affiliation with the urban mosques and in 1978 became disproportionately involved in the protests and riots of the revolution.

Corresponding to the increases in the percentages of the labor force in the modern middle class and the industrial working class, the percentage directly involved in agricultural labor declined from 47.5 percent in 1966 to 34.0 percent in 1976 (Milani 1988). Other workers in rural and urban areas were involved in providing various types of services (such as transportation, sanitation, social and community welfare, and domestic services).

Support for the Shah's Regime

During the 1963–1977 period, despite occasional violent attacks from small groups of adversaries, the shah's regime was relatively stable. His patronage system rewarded loyal businesspeople, high-ranking state administrators (who by 1977 controlled a bureaucratic network of more than 300,000 civil servants), and military leaders. In the late 1970s the army stood at 285,000 men, the air force at 100,000, and the navy at 30,000. Many officers recognized that their careers, the level of their salaries, and the prestige of their occupations depended on the vast sums the shah invested in the military.

The secret police, SAVAK, with thousands of full-time agents, tens of thousands of part-time informants, and a fearsome reputation for torture and even murder of the regime's opponents, deterred many from publicly attacking the regime. SAVAK focused mainly on countering the perceived threat from the modern middle class through gathering data on anti-shah activists, attempting to destroy the effectiveness of nonviolent anti-shah groups, and crushing the violent guerrilla groups that emerged among some college students and professional workers during the 1970s (Abrahamian 1982; Milani 1988).

U.S. interest in preserving the Iranian monarchy was apparently motivated by several factors, including concern for keeping Iran's important oil resources under the control of a friendly government. The shah's military build-up policies reduced the overall cost of oil to Western countries by returning much of Iran's oil profits to those nations in the form of billions in payment for advanced jet airplanes and other highly expensive military hardware. The shah used his powerful armed forces to "police" the Persian Gulf area, intervening in nearby Dhofar Province in Oman in 1975 and 1976 to help suppress a leftist rebellion and intimidating other potential foes of pro-Western governments in the region. The belief that the shah enjoyed the unconditional support of the United States, a nation most Iranians viewed as enormously powerful and potentially ready to intervene again in Iran as it had in 1953, helped discourage open opposition. And the perception in the latter half of the 1970s that U.S. support for the shah had weakened contributed significantly to the development of the Iranian Revolution.

The generally increasing national wealth during the years 1963–1975 and especially the accelerated growth from the early to mid-1970s contributed to regime stability by benefiting large sectors of the population, including the industrial working class (Milani 1988). The state's growing resources allowed the shah to extend medical care, education, and social services.

Opposition to the Shah

During the 1970s there were several major sources of anti-shah sentiment, reflecting distinct dissident movements among Iran's highly educated elites. The secular nationalists were drawn largely from the expanding ranks of the modern middle class and included the survivors of the old National Front. Most of the secular nationalists demanded a return to strict adherence to the 1906 constitution and genuinely free elections. Another component of secular nationalism (in the sense of opposing Western control of Iran) was Iran's Communist Party. The Tudeh, however, was tainted by its strong pro-Soviet stance. Furthermore, both the National Front and the Tudeh had little support in the countryside or among most of those who had recently migrated from rural areas to the cities (Abrahamian 1982).

The fundamentalists among the religious leadership, who advocated the concept of a government under clerical influence and faithful to traditional Islamic principles, constituted a potentially powerful adversary both to the shah's policies and eventually to the monarchy itself. The advantages the religious opposition enjoyed compared to the other anti-shah groups included the fact that the thousands of clergy constituted an organizational network permeating most classes and social groups, urban and rural. Furthermore, the masses shared a common religious value system with the clergy and did not need to be converted to a new revolutionary perspective under Islamic leadership; the fundamentalist ulama merely activated the potentially revolutionary concepts already present within Islamic ideology. A key factor in the process of mobilizing the faithful was the emergence of the charismatic, uncompromising, and widely admired anti-shah member of the religious leadership, Ayatollah Khomeini, as preeminent among the ulama (Green 1982; Hussain 1985).

The religious opposition enjoyed the support of many bazaaris, who not only tended to be strongly religious but also experienced considerable damage from certain of the shah's policies. These included the promotion of modern Western-style shopping centers to the detriment of the bazaars, urban development projects that destroyed some bazaar districts, and government price inspection teams that, in carrying out their function of combating inflation by suppressing excessive profiteering by bazaar merchants, precipitated many arrests. Many bazaaris shifted from their 1953 position of seeing the shah as a bulwark against communism to viewing him as an un-Islamic agent of corrupting foreign cultural and economic interests.

The formation of anti-shah guerrilla movements occurred after the repression of the 1963 protests. Many young activists became impatient with nonviolent techniques of resistance, such as election boycotts, strikes, and demonstrations. Some university students formed secret discussion groups and studied revolutions in countries like China, Vietnam, Cuba, and Algeria. By the early 1970s two groups developed the capacity to launch limited armed attacks against the shah's regime: the Fedayeen-e Khalq (Martyrs of the People), a secular, Marxist-oriented group, and the Mujahideen-e Khalq (Islamic Soldiers of the People), an Islamic leftist movement. The Fedayeen developed out of a union in 1970 of three Marxist groups initially organized by university students and writers in Tehran, Mashad, and Tabriz. Many of the Fedayeen were the children of modern middle-class parents who had been involved in either the Tudeh or the left wing of the National Front. Ideologically, the founders appeared to draw on the Debray-Guevara theory of the guerrilla *foco*. As one leader put it, "To inspire the people we must resort to a revolutionary armed struggle . . . to shatter the illusion that the people are powerless" (Abrahamian 1985, 156).

The Fedayeen-e Khalq initiated the guerrilla struggles of the 1970s with its February 1971 attack on security forces at the village of Seyahkal. The group carried out bank robberies, the assassination of the chief military prosecutor, and bombings of foreign corporate offices. By 1977 106 Fedayeen had died in combat and sixty-six others through execution, torture, murder, or suicide while in custody (Abrahamian 1985). Seventy-three of those killed were college students, and another fifty-four were in occupations requiring a college degree. These characteristics reflected the fact that the shah's regime succeeded, both through repression and publicly portraying them as atheistic terrorists, in limiting largely to college-educated individuals the Fedayeen-e Khalq's appeal.

The Mujahideen-e Khalq, like the Fedayeen, had its origins in the early 1960s. But many of its members were the children of parents in the highly religious traditional middle class. The Mujahideen were a manifestation of modernist Shiism and were influenced by a number of prominent Iranian Islamic figures who themselves never directly participated in the group and may not have approved of its violent actions (Abrahamian 1982; 1989).

Modernist Shiism developed as an alternative to orthodox Shiism and fundamentalism. The central themes of modernist Shiism were that Islam, if properly interpreted, could provide Iranians with a progressive ideology capable of modernizing Iran, achieving a more equitable distribution of wealth, and protecting the nation from foreign cultural domination and economic exploitation. Proponents of this view felt that their version of Islam could unify all major population groups, from those in modern occupations to the clergy, in a shared, indigenous Shia belief system. Among its major proponents was Mehdi Bazargan, who attempted to demonstrate a compatibility between scientific knowledge and Shiism. He called for a future Islamic government run not by clergy but by highly educated lay administrators and technically trained individuals who were dedicated to Shiism. An associate of Bazargan whose ideas also influenced the Mujahideen was Ayatollah Taleqani, who, "unlike most ayatollahs, . . . came from a poor family, . . . openly criticized his colleagues for being fearful of the modern world," and had ties to leftist political groups that favored a redistribution of wealth toward the poor (Abrahamian 1985, 161). Taleqani and Bazargan formed the nonviolent Islamic Liberation (Freedom) movement of Iran in 1961, which was often critical of the shah and foreign influence.

Another inspirational modernist figure for the Mujahideen was Ali Shariati, a famous Iranian sociologist and political activist who is regarded (along with Ayatollah Khomeini) as one of the "two most important persons whose writings exercised an all-pervading influence on the Iranian people" in the years leading up to the revolution (Hussain 1985, 66). Shariati, unlike several past revolutionary theorists who held that religious beliefs generally inhibited social revolution, argued that Islamic doctrine, properly interpreted, promoted and required revolution. Shariati believed that the Prophet Muhammad had intended to create a classless society but that his mission had been subverted. He asserted that "true Muslims had the duty to fight against despotic rulers, foreign exploiters, greedy capitalists, and false clergymen who use Islam as an opiate to lull masses into subservience" (Abrahamian 1985, 163).

After the 1963 repression, nine young members of Bazargan's and Taleqani's Islamic Liberation movement split off to form the Mujahideen. As one founder put it, "it was the duty of all Muslims to continue the struggle begun by the Shia Imams to create a classless society and destroy all forms of despotism and imperialism" (Abrahamian 1985, 163). The Mujahideen launched its first military actions in August 1971. In the next several months the organization lost almost all its original leadership through gun battles with the shah's forces and executions. But the group found many willing new recruits to replace losses and even expand membership, the large majority of whom were college educated, mainly within the physical sciences—unlike the Fedayeen, who were more often drawn from the humanities and the social sciences. After 1972 the Mujahideen developed an ideology more closely aligned with Marxist concepts. Many in the Tehran branch abandoned Islam as the basis of their revolutionary thought in favor of secular Marxist thinking, but most Mujahideen outside the capital continued to adhere to Islam. This division led to a split and two separate organizations after May 1975, with the secular Marxist offshoot eventually adopting the name "Paykar."

By early 1976 both Mujahideen groups and the Fedayeen, which itself was divided over the issue of the effectiveness of its previous violence, had suffered so many losses that most members decided to avoid violent combat until more favorable circumstances existed. Therefore, just prior to the mass revolutionary upsurge of 1978, there were four major guerrilla groups, two Fedayeen and two Mujahideen. "All four were well equipped to move into action and take advantage of the revolutionary situation" (Abrahamian 1985, 168).

THE SETTING FOR REVOLUTION

The development of the Iranian Revolution was in part precipitated by the fact that although the economy modernized rapidly during the 1960s and the 1970s, the country's political system did not modernize in the sense of providing new avenues of effective political participation. In contrast, the shah and his advisors in 1975 decided to combine the previous two parties into the new Resurgence Party and establish a one-party government. The purposes of this shift were to strengthen the regime through creation of a single party whose branches and activists would permeate every aspect of Iranian society and, in bringing religion and other major institutions under state control, to transform Iran from a "somewhat old-fashioned military dictatorship into a totalitarian style one-party state" (Abrahamian 1982, 441). Resurgence leaders claimed their disciplined government party would "break down traditional barriers and lead the way to a fully modern society" and, combining the best aspects of capitalism and socialism, develop a "great civilization" under the leadership of the shah, "the Light of the Aryan Race" who "guides the . . . hearts of his people" (Abrahamian 1982, 441, 442).

The shah's Resurgence Party government characterized much of the ulama as medieval reactionaries and sent a religious corps into the countryside to teach the rural masses the pro-shah version of Islam. The regime announced that in the future only state-controlled religious organizations could publish theological books and asserted state rather than clerical jurisdiction over family matters. These measures and the perception that moral evils (such as pornography, prostitution, and alcohol and drug abuse) were being spread by the shah's foreign advisors and other sources of what a large number of religious leaders viewed as contaminating Western culture pushed many of the previously passive orthodox ulama into openly opposing the shah.

Between the early 1950s and the 1970s various policies of the shah's regime in effect alienated it from almost all numerically significant social groups. When the military destroyed the Mossadeq government in 1953, the shah enjoyed the backing of not only the majority of army officers but also many from groups such as the landowning upper class, the wealthy bazaar merchants, and the religious leadership. However by the mid-1970s the shah's White Revolution had severely reduced the political influence of the landlords. Other economic measures and religious and cultural policies damaged the interests of the bazaar merchants and provoked the opposition of much of the ulama. Deprived of the support of these important groups without really winning the loyalty of the intended beneficiaries of the reforms (such as the peasant recipients of land), the shah's government depended primarily on the allegiance of the military, the state bureaucracy, Iranian industrialists, foreign investors, and the United States (Milani 1988).

Whereas lack of meaningful opportunities for political participation generated discontent within the middle classes, important economic changes promoted more widespread frustration. Income from Iran's oil dramatically increased from about $1 billion in 1968–1969 to $5 billion in 1973–1974 to $20 billion in 1975–1976. The benefits went disproportionately to the upper and modern middle classes. Inequality throughout Iran increased significantly between these classes and the mass of the population. Many of the poor did experience improvements in their lifestyle, but these were far outpaced by the wealth accruing to the upper class, whose "conspicuous consumption . . . gave rise to increasingly vocal discontent" (Keddie 1981, 174).

The shah's somewhat reckless acceleration of Iran's technical and military development after 1973 "created a host of national problems: constantly increased spending on imports; orientation of the economy toward dependence on foreigners; the huge population flow into the crowded cities; and a lack of urban low-cost housing" (Keddie 1981, 175). Because of effective energy conservation measures in the United States and Europe and the end of the Arab oil embargo, Iran's oil revenue fell behind the cost of its imports and its foreign debt began to climb rapidly. In mid-1977, the shah's regime attempted to cut expenditures and reduce the inflation rate (which had reached 30 percent) by canceling or postponing construction projects and in other ways slowing down economic development. As a result unemployment rapidly increased, and working-class wages fell, especially among semi-skilled and unskilled urban workers. As the shah's program of growth had raised expectations, the sudden worsening of conditions for many in the urban lower classes heightened mass discontent.

But even after the development of economic difficulties, the shah apparently felt secure. The nation had been, in general, prospering, becoming more educated, more technologically advanced, and far better armed. The regime was backed by the world's most powerful nation. And the shah perceived his opposition to be largely fragmented and easily countered by his security forces. Only the Islamic clergy had a mass base in all classes and an extensive organizational network. But the religious leadership appeared divided, with only a few ayatollahs—such as the exiled Khomeini—openly attacking the shah and, after 1971, calling for an end to the monarchy. The shah's false evaluation of the weakness of the ulama and decline in fundamentalist Islamic views prompted an enormously damaging measure. The puppet parliament passed a law in 1976 officially shifting Iran from an Islamic calendar, with year 1 beginning at the time of the Prophet's *hijra* (journey) from Mecca to Medina, to a monarchal calendar, with year 1 set at the founding of the Persian monarchy by Cyrus the Great. Many of the faithful viewed this change as an outrageous anti-Islamic act (Graham 1979; Milani 1988).

The shah also felt confident enough to accommodate pressure from the Carter administration to improve the human rights situation in Iran and restrain the brutality of the SAVAK in return for a continued flow of U.S. weapons. The relaxation of repression, which began in February 1977 with the freeing of 357 political prisoners, led to more demands for greater freedoms and reforms.

Thus by late 1977, after more than two decades of autocratic rule that had progressively narrowed the social base of support for the monarchy, a number of revolution-promoting conditions existed simultaneously. First, numerous discontented groups, several of which had major ideological differences among themselves, all shared an intense animosity toward the shah and the foreign imperialism they perceived he represented. This constituted the basis for the necessary degree of unity among developing revolutionary factions, none of which alone was capable of overthrowing the shah and establishing a revolutionary government. Second, there was an increase in mass discontent, which arose from inequality, regime attacks on Islamic traditions, religious authority, and the bazaar, and soaring inflation coupled with growth in unemployment and lowered working-class wages. The intensification of mass frustration coincided with the shah's temporary relaxation of repression to gratify the Carter administration. This change, along with the perception that the shah's regime no longer enjoyed the unconditional support of the United States, precipitated the release of pent-up hostility through a series of ever-larger protest demonstrations.

THE REVOLUTIONARY PROCESS

The release of political prisoners encouraged public criticism of the monarchy, mostly from discontented members of the modern middle class. In particular, on June 12, 1977, members of the National Front published 20,000 copies of an open letter calling for the shah to "desist from authoritarian rule . . . abandon . . . the single party system, permit freedom of the press and freedom of association, free all political prisoners," and establish a popularly elected government based on the 1906 constitution (Hiro 1987, 67). The following week the well-known Islamic leftist critic of the shah, Ali Shariati, died in England. In Iran it was widely believed, though not proven, that he had been poisoned by SAVAK.

By October 1977 the National Front, the Liberation movement, and the Tudeh were all stronger than they had been in years and were committed to winning more reforms. From his exile in Iraq, Ayatollah Khomeini, through his taped sermons smuggled into Iran, called on the clergy to form *komitehs* (derivative of the French word for "committees") at the mosques to organize and lead the Islamic faithful in the struggle against the shah. The suspicious October death of Khomeini's forty-five-year-old son, Mustapha, at Najaf, thought by many to have been caused by SAVAK agents, provoked sincere grief and anger among millions. Those arrested during subsequent demonstrations benefited from the new liberalization policies: they were dealt with by civilian, rather than military, courts, where most received light sentences. The lenient treatment facilitated further protests.

Ayatollah Khomeini as Revolutionary Leader

The shah and his advisors soon realized their limited but significant reforms were allowing the increasingly turbulent release of previously suppressed resentment. They decided to promote disunity among the anti-shah groups by attempting to discredit and isolate Khomeini, the shah's most hostile and adamant critic. This tactic, however, had a rather serious drawback: by singling out Khomeini the shah was enhancing the ayatollah's image as his most feared opposition figure. In effect, this aspect of the regime's strategy helped hand leadership of the revolution over to religious fundamentalists instead of the somewhat more moderate middle-class opposition movements.

The politically suicidal assault on Khomeini was launched on January 7, 1978, by means of an unsigned newspaper article (later thought to have been written by the shah's information minister) titled "Iran, and the Black and Red Reactionaries." The piece characterized Khomeini as "an adventurer, without faith, tied to the centers of colonialism" who was paid by the British to oppose the shah's reforms and policies. In addition to alleging that Khomeini was the son of a "dancing girl" and was characterized by "homosexual inclinations" (Hussain 1985, 129), the attack on Khomeini's well-known anti-imperialism appeared outrageous to most Iranians. Hundreds of theological students in the seminary city of Qom demonstrated in protest. At least ten were shot and killed. Khomeini immediately called for new demonstrations as part of the mourning procession to be held, as tradition stipulated, forty days after the deaths of the student martyrs. Many peaceful marches in commemoration of the victims took place throughout Iran on the designated day, February 18, but in Tabriz crowds attacked police stations, Resurgence Party offices, liquor stores, and large banks. Scores were killed and hundreds more wounded as troops suppressed the disorders.

Khomeini praised the uprising, and a new protest was organized for March 29, forty days after the killings in Tabriz, in order to mourn these new martyrs. On this occasion demonstrations were held in fifty-five cities and turned violent in five, with crowds attacking the same types of targets as in the earlier Tabriz rioting. Dozens of people died, prompting another set of mourning processions at which still more people lost their lives. Shaken by the repetitive and massive disorders, the shah sought to placate the opposition. On June 6 he removed the widely detested General Nemattollah Nassiri, chief of the SAVAK, and promised free elections. But whereas some prominent religious leaders appeared willing to accept the word of the shah and permit him to remain with greatly restricted powers and controlled by a proposed new and supposedly freely elected parliament, Ayatollah Khomeini was adamant that the monarchy must be overthrown (Green 1982; Keddie 1981).

On September 6 Khomeini stated, "Pay no attention to the deceptive words of the shah, his government, and its supporters for their only aim is to gain another reprieve for their satanic selves," and he called on those in the armed forces to "renew your bonds with the people and refuse to go on slaughtering your children and brothers for the sake of the whims of this Pahlavi family of bandits" (Algar 1981, 236). On September 7, 500,000 people marched in Tehran to the parliament building, chanting "Death to the shah" and "Khomeini is our leader." Thousands wore the white shrouds of martyrdom, which demonstrated their willingness to die.

The shah, deciding that his concessions were encouraging the opposition, reversed himself and imposed martial law in twelve cities. On the morning of September 8, 15,000 people gathered at Jaleh Square in Tehran, near the parliament building, largely unaware that on the previous night the shah's regime had banned public assemblies. By 8 A.M. troops equipped with tanks surrounded the square and proceeded to open fire. According to the government, eighty-six people were killed, but the opposition put the figure at three thousand (Milani 1988). To many the September 8 Black Friday Massacre seemed to prove that the shah and his regime were as brutal as ever, as Khomeini had vehemently asserted. Later in the same month staff members of Iran's Central Bank released information indicating that in the previous week 177 rich Iranians (including royal-family members and top military figures) had sent $2 billion out of the country. This news further encouraged anti-shah forces by showing that as the people rose in rebellion, the shah's regime-supporting patronage system was collapsing, and his moneyed allies were "jumping ship."

In a counterproductive move the shah pressured neighboring Iraq to expel Khomeini so as to end the ayatollah's contact with Iranians on pilgrimage to Iraq. On October 6 Khomeini flew to France, where, to the distress of the shah, he became the focus of attention of the international press. This greatly increased his ability to make his views known quickly to his followers inside Iran and function as the revolution's guiding force. Representatives of anti-shah opposition groups such as the National Front and Bazargan's and Taleqani's Liberation movement began flying to Paris to consult with Khomeini and draft coordinated policies, thereby acknowledging Khomeini as their leader (Green 1982; 1986; Keddie 1981; Milani 1988).

Disarming the Army

The ayatollah realized that the neutralization of the powerful armed forces would be a key factor in overthrowing the shah. Although Khomeini beseeched the soldiers and police not to obey orders to fire on demonstrators, he called on the faithful to confront the army fearlessly and demonstrate their willingness to sacrifice themselves. When the troops refused to fire or even joined the protesters, their actions helped accelerate the deterioration of the shah's regime by showing that it was losing control of its armed forces. If some units fired on and killed marchers, Khomeini knew that many other soldiers would be ashamed of such action and become demoralized and ready to join the revolution.

Khomeini's strategy differed radically from the armed assaults on the military by the Fedayeen-e Khalq and the Mujahideen-e Khalq. He reasoned that the approach of attacking anyone in a uniform would increase solidarity within the military and delay the fall of the shah's regime. Khomeini chose to wage a "moral attack" on Iran's armed forces. He explained, "We must fight the soldiers from within the soldiers' hearts. Face the soldier with a flower. Fight through martyrdom because the martyr is the essence of history. Let the army kill as many as it wants until the soldiers are shaken to their hearts by the massacres they have committed. Then the army will collapse, and thus you will have disarmed the army" (Hiro 1987, 100).

In late October Ayatollah Khomeini called on the oil workers to strike and cripple the regime economically. The resulting work stoppage, supported by the Tudeh, cost the shah's government $74 million a day. The shah proceeded to impose a military government on the entire nation on November 6, with the chief of staff, General Gholam Reza Azhari, as the new prime minister. During November the shah appeared to be suffering from bouts of depression over his inability to stop the uprisings. His emotional status was probably also affected by the fact that he was terminally ill from cancer; this was not to be publicly known for many months.

The shah's vacillation between repression and concessions during 1978, including his decision to make scapegoats of several of his previously faithful military and government officials to save the monarchy, reportedly dismayed and alienated many of his wealthy supporters. Their flight from Iran with millions in personal wealth speeded the deterioration of the regime.

The Soviet government, anticipating the possibility of U.S. military intervention to save the shah's regime, let it be known that such an event might result in the movement of Soviet troops into Iran in accordance with the 1921 Iran-USSR Treaty, which permitted the Soviets to send forces into Iran if another nation had already carried out such an action. The Carter administration, however, made it clear that it had no intention of sending U.S. forces to save the monarchy, further disheartening the shah (Hiro 1987).

On 10 Muharram (December 11), the anniversary of Imam Hussein's death in the seventh century, two million people, led by Ayatollah Taleqani of the Liberation movement, religious leader of the capital's faithful, and Karim Sanjabi, a major figure in the National Front, marched in Tehran. During a successful strike on December 18, five hundred army troops with tanks defected to the revolution in Tabriz, and hundreds of others defected elsewhere.

Revolutionary Victory

Confronted with almost-continuous insurrectionary conditions and December oil production falling to only 40 percent of domestic requirements, the shah made a last desperate attempt to save the monarchy. He persuaded Shahpour Bakhtiyar, a leader of the National Front, to become premier on December 29. Bakhtiyar accepted on the condition that the shah almost immediately leave the country on a "vacation" and that when he returned he would in the future act as a "constitutional monarch." But Bakhtiyar's collaboration with the doomed monarchy was so abhorrent to most of the anti-shah forces that he was not only condemned by Khomeini but also immediately expelled from membership in the National Front (Hiro 1987; Keddie 1981).

On January 16 the shah left Iran, initially for Egypt, but apparently expecting to return once conditions were right for his generals still in Iran to seize power again and invite him back in a manner similar to the 1953 overthrow of the National Front government. Under mounting popular pressure Bakhtiyar ordered the reopening of Tehran's airport, allowing the return of Ayatollah Khomeini on February 1. A reported three million people lined the streets of the capital to welcome him. The ayatollah quickly appointed a provisional government to exercise power in opposition to the Bakhtiyar regime supported by the shah's generals (Keddie 1981). On February 7 delegates from the lower-ranking personnel of the air force met with Khomeini and pledged their allegiance to him. In the following days representatives of much of the army and navy enlisted personnel and lower-level officers did the same.

Army generals sent elements of the most pro-shah branch of the military, the Imperial Guards, to suppress air force personnel who had gone over to the revolution. The airmen resisted, and thousands of civilians, including Fedayeen and Mujahideen guerrillas, joined the battle, resulting in the defeat and rout of the pro-shah forces. Guerrillas and military defectors proceeded to distribute arms from captured arsenals to tens of thousands of young people and prorevolutionary army reservists who gathered at Tehran University and volunteered to fight elements of the military still loyal to the shah or the Bakhtiyar government. On February 10 and 11, revolutionary forces attacked and defeated one of the Imperial Guard's two armored units. The rest of the military declared its neutrality. As revolutionaries seized the capital's television station, its prisons, and its police stations, Bakhtiyar fled the country.

REVOLUTIONARY IRAN

Divisions within the Revolutionary Coalition

The anti-shah groups differed on how Iran's new government should be structured and what policies it should pursue. Khomeini's fundamentalists wanted an Islamic republic led by clerics. Many lay Islamic revolutionaries in the Liberation movement, such as Bazargan, favored an Islamic state headed by Shiite laymen. Liberals in the National Front intended to create a secular parliamentary government similar to those in Western Europe. The Mujahideen-e Khalq and other Islamic leftists hoped for a significant redistribution of wealth and the establishment of an egalitarian Islamic state. The Marxist-Leninist Fedayeen-e Khalq and Tudeh saw the current revolution leading to a later secular socialist revolution. All these groups took advantage of the immediate post-shah period to express their views freely, recruit new members, stage demonstrations, and propagate their goals to the larger population.

The clerically organized pro-Khomeini movement raced to build a huge volunteer armed force, the Islamic Revolutionary Guard (IRG). Within two years this organization had expanded to 200,000. The IRG functioned to safeguard the emerging Islamic government from any potential royalist coup in the armed forces and from possible attacks by groups that participated in the revolution but did not share Khomeini's plans for Iran. Khomeini partisans purged the army of suspected pro-shah personnel. Hundreds of officers in the military and SAVAK were tried by clerical revolutionary courts controlled by Khomeini supporters, found guilty of crimes including torture, murder, and "fighting against God," and quickly executed (Hiro 1987).

Significant disagreements existed within the ulama about the future development of the economy as well as the role of clergy in government. The economic views of the ayatollahs frequently reflected their classes of origin and continuing family ties. Those from landlord or wealthy merchant families manifested the preference of these classes for maintaining an economic system that would protect their interests, and ayatollahs from less-affluent families generally expressed more concern for redistributing wealth toward the poor. The most important of the few ayatollahs from relatively poor families was Ayatollah Taleqani, the religious leader of Tehran. Taleqani, one of whose sons was a member of a Marxist-oriented guerrilla group, had ties to both the National Front and the Mujahideen-e Khalq and played an essential role in holding the revolutionary alliance together. Ayatollah Taleqani's sudden death in September 1979, apparently from natural causes, contributed to the breakdown of the revolutionary coalition.

Taleqani had also helped prevent a split between Ayatollah Khomeini and other top members of the ulama, particularly Ayatollah Shariatmadari, who had become one of the most influential clerical figures in Iran while Khomeini was in exile. Shariatmadari, representing the orthodox clerical view, did not agree with Khomeini that the Quran mandated that the clergy be in direct control of the government. Rather he held that the government was simply required not to pass laws or commit acts that violated Islamic law.

Groups opposed to the establishment of Khomeini's version of an Islamic Republic looked to Ayatollah Shariatmadari as their major ally within the religious leadership, especially after the death of Taleqani. Shariatmadari, however, suffered from tremendous disadvantages. First of all, his following tended to be limited ethnically because he was from an Azeri rather than a Persian-speaking family. Second, during the revolutionary turmoil of 1978 he had expressed a willingness to tolerate the continuation of the monarchy and to compromise with the shah and later Bakhtiyar. But Khomeini's analyses that a complete abolition of the shah's regime could be achieved through continued protest and refusal to compromise were proven correct. In fact, Khomeini's success in guiding the revolution convinced many that he must have been specially chosen and empowered by God to defeat the shah's powerful army and his evil regime. Thus Ayatollah Khomeini's views overcame Shariatmadari's criticisms (Hussain 1985; Milani 1988).

Constitution of the Islamic Republic

After the flight of the shah and the fall of the Bakhtiyar government, a situation of dual power characterized revolutionary Iran. A provisional government approved by Khomeini and headed by Bazargan technically exercised state authority. Its officials were overwhelmingly lay members of the National Front and the Liberation movement with administrative skills. Real power, however, was held by Khomeini and his clerical associates, who enjoyed the loyalty of the large majority of poor and lower-middle-class Iranians who had served as the foot soldiers of the revolution. Khomeini's followers dominated the local revolutionary *komitehs* and militias, then coalescing into the huge Islamic Revolutionary Guard. In contrast, the National Front and the Liberation movement lacked support outside the middle classes, and neither had its own militia. Whereas the Mujahideen and Fedayeen groups had thousands of members under arms, they had much less support at the grassroots level than Khomeini's fundamentalists.

Khomeini selected a group of clergy and laymen, the Islamic Revolutionary Council (IRC), to oversee government policy until a totally new government system could be established. To hasten this event, he insisted that a referendum be held almost immediately. Voters would be given only the options of declaring Yes or No to the proposal to establish an Islamic Republic (as opposed to being allowed to select a preference from several clearly defined alternate forms of government). The referendum was held on April 1, 1979, with a reported 89 percent turnout (more than twenty million people) and a 98 percent approval for the creation of an Islamic Republic.

In early August an election was held for an Assembly of Experts to draft the new constitution. Khomeini's followers had organized their own political party, the Islamic Republic Party (IRP), to compete in the vote. All the candidates for the assembly, regardless of party, had to be approved by Khomeini. The IRP won the biggest bloc of seats. The resulting constitu-

tion called for an elected parliament, including clergy and laymen who
were approved as good Muslims and supporters of the constitution before
being allowed to run, a separately and popularly elected president, and a
supreme court, the Council of Guardians, to be composed of six clerics and
six laymen selected, respectively, by the clergy and the parliament, to serve
six-year terms. The Council of Guardians was given the authority to approve candidates for parliament and to rule on whether any act of government or law passed by parliament violated either the constitution or
Islamic law (Abrahamian 1989).

The overriding theme of the constitution was the concept that ultimate
sovereignty over the political system belonged to God. Any other basis for
sovereignty, whether the people, a ruling dynasty, or conformity to some alternate ideology, was un-Islamic and unacceptable. In the Islamic Republic
God's will is expressed through the "rule of the just Islamic jurist," the
vilayat-e faqih. He is to provide advice to the parliament and the president
and has the power, at the rare times he may deem it necessary, to overrule
the government or any part of the government. The first *faqih* of the Islamic
Republic was Ayatollah Khomeini. His successors were to be selected by the
Assembly of Experts. If no single individual was perceived qualified for the
position, a committee of three or five could be selected to fill the role
(Bakhash 1984; Hussain 1985).

The establishment of the Constitution of the Islamic Republic with the inclusion of the crucial *vilayat-e faqih* principle embodied the victory of the
Shia fundamentalists over the Shia modernist and orthodox factions and the
secular groups in the revolutionary alliance. The triumph of the fundamentalists, although not at this stage complete, was due to a number of factors.
Of primary importance was Ayatollah Khomeini's role as the dominant personality of the revolution and the fact that he supported the fundamentalist
program and the IRP. As Khomeini and, consequently, the fundamentalists
enjoyed a much wider base of popular support than any of the other anti-
shah groups, the fundamentalists controlled most of the revolutionary organizations (the *komitehs* and the revolutionary courts) and possessed by far
the biggest militia, the Islamic Revolutionary Guard, to enforce their will.

The fundamentalists, however, were characterized by a potentially critical
weakness: the internal division between much of the ulama, whose considerable family economic interests were dependent on the existing pattern of
property and income relations, and the poorer majority of Iranians, who
tended to push for a further socioeconomic revolution to distribute the nation's wealth more equally. In the short run, the fundamentalists were able to
delay resolution of this issue and further strengthen their dominant position
relative to former revolutionary allies by rallying their country folk, making
themselves the true defenders of the revolution in the face of perceived external threats during the American hostage crisis and the war with Iraq.

American Hostage Crisis

A major crisis developed when on October 22, 1979, the shah was allowed to fly to New York City. Although the officially stated reason for the shah's visit was to obtain treatment for his terminal cancer, Iranian revolutionaries were not inclined to believe the shah was really ill or why, if the affliction was real, the shah could not have gotten equivalent treatment elsewhere.

Ayatollah Khomeini and other ulama viewed New York City not only as a world center of corruption and moral degradation, but also as the home of men they identified as enthusiastic shah supporters and agents of U.S. imperialism, such as the Rockefellers and Henry Kissinger. Many Iranian revolutionaries believed that a conspiracy was being hatched to restore the shah to power, possibly involving armed U.S. intervention in conjunction with a coup by antirevolutionary military figures who remained in Iran. From the confessions of several SAVAK agents it became known that certain personnel in the U.S. embassy in Tehran were courting Iranian officers and several leaders of minority ethnic groups. Consequently, a seizure of the embassy was planned in order to protest the presence of the shah in New York and possibly also to capture documents relating to CIA activities in Iran (Bakhash 1984; Hiro 1987; Hussain 1985).

On November 4 a group of 450 young militants stormed the embassy and managed to confiscate quickly many of the sought-after documents. In addition to the bonanza of information used to purge the military further and discredit critics of Khomeini, the seizure of the embassy and the holding of fifty-three U.S. officials helped to demonstrate that Khomeini's supporters were just as "anti-imperialist" as the members of the leftist Fedayeen-e Khalq and Mujahideen-e Khalq.

Those holding the hostages refused to release them unless both the shah and his wealth (in foreign investments and bank accounts) were delivered to Iran. The U.S. government refused to return the shah to stand trial, but this issue was resolved by his death on July 27, 1980.

Eventually the United States and Iran worked out a set of financial arrangements in which some of the frozen Iranian assets in the United States were used to pay U.S. business and other foreign claims on Iran's revolutionary government, with the excess, over $2 billion, made available to Iran. Resolution of the crisis may have been delayed by fundamentalist leaders, who used the confrontation with the United States to weaken their internal opponents by portraying them as disloyal to the revolution or tools of foreign imperialists, until all the major institutions of the Islamic state were firmly established (Milani 1988). In the midst of the hostage conflict the Iranian revolutionary state endured violent rebellion by the Mujahideen-e Khalq, a monumental conflict between the elected president and the parliament, and an invasion of its territory by neighboring Iraq.

Conflict Between the IRP and the Mujahideen-e Khalq

The conflict between Khomeini's state-dominating Islamic Republic Party and the Islamic Mujahideen-e Khalq was based, in part, on differing interpretations of Islam. The Mujahideen held that the Quran supported the concept that ultimate control of the government should be in the hands of the people, not the clergy, and that Muhammad had intended to create an economically egalitarian society, a notion that ran counter to the family financial interests of many of the ulama. Since the Mujahideen disagreed with the concept of clerical domination of the state, they refused to vote to confirm the new constitution.

Khomeini used the Mujahideen referendum boycott as the reason for barring the Mujahideen leader Masoud Rajavi from running as a candidate in the February 1980 presidential election. The Mujahideen responded by throwing their support to Abol Hassan Bani-Sadr, who won the election. Bani-Sadr had studied economics, sociology, and Islamic law. He was the son of an ayatollah and had been an adviser to Khomeini and a member of Khomeini's preconstitutional Islamic Revolutionary Council. The Mujahideen backed him in part because of his commitment to a redistribution of wealth and to fostering and maintaining a relatively open democratic system.

The fundamentalist clergy apparently feared the Mujahideen more than the solely Marxist groups (which, although also barred from running candidates in elections, were generally committed to supporting Khomeini for pragmatic and anti-imperialist reasons). The Mujahideen were seen as especially dangerous because they espoused Islam, which gave them a basis of appeal to Iran's masses, and because much of their membership was drawn from the younger generation of the traditional middle class, the same class that provided most of the leadership of the IRP.

The growing hostility against the Mujahideen was paralleled by increasing IRP dissatisfaction with the republic's first president, Bani-Sadr, who had been popularly elected with a 75 percent majority on February 4, 1980, over the IRP candidate (but with considerable public perception that Khomeini actually favored Bani-Sadr). When in fall 1980 President Bani-Sadr repeatedly sought to challenge members of the IRP for their restrictive interpretation of the Quran and their harassment and repression of other political parties, he provoked the animosity of the IRP-dominated parliament and the Council of Guardians. These groups were further infuriated by the president's accusation that IRG personnel were using torture on prisoners and by his exposure of the connection of both the IRP and the IRG to bands of Islamic extremists called *hezbollahis* (members of the Party of God). Some IRP members of parliament accused President Bani-Sadr of being a traitor and of causing disunity. Khomeini tried to reimpose calm by banning all public speeches. But when Bani-Sadr violated the restriction and was then declared incompetent by the parliament in June 1981, Khomeini removed him from office (Bakhash 1984; Milani 1988).

On June 28, 1981, after further violent attacks by fundamentalists on Mujahideen supporters, a massive explosion caused by thirty kilograms of dynamite placed in a building adjoining an IRP conference hall killed seventy-four top figures in the party. The Mujahideen were blamed. The Mujahideen carried out scores of assassinations and bombing attacks and in turn suffered the execution of many leaders and hundreds of other members. But they overestimated their own popularity and their ability to convey their message beyond the middle class to the poor, who were generally imbued with more traditional religious views. Thus the Mujahideen assassination campaign failed because popular support for the IRP and the religious dedication of IRP members provided for rapid replacement of murdered officeholders and, therefore, for regime stability. By the end of October 1981 the Islamic Republic had succeeded in containing internal rebellion, although air force sympathizers had managed to help both Bani-Sadr and Masoud Rajavi escape Iran.

The Iran-Iraq War

Undoubtedly the ability of the IRP government to crush or at least neutralize its opposition had much to do with the wave of nationalism that swept Iran after the Iraqi invasion on September 22, 1980. A number of factors had long fostered animosity between Iraq, at that time a nation of about twenty million, and its neighbor Iran, with about three times the population and close to four times the land area. Most Iraqis speak Arabic, while the majority of Iranians are Persian speaking. The religious composition of the two nations differs significantly, with about 63 percent of Iraqis being Shia and approximately 35 percent Sunni, whereas in Iran approximately 89 percent are Shia. A longstanding territorial controversy between Iraq and Iran concerned control over the river waterway to the Persian Gulf, the Shatt-al-Arab (the Arab River). Iran had previously forced Iraq to relinquish the east bank and had moved the international boundary between the two nations to the middle of the river. Another point of contention was rooted in the fact that Iraq was governed by the Baath Socialist Party, whose members were mostly secularly oriented Sunni Muslims. Khomeini viewed the government of Iraq as un-Islamic and called upon Iraqi Muslims, both Shia and Sunni, to establish a second Islamic republic.

Apparently Iraqi President Saddam Hussein resolved to attack Iran, not only to reclaim the east bank of the Shatt-al-Arab, but also to overthrow Iran's Islamic republican form of government, the source of inspiration for fundamentalist Islamic rebels inside Iraq. Iraqi leaders estimated that Iran's military was in disarray following the revolution and would eventually run out of spare parts to maintain and repair its U.S. military equipment, as the

United States had banned arms shipments to Iran (*New York Times*, Mar. 31, 1989, A5).

Most Iranians, however, rallied to meet the Iraqi assault. Masses of Iranian army troops and Islamic Revolutionary Guards, supported by the air force with more than four hundred combat planes, soon halted the Iraqi advance. Iran was able to obtain some replacement parts and even some new weapons from diverse sources such as Vietnam, with its stores of abandoned U.S. weaponry, the People's Republic of China, international arms dealers, U.S. companies violating the arms embargo, and the Reagan administration's covert Iran-Contra operation. The Islamic Republic, however, could not match the massive supplies of modern weapons Iraq purchased from France, the Soviet Union, and other nations with the aid of tens of billions in loans from Arab states such as Saudi Arabia and Kuwait, whose monarchs feared Iranian-inspired fundamentalist rebellions within their borders. Iran's larger population, however, permitted it to endure successfully a two-to-one disadvantage in war casualties.

By mid-1982 Iraqi forces had been driven from much of the Iranian territory they had originally occupied. Iran launched a counterinvasion of Iraq in July, demanding the overthrow of Iraq's President Saddam Hussein and huge war reparations payments as the price of peace. As Iranian forces slowly advanced, despite terrible losses to superior Iraqi air power, artillery, and armor, Iraq resorted to several desperate measures. These included attacking Iranian civilian population centers with aircraft and missiles (Iran retaliated by launching missiles into the Iraqi capital, Baghdad), use of internationally banned poison gas weapons, and in spring 1984 air attacks on Iranian oil facilities and tankers in the northern section of the Persian Gulf. Iran responded by attacking the tankers of nations aiding Iraq—Saudi Arabia and Kuwait (Iraq was transporting much of its oil by pipeline to the Mediterranean). As the threat to Europe's oil or at least oil prices increased, the Reagan administration sent U.S. naval forces to the area to protect, first, Kuwaiti tankers (reflagged and renamed as U.S. ships) and, then, other supposedly neutral vessels. These actions were viewed by some nations as, in effect, U.S. intervention in the war on Iraq's behalf. But according to Milani (1994) Washington's objective seemed to be the "mutual destruction of belligerents," similar to Great Britain's primarily sideline-observer orientation to much of World War II while Germany and the Soviet Union waged massive land warfare against each other between 1941 and 1944.

By mid-1988 several hundred thousand on both sides had perished in the conflict, many more had been wounded, and hundreds of billions of dollars had been lost or wasted due to destruction, weapons purchases, and lowered oil revenues. The Iranian economy was experiencing great difficulties, whereas the Iraqis regained some of their lost territory. Faced with the apparent impossibility of victory, Ayatollah Khomeini agreed to negotiate an end to the war in summer 1988 (*New York Times*, June 6, 1988, A1; June

20, 1988, A8). Although the fighting largely halted after 1988, the first face-to-face talks between the two countries' foreign ministers on a final peace agreement for the eight-year war did not take place until July 1990 (*New York Times*, July 6, 1990, A2). Iraq, faced with military and economic pressures from the United States and other nations because of its August invasion and occupation of Kuwait, suddenly granted Iran most of its settlement terms, possibly hoping for Iranian assistance in the confrontation with Western nations (*New York Times*, Aug. 16, 1990, A1; Jan. 6, 1991, A5).

IRAN AFTER KHOMEINI

Khomeini's apparent unwillingness to allow significant increases in freedom of political expression even after the end of the war with Iraq was illustrated in late March 1989, when he forced the resignation of Ayatollah Montazeri, whom the Assembly of Experts had previously designated as Khomeini's successor in the role of *faqih* of the Islamic Republic. Montazeri, once Khomeini's prize student, had called for greater political tolerance, charged that the revolution had failed to fulfill important promises to the people, accused the Islamic Republic's security forces of physical abuse of prisoners, and associated with critics of Khomeini's policies such as Mehdi Bazargan (*New York Times*, May 22, 1989, A1). Montazeri had also declined to support publicly Khomeini's call for the death of author Salman Rushdie for writing *The Satanic Verses*, a book considered blasphemous to Islam by the ulama.

After Khomeini's death in June 1989, the government of Iran continued to be largely in the hands of clerical politicians loyal to the ayatollah's basic concept of the Islamic Republic, but divided with respect to the degree of adherence to extreme fundamentalist principles in the face of the pragmatic requirements of domestic and foreign policymaking. On June 4, the day after Khomeini's death, the assembly of religious experts selected Hojatolislam Ali Khamenei (later elevated to Ayatollah Ali Khamenei), who had served for eight years as president of Iran, as Khomeini's successor in the role of supreme religious-political leader (*New York Times*, June 5, 1989, A1).

The selection of Ali Khamenei as Khomeini's successor in the role of *faqih* of the Islamic Republic required a change in Iran's constitution (Hunter 1993; Milani 1994). Khomeini himself had identified which parts of the constitution the twenty-five-member Assembly for Reconsideration of the Constitution would modify in 1989. The original constitution had specified that any future occupant of the role of *faqih* be both a competent administrator and a *marja* (in effect an ayatollah), a religious scholar and leader who had achieved great popularity and respect and was qualified to render judgments about religious matters independent of the views of other religious leaders. Since there was no person in Iran who was ideologically compatible with Iran's relatively youthful generation of fundamentalist revolutionaries and who also met the qualifications of being a superior administrator and a *marja*, the revised constitution dropped the requirement that future candidates for the *vilayat-e faqih* must first have attained the status of ayatollah. Following Khomeini's death, this modification permitted the selection of Khamenei, who was only a hojatolislam in clerical rank, by a 60-to-14 vote of the Assembly of Experts (Milani 1994).

The revised constitution also specified that it is the *faqih* who plays the dominant role in developing the general policy interests of the Islamic Republic and appoints the heads of the TV and radio networks. It also stipulated that the *faqih*, not the elected president, is the head of the armed forces. A major change in the constitution was the elimination of the position of parliamentary prime minister and the transferring of all of the former prime minister's powers to the executive office, that of president of the republic, which was retained from the original constitution. This measure was intended to eliminate the previous confusion and conflict inherent in having both a popularly elected executive, the president, and a powerful executive selected by parliament, a prime minister. Under the revised constitution, however, the president's authority was limited by the parliament, which was to approve all of his appointments.

With Khomeini no longer in control and the war with Iraq concluded, the possibility existed that conflict over the future course of the revolution would intensify. The result might have been a shift in government priorities regarding economic policies. Millions of Iranians wanted the government to do more to redistribute the nation's wealth. However, the framers of the Constitution of the Islamic Republic had included a provision stating that individuals had the right to private ownership as long as the property in question was the result of the owner's honest labor. High-ranking ulama on the Council of Guardians used their interpretation of this principle to block parliamentary proposals to transfer some privately owned wealth to the impoverished. Disagreement over this issue between top (generally antireform) and lower-level personnel in the Islamic Republic Party was so great that to minimize divisive confrontation, Khomeini took the extraordinary step of ordering the dissolution of the IRP in July 1987. However, with Khomeini no longer present to restrain or intimidate discontented groups, it was possible that internal popular pressures would eventually shift the ideology and policies of postrevolutionary Iran in the direction of greater redistribution of wealth and perhaps even toward economically beneficial policies of reconciliation with the United States, Europe, and Russia. The latter possibility appeared even more likely when Iranian leaders expressed gratitude for foreign assistance following a devastating earthquake in 1990, which took more than 30,000 Iranian lives.

After years of fundamentalist rule, Iranian voters, especially women and lower-income people, selected a relatively moderate cleric, Mohammad

Khatami, as president in 1997, giving him almost 70 percent of the vote. Khatami was also reelected in 2001 to serve into the year 2005. President Khatami reportedly attempted to increase the country's level of democracy, enhance the rights of women, and pursue friendlier relations with the United States and its allies. However, his ability to carry out reforms or modify Iran's foreign policy was limited by the fact that fundamentalists continued to dominate the courts, armed forces, and police. Most important, President Khatami's power as head of government was superceded by that of Iran's head of state, the fundamentalist supreme religious leader, Ayatollah Ali Khamenei. But after battling the institutionally entrenched fundamentalists for years, Iranian moderate politicians were apparently severely weakened by U.S. President George W. Bush's hostile attitude toward Iran after the September 11, 2001, terrorist attacks. In response, voters expressed preference for a new Iranian president more openly critical of Bush administration policy, fundamentalist-supported candidate Mahmoud Amadinejad, elected president in 2005.

IRAN AND THE GULF WAR

The Iraqi invasion of Kuwait in 1990 was prompted by several factors beyond Iraq's assertion that Kuwait was really a part of Iraq that had been split off by British imperialism. The Iraqis, as well as many members of the Iranian government, believed that the oil-rich monarchies of the Islamic world were in great part puppets of Western imperialism. In contrast to their often-stated support for political democracy around the world, the United States and Great Britain, in the view of both Iraq and Iran, instead supplied the weapons, military advisors, and other technological means to preserve monarchies threatened by the democratic aspirations of their subjects. The royal families of nations such as Saudi Arabia and Kuwait, beholden to Western nations for their continued existence in the face of pressures to establish republican forms of government, either secular or Islamic, served the purposes of maintaining world oil prices lower than they might otherwise be. They were also apparently available for supplying funds for projects deemed desirable by Western intelligence services, which were to be kept secret or were even banned by the Western nations' elected leaders (as in the case of the U.S. Iran-contra scandal; see chapter 6).

Relatively low oil prices helped buttress the economies of Western Europe, Japan, and the United States and thus kept internal economically motivated discontent less than it otherwise might have been. Furthermore, low oil prices, coupled with pressures to engage in an arms race, contributed to the destruction or severe weakening of several perceived threats to capitalist nations. The Soviet Union, for example, expended huge financial resources in an attempt to keep pace with the U.S. Reagan administration's arms buildup and proposed "Star Wars" program and could not simultaneously pay for the arms expenditures and tend to urgent domestic needs, in part because the USSR's revenue from its exported oil was lower than anticipated. Thus U.S. influence over the oil-rich monarchies of the Persian Gulf and their levels of oil production and oil-pricing policies may have been a key element in the economic crisis that contributed to the dismantling of the USSR and Communist Party leadership in Russia. In some ways Iraq's situation preceding its invasion of Kuwait paralleled the economic distress that was simultaneously afflicting its Soviet ally.

Iraq had powerful economic reasons to acquire control of Kuwait and its oil resources. Iraq perceived itself as having fought off an aggressive, Iranian-based, fundamentalist Islamic threat to the benefit of nonfundamentalist Arab governments. Several of these, including the Saudi Arabian and Kuwait monarchies, had loaned Iraq billions of dollars to purchase weapons while waiting on the sidelines as hundreds of thousands of Iraqis were killed or wounded in the conflict with Iran. Following the war, Iraq found itself with over $80 billion in foreign debt, much of this owed to rich Arab monarchies with much smaller populations than Iraq. To pay off these huge loans Iraq hoped to win the cooperation of its OPEC partners to raise oil prices and thereby increase Iraq's oil revenues to the point that would facilitate repayment of its loans. Instead, Saudi Arabia, Kuwait, and the United Arab Emirates (UAE) opposed higher oil prices (Milani 1994). And Kuwait and the UAE reportedly even went so far as to violate OPEC's quotas and overproduce oil so as to depress world oil prices, cut Iraq's oil income, and reduce Iraq's ability to pay off its foreign debts (Milani 1994).

The Iraqi leadership appeared to feel financially entrapped by the oil-rich monarchies that Iraq's war against Iran had helped to protect during the 1980s. Since the monarchies were supported by the United States and had cooperated in the implementation of U.S. foreign policies, Iraqi leaders perceived the Arab monarchies' oil policies as another diabolical CIA plot. Iraq attempted to use its military strength to seize Kuwait and its oil resources and in the process save its own financial future. If successful, this accomplishment would have permitted Iraq to continue its military buildup, pay its debts, improve domestic living standards, and increase its regional and world influence, since it would then control about 20 percent of the world's known oil reserves.

Fearing a more powerful Iraq, Iran was among the first nations to condemn the invasion of Kuwait and to demand an Iraqi withdrawal. Once the United States had established a large and potentially permanent military presence in Saudi Arabia, the more hard-line faction within Iran's fundamentalist clerical leadership attempted unsuccessfully to convince other Iranian leaders to enter into an anti-U.S. alliance with Iraq. Iran, however, remained effectively neutral in the military phase of the Gulf War, thereby benefiting from the U.S. rout of Iraq.

Prior to its defeat, Iraq had at least secured Iran's military neutrality by agreeing to many of Iran's demands for a final settlement of the Iran-Iraq

War. And as a result of Iraq's defeat by the U.S.-led coalition during the 1991 Gulf War, Iran's historic enemy was severely weakened. Further, in apparent gratitude for Iran's nonintervention on behalf of Iraq and Iran's support for Iraqi withdrawal from Kuwait, the U.S. Bush administration returned $200 million to Iran (for U.S. weapons that Iran had paid for before the ouster of the shah but never received) and allowed U.S. oil companies to buy a small amount of Iranian oil. By 1995 U.S. oil companies were allowed to purchase Iranian oil, as long as they sold it outside the United States, and had become the leading buyers, paying billions of dollars for approximately one-fourth of Iran's production (*New York Times*, Apr. 1, 1995, 5). But the Clinton administration was inclined to restrict trade on the grounds that Iran sponsored terrorism, opposed Middle East peace efforts, and was attempting to develop nuclear weapons.

Iraq's defeat, the subsequent U.S.-brokered Israeli-Palestinian peace agreements, and the opposition of large percentages of Arab populations to an enlarged U.S. role in the Persian Gulf may have all contributed to the continued growth of Islamic fundamentalist movements in several countries. Following the Gulf War, Iran was clearly the most powerful Islamic nation in the region. But Iran faced the likelihood of a prolonged, if not permanent, U.S. presence in the Persian Gulf, not only to contain any future Iraq problems but also because control over the Persian Gulf monarchies and their huge oil resources, upon which both Japan and Europe were highly dependent, potentially provided the United States with some significant leverage in its competition with these other economic superpowers.

Iran and Islamic Revolution Elsewhere

The central themes of Islamic fundamentalism included the concept that Islamic religious rules and moral principles must be profoundly integrated with government and must indeed permeate and influence all areas of social life. Ayatollah Khomeini and other like-minded religious leaders asserted that Islamic fundamentalism must become the dominant political ideology among both Shia and Sunni Muslims and that Iran was to be only the first of many Islamic republics. The unsuccessful attempt of some Shia Iraqis to organize a revolution in Iraq helped provoke the Iraqi government's attempt to crush the Iranian Islamic Republic. The eight-year conflict between Iran and Iraq not only resulted in hundreds of thousands of casualties and billions in economic losses, it also temporarily led to the erroneous perception among some people of Islamic fundamentalism as a uniquely Iranian or at least Shia phenomenon. Once the war was over, Islamic fundamentalism could no longer be easily depicted as a manifestation of Persian cultural and political imperialism. Advocates of fundamentalism could more effectively present their local religious movements as domestic developments in response to popular needs and aspirations.

By the end of the 1980s significant Islamic fundamentalist movements existed in Afghanistan, Algeria, Egypt, Jordan, Lebanon, Morocco, Sudan, Tunisia, Turkey, and the Arab-populated lands under Israeli control. The reasons for the growth of fundamentalism outside of Iran, apart from the easing of Arab-Iranian hostility following the end of the Iran-Iraq War, were diverse.

One powerful cause appeared to be the quest for a genuinely homegrown culture capable of instilling a sense of pride, dignity, and self-worth. The process of modernization in Muslim countries had exposed many educated persons not only to advanced technologies and managerial skills but also to foreign values and norms and relatively nonreligious lifestyles. But the largely secular ideologies, whether procapitalist or prosocialist, characteristic of the ruling elites and skilled-occupation classes of a number of Islamic societies, often appeared to offer little to the middle and lower classes except a perpetual sense of cultural and technological inferiority and the threat of the progressive erosion of cherished moral values. In contrast, the fundamentalists put forward the appealing notion of a value and belief system ordained by God and, thus, immeasurably superior to all other cultures.

Financial hardships in several Arab states also motivated many members of the middle class to turn to fundamentalism. Some apparently sought a sense of renewed moral status in compensation for reduced economic benefits and opportunities, whereas others viewed fundamentalism as a new political force through which middle-income groups, in alliance with religiously motivated persons from the lower classes, could successfully overcome the domination of privileged governing elites. The continued expansion of popular support for Islamic fundamentalism, whether a response to moral decay, cultural subversion, or economic deterioration, was exemplified in 1990 electoral victories in which fundamentalist-oriented candidates won thirty-six of eighty parliamentary seats in Jordan and the majority of the vote in Algerian local elections (*New York Times*, June 14, 1990, A1; July 1, 1990, E5).

Following the defeat of Iraq by the U.S.-led coalition in the 1991 Gulf War, Islamic fundamentalist movements continued to play important roles in several nations (Esposito 1994; *New York Times*, Oct. 23, 1994, E3). Fundamentalists exerted significant cultural and political influence in Egypt (*New York Times*, Feb. 3, 1994, A1; Feb. 11, 1994, A3). When the fundamentalist Islamic Salvation Front won the first round of parliamentary elections in Algeria in 1991, nonfundamentalist government and military officials suspended elections and outlawed the Front, leading to retaliatory bombings, assassinations, and the development of a virtual state of civil war (*New York Times*, Jan. 24, 1994, A1; Apr. 4, 1994, A1).

And a powerful Islamic fundamentalist movement arose among young, often poor Palestinians in opposition to the Israeli-Palestinian peace proposals, which were viewed by many fundamentalists and Palestinians as containing too many concessions to Israel. The Palestine Liberation Organization (PLO) had supported Iraq's unsuccessful effort to seize Kuwait and Iraq's promise to utilize oil sales revenue to aid the millions of Arab poor, including Palestinians. But Iraq's defeat not only crippled its ability to assist the PLO and the Palestinian people but also resulted in a retaliatory cutoff of aid to the Palestinians from the oil monarchies. Hamas, the Palestinian Islamic Resistance Movement, a fundamentalist organization that appeared to receive funding from international sources, some of whose members were accused of terrorism, provided much-needed assistance to thousands of poor Palestinians who felt abandoned by both the PLO and the oil-rich Arab states. A number of young Palestinians, looking forward to a happier existence in the next life and hoping to serve both God and their people, proved willing to sacrifice their own lives and take many other lives in suicidal bombing attacks against Israeli soldiers and civilians (*New York Times*, Nov. 8, 1994, A1; Jan. 25, 1995, A8; Mar. 5, 1996, A1).

Terrorist activities related to extreme elements among the Islamic fundamentalist movement also affected a number of nations outside of the Middle East by the mid-1990s, including bombings in Great Britain, France, Argentina, and Panama and against the New York World Trade Towers in 1993, along with alleged plots to attack major New York City transportation tunnels, the FBI headquarters, and possibly the UN (*New York Times*, July 29, 1994, A1; Jan. 25, 1995, A9).

IRAN, AFGHANISTAN, THE WAR ON TERROR, AND THE U.S.-LED INVASION AND OCCUPATION OF IRAQ

The triumph of Islamic fundamentalists in the Iranian Revolution against the shah's regime was widely viewed as a victory over the world's foremost superpower, the United States, which had backed the shah and whose interests, fundamentalists and others believed, the shah's government served. In particular Islamic fundamentalists (also called "Islamists") were most likely in part inspired by Islamic success in Iran to fight against the world's second greatest superpower in the 1980s. When the USSR invaded Afghanistan in 1979 to support a pro-Soviet leftist regime against Islamist rebels, tens of thousands of Islamist volunteers from many countries headed for Pakistan in order to be armed and trained and then cross the border into Afghanistan to fight Soviet and Afghan leftist forces. Among the volunteers was Osama bin Laden, a college graduate and son of a Saudi Arabian billionaire construction company owner. Bid Laden not only fought but used his money to aid the Islamist fighters and care for widows and war orphans. With the crucial asset of U.S.-supplied, shoulder-fired anti-aircraft missiles to shoot down Soviet helicopters and other low-flying aircraft, the Islamists were ultimately successful, and Soviet forces withdrew in 1989. The long, brutal conflict in Afghanistan helped foster popular unrest in the Soviet Union and decline in the legitimacy for the Communist government, contributing to its downfall and the dissolution of the USSR by the end of 1991.

The victory of Islamic forces over the Soviet Union in Afghanistan following the defeat of the United States in Iran further encouraged Islamic fundamentalists to confront not only non-Islamic nations but also governments in Islamic countries, such as those in Egypt and Saudi Arabia, that they perceived to be the allies or puppets of the United States or other non-Islamic states. In particular, Osama bin Laden and his associates organized a communication network, Al Qaeda ("the base" or "foundation"), among the tens of thousands of Arab and other Islamic volunteers who had fought in Afghanistan. After Iraq invaded Kuwait in 1990 and appeared to constitute a threat to Saudi Arabia, Osama bin Laden offered to recruit thousands of Al Qaeda members to defend Saudi Arabia against a possible Iraqi invasion. When instead the Saudi royal family decided to allow the United States to deploy its armed forces within Saudi Arabia's borders, bin Laden and many other fundamentalists were outraged at the presence of a non-Islamic country's troops near the holiest sites of Islam. Bin Laden claimed that the United States and its allies were establishing, in effect, a permanent imperialist occupation of both the religious-cultural core of Islamic nations and the oil resources of the Middle East. Al Qaeda's response, along with that of allied extremist fundamentalist groups, was to launch attacks against the United States and its interests. Among these were the 1993 truck bomb attack on the New York City World Trade Towers, the 1998 bombings of the U.S. embassies in Kenya and Tanzania, the 2000 suicide bombing of the USS *Cole*, and the 2001 destruction of the World Trade Towers and attack on the Pentagon.

In retaliation the United States, Britain, and several allies invaded and occupied first Afghanistan, which had provided training sites for Al Qaeda, and later oil-rich Iraq. But although its government had been hostile to certain U.S. policies and toward Israel, Iraq, in contrast to Afghanistan, seemed to have nothing to do with the 2001 attacks in the United States or Al Qaeda's other activities. During the U.S. occupation of Iraq, internal conflict seemed to increase, especially between Iraqi Shiites and Iraq's Arab Sunnis; a major anti-U.S. occupation insurgency developed among Arab Sunni Iraqis, and many young people from various Islamic countries, including persons affiliated with Al Qaeda, came to Iraq to resist the U.S. occupation. In the view of many observers, Iraq seemed to have replaced Afghanistan as the training ground for a new generation of Islamic fundamentalist holy warriors (Odom 2006). Bush administration policies meant that Americans who would become the victims of insurgent or Al Qaeda violence in Iraq would come mainly from the U.S.'s lower or lower middle classes. Although many U.S. citizens joined the U.S. armed forces for what they felt were patriotic reasons or to bring democracy to Iraq, some joined in part for training or future educational and career opportunities their families could not provide for them.

Following the September 11, 2001, Al Qaeda attack on the United States, President Bush in his January 2002 State of the Union message identified Iran, Iraq, and North Korea as members of an "Axis of Evil." Ironically, Iranian leaders had been cooperating with U.S. officials against the Taliban regime in Afghanistan. The Bush attack on Iran likely undermined the Iranian moderate politicians who had been enjoying significant popular support in the years before Bush's "Axis of Evil" speech. Combined with the March 2003 U.S.-led invasion and occupation of neighboring Iraq, the Bush administration's threatening orientation toward Iran probably contributed to the election of Mahmoud Ahmadinejad, a relatively hard-line Islamic fundamentalist, in Iran's 2005 presidential election. According to the BBC profile of President Ahmadinejad, "his presidential campaign focused on poverty, social justice and the distribution of wealth within Iran" (October 27, 2005). But the profile also quoted President Ahmadinejad as stating that Israel should be "wiped off the map." President Ahmadinejad also defended Iran's nuclear energy program, which the Bush administration feared could lead to the development of Iranian nuclear weapons.

Other nations suspected that Iran, following the U.S. invasion and occupation of Iraq, might be trying to develop nuclear weapons to deter the United States from subjecting Iran to a similar fate. Of further concern to the Bush administration was the belief that Iran was providing assistance to Hamas, the Palestinian religious fundamentalist movement and political party, which won the January 2006 Palestinian parliamentary election, as well as funding, training, and helping to arm Hezbollah in Lebanon. Iran was also accused of aiding Iraqi Shia militia groups, perhaps with the ultimate goal of helping to establish an actual or de facto Shia Islamic Republic in southern Iraq.

SUMMARY AND ANALYSIS

The motivation temporarily unifying diverse prorevolution groups was the desire to oust the shah, end the monarchy's corrupt patronage system, and free Iran from perceived foreign domination. Several distinct revolutionary elites developed that were committed to these goals as well as others. The fundamentalist branch of the Shia clergy believed that God, through the ulama, must govern society. This variety of elite opposition constituted potentially effective leadership for the masses because the clergy espoused an ideology and value system already shared by most Iranians. Furthermore, they constituted a network of tens of thousands with control over thousands of mosques and hundreds of bazaars as possible sites for community political organization. The fundamentalists' view that their belief system was God's creation and their plan for Iran was God's intention appealed to many: it provided poor Iranians with a sense of moral superiority to the human-created cultures and ideologies of the technologically advanced societies. As the shah became progressively identified with foreign interests, the fundamentalist clergy appeared to many to be the true representatives of Iran's traditional culture and historical identity.

Whereas the fundamentalist clergy were recruited from Iran's traditional middle class, other major revolutionary elites were derived mainly from the nation's modern middle class. But when the opportunity for revolution arose, most of the relatively secularized and Westernized anti-shah groups in this category found they were unable to effectively communicate with, much less mobilize, the Iranian masses.

Most important in determining the precise ideological direction of the anti-monarchal revolution was the fact that the movement's primary leader and most charismatic figure was a fundamentalist, Ayatollah Khomeini. Khomeini's adamant refusal to compromise with the shah despite the monarch's massive military and economic power appealed to the Iranian Shia faithful, schooled in the legendary martyrdom of Imam Hussein. Khomeini rewarded their loyalty by developing a successful "technology of revolution" tailored to the culture and psychology of Shia Iran. The ayatollah instructed the faithful to use the forty-day-interval mourning processions for the martyrs of previous demonstrations and those religious holidays commemorating sacrifice or heroic deeds as opportunities for new and ever-larger protests. He called on his followers to offer themselves in martyrdom before the shah's soldiers, knowing the shared religious significance of any resulting deaths would gradually demoralize the armed forces and ultimately destroy the coercive capacity of the monarchal regime.

When Khomeini's tactics worked, many of his country folk concluded that to defeat the shah's worldly might, the ayatollah must indeed be endowed with divine powers. Having witnessed or even participated in this fantastic achievement, many of the faithful were thereafter much inclined to seek out Khomeini's point of view on important postrevolutionary matters and follow his advice. Consequently, when conflicts developed among former revolutionary allies, Khomeini's advocacy of a political system in which both parties and candidates had to be approved by clerical leaders and in which final authority rested in the hands of the clergy ensured the defeat of alternative revolutionary elites.

The large majority of the rural population, whose expectations had been raised by the promises of the shah's White Revolution, either received no land or parcels too small to constitute viable commercial farms. Many of the poorest, who were generally strongly religious, chose to migrate to the booming cities during the 1960s and 1970s; thus at the time of the revolution 45 percent of Iran's people lived in urban areas, which would constitute the battlegrounds for the Iranian Revolution.

The mass migration to the cities produced a housing crisis. And though the standard of living did generally improve for the poor, it rose much faster for other classes, resulting in greater inequality and a sense of injustice among the urban working and lower classes. Discontent increased markedly after the mid-1970s as a result of high inflation, increased unemployment, and lowered wages. Hostility toward the shah's regime intensified because many of the shah's wealthy supporters displayed conspicuously luxuriant and lavishly expensive lifestyles and abandoned Islamic religious practices. The shah's attempt to control religion and reduce its traditional social and political influence was a cause of outrage for many, since Islam, more than providing a sense of identity, constituted the psycho-cultural mechanism through which most Iranians coped with and understood life. Once the wave of protests began in early 1978, the anger of the urban poor was heightened further by the repeated slaughter of participants.

A number of inherent flaws as well as circumstantial factors contributed to the deterioration of the coercive capacity of the shah's regime. The National Front government's effort to reduce the shah's power ended in 1953, in part because of foreign intervention. This fact impaired the legitimacy of the shah's rule and merited the profound animosity of many Iranians. Some of the shah's economic policies and attempts to modify or control religious institutions and traditions deprived his regime of the support of many landlords, bazaar merchants, and ulama who had backed his overthrow of Mossadeq's government. Without the loyalty of these groups, the existence of the shah's state depended largely on its ability to suppress opposition groups, its support from domestic and foreign businesspeople, the backing of the United States, and oil revenue, which paid for the weapons of repression, fed the shah's patronage system of military and industrial elites, and bought the temporary complacency of the masses. As the shah's regime lacked genuine popular support, it was seriously weakened after 1976, when national oil income failed to keep pace with the level of expenditure and the regime lost the capacity to improve the physical well-being of its citizens.

Undoubtedly one key factor in the deterioration of the shah's regime was his relaxation of restrictions on political activities in 1977 in reaction to pressure from the United States; moreover, he was under the mistaken impression that his popular support was much greater and his opposition much weaker than they actually were. Reduction of repressive measures and the belief that the shah no longer had the unconditional support of the United States encouraged anti-shah forces to regroup, expand, and demand increasingly far-reaching concessions, which eventually could not be met without endangering the continued existence of the monarchy. The regime was shaken by the religiously oriented confrontation tactics orchestrated by Ayatollah Khomeini, which succeeded in crippling the shah's once-mighty military machine.

The orientation of foreign powers toward the shah's government influenced the development and the success of the revolution. The Carter administration's demands for the shah to improve the human rights situation by relaxing restrictions on dissent contributed to mounting revolutionary pressures in 1977 and 1978. But even three weeks after the Black Friday Massacre of September 8, 1978, a CIA report asserted that the shah would stay "actively in power" for at least another ten years (Hiro 1987, 312). President Carter's human rights pressures on the shah, his continued support for the shah (which infuriated Khomeini and many other Iranians), and his decision not to intervene militarily to preserve the monarchy may all have been partially influenced by the incorrect assessment of the shah's ability to stay in power. The Carter administration eventually chose to accept the shah's departure rather passively. But in September 1980 Iraq attacked Iran, with the goal of putting an end to the Islamic Republic form of government. The Iraqi assault, rather than weakening the Islamic Republic, bolstered it by inspiring Iranian nationalism and prompting Iranians to rally around their revolutionary leaders.

During the 1980s Iran endured civil war; confrontation with the United States; eight years of war with Iraq, which generated hundreds of thousands of casualties and billions of dollars in losses; and finally the death of the revolution's charismatic leader, Ayatollah Khomeini. The post-Khomeini leadership of Iran faced enormous economic problems and continued hostility from the United States, ostensibly because Iran fostered Islamic-fundamentalist terrorism but probably also because Iran and its political-cultural revolution constituted a major threat to the survival of Middle Eastern governments supportive of U.S. foreign policy, including the oil-rich monarchies in the Persian Gulf, and thus, effective U.S. control over much of the region's vast and strategically important energy resources.

Following Iraq's defeat in 1991 by the U.S.-led UN coalition, Iran emerged as the most powerful Islamic power in the region. Iran, however, found itself confronted both by Israel's suspected nuclear arsenal and by likely permanent facilities available to accommodate any future U.S. interventions in Saudi Arabia, Kuwait, or other neighboring countries. But Iran's special weapon remained its role as a wellspring of inspiration for many Islamic fundamentalists around the world. The triumph of Iranian Islamic fundamentalists against the shah's regime was widely viewed as a victory over the world's number one superpower, the United States. In particular Islamic fundamentalists, including Osama bin Laden, were encouraged by Islamic success in Iran to fight against the Soviet Union in Afghanistan. The defeat of the USSR there contributed to the Communist Party's loss of power and to the disintegration of the Soviet Union in 1991.

The victory of Islamic forces in Afghanistan following the defeat of the U.S.-backed shah's regime in Iran further encouraged Islamic fundamentalists to confront other perceived threats to Islam. Osama bin Laden organized the Al Qaeda network among the tens of thousands of Islamic volunteers who had fought in Afghanistan. When after the 1990 Iraqi invasion of Kuwait the Saudi royal family allowed U.S. military forces to be stationed in Saudi Arabia, bin Laden and Al Qaeda launched attacks against the United

States, including the September 11, 2001, destruction of the World Trade Towers. After the United States invaded and occupied Iraq in 2003, Iraqi insurgents' resistance mirrored that of the Afghan Mujahideen against the Soviets in the 1980s, and their actions were augmented by those of Islamic fundamentalists who went to Iraq to fight the Americans as once others like them had flocked to Afghanistan to fight the Soviets (Bearden 2003).

IRANIAN REVOLUTION: CHRONOLOGY OF MAJOR EVENTS

1906 Iran's first constitution establishes a parliament
1926 Reza Khan founds Pahlavi dynasty
1941 Britain and the Soviet Union occupy Iran and force Reza Shah to abdicate in favor of his son, Muhammad
1953 Mossadeq's National Front government overthrown; shah establishes dictatorship
1957 SAVAK organized
1963 Protests against the shah's White Revolution; Ayatollah Khomeini jailed (expelled from Iran in 1964)
1971 Fedayeen and Mujahideen guerrilla groups are formed and launch attacks on shah's regime
1973 Arab-Israeli War and oil price rise; much of Iran's oil income used for advanced weapons
1977 Carter makes U.S. aid conditional on improved human rights situation; shah eases repression but enacts economic austerity program
1978 Shah's government slanders Ayatollah Khomeini; protesters killed by shah's forces
1979 Shah flees country on January 16; Ayatollah Khomeini returns to Iran on February 1; militants seize U.S. embassy and hostages; Constitution of the Islamic Republic ratified
1980 Iraq invades Iran in September
1981 U.S. hostages freed in January; open conflict between the IRP and the Mujahideen; Mujahideen and most other opponents of the IRP suppressed over the next two years
1988 Iran-Iraq War ends
1989 Ayatollah Khomeini dies and is succeeded by Hojatolislam Khamenei as Iran's religious leader
1990 Iraq invades Kuwait
1991 First Gulf War—U.S. and its allies defeat Iraq
1997 Moderate Mohammad Khatami elected president of Iran, defeating fundamentalist candidate
2001 September 11—Al Qaeda terrorist attacks take place against the United States

2002   January 29—In State of the Union address President George W. Bush calls Iran a member of the "Axis of Evil" nations, angering many Iranians

2003   March—United States with some allies invade and occupy Iraq

2005   Iranians elect fundamentalist-supported Mahmoud Amadinejad their new president

References and Further Readings

Abrahamian, Ervand. 1982. *Iran Between Two Revolutions*. Princeton Studies on the Near East. Princeton, NJ: Princeton University Press.

_____. 1985. "The Guerrilla Movement in Iran, 1963–77." In *Iran: A Revolution in Turmoil*, ed. Haleh Afshar. Albany: State University of New York Press.

_____. 1989. *The Iranian Mojahedin*. New Haven, CT: Yale University Press.

Algar, Hamid, trans. and annotator. 1981. *Islam and Revolution: Writings and Declarations of Imam Khomeini*. Berkeley, CA: Mizan.

Al-Qazzaz, Ayad. 2006. "Iraqi Revolution." In DeFronzo, ed., *Revolutionary Movements in World History*, 2:427–40.

Alterman, Jon B. 2001. "Iran: Came the Revolution." *Current History*, January, 27–32.

Ansari, Ali M. 2003. *Modern Iran Since 1921: The Pahlavis and After*. Upper Saddle River, NJ: Pearson Education.

Bakhash, Shaul. 1984. *The Reign of the Ayatollahs: Iran and the Islamic Revolution*. New York: Basic Books.

BBC, October 27, 2005, "Profile: Mahmoud Ahmadinejad." http://news.bbc.co.uk/2/hi/middle_east/4107270.stm (accessed April 8, 2006).

Bearden, Milt. 2003. "Iraqi Insurgents Take a Page from the Afghan 'Freedom Fighters': A Veteran of the Anti-Soviet Resistance Worries about Resourceful Foes." *New York Times*, November 9, sec. 4, 7.

Cavatorta, Francesco. 2006. "Colonialsm, Anti-Colonialism, and Neo-Colonialism." In DeFronzo, ed., *Revolutionary Movements in World History*, 1:163–68.

Cohen, Albert K. 2006. "Terrorism." In DeFronzo, ed., *Revolutionary Movements in World History*, 3:862–68.

Cole, Juan. 2006. "A 'Shiite Crescent?' The Regional Impact of the Iraq War." *Current History*, January, 20–26.

DeFronzo, James. 2006a. "Iranian Revolution." In DeFronzo, ed., *Revolutionary Movements in World History*, 2:412–27.

_____, ed. 2006b. *Revolutionary Movements in World History: From 1750 to the Present*. 3 vols. Santa Barbara, CA: ABC-CLIO.

Diba, Farhad. 1986. *Mossadegh: A Political Biography*. London: Croom Helm.

Esposito, John L. 1994. "Political Islam: Beyond the Green Menace." *Current History*, January, 19–24.

Gill, Jungyun. 2006. "Student and Youth Movements, Activism and Revolution." In DeFronzo, ed., *Revolutionary Movements in World History*, 3:848–54.

Goldstone, Jack A., ed. 1986. *Revolutions: Theoretical, Comparative, and Historical Studies*. New York: Harcourt Brace Jovanovich.

Goodson, Larry P. 2001. *Afghanistan's Endless War: State Failure, Regional Politics, and the Rise of the Taliban*. Seattle: University of Washington Press.

Graham, Robert. 1979. *Iran: The Illusion of Power*. New York: St. Martin's Press.

Green, Jerold D. 1982. *Revolution in Iran: The Politics of Countermobilization*. New York: Praeger.

_____. 1986. "Countermobilization in the Iranian Revolution." In Goldstone, ed., *Revolutions*.

Hashim, Ahmed. S. 2005. "Iraq: From Insurgency to Civil War?" *Current History*, January, 10–18.

Hiro, Dilip. 1987. *Iran Under the Ayatollahs*. London: Routledge and Kegan Paul.

Hooglund, Eric J. 1982. *Land and Revolution in Iran, 1960–1980*. Austin: University of Texas Press.

Hopkins, A. G. 2006. "The "Victory" Strategy: Grand Bargain or Grand Illusion?" *Current History*, January, 14–19.

Hunter, Shireen T. 1993. "Iran from the August 1988 Cease-Fire to the April 1992 Majlis Elections." In *The Middle East After Iraq's Invasion of Kuwait*, ed. Robert O. Freedman. Gainesville: University Press of Florida.

Hussain, Asaf. 1985. *Islamic Iran: Revolution and Counter-Revolution*. New York: St. Martin's Press.

Ibrahim, Ahmed. 2006. "The Palestinian Movement." In DeFronzo, ed., *Revolutionary Movements in World History*, 2:631–42.

Joffé, George. 2006. "Islamic Fundamentalist Revolutionary Movement." In DeFronzo, ed., *Revolutionary Movements in World History*, 2:452–64.

Katz, Mark N. 1997. *Revolutions and Revolutionary Waves*. New York: St. Martin's Press.

_____. 2002. "Osama bin Laden as Transnational Revolutionary Leader." *Current History*, February, 81–85.

_____. 2006. "Transnational Revolutionary Movements." In DeFronzo, ed., *Revolutionary Movements in World History*, 3:872–76.

Keddie, Nikki R. 1981. *Roots of Revolution: An Interpretive History of Modern Iran*. New Haven, CT: Yale University Press.

Long, David E. 1986. "Islamic Republic of Iran." In *The Government and Politics of the Middle East and North Africa*, ed. David E. Long and Bernard Reich, 60–76. Boulder: Westview Press.

McCain, John. 2006. "Stay to Win." *Current History*, January, 8–13.

Milani, Mohsen M. 1988. *The Making of Iran's Islamic Revolution: From Monarchy to Islamic Republic*. Boulder: Westview Press.

_____. 1994. *The Making of Iran's Islamic Revolution: From Monarchy to Islamic Republic*. 2nd ed. Boulder: Westview Press.

Moghadam, Val. 2006. "Afghanistan: Conflict and Civil War." In DeFronzo, ed., *Revolutionary Movements in World History*, 1:1–12.

Montgomery, Evan Braden, and Stacie L. Pettyjohn. 2006. "Ideology, Propaganda, and Revolution." In DeFronzo, ed., *Revolutionary Movements in World History*, 2:379–83.

Moshiri, Farrokh. 1991. "Iran: Islamic Revolution Against Westernization." In *Revolutions of the Late Twentieth Century*, ed. Jack A. Goldstone, Ted Robert Gurr, and Farrokh Moshiri, 116–35. Boulder: Westview Press.

Najmabadi, Afsaneh. 1987. *Land Reform and Social Change in Iran*. Salt Lake City: University of Utah Press.

New York Times, June 6, 1988, A1, "Teheran Said to Reassess the Future of Its Dream."

_____, June 20, 1988, A8, "Iraqi-Backed Army Attacks Iranian City."

_____, March 31, 1989, A5, "The War Over, Iraq's Ruler Announces Plans for Liberalization."

_____, May 22, 1989, A1, "Son of Khomeini Gains Authority."

_____, June 5, 1989, A1, "Iran Quickly Appoints Successor to Khomeini."

_____, June 14, 1990, A1, "Islamic Party in Algeria Defeats Ruling Group in Local Elections."

_____, July 1, 1990, E5, "Islamic Fundamentalism Is Winning Votes."

_____, July 6, 1990, A2, "Iran's Chief Links Aid to Better Ties."

_____, August 16, 1990, A1, "Iraq Seeks Peace with Iran, Turning Back Spoils of War in Move to End Its Isolation."

_____, January 6, 1991, A5, "Kurds Routinely, and Easily, Smuggle Food from Iran to Iraq."

_____, January 24, 1994, A1, "Islamic Rebels Gain in Fight Against Army Rule in Algeria."

_____, February 3, 1994, A1, "Fundamentalists Impose Culture on Egypt."

_____, February 11, 1994, A3, "Egypt Loses Ground to Muslim Militia and Fear."

_____, April 4, 1994, A1, "Algeria Is Said to Be Moving Toward Breakup."

_____, July 29, 1994, A1, "Iran and Allies Are Suspected in Bombwave."

_____, October 23, 1994, E3, "Islam Bent into Ideology: Vengeful Vision of Hope."

_____, November 8, 1994, A1, "Palestinian Religious Militants: Why Their Ranks Are Gaining Strength."

_____, January 25, 1995, A8, "Palestinian 'Martyrs,' All Too Willing."

_____, January 25, 1995, A9, "Clinton Orders Assets of Suspected Terrorist Groups Frozen."

_____, April 1, 1995, 5, "Christopher Proposes Tighter Curbs on Trade with Iran."

_____, March 5, 1996, A1, "4th Terror Blast in Israel Kills 12 at Mall in Tel Aviv, Nine-Day Toll Grows to 59."

Nusbaumer, Michael. 2006. "War and Revolution." In DeFronzo, ed., *Revolutionary Movements in World History*, 3:931–36.

Odom, William. 2006. "Withdraw Now." *Current History*, January, 3–7.

Rinehart, James. 2006. "Millenarianism, Religion and Revolution." In DeFronzo, ed., *Revolutionary Movements in World History*, 2:570–74.

Selected DVD, Film, and Videocassette Documentaries

See "Purchase and Rental Sources" at the end of this volume for information on how to obtain the following resources and for full names of media companies and other organizations listed here as abbreviations.

Anatomy of a Coup: The CIA in Iran. 50 min. AETV (History Undercover). CIA in Iran during the 1953 coup in support of the monarchy.

The Arming of Saudi Arabia. 1993. 60 min. Video. PBS. U.S. policy toward Saudi Arabia.

Battle for the Holy Land. 2002. 60 min. PBS. Perspectives of Israelis and Palestinians.

Greetings from Iraq. 1993. 29 min. Video. AFSC. Impact of the 1991 Gulf War and subsequent economic embargo on Iraq.

Holy War, Holy Terror. 1985. 60 min. Video. PBS. Describes Iran's Shia Islamic fundamentalism with regard to its impact on Iranians, the Middle East, and the world.

Iran. 1979. 22 min. Color film. UI, BU, UMINN, PSU, UWISC-M. Provides an overview of U.S. policy toward Iran from the 1950s to the revolution of 1979.

Iran and the Bomb. 1993. 60 min. Video. PBS. Investigations of Iranian weapons programs.

Iran: Veiled Appearances. 2002. 58 min. FRIF. Iran twenty-three years after the revolution.

Mohammed Reza Pahlavi: Politics of Oil. 1980. 24 min. Color film. BU, UIOWA, IU, UMINN, PSU, SYRU, UVEN-R. Covers the rise and fall of the shah.

Oliver's Army with Eric Mendelson. 1987. PTTV. Iran-contra operation.

Osama Bin Laden. 50 min. BIO.

Party of God. 2003. PBS Frontline. Hezbollah.

Saudi Time Bomb. 2001. 60 min. PBS Frontline. Saudi Arabia and Wahhabi international activities.

The Search for Peace in the Middle East: Yitzhak Rabin and Yasser Arafat. AETV. Twentieth Century Series.

Secret Government: The Constitution in Crisis. 1987. 90 min. SUN. Secret government activities including the Iran-Contra operation.

Soldiers of God. 1998. 46 min. Truman Library. CNN Cold War Series, Episode 20. Islamic revolutionaries and fighters in Iran and Afghanistan.

Son of Al Qaeda. 60 min. PBS Frontline. Al Qaeda associate who turned against the organization.

Women of Hezbollah. 2000. 49 min. FRIF. Women activists in Hezbollah.

8

ISLAMIC REVOLUTIONARY MOVEMENTS

By the late 1970s, after the appeal of Arab nationalist and Marxist-Leninist ideologies had declined markedly, another transnational revolutionary movement, Islamic fundamentalism, began to spread rapidly and score political victories or pose serious threats to governments. One version emerged from the Shia branch of Islam largely through the religious interpretations of Iran's Ayatollah Ruhollah Khomeini. Khomeini's call for a government in which clerical leaders would play a leading role contributed to the elimination of the Iranian monarchy and the creation of the Iranian Islamic Republic. Shia fundamentalism had significant international effects: its victory in Iran over a government backed by the United States, the most powerful nation in the world, attracted many to conservative versions of Islam and encouraged other Islamic fundamentalists, both Shia and Sunni, to aspire to achieving political goals.

Shia fundamentalism, as a significant political force, was of necessity limited to those places where the Shia were a major component of a nation's population, such as Iraq and Lebanon. But fundamentalist movements among the far more numerous Sunni began to have major political impacts from the early 1980s on, including the creation of Hamas among the Arab Palestinians in 1987, the formation of Al Qaeda in 1988 among Islamic volunteers in the Afghan war against the Soviets, and the founding of the Taliban movement in Afghanistan in 1994. The victory of Islamic fundamentalism in Iran also alerted the secular republican and monarchal governments in the Middle East to the threat of fundamentalism. Non-Islamic nations, such as the United States, either supported secular governments against the fundamentalists or in other situations supported fundamentalists against secular political leaders, depending to a large extent on the non-Islamic nations' perceived self-interests.

HISTORICAL BACKGROUND OF ISLAMIC FUNDAMENTALISM

The expression "fundamentalism" is thought to have first been applied to certain Christian groups in the United States in the 1920s who believed in a literal interpretation of the Bible (Halliday 1998; Joffé 2006.) Christian fundamentalists, for example, denied the scientifically developed theory of evolution because the Bible said that God created the world and all its creatures in six days. From this apparent origin, the term was later used to refer to religious conservatives in other faiths who also believed in a literal interpretation of their sacred texts and who advocated the transformation of government and society into greater alignment with their beliefs. In the case of Islam, it came to refer to movements that proposed replacing relatively secular governments with political systems integrating church and state and transforming society by adopting characteristics of the original Islamic community.

One enormously important Islamic fundamentalist (or Islamist) movement was launched by Muhammad al Wahhab (1705–1791), a Sunni leader who held "that no doctrine or practice originating after the end of the third Islamic century would be acceptable" (Joffé 2006). Wahhab and his followers allied with the Saud family in 1744 and proved to be of great assistance in helping the family represent its military effort to conquer other groups and create what became known as the nation of Saudi Arabia as a crusade to purify Islam. The victory of the Saud family resulted in Wahhabi Islam becoming the major form of Islam in Saudi Arabia. Requiring the continued support of the very conservative Wahhabi clergy, especially problematic after Western interests established first a technical presence to exploit the country's great oil resource and later a military deployment, the Saudi royal family provided hundreds of millions of dollars for the building of impressive mosques in Saudi Arabia and in other Islamic nations and for the funding of Islamic religious schools around the world. In many of these schools a form of conservative Islam similar to Wahhabi Islam was taught to children who often would otherwise have received little or no education at all. Tens of thousands of these children grew into the leaders of or participants in later Islamist movements.

An important event spurring the development of modern forms of Islamic fundamentalism was Napoleon's invasion and occupation of Egypt in 1798, which began the process of modern European domination of much of the Middle East and North Africa. The French victory shocked Muslims by demonstrating that Christian Europeans had achieved a marked advantage in technology, particularly in weapons. Some Islamic scholars reacted by concluding that Islamic societies had become corrupted over the passage of time and that the solution to the threat of European imperialism could be found by returning Islamic faith and practices to those of the Rashidun era, the time of the "rightly guided" caliphs. This was the period of the first four caliphs or leaders of the Islamic community, those who had personally known the Prophet Muhammad. The last of these was Ali, the Prophet's cousin and the husband of the Prophet's daughter, Fatima.

One of the central proponents of a return to the early form of Islam was Jamal al Din al Afghani (1839–1897), who began the Salafist movement. *Salaf* here refers to the "ancestors" who lived during the Rashidun period. Jamal believed and propagated the concept that returning to the Islam of the Rashidun period would revitalize and strengthen Islamic societies in the face of the European threat; within this form of Islam could be found the political and moral concepts that, if adopted, could help Islamic societies modernize and accomplish technological achievements similar to those of Europe while remaining true to Islamic values. Thus this movement was at once backward looking and forward looking in that it sought solutions to the problem of Islamic modernization in an idealized distant past.

Further impetus to Islamic fundamentalist movements was provided by the British Balfour Declaration of 1917, which advocated establishing a homeland for the Jewish people in the land called Palestine, whose residents at the time were overwhelmingly Islamic Arabs. This perceived assault of European imperialism was almost immediately followed in 1918, at the conclusion of World War I, by British and French occupation of Islamic Arab lands, which had previously been part of the Ottoman Empire. These events led to the development of another version of Islamic fundamentalism, Ikhwan Muslimin (the Muslim Brotherhood), described by some as the first explicitly political Islamic fundamentalist movement. The Muslim Brotherhood was founded by Hassan al-Banna (1906–1949) in Egypt in 1928. Its leaders advocated the nonviolent change of Islamic societies in a fundamentalist direction, but offshoots or associated movements, such as Gam'iyat Islamiyya (Islamic Groups), Islamic Jihad (Islamic Holy War), and Hamas (the Islamic Resistance Movement), sometimes turned to violence.

Joffé (2006, 456) states that the Muslim Brotherhood "became the model for all subsequent Islamist movements" among Sunni Muslims. In line with the Salafi approach, the leaders of Ikhwan Muslimin believed that the best way to strengthen Islamic societies against European domination was by resurrecting the earliest form of Islam. According to this perspective, once this transformation was achieved, Islamic societies could successfully modernize and effectively compete with Western societies. In his discussion of Islamic movements, Joffé argues against what he referred to as the Huntington (1993) and Lewis (2002) perspectives, which suggest the "doctrinal and cultural content of Islam" inherently necessitates a confrontation with Western societies (Joffé 2006, 454). Rather, Joffé asserts that the rise of Islamist revolutionary political movements followed a historical pattern in which the "profound asymmetries" between developed and developing countries were the real cause of revolutionary movements and resulting political conflict. According to this analysis, people react to domination and

exploitation by the more powerful nations by seeking within their indigenous cultural patterns an ideology that can unite people of various social
classes and backgrounds against the perceived external aggression.

Nationalism has served this purpose in a number of societies, for example, in the case of the Vietnamese and Cuban revolutions. But after the
crushing defeat of several Arab nations by Israel in the 1967 Six Day War,
Arab nationalism, which had once offered the promise of uniting into one
nation the many states whose people spoke the Arab language, lost much of
its previous appeal. Instead, revolutionary ideologies based on Islam began
to grow in popularity for several reasons. First, while also drawn from indigenous culture, Islam in theory had the potential to unite an even greater
number of people across class, racial, ethnic, and national boundaries than
Arab nationalism. Second, the commitment and spirit of self-sacrifice so important in revolutionary soldiers and supporters as they confront initially
overwhelming odds conceivably would be easier to generate with a religiously grounded ideology in which participants came to believe they were
doing God's will and could also look forward to a glorious reward after
death. Finally, as noted in chapter 7 on the Iranian Revolution, for those enduring oppression and deprivation, an Islamist-type ideology offered its adherents a level of psychological comfort that the more secularly oriented
ideologies, such as nationalism, could not provide: a sense of pride, dignity,
and self-worth deriving from the concept that they shared a value and belief
system created by God that was immeasurably superior to all other cultures,
including those of the more technologically advantaged nations.

According to Joffé (2006):

> "Islamic fundamentalist revolution" is often a culturally determined political
> response to perceived external threat. It appears to be revolutionary because
> one of its objectives is a domestic transformation of the political scene on the
> grounds that only in that way can the external threat be effectively countered:
> it had been a domestic political failure that had allowed the threat to develop
> in the first place. Indeed, this, too, is nothing new. One of the justifications for
> extreme nationalism and Fascism in Europe was that this was the only way in
> which the resources of the nation could be mobilized to counter international-
> ist cultural and political threats, whether from communism or other foreign
> conspiracies.

Joffé's analysis is consistent with Skocpol and Trimberger's structural
theory of revolution, discussed in chapter 1, which specified that the most
powerful conditions for revolution have in the past occurred in technologically inferior states when these were faced with overpowering military and
economic pressures from more-advanced nations. Inability to resist foreign
aggression reduced the perceived legitimacy of the prerevolutionary regimes,
which in many cases had fallen under the influence of the external powers.

The purpose of such revolutions, according to Skocpol and Trimberger's structural theory, was primarily political: the establishment of a new political system in a less-developed society, a system that would be better capable of resisting threats from more-advanced nations. One of the essential steps in building such a revolution was the identification and propagation of a motivational ideology for revolution, in this case Islamic fundamentalist ideology, with the capacity to unite diverse social groups in a common revolutionary effort.

Hassan al-Banna's Muslim Brotherhood was an Islamic movement intended for such a political purpose. Hassan was acting in response to foreign exploitation and to the lack of status and dignity that many Arabs and Muslims suffered. His approach emphasized personal psychological revitalization through embracing the elements of the original, pure form of Islam, which, through the exemplary behavior of Brotherhood members living morally upright lives and manifesting altruism, concern for others, and solidarity and promoting social justice among all Muslims, would help renew Islamic culture in the larger society. The cultural renewal would be a necessary step in the process of modernizing in a manner consistent with Islam and in throwing off the colonial yoke. This approach was in part meant to confront the problem that under colonial domination those Muslims who were educated in modern science and technology also typically underwent a process of secularization or conversion to the culture of the colonizing power. The Brotherhood also advocated reducing inequality and establishing a relatively equalitarian society that was perceived to be consistent with the religious culture of the earliest Muslims.

As a movement, the Muslim Brotherhood opposed the use of violence. (Candidates supportive of the Brotherhood were thought to have won as many as 88 of a total of 454 seats in the Egyptian parliamentary election of 2005 [Muslim Brotherhood—Egypt 2006].) Members of the Brotherhood became particularly concerned with the situation of the Arab Palestinians, who, under British control after World War I, believed that they were being denied the right to self-determination and that their land was being inundated by Zionist settlers intent on establishing a new homeland for the Jewish people, a goal publicly supported by the British government in its 1917 Balfour Declaration. The Brotherhood tried to provide assistance to the Palestinians during their work strikes against the British during the years 1936–1939. After the end of World War II, war broke out in 1948 between the new state of Israel, which the United Nations had voted to create in 1947, and several Arab countries. Members of the Muslim Brotherhood, who by that time were estimated to number in the hundreds of thousands, and many other Egyptians believed that the Egyptian monarchy, under British influence, refused to mount an effective military effort, contributing to Israel's victory and the flight of hundreds of thousands of Arab Palestinians from their homes. In revenge, members of an extreme faction of the

Brotherhood assassinated the Egyptian prime minister in 1948. Apparently in retaliation, secret agents of the government reportedly assassinated Hassan al-Banna in 1949. After 1948 the Egyptian government alternately banned or re-legalized the Brotherhood, but several of the Brotherhood's members, splinter factions, and associated groups carried out acts of violence.

An Egyptian member of the Muslim Brotherhood, Sayyid Qutb (1906–1966), along with Pakistani Mawlana Abu al-Mawdudi (1903–1979), who formulated similar ideas, was considered one of the major Sunni fundamentalist theoreticians of the modern era. Qutb's innovations helped transform political Islam into an explicitly revolutionary ideology by providing the religious rationale for the removal of certain Muslim leaders or governments. Qutb, according to Berman (2003), concluded that by the time of Jesus, who was regarded by Muslims as a great prophet but not himself divine, the leaders of Judaism, the guardians of God's revelations to Moses, had distorted their faith into a system of rigid ritualism. This ritualism interfered with the realization of the purpose of the rules revealed to Moses, which was to provide humankind with the proper way to integrate religion and the physical world in a manner that would both fulfill the will of God and gratify the needs inherent in human nature.

Qutb believed the Christians "went too far in rejecting Jewish teachings" (Berman 2003), in particular the code of Moses, which governed aspects of daily life. He argued that the early Christians made what he viewed as the disastrous mistake of importing "into Christianity the philosophy of the Greeks—the belief in a spiritual existence completely separate from physical life, a zone of pure spirit" (Berman 2003). According to Qutb, this theological blunder, the splitting of the "sacred from the secular," led over time to the destructive concept of the separation of church and state. Qutb believed that not only was this opposed to God's intention but such a separation necessarily failed to fulfill the needs of human nature. The result was that, despite their wealth and technology, the people of Western societies were generally unhappy and prone to anxiety, abusing drugs, and exhibiting exploitive criminal behavior.

Fortunately, according to Qutb, God provided Muhammad in the seventh century with a "new legal code" intended to properly integrate religion and the physical world. The Sharia (Islamic law), therefore, could not be replaced by moral or legal codes developed by governments. Qutb pointed to the Muslim development of the scientific method of inquiry as evidence that early Islam fostered both intellectual and scientific advances. He claimed that attacks by Christian Crusaders from the west and Mongols from the east, as well as the deterioration of the Muslim faith over time, prevented the Muslim world from exploiting its invention of the scientific method. Instead Europeans adopted this approach, leading to their great scientific and technological breakthroughs, which allowed European nations and the United States to dominate the world beginning in the nineteenth century.

This domination also permitted the European nations and the United States to begin contaminating the culture of Muslim societies, often with the collaboration of corrupt rulers, using the notion of separation of church and state. Qutb was, consequently, one of the first Muslim intellectuals to identify not only non-Islamic imperialist nations as the enemy of Islam but also supposedly Muslim rulers or governments that in reality collaborated with the imperialists.

According to Euben (2002, 369–70) "in contrast to classical doctrine . . . to endure unjust Muslim rule, Mawdudi and Qutb argue that jihad is an urgent imperative . . . between Muslims and so-called Muslims who aid and abet Western supremacy by betraying the precepts of Islamic sovereignty and opening the door to foreign corruption." The radical theological change in this new formulation is that jihad (in the sense of "holy war") can be carried out not just against aggressive foreign powers but also within the community of Islam itself. Leaders or governments that serve un-Islamic foreign interests to the detriment of the Islamic faithful must be struggled against and removed from power. According to this perspective, which Qutb developed in his famous book *Milestones*, a Muslim leader "who had transgressed Muslim precepts could be considered non-Muslim," and Muslims had a duty to wage jihad against such a leader or government as well as against external enemies.

Though faced with enormously powerful forces attempting to destroy Islam, Qutb believed that the true Islam of early Muslim society was so inherently superior to other faiths and ideologies, including in its unmatched ability to fulfill human needs and deliver happiness, that it would ultimately triumph and spread to the entire world. In *Milestones* he called upon young people to form an Islamic "vanguard" to lead the struggle against external threats and internal traitors to Islam. In response to his teachings, as well as to reported assassination attempts against government officials by members of the Muslim Brotherhood, Sayyid Qutb was imprisoned by Egyptian President Nasser's government from the mid-1950s to the mid-1960s, when he was briefly released. Although he was offered refuge in other Arab nations, Qutb refused to leave Egypt and apparently preferred to become a martyr, setting an example for his estimated three thousand students when the government executed him in 1966 (Berman 2003). Sayyid's brother, Mohammad Qutb, escaped to Saudi Arabia, where he became a professor of Islamic Studies. According to Berman, one of Mohammad Qutb's students was Osama bin Laden. It was probably no accident that bin Laden used Sayyid Qutb's term "vanguard" in referring to the nineteen men who carried out the September 11, 2001, terrorist attacks in the United States as "a group of vanguard Muslims" (Crenshaw 2001, 432).

Following Qutb's death, a number of his admirers and followers helped create Gam'iyat Islamiyya (Islamic Groups) and Islamic Jihad (Islamic Holy War), which turned to violence and some of whose members later united with Al Qaeda. Others inspired by Qutb's views assassinated Egyptian President Sadat, who had made peace with Israel, in 1981. Leaders of these Egyptian groups were also instrumental in providing an analysis that asserted that the United States itself must be attacked, since the rulers and governments they sought to overthrow were generally supported and protected by the United States. Sayyid Qutb's work, including his enormous *In the Shade of the Qur'an*, written while he was in prison, is widely viewed as a central component of the intellectual foundation for virtually all politically violent Sunni Islamic groups, including Al Qaeda.

FUNDAMENTALISM, MILLENARIANISM, AND REVOLUTIONARY POTENTIAL IN SHIA ISLAM

After the death of Muhammad, the fourth elected caliph was the Prophet's cousin, Ali, the husband of the Prophet's daughter, Fatima. Ali was admired by many as a champion of the poor, but he was assassinated in 661. Some Muslims came to believe that the Prophet had chosen Ali as his successor and that only descendants of Ali and Fatima were to lead the Islamic faithful. Those who held this view were called Shiat Ali (Partisans of Ali) or Shia. The Shia Muslims called Ali and specific male descendants of Ali and Fatima whom they believed had the right to lead Islam "imams."

The Shia considered the imams to be infallible. Other Muslims, who rejected the concept that only biological descendants of Ali and Fatima were to lead Islam and that these persons were infallible, instead held the view that only the Prophet Muhammad was infallible, along with the Word of Allah—the Quran—the most important component of the Sunna ("tradition") of Islam. According to the Sunnis, since no one after Muhammad was infallible, religious leaders could only interpret the Quran to Muslims in the unique context of each historical era.

Most Shia held that there were twelve imams. Twelver Shias believed that the last infallible imam vanished in 873. After his disappearance, there was no longer an infallible leader of Islam. But this will change when the twelfth imam, the Mahdi ("hidden imam"), returns to lead Islam. In the meantime Islamic scholars (mujtahid) were to issue opinions, authoritative but fallible, in matters concerning Islam. Since the Shia believed that at some point the twelfth imam would return to create a truly socially just Muslim society, over hundreds of years various rebellions occurred in Iran led by someone who claimed or was believed to be the Mahdi. Thus revolutionary potential was inherent in this millenarian aspect of Shiism.

According to Rinehart (2006) Shia millenarian rebellions had a recurring theme. All were led by a charismatic figure who claimed that Muslims had strayed from the guidance and laws of the Prophet. The Mahdi would reestablish true Islam among the people. Thus Shia millenarian religious movements were generally conservative or fundamentalist in nature, in the sense of leading the people back to a perceived divinely ordained religious and social system.

Ayatollah Khomeini, the main leader of the 1978–1979 Iranian Revolution, whom some believe was influenced by the ideas of Mawdudi and Qutb, had a similar fundamentalist revolutionary message and was viewed by many through the prism of Shia millenarianism as a divinely inspired holy man who was sent by God to liberate the people from the corruption of the shah's regime and the un-Islamic imperialist masters they perceived the shah's government served. Khomeini proclaimed that political power came directly from God and that the new constitution of the Islamic Republic of Iran should give supreme power to a clerically selected Islamic religious leader who represented God in the political system. Another great attraction of Ayatollah Khomeini's message to many Iranians was the sense of psychological security and moral superiority it provided to people who perceived themselves to have been exploited and humiliated both by their own prerevolutionary government and by Western imperialist powers. That is, in the face of current Western technological and military superiority, Islamic people could feel gratified in the belief that their culture was vastly morally superior to the secular, human-created cultures of the more technologically advanced societies. Khomeini's ideas and the example of the successful Iranian Revolution helped inspire the creation of the Hezbollah ("the Party of God") movement among Shia Lebanese (discussed later in this chapter).

CONTEMPORARY REVOLUTIONARY FUNDAMENTALISM IN SUNNA ISLAM: HAMAS, AL QAEDA, TALIBAN

Sunni revolutionary fundamentalist movements had the potential to become more pervasive than Shia movements because so many more nations have majority Sunni populations. But there were important differences between certain Sunni fundamentalist movements and Khomeini's Shia revolution. Ayatollah Khomeini's innovation in the 1970s was to argue that the clergy should explicitly play a dominant political role in society as representatives of Allah among the people and as interpreters of the Quran. Khomeini's revolution was primarily one of changing the nature of the political system by making the existing clergy dominant participants in a new republican political system in place of the previous monarchy (Joffé 2006). Church and state would no longer be separated. Instead, under the guidance of the clergy, both political leaders and now the political system itself would be required to conform to Islamic law.

But some Sunni Islamic movements were in certain ways even more radical than Khomeini's revolution. The Sunni Taliban movement, discussed below, imposed what some have described as "totalitarian" conditions in Afghanistan and enforced a drastically more restrictive form of Islam than that of Khomeini's Iran, particularly with regard to women. And the Sunni Al Qaeda movement, instead of acting only within the context of one nation, attempted to wage a global jihad.

Hamas of Palestine

Hamas (the Islamic Resistance Movement), was one of a number of fundamentalist-oriented Islamic organizations inspired by the Egyptian Muslim Brotherhood. As Kifner (1996, A8) notes, "typically, the Brotherhood's strategy is to fight what it sees as Westernization and corruption of Arab governments by running its own schools, hospitals and other services in order to spread its beliefs."

Hamas was founded in 1987 by Sheikh Ahmed Yasin, a teacher who had been crippled in childhood. Yasin had been supervising educational programs and social services in Gaza when the Palestine Liberation Organization (PLO) launched the first Intifada (mass participation uprising) against Israeli occupation. As Palestinian youth flocked to participate in the uprising, Yasin and his associates created Hamas apparently in order both to lend support and to provide young people with an Islamic alternative to the PLO. Article 2 of the August 18, 1988, "Covenant of the Islamic Resistance Movement" (Avalon Project 2006) stated that "the Islamic Resistance Movement is one of the wings of Moslem Brotherhood in Palestine. Moslem Brotherhood is a universal organization which constitutes the largest Islamic Movement in modern times ... characterized by its ... accurate comprehension and its complete embrace of all Islamic concepts of all aspects of life, culture, creed, politics, economics, education." The slogan of Hamas as stated in Article 8 of the Covenant was: "Allah is its target, the Prophet is its model, the Koran its constitution: Jihad is its path and death for the sake of Allah is the loftiest of its wishes."

Leaders of Hamas believed that in order to free themselves from Israeli control, the Palestinian people would have to undergo a revitalization of their faith in Islam. First, each person would have to wage "the Greater Jihad ... of the heart" (Euben 2002, 368), the internal jihad (the personal struggle "against oneself" to follow the path of God). Then each person would be able, if necessary, to engage in the lesser jihad, "the Jihad of the Sword," the struggle against the enemies of Islam, which, according to Islamic fundamentalists, also includes the requirement to resist corrupt Muslim rulers or governments.

According to Kifner (1996, A1), "in the 1970s and early in the Palestinian uprising, Israel allowed the surging Islamic movement to flourish and even covertly supported it, calculating that Muslim groups would undermine and draw support from Mr. Arafat's P.L.O., which was then the more immediate threat." But in 1989 Israel outlawed Hamas and incarcerated Sheikh Ahmed Yasin.

When the PLO supported the Iraqi invasion of Kuwait in 1990, several oil-rich Arab monarchies cut off their millions of dollars of aid to the PLO and instead reportedly provided more assistance to Hamas, which used most of the funds to expand Islamic educational and social services to the huge number of poor Palestinians. By 2003 the Palestinian Ministry of Education estimated that about 65 percent of all schools in Gaza below the level of secondary education were Islamic (Roy 2003, 16). Hamas also received funds from supporters in Europe and the United States. While the large majority of Hamas activities involved providing Palestinians with basic necessities of life and other services, Hamas also had a military wing, the Izzadin al-Qassam Brigades, named after a Muslim preacher in Haifa who in the 1930s had led rebellions against Zionist settlers and the British occupation and had died in battle in 1935. Members of the Brigade reportedly conducted numerous attacks on Israeli soldiers and civilians, including suicide and bus bombings, during the 1990s and early twenty-first century. In response, some nations labeled Hamas a terrorist organization. Israel killed a number of Hamas leaders. After a failed Israeli attempt to assassinate an important Hamas leader, Khaled Meshal, in Jordan, Israel agreed to free Sheikh Ahmed Yasin in return for the release of its captured Mossad (Israeli Intelligence) agents (Westcott 2000). But in March 2004 an Israel missile strike succeeded in killing Yasin.

Hamas opposed the U.S.-negotiated attempts at peace agreements between the Palestinians and the Israelis and refused to accept the legitimacy of the existence of the state of Israel. According to Roy (2003), the Al Aqsa Intifada, which began on September 28, 2000, provided a new opportunity for Hamas. In retaliation for both Hamas- and PLO-associated attacks, the Israelis disrupted much of the Palestinian Authority's governmental infrastructure, in part because Israel blamed the Palestinian Authority for not suppressing those Palestinians carrying out acts of violence. With the Palestinian Authority crippled, many Palestinians turned to Hamas for help. The new intifada, according to Roy (2003, 13), was in part a "response to seven years of a 'peace' process that not only deepened Palestinian dispossession and deprivation but strengthened Israel's occupation." The U.S. war on terrorism after September 11, 2001, was perceived as further strengthening Israel's freedom to deal harshly with the Palestinians and seemingly sabotage the peace process.

Over the next few years, this view, coupled with the perception of corruption within the Palestinian Authority government and the persistent widespread poverty among the Palestinians in the Gaza Strip and the West Bank, which, according to Roy (2003, 19) approached 70 percent below the poverty line and 60 percent unemployment, seemed to increase popular support for Hamas. In January 2006 Hamas won control of the Palestinian parliament, taking 74 of 132 seats, including 6 won by Hamas women candidates (Fisher 2006). But on June 30, 2006, in an attempt to win the release of a captured Israeli soldier, Israeli forces invaded Palestinian territory and captured a number of Hamas government and party officials, including approximately one-third of Palestinian Cabinet members and twenty-three Hamas members of parliament (Erlanger 2006a).

Al Qaeda and Transnational Islamic Fundamentalist Revolution

After the triumph of Islamic fundamentalists in the Iranian Revolution, Salafi Sunni Islamists were encouraged to take part in the struggle against the Soviet Union's occupation of Afghanistan, which began in 1979. The USSR had intervened there to support a pro-Soviet leftist regime threatened by an uprising of traditionalist Islamist Afghans. Thousands of volunteers from many countries traveled to Pakistan, where funds from Saudi Arabia and other nations helped pay for equipment and sustenance. The Pakistani Intelligence service provided other assistance to prepare the volunteers to cross the border into Afghanistan to attack Soviet troops and the armed forces of the Afghan leftist government.

Dr. Abdallah Azzam (1941–1989), a Palestinian-born professor who had received a Ph.D. in Islamic law from al-Azhar University in Egypt and had fought for the Palestinian cause before becoming dissatisfied with what he considered the overly secular orientation of some of its leaders, established a recruiting organization, al-Maktab al-Khidmat (MAK, the Services Office), for bringing young Islamic men to Pakistan in order to join in the conflict in neighboring Afghanistan. In Pakistan Azzam taught and advised many of the volunteers, including Osama bin Laden, the son of a Saudi Arabian construction company owner, originally from Yemen, who had become a billionaire. Azzam proclaimed that Muslims had lost their former power because they no longer waged jihad against imperialist, exploitative, and culturally subversive nations. He asserted that it was the personal responsibility of every Muslim to support or participate in jihad, including at the international level, to restore and defend true Islam. Azzam reportedly became bin Laden's primary mentor for several years during the Afghan war. Bin Laden not only fought but used his money to aid the Islamist fighters and care for war orphans and widows. Islamists ultimately won the war with the critically important aid of U.S.-supplied, shoulder-fired anti-aircraft missiles, which were used to shoot down or drive off low-flying aircraft such as Soviet helicopters. Soviet forces withdrew in 1989, but in that same year Professor Azzam was assassinated by means of a hidden bomb, possibly planted by Soviet agents or by rivals within the Islamic movement.

During the Afghan conflict, an Egyptian volunteer, Ayman al-Zawahiri, became a close associate of Osama bin Laden. Zawahiri was born to a prominent Egyptian family, some of whose members had been nationally known educators and physicians. Ayman al-Zawahiri was a brilliant student who became a medical doctor. According to family members, as a child he became very interested in religion. At about age fifteen he joined the Muslim Brotherhood. Later he became involved in the more radical and violence-prone Egyptian Islamic Jihad. When Egyptian President Sadat was assassinated by Muslim fundamentalists in 1981, Zawahiri was arrested, along with hundreds of others. Charismatic and fluent in English, he became a spokesperson for many of those imprisoned. While not proven to have participated in the assassination, he was convicted of illegal possession of weapons and sentenced to three years in prison, where he suffered torture. After his release, Zawahiri traveled to Peshawar, Pakistan, where he reportedly worked as a surgeon for Islamic fighters wounded in the holy war against Soviet forces and the leftist Afghan government. In the context of the Afghan war, Zawahiri met bin Laden and also worked with Azzam. Zawahiri reportedly had a significant effect on bin Laden in advocating to him the concept that the United States should be attacked directly, since it provided the crucial support and protection for corrupt and despotic regimes in Muslim countries, such as the Arab monarchies, as well as for Israel.

The victory of Islamic forces over the Soviet Union in Afghanistan following the defeat of the U.S.-backed government of the shah in Iran further encouraged Islamic fundamentalists to confront not only non-Islamic nations but also governments in Islamic countries, such as those in Egypt and Saudi Arabia, which they perceived to be the allies or puppets of the United States or other non-Islamic states. Osama bin Laden and his associates in 1988 organized a database and communication network for the thousands of foreign volunteers, sometimes referred to as the Afghan Arabs, who had fought in Afghanistan and survived the conflict. This network was later called Al Qaeda ("the base" or "foundation"). Soon after the Soviets withdrew from Afghanistan, bin Laden returned to Saudi Arabia, where he was initially treated as a hero. But shortly after he returned home, Iraq invaded Kuwait in 1990 and appeared to constitute a threat to Saudi Arabia. Strongly opposed to the secular Baath Party government of Iraq and President Saddam Hussein, bin Laden offered to recruit thousands of Al Qaeda members to defend Saudi Arabia against a potential Iraqi invasion, possibly as many as 35,000 (Joffé 2006, 460). But the Saudi royal family decided to decline bin Laden's offer and instead allowed the United States to deploy large forces to Saudi Arabia and use the country as a base of operations against Iraq and for a possible counterinvasion of Kuwait.

The Saudi monarchy's decision may have been based on several factors. First, it is highly questionable whether bin Laden's forces could have made much difference in the face of a major invasion from Iraq. Second, Al Qaeda forces probably could not have aided significantly in an effort to force the Iraqis to leave Kuwait. Third, the Saudi royal family was highly dependent on the United States for military equipment and training for its armed forces and for other types of assistance and would certainly have been reluctant to turn down the U.S. request to use Saudi territory to wage war against Iraq. Fourth, neither the United States nor the Saudi Arabian monarchy wanted to see a re-concentration of Al Qaeda forces in oil-rich and strategically important Saudi Arabia.

Some observers believe that after the Afghan war the United States forced Pakistan to send the foreign Islamic volunteers back to their home countries or at least out of Pakistan once their desired function of defeating Soviet forces had been accomplished. The idea of reconstituting tens of thousands of battle-hardened Islamic fundamentalist fighters, brimming with self-confidence after defeating the Soviets, on Saudi Arabian territory, undoubtedly worried, if not terrified, the royal family and its U.S. and British allies. The Salafi-oriented Al Qaeda leadership was inclined to favor replacing despotic monarchies with a clerically dominated Islamic form of government. There was probably considerable concern in the royal family and Washington that once the Iraqi threat was neutralized, or even before, an Al Qaeda fundamentalist army in Saudi Arabia could have turned on the pro-U.S. royal family.

Bin Laden and many other fundamentalists were outraged at what they perceived as the occupation of the nation with the holiest sites of Islam by a non-Islamic country's armed forces. Having just fought a long and costly war (especially in terms of the many lives lost) to drive the Soviets from one Islamic nation, the fundamentalists were confronted with what they viewed as the betrayal by the Saudi royal family allowing another "infidel" army to occupy the religiously sacred territory of Arabia. Bin Laden claimed that the United States was establishing a permanent occupation and military domination of both the religious-cultural core of Islam and the oil resources of the Middle East. For voicing opposition to the Saudi monarchy's policies, he was forced to leave the country. He traveled to Sudan where, for a number of years, in addition to his Al Qaeda activities, he established and oversaw several businesses. In 1996 he left Sudan for Afghanistan. Al Qaeda, along with allied Salafi-led Islamist groups, launched a series of attacks against the United States and its interests, including the 1993 truck bomb attack on the New York City World Trade Towers.

In February 1998 Osama bin Laden, his second in command, Ayman al-Zawahiri, and the leaders of a number of other Islamist extremist organizations from several nations announced the formation of the Islamic World Front for the Struggle Against the Jews and the Crusaders, an international global jihad alliance. By this point it is thought that members of al-Zawahiri's Egyptian Islamic Jihad had not only merged with but assumed major leadership positions within Al Qaeda. In August 1998 Al Qaeda associates bombed the U.S. embassies in Kenya and Tanzania. In 2000 suicide bombers, using a small boat, struck the USS *Cole*. An apparent Al Qaeda plot to bomb Los Angeles International Airport at the end of the same year was prevented. And on September 11, 2001, Al Qaeda associates carried out what has been described as the most destructive terrorist attack in history by using hijacked passenger airliners to destroy the New York World Trade Towers and to attack the Pentagon.

The United States, Britain, and several allies invaded and occupied Afghanistan, beginning in October 2001, and ousted the Taliban regime, which had provided refuge for bin Laden and training sites for Al Qaeda. In March 2003, without the support of the United Nations and justifying the action on what appears to have been false information concerning a nonexistent nuclear threat and apparently never found weapons of mass destruction, the United States, Britain, and a number of other nations invaded and occupied Iraq.

Although its government had been hostile to certain U.S. policies and toward Israel, Iraq, in contrast to Afghanistan, seemed to have had nothing to do with the 2001 attacks in the United States or Al Qaeda's other activities. During the U.S. occupation of Iraq, internal conflict increased, especially between Iraqi Shiites and Iraq's Arab Sunnis, a major anti-U.S. occupation insurgency developed among Arab Sunni Iraqis, and many young people from various Islamic countries came to Iraq to resist the foreign occupation, as once volunteers had poured into Afghanistan to fight the Soviets. Iraq seemed to have replaced Afghanistan as the training ground and inspiration for a new generation of Islamic fundamentalist holy warriors (Odom 2006), apparently increasing the threat of terrorism (Mazzetti 2006).

By 2006 the structure of the Al Qaeda–led fundamentalist alliance was thought to be highly decentralized, involving groups with somewhat varying versions of Islam. Top leaders such as Osama bin Laden and Ayman al-Zawahiri were in hiding, possibly in relatively remote mountainous areas of Pakistan or Afghanistan, making communication with many of their followers very difficult. It seemed that often bin Laden or al-Zawahiri relied on sending messages or encouragement to followers through internationally broadcast video or audio recordings. This suggested that Al Qaeda, rather than being a tightly organized hierarchal organization, might more accurately be viewed as a transnational social movement attempting to spread and popularize its ideas to millions of Muslims who were expected to organize and act with little or no direct Al Qaeda assistance.

Taliban of Afghanistan

The development of the Taliban ("religious students" or "students of the Book," the Quran) movement, its military victories in most of Afghanistan during the years 1994–1996, and its rule over almost 90 percent of the country for four years were due to several simultaneously occurring factors. These included, first, the education in the years before 1994 of tens of thousands of young men in fundamentalist-oriented Islamist schools, *madrasas*, affiliated with the Deobandi form of Islam. Deobandi Islam had apparently originated in northern India and advocated a purified form of Islam similar to that of the Wahhabis of Saudi Arabia. The intellectual father of the Deobandi movement, Shah Waliullah, was apparently inspired by the founder of Wahhabism, Muhammad ibn Abdul Wahhab (Rubin 1999, 82). Thus from the beginning of the Deobandi movement there was a strong link to Wahhabi Islam. Furthermore, there is some indication that Wahhabi missionaries were sent to northern India during the British colonial period to aid Islamic residents in protecting their culture from British influences. Although from different *madhabs* or legal schools of Sunni Islam (the Deobandi are of the Hanafi school, and the Wahhabi are of the Hanbali school), the Deobandis were very "sympathetic to the Wahhabi creed" (Rashid 2000, 90). This was also partly due to the fact that funds from Saudi Arabia were used to support many *madrasas* in Pakistan and Afghanistan favorable toward Wahhabi concepts, such as those run by the Deobandi clergy.

The billions of dollars that the Saudis spent in spreading Wahhabi Islam around the world through thousands of Wahhabi missionaries and through supporting religious schools and mosques, including in Pakistan and Afghanistan, served several useful functions for the Saudi royal family. It helped secure the Wahhabi clergy's support or at least tolerance for the Saudi monarchy, despite its cooperation with and dependence on the United States; it exported to other countries many young Saudi Wahhabi clergy who might otherwise have caused problems for the regime at home; and it helped counter the international influence of Shia fundamentalism, which had increased following the Shia victory over the U.S.-backed monarchy of Iran in 1979. Some of the men schooled in the Deobandi *madrasas* participated in the war against the Soviet occupation of Afghanistan, a war that depended on substantial aid from Saudi Arabia, as well as assistance from Pakistan and weapons and CIA agents from the United States. But many more younger students, filled with religious zeal and idealism from their years in the *madrasas*, would fill the ranks of the Taliban (Gill 2006; Rashid 2000).

A second key element in the rise and temporary victory of the Taliban was the terrible civil war conditions, banditry, lawlessness, and economic disruption that characterized certain areas of Afghanistan after the departure of Soviet forces in 1989. This situation created a popular demand for some force to provide public security and deter and punish criminals, insure a stable and effective environment for transportation and commerce, and unify the country under honest government. When the Taliban began to display these characteristics beginning in 1994, many people welcomed the movement and the new Taliban regime.

Finally, Pakistan provided assistance to the Taliban (Rubin 1999), which was extremely important, especially for its early military victories. These gave the Taliban the opportunity to demonstrate its other capabilities to people in the areas it secured, causing support to develop for the movement in other regions, which helped to bring about new Taliban triumphs. The Pakistanis appeared interested in promoting the Taliban for at least two major reasons. First, Pakistan hoped to benefit from energy resources and resource transportation from countries to the north of Afghanistan, such as the natural gas of Turmenistan. But the ability to build pipelines required a cessation of fighting in Afghanistan, law and order, and an end to the multiple tolls different militias or criminal groups charged trucks on the roadways. The Taliban were apparently intended by Pakistan's intelligence service to accomplish these goals. Furthermore, since Taliban members were largely from the Pashtun ethnic group, the largest in Afghanistan at about 45 percent of the population (also a significant ethnic component of Pakistan's population) and since a future Taliban government would likely be grateful for assistance provided by Pakistan, the Pakistan government probably anticipated that it would then be able to count on a friendly regime to its west. This could have been helpful to Pakistan in any future conflict with its much bigger long-time rival, India.

With Pakistani assistance, the Taliban began its military campaign by taking the transportation depot town of Spin Baldak near the Afghanistan-Pakistan border in October 1994. Then the Taliban demonstrated that it could assure clear passage along the length of road it controlled from Pakistan. In November the Taliban took Afghanistan's second largest city, Kandahar, after about two days of fighting. In the words of Ahmed Rashid (2000, 29), "the Taliban immediately implemented the strictest interpretation of Sharia (Islamic) law ever seen in the Muslim world. They closed down girls' schools and banned women from working outside the home, smashed TV sets, forbade a whole array of sports and recreational activities and ordered all men to grow long beards." As the Taliban enforced the law and severely punished criminals, collected firearms from the general population to suppress armed conflict among tribal or ethnic groups, and reestablished conditions for businesses and commerce to function, the movement's popularity grew among many Afghanis.

The Taliban took the capital, Kabul, in September 1996 and imposed their extremely restrictive form of Sharia rule. They established a government under the leadership of Mullah Mohammad Umar, the leader of the group of *madrasa* teachers and students that had created the Taliban movement at Kandahar in 1994. Eventually the Taliban controlled approximately 85 to 90 percent of Afghanistan. Only the Tajik-populated area in the northeastern part of the country, under the Northern Alliance led by Ahmed Shah Massoud, continued to effectively resist the Taliban. On September 9, 2001, two suicide bombers, most likely associated with either Al Qaeda or the Taliban or both, posing as journalists coming to interview Massoud, assassinated him with a bomb concealed in a camera. This was possibly an effort by Al Qaeda to weaken the Northern Alliance before expected retaliation from the United States after the planned September 11 attacks.

In May 1996 Osama bin Laden, the veteran of the Afghan war against the Soviets, returned to the country as the guest of the Taliban. The Taliban allowed bin Laden to set up training camps for hundreds of Islamic volunteers who came to Afghanistan to prepare for Al Qaeda–inspired attacks directed against other nations, including the United States. Bin Laden reportedly convinced Taliban leaders that the United States, which supported Israel and what he viewed as corrupt governments in Muslim countries, should be a central target of jihad.

Following the September 11, 2001, Al Qaeda terrorist attacks against the United States, President Bush gave an ultimatum to the Taliban leadership to turn over bin Laden and Al Qaeda members in Afghanistan to the United States. When the Taliban leadership refused, the U.S. military used air attacks, U.S. special forces, and the anti-Taliban Northern Alliance in its attack on Taliban and Al Qaeda forces in Afghanistan in October 2001. The Taliban were driven from power in the major cities and much of the countryside, but bin Laden and Mullah Umar escaped capture. Certain rural and mountainous areas of Pashtun-populated sections of Afghanistan continued to be supportive of the Taliban and to oppose the new U.S.-assisted government in Kabul. In 2006 the Taliban seemed to still have the capacity to wage at least limited war in long-suffering Afghanistan.

THE WAR IN IRAQ

On March 20, 2003, U.S.- and British-led forces invaded Iraq. An assortment of reasons were used to justify the invasion, including claims that Iraq possessed weapons of mass destruction and, despite the fact that Osama bin Laden had disapproved of Saddam Hussein and the relatively secular government in Iraq, that the Iraqis had somehow been involved with the September 11, 2001, attacks by Al Qaeda. Later investigations seemed to indicate that the claims were false. But in the post–9/11 war on terrorism atmosphere in the United States these charges seemed to play a role in relation to the Iraq War similar to that played by the Gulf of Tonkin incident in relation to the Vietnam War. Both helped stampede the U.S. Congress into passing a resolution that provided the legal basis for the president to take the country to war (see chapter 4).

As U.S. companies were awarded contracts to do work in occupied Iraq, and the country's oil seemed to be, in effect, under U.S. control, the new justification for maintaining military occupation was to make sure that the country succeeded in establishing a stable democratic system rather than withdrawing while it still endured the insurgent, interreligious, and interethnic violence that followed the invasion. The resistance insurgency that developed against foreign occupation was multifaceted, varying significantly in motives, ideology, goals, and tactics. By 2006 at least eleven major insurgent organizations or alliances existed. Possibly as many as thirty or forty smaller insurgent groups, some splinter factions from the large organizations, also operated. The estimated number of active insurgents ranged "from a few thousand to more than 50,000" (Finer 2006). Approximately 90 percent of the insurgents were thought to be Sunni, and 90 percent or more were thought to be Iraqi rather than foreign volunteers, although the

Islamic foreign fighters were apparently overrepresented among those who engaged in suicide bombing attacks.

The primary motivations offered by the Sunni insurgents for their armed resistance seemed to be either "patriotism or Salafi ... religious fervour" (Guidère and Harling 2006). In addition to the armed, mostly Sunni insurgents, there were many thousands in Shia militias apparently attempting to protect Shia neighborhoods, promote Shia dominance in the southern areas of Iraq, or in some cases engage in sectarian conflict with Sunni groups. The U.S.-led invasion removed the Saddam Hussein regime and ended decades of Sunni domination of government (about 35 percent of the population was Sunni, while more than 60 percent of Iraqis were Shia). But the Shia seemed overrepresented in the new occupation-sponsored Iraqi army and police forces. Both Shia and Sunni Iraqis were motivated to join the new armed forces by the terrible economic situation in Iraq and the fact that occupation authorities had disbanded the country's old army, significantly increasing the number of the unemployed by hundreds of thousands.

Iraq War: Nationalist Insurgents

Virtually as soon as the U.S.-led occupation of Iraq began, so did insurgent resistance. Many of the original insurgents were members of Saddam Hussein's Baath Party, including many former military and intelligence officers. Some of these may have hoped to reinstall a Baath Party government. But after Saddam Hussein was captured on December 13, 2003, many Baathists began to lose hope of the party or Hussein regaining power. Since the Baathists were also staunch nationalists, many of those who continued to participate in the insurgency shifted primarily to the goal of fighting to drive the occupying foreign forces out and establishing conditions for what they would consider a government that was the product of Iraqi self-determination rather than a creature of the foreign occupation. Similarly, they apparently intended to punish foreign corporations, which they viewed as stealing Iraq's oil for the benefit of the invading powers or Israel. Other nationalists fought because they had family members or friends who had been killed as a result of the invasion or the actions of occupation forces against insurgents. The Baathist and nationalist insurgents were estimated to have targeted either U.S. forces or non-Iraqi contractors in the large majority of their attacks (Lehrer 2006). Some former Baathist Party militants, however, decided to join one of the several Islamic-oriented insurgent movements.

Iraq War: Sunni Islamic Insurgents

Some Iraqi Sunnis were members of the Iraqi branch of the Muslim Brotherhood, which advocated that Iraq should be freed from non-Islamic influences, the Iraqi people should adopt the authentic form of Islam that the

Brotherhood believed existed early in Islam's history, and Iraq should be transformed into an Islamic republic.

In addition to the indigenous Iraqi Salafi Sunni insurgents, hundreds of foreign Islamic volunteers began to cross into Iraq from Syria, Jordan, and Saudi Arabia, many of whom were Wahhabi-schooled Saudi Arabian citizens. One of the Jordanian fighters was Abu Musab al-Zarqawi, who led a major group of foreign Islamist volunteers that began to identify itself as a branch of the Al Qaeda movement. Whereas the nationalist-oriented insurgents and Iraqi Sunni Islamic insurgents tended to attack occupation forces by means of roadside bombs, ambushes, mortars, and rifle-propelled grenades, the foreign Islamic fighters were more prone to engaging in suicide bombing attacks ("martyrdom missions") than other fighters. The Zarqawi-led group was also blamed for some of the most brutal attacks and acts of violence of the insurgency. These included bombing attacks killing many civilians. Zarqawi's followers were accused of targeting Shia civilians and mosques in an attempt to provoke a civil war between Sunni and Shia Iraqis, although it is not entirely clear how such a civil war could have led to the end of the occupation.

Many nationalist and Islamic Iraqi insurgents strongly condemned the bombings of civilians, whether the victims were Sunni or Shia, and the brutal beheadings of some captured hostages as unjustified and counterproductive. Even the leaders of Al Qaeda criticized some of these actions. Some Iraqi insurgents were thought to have attacked and killed a number of foreign fighters to prevent them from carrying out bombings or executions of civilians or to punish them for such brutality. But as the insurgency continued, there was some evidence that various insurgent organizations had increased their levels of cooperation with one another and that the Al Qaeda–linked groups actually had come to include many indigenous Iraqis. Some observers thought that this might have been due to a need for money, which some of the Islamist groups could supply from foreign sources. Despite their earlier criticisms both top leaders of Al Qaeda, Osama bin Laden and Ayman al-Zawahiri, issued audio recordings praising Zarqawi as a martyr after he was killed by a U.S. air strike on June 7, 2006.

Iraq War: Shia Fundamentalists

Juan Cole (2006) argues that the Bush administration's invasion of Iraq and overthrow of the Baath Party government there may have set in motion a second Shia Islamic Fundamentalist Revolution (the first being the Iranian Revolution of 1979).

As noted in chapter 7 on the Iranian Revolution, Ayatollah Khomeini considered both the secular republican form of government, such as that in Egypt or that in Iraq led by Saddam Hussein, and the monarchies in countries such as in Saudi Arabia, Jordan, and Kuwait, to be un-Islamic forms of government; he called for their replacement with Islamic republics in which clerical leaders would play a dominant role and in which church and state would be integrated. Since Iraq's population had a Shia majority, Iraq seemed the most likely candidate for a second Islamic Republic. Some members of the Shia Iraqi Dawa Party, which had formed in the 1950s to counter the appeal to Shia young people of both the Baath Socialist Party and the Iraqi Communist Party, were accused of organizing a fundamentalist rebellion against the Iraqi government. This appeared to have been one of the reasons for Saddam Hussein's war with Iran during the years 1980–1988, in which Iraq's effort was backed by Saudi Arabia, Jordan, other Arab countries, and, according to Cole (2006), the United States. Although Iraq's invasion did not overthrow the Iranian Islamic Republic but instead appeared to strengthen it, Iraq's military effort was thought to have temporarily slowed the spread of Shia Islamic revolutionary movements to other countries. As also noted in chapter 7, the economic consequences of that war contributed to Iraq's invasion of Kuwait in 1990. This action, in turn, led to the first Gulf War and later, coupled with the U.S. reaction to the September 11, 2001, terrorist attacks, to the Bush administration's decision to invade Iraq and occupy the country.

But the end of the secular Baath Party regime in Iraq unleashed the revolutionary potential of Iraq's Shia majority and encouraged Shia movements in other countries in the region. Throughout much of southern Iraq as well as in other Shia-populated areas and sections of Iraqi cities, Shia men formed into armed militias, some of whose personnel had reportedly been trained by Iran's Islamic Revolutionary Guards. The Shia militias were often under the authority of one of three Shia organizations—the Dawa Party, the Supreme Council for Islamic Revolution in Iraq (SCIRI), or Shiite cleric Moqtada al-Sadr's Mahdi Army. Ultimately these three groups entered into an electoral alliance (Finer and Fekeiki 2005), the United Iraqi Alliance, in the U.S.-sponsored Iraqi elections of December 2005. This Shia alliance won 128 of the 275 seats in the national assembly, the Council of Representatives, and was able to form a coalition government with Iraq's Kurdish Alliance. Shia alliances also won in eleven of the country's eighteen provinces in the January 2006 provincial elections.

The parliament proceeded to write a constitution that "stipulated that Islam is the religion of state and that civil parliament could pass no legislation that contravened established Islamic laws" (Cole 2006, 21). To some observers this represented the achievement of the central fundamentalist goal of the integration of church and state in Iraq and the ultimate triumph of Khomeini's ideas. The new Shia-dominated government in Iraq seemed to serve as an inspiration to other Shia groups in the Middle East, such as the Shia Lebanese Hezbollah Party; the Shia minority of Saudi Arabia, which resides primarily in its oil-rich Eastern Province; and the Shia majority of Bahrain, ruled in 2006 by a Sunni monarch.

Iraq War: The Future of Iraq?

The U.S.-led invasion of Iraq in 2003 may ultimately have any of the following consequences, which are not necessarily mutually exclusive: a state of long-term civil war, in particular between segments of the Sunni and Shia population for reasons such as the unwillingness of Sunnis to accept a state dominated by Shia religious groups or what they might view as rule by an Iranian-allied or -controlled regime; the fragmentation of Iraq into separate Sunni Kurdish, Sunni Arab, and Shia Arab states; the existence of Iraq as a partial or "guided" democracy in reality controlled ultimately by the United States; and the continuous U.S. military occupation of all or part of Iraq.

One problem with ending the civil conflict through dividing Iraq into three new countries is that if the approximately 18 percent of Iraq's population that is Kurdish forms an independent Kurdish nation, it would almost certainly serve as an encouragement and as a base of support for the Kurds in Turkey and Iran and possibly Syria to attempt to break off from those countries to form a united Kurdistan. Of some concern to the United States and Israel is that an independent Shia nation in the territory of southern Iraq, in which major oil resources are located, would probably be closely allied with Iran.

Despite the fact that one stated goal of U.S. and British authorities in invading and occupying Iraq was to establish a democratic government, this could ultimately prove costly or unacceptable to the United States. Although many Shia initially outwardly welcomed the U.S.-led invasion, there are major sources of hostility toward the United States within Iraq's Shia population. First, some Shia clerics in Iraq oppose what they view as U.S. imperialism, including cultural corruption emanating from the United States, as did the Iranian revolutionary leader Ayatollah Khomeini. Second, many Shia Iraqis bitterly resent the fact that when they rose in rebellion against Saddam Hussein's regime in March and April 1991, responding to what they perceived as the call of President George H. W. Bush for the uprising after the Iraqi defeat in the first Gulf War, the United States appeared to allow Hussein's force to repress the rebellion "with great brutality" (Cole 2006, 24). So the willingness of many Shia leaders to cooperate with the U.S. occupation was likely only temporary. Many in the sizable Sunni minority consider the U.S.-led invasion to have been an unjustified aggression in violation of international law. Thus one of the few things that many Sunni and Shia Iraqis have in common is their animosity toward the United States. Handing over the country for full democratic rule by Iraq's people could result in an elected government in control of the country's oil resources that is extremely hostile to the United States.

In consideration of this possibility, there will likely be a strong inclination on the part of some in the U.S. government to maintain a permanent military occupation of Iraq and allow only a U.S.-censored form of self-government. Evidence of this type of a plan for the future of Iraq might be found in an aspect of the Iraqi legal system in 2006 that specified that U.S. soldiers in Iraq charged with crimes against Iraqis could only be dealt with and punished by U.S. authorities. As noted in chapter 7, this type of legal arrangement in Iran under the U.S.-supported government of the shah was strongly condemned by Ayatollah Khomeini as evidence that the shah's government was a puppet regime of the United States in the years leading up to the Iranian Revolution. In a U.S.-controlled Iraqi "guided democracy," a religiously dominated Iraqi government would likely be allowed to enforce Islamic religious law, particularly in certain Shia-dominated parts of the country (which in certain aspects, such as the potential curtailment of women's rights, would seem to be in clear contradiction of the human rights ideals publicly advocated by the U.S. government) in return for effective control of Iraq's oil by the U.S. government or U.S. corporations. In all likelihood, most Iraqis, including many Shia Iraqis, would find it difficult to peacefully accommodate such a situation.

HEZBOLLAH AND THE WAR WITH ISRAEL

One of the significant impacts of the Iranian Revolution was its contribution to the formation in 1982 of a militant Islamic organization, the Hezbollah ("Party of God"), among the approximately 35 to 40 percent of Lebanon's population that is Shia. The immediate impetus for the creation of Hezbollah was the Israeli invasion and occupation of southern Lebanon. The Israeli Defense Force (IDF) entered Lebanon in 1982 in an attempt to stop attacks into northern Israel by guerrillas of the PLO. Eventually, Israel occupied much of the country, including the territory around Beirut, and forced the departure of PLO forces from Lebanon. However, the IDF then allowed a Lebanese Christian Phalange militia to enter the Palestinian Sabra and Shatila refugee camps on September 16 to search for any remaining PLO fighters. The Phalangists reportedly killed somewhere between 460 and 3,500 people, depending on the source, including women and children. This massacre of unarmed Palestinians enraged many Lebanese against both the Christian extremists and the Israeli occupying forces.

Israel continued to occupy southern Lebanon for eighteen years, until 2000, and in the process employed a Christian-Druze militia, the South Lebanon Army (SLA), accused of torture and murder, in efforts to control the area. The Israeli invasion and occupation, while bringing about the departure of the PLO, resulted in the creation among Lebanese Shia of a new threat to Israel, Hezbollah. With the aid of an estimated 1,500 to two thousand Iranian Islamic Revolutionary Guards, who came to Lebanon to train Lebanese Shia volunteers to fight the Israeli occupation, Hezbollah's armed wing engaged in a number of violent actions against the SLA, the Israelis, and other foreign forces viewed by Hezbollah as hostile to Lebanon's Islamic residents or allied with Israel.

Hezbollah was thought to be responsible for the kidnapping of a number of U.S. citizens during the 1980s, including several who were apparently released through Iranian influence on Hezbollah as part of the Iran-Contra deal (see chapters 6 and 7). Hezbollah members were also thought to have carried out suicide attacks against Americans in Lebanon, including the April 18, 1983, bombing of the U.S. embassy in Beirut that killed sixty-three people and the October 23, 1983, barracks bombing that killed 241 U.S. Marines. U.S. forces later withdrew from Lebanon. During the 1982–2000 Israeli occupation of south Lebanon, Hezbollah, thought to have received major assistance and funding from Shia Iran and from Syria, became the most effective Lebanese force resisting Israeli occupation. The links between largely Sunni Syria and Shia Hezbollah and predominantly Shia Iran may in part be due to the fact that Syria's top governing elite is disproportionately Alawi, a form of Islam that is closely related to Shiism.

When the Israelis agreed to withdraw from Lebanon in 2000, most observers thought that this was partly because of continuous casualties sustained by the IDF from Hezbollah attacks. Many viewed Hezbollah as the first Arab army to ever accomplish such a victory against the Israeli armed forces. As a result, its popularity appeared to increase significantly. Hezbollah, however, was far from just a military organization. Its civilian sector provided educational and social services to tens of thousands of grateful Lebanese. For some time Hezbollah advocated transforming Lebanon into an Islamic Republic like Iran. But in the face of opposition from the large Christian minority, about 39 percent of the population, most in the Hezbollah leadership may have permanently or at least temporarily abandoned this goal. Hezbollah developed significant electoral support and in 2005, as a political party, won twenty-three of 128 seats in the Lebanese parliament. Two members of the party were appointed to cabinet positions.

Under the leadership of Sheik Hassan Nasrallah, Hezbollah was strongly critical of both Osama bin Laden's September 11, 2001, attack on the United States (because it resulted in the death of many innocent people) and many of the bombings and executions in Iraq, which took the lives of civilians after the 2003 U.S.-led invasion. Hezbollah also condemned the Sunni Taliban regime in Afghanistan as a repressive and "very hideous example of an Islamic state" (Wright 2006).

Hezbollah, however, developed a level of cooperation with Sunni Hamas and other Palestinian organizations. Hezbollah leaders did not accept the existence of the state of Israel and referred to it with expressions such as "the Zionist entity." Hezbollah (Wescott 2002) indicated that it was "ready to open a second front against Israel" in support of the Palestinians. After several Palestinians tunneled their way from Gaza to an Israeli outpost, killed two Israeli soldiers, and captured a third, Israeli forces invaded Gaza at the end of June 2006 and seized many Hamas members of the Palestinian government. Possibly in response to the Israeli invasion of Gaza (Erlanger

2006b) and also apparently as part of an effort to force the return of a number of Lebanese people from Israeli captivity, Hezbollah guerrillas crossed into Israel on July 12, killed eight Israeli soldiers, and captured two others. Israeli forces then attacked into Lebanon, carrying out air and artillery bombardments and then a ground invasion of southern Lebanon. Hezbollah launched about 150 to two hundred rockets into Israel almost each day of the conflict. Hezbollah's popularity surged within much of the Islamic world, and the war between Israel and Hezbollah threatened to involve the allies of Hezbollah, Iran and Syria. During the conflict Israel destroyed much of Lebanon's infrastructure, which elicited criticism from the governments of a number of nations.

After thirty-three days of violence, death, and destruction, the conflict between Hezbollah and Israel subsided on August 14, when a cease-fire negotiated by the United Nations went into effect. By that point approximately 1,150 Lebanese, mainly civilians, perished, while about 150 Israelis, mostly soldiers, died (Erlanger 2006b). The Israeli military estimated that it killed about five hundred Hezbollah fighters, but Hezbollah indicated that the real number was lower.

Both sides claimed to have won. Israel believed that Hezbollah had been significantly weakened and anticipated that as the result of the war the Lebanese government would be strengthened and under international pressure to disarm Hezbollah or at least to prevent Hezbollah from operating as an armed force in southern Lebanon between the Litani River and the Israeli border. This area, according to the cease-fire agreement, was to be patrolled by both the Lebanese army and United Nations troops.

To many observers, however, Hezbollah seemed to emerge politically strengthened, despite the losses it suffered. Hezbollah's prowess in battle and its ability to launch several thousand rockets into Israel damaged the myth of Israeli military invincibility and bolstered the pride and sense of dignity of millions of Arabs and Muslims. The expectation that the Lebanese government and military would be strengthened relative to Hezbollah was questionable, especially since some anticipated that Hezbollah's military performance against Israel would give it an even larger role in the Lebanese government and since much of the Lebanese armed forces were Shia and apparently sympathetic to Hezbollah.

The popularity of Hezbollah leader Sheik Hassan Nasrallah soared internationally, while anger against Israel's seeming collective punishment inflicted on Lebanon appeared widespread. The example of Hezbollah in the war with Israel was thought likely to accelerate the growth of political Islamic movements and motivate thousands of young Muslims to join Hezbollah or similar organizations. According to Slackman (2006), "the lesson learned by many Arabs from the war in Lebanon is that an Islamic movement, in this case Hezbollah, restored dignity and honor to a bruised and battered identity."

In a world in which the technology of war available to perceived imperialist nations continues to improve and existing elites in Islamic countries are viewed as corrupted by collaboration with those powers or with international profit-driven corporations, among the most effective resistance movements possible may increasingly be those whose participants are religiously driven soldiers. Such soldiers are relatively unafraid to die, their ranks are soon replenished by highly motivated volunteers, and their leaders' religious commitment makes them less susceptible to the financial inducements offered by foreign interests.

Summary and Analysis

The Salafi movement, which advocated returning to an early "pure" form of Islam that would protect Islamic peoples from the corrupting influences and domination of non-Islamic nations, developed in the nineteenth century in response to European military conquest and technological superiority. Another religious movement with similar ideas had been formulated earlier by Mohammad Wahhabi. A modern manifestation of what some historians regard as a form of the Salafi perspective was the Muslim Brotherhood, founded in Egypt in 1928. A member of the Egyptian Muslim Brotherhood, Sayyid Qutb, opposed the previous notion that the government of unjust Muslim rulers should be endured. In contrast, Qutb defined such regimes, especially those serving the interests of non-Islamic imperialist countries, as non-Muslim governments that true Muslims were required to overthrow. Branches of the Muslim Brotherhood were established in a number of Sunni Islamic countries. Some groups that split off from or were inspired by the Muslim Brotherhood engaged in violence, such as the Egyptian Islamic Holy War and the armed wing of Hamas, the Izzadin al-Qassam Brigades.

A form of Shia fundamentalism was put forth by Ayatollah Khomeini, who some believe was inspired in part by the writings of Qutb. Khomeini specifically defined secular republics and monarchies as un-Islamic forms of government and, similar to Qutb and the Sunni Salafi fundamentalists, rejected the concept of the separation of church and state. The 1978–1979 Khomeini-led Iranian Revolution resulted in the establishment of the first modern Islamic Republic in which church and state were integrated under clerical leadership. The success of the Iranian Revolution in overthrowing a U.S.-supported monarchy with an enormous military and supply of weapons encouraged Islamic fundamentalists, both Shia and Sunni.

The next major victory for Islamic fundamentalism occurred during the 1980s, when Sunni Islamic resistance fighters defeated the Soviet occupation of Afghanistan. Foreign Islamic volunteers in the Afghan war against the Soviets, including Osama bin Laden and Ayman al-Zawahiri, organized a communications network among the thousands of volunteers in 1988 that came to be called Al Qaeda. After U.S. forces were deployed in large numbers to Saudi Arabia in the early 1990s, Al Qaeda and allied Salafi movements launched what they described as a global holy war on behalf of Islam, one that included many acts of violence, such as the September 11, 2001, terrorist attacks in the United States.

Another consequence of the Afghan war was the formation of the Taliban and its establishment of the most conservative and repressive Islamic regime in modern history. Because the Taliban provided bases for Al Qaeda in Afghanistan, the United States led military actions to drive them from power at the end of 2001. But while Taliban rule was overthrown, another Sunni fundamentalist movement, Hamas, gained power through the Palestinian parliamentary election of 2006.

As part of its response to the September 11, 2001, terrorist attacks on the United States, the George W. Bush administration made the controversial and generally internationally unpopular decision to invade and occupy Iraq. While the United States was successful in ousting Saddam Hussein and his Baath Party government and then holding elections for a new Iraqi parliament in December 2005, Iraq in 2006 was still characterized by an insurgency against occupation forces and a high level of sectarian violence. In the view of many it had become a new cause of and training ground for terrorists intent on attacking the United States.

An earlier Israeli invasion and occupation of southern Lebanon during 1982–2000 had led to the creation of a Shia Lebanese military, political, and social welfare organization, Hezbollah. As the conflict in Iraq continued, war broke out on July 12, 2006, between Hezbollah and Israel. The ability of Hezbollah to resist the new Israeli invasion of southern Lebanon and to attack Israel with thousands of rockets seemed to bolster the pride of many Arabs and Muslims around the world and appeared likely to increase even further the attraction of politically oriented Islamic movements.

As in the analyses of other revolutions, the five factors crucial to the development of revolutionary movements can be applied in assessing the development and success or failures of Islamic revolutionary movements.

Large sectors of the populations of some Muslim nations historically suffered from poverty, economic exploitation, and often political oppression. Mass discontent in some of these societies was heightened by foreign invasion and occupation, which motivated people to be receptive to revolutionary ideologies that might offer a solution to their plight. Many of the Afghan people whose nation was occupied by the Soviets, then devastated by years of war and destruction, followed by more years of civil turmoil and lawlessness, became attracted to the Taliban's brand of Islam, since the Taliban at least restored some level of peace and social order. The Arab Palestinians, many of whom have suffered from long-term poverty and occupation as well as control by a foreign power, eventually turned to the ideas of Hamas and voted the fundamentalist movement into power in 2006.

A prerequisite for the development of revolutionary ideologies and organizations within Islam was the existence of a dissident elite. In the case of Islamic revolutionary movements, the dissident elite often came from the ranks of religious scholars or clergy who responded to social injustice, moral corruption, and imperialism with Salafi-like revolutionary ideologies that called for the restoration of the form of Islam that existed in the early decades of the Islamic faith. Such a religiously based ideology could, and in some cases did, provide the unifying motivational factor necessary to unite people of different social classes in a revolutionary movement.

For a number of prerevolutionary Muslim societies, the fourth and fifth factors of state collapse and world permissiveness are interrelated. Some Muslim countries, in particular certain of those still governed by monarchies, relied significantly on foreign support from non-Islamic nations to resist revolutionary movements seeking their overthrow. As noted in chapter 7, the Carter administration's international human rights policy, which required the Iranian monarch to improve the treatment of his own people as a condition of continued U.S. aid, weakened the shah's government, contributing to its ultimate collapse and the victory of Shia fundamentalist revolution there. In the case of Afghanistan the Soviet-backed government that preceded the Sunni Islamic revolution of the Taliban could not survive once the Soviets, partly for their own domestic reasons, decided to withdraw their military forces in 1989. Islamic revolutionary movements in a number of countries have not yet succeeded in part because of the support provided to existing governments by the United States and other nations. The election in the United States of another administration with foreign policies similar to those of the Carter administration might weaken some governments in Muslim countries enough to permit new victories for Islamic revolutionary movements.

ISLAMIC REVOLUTIONARY MOVEMENTS: CHRONOLOGY OF MAJOR EVENTS

571–632	The life span of the Prophet Muhammad, whose leadership and teachings inspire one of the greatest religious movements in history
632–661	The "Rashidun" or reigns of the Rightly Guided Caliphs, the period from the death of the Prophet to the death of Ali, the last of the four leaders of Islam who had personally known Muhammad
680	Death of Hussein, son of Ali, in battle at Karbala; some adherents of Islam, the Shia (Shiat Ali, or "Partisans of Ali") come to believe that only certain male descendants of Ali and his wife, the Prophet's daughter, Fatima, should rule Islam; by the twenty-first century, it is estimated that Shia are

somewhat less than 20 percent of Islam, while over 80 percent are Sunni

1744 Saud family allies with Muhammad ibn Abdul Wahhab, the religious leader of an Islamic purification movement; the alliance helps the Saud family to conquer what becomes known as Saudi Arabia and leads to Wahhabi Islam, a very conservative form of Islam, becoming dominant there

1798 Napoleon conquers Egypt, shocking the Islamic world with the reality of European technological superiority

1860s Jamal al-Din al Afghani begins the Salafi movement, which emphasizes the idea that the Islamic world could modernize and successfully confront European nations by first returning to the culture and concepts of the *salaf* ("ancestors"), the original version of Islam of the Rashidun period

1917 British Balfour Declaration supports the Zionist movement to create a homeland for the Jewish people in then overwhelmingly Islamic Palestine

1928 Hassan al-Banna creates the first modern Islamic political movement, the Ikhwan Muslimin, the Muslim Brotherhood, in Egypt

1947–1948 United Nations creates the state of Israel

1948 First Arab-Israeli War results in hundreds of thousands of Arab Palestinian refugees

1967 Israel's devastating victory over Egypt, Jordan. and Syria in the "Six Day War"

1979 Iranian Revolution ousts the pro-U.S. monarchy

1979–1989 Soviets occupy Afghanistan, and in response tens of thousands of volunteers, including Osama bin Laden, from dozens of countries join Afghan Islamic fighters in combating the army of the leftist Afghan government and Soviet military, which is forced to withdraw in 1989

1981 Islamic extremists assassinate President Sadat of Egypt

1982 Israeli army invades Lebanon to evict Palestine Liberation Organization forces there, but in reaction Shia Lebanese create Hezbollah to resist the occupation and force the Israeli military to withdraw from the country

1987 Hamas (Islamic Resistance Movement), inspired by the Muslim Brotherhood branch in Palestine, is founded among Palestinian Arabs by Sheikh Ahmed Yasin

1988 Osama bin Laden and his associates create Al Qaeda, "the base," an organizational and communications network among Islamic foreign volunteers in Afghanistan

1989 Soviets withdraw from Afghanistan

1990	Iraq invades Kuwait
1990–1991	US. increases its military deployment to Saudi Arabia
1991	Iraq defeated by the United States, Britain, and their allies in the First Gulf War
1993	Islamic extremists use a truck bomb to attack the New York World Trade Towers
1994–1996	Taliban emerges in Afghanistan and wins control of most of the country
1996	May—Osama bin Laden returns to Afghanistan
1998 Feb.	Al Qaeda leaders form Islamic World Front (global jihad alliance)
1998 Aug.	U.S. embassies in Kenya and Tanzania are attacked by Al Qaeda associates using vehicle bombs
2001	September 11—Al Qaeda attacks the New York World Trade Towers and the Pentagon in Washington, DC
2001	October 7—The United States and its allies begin military operations against Al Qaeda and the Taliban in Afghanistan and soon oust the Taliban regime
2003	March 20—U.S., British, and allied forces begin an invasion and occupation of Iraq
2004	Israel assassinates Sheikh Ahmed Yasin, founder of Hamas
2006	January—Hamas wins control of the Palestinian parliament in the legislative election
2006	July 12—War breaks out between Hezbollah and Israel
2006	August 14—Hezbollah-Israel cease-fire with both sides claiming victory

References and Further Readings

Abrahamian, Ervand. 1982. *Iran Between Two Revolutions*. Princeton Studies on the Near East. Princeton, NJ: Princeton University Press.

_____. 1989. *The Iranian Mojahedin*. New Haven, CT: Yale University Press.

Algar, Hamid. 1981. *Islam and Revolution: Writings and Declarations of Imam Khomeini*. Berkeley, CA: Mizan.

Al-Qazzaz, Ayad. 2006. "Iraq Revolution." In DeFronzo, ed., *Revolutionary Movements in World History*, 2:427–40.

Ansari, Ali M. 2003. *Modern Iran Since 1921: The Pahlavis and After*. London: Pearson Education.

Avalon Project. 2006. "The Covenant of the Islamic Resistance Movement." Yale University Law School. http://www.yale.edu/lawweb/avalon/mideast/hamas.htm.

Bakhash, Shaul. 1984. *The Reign of the Ayatollahs: Iran and the Islamic Revolution*. New York: Basic Books.

Berman, Paul. 2003. "The Philosopher of Islamic Terror." *New York Times*, March 23.

Brown, Nathan J. 2003. *Palestinian Politics after the Oslo Accords: Resuming Arab Palestine*. Berkeley: University of California Press.

Burke, Jason. 2003. *Al-Qaeda: Casting a Shadow of Terror*. London: I. B. Tauris.

Chehab, Zaki. 2005. *Inside the Resistance: The Iraqi Insurgency and the Future of the Middle East*. New York: Thunder's Mouth Press/Nations Books.

Clancy-Smith, Julia. 1998. "Islamic Anti-Colonial Revolts of the Nineteenth Century." In Goldstone, ed., *The Encyclopedia of Political Revolutions*, 260–63.

Cohen, Albert K. 2006. "Terrorism." In DeFronzo, ed., *Revolutionary Movements in World History*, 3:862–68.

Cole, Juan. 2006. "A 'Shiite Crescent?' The Regional Impact of the Iraq War." *Current History*, January, 20–26.

Coll, Steve. 2004. *Ghost Wars: The Secret History of the CIA, Afghanistan, and Bin Laden, from the Soviet Invasion to September 10, 2001*. New York: Penguin Books.

Combs, Cindy C. 2005. *Terrorism in the Twenty-First Century*. 4th ed. Upper Saddle River, NJ: Prentice-Hall.

Crenshaw, Martha. 2001. "Why America? The Globalization of Civil War." *Current History*, December, 425–32.

DeFronzo, James. 2006a. "The Iranian Revolution." In DeFronzo, ed., *Revolutionary Movements in World History*, 2:412–27.

———, ed. 2006b. *Revolutionary Movements in World History: From 1750 to the Present*. 3 vols. Santa Barbara, CA: ABC-CLIO.

Denoeux, Guilain. 2002. "The Forgotten Swamp: Navigating Political Islam." *Middle East Policy Council*, June. http://www.mepc.org/journal_vol19/0206_denoeux.asp.

Erlanger, Steven. 2006a. "Seizures Show New Israel Line Against Hamas." *New York Times*, June 30. http://www.nytimes.com/2006/06/30/world/middleeast/30palestinians.html.

———. 2006b. "Lebanon Cease-Fire Begins After Day of Fierce Attacks." *New York Times*, August 14.

Euben, Roxanne L. 2002. "Jihad and Political Violence." *Current History*, November, 365–76.

Farsoun, Samih K., with Christina E. Zacharia. 1997. *Palestine and the Palestinians*. Boulder: Westview Press.

Finer, Jonathan. 2006. "Iraq's Insurgents: Who's Who." *Washington Post*, March 19.

Finer, Jonathan, and Omar Fekeiki. 2005. "Iraqi Shiite Groups Form Election Alliance." *Washington Post*, October 28.

Fisher, Ian. 2006. "Women, Secret Hamas Strength, Win Votes at Polls and New Role." *New York Times*, February 3. http://www.nytimes.com/2006/02/03/international/middleeast/03women.html.

Gill, Jungyun. 2006. "Student and Youth Movements, Activism and Revolution." In DeFronzo, ed., *Revolutionary Movements in World History*, 3:848–54.

Goldstone, Jack A., ed. 1998. *The Encyclopedia of Political Revolutions*. Washington, DC: Congressional Quarterly Press.

Goodson, Larry P. 2001. *Afghanistan's Endless War: State Failure, Regional Politics, and the Rise of the Taliban*. Seattle: University of Washington Press.

Guidère, Mathieu, and Peter Harling. 2006. "'Withdraw, Move on, Rampage': Iraq's Resistance Evolves." *Le Monde Diplomatique*, May. http://mondediplo.com/2006/05/02irak.

Gunaratna, Rohan. 2002. *Inside al-Qaeda: Global Network of Terror*. New York: Columbia University Press.

Halliday, Fred. 1995. *Islam and the Myth of Confrontation: Religion and Politics in the Middle East.* London: I. B. Tauris.

_____. 1998. "Islamic Fundamentalism." In Goldstone, ed., *The Encyclopedia of Political Revolutions,* 263–65.

Halper, Stefan, and Jonathan Clarke. 2004. *America Alone: The Neo-Conservatives and the Global Order.* Cambridge, UK: Cambridge University Press.

Harub, Khalid. 2000. *Hamas: Political Thought and Practice.* Washington, DC: Institute for Palestine Studies.

Hashim, Ahmed. 2006. *Insurgency and Counter-Insurgency in Iraq.* Crises in World Politics. Ithaca, NY: Cornell University Press.

Hiro, Dilip. 1987. *Iran Under the Ayatollahs.* London: Routledge and Kegan Paul.

Howard, Russell D., and Reid L. Sawyer, eds. 2002. *Terrorism and Counterterrorism: Understanding the New Security Environment.* Guilford, CT: McGraw-Hill.

Huntington, S. P. 1993. "The Clash of Civilizations." *Foreign Affairs* 72:28–50.

Hussain, Asaf. 1985. *Islamic Iran: Revolution and Counter-Revolution.* New York: St. Martin's Press.

Ibrahim, Ahmed H. 2006. "The Palestinian Movement." In DeFronzo, ed., *Revolutionary Movements in World History,* 2:631–42.

Joffé , E. G. H. 2000. *International Implications of Domestic Security.* Lisbon: EuroMeSCo Paper No. 9, IEEI.

_____. 2004. *Global Terrorism.* Lisbon: EuroMeSCo Paper No. 30, IEEI.

_____. 2006. "Islamic Fundamentalist Revolutionary Movements." In DeFronzo, ed., *Revolutionary Movements in World History,* 2:452–64.

Kaplan, Eran. 2006. "Zionist Revolution and the State of Israel." In DeFronzo, ed., *Revolutionary Movements in World History,* 3:994–1004.

Katz, Mark N. 2002. "Osama bin Laden as Transnational Revolutionary Leader." *Current History,* February, 81–85.

_____. 2006. "Transnational Revolutionary Movements" In DeFronzo, ed., *Revolutionary Movements in World History,* 3:872–76.

Keddie, Nikki R. 1981. *Roots of Revolution: An Interpretive History of Modern Iran.* New Haven, CT: Yale University Press.

_____. 1998. "Islamic Pre-Colonial Revolts of the Eighteenth and Nineteenth Centuries." In Goldstone, ed., *The Encyclopedia of Political Revolutions,* 265–66.

Khalidi, Rashid. 1997. *Palestinian Identity: The Construction of Modern National Consciousness.* New York: Columbia University Press.

Kifner, John. 1996. "Aims and Arms: Tactics in a Holy War." *New York Times,* March 15, A1, 8, 10–11.

_____. 2006. "Hezbollah Leads Work to Rebuild, Gaining Stature." *New York Times,* April 16.

Knickmeyer, Ellen, and Jonathan Finer. 2006. "Insurgent Leader Al-Zarqawi Killed in Iraq." *Washington Post,* June 8.

Lacey, Robert. 1981. *The Kingdom: Arabia and the House of Saud.* New York: Harcourt Brace Jovanovich.

Lehrer, Jim. 2006. "Who's Behind the Violence in Iraq?" *NewsHour Extra,* June 12. http://www.pbs.org/newshour/extra.

Lewis, Bernard. 2002. *What Went Wrong? Western Impact and Middle Eastern Response.* London: Weidenfeld and Nicholson.

_____. 2003. *The Crisis of Islam: Holy War and Unholy Terror.* London: Weidenfeld & Nicholson.

Lieven, Anatol. 2006. "Chechen Revolt against Russia." In DeFronzo, ed., *Revolutionary Movements in World History*, 1:99–107.

Malley, William, ed. 1998. *Fundamentalism Reborn? Afghanistan and the Taliban.* New York: New York University Press.

Mazzetti, Mark. 2006. "Spy Agencies Say Iraq War Worsens Terrorism Threat." *New York Times*, September 24. http://www.nytimes.com/2006/09/24/world/middleeast/24terror.html.

Milani, Moshen M. 1994. *The Making of Iran's Islamic Revolution: From Monarchy to Islamic Republic.* Boulder: Westview Press.

Moghadam, Valentine M. 2006. "Afghanistan: Conflict and Civil War." In DeFronzo, ed., *Revolutionary Movements in World History*, 1:1–12.

Moshiri, Farrokh. 1991. "Iran: Islamic Revolution against Westernization." In *Revolutions of the Late Twentieth Century*, ed. Jack A. Goldstone, Ted Robert Gurr, and Farrokh Moshiri, 116–35. Boulder: Westview Press.

Muslim Brotherhood—Egypt. 2006. http://lexicorient.com/e.o/mus_br_egypt.htm.

Odom, William. 2006. "Withdraw Now." *Current History*, January, 3–7.

Rapoport, David. C. 2001. "The Fourth Wave: September 11 in the History of Terrorism." *Current History*, December, 419–24.

Rashid, Ahmed. 2000. *Taliban: Militant Islam, Oil, and the New Great Game in Central Asia.* New Haven, CT: Yale University Press.

Rifat, Ali, and Hala Jaber. 2006. "Key Insurgents Vow to Reject Iraq Peace Plan." *The [London] Times*, June 25. http://www.timesonline.co.uk.

Rinehart, James F. 2006. "Millenarianism, Religion and Revolution." In DeFronzo, ed., *Revolutionary Movements in World History*, 2:570–74.

Rodell, Paul. 2006. "Philippine Muslim Separatist Rebellions." In DeFronzo, ed., *Revolutionary Movements in World History*, 2:678–88.

Roy, Sara. 2003. "Hamas and the Transformation(s) of Political Islam in Palestine." *Current History*, January, 13–20.

Rubin, Barnett R. 1999. "Afghanistan Under the Taliban." *Current History*, February, 79–91.

Safran, Nadav. 1985. *Saudi Arabia: The Ceaseless Quest for Security.* Cambridge, MA: Belknap Press of Harvard University Press.

Said, Edward. 1991. "Reflection on Twenty Years of Palestinian History." *Journal of Palestine Studies* 20 (4): 5–22.

_____. 1994. *The Politics of Dispossession: The Struggle for Palestinian Self-Determination.* New York: Random House.

Skocpol, Theda. 1979. *States and Social Revolutions: A Comparison of France, Russia, and China.* Cambridge, UK: Cambridge University Press.

Skocpol, Theda, and Ellen Kay Trimberger. 1978. "Revolutions and the World Historical Development of Capitalism." *Berkeley Journal of Sociology* 22: 101–13.

Slackman, Michael. 2006. "And Now, Islam Trumps Arabism." *New York Times*, August 20, 4:1, 3.

Smith, Charles D. 2004. *Palestine and the Arab-Israeli Conflict: A History with Documents.* Boston: Bedford/St. Martin's Press.

Volpi, Frederic. 2006. "The Algerian Islamic Revolt." In DeFronzo, ed., *Revolutionary Movements in World History*, 1:19–36.

Vujaèic, Veljko. 2006. "Yugoslavia: Dissolution." In DeFronzo, ed., *Revolutionary Movements in World History*, 3:963–74.
Westcott, Kathryn. 2000. "Who Are Hamas?" BBC News, October 19. http://news.bbc.co.uk/1/hi/world/middle_east/978626.stm.
_____. 2002. "Who Are Hezbollah?" BBC News, April 4. http://news.bbc.co.uk/1/hi/world/middle_east/1908671.stm.
Wiktorowicz, Q. 2001. "The New Global Threat: Transnational Salafis and Jihad." *Middle East Policy Council* 8 (4):18–38. http://www.mepc.org/journal_vol8/0112_wiktorowicz.asp.
Wright, Robin. 2006. "Inside the Mind of Hezbollah." *Washington Post*, July 16.

Selected DVD, Film, and Videocassette Documentaries

See "Purchase and Rental Sources" at the end of this volume for information on how to obtain the following resources and for full names of media companies and other organizations listed here as abbreviations.

Afghanistan Unveiled. 2004. ITVS. The lives of women during the rule of the Taliban.
The Arming of Saudi Arabia. 1993. 60 min. Video. PBS. U.S. policy toward Saudi Arabia.
Battle for the Holy Land. 2002. 60 min. PBS. Perspectives of Israelis and Palestinians.
Holy War, Holy Terror. 1985. 60 min. Video. PBS. Describes Iran's Shia Islamic fundamentalism with regard to its impact on Iranians, the Middle East, and the world.
Hunting Bin Laden. 2001. 60 min. Video. PBS. Describes bin Laden, the Al Qaeda leader.
The Insurgency. 2006. PBS Frontline. Investigation of aspects of the Iraqi insurgency including interviews with insurgents.
Iran: Veiled Appearances. 2002. 58 min. FRIF. Iran twenty-three years after the revolution.
Osama Bin Laden. 50 min. BIO.
Party of God. 2003. PBS Frontline. Hezbollah.
Return of the Taliban. 2006. 60 min. PBS *Frontline*. Taliban resurgence following the 2001 U.S.-led overthrow of the Taliban regime.
Saudi Time Bomb. 2001. 60 min. PBS Frontline. Saudi Arabia and Wahhabi international activities.
Soldiers of God. 1998. 46 min. CNN Cold War Series, Episode 20. Truman Library. Islamic revolutionaries and fighters in Iran and Afghanistan.
Son of Al Qaeda. 60 min. PBS Frontline. Al Qaeda associate who turned against the organization.
Women of Hezbollah. 2000. 49 min. FRIF. Women activists in Hezbollah.

9

SOUTH AFRICA

The Russian, Chinese, Vietnamese, Cuban, Nicaraguan, and Iranian revolutions aimed to overthrow dictatorships, perceived foreign imperialism, and unjust economic systems. Efforts for social change in southern Africa, however, confronted the further and more profound obstacle of institutionally and culturally embedded racism. In the late twentieth century only one major nation claimed the distinction of awarding political rights on the basis of race: the Republic of South Africa. The white minority had confirmed its control of the mineral-rich country through the passage of a set of laws during the years 1948–1960 reinforcing race separation under the label "apartheid." In the 1950s massive peaceful protests against white minority rule were severely repressed, as were attempts at rebellion from the 1960s on. In the 1990s movements opposing apartheid finally achieved access to state power through the national elections of 1994 but continued to struggle to establish the unity and commitment necessary to accomplish a revolutionary transformation of South Africa's economic and social systems.

GEOGRAPHY AND POPULATION

South Africa has a land area of 471,008 square miles (1,219,912 square kilometers) bounded by the Atlantic on the west, the Indian Ocean on the south and east, Namibia in the northwest, Botswana and Zimbabwe in the north, and Mozambique and Swaziland in the northeast. The independent kingdom of Lesotho is an enclave totally encompassed by South African territory in the southeast. Much of the interior is a high plateau or veld, half of which averages 4,000 feet (1,219 meters). The Drakensberg Mountains rise to 11,000 feet (3,350 meters) in the east. The longest river is the Orange, which begins in Lesotho and flows westward 1,300 miles (2,092 kilometers) to the Atlantic. South Africa possesses large gold, diamond, platinum, uranium, and other important mineral deposits. The country's population was estimated at about 47.4 million in 2006, of which approximately 79.5 percent was of indigenous African ancestry, 9.2 percent of European ancestry, 2.5 percent Asian (mostly persons of Indian ancestry), and 8.9 percent of mixed racial ancestry (identified as "colored" in South African society before 1994).

Prior to the establishment of a Dutch settlement at the Cape of Good Hope in 1652, a number of African peoples inhabited the territories that eventually were to become the Republic of South Africa. The San (whom the colonists called Bushmen) were located in the Cape area. The San had a hunter-gatherer economy based on the abundant game, fish, vegetables, and fruits of the region. They roamed parts of southwestern Africa in bands as small as twenty-five to as large as three hundred. The San, like the other major group in the area, the Khoi (whom the colonists called Hottentots), spoke a "click language" (characterized by clicking sounds). The Khoi, however, made use of domesticated animals, sheep, and large herds of cattle. They lived in villages varying in size from five hundred to two thousand over a large territory that stretched from the Cape as far as 500 miles (800 kilometers) to the east and 190 miles (300 kilometers) to the north.

Other peoples in southern Africa were technologically more advanced than the San and the Khoi in that they used iron tools and engaged in agriculture as well as cattle and sheep herding. Most of these groups have been classified by linguists as Bantu speaking. In this sense the expression "Bantu" was used to refer to an African language category that had several major subdivisions. "Bantu" appears to have been derived from the Zulu word "abantu," which means "people." White colonists later applied the expression in a derogatory sense to all indigenous Africans (Danaher 1984; North 1985).

In the area from the Drakensberg Mountains to the Indian Ocean lived the Nguni-speaking groups of the Bantu linguistic category. These included the Xhosa and the Zulu. Much of the territory of southern Africa to the north of the Orange River was inhabited by the Sotho-Tswana groups, whose Bantu dialects were mutually intelligible. In addition, a number of smaller groups whose languages were included in the Bantu family inhabited various parts of South Africa.

DUTCH AND BRITISH COLONIZATION

After the Dutch East India Company set up a naval refreshment facility at the Cape of Good Hope in 1652 for their ships in transit to and from Asia, some of the company's employees were encouraged to establish farms and cattle herds to help provision the trading vessels. Early white settlers were overwhelmingly Dutch but also included some Germans and significant numbers of French and Belgian Huguenots (Calvinist Protestants). Although the Huguenots constituted about one-sixth of the late-seventeenth-century white settler population, they adopted the Dutch language and affiliated with the Protestant Dutch Reformed Church. Over time, the colonists sharing the Dutch culture added some African expressions and other modifications to their speech, which came to constitute a new Dutch dialect called "Afrikaans," and referred to themselves as "Afrikaners." The colony's farmers were called "Boers." These people obtained land and cattle from the surrounding Khoi, initially through purchase and trade. But when the Khoi resisted, the settlers resorted to warfare. After several decades many of the San and the Khoi had been transformed into a destitute class whose members could only survive through accepting the role of servant or slave to the white colonists (Magubane 1979; Magubane and Mandaza 1988; Omer-Cooper 1987).

In 1806 Great Britain, to facilitate trade with its Asian interests, seized Holland's Cape Colony. About five thousand English settlers arrived in 1820. Many Afrikaans-speaking inhabitants resented British domination and the increasing use of English in the colony. Furthermore, young Afrikaners who sought to establish large farms—of a thousand or more acres—found their goal to be less and less attainable as the Cape became more heavily populated. Finally, in 1834 many Afrikaners were outraged at the British abolition of slavery. Thousands decided to head for other territories as yet free from British control. A series of large settler expeditions, collectively referred to as the Great Trek, set out from the Cape from 1836 to 1856. The heavily armed wagon trains generally avoided the most densely populated areas and well-organized African groups, such as the Xhosa along the coast, and turned into the interior to regions that had recently been partially depopulated by episodes of intense warfare among the Africans. English merchants provided much of the equipment, weapons, and ammunition that the trekkers used to defeat, dispossess, and subjugate the inhabitants of the territories they invaded (Magubane 1979; Wheatcroft 1986).

Eventually, those Afrikaners who trekked (most had stayed behind at the Cape) succeeded in establishing two land-locked Afrikaner states independent of British rule, the Orange Free State, between the Orange and Vaal rivers; and the much larger Transvaal Republic (also called the South African Republic), to the north of the Vaal. The British, in part discouraged by the potential cost of militarily subduing and then administering the republics, were temporarily content to tolerate their existence. The discovery of diamonds at British-controlled Kimberley, near the border between Cape Colony and the Orange Free State, in 1867 and the economically much more significant discovery of vast gold deposits in the Transvaal in 1886 prompted Britain's leaders to seek the incorporation of the Afrikaner republics into a united South Africa, along with the Cape Colony and the colony of Natal on the eastern coast, under a pro-British regime.

In the years after the gold find, thousands of Britons arrived in the Transvaal to mine the precious metal. It soon became clear that the ore, though abundant, was of generally moderate-to-poor quality, meaning that enormous quantities had to be extracted and processed. Furthermore, much of the gold was located far below the surface, necessitating the construction of expensive deep mines. The exploitation of the huge gold resource was to require major capital investments and cheap, plentiful labor to ensure large profits.

British miners and businesspeople, who by the 1890s were generating most of the Transvaal's export income, were referred to as "outlanders" and were not allowed to vote. British authorities rejected a compromise for an eventual extension of the vote to British residents of the Transvaal and provoked war with the republics in 1899. Mounted Boer guerrilla fighters numbering up to 40,000 waged an effective resistance, forcing the commitment of a quarter of a million British troops to the conflict. British authorities forcibly removed Afrikaner farm families to concentration camps, where 25,000 women and children perished from disease, and destroyed many farms to deprive guerrillas of sustenance. The British also detained the Boers' African servants and workers in separate concentration camps, where similar numbers died (Omer-Cooper 1987).

Many Africans denied provisions to Boer troops and even at times attacked Boer commandos, anticipating that British victory would result in the extension of political rights to nonwhites. African opposition was instrumental in forcing the Boers to accept British peace terms (Omer-Cooper 1987; Warwick 1983). But in an attempt to convince the Boers to agree to the 1902 peace proposal, the British promised not to grant political equality to nonwhites, thus betraying African loyalty and wartime sacrifices (the Boers often executed Africans who aided the British). British authorities even arrested native Africans for violating the Transvaal's laws by burning their mandatory "work passes" and obliged them to continue working at low wages in the mines, owned largely by British interests (Magubane 1979; Omer-Cooper 1987; Wheatcroft 1986).

In 1905 the Liberal Party won control of the British Parliament from the Conservatives and proposed a policy of reconciliation with the Boers in which the formerly independent republics would quickly be returned to self-government within the framework of a union with the British-dominated Cape and Natal colonies. The constitution of the Union of South Africa, approved by 1910 by the legislatures of the four states and the British Parliament, limited the vote to white males except in the Cape, where certain economically prosperous nonwhite men retained the franchise (these constituted at the time about one-seventh of all Cape voters). British Liberals apparently adopted the optimistic but incorrect view that the Cape system would serve as a model to the three other members of the union. Instead, white South African leaders eliminated nonwhite Cape voting rights by denying the vote to Cape indigenous Africans in 1936 and Cape residents of mixed race in 1956 (Radu 1987). Thus the measures taken by the British in resolving the Boer War resulted in the establishment of a virtually all-white state structure, which both constituted a major continuous cause for non-white mass discontent and provided a motivation for overthrowing the white regime, a motivation that conceivably could unify nonwhite population groups in a revolutionary effort.

At the point of formation of the Union of South Africa, mining and other major developing industries, along with the professions, were dominated by whites of British ancestry. Although some Afrikaners were involved in trades or other businesses, they were predominantly farmers. But as a result of the devastation of the Boer War and later taxation, thousands of Afrikaners were forced to sell or abandon their farms, often to expanding agribusiness interests, and seek employment in the mines or in the urban industries. This massive movement of thousands of former Afrikaner farmers from the countryside to the mining and urban areas after the Boer War was called the Second Great Trek. Thus much of the Afrikaans-speaking majority of the white population (approximately 60 percent of the whites) came to constitute an impoverished working class. These Afrikaners were especially prone to maintaining their ideology of racial superiority both as a source of psychological status and as a justification for preventing nonwhites from competing economically on an equal footing with whites or from having access to political power (Magubane 1979; Omer-Cooper 1987; Thompson 1985). Afrikaner leaders attempted to gain control of South Africa's new government by convincing all Afrikaners, who were a majority of the white voters, to support the (Afrikaner) Nationalist Party founded in 1914.

The British, in general, tended to be more liberal than the Afrikaners, as reflected by the extension of the vote to some nonwhites in the Cape Colony. British missionaries converted many Africans to Christianity and provided educational opportunities for limited numbers. But certain British colonial authorities not only held personal beliefs in white racial superiority but also took actions at various points to crush nonwhite opposition and capacities for self-sufficiency. These included the British-precipitated Zulu War in the 1870s, which (though later condemned in England, especially after initial Zulu victories resulted in the deaths of many British soldiers) led to the subjugation of the Zulu and their availability as laborers for various white-owned industries. Later British authorities imposed taxation measures that coerced hundreds of thousands of indigenous Africans to seek employment in mining, industry, or other jobs at which they could earn the money to pay taxes and otherwise survive in the increasingly white-structured economic environment (Omer-Cooper 1987).

THE UNION OF SOUTH AFRICA

After 1910 a national parliament elected exclusively by whites, except in the Cape Province, governed South Africa as a member of the British Commonwealth. Early parliaments were dominated by parties and coalitions that generally promoted reconciliation among the nation's whites. However, during World War I thousands of Afrikaners protested against South Africa's alliance with Britain and its seizure of German-occupied Southwest Africa (Namibia). After the war, which drew many more black South Africans into the industrial labor force and, consequently, into competition with whites, many white workers, objecting to their own poor working conditions and to advances by nonwhites, staged strikes and even violent protests. Government forces killed scores of white workers. Partly as a result, the white workers' Labor Party formed an alliance with the National Party (then supported largely by Afrikaner farmers and businesspeople) and during the 1920s helped pass a series of laws further restricting the rights of nonwhites. The Labor Party, however, was soon weakened by internal conflict between those members who proposed cooperation with nonwhite workers and others who maintained segregationist attitudes. The National Party continued to gain support under the leadership of a former official of the Orange Free State, J. B. Hertzog.

Hertzog's government (first elected in 1924) took measures to improve employment opportunities for Afrikaner whites, such as the creation in 1928 of the state-owned Iron and Steel Corporation (ISCOR), and assisted other Afrikaner-controlled industries by imposing special protective tariffs. These and other businesses were required to reserve certain types of jobs for whites only and employ specific quotas of white workers. Many Afrikaners, believing that continued political association with Britain would gradually erode Afrikaner culture and perhaps even lead to a liberalization of race policy, favored withdrawal from the Commonwealth. Afrikaner nationalism was embodied in the growth of a covert Afrikaner organization called the Broederbond, which set up secret cells in major economic, cultural, and governmental institutions throughout the nation as well as in the armed forces (Giliomee 1980; Omer-Cooper 1987).

The worldwide Great Depression had a devastating effect on South Africa, worsened by the fact that until 1933 South Africa refused, unlike the rest of the world, to abandon the gold standard. In 1934 Hertzog's National Party and the party supported by many whites of British descent, the South Africa Party, led by a more moderate Afrikaner, Jan Smuts, joined forces to form the United Party, which then enjoyed a large majority in the parliament. Those English-speaking whites who opposed the United Party organized the Dominion Party, whereas those Afrikaners objecting to unifying politically with British interests formed the much more important Purified National Party (which later was known simply as the National Party), under D. F. Malan (Omeara 1983; Omer-Cooper 1987).

As World War II began, the United Party experienced internal conflict. Hertzog and many of his Afrikaner followers favored neutrality. But Smuts, with his Afrikaner associates and the English-speaking members of the United Party, supported by the smaller Dominion and Labor parties,

SOUTH AFRICA (before 1994)

obtained a majority in the parliament in favor of entering the war on Britain's side. As a result, thousands of South Africans of all races served in the war, although only whites were allowed to bear arms (nonwhites performed support functions). Some Afrikaners espoused pro-German views because they approved the Nazi doctrine of Aryan racial superiority. A number engaged in sabotage of military facilities, and some were incarcerated for the duration of the conflict.

The war caused a tremendous boom in and transformation of the South African economy. At the onset of the conflict South Africa's wealth was derived primarily from mining. But at the conclusion manufacturing was foremost. The war had stimulated South Africa to develop the capacity to build much of the machinery and equipment it had formerly imported. Furthermore, in the absence of the many whites serving in the armed forces, a massive influx of indigenous Africans into mining and urban industry occurred.

After the conclusion of World War II the United Party, under Smuts, was confident of victory in the 1948 election for parliament. However, most Afrikaners and some English-speaking whites had become dissatisfied over certain issues. United Party leaders had proposed permanent urban residency for the Africans, who by that point were extensively employed in industry. Thousands of returning whites feared not only racial integration but also increased economic competition from blacks if the United Party retained power (Lazerson 1994; Omeara 1983; Omer-Cooper 1987). Also Afrikaner farmers blamed the United Party for a shortage of low-cost African agricultural laborers. Others were concerned with the growth during wartime of groups opposed to the racially based political system; they were especially wary of the South African Communist Party, which had increased its influence in the labor movement.

All these factors combined to heighten the popularity of the concept of continued and increased apartheid ("separateness" of the races) championed by Malan's National Party. According to apartheid doctrine, each race and nation has its own distinct cultural identity and has been created to achieve a unique destiny laid down by God. Therefore each race must be kept pure and allowed to develop freely along its own lines because "excessive contact between races, above all interbreeding, would corrupt and destroy the inner potential of both races" (Omer-Cooper 1987, 190). Whites' fear of liberalization of racial policies provided the revived National Party with a narrow victory in the momentous 1948 election.

THE APARTHEID STATE

Malan's new National Party government immediately moved to implement a series of laws intended to increase and systematize separation not only among the four official "racial" categories of white, colored, Asian (Indian), and black, but also among the major ethnic, or tribal, groups within the huge indigenous African majority. Legislation formalizing apartheid included the Population Registration Act (mandating official racial classification of all South Africans) and the Prohibition of Mixed Marriages Act. The Suppression of Communism Act, passed in 1950, not only banned the South African Communist Party but also permitted the punishment of anyone working to implement the supposedly "Communist doctrine" of racial equality (Davis 1987; Omer-Cooper 1987). Thus the government created a powerful coercive tool to protect the white-controlled state by severely punishing opponents of apartheid as "Communists" and "traitors."

The 1952 Native Laws Amendment Act restricted native Africans' right to permanent residency in towns and urban areas largely to those who had previously resided and been employed in a particular town for a period of fifteen or more years. The select group of Africans in this category, though, could not move to any other urban area and could be removed from the town if authorities determined they were unemployed for long periods or were judged harmful to the public good. All other indigenous Africans were permitted to reside only temporarily in urban areas (in designated locations usually remote from the white cities) as long as they were employed and had received the necessary clearance. But they officially held permanent residency only in their "tribal homelands."

The South African government had previously, through the 1913 Native Land Act and the 1936 Native Trust and Land Act, allotted 13.5 percent of South Africa's territory as tribal homelands or "Bantustans," which were to serve as the only truly permanent residences for most of the country's population. The ten homelands, which on average had close to half of their supposed populations living in the "white" 86.5 percent of South Africa, included Basotho-Qwaqwa of the Southern Sotho, Bophuthatswana of the Tswana, Ciskei of the Xhosa, Gazakulu of the Shangaana, KaNgwane of the Ngwane, KwaNdebele of the Ndebele, KwaZulu of the Zulu, Lebowa of the Northern Sotho, Transkei of the Xhosa, and Venda of the Venda (Magubane 1979; Omer-Cooper 1987). Most Bantustans possessed little in the way of mineral wealth or industrial or transportation infrastructure. They functioned primarily as sources of cheap labor for white industry, business, and domestic service, and depositories for the elderly, the infirm, and surplus labor. Many migrant workers were not permitted to bring their families with them to white areas and were often required to live in barracks-like conditions that fostered alcohol abuse and crime. Hundreds of thousands of native African women were forced to surrender care of their own children to others as the condition of employment as domestics in white homes, where, ironically, they played a major role in raising and tending to their employers' children.

The 1952 Pass Law required indigenous Africans to carry in a single mandatory passbook a personal photograph and information on place of birth, employment history, payments of taxes, and record of police contacts.

The 1956 Native Resettlement Act helped resegregate blacks after years of urban expansion had created situations in which previously black areas had become surrounded by white residential developments. Many indigenous Africans were uprooted from these enclaves and forced to take up residency in new government-built townships, such as those southwest of Johannesburg (known by the acronym for South Western Townships, Soweto, eventually inhabited by more than one million people).

Other laws restricted education for nonwhites so that they would be trained only in the skills necessary to serve their tribal kin in the Bantustans and "perform the labouring roles which might be required of them by whites" (Omer-Cooper 1987, 201). By 1961 the National Party government had succeeded in enacting into law all the measures that constituted its original white supremacist form of apartheid. This system not only perpetuated separation of the races but also guaranteed the lion's share of the nation's growing wealth to the white minority, eventually virtually eliminating poverty among whites. The National Party also renamed the nation in 1960 the Republic of South Africa and withdrew it from the British Commonwealth. These events, in a sense, reversed the outcome of the 1899–1902 Boer War.

Changes in the Apartheid System

After 1959 the apartheid system underwent several modifications. As most former African colonies achieved independence from European domination, South Africa attempted to influence the emerging states through offers of technical assistance and trade. One purpose of the new tactic was to deflect criticism and increasing anti-apartheid animosity emanating from the United Nations. As newly independent Asian and African nations were admitted to its ranks, that body was becoming less dominated by the European nations (which in the past had seemed relatively tolerant of South African racism). The white regime also sensed that good relations with the other nations of the continent would provide nearby and ready markets for the exports generated by its growing manufacturing sector.

Greater reliance on manufacturing and increasing technological sophistication, along with white social mobility out of the working class and into white-collar occupations, resulted in changes in the nature of the demands for nonwhite labor. Previously mining and industry had utilized mainly unskilled or semi-skilled nonwhites. Now the economy needed larger numbers of skilled nonwhite workers who could reliably carry out their jobs over an extended period. Finally, the increasing internal protests against apartheid since World War II, progressing from peaceful campaigns of defiance to armed resistance, and punctuated by internationally condemned episodes of violent repression, also prompted significant policy alterations (Danaher 1984; 1987; Omer-Cooper 1987).

SOUTH AFRICAN TRIBAL HOMELANDS (before 1994)

The three major innovations engineered by the white regime between 1960 and 1990 included pursuing separate development toward political independence for the tribal homelands, promoting processes intended to result in a more highly skilled and stable nonwhite labor force, and in 1983 enacting a new constitution intended to co-opt Indians and South Africans of mixed racial descent (coloreds) into an alliance with whites and in opposition to the indigenous African majority (Danaher 1984; Greenberg 1987; Omer-Cooper 1987).

Prior to 1959, the South African government intended that the native homelands would develop local self-government along tribal lines but would still remain under the jurisdiction of the white republic. However, theoreticians within the National Party eventually succeeded in winning support for the argument that South Africa could both achieve wider international acceptance and divide or blunt internal opposition by pushing a policy of full independence for the homelands. Publicly the white regime began to assert that it now recognized that indigenous Africans had the capability to organize and govern modern nation-states. But the result of successfully establishing the homelands as independent states would be to transform the basis for economic and political discrimination against Africans from that of racism to that of citizenship. The millions of indigenous Africans employed in South African industries, businesses, and households would in the future be classified as foreign migrant labor; their lack of entitlement to the rights of South Africans would be based on nationality, not race (Danaher 1984; Magubane 1979; Omer-Cooper 1987).

Furthermore, National Party leaders anticipated that the development of independent homeland government administrations, service bureaucracies, and economic enterprises would provide opportunities for social mobility for educated indigenous Africans blocked from participating in the republic's government or from playing major roles in other institutions, thus minimizing African elite discontent. Additional potential benefits to the white community included the probability that frustrated blacks would in the future target their own homeland governments for protest actions rather than white authorities. Granting independence along tribal lines was also thought likely to heighten competitiveness and hostility among black ethnic groups, thereby presenting whites with a divided and more easily controlled black population, whose tribal animosities might override the motivation to unite against apartheid. As most of the homelands lacked both industrial infrastructure and known significant mineral wealth and some were actually composed of several noncontiguous parcels separated by the republic's territory, they would remain economically dependent on the white-controlled state and could be easily intimidated by South Africa's overpowering military.

Business leaders reacted to the growing shortage of skilled workers by pressuring the government to open many previously restricted jobs to nonwhites. Furthermore, in seeking a stable and reliable skilled workforce, the white regime by the 1980s had granted many Africans virtual permanent residency outside the homelands by successively allowing them the right to lease houses in segregated urban townships for thirty years and then ninety years, finally permitting them the right to purchase homes. Furthermore, to promote emotional stability among African skilled workers, the regime eventually allowed many to have their families live with them. In 1970 before the stabilization-of-workers program had begun at the Kimberley diamond mines, 86 percent of the workforce was composed of migrants, whereas in 1979, after the new program had been in effect for seven years, 62 percent of the mine workers were stabilized, and only 38 percent were migrants (Omer-Cooper 1987).

The need to reduce the incidence of wildcat strikes and in general provide mechanisms through which business and government could communicate with and exercise influence over the increasingly skilled and difficult-to-replace workforce prompted the government to permit the legal existence of black labor unions after 1979, provided they did not engage in "political" activity (Davis 1987; Kerson 1987). To meet the demand for highly trained technicians of all races, segregated nonwhite colleges and universities were expanded, and white universities were opened to those needing courses not available at nonwhite institutions. In 1986 the white regime finally abolished the Pass Law and permitted the freer movement of African workers to black urban districts (*New York Times*, June 27, 1988, A1).

White voters in 1983 approved a new "multiracial" constitution that supposedly offered a "share of power" to coloreds and Indians, to the exclusions of the indigenous African majority. The reorganized three-part legislature included a white House of Assembly, with 166 members; a colored House of Representatives, with 85 members; and an Indian House of Delegates, with 45 members. The president of the republic, selected by an Electoral College composed of 88 members (50 elected by the white parliament, 25 by the colored, and 13 by the Indians), enjoyed greatly expanded executive powers under the new constitution. Individual parliaments were to deal with matters particular to their racial groups and jointly with matters of "common interest" (Danaher 1984, 23), as determined by the president of the republic. Although some viewed the constitution as a step forward, many others considered it a mechanism for preserving white domination and strengthening the coercive capacity of the regime. Large numbers of mixed race and Indian South Africans reportedly refused to register to vote in elections under the new constitution, and of those who did register, only 30 percent of coloreds and 20 percent of Indians actually took part in the first parliamentary elections. The new political system particularly infuriated many members of the totally excluded black population and precipitated the most widespread series of protests since the 1976 Soweto uprising (Danaher 1984; Davis 1987; Omer-Cooper 1987).

OPPOSITION TO APARTHEID

The defeat of Chief Bambatha's 1903 rebellion against taxation and white-supported collaborationist tribal leaders has been widely cited as the last of the traditional wars of resistance against white domination in South Africa. But in 1912, following the rejection of the concept of political equality for nonwhites by the victorious British, an important African movement opposed to white domination was organized, the African National Congress (ANC), originally called the South African Natives' National Congress. This group, established largely by Western-schooled black professionals, businesspeople, and prosperous farmers, whose education was often the product of Christian missionary efforts, was the "first modern, nontribal organization of blacks formed to discuss black interests under white rule" (Davis 1987, 3). The early ANC was resigned to the at-least-temporary reality of white minority rule but was committed to working against laws promoting racial discrimination and for an extension of the benefits of modern education and technology to the larger population. The group proclaimed its support for a future nonracial political system in which all South Africa's peoples would enjoy equal rights in a European-style democratic state. ANC leaders originally hoped that peaceful protest and legal efforts, coupled with anticipated international pressure from Britain, other democratic nations, and the worldwide Christian church, would bring about a reorganization of South Africa along nonracial lines. But during its early years the ANC remained largely an elitist, middle-class group, somewhat isolated culturally from the traditional lifestyles of the majority of Africans (Davis 1987; Omer-Cooper 1987).

During World War II, as South Africa joined the side of the Allies against Nazi Germany with its doctrine of racial supremacy, ANC leaders voted to support the war effort in the expectation that victory would result in a reduction of racism and an extension of political rights at home. The results of the 1948 election, which brought the Afrikaner National Party to power, reversed the small level of wartime liberalization and led quickly to the passage of a series of laws that reaffirmed and systematized racial segregation, also precipitated the more militant younger generation's ascendancy to leadership of the ANC. The youthful activists favored the mobilization of mass-protest movements instead of the previous exclusive reliance on negotiation and moral appeals to white leaders, who in reality seemed primarily concerned with appeasing the racially biased elements within their existing electorate.

On June 26, 1952, the ANC, together with the anti-apartheid South African Indian Congress (SAIC), launched the Defiance Campaign. This action involved the planned violation of segregation laws by volunteers in several cities, who passively submitted to arrest. The campaign quickly generated large-scale popular support among nonwhites, and ANC membership, which had been 4,500 in 1947, rapidly increased to 100,000. But among the many recruits were scores of paid government agents (some motivated in part by opposition to the ANC's nontribal orientation), whose information regarding the movement's leadership helped the white government's efforts at repression. In August and September the white regime arrested ANC and SAIC leaders and accused them of violation of the Suppression of Communism Act, which banned working for racial equality. Then in mid-October in response to government actions, spontaneous riots broke out in several cities; the riots were violently crushed. As a result of the mass arrests of leaders and the smashing of riots, the Defiance Campaign collapsed (Davis 1987; Omer-Cooper 1987). In reaction, Nelson Mandela, a young lawyer of Xhosa ancestry who was an architect of the Defiance Campaign, began the construction of a secretive cellular network within the ANC, the elements of which in the future would continue to provide leadership at the local level regardless of whether top leaders or any components of the overall organization were eliminated (Benson 1986; Davis 1987).

The ANC and the SACP

The ANC received instruction in organizing an internal underground network from members of the illegal South African Communist Party (SACP). The SACP had been founded among exploited white workers in 1921 and, reflecting the racist attitudes of many whites, initially avoided working with blacks. But well before the 1950s the SACP had officially committed itself to organizing black laborers and to working for racial equality. SACP activists played significant roles in some labor unions and in several protests against the regime. They perceived that the ANC had the capability to organize and guide the development of a mass movement to bring an end to white rule. In the original SACP view, such an event would lead to a second revolutionary transition to "a socialist South Africa, laying the foundations of a classless, communist society" (Davis 1987, 10). The SACP's estimated membership of 2,000 in 1950 included 150 whites and 250 Indians (Davis 1987; Karis 1986/1987; Lazerson 1994). Outside of the small number of whites in the SACP, however, the percentage of the nation's white elite committed to overturning apartheid through a revolutionary effort remained close to zero.

The ANC's attitude toward the SACP shifted over time. From the 1920s through the 1940s many ANC members opposed working with the SACP (Karis 1986/1987; Mandela 1994). ANC leaders Nelson Mandela and Oliver Tambo in the late 1940s even proposed expelling SACP members from the ANC. But the post–World War II National Party government's apartheid program and, in particular, its implementation of broad repressive policies under the Suppression of Communism Act of 1950, which mandated that anyone working for racial equality could be punished for advocating communism, tended to promote cooperation between the ANC and the SACP.

When the ANC itself was outlawed in 1960, the organization became more dependent on assistance from the SACP. SACP members helped establish the critically important secret leadership network of ANC militants inside South Africa, obtained financial and military aid for the ANC from the Soviet Union and other Communist Party–dominated states, and provided information on the South African government, military, and economic installations that was gathered either by SACP members or by the Soviet Union (Davis 1987; Karis 1986/1987; Magubane 1979). And the SACP's characterization of South Africa's system as a form of European imperialist exploitation of Africa appeared increasingly valid to many ANC members, whose peaceful efforts at change were crushed within the country while many capitalist nations cooperated with the white government and refused to help the ANC.

By the end of 1969 the ANC began to accept nonindigenous South African Communists into its ranks, and in 1985 the ANC National Executive Committee was opened to all races. At that time the number of SACP members on the thirty-three-person ANC Executive Committee was estimated to be at least three to as many as twenty-three (Karis 1986/1987; Radu 1987; *New York Times*, Nov. 11, 1990, A15). However, ANC leaders and most informed observers asserted that the ANC represented a broad coalition of interests and ideologies within South Africa, was not controlled by Communists, and publicly called for a multiparty, nonracial political democracy.

The ANC and the Freedom Charter

The ANC and other groups participated in a Congress of the People at Kliptown in June 1955, involving a mass meeting of three thousand people of all races. Those present voted to adopt a Freedom Charter, which asserted that the wealth of South Africa belonged to all its inhabitants and demanded the elimination of apartheid and the establishment of a nonracial democracy. In addition to calling for a more equitable distribution of land, profits, and other forms of wealth and equal access to education and employment opportunities, further goals proclaimed in the charter included:

> The mineral wealth beneath the soil, the banks and monopoly industry shall be transferred to the ownership of the people as a whole; . . . other industries and trade shall be controlled to assist the well-being of the people. . . . The police force and army shall be open to all on an equal basis and shall be helpers and protectors of the people. . . . Free medical [treatment] and hospitalization shall be provided for all with special care for mothers and young children. . . . Peace and friendship amongst all our people shall be secured by upholding the equal rights, opportunities and status of all. (Congress of the People [1955] 1987, 209, 210, 211)

The white regime reacted harshly to the Freedom Charter and the mammoth Kliptown interracial effort to undermine apartheid. On December 5, 1956, after months of gathering information on activists, the government arrested scores of leaders of participating groups and accused them of treason. The proceedings of the so-called Treason Trial continued until November 29, 1961, with all the defendants found not guilty. However, the government had succeeded in not only imprisoning key leaders for extended periods but also financially and occupationally injuring those apprehended so as to deter future potential activists.

The ANC and the PAC

Long-standing controversies within the ANC over the issues of multiracial cooperation to end white domination, the role of the SACP in the ANC, and reliance on funding from non-African countries that were dominated by Communist parties resulted in a major defection from the ANC and the establishment in April 1959 of the Pan-Africanist Congress (PAC), the second South African liberation group officially recognized by the United Nations (the first was the ANC). The founders of the PAC, which like the ANC supported the eventual establishment of a nonracial government, argued that South Africa must be freed from the bonds of apartheid primarily through black militancy, not through the ANC multiracial cooperation approach, which, according to the PAC, was being subverted by its Communist members and was too greatly influenced by the non-African nations from which it obtained much of its funds and weapons. The PAC advocated the "black nationalist" view that the psychology of black South Africans, theoretically crippled by decades of oppression and humiliation at the hands of whites, could only be rejuvenated by having the nation's blacks "act alone in reclaiming South Africa from white domination" (Davis 1987, 11). The PAC's ideology gained popularity because it enhanced feelings of pride and importance among many young Africans and engendered a special sense of mission.

Both the ANC and the PAC planned to launch a campaign against the nation's Pass Law in spring 1960. The leaders of the PAC, however, decided to begin their protest movement on March 21, ten days before the scheduled start of the ANC antipass drive. At Sharpeville on the morning of March 21, a large number of people gathered without their pass documents to await arrest. Some police, possibly fearing for their own safety, opened fire on the crowd, killing sixty-seven, most of whom were shot in the back as they tried to flee. Police shootings at other locations also resulted in deaths and scores of injuries. The killings precipitated riots by tens of thousands in the black townships outside the white cities and industrial centers they served. On April 8 the South African government outlawed both the ANC and the PAC. Because the ANC had succeeded over a number of years in building an underground network, it was less devastated than the

PAC, which, partly owing to its recent creation, had virtually no clandestine organizational structure and was almost eliminated (Adam 1988; Davis 1987; Schlemmer 1988).

The ANC and Armed Resistance

Elements of the ANC, under the youthful leadership of Nelson Mandela, made one last attempt to convince the white government to accept peaceful change. They demanded a national convention of all races be called to draft a new nonracial constitution. When the white regime rejected this concept, the ANC militants reluctantly resolved to abandon their organization's long-held commitment to nonviolent protest and begin a campaign of selective sabotage. Because the shift in tactics was resisted by the older and more moderate members of the ANC, the younger activists formed a semi-independent but ANC-associated military organization called Umkhonto we Sizwe (Zulu for "Spear of the Nation"). The aim of Umkhonto was to carry out sabotage of important transportation, communication, and industrial facilities in order both to inflict injury on the nation's white-owned economy and to frighten off foreign investors, thereby pressuring the government into serious negotiations with the ANC (Davis 1987; Mandela 1994; Omer-Cooper 1987). Members of the South African Communist Party with military experience began to train young South Africans in the use of bombs, grenades, and other weapons and succeeded in obtaining military assistance from the Soviet Union. Western countries, dependent on South Africa for important minerals, such as platinum and chromium, and generally favorably influenced by South Africa's strong anti-Communist stance, refused to provide military aid to the ANC, although by the 1980s several Western European nations were assisting through cash donations and in other nonmilitary ways.

The Umkhonto sabotage campaign was begun on December 16, 1961, to counter the Afrikaner celebration of an 1838 Boer victory over a Zulu army at "Blood River" during the Great Trek. Over several months scores of targets were hit by dynamite bombs or mines, but the damage inflicted was usually slight. Furthermore, the public was generally not informed regarding the political purpose of the attacks or of the link between Umkhonto and the much better known ANC. In August 1962 Mandela was captured, reportedly with the aid of information supplied to the white South African government by the CIA (*New York Times*, June 10, 1990, A15), and later tried for trying to violently overthrow the government of South Africa; he was given a life sentence. By the end of 1963 the Umkhonto sabotage effort had been largely crushed. A sabotage-assassination campaign begun by PAC extremists was also smashed. The ANC's leadership concluded that before another large-scale armed assault was attempted, the ANC underground "would have to be purged of counter-espionage agents and made secure" and that a military command center outside South Africa would have to be

established to plan, coordinate, and order operations "without fear of capture" (Davis 1987, 21).

Revolutionary Changes among South Africa's Neighbors

In the mid-1970s major political changes to the north of South Africa appeared to improve the chances for anti-apartheid movements and certainly
had the effect of both encouraging militancy among nonwhites and alarm-
ing the white minority. After more than a dozen years of unsuccessful attempts to repress nationalist guerrilla movements in its Angola and
Mozambique colonies, Portugal experienced its own revolution. Leftist-
oriented Portuguese soldiers, disillusioned by decades of right-wing military
dictatorship and the futile and wasteful colonial wars, and in part inspired
by the ideology of the African revolutionaries they had struggled against,
overthrew their nation's authoritarian regime. The new left-leaning Portuguese government soon granted independence to Angola and Mozambique. In both nations leftist-oriented movements, extremely hostile to the
apartheid state to the south, achieved dominance (Mabeko-Tali 2006;
Newitt 2006). For the first time, countries geographically close to South
Africa appeared ready to lend support to a large-scale revolutionary effort.

Within a few more years nationalist guerrilla movements in another
nearby country, Zimbabwe (formerly called Rhodesia, after the wealthy
white British expansionist, Cecil Rhodes), succeeded with the aid of international pressure in forcing a negotiated end to the rule of its then approximately 4 percent white minority (Rubert 2006). In the April 18, 1980,
election for a national parliament, the ZANU (the Zimbabwe African National Union), the party of the self-proclaimed Marxist and "most radical of
the contenders," Robert Mugabe, won a resounding victory (Omer-Cooper
1987, 234). The new government, under black majority rule, encouraged
whites to remain but declared its commitment to helping to overturn white
minority rule in South Africa.

The Black Consciousness Movement and the Soweto Uprisings

Prior to the changes in Angola, Mozambique, and Zimbabwe, a new ac-
tivist movement had been organized by young blacks at Bloemfontein in
South Africa in August 1971. Steve Biko was selected as leader of the new
Black Consciousness Movement. The BCM, inspired in part by the Black
Power movement in the United States, was mainly influenced by earlier
African nationalist ideology, such as that formulated by PAC leaders. The
militants of the BCM asserted the need for blacks to lead the anti-apartheid
movement but proposed to rely on legal means to attain their goals. This
meant that the BCM was to avoid the ANC and PAC campaigns of civil disobedience and their later armed struggles. BCM leaders began "a scrupu-
lously law-abiding education and community action campaign designed to

work at the grass-roots level toward building a psychology of self-reliance among blacks" (Davis 1987, 25).

According to the BCM the pressure of a politically aroused, unified, and determined black majority, the anticipated result of the BCM program, would persuade the white government to seriously negotiate a restructuring of South African society. Wherever the BCM set up local organizations, whether community action groups, labor unions, or political education seminars, only blacks were allowed to participate. As the BCM advocated strict legality and seemed to employ its own form of apartheid rather than embrace the supposedly "Communist" method of multiracial cooperation to attain a nonracial state, the white regime temporarily tolerated the development of the movement (Omer-Cooper 1987). The apartheid government may have hoped that the BCM would draw potential recruits away from what it perceived as the more radical and more dangerous ANC and PAC. But the BCM failed to build a significant mass-organizational network, relying instead on a relatively small elite of educated middle-class individuals for guidance. The BCM raised expectations through its leaders' public speeches eliciting black pride and self-confidence and by instilling a belief that sweeping change could be accomplished through the legal structures existing within the apartheid state. Since the group rejected the concept of an extralegal confrontational approach to dealing with the white regime, it was not prepared to coordinate the protests generated by the mass frustration that resulted when white authorities ignored peaceful demands for change (Davis 1987).

The efforts of the ANC, PAC, and BCM helped motivate a new defiance campaign by the schoolchildren of the massive black township of Soweto in 1976. The protest was directed against a law requiring that black students "not only learn Afrikaans as a language as well as English but accept it as the media of instruction through which they would have to learn other key subjects like mathematics"; many viewed this rule as constituting "an intolerable, artificial obstacle to their struggle for advancement" (Omer-Cooper 1987, 224). In June 1976 Soweto schoolchildren began large-scale protests. When the police used force to suppress the demonstrations, rioting broke out and spread to other towns in the Transvaal as well as to cities in Natal, the Cape, the Orange Free State, and the homelands.

The wave of riots constituted the largest black rebellion in twentieth-century South Africa. Unlike earlier outbreaks, such as that following the 1961 Sharpeville massacre, the Soweto rebellion was not quickly crushed, despite vicious police and military violence, but continued for months. At least six hundred people, mostly young students, were shot to death by state forces during the conflict. The white regime arrested hundreds of suspected leaders of the protest, dozens of whom died in police custody from supposed "suicides," "hunger strikes," and "unexplained causes" (Brewer

1986). In September 1977 the nationally known leader of the BCM, Steve Biko, was arrested and then beaten to death by police. Thousands of young people, however, fled the townships and South Africa, and many joined ANC guerrilla forces organized in the anti-apartheid states to the north (Brewer 1986; Davis 1987). The Soweto uprisings infused the ANC with a new generation of radicalized youth and intensified mass frustration with the white regime and support for violent revolution throughout many sectors of the African population.

Other young militants were drawn to the surviving elements of the PAC, which shared the black nationalist orientation of the shattered Black Consciousness Movement, and formed the Azania People's Liberation Army, many of whose members were quickly arrested, as the PAC had been successfully infiltrated by government agents. The post-Soweto repression crushed all major contenders for leadership of the black opposition—except the longer established and more secretively organized ANC—and persuaded many more nonwhite South Africans "of the futility of above-ground, peaceful opposition" (Davis 1987, 33).

After 1978 "the story of the black military opposition in the Republic is largely the story of the ANC and its allies" (Davis 1987, 33). The ANC in the early 1980s was able to commence a relatively sustained guerrilla effort, beginning with bombings of major South African oil facilities. The dominant view within the ANC was that although armed resistance could not result in a military victory in the near future, given the strength of the white regime's army and security forces, it could increase the costs of maintaining apartheid and, along with other factors, help pressure Pretoria into serious negotiations toward establishment of a nonracial democracy (Adam 1988).

Opposition to White Domination in the 1980s

The 1983 adoption of the new multiracial constitution by the white minority, which was widely interpreted as an attempt to co-opt the colored and Indian minorities while maintaining control firmly in the hands of whites, precipitated a massive intensification of protest. A major new—initially legal—anti-apartheid organization was established in August 1983, when 12,000 delegates convened in Cape Town to form the United Democratic Front (UDF, later renamed the "Mass Democratic Movement" in an effort to circumvent government repressive measures) to oppose the approaching white referendum on the multiracial constitution. The organizational concept of the UDF involved the notion of linking the many local anti-apartheid groups together through a countrywide board of directors that could set national policy objectives, suggest tactics, and offer coordination. "By the end of 1986, some seven hundred community bodies had affiliated with the umbrella-like UDF," including civic organizations, "women's groups, labor unions, youth leagues, and religious councils" (Davis 1987, 87).

Although the UDF declared itself independent of the illegal African National Congress, the UDF's goals for the future of South Africa appeared to be almost identical to those of the ANC. Most of the UDF's member groups supported the ANC and accepted the Freedom Charter, and several national and local leaders of the UDF acknowledged at least past membership in the ANC. The UDF differed from the ANC in terms of its publicly accepted range of tactics, which excluded violence. However, in 1988 the white government declared the UDF, then claiming three million members in more than six hundred affiliated community organizations, illegal (*New York Times*, Feb. 25, 1988, A1). In addition to the UDF, a major new union federation, the Congress of South African Trade Unions (COSATU), was established at Durban in December 1985. Similar in structure to the UDF, COSATU also declared its independence of the ANC, while expressing many of the same goals, and "announced socialist aims and principles" (Davis 1987, 102). Within several months thirty unions, representing 600,000 workers, had joined COSATU (membership would reportedly reach approximately one million by 1990), the largest union association in South Africa's history.

ANC leaders decided that rather than attempt the difficult task of organizing large numbers of South Africans directly into the illegal ANC, they would "federate" with like-minded legal organizations. In return for the cooperation and support of the UDF, COSATU, and associated groups, the ANC had to accept the significant degree of ideological variation characterizing the allied organizations, a decentralized authority structure, and a possibly reduced role for the ANC itself in the anti-apartheid struggle. But federation presented the possibility of genuinely united, massive participation in a coordinated effort to overturn white domination through measures including labor strikes, boycotts of white businesses, and military actions involving the sabotage of key economic installations as well as violent attacks on the military instruments of white oppression.

The ANC also called on nations trading with South Africa to boycott the republic and to convince or coerce their citizens to remove their investments from South Africa or from companies doing business in South Africa to help damage the economy and force change. The ANC hoped that its supporters would make the black townships ungovernable for the white-approved, often collaborationist township councils (whose members achieved power through elections in which generally less than 20 percent of those eligible voted) and that the townships could be turned into relatively secure bases for ANC activities. By 1986 many councils had been effectively replaced by local popular committees typically favorable to the ANC. The African National Congress and allied groups in the 1980s were estimated to enjoy the backing of about 50 percent of the black population (40 percent of the overall South African population), making it the single most widely supported political group in the nation (Davis 1987).

One rough gauge of the relative strengths of the ANC and the PAC in 1990 was size of the labor union federations affiliated with each organization. The Congress of South African Trade Unions, whose leaders tended to identify with the aims of the ANC, claimed approximately one million members, while the pro-PAC National Council of Trade Unions had about 150,000 (*New York Times*, March 4, 1990, A14). A further indication of popular allegiance to the ANC was the fact that an estimated 70 percent of native African workers participated in the nationwide strike called by the Mass Democratic movement to protest the 1989 South African elections (*U.S. News and World Report*, Sept. 18, 1989, 52).

Support for the ANC and other organizations working for change was motivated not only by widespread opposition to apartheid but also by economic hardships afflicting enormous numbers of nonwhites. In the 1980s white per capita income was more than four times that of Indians or individuals of mixed racial ancestry and over eight times that of native Africans (Seedat 1987a; 1987b). Unemployment among native Africans was over 20 percent. And the impact of unemployment or employment at relatively low wages included a level of undernourishment for indigenous African children estimated at between 10 percent and 30 percent (Le Roux 1988).

Inkatha

A major rival to the ANC and its allied groups among the Zulu in Natal Province was Inkatha yeNkululeko yeSizwe (National Cultural Liberation movement). Its most prominent figure was Chief Gatsa Buthelezi, head of the most populous homeland, KwaZulu, to which more than six million black South Africans were assigned, whether residents there or working in white areas. Inkatha, a Zulu cultural organization revived by Buthelezi in 1975, had 100,000 members by 1977 and claimed 1,700,000 by 1990. Despite the fact that Inkatha was opened to participation by non-Zulu blacks in 1979, the organization continued to draw mostly from Zulus living in rural areas in KwaZulu or other parts of rural Natal. Inkatha's "political culture was dominated by the personality cult surrounding Buthelezi's populist leadership, and by the traditions of Zulu power" (Davis 1987, 107).

While formally opposing apartheid, Buthelezi and other Inkatha leaders criticized the ANC for, in their view, advocating "socialism" as opposed to "free enterprise"; for demanding a one person, one vote democratic political system for South Africa instead of being "flexible" enough to consider other forms of sharing power with whites; and for resorting to armed resistance rather than continuing to utilize nonviolent means to pressure the white regime to accept reforms. Buthelezi also rejected ANC calls for other nations to disinvest in South Africa as a way of helping to coerce the white minority economically to enact positive changes; he instead promoted foreign investment in order, in his view, to further develop the nation's economy and thereby provide more jobs and opportunities for nonwhites. In opinion surveys conducted during the 1980s, the KwaZulu chief's followers, much to the pleasure of the white government, reflected their leader's relative conservatism: generally only small percentages of pro-Inkatha blacks favored the use of strikes, divestiture, or violence against the white regime in comparison to large majorities among ANC-UDF supporters (Bernstein and Godsell 1988; Davis 1987).

Buthelezi's position of leadership in KwaZulu was, in part, the result of the white regime's homeland policy, intended to separate blacks not only from whites, coloreds, and Indians, but also from other Africans by emphasizing tribal differences. In KwaZulu, where unemployment levels were high, the jobs and opportunities for economic and social mobility that Buthelezi could provide to thousands both through his control of the homeland administration and his influence over Inkatha's staff hiring constituted a major patronage-dispensing base of his power. Unlike several other homeland leaders, however, he had refused to accommodate white demands that he accept full independence for the several geographically separated territories that together constituted KwaZulu. Instead he proposed an experiment in which Zulus, Natal Indians, and coloreds would have some role, along with whites, in the governing of Natal Province. Buthelezi's opposition to total independence for KwaZulu partially shielded him from being perceived as simply a puppet of white rulers. His prestige was further enhanced by the coverage his public statements received in the white media, which portrayed him as a relatively responsible and reasonable adversary and advocate of black aspirations.

Comparatively favorable white attitudes toward Buthelezi in part resulted from his rejection of ANC violence: he instructed his followers to "avoid at all costs being made cannon fodder by people who want to use our corpses to stand on in order to be seen as leaders" (Davis 1987, 108). But seemingly in contrast with his condemnation of armed attacks directed at the white regime or its agents, Buthelezi's Inkatha became widely known as an organization willing to use violence in the conflict between Inkatha members and supporters of the ANC (*New York Times*, Apr. 22, 1990, A3; Aug. 22, 1990, A7). Inkatha's influence in the 1980s and early 1990s was limited primarily to Natal Province and other locations with large numbers of Zulu immigrants from rural backgrounds, whereas the ANC and its allied organizations enjoyed wide support in nonwhite urban areas throughout South Africa. Buthelezi in July 1990 announced that Inkatha was being reorganized as a political party, the Inkatha Freedom Party, in anticipation of participation in a reformed South African political system (*New York Times*, July 15, 1990, A5).

White Opposition to Aspects of Apartheid

Several significant groups within the white community expressed support for an end to major aspects of the apartheid system. The greatest movement away from apartheid through 1989 had occurred in the economic sector. Major elements of the nation's white business community, responding to the economy's need for an expanded, stable, skilled workforce, convinced government officials to alter legal codes in order to achieve this goal. The changes included opening new occupational categories to nonwhites, legalization of indigenous African labor unions, and the 1986 repealing of the Pass Laws (Bernstein and Godsell 1988). Some business leaders asked the government to negotiate with the ANC, and several called for the establishment of a nonracial democracy.

Another major source of white opposition to apartheid was the Progressive Federal Party, which, drawing support disproportionately from middle- and upper-middle-income whites, had for thirty years fought for greater civil and political rights for the nonwhite majority. In April 1989 this group joined with two smaller political parties to create a united left-wing opposition to the National Party government. The result was the new Democratic Party, which in the 1989 national election won about 20 percent of the vote and thirty-three positions in the 166-seat white parliament (*New York Times*, Sept. 8, 1989, A8). The Democratic Party advocated "a true democracy which rejects race as its basis and protects the human dignity and liberty of all its citizens" (*New York Times*, Apr. 9, 1989, 6).

A third element of white society, the South African Dutch Reformed Church, which long helped provide ideological justifications for white domination, officially moved to express opposition to apartheid. In 1986 leaders of the church, which at that time included 80 percent of white legislators among its 1.7 million members, declared racism to be a sin "and opened its membership to Christians of all races" (Berger and Godsell 1988b, 298).

COUNTERINSURGENCY STRATEGIES OF THE REGIME IN THE 1980S

In attempting to cope with movements in favor of nonracial democracy, over several decades white leaders developed a comprehensive and integrated strategy. The plans included coordination of governmental policy, the economy, mass media, the military, and police in such a way as to sustain or increase divisions among the black majority, co-opt nonwhite elite elements by providing them with channels of economic and social mobility in return for their collaboration in the maintenance of white dominance, and use of selective violence against rebellious groups or individuals.

The 1983 constitution vested potentially dictatorial powers in the president, who was therefore able to act decisively in "emergencies" regardless of any divisions within the white establishment. A major split within the white elite existed between the "moderates" (mainly members of the National Party, which had engineered the 1983 supposedly power-sharing multiracial constitution and won 48 percent of the vote in the 1989 election and ninety-three seats in the white parliament) and the "conservatives" (largely associated with the Conservative Party, the product of a schism in the National Party), who were generally opposed to any concessions to nonwhites (Brewer 1986; Davis 1987). The Conservative party obtained 31 percent of the vote in 1989 and thirty-nine parliamentary seats. Voter analyses in the 1980s indicated that the Conservative Party drew support disproportionately from lower-middle-class and lower-income whites, many of whom probably felt that their economic interests and status in society would be threatened by a weakening of the apartheid system (Schlemmer 1988). The primary disagreement among most white leaders during much of the 1980s appeared to be not over the issue of whether to prevent the advent of black majority rule but rather of how to prevent it: through emphasis on the co-opting reforms advocated by the moderates or through the repression stressed by the conservatives. In general, the major component of the white elite recognized the necessity of reducing apartheid barriers in the labor market in order to ensure future economic growth, but "in the social domain, and more emphatically in politics, racial division and white racial hegemony" were to be maintained (Berger and Godsell 1988b, 281).

The South African Defense Force (SADF) was capable of quickly mobilizing more than 70,000 men at any one time and more, if necessary, from its sizable reserves (almost all white men were required to undergo military training). Through much of the 1980s about 5 percent of the regular SADF personnel were nonwhites, often organized into units separated on the basis of tribal membership, in part in order to ensure that military service reinforced rather than reduced the significance of ethnicity. Recruits for the non-white units, carefully screened to admit only those with anti-leftist views or with strong tendencies toward tribal identification or other antirevolutionary political attitudes acceptable to white officials, were apparently attracted to military service primarily by significant financial incentives within the context of relatively high nonwhite unemployment rates (Davis 1987). Since the army was overwhelmingly white, it was virtually impossible to conceive of a situation in which significant segments of the military would defect from the white-dominated state to the side of the almost entirely non-white revolutionary movement. The South African Defense Force was supplemented by 75,000 police, approximately half of whom were white and half nonwhite (*New York Times*, Jan. 6, 1991, A9).

After signs of nuclear blasts were detected in the South Atlantic during South African naval exercises, followed by evidence of radioactive fallout, many authoritative observers concluded that South Africa must possess at least a small number of nuclear explosive devices. Other forms of military pressure against neighboring black revolutionary states, including military incursions by South African troops and support for rebel groups opposing leftist African governments, contributed to forcing several pro-ANC countries to deny the ANC bases on their territories (Davis 1987; Nolutshungu 1988). In return South Africa pledged to cease its hostile actions and reduce aid for counterrevolutionary forces.

The white regime could generally count on the six homeland armies it had trained and staffed, in part with white officers, not only to help repress ANC activities but also to intervene to control political developments within the homelands that might be viewed as detrimental to the interests of the white regime. Homeland constitutions often granted the rulers, initially selected by the white regime to head a particular supposedly "independent" homeland, the right to appoint a significant proportion of the homeland's parliament or in other ways reserve a large number of seats for tribal chauvinists or other individuals willing to collaborate with Pretoria. This resulted in elections in which the candidate favored by the white regime lost as much as 70 percent of the homeland vote but continued to rule because he still controlled the homeland parliament (Davis 1987).

REFORMING APARTHEID

By the mid-1980s a number of changes had occurred that in effect began to eliminate significant aspects of the apartheid system (*New York Times*, Mar. 12, 1989, E2). The modifications included the 1983 measure allowing the residents of black townships to buy rather than rent their homes, the 1985 governmental acceptance of the right of individuals of different racial designations to marry or live together, the 1986 retraction of the Pass Laws for indigenous Africans, and the 1990 opening of public hospitals to patients of all races (*New York Times*, May 17, 1990, A1). Many movie theaters, sports events, restaurants, and airline flights were made accessible to all people who could afford them. And many skilled job categories were opened to indigenous Africans because of labor shortages. But white workers still earned considerably more than black, and the segregated educational system spent 5.5 times more on a white child than on a black child. The government granted legal status to a few integrated neighborhoods in response to a housing shortage, and in Cape Town, the traditionally most liberal of South Africa's major urban areas, the city council in 1989 requested permission from the national government to be allowed to abolish local residential segregation (*New York Times*, Mar. 28, 1989, A4).

The regime permitted the parents of students in all-white public schools to vote on the issue of desegregation. The requirements for integration were that 80 percent of a school's parents had to participate and that at least 72 percent vote in favor of the new admissions policy. The results were that approximately 10 percent of previously all-white public schools admitted at least some nonwhite students during January 1991 (*New York Times*, Jan. 10, 1991, A3). Despite these developments most of the nonwhite population continued to demand substantially greater change.

The ANC, supported by the countries of the Organization of African Unity, called for "negotiations and elections leading to majority rule in South Africa" (*New York Times*, Aug. 22, 1989, A8). ANC conditions for the opening of talks with the white government included asking Pretoria to lift the nation's state of emergency, releasing political prisoners, legalizing all anti-apartheid political organizations, withdrawing government troops from the black townships, and halting trials and executions. In contrast, the white, predominantly Afrikaner Conservative Party was the only major political group that advocated the 1950s form of apartheid.

Leaders of the National Party stated during the 1989 election campaign that they were committed to moving the nation further away from its original apartheid system. President F. W. de Klerk went so far as to announce that the National Party intended gradually to alter the nation's political system from the situation of white dominance to one that would involve wider power sharing among the country's designated racial groups (*African News*, Aug. 1989, 14). But since he also asserted that the evolutionary transformation he foresaw would not permit the possibility of indigenous African majority rule, many viewed his proposal as mainly another set of reforms intended to modify the structure of white dominance in significant ways while retaining white control of the economy, the security forces, and, ultimately, the political system (*New York Times*, July 23, 1989, E2).

Many residents of South Africa, however, rejected the establishment of any political structure other than one that would permit the peoples of the nation absolutely equal rights of political participation and responsibility. And critics of the National Party government asserted that a valid departure from the system of apartheid must also involve a shift from exclusive white control of the security forces and the major economic institutions. Many believed that any significant attempt to increase economic equality could occur only if a postapartheid government intervened to weaken or break white minority domination of the economy. That move could open new opportunities for nonwhites in state-owned industries or even in other major economic concerns that could conceivably be nationalized. Such a program would be analogous to the government effort to raise the economic status of the Afrikaners in the British-dominated South African economy in the decades immediately following the Boer War.

The South African government, however, began to sell state-owned corporations, enterprises, and facilities to private concerns and individuals, including its Iron and Steel Corporation (ISCOR) in 1989. By fall 1990 the ANC, COSATU, and other major anti-apartheid organizations had vigorously condemned the regime's privatization of state property as an attempt to deprive a future democratically elected nonracial government of the resources necessary to distribute wealth and economic opportunities more equitably (*New York Times*, Nov. 13, 1990, A10). The result of the process, if continued, would be to place in the hands of affluent whites industries and other capital that would have been owned collectively by all South Africans. In response to protests, South African officials stated that they would suspend further plans to sell publicly held assets.

The mere dismantling of major apartheid laws might be of limited significance to the majority of impoverished nonwhites unless accompanied by governmental measures to redistribute wealth. For example, the repeal by South African authorities of the Land Acts of 1913 and 1936, which had assigned approximately 87 percent of the nation's land to the white minority, did not insure that most of the millions of people from whose parents huge territories had been taken would have the money to exercise their new right to buy land throughout the country (*New York Times*, Jan. 4, 1991, A4). The majority that lacked property could only benefit significantly if additional government action provided them with land parcels either free or at very low cost.

One significant fear among some anti-apartheid activists who demanded a restructuring of both the economic and the political systems was that without economic reorganization the white regime might attempt to co-opt the minority of middle-class native Africans into a new governing coalition, as it had once tried to do with Asians and persons of mixed racial ancestry through adoption of the 1983 multiracial constitution. In such a hypothetical arrangement virtually the entire white population would be joined with relatively affluent nonwhites in a ruling alliance, which would then economically and politically dominate and exploit the almost exclusively nonwhite industrial and agricultural working classes.

At the outset of the 1990s South Africa embarked on what appeared to be an irreversible path of change. Those advocating a full departure from the system of white domination, however, had to confront the dilemma of how to improve the economic and social conditions of the nation's majority significantly without at the same time precipitating the departure of large numbers of whites possessing technical knowledge, managerial skills, and investment capital important to the nation's and the continent's future development.

In February 1990 the National Party administration of F. W. de Klerk took a major step toward the resolution of South Africa's civil conflict by releasing the famous ANC leader Nelson Mandela, after more than twenty-seven years of imprisonment (*New York Times*, Feb. 12, 1990, A1). The government also legalized the previously banned African National Congress, the South African Communist Party, and other anti-apartheid organizations. In March 1990 Namibia, the country between South Africa and

Angola, achieved independence after seventy-five years of South African occupation (*New York Times*, Mar. 21, 1990, A1).

Once out of prison, Nelson Mandela was elected by ANC officials as deputy president of the organization (the president was the ailing Oliver Tambo). After substantial discussions with other ANC leaders, Mandela called for continued international economic sanctions against South Africa until the establishment of a new democracy with equal rights of political participation for all the nation's peoples. Although also demanding a restructuring of the economy, Mandela noted, especially during his June 1990 visit to the United States, that economic reform need not necessarily involve extensive nationalizations if other measures could assure the desired benefits of improving the welfare and protecting the interests of the nonwhite majority (*New York Times*, June 22, 1990, A20; June 27, 1990, A11).

Mandela, while diligently promoting the goals of the ANC and the anti-apartheid movement, provoked some measure of controversy by reconfirming the ANC's friendly relations with Cuba, Libya, and the Palestine Liberation Organization, and the ANC's alliance with the South African Communist Party. These governments and organizations had long provided valuable assistance to the ANC's struggle against racism in Africa. The ANC expressed particular gratitude for Cuban efforts not only in aiding the ANC but also in combating white South African intervention in Angola and in helping to achieve independence for Namibia.

President de Klerk offered to negotiate the formulation of a new constitution for South Africa that would provide national political power for indigenous Africans (*New York Times*, Apr. 18, 1990, A5; June 28, 1990, A22). And as talks progressed, the ANC in August 1990 announced the suspension of its armed struggle against the South African regime (*New York Times*, Aug. 12, 1990, E4). But de Klerk and other National Party leaders consistently refused to accept the ANC's demand for a totally nonracial, one person, one vote political system. Agreement on a new South African constitution, consequently, necessitated a shift in the views of the major political organizations representing whites or nonwhites or both.

THE DISMANTLING OF APARTHEID

The various participating parties during years of negotiations for a new political system pushed for often-conflicting goals (Grundy 1993; Jost 1994). The ANC held out for a one person, one vote, nonracial democracy at the national level and a strong central government capable of organizing and carrying out policies to provide dramatic improvements in educational, housing, and economic opportunities for the country's nonwhite majority. The National Party, Inkatha, die-hard Afrikaner nationalists, and tribal homeland authorities tended to demand a federal system that would be characterized by relatively strong provincial government powers capable of defending local and minority interests. These groups also pushed for a division of the country into a larger number of smaller provinces in which locally concentrated ethnic minorities could exercise influence or even dominance.

The parties and groups not allied with the ANC also supported an agreement specifying that adoption of a new constitution or constitutional amendments would require a supermajority of 75 percent either of a parliament in which seats were awarded proportionally by popular vote or in a popular referendum. This proposal would, it was thought, enable the non-ANC political parties to block the enactment of a constitution or constitutional amendments that they considered oppressive or otherwise unacceptable. Inkatha leaders demanded and received continuation of the Zulu hereditary monarchy as part of the price for their participation in elections. All parties to negotiations appeared concerned with safeguarding the economic benefits enjoyed by the more privileged groups, classes, and elites in South African society, evidently as a way of deterring any large elite segment from either organizing significant mass opposition to a final agreement or leaving the country and depriving it of their valuable resources and skills (*New York Times*, May 15, 1994, 14; June 4, 1994, 1; May 8, 1995, A19).

During the negotiation process, violence and political and economic protests continued. Thousands died in lethal attacks between Inkatha and ANC supporters. In particular, evidence arose that elements within South Africa's white military and police leaderships assisted Inkatha extremists in carrying out and escaping punishment for massacres of ANC sympathizers (*New York Times*, Mar. 19, 1994, 1; Mar. 20, 1994, 10; Feb. 20, 1995, A7). White nationalist fanatics planted bombs and assassinated some ANC leaders, in particular Chris Hani in 1993, who had led the ANC guerrilla group, Spear of the Nation, and was serving as chairperson of the South African Communist Party.

The ANC's future development and policy objectives may have been significantly affected by the loss of these leaders. However, the ANC's position in negotiations was strengthened by its popular support and more specifically by economically damaging strikes and demonstrations by the Congress of South African Trade Unions in support of ANC demands (Jost 1994).

Negotiations finally resulted in agreement on a temporary five-year constitution for South Africa under which the 1994 elections could be held. The temporary constitution was structured so as to insure that the 1994 elections would result in a government of national unity that would, ideally, be a manifestation of democratic process and capable of moving toward significant social change while avoiding extreme measures and reducing internal domestic conflict. Under the constitution the country was divided into nine provinces from the original four, primarily by subdividing the former Transvaal and Cape Provinces. The new legislature consisted of a National Assembly with four hundred members and a National Council of Provinces of ninety. National Assembly seats were awarded on the basis of the proportion of popular vote received by each political party (Jost 1994). The citizens of each of the nine provinces elected ten members of the National Council of Provinces. The four-hundred-member National Assembly was to carry out the function of selecting the president. The constitution provided for multiple deputy presidents, one for each political party that received at least 20 percent of the popular vote. The president was to have a twenty-seven-member cabinet, with any party that received at least 5 percent of the popular vote entitled to at least one cabinet position.

All tribal homeland governments, including the supposedly independent homeland states, were eliminated, and their bureaucracies were incorporated into the new South African government. Similarly, the anti-apartheid guerrilla armies were merged with the much larger South African Defense Force (Nathan 1994). According to the temporary constitution, constitutional amendments or a whole new constitution had to be approved by either a two-thirds vote of the legislature or a 60 percent approval by direct popular vote. The temporary constitution also included a basic bill of rights.

In the 1994 election the ANC received approximately 63 percent of the popular vote, the National Party received 20 percent, and the Inkatha Freedom party about 10 percent. Other parties received the remaining 7 percent, including about 1.5 percent for the PAC. The parliament selected Nelson Mandela of the ANC as president; Thabo Mbeki, also of the ANC, as first deputy president; and F. W. de Klerk of the National Party, the former president, as second deputy president ("South Africa's New Leadership" 1994; *New York Times*, May 3, 1994, A1; May 11, 1994, A1; June 20, 1994, A7; Norment 1994; Watson, Contreras, and Hammer 1994).

President Mandela and his government, facing the massive inequalities between indigenous Africans and whites and over 40 percent unemployment among indigenous Africans, proposed a five-year "Reconstruction and Development Plan." The plan called for the government to provide a minimum of ten years of free education for all children, the creation of 2.5 million public works jobs, the building of one million new homes, the electrification of another 2.5 million residences, and the redistribution of about 30 percent of the country's arable land. The cost of achieving the goals of the five-year reconstruction plan was initially estimated at $11 billion by the ANC, but up to $165 billion by ANC critics (*New York Times*, Apr. 21, 1994, A10; July 29, 1994, A6; Aug. 19, 1994, A3; Dec. 4, 1994, E7; Apr. 27, 1995, A1).

To accomplish these goals through peaceful democratic methods within the context of the post–Cold War "new world order," the ANC leadership encouraged foreign investment and even entertained the possible economic and efficiency benefits of privatizing certain state industries. This shift in ANC as well as SACP policies most likely reflected the fact that by the mid-1990s virtually all the wealthy advanced nations of the world with whom South Africa traded and from whom South Africa received technological and other assistance were firmly committed to capitalist economic systems and trade relations. South Africa, therefore, even though governed by the

SOUTH AFRICA (after 1994)

ANC with SACP participation, was strongly influenced to structure its economy according to the rules of capitalist economic development.

The apparent modifications in the ideology of the former liberation movement and the gradualism and moderation of its reconstruction and redistribution plans led some critics within the ANC to openly question whether the anti-apartheid liberation movement had taken over white South Africa or whether white South Africa and the international capitalist system had taken over the liberation movement.

On May 8, 1996, more than 85 percent of South Africa's national legislators voted to adopt and gradually implement over a three-year period a new constitution that retained several major features of the 1994 interim constitution, such as the four-hundred-member National Assembly and the ninety-member National Council of Provinces (*New York Times*, May 9, 1996, A1). While assigning to the nine provincial governments exclusive control over provincial planning, sports, recreation, and roads, the new charter provided for a relatively strong presidency and central government and dispensed with the interim constitution's stipulation that some positions in the presidential cabinet be reserved for all political parties that received at least 5 percent of the popular vote. The 1996 document also established an independent judiciary crowned by the Constitutional Court, whose eleven members were appointed by the nation's president. A major feature of the new constitution was its Bill of Rights, which not only guaranteed freedom of speech, movement, and political activity and banned discrimination on the basis of race, gender, sexual orientation, age, pregnancy, or marital status, but also supported every citizen's right to adequate housing, food, water, education, and health care.

SOUTH AFRICA AFTER APARTHEID

Economy

South Africa's economy after apartheid had several attributes of a relatively advanced capitalist system, including enormous quantities of natural resources, and effective energy, transportation, communications, and financial sectors. The annual increase in GDP in 2005 was estimated to have been almost 5 percent. However, this level of growth was viewed as insufficient to allow the country to overcome its several substantial problems. These included a very high unemployment rate—estimated at 26.7 percent in September 2005 (Statistics South Africa 2006), about half of the population living below the poverty line, and one of the most extreme situations of income inequality in the world (Lawson 2005, 160). Among households with incomes in the highest 10 percent, average income was about forty-two times the average for households in the lowest 10 percent.

This situation in part reflected the fact that the South African Revolution was largely political and social in nature but did not encompass much in the way of a socioeconomic transformation or redistribution of wealth or resources. According to Antoinette Handley, in 2004 "Black Africans, who made up 75 percent of the population, are generally considered to own between 2 percent to 7 percent of capitalization in terms of stock shares" (2004, 200). So the economy was still overwhelmingly dominated by whites. Social mobility was more possible for nonwhite South Africans after 1994, but those best prepared to benefit from the postapartheid system were those with already high educational levels and other predemocracy advantages. Since the revolution did not involve a sweeping redistribution of wealth and resources toward the poor mass of the population, the only alternative was to try to accelerate development of the existing capitalist system to the point at which it could generate opportunities for less-fortunate citizens to work their way out of poverty. As of 2006 the needed pace of development had not been achieved.

The ANC governments after 1994 did attempt to enact measures to alleviate the worst economic sources of misery and social discontent. They tripled the number of recipients of social grants (child support, old age assistance, disability aid) and established seven hundred new health clinics (Lawson 2005, 159–60). They also increased the availability of housing, electricity, and clean water. According to Handley (2004, 198–99), "the percentage of households with access to clean water rose from 60 percent in 1996 to 85 percent in 2001 and those with sanitation from 49 percent in 1994 to 63 percent in 2003. The proportion of households with electricity rose from 32 percent in 1996 to 70 percent in 2001." The South African government also provided free medical care to pregnant women and to children under the age of five. Handley notes that the ANC-dominated government was able to provide one million new homes. The postapartheid government expanded educational opportunities, but as in most societies the schools and teachers available to many children from low-income backgrounds often seemed greatly inferior on the average to the schools and teachers of most middle- and upper-class children.

One of the most important antipoverty measures enacted in the 1990s was actually initiated by the white National Party shortly before the first nonracial democratic election of 1994 in an apparent attempt to attract more votes from nonwhite persons and poor people to the party. The National Party government carried out racial equalization of pensions for elderly persons, raising those of nonwhites to the level that whites had received. This act immediately boosted state pensions for elderly indigenous Africans to about "$90 per month, or roughly twice the median black income" (Handley 2004, 199). Since many South Africans are bound to and committed to the well-being of the members of their extended family network, this dramatic increase in pensions benefited many non-elderly persons and is thought to have contributed to improving the nutrition and health of hundreds of thousands of children. But the cost of maintaining the state pension system and also coping with the enormous AIDS problem threatened to overwhelm the government's budget.

The AIDS Catastrophe

South Africa's extensive poverty and flawed educational system likely contributed to the development of the country's AIDS epidemic, which constituted simultaneously a gigantic medical problem, a huge drain on the state's economic resources, and an immense human rights disaster. An estimated 10 to 11 percent of South Africa's population was infected with the HIV virus in the first decade of the twenty-first century (Lawson 2005, 163). In certain age categories the proportion infected was much higher. A national health study found that whereas perhaps less than 1 percent of pregnant women were infected with HIV in 1990, the percentage had risen to about 25 percent in 2001 (Cauvin 2002). According to a later survey, this percentage rose to 29.5 percent in 2004 (Noble 2006). Noble also reports that, whereas the number of deaths in the 25–49 age range in South Africa was about 58 percent of those over fifty in 1997, in the year 2002 this percentage had increased to about 95 percent. In other words, by 2002 the number of people dying annually ages twenty-five to forty-nine was about the same as for all South Africans age fifty years or older. Handley (2004, 197) reports that the AIDS epidemic was predicted to reduce the "life expectancy of black South Africans to 40 years."

Some ANC leaders, in particular Thabo Mbeki, were accused first of not understanding the nature or seriousness of the HIV/AIDS threat and of then taking years to respond effectively. Handley (2004) suggests that the slowness of ANC leaders to react to the AIDS epidemic was probably due to the fact that the disease appeared on the scene just as the ANC was defeating the apartheid system; about to gain control of the state and its resources, ANC leaders were focused on preparing to launch their program of social reforms to improve the lives of South Africa's millions of poor people. There was an apparent reluctance to heed warning signs of the AIDS problem because early government recognition of the disease and its devastating consequences could have meant an immediate diversion of state funds to combat the medical emergency rather than being used to deal with the people's pressing economic and social needs. The poor, however, were far from the only victims of AIDS. Chief Mangosuthu ("Gatsha") Buthelezi's son died of AIDS in 2004 and Nelson Mandela's son in 2005.

Crime

Since the late 1970s South Africa has had one of the highest homicide rates in the world (the number of homicide victims per one hundred thousand residents). The official South African homicide rate reached its highest recorded level of about sixty-seven in 1994. After that year the homicide rate generally declined. By 2004 the homicide rate was about forty (South African Police Service 2006), but this was still about seven times the U.S.

homicide rate of 5.5 that year. Other violent crime rates in South Africa, such as attempted murder, assault, and rape, were also far above those of most other countries.

High levels of violent crime were thought to have been the product of a combination of factors, such as extreme economic inequality, racial strife, ethnic or political conflict among indigenous Africans, wide availability of guns, rapid social change, and a sense of frustration on the part of many poor people who realized that the end of apartheid had really not changed much in their lives. Once the ANC had adopted neoliberal economic policies, there seemed no longer any hope in deliverance through participation in a viable revolutionary movement. As in most countries, the victims of violent crimes as well as the offenders were disproportionately poor and young (Louw and Shaw 1997). Property crime rates known to police in South Africa, unlike violent crime rates, were not notably higher than those in other countries. This may have been due to the fact that the homes of the affluent with the most valuable possessions were usually residentially segregated from poor areas and were typically well protected, often by private guards. CNN and Reuters reported that in 2006 there were almost three private security personnel for every one publicly employed police officer.

The validity of using property crime rates and most violent crime rates generated from police data to assess trends over time is questionable because the rates are vulnerable to increases or decreases in the willingness of people to report crimes to police. Willingness to report crimes can be influenced by changes in government, level of trust in the effectiveness of police, fear of retaliation from offenders, and other factors. The nature of homicide, however, makes the rate of this offense a relatively valid measure of the risk of homicide victimization from one point in time to another. Data analyzed by Thomson (2004, 10) indicated that homicide rates in South Africa were relatively low in the early 1970s but then started climbing, especially after the 1976 Soweto uprising. Then rates increased again around the time of the implementation of the 1983 multiracial constitution, another period of heightened anti-apartheid protest.

After 1991, when conflict and negotiations were taking place in regard to the creation of the postapartheid political system, the homicide rate climbed to its highest levels in 1994 and 1995 and then began a fairly steady decline despite the abolition of the death penalty. The reasons for the decline were not widely agreed upon but may have included the reduction in lethal conflict between Inkatha and ANC supporters, improved welfare measures alleviating for many people the worst miseries of poverty, the impact of the AIDS epidemic in causing the death of massive numbers of young adults (some of whom might have been homicide victims or offenders), expanded educational opportunities, and improved medical services saving the lives of attempted murder victims who in the past would have died and been classified as homicide victims.

Political Developments

To reduce the likelihood of continued political, racial, and ethnic conflict after the end of apartheid and enhance the probability that the postapartheid political system would be successful, the new democratically elected government created the Truth and Reconciliation Commission. It convened for the first time in January 1996. One of its main purposes was to reveal the truth about murders, disappearances, and bombings committed by defenders as well as opponents of apartheid in the hope that this process would help bring about reconciliation among all of South Africa's people. Many persons who committed acts of violence during the anti-apartheid conflict were offered immunity from criminal prosecution by the government if they confessed to their actions. Those taking advantage of the opportunity offered by the commission included some members of the former white security forces who admitted to killings and other human rights abuses. According to Lawson (2005, 169), about seven thousand people applied to the commission for amnesty from criminal charges.

In the 1999 election, the second postapartheid democratic election, the ANC's share of the popular vote increased to 66.4 percent. But so many people were apparently disappointed by the failure of the ANC-led government to do more to reduce inequality, improve lives more significantly, and cope more effectively with important problems like the AIDS epidemic that the total number of people voting in 1999 was 3.5 million less than in 1994. In fact, though increasing the size of its parliamentary majority, the ANC actually received 1.6 million fewer votes than it did in 1994. Thabo Mbeki of the ANC, who had served as first vice president, replaced Nelson Mandela as president of South Africa.

In the 2004 election, the percentage of the vote going to the ANC increased further to 69.7 percent, and its actual vote total increased by about 279,000 over what it received in 1999. President Mbeki was elected to a second term as president. But at the same time the total of votes cast for all parties declined by about 360,000. Public opinion surveys indicated that people were least satisfied with regard to the government's performance in fostering the creation of jobs and in combating crime but somewhat more satisfied with regard to improvements in health care and education. The percentage of votes going to the once powerful National Party (called the New National Party in this election), which had installed the modern apartheid system and dominated the country from 1948 to 1994, declined to about 1.7 percent. This poor result led to its disbanding in 2005.

Within the ruling ANC serious divisions arose over issues such as the government's AIDS policy, inequality, unemployment, and the issue of whether to further privatize state-owned enterprises. Some opposed what they viewed as the emergence of a ruling alliance between the small minority of well-to-do indigenous Africans and wealthy whites who overwhelmingly possessed the shares of South Africa's privately owned companies and dominated the economy. Criticisms of ANC moderate leaders often came from SACP and COSATU members within the ANC. President Mbeki was accused of, among other things, at first ignoring and then ineptly responding to the AIDS crisis and of not doing enough to protect the interests of South Africa's workers who were so essential to the creation of the democratic system and the victory of the ANC. Some of the discontented within the ANC apparently even considered the possibility of creating a new political party to the left of the ANC.

SUMMARY AND ANALYSIS

The white-dominated state in South Africa had its origin in the Dutch settlement of the Cape in the seventeenth century. The Afrikaners justified their conquests and repeated confiscations of the wealth of native peoples as a religious mission: whites were acting to fulfill God's plan for a Christian South Africa. After gold deposits were discovered in the Transvaal, the British conquered the Boers and unified South Africa into a single white-dominated state.

Afrikaners, many impoverished by the effects of the Boer War or British economic policies, constituted the bulk of the white working class, which intensely feared social and economic integration with the country's nonwhite masses. Afrikaner nationalism, inflamed by the migration of tens of thousands of blacks to urban areas during World War II and into jobs previously reserved for whites, achieved the unity necessary to win the national elections in 1948. Over the next twelve years the apartheid system was formally established. It confirmed past segregationist policies and reversed much of the limited integration that had previously occurred. Despite numerous internal and external pressures, the white regime continued to endure with the help of several factors: the support of the large majority of the white population; a well-trained, technologically advanced, and extremely loyal military machine; a successful policy of selectively co-opting, dividing, or repressing elements of the nonwhite majority to facilitate control; and the cooperation, even if sometimes covert, of the major Western powers in need of South Africa's important mineral resources.

South Africa's system of white domination provided the potentially key factor for the development of a successful revolutionary movement, the motivation for the huge nonwhite majority to join together in a mutual effort to establish a truly representative, nonracial government. But the achievement of the necessary degree of unity among those opposed to apartheid was impeded by divisions over issues such as whether goals should be pursued violently or through nonviolent methods, or whether the movement should demand a one person, one vote democracy or should settle for some other form of power sharing that would allow whites to retain at least temporarily a disproportionate control of government. Other divisive concerns included persisting tribal rivalries, the issue of whether the homelands should maintain any significant level of autonomy in the postapartheid state, and the degree of socialization of the postapartheid economic system.

Mass discontent among the majority of South Africans had its obvious origin in the European conquests and seizure of the nation's wealth. Traditional forms of rebellion against white invaders, such as those of the Xhosa and the Zulu, were unsuccessful. Although European exploitation of the country's resources improved the living conditions of many nonwhite South Africans relative to the residents of other African states, the distorted levels of inequality between whites and nonwhites and the humiliation imposed by various aspects of the racially oriented political, economic, social, and cultural systems constituted powerful sources of modern discontent.

South Africa was distinguished in part by the fact that its educated elites were separated along racial and ethnic lines. Although by the time of the 1989 parliamentary elections the majority of white political leaders (those of the National and Democratic parties) at least publicly supported an end of the 1950s-style apartheid system, an even larger majority of white political leaders (those of the National and Conservative parties) resisted the creation of a political system that would allow the possibility of indigenous African majority rule.

Nonwhite educated elites organized a series of movements to end white minority rule. Virtually all of these, inspired by somewhat varying ideologies, initially attempted to use legal means or at least methods of nonviolent civil disobedience to motivate whites morally to negotiate reform. When they appeared to be gaining strength, such movements were crushed by the white regime, convincing many among the nonwhite elites that South Africa would change only in response to the successful use of revolutionary violence. In the 1960s and the 1970s leaders of the black nationalist Pan-Africanist Congress and Black Consciousness Movement argued that only the efforts of the black population acting alone could result in a simultaneous dismantling of the racist system and a restoration of psychological strength (pride and positive self-esteem) among indigenous Africans.

Another movement against apartheid was made up almost completely of Zulu membership. Chief Buthelezi's Inkatha organization, founded in 1974, never provoked violent white repression, since its goals, at least in the short run, appeared consistent with the white aim of maintaining not only racial separation but also tribal disunity among blacks, and since it opposed the concept of armed revolution. Though powerful in KwaZulu and Natal and often a significant force in areas with large numbers of Zulu immigrants, Inkatha remained mainly a regional organization following an ideology and a leader viewed as collaborationist by many Africans.

The African National Congress, along with its allied groups, such as the Congress of South African Trade Unions, appeared to be the strongest, best organized, and most widely supported of the anti-apartheid groups. The original members of the group, founded in 1912, attempted to appeal to successive white governments on philosophical, religious, and moral grounds to grant concessions to the nonwhite majority. The ANC advocated the goal of a nonracial, one person, one vote democracy, and eventually attempted to achieved this goal through an interracial movement. The political tactics employed by the ANC until the 1950s were generally peaceful, legal, and nonconfrontational. But following the perceived betrayal of ANC support for South Africa's role in the World War II struggle against German Nazi racism, the younger generation of ANC militants, led by individuals such as Nelson Mandela, decided to organize campaigns of mass civil disobedience in defiance of racist laws. After several such efforts were repressed in the 1950s, plans were laid for the development of an ANC underground network and the organization of a revolutionary armed force to employ selective violence against the white regime.

Foreign involvement in South Africa historically served primarily to assist the survival of the racially organized, white-dominated state. The British declined to push for a nonracial democratic system after their victory over the Boers in 1902 not only because of a desire to end self-destructive violent conflict within the white community but also to ensure a continuous supply of very cheap nonwhite labor for British enterprises. Throughout most of the twentieth century Britain, other Western European nations, and the United States continued to trade with South Africa and overtly or covertly supply weapons or weapon technologies to the white regime in exchange for the republic's strategically important mineral resources and its hostility toward Communist Party–led states or movements (Cran 1979). Until the latter part of the twentieth century, when a genuine and significant commitment by much of the international community to end apartheid developed, only countries dominated by Communist parties and a few liberal Western European nations and African states provided significant aid to anti-apartheid revolutionary forces.

At the beginning of the 1990s several factors precipitated a rapid political transformation of South Africa. The end of the cold war and the disintegration of the USSR reduced the fear of leftist elements in the ANC both among major leaders of the white South African National Party and among the governments of foreign powers that once dreaded the possibility that South Africa's critical resources might fall into unfriendly hands. Trade restrictions imposed by many nations against South Africa's white government and strikes by large numbers of nonwhite South African workers economically pressured South Africa's business community and state officials to enter into an agreement with the ANC and other anti-apartheid groups to politically democratize the country. After years of negotiations, a transitional five-year political system permitted the election of an ANC majority to a new parliament and the election of the country's first nonwhite president, Nelson

Mandela. The final outcome of this process and the extent to which political change would result in substantial economic and social change remained issues for future resolution.

In the dozen years following the end of apartheid, South Africans of all races had the legal right to enjoy previously denied freedoms. But millions lacked the economic means to do so to any substantial degree. Approximately one-half of the population lived in poverty, and about one-quarter lacked jobs. The level of income inequality was enormous, especially striking given the leftist history of the ANC and the fact that a significant minority of its members in the National Assembly were also members of the South African Communist Party. In 2006 South Africa also faced the necessity of coping with the nation's immense AIDS problem. While the country's economy grew at a relatively strong pace in the twenty-first century, most political leaders and observers believed that considerably higher levels of growth were necessary to provide the means to effectively cope with the nation's range of serious problems. Significant divisions appeared to develop within the ANC over a number of issues. But around the world people continued to be inspired by and admire South Africa's anti-apartheid movement and the sacrifice and charismatic qualities of its central leaders, especially Nelson Mandela.

SOUTH AFRICA: CHRONOLOGY OF MAJOR EVENTS

1652	Dutch begin settlement and conquest of South Africa
1806	Britain assumes control of the Dutch settlement
1836–1856	Great Trek of many Afrikaners inland to establish independent Boer republics
1899–1902	British wage and win Boer War
1910	Union of South Africa established
1912	African National Congress (ANC) founded
1913	Native Land Act limits access to land for large majority of South Africans
1914	Afrikaner National Party founded
1948	National Party wins elections and begins process of reinforcing separation of races, which it calls "apartheid"
1950	Suppression of Communism Act and the Group Areas Act (Limiting people's residences and businesses to their racial areas)
1952	ANC and South African Indian Congress launch Defiance Campaign
1955	Congress of the People proclaims Freedom Charter
1959	Pan-Africanist Congress (PAC) established
1960	Sharpeville Massacre; ANC and PAC declared illegal
1961	ANC organizes Spear of the Nation and launches limited armed resistance

1962   Mandela arrested and eventually sentenced to life in prison
1976   Soweto uprisings
1983   Multiracial constitution approved by white voters; United Democratic Front organized
1984   Sustained protests against constitution begin
1985   Congress of South African Trade Unions organized
1989   F. W. de Klerk becomes president of South Africa and pledges to end apartheid
1990   Mandela released from prison; antiapartheid organizations re-legalized; ANC ends violent resistance to South African regime; government leaders announce plans to develop a new constitution; repeated violent conflict between ANC and Inkatha supporters
1994   ANC wins first fully democratic elections in South Africa
1996   New South African constitution adopted
1999   Second postapartheid election won by the ANC with a larger percentage of the vote, but voter participation declines significantly; Thabo Mbeki of the ANC succeeds Nelson Mandela as president of South Africa
2004   Third postapartheid election won by the ANC with an even larger majority of the vote; Thabo Mbeki reelected president
2005   National Party disbands

References and Further Readings

Adam, Heribert. 1988. "Exile and Resistance: The African National Congress, the South African Communist Party, and the Pan African Congress." In Berger and Godsell, eds., *A Future South Africa.*

African News, August 1989, 14, "We're Changing, Government Says."

Benson, Mary. 1986. *Nelson Mandela.* New York: W. W. Norton.

Berger, Peter, and Bobby Godsell, eds. 1988a. *A Future South Africa: Visions, Strategies, and Realities.* Boulder: Westview Press.

———. 1988b. "South Africa in Comparative Context." In Berger and Godsell, eds., *A Future South Africa.*

Bernstein, Ann, and Bobby Godsell. 1988. "The Incrementalists." In Berger and Godsell, eds., *A Future South Africa.*

Brewer, John D. 1986. *After Soweto: An Unfinished Journey.* Oxford: Clarendon Press.

Cauvin, Henri E. 2002. "H.I.V. Survey in South Africa Suggests Plateau in Infections." *New York Times*, June 11.

Cavatorta, Francesco. 2006. "Colonialism, Anti-Colonialism, and Neo-Colonialism." In DeFronzo, ed., *Revolutionary Movements in World History*, 1:163–68.

CNN, April 6, 2006, "Crime, private security boom in South Africa." http://www.cnn.com/2006/WORLD/africa/04/06/safrica.crime.reut/index.html.

Congress of the People. [1955] 1987. "The Freedom Charter." In Mermelstein, ed., *The Anti-Apartheid Reader.*

Cran, William. 1979. *Hot Shells: U.S. Arms for South Africa*. Boston: WGBH Transcripts.

Crawford, Neta. 1998. "South African Antiapartheid Revolts and Reform." In *The Encyclopedia of Political Revolutions*, ed. Jack A. Goldstone, 446–50. Washington, DC: Congressional Quarterly Press.

Danaher, Kevin. 1984. *In Whose Interest? A Guide to U.S.–South Africa Relations*. Washington, DC: Institute for Policy Studies.

_____. 1987. "Neo-Apartheid: Reform in South Africa." In Mermelstein, ed., *The Anti-Apartheid Reader*.

Davis, Stephen M. 1987. *Apartheid's Rebels: Inside South Africa's Hidden War*. New Haven, CT: Yale University Press.

DeFronzo, James. 2006a. "Cuban Revolution." In DeFronzo, ed., *Revolutionary Movements in World History*, 1:177–91.

_____, ed. 2006b. *Revolutionary Movements in World History: From 1750 to the Present*. 3 vols. Santa Barbara, CA: ABC-CLIO.

_____. 2006c. "South African Revolution." In DeFronzo, ed., *Revolutionary Movements in World History*, 3:784–801.

Giliomee, Hermann. 1980. "The National Party and the Afrikaner Broederbond." In Price and Rosberg, eds., *The Apartheid Regime*.

Gill, Jungyun. 2006. "Student and Youth Movements, Activism and Revolution." In DeFronzo, ed., *Revolutionary Movements in World History*, 3:848–54.

Glaser, Daryl. 2001. *Politics and Society in South Africa*. Thousand Oaks, CA: Sage.

Gocking, Roger. 2006. "Ghana's Independence Revolution: Decolonizing the Model Colony." In DeFronzo, ed., *Revolutionary Movements in World History*, 1:307–15.

Greenberg, Stanley. 1987. "Economic Growth and Political Change: The South African Case." In Mermelstein, ed., *The Anti-Apartheid Reader*.

Grundy, Kenneth W. 1993. "South Africa's Tortuous Transition." *Current History*, May, 229–33.

Handley, Antoinette. 2004. "The New South Africa, A Decade Later." *Current History*, May, 195–201.

James, Frank. 1994. "The Black Middle Class." *Ebony*, August, 92–94, 96.

Jost, Kenneth. 1994. "South Africa's Future." *Congressional Quarterly Researcher*, January, 24–48.

Karis, Thomas. 1986/1987. "South African Liberation: The Communist Factor." *Foreign Affairs*, Winter, 267–87.

Kerson, Roger. 1987. "The Emergence of Powerful Black Unions." In Mermelstein, ed., *The Anti-Apartheid Reader*.

Lawson, George. 2005. *Negotiated Revolutions: The Czech Republic, South Africa and Chile*. Burlington, VT: Ashgate Publishing.

Lazerson, Joshua N. 1994. *Against the Tide: Whites in the Struggle Against Apartheid*. Mayibuye History and Literature 50. Boulder: Westview Press.

Le Roux, Peter. 1988. "The Economics of Conflict and Negotiation." In Berger and Godsell, eds., *A Future South Africa*.

Lobban, Richard, and Paul Saucier. 2006. "Guinea-Bissau Independence Revolution." In DeFronzo, ed., *Revolutionary Movements in World History*, 1:340–47.

Louw, Antoinette, and Mark Shaw. 1997. "Measuring the Unequal Impact of Crime." http://www.iss.co.za/Pubs/Monographs/No14/Part1.html.

Mabeko-Tali, Jean-Michel. 2006. "Angolan Revolution." In DeFronzo, ed., *Revolutionary Movements in World History*, 1:61–70.

Magubane, Bernard. 1979. *The Political Economy of Race and Class in South Africa*. New York: Monthly Review Press.

Magubane, Bernard, and Ibbo Mandaza, eds. 1988. *Whither South Africa?* Trenton, NJ: Africa World Press.

Maltz, Gideon. 2006. "Zimbabwe After Mugabe." *Current History*, May, 214–18.

Mandela, Nelson. 1994. *Long Walk to Freedom: The Autobiography of Nelson Mandela*. Boston: Little, Brown.

Marais, Hein. 1998. *South Africa, Limits To Change: The Political Economy of Transformation*. Cape Town, South Africa: University of Cape Town Press.

Meldrum, Andrew. 2006. "South Africa On Trial." *Current History*, May, 209–13.

Mermelstein, David, ed. 1987. *The Anti-Apartheid Reader: The Struggle Against White Racist Rule in South Africa*. New York: Grove Press.

Nathan, Laurie. 1994. "Merging the Military." *Work in Progress* 95 (February /March): 3–4.

Newitt, Malyn. 2006. "Mozambique Revolution." In DeFronzo, ed., *Revolutionary Movements in World History*, 2:575–82.

New York Times, February 25, 1988, A1, "South Africa Bans Most Anti-Apartheid Activities."

_____, June 27, 1988, A1, "Pretoria Pass Law Dies, But Spirit Lives."

_____, March 5, 1989, 4, "South Africa Racial Toll Put at More Than 4,000."

_____, March 12, 1989, E2, "Apartheid Frays at the Edges, But Its Core Is Unchanged."

_____, March 28, 1989, A4, "A Cradle of Apartheid Looks for a Way Around It."

_____, April 9, 1989, 6, "New Party Meets in South Africa."

_____, July 23, 1989, E2, "Seeing Change, Apartheid's Foes Seek a Path of Less Resistance."

_____, August 22, 1989, A8, "South African Rebel Blueprint Is Backed by Continent Group."

_____, September 8, 1989, A8, "Pretoria Leader Sees Mandate for a Change in Racial Policy."

_____, February 12, 1990, A1, "Mandela Freed, Urges Step-up in Pressure to End White Rule."

_____, March 4, 1990, A14, "Rival Congress Wants No Talks with Pretoria."

_____, March 21, 1990, A1, "Namibia Achieves Independence After 75 Years of Pretoria's Rule."

_____, April 18, 1990, A5, "De Klerk Endorses Sharing of Power."

_____, April 22, 1990, A3, "Neutrality Has Its Dangers in the Blood Feuds of a South African Province."

_____, May 3, 1990, A1, "South Africans Open Black-White Talks."

_____, May 17, 1990, A1, "South Africa to Admit All Races as Patients to Its Public Hospitals."

_____, June 8, 1990, A1, "South Africa Ends Emergency Decree in 3 of 4 Provinces."

_____, June 10, 1990, A15, "CIA Tie Reported in Mandela Arrest."

_____, June 22, 1990, A20, "Mandela Says Movement Does Not See Socialism as the Only Route."

_____, June 27, 1990, A11, "Mandela Invokes Struggles of U.S., Rousing Congress."

_____, June 28, 1990, A22, "De Klerk, Addressing Blacks, Speaks of a New Constitution."

_____, July 15, 1990, A5, "Zulu Chief Turning Movement into Political Party."

_____, August 12, 1990, E4, "Who Speaks for Whom in South Africa?"

_____, August 22, 1990, A7, "In South Africa, Joint Plea to End Black Strife."

_____, October 19, 1990, A3, "De Klerk Lifts Emergency Rule in Natal."

_____, November 11, 1990, A15, "South Africa: A Communist Looks Ahead."

_____, November 13, 1990, A10, "Pretoria Retreats on Privatization."

_____, January 4, 1991, A4, "As Apartheid Fades, Uprooted Try to Go Home."

_____, January 6, 1991, A9, "Crime Overwhelms Pretoria's Police."

_____, January 10, 1991, A3, "South Africa Integrates Some Schools."

_____, March 19, 1994, 1, "Inquest Finds South Africa Police Aided Zulus in Terror Campaign."

_____, March 20, 1994, 10, "War to Keep Apartheid Spawned Terror Network."

_____, April 21, 1994, A10, "Blacks and Whites Wonder, Will Apartheid's Wrongs Now Be Reversed?"

_____, May 3, 1994, A1, "Mandela Proclaims a Victory: South Africa Is 'Free At Last'!"

_____, May 11, 1994, A1, "South Africans Hail President Mandela; First Black Leader Pledges Racial Unity."

_____, May 15, 1994, 14, "Mandela's Inheritance: Bloated Bureaucracy."

_____, June 4, 1994, 1, "Same Old Bureaucracy Serves a New South Africa."

_____, June 20, 1994, A7, "Zulu Royalists Win Control of Homeland, But They Forfeit Their King's Allegiance."

_____, July 29, 1994, A6, "Back to the Land: South African Blacks Walk a Legal and Economic Maze."

_____, August 19, 1994, A3, "Mandela's First 100 Days: 'On Course,' He Says."

_____, September 27, 1994, A3, "Growing Peril on South African Roads: Wave of Car Jackings."

_____, December 4, 1994, E7, "Apartheid's Fading Communist Foe Wins Mortgages for the Masses."

_____, December 28, 1994, A7, "Apartheid's Gone, and Anything Goes."

_____, February 20, 1995, A7, "A Glimpse of Apartheid's Dying Sting."

_____, March 29, 1995, A10, "Mandela Against Mandela."

_____, April 27, 1995, A1, "After Apartheid, Change Lags Behind Expectations."

_____, May 8, 1995, A19, "How Mandela Wooed Businessmen."

_____, May 9, 1996, A1, "A New Charter Wins Adoption in South Africa."

Noble, Rob. 2006. "South Africa HIV/AIDS Statistics." http://www.avert.org /safricastats.htm.

Nolutshungu, Sam C. 1988. "The South African State and Africa." In Magubane and Mandaza, eds., *Whither South Africa?*

Norment, Lynn. 1994. "The Women of South Africa." *Ebony*, August, 98–100, 134.

North, James. 1985. *Freedom Rising*. New York: Macmillan.

Omeara, Dan. 1983. *Volkskapitalisme: Class, Capital, and Ideology of Afrikaner Nationalism, 1934–1948*. Cambridge, UK: Cambridge University Press.

Omer-Cooper, J. D. 1987. *History of Southern Africa*. London: James Curry.

Price, Robert M., and Carl G. Rosberg, eds. 1980. *The Apartheid Regime: Political Power and Racial Domination.* Research Series 43. Berkeley: University of California Press.

Radu, Michael. 1987. "The African National Congress: Cadres and Credo." *Problems of Communism,* July–August, 58–75.

Rubert, Steven C. 2006. "Zimbabwean Revolution." In DeFronzo, ed., *Revolutionary Movements in World History,* 3:984–94.

Schlemmer, Lawrence. 1980. "The Stirring Giant: Observations on the Inkatha and Other Black Political Movements in South Africa." In Price and Rosberg, eds., *The Apartheid Regime.*

_____. 1988. "South Africa's National Party Government." In Berger and Godsell, eds., *A Future South Africa.*

Seedat, Aziza. 1987a. "Health in Apartheid Africa." In Mermelstein, ed., *The Anti-Apartheid Reader.*

_____. 1987b. "Poverty in South Africa." In Mermelstein, ed., *The Anti-Apartheid Reader.*

South African Police Service. 2006. www.saps.gov.za.

"South Africa's New Leadership." 1994. *Ebony,* August, 86, 88, 90, 100.

Statistics South Africa. 2006. http://statsa.gov.za (accessed September 6, 2006).

Thompson, Leonard. 1985. *The Political Mythology of Apartheid.* New Haven, CT: Yale University Press.

_____. 2001. *A History of South Africa.* 3rd ed. New Haven, CT: Yale University Press.

Thomson, J. D. S. 2004. "A Murderous Legacy." *South Africa Crime Quarterly* 7 (March): 9–14.

U.S. News and World Report, September 18, 1989, 52, "No Time to Dawdle."

Warwick, Peter. 1983. *Black People and the South African War 1899–1902.* Cambridge, UK: Cambridge University Press.

Watson, Russell, Joseph Contreras, and Joshua Hammer. 1994. "Black Power." *Time,* May 9, 34–35, 36, 38, 39.

Wheatcroft, Geoffrey. 1986. *The Randlords.* New York: Atheneum.

Wilson, Richard A., and Chris Arup. 2001. *The Politics of Truth and Reconciliation in South Africa: Legitimizing the Post-Apartheid State.* Cambridge, UK: Cambridge University Press.

Wood, Elizabeth. 2000. *Forging Democracy From Below: Insurgent Transitions in South Africa and El Salvador.* Cambridge: Cambridge University Press.

Worden, Nigel. 2000. *Making of Modern South Africa: Conquest, Segregation, and Apartheid.* Oxford, UK: Blackwell Publishing.

Selected DVD, Film, and Videocassette Documentaries

See "Purchase and Rental Sources" at the end of this volume for information on how to obtain the following resources and for full names of media companies and other organizations listed here as abbreviations.

Amandla! A Revolution in Four Part Harmony. 2002. 103 min. Indie. The power of music in the revolution against apartheid.

Apartheid's Last Stand. 1993. 60 min. Video. PBD. Dismantling of apartheid and social conflict in South Africa.

Biko: Breaking the Silence. 1988. 52 min. Video. AFSC, SAMC. Describes the life of Steve Biko and the impact on South Africa of the Black Consciousness Movement he led.

Chain of Tears. 1989. 50 min. Video. SAMC. Describes the impacts of war and violence on the children of South Africa, Angola, and Mozambique.

Changing This Country. 1988. 58 min. Video. SAMC. Describes how South African labor unions organized to combat exploitation and became the most powerful internal opposition force against apartheid.

Children of Apartheid. 1987. 50 min. Video. AFSC, SAMC. This documentary, narrated by Walter Cronkite, explores the contrasts between and divisions among white and nonwhite youth in South Africa.

Classified People. 1987. 55 min. Video. AFSC. Explains how racial classification in South Africa affected many aspects of how people lived and interacted.

Cry of Reason: An Afrikaner Speaks Out. 1987. 58 min. Video. AFSC, SAMC. Describes the extraordinary transformation of a clergyman who, after living and preaching among South Africa's pro-apartheid wealthy elite, left his affluent congregation to join the anti-apartheid movement and establish a new nonracial ministry.

The Deadline. 1996. 52 min. FRIF. Development of the 1996 constitution of South Africa.

Generations of Resistance. 1980. 52 min. 16mm color film. AFSC, SAMC. Describes the forms and methods of resistance to apartheid during the twentieth century.

Good Guys, Bad Guys. 1998. 46 min. CNN Cold War Series, Episode 17. Truman Library. Cold war conflict in the Third World, including Angola and South African and Cuban military involvement there.

Land Affairs. 1995. 26 min. FRIF. Indigenous South Africans demand return of land owned by whites.

Last Grave at Dimbaza. 1974. 55 min. Color film. AFSC. Documentary of the oppression caused by apartheid in South Africa.

The Long Walk of Nelson Mandela. 120 min. PBS. Life of the legendary anti-apartheid leader and first president of postapartheid South Africa.

Maids and Madames. 1986. 52 min. Video. AFSC, Filmakers Library. Describes the relationships between white women and the more than one million indigenous African women who work for them as domestic servants, typically forced to leave the raising of their own children to others while caring for their employers' offspring.

Mandela: Free at Last. 1990. 79 min. Video. AFSC. Mandela's life and struggle in the context of apartheid and the poverty and hardships of the large majority of South Africans.

Mandela: Son of Africa, Father of a Nation. 1997. 118 min. Indie.

Mandela's Fight for Freedom. 1995. 150 min. DCTV.

Nelson Mandela: Journey to Freedom. 50 min. AETV.

Regopstaan's Dream. 2000. 52 min. FRIF. Indigenous people struggle to regain their lands.

Rights and Wrongs: South Africa. 1994. 26 min. Video. AFSC. Mandela's election and continuing social conflicts.

Samora Machel, Son of Africa. 1989. 28 min. FRIF. Interview with Samora Machel, leader of the Mozambique Revolution.

Spear of the Nation: History of the African National Congress. 1986. 50 min. Video. SAMC. Documentary of the development of the ANC and its changing and varied means of opposing apartheid.

Twelve Disciples of Nelson Mandela. 70 min. ITVS.

White Laager. 1978. 58 min. DVD. AFSC. Documentary on the white settlement of South Africa, the development of Afrikaner nationalism, and the establishment of the apartheid system.

World Revolutions for Students: The South African Anti-Apartheid Movement. 2005. 23 min. LVC.

10

CONCLUSIONS

The opening chapter presented five major factors that have played essential and interdependent roles in the success of revolutionary movements throughout history: the development of mass frustration; the existence of elite dissident movements; the presence of a unifying motivation that brings together different classes or social groups in support of revolution; a severe political crisis that erodes the administrative and coercive capacity of the state; and an international environment permissive of revolution. The revolutions and the revolutionary conflicts covered in this volume illustrate the importance of the five factors in varied contexts. Internal societal characteristics and the interrelationship between the subject societies and other nations of the world helped determine which of the factors was most central to the success of individual revolutionary movements.

SOME COMPARISONS AMONG THE CASE STUDIES

In the case of the 1917 Russian Revolution the deterioration and collapse of the state was of primary significance. Lenin and other Bolsheviks correctly anticipated that the defeat of Russia during World War I would create a crisis of legitimacy and competency for the czarist regime much greater than that which followed Russia's loss to Japan in 1904. Taking advantage of the disintegration of czarist authority and mass military mutiny, the revolutionists bypassed the stages of historical development described in Marx's model and attempted to establish a socialist society.

In comparison to the Russian situation, Chinese revolutionaries, following the overthrow of the Manchu dynasty, confronted a stronger antirevolutionary state in the form of an alliance among former imperial officers, warlords, landlords, and coastal commercial elites. China's revolution would win last in the centers of state power, the cities. The Chinese Revolution, once under the leadership of Mao and like-minded associates, succeeded primarily because of the profound discontent of China's people, reflected in centuries of peasant rebellions against landlord avarice or excessive taxation and in uprisings against humiliating foreign invasions and occupations. Intensification of mass frustration in the twentieth century resulted from hardships caused both by the increasingly impersonal and exploitive relations between landlords and poor peasants under the Guomindang and by the Japanese invasion, which further inflamed nationalist passions. The course of the war displayed the incompetence, moral shallowness, and even collaboration of prerevolutionary elites with Japanese authorities and helped propel the Chinese Revolution to victory.

Vietnam's Revolution was distinguished by the dominant theme of resistance to centuries of foreign invasion and exploitation. Nationalism unified diverse social groups in the revolutionary effort. In Vietnam only one of many anticolonial movements displayed the capacity to organize a successful revolution, the Communist-led Viet Minh. This group's assets included a revolutionary policy of redistributing wealth, especially land, to the poor and the general independence of the revolutionary movement from foreign sponsorship. Non-Communist Vietnamese leaders or groups that aspired to play a nationalist role had relatively narrow bases of support and typically depended on substantial foreign assistance, thereby betraying any believable claim to genuine nationalism. Furthermore, the individuals in such groups tended to display the self-centeredness and material concerns characteristic of the upper classes of their sponsoring countries, rather than the spirit of self-sacrifice often essential to the success of a revolutionary effort.

The Cuban, Nicaraguan, and Iranian revolutions were like the Vietnamese in the sense of being viewed by many of their participants as national liberation movements. Whereas the Vietnamese Revolution began against colonial control by France, the latter three revolutions were directed against governments that many termed "neocolonialist": technically independent but perceived to be functioning in reality as instruments of foreign exploitation. Revolutionaries in all three countries also appealed to their fellow countrymen and women to rally behind efforts to oust notorious personalized dictatorial regimes.

Unlike Vietnam, however, leadership for the revolutions in Cuba, Nicaragua, and Iran was not provided by the existing prerevolutionary Communist parties, all of which had limited appeal and initially opposed armed rebellion as a means of political transformation. The Cuban Revolution benefited from a situation in which the prerevolutionary regime lacked legitimacy, having seized power in 1952, and was largely unprepared for the rural guerrilla tactics employed by Castro's forces. Cuba was further distinguished by the existence of a clearly identifiable and towering revolutionary leader whose concepts dictated the country's future course of development.

Nicaraguan revolutionary leaders faced a military opposition specially trained in counterinsurgency warfare and at first unconditionally backed by the United States. Experiencing more than a decade of failure in its attempts to overthrow Somoza, the FSLN temporarily fragmented over future strategy and tactics. One faction, the so-called FSLN Third Force (Christian Wing), developed the approach best suited to Nicaragua's strong religious culture and to taking advantage of the popularity of liberation theology. The Third Force transformed the FSLN into a broad coalition of anti-Somoza, socially progressive, and reform-minded Nicaraguans. After the victory the revolutionary government, profiting from knowledge of the early mistakes made by Cubans after their 1959 revolution, maintained a strong private sector in the economy and contributed to the development of a pluralistic democratic political system.

Iran's nationalistic, anti-shah revolution was, like the Cuban, ultimately dominated and shaped by a charismatic and commanding revolutionary leader, Ayatollah Khomeini. Khomeini mobilized the single major Iranian social institution, Shia fundamentalism, that could unquestionably be perceived as free from foreign ideological taint or assistance and, consequently, be recognized by the large mass of strongly religious Iranians as a legitimate nationalist force (although Khomeini vehemently argued the revolution was religious, not nationalist). Reminiscent of the Russian czar's overthrow, the shah's military and government disintegrated in the face of repeated urban demonstrations and insurrections. The ayatollah, having guided the revolution to victory, was then in position to influence greatly the formulation of the nation's postrevolutionary political, social, and economic systems.

The success of the Iranian Revolution encouraged Islamic movements, both Shia and Sunni, in other societies. Modern Sunni fundamentalist movements often derived their theological and social principles and revolutionary concepts from one of three similar bodies of thought: Wahhabism, Salafism, and the philosophy of the Muslim Brotherhood. All of these traditions advocated a revitalization of Muslim societies by a return to the pure form of Islam thought to have characterized the earliest historical period of the Islamic community. The momentous conflict in Afghanistan following the Soviet military intervention in 1979 ultimately gave rise to two related Sunni fundamentalist revolutionary movements, the Taliban and Al Qaeda. The Taliban movement developed in and directly affected one nation, Afghanistan. Taliban victory in most of the country in 1996 resulted in the institution of the most conservative and repressive Islamic regime in modern times. The other fundamentalist movement arising out of the Afghan War, Al Qaeda, first organized among the thousands of foreign volunteers from many countries who came to fight in Afghanistan, was by its nature and its ideology internationalist or "transnational." Its leaders sought to wage a global jihad against what they viewed as the enemies of Islam and Islamic peoples. The response of the United States, Britain, and a number of other nations to attacks by Al Qaeda led to new wars in Afghanistan and Iraq, attempts to construct more democratic political systems, and insurrections against foreign occupation.

Of all the societies covered in this volume, South Africa was the one characterized by the deepest social divisions and the one in which the revolutionary movement was in greatest need of mass commitment to a unifying revolutionary goal, the creation of a nonracial political system. Barriers to the sufficient realization of this element of the revolutionary process included ethnic and class differences within the nonwhite population. But the most important impediment had been the unwillingness of a majority of white South Africans, who had constituted the basis of the prerevolutionary state and armed forces, to support the transformation to a nonracial society. As anticipated in the first edition of this book, this conversion required continuous pressure and encouragement from internal as well as external opponents of apartheid coupled with negotiations in which the emergent revolutionary leadership attempted to assure South Africans of European ancestry that they would not be persecuted or severely penalized in an open democratic system by the nonwhite majority.

In 1994 this process led to the first national elections in which all South Africans could vote, the election of a nonwhite majority in the new parliament, an indigenous African president, and a government of national unity under a five-year temporary constitution. Though leaders of most major political groups announced the end of apartheid, what this would mean in terms of future economic structure and political and social systems was still very much in question. By 1995 South Africa's new government had opened public schools to all groups and abolished the laws requiring the social segregation of different races. But abolishment of socially restrictive apartheid laws and the ascendancy of indigenous Africans and other nonwhites to national political leadership need not signify a truly comprehensive revolution unless these changes are eventually accompanied by sweeping socioeconomic restructuring and development resulting in far more equality of opportunity among South Africa's people. If the ownership of wealth continues to be concentrated largely in white hands, South Africa will remain a highly divided society with social cleavages based primarily on class and culture but with an accompanying racial segregation of most of the country's population as a necessary consequence of persisting economic inequality.

INADEQUACIES IN THE THEORIES OF REVOLUTION

Chapters 2 through 9 explored the five essential factors affecting the success of revolutionary movements in different societies. Since the importance of these elements has been repeatedly demonstrated, it may be instructive to assess the capabilities as well as the limitations of general theories of revolution to account for their development. Chapter 1 described the core features of the Marxist, frustration-aggression, systems, modernization, and structural theories of revolution and noted that the first four theories neglected consideration of the necessary unifying motivation factor for revolutionary success. The Skocpol and Trimberger structural theory, though concerned primarily with explaining the factor of state deterioration, implicitly identified a logical basis for the development of a unifying motivation for revolution, international conflict and competition, which could provoke heightened feelings of nationalism among all classes in a society threatened by more powerful countries. All five theories, however, ignored the world permissiveness aspect of successful revolutions.

The reasons for these serious oversights may include the fact that the internal logical structure of several of the general theories implies an overly rational and materialistic basis for revolution. The Marxist, frustration-aggression, systems, and modernization theories suggest that the major cause of frustration is a lack of satisfaction of material needs or expectations. This emphasis, however, tends to promote theoretical omission of the necessary unifying element because such a factor must transcend economic considerations in order to bond together social groups whose economic interests are often nonidentical and sometimes even in conflict. Analyses of past revolutions indicate that key unifying factors have been nonrational in a strict economic sense and appealed for movement support on moral and emotional bases. For the majority of revolutions examined in this volume, a major unifying element was nationalism. This is a sentiment not necessarily identical to the gratification of economic aspirations, but rather one that involves a passionate need to rally in solidarity with one's country folk and to fulfill that part of one's self-identity and self-esteem that derives from membership in a particular national group.

The Skocpol and Trimberger structural theory, in contrast, does provide a logical framework for explaining the development of nationalism by focusing on the role of competition and conflict among countries at different levels of technological and economic strength. According to this structural theory, just as a society's government, often the most immediate target for revolutionary transformation, is not defined as an entity reducible to the interests of an individual economic class, similarly the driving engine of revolution, mass participation, is not exclusively the expression of a single class's aspirations. Rather, popular involvement and support for revolution can be viewed in part as a manifestation of most of the population's mobilization against a foreign adversary. The effort to overthrow a domestic government that is perceived as either unable or unwilling to defend the nation against exploitation by a foreign power can be interpreted as functionally the central component of the war against the external enemy itself. Thus, unlike the more limited Marxist, frustration-aggression, systems, and modernization theories, the Skocpol and Trimberger structural perspective provides a possible explanation for the occurrence of the necessary unifying motivation for revolution. As noted in chapter 8, the Skocpol and Trimberger structural theory can also be applied to a collection of nations sharing the same religious tradition, in which case common religious identity (such as Islam), rather than nationalism, can play the role of uniting not only people of different classes but also people of different countries in a transnational revolutionary effort.

Lack of theoretical inclusion of the world permissiveness factor has probably resulted from the difficulty of identifying a scientific basis for predicting this element of the revolutionary situation. In modern history the willingness of major powers, such as the United States and the USSR, to stand aside and allow revolutions to occur appeared very dependent on the idiosyncrasies and personal philosophies of top government leaders, in particular Jimmy Carter (Nicaragua and Iran) and Mikhail Gorbachev (Eastern Europe). In other cases, powerful nations have chosen not to intervene effectively or to stop interventions and allow revolutions to succeed because of lack of internal popular support for such interventions; fear of provoking war with or economic sanctions by disapproving countries; military, economic, or other internal strife that made effective intervention impossible; or, in some cases, opposition to the government a revolution seeks to overthrow. Just as some students of revolution have argued that the circumstances giving rise to individual revolutions are too unique to particular societies to be validly depicted in any general theory of revolution, it might also be argued that the causes of international permissiveness toward revolution have simply been so varied as to defy incorporation into any existing theoretical framework.

REVOLUTIONS OF THE FUTURE?

The great reduction in East-West hostility in the 1990s constituted a potentially far-reaching increase in international permissiveness for revolutionary change. Many societies had been characterized by both mass and elite discontent, but until the 1990s proponents of revolution were restrained by the perception of a high probability of external intervention, as well as internal repression, "justified" by the need to counter the threat of communist or capitalist "aggression." Without the restraint of the previously intense East-West conflict, many peoples were at least temporarily freer to consider significant or even sweeping economic, political, or other social change as a means of coping with serious domestic social problems.

In the twenty-first century there are a number of potential sites for further revolutions. Many nations in various parts of the world are dominated by authoritarian governments, including monarchies, or are characterized by extreme levels of economic inequality, or both. Selbin (2001) notes that in a number of countries inequality and poverty were increasing and logically the motivation for revolution in those nations might also have grown in response. In Colombia, Chiapas, and Nepal, armed leftist guerrillas resisted the established governments. In the Middle East various movements aimed at political or social transformations. Some of these targeted the remaining monarchies in the area or other forms of government viewed as unsatisfactory and aspired to create either European-style democracies or Islamic Republics. Members of Islamic fundamentalist movements battled government forces in Afghanistan (where the ousted Taliban sought to regain power), Chechnya, Egypt, and in U.S.- and British-occupied Iraq, some with the goal of driving out invaders and expelling or punishing collaborators and some with the intention of establishing more theologically infused governmental and social systems.

Extremists appeared prepared to strike against the interests of nations they viewed as supporting governments they sought to overthrow, leading to attempts at or actual terrorist attacks in Canada, France, Great Britain, Egypt, Indonesia, Russia, and Spain, as well as the September 11, 2001, attacks on the World Trade Center and Pentagon in the United States, following apparent earlier plots to bomb FBI headquarters and the Holland and Lincoln tunnels in New York. The intensified U.S. war on terrorism after the 9/11 attacks appeared to once again alter the international permissiveness factor for revolution, as the George W. Bush administration appeared willing to use not only economic pressure but force, including invasion and occupation, against governments viewed as harboring terrorists or perceived to be threats to the security of the United States.

In Asia millions confronted the tasks of democratizing China, Vietnam, Burma, North Korea, and other nations. Many Latin American and Caribbean peoples faced the monumental problems of dealing with enormous foreign debts, reducing domestic inequality and poverty, accomplishing the genuine democratization of political systems, and, in some cases, dealing with powerful drug trafficking organizations. In the post-Soviet era large numbers of people in Eastern Europe, Russia, and other nations of the former USSR expressed intense discontent with governmental and/or economic policies blamed for generating inequality of opportunity and wealth and greatly increasing levels of organized and street crime, drug abuse, and other social problems; they continued to search for alternatives.

In many societies people continued to suffer abysmal violations of human rights, including massive levels of poverty, crime, international human trafficking, and child abuse. It should be expected that, given the chance, those experiencing such problems might opt for radical change. Genuine democracy, unrestrained and free from intimidation by other nations or external economic forces, has the potential to be an instrument of popular revolution in countries where most people suffer from limited opportunity and perceive themselves to be exploited. By 2006 rejuvenated political democracies in several Latin American nations led to the election of leaders publicly committed to sweeping change on behalf of their nations' poor and to curbing what they viewed as socially and morally destructive neoliberal economic policies.

Revolution—meaning, according to our definition, structural social change—may be carried out in some cases through the ballot box. Social movement leaders who formulate themes of moral and community renewal and devise new forms of society in attempts to combine the promise of equal opportunity and freedom from want historically emphasized by socialism with the call for individual fulfillment stressed by capitalism will likely continue to attract supporters and inspire the political mobilization of many people with the call to revolution.

References and Further Readings

DeFronzo, James. 2006a. "Introduction." In DeFronzo, ed., *Revolutionary Movements in World History*, xix–xxii. Santa Barbara, CA: ABC-CLIO.

_____, ed. 2006b. *Revolutionary Movements in World History: From 1750 to the Present*. 3 vols. Santa Barbara, CA: ABC-CLIO.

Selbin, Eric. 2001. "Same as It Ever Was: The Future of Revolution at the End of the Century." In *Revolution: International Dimensions*, ed. Mark N. Katz, 284–97. Washington, DC: Congressional Quarterly Press.

Purchase and Rental Sources

AEMS: Asian Educational Media Service, http://www.aems.uiuc.edu

AETV: Arts and Entertainment Television, http://www.aetv.com

AFSC: American Friends Service Committee, 2161 Massachusetts Ave., Cambridge, MA 02140; 617-497-5273; http://www.afsc.org/resources/video-film.htm

Amazon.com: http://www.amazon.com

BBC: British Broadcasting Company, http://www.bbc.co.uk/bbcfour/documentaries

BIO: Biography, http://www.biography.com

BU: Boston University, Krasker Memorial Film Library, 985 Commonwealth Ave., Boston, MA 02215; 617-353-8112; http://www.bu.edu/media/krasker.html

CNR: California Newsreel, http://www.newsreel.org

CWU: Central Washington University Media Library Services–IMC, Ellensberg, WA 89826; 509-963-2861; http://www.lib.cwu.edu/media/

DCTV: Discovery Times Channel, http://www.dctvny.org

EMC: Educational Media Collection, http://www.css.washington.edu/emc/index.php

Filmakers: Filmakers Library, 124 East 40th St., New York, NY 10016; 212-808-4980; http://www.filmakers.com

Films Inc.: Films Incorporated, 5547 N. Ravenswood, Chicago, IL 60640; 800-323-4222

FRIF: First Run Icarus Films, http://www.frif.com

HC: History Channel, http://www.historychannel.com

Indie: Indie Docs, www.indiedocs.com

ISU: Iowa State University Media Resource Center, 121 Pearson Hall, Ames, IA 50011; 515-294-8022

ITVS: Independent Television Service, http://www.itvs.org

IU: Indiana University Audio Visual Center, Bloomington, IN 47405

KSU: Kent State University Audio Visual Services, 330 University Library, Kent, OH 44242; 330-672-3456

LVC: Library Video Company, www.libraryvideo.com

NAATA: National Asian American Telecommunications Association, http://www.capaa.wa.gov/naata.html

PBS: Public Broadcasting Service, 1320 Bradock Pl., Alexandria, VA 22314; 800-344-3337 and 800-328-7271 (for ordering videos); http://www.pbs.org

PSU: Pennsylvania State University Audio Visual Services, Special Services Building, University Park, PA 16802

PU: Purdue University Audio Visual Center, West Lafayette, IN 47907

SAMC: Southern African Media Center, Resolution Inc./California Newsreel, 149 Ninth St. #420, San Francisco, CA 94103; http://www.newsreel.org

SEG: Sterling Entertainment Group, http://www.sterlingentertainmentgroup.com

SUN: Sunrise Media LLC, http://www.sunrisemedia.tv/films

SUNY-B: State University of New York at Buffalo, Educational Communications Center, Media Library, 24 Capen Hall, Buffalo, NY 14260

SYRU: Syracuse University Film Rental Center, 1455 E. Colvin St., Syracuse, NY 13210; 315-479-6631; http://library.syr.edu/information/media/film/main.htm

Truman Library: http://www.trumanlibrary.org/educ/video.htm

UARIZ: University of Arizona Film Library, 1325 E. Speedway, Tucson, AZ 85721; http://www.library.arizona.edu

UC-B: University of California/Berkeley, Extension Media Center, 2223 Fulton St., Campus Box 379, Berkeley, CA 94720; http://www.lib.berkeley.edu/MRC

UI: University of Illinois/Urbana, University Film Center, 1325 S. Oak St., Champaign, IL 61820; http://www.library.uiuc.edu

UIOWA: University of Iowa Audiovisual Center, C-5 East Hall, Iowa City, IA 52242; http://www.uiowa.edu/~avcenter

UMINN: University of Minnesota Audio Visual Services, 3300 University Ave., S.E., Minneapolis, MN 55414; http://www.classroom.umn.edu/cts/avrental

UMISSOURI: University of Missouri/Columbia, Academic Support Center, 505 East Stewart Rd., Columbia, MO 65211; http://www.missouri.edu/~ascwww

UMONT: University of Montana Instructional Materials Services, Missoula, MT 59812; http://www.libcat.lib.umt.edu

UNEV-R: University of Nevada/Reno, Film Library, Getchell Library, Reno, NV 89557; 775-784-6037; http://www.innopac.library.unr.edu/search/X

USF: University of South Florida, Film Library, 402 Fowler Ave., Tampa, FL 33620; http://www.lib.usf.edu

UT-A: University of Texas/Austin, Film Library, P.O. Box W, Austin, TX 78712; http://www.lib.utexas.edu

UT-D: University of Texas at Dallas, Media Services, P.O. Box 643, Richardson, TX 75083; http://www.utdallas.edu/library

UWASH: University of Washington Instructional Media Services, Seattle, WA 98195; http://www.lib.washington.edu

UWISC-M: University of Wisconsin/Madison, Bureau of Audio-Visual Instruction, 1327 University Ave., Madison, WI 53701; http://www.library.wisc.edu

UWY: University of Wyoming, Audio Visual Services, Laramie, WY 82071; 307-766-3184; http://www-lib.uwyo.edu

WMM: Women Make Movies, http://www.wmm.com

WSU: Washington State University, 4930 Academic Media Services, Pullman, WA 99164-5604; 509-335-4535; http://www.wsulibs.wsu.edu

About the Book and Author

The rise of Islamic fundamentalist revolutionary movements, the conflict in Iraq, the surge of leftist political movements in Latin America led by Venezuela's example, and updates of the chapters on Russia, China, Vietnam, Cuba, Nicaragua, Iran, and South Africa are some of the main features of this third edition of *Revolutions and Revolutionary Movements*. With crucial insights and indispensable information concerning modern-day political upheavals, the third edition of this widely used book provides a representative cross section of many of the most significant revolutions of the modern era. Students can trace the historical development of eight revolutions using a five-factor analytical framework. Attention is devoted to clearly explaining all relevant concepts and events, the roles of key leaders, and the interrelation of each revolutionary movement with international economic and political developments and conflicts, including World Wars I and II, the cold war, and the War on Terror; eleven orienting maps are provided, and summary and analysis sections, suggested readings, chronologies, and updated lists of documentary resources with purchase and rental sources complete each presentation.

A compact handbook of revolution that encompasses history, politics, theory, societal and cultural diversity, and connections to current and future events, this revised edition of a proven text gives students the background they need to understand not only the dramatic events of the past but also those certain to rock the twenty-first century.

James DeFronzo of the University of Connecticut at Storrs is also the editor of *Revolutionary Movements in World History: From 1750 to the Present* (2006), a three-volume encyclopedia, as well as the author of many articles on criminology, revolutionary movements, gender issues, social stratification, and demography. More than seven thousand students have completed his Revolutionary Movements course, from which this book was developed.

Index

Acquired Immune Deficiency Syndrome
(AIDS), xv, 68, 393–397, 400, 404
Adleman, David E., 15, 27
Afghanistan, vii, 1, 4, 17, 276, 313–316,
319–320, 322, 324–325, 341–342,
348, 350–355, 357–358, 411, 415
African National Congress (ANC), xv, 217,
372–383, 385, 386, 388–390,
392–397, 398–401, 404, 406
and Cuba, 388
Executive Committee, 374
and Libya, 388
and the Palestine Liberation Organization,
388
and the Soviet Union, 376
and Western European nations, 376
Afrikaans. See South Africa
Afrikaners. See South Africa
Aguila, Juan, 227
AIDS. See Acquired Immune Deficiency
Syndrome
ALBA. See Bolivarian Alternative for the
Americas
Alexander II, Czar, 36–37
Alexander III, Czar, 39
Algeria, 292, 313, 323, 357
civil war, 313
Islamic Salvation front, 313
Ali, Imam, 277, 332
Allende, Salvador, 214–219, 226–227, 231, 258
Alliance for Progress, 212
Al Qaeda, 4, 315–316, 319–320, 324–325,
332–334, 336–339, 341–342, 344,
350–351, 353–355, 358, 411

Amnesty International, 117, 244
Anarchism, 36, 80
ANC. See African National Congress
Anglo Iranian Oil Company, 283
Anglo Persian Oil Company, 278
Angola, xvi, 123, 190, 216–217, 226, 229,
377, 388, 402, 405–406
Annam. See Vietnam
Anti-Bolshevik armies, 48
Anti-Taiping Manchu Ever-Victorious Army,
90
Apartheid, 217, 226, 359, 366–368, 370,
372–375, 377–381, 383–388, 390,
392–406, 412
Arab-Israeli War, 288, 320, 353
Arab Oil Embargo of 1973, 57, 295
Arawak Indians. See Cuba
Arbenz Guzman, Jacobo, 203–204
ARDE. See Democratic Revolutionary Alliance
Arevalo Bermejo, Juan Jose, 203
Argentina, 203, 212, 216, 219, 246, 253, 314
Army of the Republic of Vietnam (ARVN), xv,
164. See also Vietnam, South military
ARVN. See Army of the Republic of Vietnam
Assembly of Experts of the Islamic Republic of
Iran. See Iran
August Revolution. See Vietnam
Austro-Hungarian Empire, 42, 69
Aylwin, Patricio, 216
Azania People's Liberation Army, 379
Azerbaijan, 276, 281
Azhari, Gholam Reza, 299

Bachelet, Michelle, 218

Bakhtiyar, Shahpour, 300, 302
Bakunin, Mikhail, 36–37. *See also* Anarchism
Bambatha, Chief, 372
Bani-Sadr, Abol Hassan, 305–306
Bantustans (tribal homelands). *See* South Africa
Bao Dai, 158, 161, 164–165, 181
Barricada, 250
Basotho-Qwaqwa, 367
Batista, Fulgencio, 15, 189, 196–197,
    199–202, 204–208, 223–225, 233
Bayo, Alberto, 202
Bay of Pigs, 209–211, 225–226,231
Bazargan, Mehdi, 292–293, 298,
    301–302,324
BCM. *See* Black Consciousness Movement
Bedel, Berkley, 256
Bermeudez, Enrique, 262
Binford, Leigh, 9, 22, 27, 227, 271
Binh Xuyen criminal mafia. *See* Vietnam
Bin Laden, Osama, 229, 314–315, 319,322,
    324, 331, 336–339, 341–342, 344,
    348, 350, 353–354, 356, 358
Biko, Steve, 377, 379, 405
Black Consciousness Movement (BCM), xv,
    377, 379, 398, 405
Black Friday Massacre 298, 335
Black Power Movement, 377
"Blood River", 376
Bloody Sunday, 41
Boers. *See* South Africa
Bolivia, 214, 219, 226–227, 231
Bolivarian Alternative for the Americas
    (ALBA), 219, 227
Bolshevik Revolution, 17, 34, 47–48,75, 82,
    199, 278
Bolsheviks. *See* Russian Social Democratic Party
Bophuthatswana, 367
Borge, Tomas, 241–242
Borodin, Mikhail, 152
Bosnia-Hercegovina, 69–70
    and ethnic cleansing, 70, 72
    Muslim-Croat "federation," 72
Boxer Rebellion, 125, 134
Brazil, 123, 125, 131, 190, 212, 219
Brezhnev, Leonid, 56
Brezhnev Doctrine, 56, 58
Brinton, Crane, 22, 27
British Commonwealth, 363, 368
Broederbond, 364, 402
Brunei, 256
Buddhism, 90, 138, 144, 169, 186
"Build Socialism in One Country First!"
    (slogan). *See* Stalin, Joseph
Bulgaria, 18, 20, 58, 79

Bush, George H.W., 178, 233, 252, 259, 261,
    264, 312
Bush, George W., 67, 175, 219, 221–223, 230,
    267, 310, 315–316, 321, 342,
    344–346, 351, 415
Buthelezi, Gatsa, 381–382, 394, 398
Byrne, Malcolm, 21, 28

Cable News Network (CNN), xv, 81, 113,
    134, 188, 227, 232, 254, 271, 324,
    358, 395, 401, 406
Cambodia, 137–140, 149, 161, 172, 176–180,
    183–188
Constituent Assembly, 43–45, 49, 62, 179
Canada, 84, 162, 221, 229, 248, 415
Cao Dai. *See* Vietnam
Cape Colony, 361, 363
Capitalism, 6, 8, 13, 23, 31, 38–39, 47, 52,
    63, 79, 97, 110, 114, 122, 132, 135,
    192, 229, 294, 357, 416
Carter, Jimmy, administration, 225, 244, 246,
    252, 268, 270, 296, 299, 318–319,
    352, 414
Castro, Angel, 200
Castro, Fidel, 14, 189–190, 197, 200–212,
    214, 219–220, 222–224, 226,
    229–232, 410
Castro, Raul, 202
Catechism of the Revolutionary, 37. *See also*
    Anarchism
Cavatorta, Francesco, 15, 28, 130, 321, 401
CDRs. *See* Committees for Defense of the
    Revolution
CDSs. *See* Sandinista Defense committees
Central America Free Trade Agreement
    (CAFTA), xv, 267
Central Intelligence Agency (CIA), xv, 155,
    162, 174, 184,187, 203–204,
    207–212, 214–216, 225–227,
    231–233, 253–258, 265, 273–274,
    284–285, 304, 311, 319, 323, 340,
    355, 376, 403
    and Chile, 214–215, 258, 265
    contra manual, 255
    and Cuba, 208–212, 253
    and Guatemala, 203, 210, 253
    and Iran, 284–285, 304
    and Nicaragua, 253–257
    and South Africa, 376
    and Vietnam, 155
Chamorro Cardenal, Pedro Joaquin, 245, 250,
    260, 268, 270
Chamorro Cardenal, Xavier, 250
Chamorro, Carlos Fernando, 250

Marxism-Leninism, 206–207,211–212, 214, 223
and Mexico, 190, 202–203, 209, 221, 229
missile crisis, 211, 226, 231–232
National Assembly 223, 226
nationalism, 194–195, 211, 224
and Organization of Non-Aligned States, 190
and organized crime, 197, 209, 224
and Olympics, 190
Oriente Province, 204
Orthodox party, 197, 201–202, 225
peasants, 196, 203–204, 214
political system, 191–192, 194–197, 206–208, 220–223
Pope John Paul II, 226
population, 191
revolutionary factors,
  and elite dissidence, 200–202, 224
  and mass frustration, 195–196, 198–200, 224
  and permissive world context, 205, 224–225
  and severe state crisis, 198, 205–206, 224
  and unifying motivation, 189, 224
Revolutionary Instruction Schools, 207
and slaves, 191
and Spain, 192, 194, 221, 234
sugar industry, 194,
Sugar Workers Federation, 200
and UN, votes against U.S. economic embargo, 221
and U.S., 189–190, 194–196, 198, 205–212, 219, 221–222, 224–226
and USSR, 209–211, 217, 220, 225
and Venezuela, 219–220, 225
Cung, Nguyen Sinh (Ho Chi Minh), 150
Cyrus the Great, 276, 295
Czechoslovakia, 5, 17–18, 27, 56, 58, 76, 150, 209

Davies, James, 12, 24, 28
Death squads, 9, 255
Debray, Regis, 212–213, 228, 292
de Cespedes, Carlos M., 196
Decolonization, 16, 152
Defiance Campaign. *See* South Africa
de Klerk, F. W., 386–388, 390, 401, 403–404
Democratic Conservative party (PCD), xvi, 251, 254, 257
Democratic Revolutionary alliance (ARDE), xv, 254
Deng Xiaoping (Teng Hsiao-ping), 112, 120–121, 126, 133

Four cardinal principles, 120
Dhofar, 290
Dictatorship of the Proletariat, 23, 39–40, 55, 173
Diem, Ngo Dinh, 164–168, 181, 183
Dienbienphu, 161–162
Doumer, Paul, 140, 142
Dowager Empress. *See* Ci Xi
DR. *See* Revolutionary Directorate
Duiker, William, 147, 150–152, 162, 166–167, 169, 173, 177, 179, 184
Duma, 41, 43
Dunn, John, 16, 28, 50, 77, 103, 131, 156, 184
Dutch East India Company, 360

Eastern Europe v, ix, 1–3, 18, 33, 37, 39, 41, 43, 45, 47, 49, 51, 53, 55–60, 62–63, 65, 67, 69, 71–73, 75, 77–82, 102, 121, 126, 131, 133, 173–175, 190, 209, 217, 221, 225, 248, 252, 257, 259, 414–415
  and nationalism, 55–59, 62–65, 69–73
  and revolution, 2, 55–59, 62–65, 69–73, 75
East Germany, 18, 58, 126
East-West conflict, 264, 414
economic shock therapy, 65, 118
Egypt, 21, 31, 56, 300, 313, 315, 323, 326–327, 329–332, 334, 336–338, 344, 350, 353–354, 357, 415
Eisenhower, Dwight, administration, 164, 203, 205, 209–210, 224–225, 283
Eisenstadt, S. N., 13, 17, 28
Elite dissidence, 10, 12–14, 19, 26, 95, 352. *See also* revolution under China, Cuba, Iran, Islamic Revolutionary Movements, Nicaragua, Russia, South Africa, Vietnam
El Nuevo Diario, 250
El Salvador, 9, 17–19, 21–22, 27, 30–31, 216–217, 222, 229–232, 252, 264, 271, 405
  civil war, 22
  U.S. intervention, 22
Engels, Frederick, 13, 23, 28, 30–31, 38, 51, 78
Estonia, 58

Fascism, 70, 203, 238, 328
Fatima, 276–277, 327, 332, 352
FDN. *See* Nicaraguan Democratic force
February Revolution, 42, 78
Fedayeen-e Khalq, 292, 299, 301, 304

Nicaragua (continued)
Bolaños, Enrique, 267
brown shirts, 238
canal, 236
Catholic Church, 249–250
Council of Bishops, 249
Popular Church, 249
and Central American Common Market, 239
and Central American nations, 252
and Chile, 253, 258, 264–266, 273
and civil liberties, 243, 258–259, 269
classes, 239–240
Communist Party (originally called Nicaraguan Socialist Party), 238, 241, 242, 259
Conservative Party, 259, 267
Costa Rica, 245, 253–254
Council of State, 250–215
and Cuba, 233, 239, 242, 244–245, 248–249, 252–253, 257, 259, 264, 265, 271
earthquake of 1972, 236, 240, 243, 268
and Eastern European nations, 248, 252, 257, 259
economy, 239–240, 255, 257, 260
election of 1984, 257–258
election of 1990, 259, 261, 269, 274
and El Salvador, 264
geography, 233–234
and Granada, 234
and Great Britain, 234
and the Great Depression, 237
health, 247–248, 251, 255, 269, 271–272
and Honduras, 234, 246, 253–256, 259
imperialism, 249, 263
Indigenous population, 233–234, 236–237, 251–252, 254, 271
Miskito, 234, 255, 259
Rama, 234
Sumu, 251
inequality, 240
and Iran-contra operation, 256, 274
and Japan, 236, 252
Jarquín, Edmundo, 267
land reform, 248
León, 234
Liberal Constitutionalist Party (PLC), 266–267
Liberal National Party, 244
Liberal Party, 234, 234, 259
military, 233, 236–238, 241–247, 253–254, 256, 263, 265,269–270
draft, 249, 260, 269

Nicaraguan Army, 249, 264, 272
Sandinista People's Army, 241, 256, 263, 265
mining of harbors in, 256
Montealegre, Eduardo, 267
Moravian Protestant Church, 251
and multinational corporations, 265–266
National Guard, 233, 236–238, 241–247, 253–254, 269–270
nationalism, 233, 237, 241, 270
National Literacy Campaign of 1980, 249
National Opposition union (UNO), xvi, 259–260, 262–264, 269
and neoliberal economic policies, 262, 266
pacto, el, 266
and Panama, 236, 245
Pastora, Edén, 245, 253–254, 267, 271–272
peace agreement of 1989, 259, 261, 270
peasants, 239–240
political parties, 234, 236–238, 241–242, 244–245, 247–248, 250–253, 257–260, 265–266, 269, 272
political system, 233, 247, 264–265, 268
pope's visit to, 249–250
population, 233–234, 239–240, 243, 244, 257, 260, 263, 266–267, 269
public opinion surveys in, 256, 260, 263, 267
revolutionary factors,
and elite dissidence, 241–243, 268
and mass frustration, 243–244, 215–216, 268
and permissive world context, 244, 246, 268–269
and severe state crisis, 244, 246, 268–269
and unifying motivation, 243–246, 268
Sandinista Front for National Liberation (FSLN), 233, 241–274
Sandinista Renewal Movement, xvi, 263, 264, 267
and Spain, 234
state of siege, 244, 268, 270
Superior Council of Private Enterprise (COSEP), xv, 249–250
as target of low intensity warfare, 269, 271
and the UN, 255–256, 259
and U.S., 233–234, 236–239, 244–246, 252–259, 261–262, 264–265, 267–270
and USSR, 238, 242, 252, 257, 259, 264